FIRST PRINCIPLES OF INSTRUCTION

M. DAVID MERRILL
PROFESSOR EMERITUS
UTAH STATE UNIVERSITY

Identifying and Designing Effective, Efficient, and Engaging Instruction

A Wiley Imprint
www.pfeiffer.com

Cover Image: © Realeoni/Getty Images RF
Cover Design: Jeff Puda

Published by Pfeiffer
An Imprint of Wiley
One Montgomery Street, Suite 1200, San Francisco, CA 94104-4594. www.Pfeiffer.com

For additional copies/bulk purchases of this book in the U.S. please contact 800–274–4434.

Pfeiffer books and products are available through most bookstores. To contact Pfeiffer directly call our Customer Care Department within the U.S. at 800-274-4434, outside the U.S. at 317-572-3985, fax 317-572-4002, or visit www.pfeiffer.com.

Pfeiffer publishes in a variety of print and electronic formats and by print-on-demand. Some material included with standard print versions of this book may not be included in e-books or in print-on-demand. If this book refers to media such as a CD or DVD that is not included in the version you purchased, you may download this material at http://booksupport.wiley.com. For more information about Wiley products, visit www.wiley.com.

Library of Congress Cataloging-in-Publication Data

Merrill, M. David, 1937-

First principles of instruction : assessing and designing effective, efficient, and engaging instruction / M. David Merrill.

p. cm.

Includes bibliographical references and index.

ISBN 978-0-470-90040-6 (pbk.) ISBN 978-1-118-22119-8 (ebk.)

ISBN 978-1-118-23502-7 (ebk.) ISBN 978-1-118-25958-0 (ebk.)

1. Instructional systems—Design. 2. Educational technology. I. Title.

LB1028.38.M468 2013

371.3—dc23

2012023040

Acquiring Editor: Matthew Davis
Production Editor: Robin Stephanie Lloyd
Editorial Assistant: Michael Zelenko
Development: Susan Rachmeler
Editor: Rebecca Taff
Manufacturing Supervisor: Becky Morgan

Printed in the United States of America

FIRST EDITION

HB Printing 10 9 8 7 6 5 4 3 2 1

ABOUT THIS BOOK

WHY IS THIS TOPIC IMPORTANT?

If you are reading this book you are probably an instructional professional charged with identifying or designing instruction. The first principles of instruction, as outlined in this book, provide guidance to assist you in evaluating existing instruction to determine the degree to which it is effective, efficient, and engaging. The principles also provide guidance for designing instruction that will promote the ability of your learners to more quickly and successfully solve real-world problems and complete complex real-world tasks.

WHAT CAN YOU ACHIEVE WITH THIS BOOK?

In Part I of this book you will find prescriptions and checklists that you can use to evaluate the potential effectiveness, efficiency, and appeal of existing instruction. In Part II you will find a problem-centered model that you can use to design more effective, efficient, and engaging instruction.

HOW IS THIS BOOK ORGANIZED?

The first part of this book describes subject-matter content and instructional interaction. Instructional interaction and subject-matter content are then combined to provide prescriptive instructional strategies for promoting different types of instructional outcomes. These different instructional strategies are then combined in an integrated strategy for teaching problem-solving.

Part I concludes by prescribing an instructional sequence consisting of a progression of increasingly complex problems.

Part II demonstrates a problem-centered approach to instructional design and the use of a functional prototype as a design tool.

Part III contains research supporting First Principles of Instruction and some predictions about the future of the field.

The Instructor's Guide for *First Principles of Instruction* contains chapter-specific teaching materials, including presentations, discussion materials, example documents, and related teaching tools. The Instructor's Guide is available free online. If you would like to download the Guide, please visit: www.wiley.com /college/merrill.

CONTENTS

List of Figures and Tables vii

Online Premium Content xiii

Acknowledgments xvii

Preface xix

Part I Identifying E^3 Instruction **1**

Chapter 1 **What Are the Problems with Instruction?** **5**

Chapter 2 **First Principles of Instruction** **19**

Chapter 3 **Instructional Content** **47**

Chapter 4 **Instructional Interaction** **69**

Chapter 5 **Instructional Strategies** **87**

Chapter 6 **Instructional Strategies for Problem Solving** **121**

Chapter 7 **Problem-Centered Instructional Strategy** **149**

Chapter 8 **Enhancing Instructional Strategies with Structural Frameworks and Learner Interaction** **171**

Chapter 9 **Multimedia Implementation of Instructional Strategies** **191**

Chapter 10 **Critiquing Instructional Strategies in Existing Instruction** **219**

Part II Designing E^3 Instruction **247**

Chapter 11 **A Pebble-in-the-Pond Model for Instructional Design** **249**

Chapter 12 **Designing Functional Prototypes** **273**

Chapter 13 **Design a Problem Prototype** **299**

Chapter 14 **Design a Problem Progression** **315**

Chapter 15 **Design Strategies for Component Skills** **325**

Chapter 16 **Design Structural Framework and Peer-interaction Strategy Enhancements** **339**

Chapter 17 **Finalize the Functional Prototype** **353**

Chapter 18 **Design Assessment and Evaluation** **369**

Chapter 19 **The Pebble-in-the-Pond Instructional Design Checklist** **381**

Part III Support for First Principles of Instruction **393**

Chapter 20 **Indirect Support for First Principles of Instruction** **395**

Chapter 21 **Direct Research Support for First Principles of Instruction** **417**

Chapter 22 **First Principles of Instruction and the Future** **437**

Appendix Adding Assessment Capabilities to PowerPoint **451**

Glossary **461**

References **469**

About the Author **477**

Index **479**

LIST OF FIGURES AND TABLES

FIGURES

Figure I-1	Content Organization for *First Principles of Instruction* Part 1	1
Figure 1-1	Information Only—Textbook Online	9
Figure 1-2	Information Plus Remember-Question	9
Figure 1-3	Information with No Examples	10
Figure 1-4	Insufficient Examples and Missing Application	11
Figure 1-5	Tell-and-Ask Instruction	12
Figure 1-6	Remember-What-I-Told-You Questions	13
Figure 1-7	Too Much Guidance	14
Figure 1-8	Reading Online Text	15
Figure 1-9	Ineffective Game	16
Figure 2-1	First Principles of Instruction	22
Figure 2-2	Opening Interactive Scenario—Activation	31
Figure 2-3	Lesson 2—Accident Prevention—Activation	33
Figure 2-4	Case Study Simulation Interface	34
Figure 2-5	Guided Case Study—Demonstrate Problem	35
Figure 2-6	Tutorials—DRABC and Facial Injuries—Demonstration Application for Component Skills	37
Figure 2-7	Case Study—Bleeding Nose—Problem Application	40
Figure 3-1	Content for Information-About Component Skill—Famous Presidents	50
Figure 3-2	Content for Part-of Component Skill—Utah Counties	51
Figure 3-3	Content for Kind-of Component Skill—Elements of Art	52
Figure 3-4	Content for How-to Component Skill—Spreadsheets	52
Figure 3-5	Content for What-Happens Component Skill—Gantt Charts	54
Figure 3-6	Information and Portrayal Compared	55
Figure 3-7	Content for Kind-of Component Skill—Grammar Adverbs	58
Figure 3-8	Content for Kind-of Component Skill—Interview	58
Figure 3-9	Content for Coordinate Kind-of Component Skill—Sailboats	59
Figure 3-10	Example and Non-Example Comparison	60
Figure 3-11	Example and Pseudo Example Comparison	61
Figure 3-12	Content for How-to Component Skill—Sales	63
Figure 3-13	Content for What-Happens Component Skill—Properties of Water	64
Figure 3-14	Content for What-Happens Component Skill—Interview	65
Figure 4-1	Often Used *Tell-and-Ask* Instructional Interaction	72
Figure 4-2	*Tell-and-Show* Instructional Interaction—Skate Board Ollie	73
Figure 4-3	*Tell-and-Show* or Demonstration Instructional Events Involving Simulation—Focal Length	74

Figure 4-4 *Simon-Says* Instructional Interaction—Excel 75
Figure 4-5 *Do* Instructional Interaction, Kind-of Component Skill—Photography 76
Figure 4-6 *Do* Instructional Interaction, How-to Component Skill—Spreadsheet 76
Figure 4-7 *Do* Instructional Interaction, What-Happens Component Skill—Newton's Laws 77
Figure 4-8 Attention-Focusing Guidance—Gantt Charts 78
Figure 4-9 Matching Guidance—Grammar Adverbs 80
Figure 4-10 Divergent Guidance Contrasted with Convergent Examples—Grammar Adverbs 81
Figure 4-11 Range-of-Difficulty—Grammar Adverbs 81
Figure 4-12 Coaching and Corrective Feedback—Grammar Adverbs 83
Figure 4-13 Intrinsic Feedback—Spreadsheets 84
Figure 5-1 Information-About Instructional Strategy—Famous Presidents 91
Figure 5-2 Part-of Instructional Strategy—Utah Counties 94
Figure 5-3 Kind-of Instructional Strategy—Job Counseling 96
Figure 5-4 Kind-of Instructional Strategy—Photography Rule of Thirds 98
Figure 5-5 Kind-of Instructional Strategy—Coordinate Concept Poetic Meter 102
Figure 5-6 How-to Instructional Strategy—Spreadsheets 108
Figure 5-7 What-Happens Instructional Strategy—Experiential Environment Momentum 113
Figure 5-8 Goal for Problem 1 Momentum Experiential Environment 113
Figure 5-9 Audio Directions for Problem 1 Momentum Experiential Environment 114
Figure 5-10 Reflection Questions for Problem 1 Momentum Experiential Environment 115
Figure 5-11 Summary for Problem 1 Momentum Experiential Environment 115
Figure 5-12 Problem 2 for Momentum Experiential Environment 116
Figure 5-13 Goal for Problem 2 Momentum Experiential Environment 116
Figure 5-14 Audio Explanation for Problem 2 Momentum Experiential Environment 116
Figure 5-15 Reflection Questions for Problem 2 Momentum Experiential Environment 117
Figure 5-16 Summary for Problem 2 Momentum Experiential Environment 117
Figure 6-1 Content Elements for What-Happens Component Skill 122
Figure 6-2 Typical Content Elements for How-to Component Skill 122
Figure 6-3 Steps Bring About Conditions That Lead to the Consequence 123
Figure 6-4 Content Elements for a Problem-Solving Event 124
Figure 6-5 A Problem-Solving Event—A Warm Greeting 125
Figure 6-6 Content Elements for the Problem-Solving Event—A Warm Greeting 126
Figure 6-7 Content Elements for a Whole Problem 127
Figure 6-8 Content Elements for the Whole Problem of Selling Furniture 128
Figure 6-9 Problem-Solving Events Nested in the Larger Problem-Solving Event—A Friendly Approach 129
Figure 6-10 Example of a Whole Problem—Selling Furniture 131
Figure 6-11 Instructional Strategy for Demonstrating the Whole Problem—Selling Furniture 135

Figure 6-12 Instructional Strategy for Problem-Solving Event—A Friendly Approach 137
Figure 6-13 Final Application for Selling Furniture 146
Figure 7-1 A Topic-Centered Instructional Strategy 150
Figure 7-2 A Problem-Centered Instructional Strategy 151
Figure 7-3 Problem-Solving Event Diagram Showing Major Content Elements for Entrepreneurship 155
Figure 7-4 Interface for Entrepreneur Course 157
Figure 7-5 Entrepreneur Pig Farm Introduction 158
Figure 7-6 Instructional Events for Business Opportunity—Pig Farm 158
Figure 7-7 Instructional Events for Business Opportunity—Carpet Cleaning 159
Figure 7-8 Instructional Events for Business Opportunity—Cell Phone Business 160
Figure 7-9 Instructional Events for Business Opportunity—Restaurant 162
Figure 7-10 Instructional Events for Business Opportunity—Own Business 163
Figure 7-11 Problem Progression for Biology 100—Process of Science 163
Figure 7-12 Instructional-Event Sequence for Biology 100 167
Figure 8-1 Mnemonic as a Structural Framework—Sportsmanship 174
Figure 8-2 Straightforward Lesson on Transistors 176
Figure 8-3 Analogy as a Structural Framework—Transistors 178
Figure 8-4 Checklist Summary Frame as a Structural Framework—Persuasive Essay 181
Figure 8-5 Effective Peer-Interaction 187
Figure 9-1 Abbreviated Text with Audio Elaboration 194
Figure 9-2 Use of Audio to Elaborate Graphics Rather Than On-Screen Text 195
Figure 9-3 Relevant Use of Color to Emphasize a Property 196
Figure 9-4 Alternative Representation of Information 196
Figure 9-5 Text for Showing Defining Properties 197
Figure 9-6 Animation to Show Operation of Locomotive Walschaert Valve Gear 199
Figure 9-7 Use of Color to Focus Attention 200
Figure 9-8 Format for Course Organization—Entrepreneur Course 202
Figure 9-9 Using Font to Differentiate Elements of an Instructional Event 202
Figure 9-10 Examples of Conventional Navigation Buttons 204
Figure 9-11 What-Happens Response Control 208
Figure 9-12 Simple Circuit Simulation—Ohm's Law 209
Figure 9-13 Learner Control of Instructional Events 211
Figure 9-14 Multimedia Implementation for Entrepreneur Course 215
Figure 10-1 How-to Skill—Coconut Leaf Weaving 227
Figure 10-2 What-Happens Skill—Focal Length 229
Figure 10-3 Whole Problem Module—Photographic Exposure 231
Figure II-1 The Pebble-in-the-Pond Model for Instructional Design 247
Figure 11-1 Instructional Systems Design 251
Figure 11-2 A Pebble-in-the-Pond Model for Instructional Design 252
Figure 11-3 Identify the Problem 254
Figure 11-4 Demonstrate the Problem Solution 255
Figure 11-5 Problem Application 255
Figure 11-6 Progression of Problems 256
Figure 11-7 Demonstration for Problems 1 and 2 in the Progression 257

Figure 11-8 Prompted Applications for Problems 3 and 4 in the Progression 258
Figure 11-9 Unprompted Application for Problem 5 in the Progression 258
Figure 11-10 Application for Problems 6, 7, and 8 in the Progression 258
Figure 11-11 Branching to Component Skill Instruction 260
Figure 11-12 Component Skill Instruction for Entering Formulas 261
Figure 11-13 Structural Framework for Excel Course 263
Figure 11-14 Guided Demonstration Using Structural Framework for Component Skills 263
Figure 11-15 Guided Demonstration Using Structural Framework for Problem 264
Figure 11-16 Coached Problem Application Using Structural Framework 265
Figure 12-1 Demonstration Animation for Functional Prototype 278
Figure 12-2 Functional Prototype for Application for Famous Presidents 279
Figure 12-3 Slide Master for Famous Presidents Demonstration 281
Figure 12-4 Information-About Application for Famous Presidents 283
Figure 12-5 Slide Master for Information-About Application 283
Figure 12-6 Another Information-About Application for Famous Presidents 284
Figure 12-7 Kind-of Demonstration Instructional Event for Rule of Thirds 285
Figure 12-8 Slide Master for Kind-of Demonstration Instructional Event 285
Figure 12-9 Kind-of Demonstration Instructional Event with Multiple Examples 286
Figure 12-10 Slide Master for Kind-of Multiple Examples Demonstration 287
Figure 12-11 Kind-of Application Instructional Event for Rule of Thirds 287
Figure 12-12 Slide Master for Kind-of Application 288
Figure 12-13 A How-to One-Step Demonstration Instructional Event for Furniture Sales 289
Figure 12-14 Slide Master for How-to Demonstration 290
Figure 12-15 Slide Master for Active How-to Demonstration 291
Figure 12-16 Slide Master for How-to Application 291
Figure 12-17 What-Happens Demonstration for Aperture and Focal Length 292
Figure 12-18 Slide Master for What-Happens Application 293
Figure 12-19 What-Happens Dialog Simulation for Car Sales 294
Figure 12-20 What-Happens Dialog Simulation 295
Figure 12-21 Slide Master for What-Happens Dialog Simulation 295
Figure 13-1 Prototype Problem Demonstration for Photographic Composition 302
Figure 13-2 Prototype Problem Application for Photographic Composition 304
Figure 13-3 Problem-Solving-Event Chart for Photographic Composition 305
Figure 13-4 Prototype Demonstration of Steps for Photographic Composition 306
Figure 14-1 Sample Problem Portrayals for Photographic Composition 317
Figure 14-2 Component Skills Matrix for Photographic Composition 318
Figure 14-3 Modify the Progression by Adding a Photograph 321
Figure 15-1 Prototype Demonstration for Photograph D (Portrayal 1) 328
Figure 15-2 Prototype Application/Demonstration for Photograph E (Portrayal 2) 329
Figure 15-3 Prototype Application/Demonstration for Photograph F (Portrayal 3) 330
Figure 15-4 Prototype Application/Demonstration for Photograph C (Portrayal 4) 331

Figure 15-5 Prototype Application/Demonstration for Photograph A (Portrayal 5) 332
Figure 15-6 Culminating Prototype Application for Photograph B (Portrayal 6) 333
Figure 16-1 Structural Framework for Photographic Composition 342
Figure 16-2 Presentation Guidance Based on Structural Framework 343
Figure 16-3 Application Coaching Based on Structural Framework 344
Figure 16-4 Feedback for Photographic Composition Application 345
Figure 16-5 Reflection Based on Structural Framework 346
Figure 17-1 Course Organization for Photographic Composition—Module 1 356
Figure 17-2 Application Slide for Photographic Composition 357
Figure 17-3 Application Slide for Photographic Composition 357
Figure 17-4 Application Slide for Photographic Composition 358
Figure 17-5 Title Page for Photographic Composition 358
Figure 17-6 Introduction Slide for Photographic Composition 359
Figure 17-7 Course Organization and Menu for Photographic Composition 360
Figure 17-8 Photographic Composition Summary and Checklist 361
Figure 17-9 Location Indicator and Within-Slide Navigation 363
Figure 17-10 Within- and Between-Slide Navigation 365
Figure 18-1 Revision of Application Slides in the Functional Prototype 373
Figure 18-2 Slide Master for Application Slides for Photographic Composition 375
Figure 18-3 Questionnaire Slide for Photographic Composition 376
Figure 18-4 Alternative Treatments for Audio Guidance Versus Text Guidance 378
Figure 20-1 Learning Cycle of Star Legacy 408
Figure 20-2 4-MAT Cycle of Learning 409
Figure 21-1 Instructional Events from an Off-the-Shelf Topic-Centered Tutorial 418
Figure 21-2 Sample Quiz Items from an Off-the-Shelf Topic-Centered Course 419
Figure 21-3 Problem-Centered Demonstration Strategy—Problem 1 421
Figure 21-4 Flash Programming Task 1—Create Animal Slide Show 426
Figure 21-5 Flash Programming Task 2—Create a Virtual "Petting Zoo" 427
Figure 21-6 Topic-Centered Instructional How-to Demonstration Event 427
Figure 21-7 Task-Centered Instructional How-to Demonstration Event 428
Figure 21-8 Sequence of Topics in Flash Programming Treatment Conditions 429

TABLES

Table 3-1 Content Information and Portrayal Elements 49
Table 4-1 Instructional Interactions 85
Table 5-1 Instructional Strategies for Component Skills 89
Table 6-1 Prescribed Instructional Events for a Problem-Solving Event 124
Table 6-2 Prescribed Instructional Events for a Whole Problem 129
Table 7-1 Distribution of Instructional Events Across Problems 153
Table 7-2 Prescribed Instructional Events for a Problem-Solving Event 155

Table 7-3 Entrepreneur Instructional Events Distributed Across Different Problems 156
Table 9-1 Multimedia Checklist 214
Table 10-1 Information-About Strategy Checklist 221
Table 10-2 Summary Critique for Figure 5-1—Famous Presidents 222
Table 10-3 Part-of Strategy Checklist 222
Table 10-4 Summary Critique for Figure 5-2—Utah Counties 222
Table 10-5 Kind-of Strategy Checklist 223
Table 10-6 Summary Critique for Figure 5-4—Rule of Thirds 224
Table 10-7 Summary Critique for Figure 5-3—Helping Relationship 224
Table 10-8 How-to Strategy Checklist 225
Table 10-9 Summary Critique for Figure 5-6—Spreadsheets 226
Table 10-10 Summary Critique for Figure 10-1—Leaf Weaving 228
Table 10-11 What-Happens Strategy Checklist 229
Table 10-12 Summary Critique for Figure 10-2—Focal Length 229
Table 10-13 Content Elements for Whole Problem—Photographic Exposure 237
Table 10-14 Course Critique Checklist for Whole Problem 238
Table 10-15 Course Critique Checklist for Photographic Exposure 240
Table 13-1 Prescribed Instructional Events to Demonstrate a Whole Problem 306
Table 13-2 Prescribed Instructional Events for Whole-Problem Application 307
Table 15-1 Instructional Event Table for Photographic Composition for Individuals 326
Table 15-2 Checklist for Prescribed Instructional Events for Component Skills 327
Table 15-3 Checklist for Component Skills in Photograph Composition for Individuals 335
Table 16-1 Directions for Peer-Sharing for Photographic Composition 348
Table 16-2 Peer-Discussion and Peer-Critique Rubric for Photographic Composition 349
Table 16-3 Peer-Discussion Activity for Photographic Composition 349
Table 16-4 Peer-Collaboration Activity for Photographic Composition 349
Table 16-5 Peer-Critique Activity for Photographic Composition 350
Table 19-1 Pebble-in-the-Pond Instructional Design Checklist 382
Table 20-1 Theories Reviewed by Gardner 414
Table 21-1 First Three Problems in Problem Progression 420
Table 21-2 Detailed Directions for Coached Application Problems 3 and 4 422
Table 21-3 Directions for Problem 5 423
Table 21-4 Directions for a Final Spreadsheet Problem to Evaluate Learner Performance 424
Table 21-5 Teaching and Learning Quality Scales 431
Table 21-6 Use of First Principles of Instruction in Marriage Relations Courses (Possible Score = 15) 434
Table 22-1 The Science and Technology of Instructional Design 440
Table A-1 Visual Basic Macros for PowerPoint Assessment 453
Table A-2 Sample Data File 458

ONLINE PREMIUM CONTENT

The following materials are available for FREE with the purchase of this book at:
www.pfeiffer.com/go/principlesofinstruction
Password: professional

FIRST PRINCIPLES OF INSTRUCTION

Online Premium Content

The book *First Principles of instruction* includes guides and checklists for identifying and designing effective, efficient, and engaging (e^3) instruction. For your convenience this site contains four evaluation and design tools: guides, checklists, PowerPoint tutorials, and a PowerPoint functional prototype demonstration. These tools can be downloaded for your use.

Guides contain prescriptions for instructional strategies for component skills, for whole problems and for whole modules or courses. The guides usually include a graphic representation of these prescriptions plus directions for identifying the use of First Principles in existing instruction or for designing new e^3 instruction based on First Principles.

The Checklists are Microsoft Word forms. These forms are saved in Microsoft Word template format (.dotx). If you save these checklists files to your template file you can then open a form to use on your computer for purposes of evaluating existing or your own instructional modules or courses. These forms are write-protected but not password protected. This will prevent you from accidently corrupting a given form. If you wish to modify the form you can stop the protection to make your modifications.

While this book does not advocate the use of any particular rapid prototyping tool for designing a functional prototype, it does demonstrate the design of a functional prototype using Microsoft PowerPoint 10. This tool was chosen because it is readily available, inexpensive compared to other authoring tools, and contains some very useful features for designing functional prototypes. The PowerPoint tutorials and demonstration functional prototype are all programmed in Microsoft PowerPoint 10. You can download PowerPoint presentations for these files, which can be modified and used as a starting point for your own functional prototype.

These instructional tools are indexed here in three different formats. First, the tools are listed by category: Posters, Guides, Checklists, Tutorials and Prototype Demonstration. Second, the tools are referenced according to the chapters in the book in which the principle or prescriptions are described and illustrated. Third, Checklist 5 cross-references the guides, checklists, and tutorials appropriate for the steps in Pebble-in-the-Pond instructional design. The instructor guide associated with *First Principles of Instruction* also indicates where these tools can be useful in a course on instructional design based on First Principles of Instruction.

FIRST PRINCIPLES OF INSTRUCTION

Tools for Identifying and Designing e^3 Instruction

Posters

Poster 1: First Principles of Instruction
Poster 2: A Pebble-in-the-Pond Model for Instructional Design

Guides

Guide 1: Instructional Strategies for Component Skills (See Table 5-1)
Guide 2: Problem-Solving-Event Analysis (See Figure 6-7 and Table 13-3)
Guide 3: Problem-Centered Instructional Strategy (See Figure 7-2)
Guide 4: Problem-Progression and Component Skills Matrix (See Figure 14-2)
Guide 5: Instructional Event Table (See Table 7-1 and Table 15-1)
Guide 6: Effective Peer Interaction (See Figure 8-5)

Checklists

Checklist 1: Component Skills (See Tables 10-1 Through 10-11)
Checklist 2: Problem Demonstration and Application (See Table 6-2 and Tables 13-1 and 13-2)
Checklist 3: Multimedia (See Table 9-1)
Checklist 4: Course Critique (See Table 10-4)
Checklist 5: Pebble-in-the-Pond Instructional Design (See Table 19-1)

Tutorials

Tutorial 1: Using PowerPoint for Developing a Functional Prototype (video)
Tutorial 2: Instructional Strategy Templates (PowerPoint with video)*
Tutorial 3: Adding Macros to a Functional Prototype (PowerPoint)*

Demonstration

Functional Prototype Photographic Composition—Improving Your Photographs (PowerPoint)*

*Please note that these documents are provided in Office 2010 format, and only play correctly in Office 2010. To view the presentation after downloading, click Slide Show, then From Beginning.

First Principles Tools by Chapter

Chapter	Title	Table or Figure	First Principle Tool
2	First Principles of Instruction		Poster: First Principles of Instruction
			List: First Principles of Instruction
3 to 5	Instructional Content, Interaction, and Strategies	Table 5-1	Guide 1: Instructional Strategies for Component Skills
		Tables 10-1 through 10-11	Checklist 1: Component Skills
6	Instructional Strategies for Problem Solving	Tables 6-2, 13-1, and 13-2	Checklist 2: Problem Demonstration and Application
		Figure 6-7, Table 13-3	Guide 2: Problem-Solving Event Analysis
7	A Problem-Centered Instructional Strategy	Figure 7-2	Guide 3: Problem-Centered Instructional Strategy
		Figure 14-2	Guide 4: Problem Progression and Component Skills Matrix
		Tables 7-1 and 15-1	Guide 5: Instructional Event Table
8	Enhancing Instructional Strategies ...	Figure 8-5	Guide 6: Effective Peer Interaction
9	Multimedia Implementation of Instructional Strategies	Table 9-1	Checklist 3: Multimedia
10	Critiquing Instructional Strategies in Existing Instruction	Tables 10-1 through 10-11	Checklist 1: Component Skills
		Table 10-14	Checklist 4: Course Critique
	Part 2: Designing e^3 Instruction		Functional Prototype Demonstration: Photographic Composition—Improving Your Photographs
11	Pebble-in-the-Pond Model for Instructional Design	Figure 11-2	Poster: A Pebble-in-the-Pond Model for Instructional Design
12	Designing Functional Prototypes		Tutorial 1: Using PowerPoint for Developing a Functional Prototype
			Tutorial 2: Instructional Strategy Templates
13	Design a Problem Prototype	Tables 5-2, 13-1, and 13-2	Checklist 2: Problem Demonstration and Application
		Figure 6-7 and Table 13-3	Guide 2: Problem-Solving Event Analysis
14	Design a Problem Progression	Figure 7-2	Guide 3: Problem-Centered Instructional Strategy
		Figure 14-2	Guide 4: Problem Progression and Component Skills Matrix
15	Design Strategies for Component Skills	Tables 7-1 and 15-1	Guide 5: Instructional Event Table
			Checklist 1: Component Skills
			Guide 1: Instructional Strategies for Component Skills
16	Design Enhancements	Figure 8-5	Guide 6: Effective Peer Interaction
17	Finalize the Functional Prototype	Table 9-1	Checklist 3: Multimedia
18	Design Assessment and Evaluation		Tutorial 3: Adding Macros to Functional Prototypes
19	The Pebble-in-the-Pond Instructional Design Checklist	Table 19-1	Checklist 5: Pebble-in-the-Pond Instructional Design

About Pfeiffer

Pfeiffer serves the professional development and hands-on resource needs of training and human resource practitioners and gives them products to do their jobs better. We deliver proven ideas and solutions from experts in HR development and HR management, and we offer effective and customizable tools to improve workplace performance. From novice to seasoned professional, Pfeiffer is the source you can trust to make yourself and your organization more successful.

Essential Knowledge Pfeiffer produces insightful, practical, and comprehensive materials on topics that matter the most to training and HR professionals. Our Essential Knowledge resources translate the expertise of seasoned professionals into practical, how-to guidance on critical workplace issues and problems. These resources are supported by case studies, worksheets, and job aids and are frequently supplemented with CD-ROMs, websites, and other means of making the content easier to read, understand, and use.

Essential Tools Pfeiffer's Essential Tools resources save time and expense by offering proven, ready-to-use materials—including exercises, activities, games, instruments, and assessments—for use during a training or team-learning event. These resources are frequently offered in looseleaf or CD-ROM format to facilitate copying and customization of the material.

Pfeiffer also recognizes the remarkable power of new technologies in expanding the reach and effectiveness of training. While e-hype has often created whizbang solutions in search of a problem, we are dedicated to bringing convenience and enhancements to proven training solutions. All our e-tools comply with rigorous functionality standards. The most appropriate technology wrapped around essential content yields the perfect solution for today's on-the-go trainers and human resource professionals.

Essential resources for training and HR professionals

ACKNOWLEDGMENTS

The principles, prescriptions, and suggestions in this book have been influenced by many sources. While it is impossible to acknowledge everyone, I would nevertheless like to recognize some of the most obvious influences. I have tried to represent what I have learned from the theories, research, and practice of the many instructional professionals with whom I have interacted all over the world. It has been my great pleasure to have presented and discussed effective, efficient, and engaging instruction in instructional environments found in business, government, the military, and all levels of education. These interactions have shaped my thinking and influenced what is presented in this book.

Perhaps the greatest influence on my thinking is the interaction I have had with the hundreds of students it has been my pleasure to mentor and to learn from. I have often been asked why I stayed in higher education when I had many opportunities to enter the training world in business for considerably more salary. My answer has always been the same: because of the opportunity each school year to interact with another group of very intelligent future leaders.

The work of some of these students is represented here. Letter Press Software is an award-winning developer of outstanding instructional materials. Mark Lacy, Leston Drake, and Mike Peterson and their associates have consistently applied, modified, and experimented with the ideas I tried to help them understand when they were my students and in consulting with their company. Their courses under the copyright of The Furniture Training Company and Down Load Learning represent some of the important course examples included here.

Anne Mendenhall served as an instructional designer working with me at Brigham Young University–Hawaii. She directed the faculty and students who designed the Entrepreneur course, which is the example of problem-centered instruction described herein.

Students and colleagues at Brigham Young University, Utah State University, Florida State University, and the University of Hawaii all designed modules and course segments that have provided illustrations included here. I only wish that there were room to include all of these excellent examples for you to explore. Thanks to David Bybee, Michael Cheney, Ariana Eichelberger, Greg Francom, Christopher Gardner, Gregory Gibson, Dean Hammond, Susan Joworowski, Ross Jung, Dallen Miller, Michah Murdock, Dewi Padmo, Kristanti Puspitasari, Rinat Rosenberg-Kima, Michael Shoneman, Jonathan Tan, Robert Tennyson, Garren Venzon, and Sri Wahyuni for permitting me to show some of their work as examples of e^3 instruction.

I have also included examples of e^3 instruction from other designers who were not students but who nevertheless have implemented the ideas represented by First Principles of Instruction in their work. Thanks to St. John's Ambulance of Australia for allowing me to describe their course in First Aid and to Martha Legare of the Gantt Group for the Gantt Chart module.

The manuscript for this book was significantly improved by the very insightful suggestions made by our reviewers. I was impressed with the extra effort and thorough analysis they provided. They caused me to have a number of "Why didn't I think of that?" experiences. Many thanks to Brian R. Belland, Ruth Clark, Norman Gustafson, Ellen S. Hoffman, Monica W. Tracey, Wilhelmina C. Savenye, Katsuaki Suzuki, and Stuart H. Weinstein.

Because of the excellent detailed suggestions, both editorial and substantive, provided by Susan Rachmeler, senior development editor at Pfeiffer, this book is far better than it would have been without her collaboration. Thank you, Susan.

Finally, a debt of gratitude to my wife Kathleen for her patience for the serious neglect of her "Honey Do" list during the writing of this book. Without her encouragement this book may never have been written. I am grateful for her gentle prompting after a presentation where I had promised the participants that I was writing a book. "You've been telling folks that you are writing a book, but I don't see you doing any writing. You are not getting any younger." Her comment was the stimulus I needed to get serious and actually write the book. Thank you, Kate.

PREFACE

WHAT IS THIS BOOK ABOUT?

This book is about instruction and how to promote learning by implementing established principles of instruction through appropriate instructional strategies. We are surrounded by instruction. We spend most of our early years in school. If you are reading this book, you probably went to a college or university. When you accepted a new job, you probably spent some time in training. If you are part of the military, you spend a significant amount of time in training. Education and training are a predominant part of our lives.

Is all of this education and training of equal value? Does all of this time spent learning always result in better skills? If you are reading this book, you probably have some responsibility to identify education or training products that work. But how can you tell whether a given instructional product will really teach? A beautiful cover does not always identify a good book. Professional multimedia does not always indicate effective instruction. What is required for good instruction that teaches? This book will help answer these important questions.

If you are reading this book, you may also have responsibility to develop instruction. There are many available guides for designing and developing education and training materials. Even following these recommended procedures sometimes results in instruction that fails its goal of providing learners with desired skills. How can we increase the probability that our educational or training materials will really help our students acquire desired knowledge and skill?

I have spent more than forty years searching for ways to make instruction maximally engaging, effective, and efficient (see Merrill, 2008). With the growing popularity of e-learning, it occurred to me that the *e* should mean more than *electronic.* If we are going to call it *e-learning,* shouldn't it be *effective, efficient,* and *engaging*? In this book I call this e^3 learning or e^3 instruction. But saying "e to the third power" is more than a bit awkward so I just call it e-three instruction. However, the principles in this book are not limited to online or electronic learning but apply to all instructional environments, including instructor-led, online, distance learning, and the many other forms of instruction. This book was written to help you identify and design e^3 instruction in all instructional settings, for learners of any age, and for all subject-matter areas, both in training and education.

In the late 1990s, I decided to identify basic instructional principles that are fundamental to e^3 instruction. I searched instructional design theory and instructional research, and reviewed the practice of many effective instructional designers to see whether I could find a set of such fundamental principles. I wanted principles that applied to all kinds of instruction, principles that were fundamental to different theoretical orientations, principles that applied to different learner populations, and principles on which most instructional theorists and experienced designers would agree. In 2002, I published a paper in *Educational Technology Research and Development* titled First Principles of Instruction (Merrill, 2002a).

I am pleased that many instructional professionals and students have found these principles to be of value in identifying and designing e^3 instruction. However, I have also learned that, while these principles seem obvious to many professionals, applying them to the identification and designing of e^3 instruction is a bit more complex. This book was written to bring these principles up-to-date, to provide a more complete explanation of these principles, and to illustrate some possible ways to apply First Principles of Instruction.

WHO SHOULD READ THIS BOOK?

Are you an administrator or supervisor charged with finding courses, workshops, or other instructional products that will enable your employees to gain the skills they need to perform their job? Are you an instructional professional employed to design education or training materials for your organization? Are you an instructor who must identify or create instructional materials for your students? Are you a student seeking to acquire instructional design skills to pursue a career in designing instructional materials?

If you answered yes to any of the above questions, this book will be a valuable guide to help you carry out your responsibilities to identify, revise, or design more effective, efficient, and engaging instructional products.

HOW IS THIS BOOK ORGANIZED?

This book has three parts. *Part I: Identifying e^3 Instruction*, describes First Principles of Instruction and then provides guidance in how to use these principles to critique existing instructional courses, modules, or lessons to predict their potential effectiveness, efficiency, and engagement. *Part II: Designing e^3 Instruction*, provides guidance in how to design instruction that implements First Principles of Instruction. *Part III:, Support for First Principles of Instruction*, presents research support for First Principles of Instruction, compares the principles and prescriptions contained in this book with other instructional design theories and practices, and suggests ways for you to extend these principles and evaluate their application in your own instructional environment.

To facilitate your study of First Principles and the strategies that implement these principles, each chapter has several special features. Each chapter begins with an organization figure that identifies the primary topic presented in the chapter and how it relates to the previous and subsequent chapters in each section of the book. This figure is followed by a *Quick Look* section that provides a set of instructional design questions answered by the chapter. The chapter then has a *Key Words* section that defines some of the special vocabulary introduced in the chapter. These key words are also included in the Glossary at the end of the book.

The chapters contain many tables and figures that present instructional segments that demonstrate the concepts or strategies presented in the chapter. Don't skip over these examples! A key principle of e^3 instruction is demonstration or show-me. I have tried to include a wide variety of different courses from different disciplines and for different age groups to demonstrate the application of first principles in actual courses. You will understand the strategies presented in this book much better if you carefully study these examples.

Each chapter concludes with an *Application* section that suggests ways for you to apply the skills you have acquired from the chapter; a *Principles and Strategies* section that summarizes the principle that is elaborated in the chapter and the strategies that are presented as a way to implement this principle; a *To Learn More* section that includes references to other sources that are related to the ideas presented in the chapter; and, finally, a short *Coming Next* section introduces the next chapter and how it builds on the current chapter.

This book introduces a considerable amount of special vocabulary for describing instructional content, interaction, and strategies. There is an extensive Glossary at the end of the book that brings all of these new terms together with their definitions. Some of these terms are everyday words used in special ways in this book. You are encouraged to refer to this Glossary section as you read to be sure that your interpretation of a given term is consistent with its use in this book.

Key references have been cited throughout the book; however, because the target audience is instructional professionals rather than scholars, I have not provided an exhaustive set of references in support of all of the prescriptions and guidelines included. Part III of this book does provide a summary of some of the research support for First Principles of Instruction and a comparison of First Principles of Instruction with instructional design prescriptions recommended by other scholars. The complete citations for all of these references are included in the References section at the end of the book.

WHAT IS THE APPROACH OF THIS BOOK?

This book is a how-to book—how-to identify e^3 instruction and how-to design e^3 instruction. It is, first, a set of instructional principles and, second, a set of recommended instructional strategies for implementing these principles. An instructional principle is a relationship that relates learning to underlying properties of the instruction designed to promote learning. An instructional strategy is a particular procedure for implementing a principle. Principles can be implemented in a wide variety of different ways. The instructional strategies included in this book represent only some of the methods that appropriately implement First Principles of Instruction.

This book includes three different levels of discourse: principles, prescriptions, and practices. *Principles* are relationships that apply to a wide variety of settings, to a wide variety of populations, and to a wide variety of different instructional approaches. But principles are abstract and, because they are so widely applicable, can easily be misinterpreted and inappropriately applied. Principles can be implemented with a variety of prescriptions. This book presents a set of *prescriptions* that I have found lead to e^3 learning experiences. You should keep in mind that the prescriptions presented in this book are only one way to implement these principles, not the only way. Finally, even prescriptions tend to be abstract and are best understood when illustrated with actual instructional events. The third level of discourse in this book is a wide variety of examples of *practices* that attempt to illustrate the recommended prescriptions for implementing First Principles of Instruction. I hope there is a sufficient variety of such examples that you will be able to extrapolate to your own situation and find ways to implement the prescriptions and most importantly the principles presented here. I hope that this book serves as a catalyst for you to develop your own effective, efficient, and engaging instructional practices and your own customized prescriptions that you find implement effective, efficient, and engaging instruction in your learning environment.

In order to provide prescriptions that can be used to implement First Principles of Instruction, I have taken a very systematic approach. I first suggest a vocabulary to describe instructional content. I then suggest a vocabulary to describe instructional interaction. I then use this technical vocabulary to suggest instructional strategies for different types of instructional outcomes. These instructional strategies are then combined to suggest an integrated strategy for providing instruction for problem solving. Finally, this problem-solving strategy is expanded to a problem-centered approach involving learners in solving a progression of increasingly complex problems. My purpose for taking this detailed systematic approach is to provide guidance that is precise and unambiguous. I hope you will find the guidelines presented here of value in your own efforts to identify or design e^3 instruction.

M. David Merrill

To Harvey B. Black
1926—2011
my colleague, my mentor, my friend

FIRST PRINCIPLES OF INSTRUCTION

PART

I

IDENTIFYING E^3 INSTRUCTION

Part I describes *First Principles of Instruction* and then provides guidance in how to use these principles to critique existing instructional courses, modules, or lessons to predict their potential effectiveness, efficiency, and engagement. Figure I-1 is the organization of the content for Part I of this book.

FIGURE I-1 Content Organization for *First Principles of Instruction* Part I

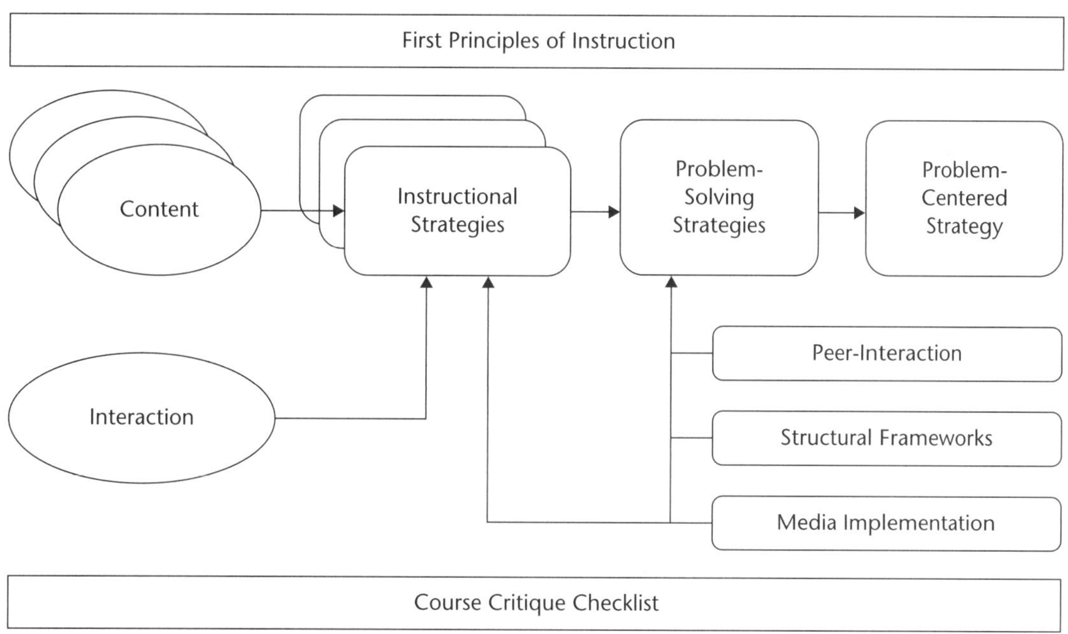

Chapter 1, What Are the Problems with Instruction? (not represented in Figure I-1). This chapter raises a number of frequently asked questions about instruction. It also identifies some common instructional mistakes and poses questions about these mistakes for you to consider. The principles and prescriptions of this book will help you recognize and avoid these mistakes, both in the instructional products you select and in those you design.

Chapter 2, First Principles of Instruction. This chapter demonstrates five categories of instructional activities that promote effective, efficient, and engaging (e^3) learning: demonstration, application, problem-centered, activation, and integration. Each of these principles is explained and their application in a sample course is illustrated. The subsequent chapters then elaborate on these principles and provide possible prescriptions and examples for how these principles might be implemented.

Chapter 3, Instructional Content. This chapter demonstrates five types of component skill that are required to solve a complex problem—*information-about, part-of, kind-of, how-to,* and *what-happens.* For each of these different types of skill, this chapter identifies and illustrates the content elements required for this skill. To acquire a specific type of component skill, e^3 instruction must include the content elements that are consistent with this type of skill.

Chapter 4, Instructional Interaction. This chapter demonstrates instructional modes of *tell, show, ask,* and *do* that, when combined with content elements, form instructional events. The chapter also demonstrates other essential features of the demonstration principle, including guidance and effective multimedia implementation; it also demonstrates other essential features of application principle, including coaching and feedback.

Chapter 5, Instructional Strategies. This chapter demonstrates how instructional content and interaction are combined into prescribed sets of instructional events that implement First Principles of Instruction for the five types of component skill.

Chapter 6, Instructional Strategies for Problem Solving. This chapter demonstrates how instructional strategies for individual skills all work together in a coordinated way to provide an integrated instructional strategy for problem solving. This chapter then prescribes a set of instructional events that enable learners to acquire all of the component skills that comprise the whole problem.

Chapter 7, Problem-Centered Instructional Strategy. This chapter contrasts topic-oriented courses with courses organized around a progression of whole problems. This chapter demonstrates how the instructional events appropriate for teaching a whole problem can be distributed across a progression of problems to apply a *tell–show–do* instructional strategy to a whole module or course.

Chapter 8, Enhancing Instructional Strategies with Structural Frameworks and Learner Interaction. This chapter demonstrates several effective ways to use a structural framework to provide learner guidance during demonstration and coaching during application to help learners acquire the content required for their new skills. This chapter also demonstrates how to integrate social interaction into e^3 instruction, including peer-sharing, peer-discussion, peer-collaboration, and peer-critique.

Chapter 9, Multimedia Implementation of Instructional Strategies. This chapter demonstrates effective ways to use multimedia to implement the instructional strategies described in previous chapters, to provide effective navigation, and to provide effective learner interaction.

Chapter 10, Critiquing Instructional Strategies in Existing Instruction. This chapter is the culminating chapter for *Part 1, Identifying e^3 Instruction.* This chapter demonstrates a set of checklists that will facilitate your evaluation of existing lessons, modules, or courses. There is a checklist for each type of component skill as well as for the evaluation of instruction that teaches whole problems. These checklists help you determine whether the principles and strategies that have been introduced in the previous chapters are appropriately implemented in the instruction you are evaluating. The checklists also suggest a way to assign an e^3 score to a given lesson, module, or whole course.

The arrows in Figure I-1 emphasize how the ideas in these individual chapters build on one another. Instructional interaction combines with instructional content to create instructional strategies for different kinds of skill. The strategies for these individual skills all combine to create an integrated instructional strategy for problem solving. This problem-solving strategy is repeated for each problem in a progression of increasingly complex problems in a problem-centered instructional strategy. A problem-solving instructional strategy is enhanced by peer interaction and structural frameworks. Media implementation is required for both instructional strategies for individual skills and for a problem-solving instructional strategy.

CHAPTER 1

WHAT ARE THE PROBLEMS WITH INSTRUCTION?

Quick Look

This book is about instruction and how to promote learning by implementing established principles of instruction through appropriate instructional strategies. The instructional design problem is how to recognize effective instruction and how to design new effective, efficient, and engaging instruction.

To provide a context for this problem, this chapter raises a number of frequently asked questions about instruction. It also identifies some common instructional mistakes and poses questions about these mistakes for you to consider. As you study the material in the remainder of this book, you will find ideas to help you answer these questions when you encounter them in your own instructional design efforts.

This chapter poses the following questions: What is instruction? How is it different from learning? What is training? Is it different from education? Do today's technologies require new instructional strategies? Have learners changed? What are some common instructional mistakes? Is information instruction? Where are the examples? Where is the application? What do learners already know? How much help is too much? Does reading online text facilitate learning? Does learner interaction facilitate learning? Do educational games facilitate learning? What are the problems for instructional professionals?

INTRODUCTION

Instruction is so prevalent in our society that I suspect that all of us think we know what we mean by the word "instruction." But do we? In this chapter I will provide a brief definition of instruction and I will contrast education and training. Some are suggesting that the availability of new technologies require learners to learn differently. Do they? Have learners really changed? This chapter briefly addresses these concerns. Learning is all around us, but is it always effective? This chapter identifies a few of the most common instructional mistakes, including the abundance of information with little or no examples and practice. It addresses the need to start with what learners already know. It suggests that some of the common media implementations of instruction may actually interfere with rather than facilitate learning. Finally, it suggests that the primary problems for an instructional professional are how to recognize e^3 instruction and how to revise existing instruction or design new e^3 instruction.

WHAT IS INSTRUCTION?

Learning always occurs, although it may be incidental, and it is not necessarily goal-directed. On the other hand, instruction is a goal-directed activity. Instruction is a deliberate attempt to structure a learning environment so that students will acquire specified knowledge or skill. The purpose of instruction is to promote learning. *Promote* means that the learning is more efficient, effective, and engaging than learning that might occur without this intervention. Obviously, we are all incidental learners, but incidental learners are unlikely to have either the previous knowledge of the content or sufficient skill in applying principles of instruction to efficiently direct their own learning. When it is necessary to acquire specific knowledge and skill, directing our own learning is likely to be extremely inefficient and may even lead to chaos. The purpose of instructional design is to ensure that the resulting instructional product really does promote e^3—effective, efficient, and engaging—learning.

Does this definition mean that instruction is always an instructor-directed activity? Certainly not! Learners can select the goals to be accomplished either from a menu of options or in more open-ended learning situations. But selecting goals is significantly different from selecting the learning strategies to accomplish these goals. Research on learner control has demonstrated that only learners with high previous knowledge or highly developed metacognitive skills are effective in directing their own learning (Clark & Mayer, 2003, 2008; Merrill, 1980a, 1984). Does this mean that only tutorial instruction is effective instruction? Again, certainly not! However, it does mean that when there are more open learning environments, there is even a greater need to be sure that the learners are guided by established principles of instruction. This book is about these established principles of instruction.

IS TRAINING EDUCATION?

Direct instruction is often equated with training, and training is contrasted with education. Training is seen as the less desirable option, appropriate only for vocational education in the workplace. But is this a meaningful contrast? The best education always involves some training. The best training always involves some education. Training is involved with the acquisition of specific knowledge and skill. Some would say that the world changes so fast that the skill needed is how to acquire skills rather than the skills themselves. But isn't learning how to acquire skill itself a skill? Don't we learn how to acquire skill by acquiring specific skill? Is it possible to acquire the ability to acquire skill in the abstract without learning some specific skill? If education is the development of the whole person or the development of character, don't these goals also require the acquisition of knowledge and skill?

This book does not distinguish between education and training. The principles and strategies described and illustrated are appropriate for both. The principles and strategies in this book promote appropriate active learning, interaction among learners, and instruction in both educational and training environments.

DO TODAY'S TECHNOLOGIES REQUIRE NEW INSTRUCTIONAL STRATEGIES?

While today's opportunities and contexts for learning are far more varied than they were only a decade or two ago, the underlying learning mechanisms of individual learners have not changed. It is important as we explore these different learning opportunities that we don't naïvely assume that because the landscape has changed dramatically the learners have also changed. There are fundamental instructional strategies, determined primarily by the type of content to be taught rather than by learning styles or by the form of instruction, that are necessary for effective, efficient, and engaging learning of specified knowledge and skill to occur. While their implementation may be radically different, those learning strategies that best promoted learning in the past are those learning strategies that will best promote learning in the future.

The principles and strategies presented in this book apply just as well to instruction delivered in traditional schools as in today's high-tech learning environments. However, with the ready availability of multimedia tools, the implementation of these strategies can be accomplished much more effectively and efficiently than was feasible for an earlier generation.

This book makes the following assumptions about instructional principles and strategies: Appropriate instructional principles can be discovered. There are known instructional strategies that implement these principles. If an instructional experience or environment does not implement instructional strategies that are required for the acquisition of the desired knowledge or skill, then effective, efficient, and engaging learning of the desired outcome will not occur (Merrill, Drake, Lacy, & Pratt, 1996).

HAVE LEARNERS CHANGED?

There is much discussion that because of technology today's young people may learn much differently from the way their parents or grandparents did. I am not naïve about the dramatic changes that have occurred in the instructional environment over the past few decades. The opportunities for learning and instruction are certainly much more varied than they were a generation ago. The amount of information available is many times greater than was true for previous generations. The easy access to information via the Internet that we currently enjoy would have been inconceivable to our parents and grandparents. But it is important that we ask ourselves: What has changed and what has remained the same? Does this mean that learners today learn differently from their parents or grandparents? Does this mean that the basic mechanisms of learning have changed?

There is no argument that the sheer volume of available information is significantly greater than for any previous generation. There is no question that there are many more forms of instruction than the traditional schooling of only a couple of generations ago. However, in spite of these dramatic changes in the learning environment, it is unlikely that young people have significantly different learning mechanisms than their parents have. Adaptation by evolution takes thousands of years, not a single generation.

This book makes the following assumption about learners: The basic learning mechanisms of learners today are not significantly different from those of a decade ago, a generation ago, or a century ago (Merrill, Drake, Lacy, & Pratt, 1996).

WHAT ARE SOME COMMON INSTRUCTIONAL MISTAKES?

Perhaps the greatest impediment to e^3 instruction is that too often the only requirement to be a teacher or a trainer is subject-matter expertise. It is assumed that if you know the content, you can teach. Technology is so easy to use that almost anyone can put information on the Internet and call it instruction. However, instruction is unlikely to be effective if it is not carefully designed. This book will help you recognize ineffective instruction, help you find ways to improve this instruction, and help you design instruction that avoids some of the most common instructional mistakes. Unfortunately, it is easy to find ineffective instruction. You have probably endured boring, ineffective courses in your own education. While observing live instruction is not always convenient, it is easy to find instruction on the Internet. There are many free courses available as well as thousands of courses for credit in almost any conceivable area of interest. Take a close look at several of these courses. Too often, what are you likely to find? Many courses present lots of information with little or no other instructional interaction. Many courses fail to demonstrate the skills being taught. Courses that involve only remember-level practice with no opportunity to apply what has been learned. Attempts at motivation that actually increase the learning effort for the learner, making skill acquisition less likely rather than more likely. Lack of guidance and coaching to facilitate skill acquisition or coaching that continues throughout application that interferes with learners' ability to solve problems without this extra help. Courses that use extensive multimedia, but often in a way that fails to promote learning and in many cases actually interferes with learning. Social networking that promotes interaction among learners, but too often does not contribute to learning. Courses that employ educational games that too often fail to motivate and fail to contribute to learning.

The instructional principles and recommended strategies in this book will assist you in identifying these instructional problems in existing instruction and help you to avoid them in the design of new instruction.

IS INFORMATION INSTRUCTION?

By far the most common instructional problem is presenting information and calling it instruction. If you take a look at existing instructional materials, what are you most likely to find? Pages of text, lots of information. Many courses are merely books online. Sometimes there are *remember-what-I-told-you* questions to "check your understanding." This was once called *shovelware,* that is, take some information and shovel it onto the Internet. Is it valuable to have access to so much information? Of course! Is it instruction? No! Information is not instruction. Instruction involves more than merely presenting information, even if the author adds a few remember questions to the information.

One of the most prevalent forms of online instruction is providing a textbook online. Figure 1-1 shows a small statement similar to those from an online first aid course that is comprised of a frequently used first aid manual. Although having the information available online is convenient, it does not make for engaging instruction. Online electronic reference materials are not instruction. What would be required to convert this online text to instruction? Figure 1-2 illustrates an information plus remember-questions course. This course contains much very good information and links to related websites. It also includes some activities for learners that require them to apply some of the ideas presented. Nevertheless, it still illustrates the predominate form of online instruction that is primarily text plus remember-questions.

FIGURE 1-1 Information Only—Textbook Online

First Aid Course	
The following snippet is based on a first aid course that is merely a first aid manual put online. It describes a common first aid problem and then describes a solution. The solution is sometimes accompanied with an illustration. Is this instruction or information?	
Minor Eye Injuries An eye injury is when a small foreign object strikes the eye or sticks to its surface. A bloodshot eye or urge to rub the eye may be a sign of an eye injury.	**Care and Treatment** • Irrigate the eye and wash the object out. • If this fails, touch the corner of a clean wet cloth to the object and lift it off the surface. • Refer to medical aid if vision is affected. • Cover the affected eye if appropriate. • Avoid pushing the object around the eye's surface. • Only use eye drops if prescribed by a doctor.

Paraphrased material based on an online First Aid Course. Source unknown.

FIGURE 1-2 Information Plus Remember-Question

Gardening	
The following segment is from a gardening course that provides lots of information and is accompanied by remember-questions. The objective for this segment is techniques to make full use of available growing space. The left column includes only a very small snippet of the text to give you a flavor of what is included. The actual text for this segment is five pages long. The right column is one of the questions following the segment.	
Succession cropping means growing an early crop followed by a later crop in the same area. . . . An example of succession cropping: plant cool crops first, then the warm crops in the same space after harvesting the cool crops. So what is a cool crop and what is a warm crop? [A description of the characteristics of warm and cool crops follows with a list of each type of plant for a vegetable garden.]	Did you grasp the facts? 6. An example of succession cropping is when a. You plant two crops together at the same time. b. You plant two crops in the same planting area, one right after another in the same growing season, an early crop followed by a late-season crop. c. You plant the same crop in a different part of the garden each season.

From *Planning and Preparing Your Garden.* http://ce.byu.edu.

WHERE ARE THE EXAMPLES?

When I'm asked to review course material, my approach is to immediately turn to Module 3 of the material. By then the course is usually into the heart of the content and the introductory material is finished. What do I look for first? Examples. Does the content include examples, demonstrations, or simulations of the ideas being taught? Every elementary teacher knows that for children to learn they need to have hands-on experience. As children get older, we often resort to verbal communication and assume that this is sufficient for learning to occur. But we are all children when we encounter a new content area; we need to see what is being taught, not just told. Way too much existing instruction is merely *Tell* without sufficient *Show.*

Figure 1-3 is a short segment on Federalism from a course on the Constitution. This segment is a very clear statement of the division of responsibilities between the federal government and the states. However, none of the rights stated are illustrated. Can learners really understand these rights without seeing examples? What is an instance when a state may treat a nonresident of the state differently from a resident in violation of the law? What is an instance when the federal government regulates interstate commerce? Would understanding of these rights be significantly increased if these various rights were illustrated with actual situations?

FIGURE 1-3 Information with No Examples

Federalism

In addition to separating the powers of the national government into three distinct branches, the Constitution also divides powers between national government and state governments. The Constitution grants specific powers to the national government, such as the authority to regulate interstate commerce and to print and coin money. Other powers are reserved to the states.

In the American *federal* system there are multiple levels of government that perform a wide variety of functions. There are few powers that are held and exercised exclusively by only one level of government. In almost every instance, powers are shared by overlapping levels of government.

The national government does, however, have *exclusive authority* over several important areas of national policy. These areas include the power to

- borrow money on the credit of the United States.
- raise and support armies and provide and maintain a navy.
- declare war.
- regulate commerce with foreign nations and among the states.
- issue patents and copyrights.
- resolve disputes between the states.

The Constitution also establishes that where state and national laws conflict, the state law or laws in question shall be invalid. In the federal system, the national government is supreme.

Shared Powers in the Federal System

There are several shared powers that the national and state governments exercise jointly:

- laying and collecting taxes
- passing, enforcing, and adjudicating the laws of the land
- protecting the environment and civil rights
- promoting economic development

Powers Forbidden to the States

The Constitution includes several prohibitions on state behavior. Most notably states cannot

- make treaties with foreign governments.
- print or coin their own money.
- overrule civil judgments (such as divorce settlements) of courts in other states.
- treat nonresidents differently from residents (except for charging nonresidents more for tuition to attend state colleges and universities).
- refuse extradition requests from other states (if someone is charged with a crime in another state, a state must surrender the suspect to the state where the crime was committed).
- wage war against other states or nations.

From *The Citizen's Guide to American Politics.* http://ce.byu.edu.

Figure 1-4, from a course on strengthening marriage, illustrates instruction to help learners discriminate between *worth* and *worthiness*. Each of these abstract terms is defined and a single example cited. Is a single example sufficient to help learners grasp the difference between these two abstract ideas? Would some specific situations involving contemporaries with the learners help them grasp the difference between these ideas?

FIGURE 1-4 Insufficient Examples and Missing Application

Worth and Worthiness

The following idea is from a course on Strengthening Marriage. The lesson is on developing a sense of identity. The concept being taught is to contrast worth and worthiness. The left column defines related terms. The right column provides an example of each term, but, unfortunately, like many courses, this course fails to provide adequate examples to clearly distinguish among the terms.

Many terms identify ways that we feel about ourselves, such as self-concept, self-worth, self-esteem, and worthiness. Although you often hear people use these words interchangeably, it is helpful to differentiate among them.

Worthiness	Worth
Is dependent on obedience	Is inherent and never changes
Is dependent on our agency, coupled with the Lord's grace	Cannot be affected by people
Is dependent on what we do in our lives	Cannot be increased, decreased, or destroyed
	Is independent of our actions

Term	Definition	Example
Self-concept	The mental image you have of yourself.	"I have curly red hair and I like to cook."
Self-esteem	Confidence and satisfaction in yourself; how well you like yourself.	"I feel pretty good about how well I do in school."
Self-worth	A sense of your inherent, unchanging value as a child of God.	"Knowing I am a daughter of my Heavenly Father helps me feel loved and understood."
Worthiness	A condition resulting when you correctly use your agency to obey God's commandments; unworthiness is the condition that follows disobedience.	"I know I shouldn't have been so rude to him yesterday, I really feel bad about it now."

True/False

1. Our individual worth is absolute.
   - ❍ True
   - ❍ False
2. Individual worth cannot be increased or decreased.
   - ❍ True
   - ❍ False

From *Strengthening Marriage and Family*. http://ce.byu.edu.

WHERE IS THE APPLICATION?

When I review instruction, what is the next instructional element I seek? Application. Does the instruction provide an opportunity for learners to use the knowledge and skill they have acquired to solve a new problem or do a new task? Answering multiple-choice, short-answer, or matching questions that merely require learners to remember what they read or what they heard in a lecture is not application. If "information only" is the first major problem with too much current instruction, the second greatest offender is that this instruction is characterized by remember-what-I-told-you questions rather than application.

In Figure 1-4, the practice illustrated in the last row merely requires memory and not application. Does remembering the definitions demonstrate that learners know the difference between *worth* and *worthiness*? What would be appropriate application to demonstrate that learners really understand the difference between *worth* and *worthiness*? Would having learners judge specific scenarios to determine whether there was a problem with a sense of worth or a sense of worthiness help them grasp this difference?

Figure 1-5 is a representation of a single display from a course on office safety. This course is an illustrated lecture on the Internet. Following each lesson in this course, students are asked to answer five multiple-choice or short-answer, remember-what-I-told-you questions. Figure 1-5 lists a couple of sample questions for one segment in this course. Of course, there is a place for *tell-and-ask* instruction. However, *tell-and-ask* falls short of enabling learners to acquire the desired skills. Appropriate application exercises would better assess whether or not learners have acquired the skill of promoting office safety. Rather than merely asking learners to remember the rules, would better application activities require them to make adjustments in a real or simulated office? Could such an application exercise require learners to first recognize a problem and then take corrective action? Rather than merely remembering the general rule, they would have to apply the rule in a specific situation. It should be obvious to the reader that applying the rules of office safety in several different situations would be an even more effective application.

FIGURE 1-5 Tell-and-Ask Instruction

<table>
<tr><th colspan="3">Office Safety</th></tr>
<tr><td colspan="3">This short segment of Tell-and-Ask instruction is a description of an online course on office safety. The three columns below describe the animated display. The numbers indicate the sequence of appearance for the various elements of the display. The last row is a sample of the questions included in the quiz following this segment.</td></tr>
<tr><td>Audio</td><td>Bullets</td><td>Graphic</td></tr>
<tr><td>[1] High levels of noise can come from computer printers, large copy machines, and other types of office equipment and
[2] can be damaging to your hearing as well as adding stress to the work environment.
[3] Ways to reduce office equipment noise include: relocating equipment to other rooms, using insulating dividers or pads around equipment or workers to lessen the noise level, installing carpet and draperies to absorb sound, and wearing protection such as ear plugs and ear muffs.</td><td>[1] High levels of noise can come from:
Computer printers
Copy machines
Other types of equipment
[2] High levels of noise can damage hearing and add stress.
[3] Ways to reduce noise include:
Relocating equipment
Using insulating dividers or pads
Installing carpet and drapes
Wearing protection</td><td>[1] pictures of office equipment
[2] picture of an ear
[3] picture of ear plugs</td></tr>
<tr><td colspan="3">Quiz

Select the appropriate answer for each question or enter the answer in the blank provided. When you are finished, click the button to submit your answers, register your answers, and find out your score.
1. Which methods below identify ways to reduce office equipment noise?
a. Relocating equipment to other rooms.
b. Using insulating dividers or pads.
c. Installing carpet and drapes.
d. All of the above.
2. Which method below can reduce office noise?
a. Install insulating dividers around equipment.
b. Install linoleum instead of carpet around equipment.</td></tr>
</table>

Based on an online course on Office Safety. Source unknown.

Figure 1-6 is a sample of remember-what-I-told-you questions from a variety of free courses from the online offerings of a major university. It should be noted that some of these courses also include application questions as well. But too many courses limit their practice to remember-level questions that do not require application.

FIGURE 1-6 Remember-What-I-Told-You Questions

Remember-What-I-Told-You Questions	
In each of the following rows I have selected a sample remember-question from a wide variety of courses offered free on the continuing education website of a major university.	
Astronomy	True or False A large grouping of stars is called a galaxy. T F
Government	What is a progressive tax system? Essay
Family Life	Which of the following best describes a relationship? a. It is the context for meeting basic human needs. b. It is the context for accomplishing personal goals. c. It is the context for developing faith and charity. d. It is the context for nurturing success and stability.
Genealogy	If you are just starting to identify your ancestors, you should start by finding information about: a. Yourself and your family b. Your third great-grandmother c. Your cousins d. Your uncles and aunts
Gardening	Which of the following is not a characteristic of the ideal garden? a. established on level ground on terrace b. established in the sunniest area of your yard c. contains foods desired most by you and your family d. walking space covers the same amount of ground as planting space

From various free courses available from ce.byu.edu.

WHAT DO LEARNERS ALREADY KNOW?

Learning needs to start with what learners already know. Learning needs to build on existing mental models of the world. A very common motivational technique is to build a course around a theme. Do such themes contribute to learning?

I came across a course for which the menu screen depicts a medieval scholar leafing through an ancient manuscript. His hand is on a stack of scrolls. In front of the scholar is a set of medieval buildings, including a castle labeled *simulation workshop* surrounded by four other medieval buildings labeled *library*, *learning center*, *examination center*, and *café*. Clicking on these various buildings takes the learner to the different activities of the course. The name of the course appears in the small window at the lower center of the illustration.

What do you think of when you see a medieval monk with scrolls? What does a castle or other medieval building activate in your mind? What mental models are activated by this medieval illustration? What do you think that this course is about? I was surprised to learn that the course was for insurance adjusters, those who would estimate damage to an automobile that had been in an accident. Is the medieval theme related to the topic of the course? The designers of this course assume that a theme is motivating for the learners. Does this unrelated theme motivate the learner? Or does this unrelated theme make learning more difficult? The medieval theme is carried throughout the instruction in various learning activities. For example, the course contains a game in which knights joust with each other. The knights advance when the learner determines the correct estimation for a damaged part of an automobile.

The medieval theme of this course activates a mental model in the head of the learner. The mental model activated by the medieval theme is unlikely to have anything to do with estimating damage to automobiles. Learners have limited capacity for mental processing. This course requires that learners simultaneously activate two different, unrelated mental models: medieval mental model and automobile damage mental model. Trying to work with two mental models simultaneously significantly increases cognitive load. The result is that any increase in motivation is more than offset by an increase in learning difficulty because of the increase in cognitive load. Unrelated themes make learning the intended content more difficult.

HOW MUCH HELP IS TOO MUCH?

Figure 1-7 illustrates the procedure for teaching a command in Excel from a popular computer application course. The procedure illustrated to guide learners is repeated for each command in the program. Do you think learners will remember where to push the next time? The excessive guidance as to what to do next is probably an exercise in following directions rather than learning Excel. This is an example of too much guidance. Guidance is an important principle, but effective guidance must be gradually reduced or learners will come to rely on the guidance rather than processing the information.

FIGURE 1-7 Too Much Guidance

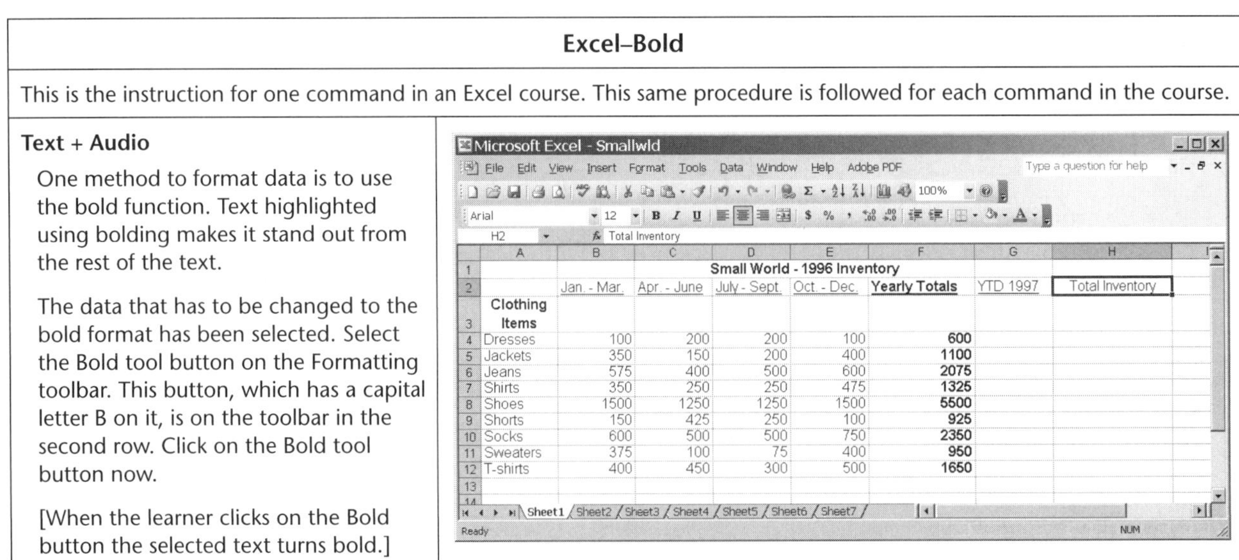

Excel–Bold

This is the instruction for one command in an Excel course. This same procedure is followed for each command in the course.

Text + Audio

One method to format data is to use the bold function. Text highlighted using bolding makes it stand out from the rest of the text.

The data that has to be changed to the bold format has been selected. Select the Bold tool button on the Formatting toolbar. This button, which has a capital letter B on it, is on the toolbar in the second row. Click on the Bold tool button now.

[When the learner clicks on the Bold button the selected text turns bold.]

Based on popular Excel course by NETg.

DOES READING ONLINE TEXT FACILITATE LEARNING?

Figure 1-8 is one display from an online course on workplace safety. When this display is presented, an audio message reads the text at the left to the learner. As the text is read, the graphic at the right changes to correspond to the text, as indicated in the right column. When text is being read out loud, where does the learner look? Probably not at the image. Most learners follow the written text as it is being read. Humans are linear processors. We cannot look at two things at the same time. When our eyes are focused on the text, we cannot simultaneously look at the graphic. If we glance at the graphic, we lose our place in the text. Research has shown that when a presentation contains three elements—graphic, text, and audio reading—that there is a decrement in learning (R.E. Mayer, 2001). It is better to have the graphic with audio and no text or the text and graphic with no audio than it is to have all three. Yet how often do e-learning courses read the text to learners, even when there is a graphic on the screen? Violating known principles of multimedia instruction interferes with learning.

FIGURE 1-8 Reading Online Text

Workplace Safety—Posture	
Text and Audio	**Graphics**
To understand back injury, you must first understand the back. The back consists of [1] 300 muscles, 33 vertebrae, and 30 spinal disks. [2] The spinal disks, gel-filled pads, fit between the vertebrae to form the spine, which protects the fragile spinal cord. From the spinal cord, nerve roots extend out into the body. If a disk becomes ruptured, also called a herniated disk, it can cause the spine to compress and pinch the nerve roots, causing pain. The best way to prevent this from occurring is to exercise, including stretching, and follow safe lifting and other ergonomic practices.	[1] drawing of muscles of back [2] drawing of vertebrae and disks

From an online course on Workplace Safety. Source unknown.

DOES LEARNER INTERACTION FACILITATE LEARNING?

If you are older, you probably remember being scolded for talking to other students in your class. But recent practice suggests that students might learn better when they collaborate with one another. Communities of learners are very popular, especially those that utilize online discussion boards. But do these online discussions contribute to learning? Is the number of posts per student a measure of learning? When some students fail to post does that mean they are not participating? Does failure to post mean that the student is not learning? Can students engage in meaningful discussion with minimal guidance? What kind of assignments lead to increased learning as a result of learner interacting with each other? This book will demonstrate effective learner interaction that can increase learning when it is guided and helps reinforce effective instructional strategies.

DO EDUCATIONAL GAMES FACILITATE LEARNING?

The soccer game depicted in Figure 1-9 is designed to teach English vocabulary to non-English speaking youth. An auditory message in their native language instructs learners to "Find the word *red*" by clicking on the speaker icon below each player and listening to the spoken word. The game can be used for any type of vocabulary matching; in this case the words are color words. When the learners hear the matching word, they are directed to click on the corresponding player. If they are correct, the player scores and the goalie pounds his fists on the ground. If they are incorrect, the player misses the net and the goalie jumps up and down in celebration. Each response is timed and a running score is kept for the student.

FIGURE 1-9 Ineffective Game

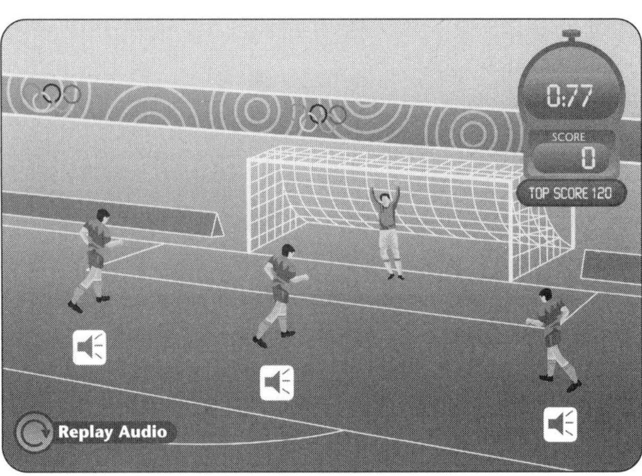

From an unpublished prototype course developed for the U.S. Office of Education.

Obviously, the purpose of this edutainment game is to find a way to motivate the student to learn the vocabulary words. Do you think that learners will find this game motivating? How many times is it entertaining to see the goalie pound the ground when the player scores? Repetitive feedback becomes boring. Is it more fun to see the goalie upset when there is a score or to see him celebrate when the ball misses the net? Too many so-called educational games violate the basic rules of effective games: provide a challenge, allow for increasing skill levels, and provide competition. The result is a boring exercise for which the learner quickly loses interest. Poorly designed games, far from motivating, actually create boredom and appear, even to young learners, to be irrelevant.

Game-like activities do have a place. What are the characteristics of an effective educational game? Many courses are now incorporating forms of simulation in which learners have an opportunity to manipulate virtual representation of devices. Some courses now incorporate experiential environments in which learners can visit virtual locations and participate in virtual activities representative of those activities they might encounter in the real world. Are these simulation-type activities effective? Many attempts at simulations and experiential environments in educational materials fall short and fail to teach the desired skill. What are the characteristics of an effective simulation? How real do these environments have to be to be instructionally effective? This book will demonstrate some effective use of simulations that implement effective instructional strategies.

WHAT ARE THE PROBLEMS FOR INSTRUCTIONAL PROFESSIONALS?

A primary theme of this book is problem-centered instruction. The primary purpose of any module or course should be to help learners acquire the skills necessary to solve a real-world problem. As instructional professionals, we have two major problems to solve: first, identifying e^3 instruction when we find it, and second, revising inadequate instruction or designing new e^3 instruction.

First Principles of Instruction and the prescriptions described and illustrated in this book will help you acquire the skills necessary to solve these instructional problems. These skills will help you avoid some of the instructional mistakes that have been identified in this introductory chapter.

PRINCIPLES AND PRESCRIPTIONS

- Information alone is not instruction.
- Too much instruction is merely *Tell* without sufficient *Show.*
- Tell-and-ask instruction does not enable learners to acquire problem-solving skills.
- Unrelated themes make learning the intended content more difficult.
- Excessive guidance interferes with learning.
- Information should be presented by audio or text, but not both.
- Learner interaction can increase learning when it is guided and reinforces effective instructional strategies.
- Games and simulation are effective when they implement effective instructional strategies.

APPLICATION

Go to the Internet. Review courses from different disciplines, aimed at different learner populations, and that use different instructional approaches. What were some of the instructional mistakes that you found? What other instructional mistakes did you find that were not described in this chapter? What effective instructional strategies did you observe? You may want to keep track of the courses you review so that you can visit them later as you acquire the skills for applying what you learn in *First Principles of Instruction.*

COMING NEXT

The instructional mistakes identified in this chapter indicate a failure to apply First Principles of Instruction. Chapter 2, which is the foundation for the rest of this volume, provides an overview of First Principles of Instruction.

CHAPTER 2

FIRST PRINCIPLES OF INSTRUCTION

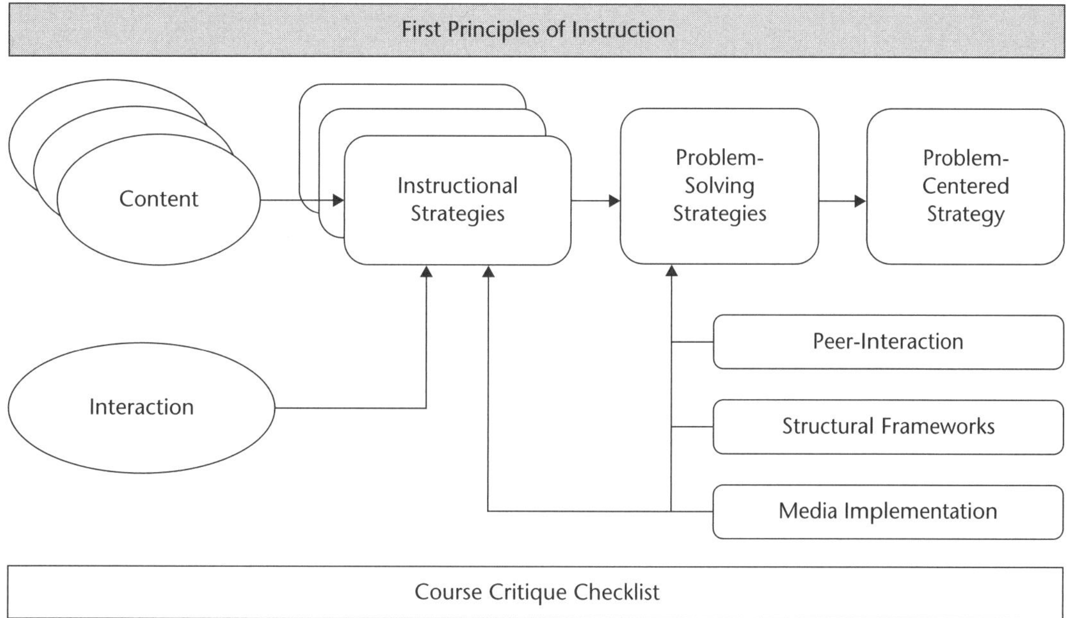

Quick Look

This chapter introduces and describes First Principles of Instruction. These principles form the foundation for the rest of this book. This chapter answers the following questions: Where did First Principles of Instruction come from? What are the First Principles of Instruction? What is the demonstration principle? What is the application principle? What is the problem-centered principle? What is the activation principle? What is the integration principle? How can we evaluate complex problem solving? Can you show me a course that implements First Principles of Instruction?

Key Words

Principle: a relationship that is always true under appropriate conditions, regardless of the methods or models used to implement the principle.

Problem-Centered Principle: learning is promoted when learners acquire skill in the context of real-world problems.

Activation Principle: learning is promoted when learners recall existing knowledge and skill as a foundation for new skills.
Demonstration Principle: learning is promoted when learners are shown the skill to be learned.
Application Principle: learning is promoted when learners use their newly acquired skill to solve problems.
Integration Principle: learning is promoted when learners reflect on, discuss, and defend their newly acquired skill.
Level-0 Instructional Strategy: information-only.
Level-1 Instructional Strategy: information plus demonstration.
Level-2 Instructional Strategy: information plus demonstration plus application.
Level-3 Instructional Strategy: problem-centered information, demonstration, and application.
Mental Model: an internal representation of some phenomena in the real world.
Intrinsic Feedback: an instructional interaction that shows the learner the consequence of his or her response.
Corrective Feedback: information following a response indicating the correct response and why it is the correct response.

INTRODUCTION

Recent years have seen a proliferation of instructional design theories and models. A series of important books titled *Instructional Design Theories and Models* (Reigeluth, 1983, 1999a, 1999b; Reigeluth & Carr-Chellman, 2009) provided an opportunity for a variety of different instructional design theorists to summarize their various ideas about instruction. The instructional design theories described in these sources vary from basic descriptive laws about learning to broad curriculum programs that concentrate on what is taught rather than on how to teach. Do these design theories and models have fundamental underlying principles in common? If so, what are these underlying first principles? This book, *First Principles of Instruction*, identifies a set of instructional design principles on which these various design theories and models are in essential agreement. While these principles are not new, it is surprising the extent to which they are not implemented.

For purposes of this work, a *principle* is defined as a relationship that is always true under appropriate conditions regardless of the methods or models used to implement this principle. Principles are not, in and of themselves, a model or method of instruction, but rather relationships that may underlie any model or method. These principles can be implemented in a variety of ways by different models and methods of instruction. However, the effectiveness, efficiency, and engagement of a particular model or method of instruction are in large part a function of the degree to which these principles are implemented.

Over several years, I reviewed instructional design theories, models, and research. From these sources I abstracted a set of interrelated prescriptive instructional design principles (Merrill 2002a, 2009b). Not all of the sources cited empirical support for these principles. However, I assumed, perhaps without sufficient justification, that if a principle is included in several instructional design theories and is used by a number of successful instructional designers, that the principle has been found either through experience or empirical research to be valid.

To be included as a First Principle, it had to be included in some of the instructional design theories that I reviewed. The principle had to promote more effective, efficient, or engaging learning. When the principle had been subjected to careful study, it had to be supported by the research. The principle had to be general so that it applies to any delivery system or any instructional architecture. *Instructional architecture* refers to the instructional approach, including direct methods, tutorial methods, experiential methods, and exploratory methods (R. C. Clark, 2003). The principles had to be design-oriented, that is, they are principles about instruction that have direct relevance for how the instruction is designed to promote learning activities, rather than activities that learners may use on their own while learning. They relate to identifying and creating learning environments and products rather than describing how learners acquire knowledge and skill from these environments or products.

While these principles can be found in a number of different instructional design theories, the terms used to state these principles may differ from the terms used in this book. Nevertheless, it is assumed that the authors of these theories would agree that these principles are necessary for effective, efficient, and engaging instruction. If this assumption is true, then it is hypothesized that when a given instructional program or practice fails to appropriately implement one or more of these First Principles, there will be a decrement in learning and performance. Obviously, the support for this hypothesis can only come from evaluation studies for a given instructional product or research comparing the use and misuse of these principles.

Many current instructional theories and models suggest that the most effective learning products or environments are those that are problem-centered and involve learners in four distinct phases of learning: (1) *activation* of prior experience, (2) *demonstration* of skills, (3) *application* of skills, and (4) *integration* of these skills into real-world activities. Too much instructional practice concentrates primarily on the demonstration phase and ignores the other phases in this cycle of learning.

Most of the theories that were reviewed to identify these principles emphasize *problem*-centered instruction and include some if not all of these four phases of effective instruction. Figure 2-1 provides a conceptual framework for stating and relating the first principles of instruction. This figure, which should be read clockwise, represents a four-phase cycle of instruction—activation, demonstration, application, integration. The *problem-centered principle* indicates that this cycle of instruction is most effective in the context of learning to solve real-world problems or do real-world tasks. Following are concise descriptions of each of these five principles:

- *Problem-Centered:* Learning is promoted when learners acquire skill in the context of real-world problems.
- *Activation:* Learning is promoted when learners activate existing knowledge and skill as a foundation for new skills.
- *Demonstration:* Learning is promoted when learners observe a demonstration of the skill to be learned.
- *Application:* Learning is promoted when learners apply their newly acquired skill to solve problems.
- *Integration:* Learning is promoted when learners reflect on, discuss, and defend their newly acquired skill.

FIGURE 2-1 First Principles of Instruction

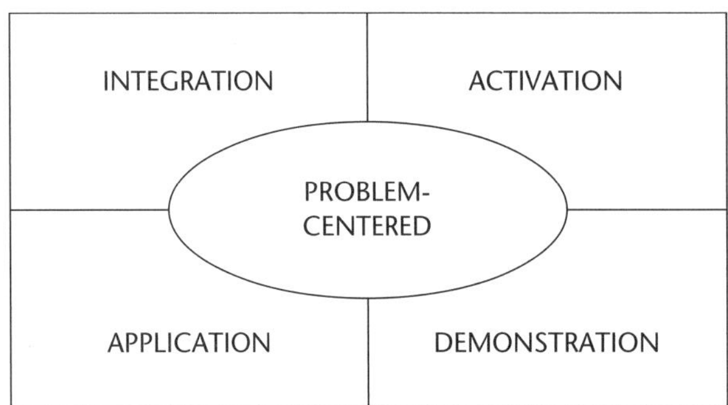

Some theories make a distinction between problems and tasks. Solving a problem results in a solution; doing a task results in some artifact. While there are differences between problems and tasks, in this book I have used the term *problem* to refer to both complex problems to be solved and complex tasks to be executed.

Some theories make a distinction between knowledge and skill. Knowledge refers to what is known and skill refers to using the knowledge to accomplish some task or solve some problem. In this book, I have used the term *skill* to refer to a combination of knowledge and skill.

FIRST PRINCIPLES OF INSTRUCTION AND LEVELS OF INSTRUCTIONAL STRATEGY

I'm often asked which of the First Principles of Instruction is most important. If I can't implement all of the First Principles, which principles should I design first? Are these principles of equal value? Do they contribute equally to learning effectiveness or efficiency? Are some of these principles more fundamental than others? How are these principles related to one another? What is the relative contribution of these principles to the acquisition of the skill and knowledge necessary to complete complex problems? The next section of this chapter explains each of the principles and suggests the relative contribution of these principles to performance on complex problems. The successive application of these First Principles of Instruction defines increasingly effective levels of instructional strategy. Application of the *demonstration principle* represents the first level of effectiveness, including *application principle* defines the second level, and including the *problem-centered principle* defines the third level. Adding the *activation principle* and the *integration principle* adds additional effectiveness enhancements to the instruction.

Information-Only (Level 0)

Presenting information-only is a level 0 baseline instructional strategy Too much instruction is presentation-oriented. There are many tools to enable us to make beautiful and, if used appropriately, effective presentation. Almost anyone can now create a multimedia presentation using tools such as PowerPoint. Incorporating music, audio, graphics, video, and animation into a presentation is no longer the challenge it once was. However, a surprising number of presentations resort to bullet points and talk. The assumption seems to be that, if instruction merely provides information, folks will be able to understand this information, remember this information, and, more importantly, use this information to solve complex problems. Unfortunately, such is not the case.

Information-only includes presentation alone or presentation plus recall. An information presentation tells learners associations among two or more pieces of information; the name and description of one or more parts; the defining characteristics of a class of objects, situations, or processes; the steps and sequence to carry out a procedure; or the conditions and consequence for the events in a process. Recall asks learners to remember the information that was presented. Information-only instructional strategies are very common in all educational environments whether schools, industry, or government. Information-only instructional strategies are very efficient for conveying large amounts of information but are subject to significant forgetting and are ineffective in promoting performance on complex problems.

Demonstration (Level 1)

A level 1 instructional strategy consists of information plus demonstration. Far too much instruction is merely *Tell* rather than *Show*. The word *demonstration* was carefully selected to reflect the fact that this principle is not about presenting information but rather about showing learners what to do to apply this information to specific situations. A *demonstration* is one or more worked examples of all or part of the problem that shows how the information is applied to specific situations. The demonstration principle states that:

> *Learning is promoted when learners observe a demonstration of the knowledge and skill to be learned.*

Consistent There are different kinds of skill to learn. Each kind of skill requires unique content elements; each kind of skill requires unique presentation strategies. The demonstration for one type of skill is different from the demonstration for a different type of skill. To be effective, the demonstration must be consistent with the kind of problem: location with respect to the whole for parts (*part-of*); examples of the various categories for concepts (*kind-of*); showing the execution of the steps together with the consequence for a procedure (*how-to*); and illustrating a specific process by showing the portrayal of the conditions and consequence (*what-happens*). Learning is promoted only when the demonstration is *consistent* with the type of skill being promoted. The consistency criterion is more critical than guidance or effective multimedia because if the presentation is inconsistent with the type of skill being promoted, then it doesn't matter whether there is learner guidance or whether the media appropriately implements instructional events. The consistency corollary states:

> *Learning is promoted when learners observe a demonstration of the skills to be learned that is consistent with the type of content being taught.*

Guidance Presenting information and showing its application to specific situations are the fundamental instructional events of an instructional strategy. However, the relationship of the information to the specific applications may not be clear to learners. Guidance provides direction to learners for processing the information and for attending to the critical aspects of the demonstration in a specific situation. Guidance may also provide directions to learners for relating the information and its application to a previously acquired skill or knowledge structure. Appropriate guidance enhances the learning that results from a demonstration. The guidance corollary states:

> *Learning from demonstrations is enhanced when learners are guided to relate general information or an organizing structure to specific instances.*

Multimedia Because it is so easy to include, the multimedia in instructional products too often fails to enhance learning and in some instances actually interferes with learning. Too often graphics have little relevance to the content being taught. Too often video and animation are used merely to make the instruction more attractive, with the hope of increasing the interest of learners in the material. The appropriate use of multimedia is to implement prescribed instructional events. When multimedia is used merely to provide interest or make the instruction more attractive, then it is more likely to distract from rather than promote learning. The multimedia corollary states:

> *Learning is promoted when multimedia implements prescribed instructional events and functions.*

If you have the opportunity to revise a level 0, information-only instructional strategy, you will obtain a significant increment in learning by adding appropriate demonstration to illustrate the information presented. The demonstration principle is elaborated in Chapter 5 and Chapter 9.

Application (Level 2)

A level 2 instructional strategy adds application to an information plus demonstration strategy. It is surprising to me that even though there is almost universal agreement on the importance of applying knowledge to real-world problems, so much instruction merely includes a few multiple-choice questions that are labeled practice. Such remember-what-you-were-told questions do little to promote learning. Skill development occurs when learners have an opportunity to do it, to apply the skill they have acquired to a variety of specific problems. Remembering information is not application; remembering information seldom prepares learners for applying their skill in real-world situations. *Application* requires learners to use their skill to complete specific problems. Consistent application for *kinds-of* problems is to sort examples into appropriate categories; for *how-to* problems, it is to execute a series of steps; and for *what-happens* problems, it is to predict a consequence given a set of conditions or find faulted conditions given an unexpected consequence.

Given information plus consistent demonstration assists the learners to form an appropriate mental model of the skill to be acquired. A *mental model* is an internal representation of some phenomena in the real world and how it works (R.E. Mayer, 1992a). Using this skill to do a new problem requires learners to check the completeness and adequacy of their mental model for solving the problem. When errors result and these are followed by corrective feedback, then learners can adjust their mental model. The initial application usually results in the most dramatic adjustment of the mental model. If a mental model is incomplete or inadequate, then learners may be unable to complete the problem. If the problem is too similar to problems that were demonstrated, then learners merely do the problem but engage in very little reconstruction of their mental model. The challenge is to find new problems for application that challenge the student but are not so challenging that the mental model is inadequate to complete the problem. The application principle states:

> *Learning is promoted when learners apply their newly acquired knowledge and skill.*

Consistent The word *consistent* is just as important for application as it is for demonstration. Just as there are different content elements for presentation and learner guidance appropriate for different kinds of skill acquisition, so there are different kinds of content elements appropriate for application for different kinds of skill. Engaging in application that is inconsistent with the desired instructional goal will do little to improve performance. Learning is promoted when the application is consistent with the type of skill to be acquired. The consistency criterion is critical. If the application is inconsistent with the intended goals of the instruction, then it will be ineffective and it doesn't matter whether or not there is appropriate coaching and feedback. The consistency corollary states:

> *Learning is promoted when learners engage in application of their newly acquired knowledge and skill that is consistent with the type of content being taught.*

Feedback Feedback has long been recognized as a critical aspect of practice. Practice without feedback does little to improve performance. The same is true for application. There are many forms of feedback, but when learners are applying information to the solution of a specific problem, right-wrong feedback is insufficient. The most effective form of feedback, called *intrinsic feedback,* is enabling learners to observe the consequence of their action. Another form of effective feedback, called *corrective feedback,* provides a demonstration of how learners should have performed the action. Feedback may be considered a form of guidance after the fact, guidance after having attempted to apply information to the accomplishment of a specific problem. The feedback corollary states:

> *Learning from an application is effective only when learners receive intrinsic or corrective feedback.*

Coaching *Coaching* means that the instruction or instructor does some of the cognitive processing for the student. Such coaching often takes the form of hints. A simple problem may require only a single hint, but complex problems may require a series of more and more complete hints.

Coaching can help learners select the part of the information that is relevant during the application, recall previous knowledge that can be used to help them solve the problem, and use a mental framework to help solve the problem. Coaching is most effective early in the application sequence, but as learners gain more experience in solving problems, this help should be gradually withdrawn so that learners are solving problems on their own without additional help. The coaching corollary states:

> *Learning from an application is enhanced when learners are coached and when this coaching is gradually withdrawn for each subsequent problem.*

When you encounter a level 1, information plus demonstration, instructional strategy, you will obtain an additional significant increase in learning by adding appropriate application to the instruction. The application principle is elaborated in Chapter 5.

Problem-Centered (Level 3)

A level 3 instructional strategy adds a problem-centered strategy to demonstration and application. The use of the word *problem* includes a wide range of activities, the most critical characteristic being that the activity is some whole problem rather than only components of a problem and that the problem is representative of the problems learners will encounter in the world following instruction. A problem-centered instructional strategy combines problem solving with more conventional instruction on the skills required to solve the problem. Learners are shown a problem solution, are explicitly taught the skills required to solve the problem, and are then given the opportunity to apply these skills to a new problem.

A problem-centered approach differs from problem-based learning or case-based learning as they are typically described in the instructional literature. A problem-centered approach is much more structured. It involves presenting a specific whole complex problem to the learners, demonstrating a successful completion of the problem, providing information plus demonstration plus application for each of the component skills required by the problem, and then showing learners how these component skills apply to the problem.

When instructional components are decontextualized, students are often admonished with "You won't understand this now, but later it will be very important to you." As a result, the motivation to learn the material is significantly reduced. Further, when learners must retain many component skills without a context for their use, they must often resort to associative memory and are likely to forget or fail to recognize the relevance of the information when confronted with the whole problem and thus be unable to retrieve the required information when it is needed. At best they will construct a mental model for the individual skills. They are unlikely to incorporate the component skill into a mental model for the whole complex problem. When instructional components are presented just in time for their application to a complex problem, then the need for the knowledge or skill is apparent and the motivation to learn the skill is increased. When the components are immediately applied to a complex problem, then the student can construct a mental model for the whole problem rather than separate mental models for the individual instructional components. The problem-centered principle states:

> *Learning is promoted when learners acquire knowledge and skill in the context of real-world problems or tasks.*

Problem-Centered A problem-centered instructional strategy that consists of a single complex problem may be an effective strategy, but a single problem is far less effective than a progression of increasingly more complex problems. A family of complex problems, while sharing many similarities, is also characterized by subtle differences. Learning to complete a single problem leaves learners with only one view of the problem and, when confronted with a problem from the same family but with differences from the original learning problem, they may fail to recognize that it is from the same family of problems or they may not have sufficiently tuned their mental model to enable them to adjust the solution process to accommodate the differences found in the problem. If the training problem is a less complex problem than a new problem, then learners may not have developed the nuanced mental model necessary to tackle the more complex problem. When they attempt to solve a progression of increasingly more complex problems, learners are able to continually improve their mental model. Then, when confronted with a different or more complex problem from the same family, they are more likely to be able to move forward toward problem completion. The problem-centered corollary states:

> *Learning is promoted when learners engage in a problem-centered instructional strategy in which component skills are taught in the context of a simple-to-complex progression of whole real-world problems.*

A level 2 strategy consisting of information plus demonstration plus application is often an effective instructional strategy that results in significant learning. However, an even greater increase in learning, and especially in engagement, will result from converting level 2 instruction to a level 3 problem-centered instructional strategy by having learners learn component skills in the context of a progression of real-world problems. The problem-centered principle is elaborated on in Chapters 6 and 7.

Activation It has long been a tenant of education to start where the child is. Elementary school teachers understand this phenomenon and spend considerable time providing experiences upon which later learning can be built. As learners mature, the educational system seems to feel that providing relevant experience prior to instruction is no longer necessary. Consequently, learners must resort to memorizing the material presented because they lack previous mental models based on experience that can be used to structure the new knowledge. Too often instruction jumps immediately into the new material without laying a sufficient foundation for the learners. If learners have had relevant experience, then the first phase of learning is to be sure that this relevant information is activated, ready for use as a foundation for the new knowledge. If learners have not had sufficient relevant experience, then the first phase of learning a new skill should be to provide real-world or simulated experience that they can use as a foundation for the new knowledge. Too much instruction starts with abstract representations for which learners have insufficient foundation.

When learners feel that they already know some of the material to be taught, then their existing experience can be activated by an appropriate opportunity to demonstrate what they already know. When they don't feel that they know the material, requiring learners to complete an information-oriented pretest of the material to be taught is frustrating to them and not productive in activating prior experience. A simple recall of information is seldom effective as an activating experience (Andre, 1997).

Adding activation to an information-only strategy may promote an increment in performance if the learner has developed a relevant mental model from his or her previous experience. This mental model can then be used as the basis for the construction of a revised mental model given the information. The more familiar the new problem is to previously learned problems, the larger the affect from activation of this previous learning. Unfamiliar new problems, for which the previous experience is only tangentially related, are less likely to promote an increment in performance. Activating the recall of a relevant mental model, when added to level 1, level 2, or level 3 instructional strategies, facilitates the formation of a revised mental model by allowing learners to build on an existing mental model. On the other hand, activating an inappropriate mental model by activating experience that is not relevant may actually promote a decrement in performance. The activation principles states:

> *Learning is promoted when learners activate a mental model of their prior knowledge and skill as a foundation for new skills.*

Structure Associative memory is that memory used to relate ideas to other ideas and is subject to rapid forgetting. Mental models, on the other hand, are representations of how the world works and allow learners to make sense of their world. Associative memory is insufficient for solving complex problems. Complex problems require learners to build their new skill on some previously acquired mental model that organizes the diverse skills required into some interrelated whole. When left on their own, learners often activate an inappropriate mental model, thus increasing the mental effort required to acquire the integrated set of skills necessary for solving the problem. Building on an inappropriate mental model often results in misconceptions that show up as errors when learners attempt to complete a new problem. Directing learners to recall past relevant experience and checking this recollection for relevance to the problem under consideration are more likely to activate an appropriate mental model that facilitates the acquisition of the new set of interrelated skills (R.E. Mayer, 1992a).

Activation is more than merely helping learners recall previous experience or providing relevant experience. Activation also involves stimulating those mental models that can be modified to enable learners to incorporate the new knowledge into their existing knowledge. This internal representation can be used as a framework for organizing new content. If a learner has a mental model that can be used to organize the new knowledge and skill, then he or she should be encouraged to activate this mental model. However, learners are often not efficient in constructing frameworks that they can use to organize their newly acquired skills. Left on their own, they often use inefficient or even inappropriate organizational schemes. If the learner's mental model is insufficient to adequately organize the new knowledge, then learning can only be facilitated if the instruction provides a structure that learners can use to build the required organizational mental model for the new knowledge. The structure corollary states:

> *Learning is promoted when learners recall or acquire a framework or structure for organizing the new knowledge, when the structure is the basis for guidance during demonstration, coaching during application, and reflection during integration.*

The activation principle is elaborated on in Chapter 8.

Integration Learning occurs when learners do more than merely acquire the desired skill. Learning requires a modification of existing mental models and an integration of the new skill into the skills learners have already acquired. Effective instruction provides an opportunity for learners to reflect on how the new skill relates to what they already know. Effective instruction provides an opportunity for learners to explain their new skill to others and to defend what they know when it is challenged. Reflection, discussion, and defense of new ideas help learners integrate the new skill in a way that its retention and future application is more certain. The integration principle states:

> *Learning is promoted when learners reflect on, discuss, and defend their newly acquired knowledge and skill.*

Peer-Collaboration and Peer-Critique I am often asked, "Where is the motivation principle?" These are principles about design, about the instruction to be presented to learners. Motivation is a state of the learner. Carefully designed instruction should result in motivation, which for this book is labeled *engaging*. Motivation is often misunderstood. While flashy media and high production quality may grab attention, these are not the factors that result in motivation. Motivation is an outcome of learning. People love to learn.

The most motivating of all events is when people realize that they can solve a problem or perform a task that they couldn't do before. Learning is the most motivating of all activities when learners can observe their progress. Whenever learners acquire a new skill, the first desire is to show another person their newly acquired ability. One of the main attractions of computer games is the increasing skill level that is apparent to the player. Effective instruction must provide an opportunity for learners to demonstrate their newly acquired skills. The key exclamation is, "Watch me! See what I can do!"

Carefully structured peer-collaboration and peer-critique require learners to share what they have learned—to go public with their work. Rather than merely turning in their problem solutions or task performance to the instructor, effective instruction requires learners to share their work with their classmates. The first level of sharing might be with a collaboration team whose members work together to solve a problem or do a task. If appropriately structured, this collaboration requires reflection and discussion of a learner's newly acquired knowledge and skill. The second level of sharing is for selected classmates to critique their work. Appropriately structured peer-critique requires learners to defend their newly acquired skill and its application. Peer-collaboration and peer-critique are most effective when learners are proud of their work and want to show off their newly acquired skills. The purpose of e^3 instruction is to promote this skill acquisition. The Peer-Collaboration and Peer-Critique corollary states:

> *Learning is promoted when learners integrate their new knowledge into their everyday lives by being required to reflect on, discuss, or defend their new knowledge or skill via peer-collaboration and peer-critique.*

The integration principle is elaborated on in Chapter 8.

EVALUATING COMPLEX PROBLEM SOLVING

The principles identified in this book are believed to facilitate learning in most instructional situations. However, the increased learning that results from these First Principles of Instruction will probably not be detected by assessment techniques that require only recall of information. The performance enhancements promoted by these principles will be most evident in performance on complex problems. Complex problems require learners to produce an artifact or develop a solution. Such problems require a variety of different kinds of knowledge and skill all brought together in an interrelated way. Complex problems allow for many levels of performance. At first the learner may only be able to complete simple versions of the problem. As skill increases, the learner can complete more and more complex versions of the problem. In solving problems, early solutions may be unsophisticated and may consider only a portion of the factors involved. As the learner gains skill, the solutions become more elegant, more complex, and take into consideration more and more factors. Measurement of problem performance must reflect this gradual acquisition of skill (see Bunderson, 2006).

What are some possible procedures for designing scaled measurement of performance level in complex problems? The following paragraphs suggest a few possibilities.

1. Identify a progression of problems, arranged so that the number or complexity of activities required for completion increases incrementally. For each problem in the progression, establish a checklist for acceptable performance. The learner completes the problems in succession until he or she is unable to complete a problem. Appropriate scoring measures the highest level in the progression of problems at which the student completed the whole problem in an acceptable manner.
2. Learners are given a problem with various levels of coaching available. When the learner is unable to proceed, the first level of coaching is provided. If the learner still has difficulty, the second level of coaching is provided, and so forth until the learner is able to complete the problem. The score is an inverse of the amount of successively more elaborate coaching required for the student to solve the problem or complete the problem. In this case it is not a progression of problems that is scaled but the amount of help required within a problem.
3. It may be possible to use a single nested complex problem to assess increasing levels of performance. This is similar to the problem progression previously described, but in this situation solving the problem or completing the problem can proceed incrementally. Each stage toward the complete solution requires an incremental increase in expertise. A student is scored on the number of stages completed toward the problem solution.

DEMONSTRATION COURSE—FIRST AID

In this section, I'll review a course—created by Australian First Aid—that incorporates First Principles of Instruction. While this course is a good example, it could still be improved. The objective is stated as follows: "The aims of this course are to provide you with the confidence and skills to treat the injured in a range of emergency situations." The course consists of four introductory lessons: (1) Aims of First Aid, (2) Accident Prevention, (3) First Aid Essentials, and (4) The First Aid

Kit; twenty-nine tutorials that provide instruction in specific first aid procedures; two guided case studies demonstrating first aid in real-world emergency situations; twenty practice case studies that require learners to demonstrate first aid skills in simulated real-world emergency situations; ten test case studies; and four supplementary test case studies.

Learners must complete each of the four lessons before they can begin the practice case studies. The guided case studies teach learners how to navigate the simulations in the case studies. The tutorials cover the skills needed for the case studies. Before each case study, learners are given a list of the tutorials that they should complete before undertaking the case study. Learners can complete the tutorials and practice case studies in any order. Learners must complete all twenty of the practice case studies before they can begin the test case studies.

This section describes a few selected segments of this course to illustrate the First Principles of Instruction that make this an example of e^3 instruction. The following paragraphs describe and illustrate an opening simulation, a lesson on accident prevention, a guided case study, a tutorial on the DRABC procedure, a tutorial on facial injuries, and an application case study on bleeding noses. This demonstration is designed to help you start to apply First Principles of Instruction. Each segment is described and then followed by some questions to encourage you to think about how First Principles were applied in the segment. You will learn more if you try to answer these questions before reading my comments at the end of each section.

Opening Simulation

After registration, the course begins with a brief interactive scenario, the design for which is presented in Figure 2-2. The figure shows the learner's actions and the systems responses to it. What is the purpose of this opening scenario? Does it help learners recall emergency situations from their own experience where first aid was needed? Does it provide a reason why learners may want to take the course? Does it help motivate learners to acquire the skills taught in the course?

Did you remember the cycle of learning that starts with activation? What prior experience is it likely that learners have that is relevant to this course? Does the opening scenario help them recall this relevant experience? What is a probable mental model that a learner taking this course might already have? Does this simulation help the learner activate this mental model?

FIGURE 2-2 Opening Interactive Scenario—Activation

First Aid Introduction			
#	Learner Action	System Response	
1	Click on Next button after registration.	**Audio:** I'm a qualified first aider but I need your help. Could you find a phone box and call for an ambulance. This woman is unconscious, but she is breathing. She needs medical help urgently.	

(continued)

FIGURE 2-2 *Continued*

2	Click the Forward arrow	**Text** [overlays photo]: Will you need to place coins or a phone card in the public telephone? **Buttons:** YES NO	**Graphic:** Close-up photograph of a public phone in a phone booth.
3	Click NO	**Audio:** Call for help by clicking on the buttons on the telephone to call the correct number.	
4	Click any numbers other than 000	**Text:** Incorrect. You have dialed xxx. In Australia, you must dial 000 to get emergency service. Please dial 000.	
5	Click numbers on phone 000	**Audio:** Which emergency service do you require?	**Buttons:** Fire Brigade Ambulance Police
6	Click button Ambulance	**Audio:** Tone. Ambulance service. Don't hang up until I tell you! What is your location with nearest cross-street?	**Graphic:** Information card displayed near the telephone, which includes the address, phone number, and other information. **Buttons:** Three choices for the address and cross-street
7	Click button Martin Place near Elizabeth Street	**Audio:** How many casualties are involved?	**Buttons:** One Two Three
8	Click button One	**Audio:** What type of injuries?	**Buttons:** Possible heart attack Collapsed in street Unconscious but breathing
9	Click button Unconscious but breathing	**Audio:** Are any other emergency services required?	**Buttons:** YES NO
10	Click button NO	**Audio:** What is the number of the phone you are calling from?	**Buttons:** 02 309 019P2 02 309 0192 02 309 091P2
11	Click button 02 309 019P2	**Audio:** An ambulance is on its way. You may hang up now. Siren sounds.	
12	**Narrator Audio:** The importance of the part you have just played in this simulated first aid emergency should never be underestimated. But the reality is that there will always be more bystanders than effective first aiders. Completion of this exciting CD-ROM package accompanied by qualified trainers during a special one-day practical course conducted by St. John's Ambulance will equip you with skills and knowledge to provide life-saving first aid to the injured or acutely ill. First aid is one of the most important of all life skills. Acute illness or sudden injury has no respect for age or status, place, or time, and many of us will be called upon to deal with emergencies among our family, friends, or even total strangers.		

My comments: Most learners have probably witnessed an accident where first aid was required. The opening scenario presents a somewhat typical situation with the hope that it will help learners recall similar situations that they may have witnessed. Many learners will already have at least a minimal idea of what to do in case of an accident. The opening scenario may help them activate this mental model, and then the steps illustrated in the scenario can help them compare their own mental models with the steps taken in the scenario. This scenario illustrates an appropriate activation instructional event.

Lesson 2—Accident Prevention

Figure 2-3 illustrates the design of Lesson 2—Accident Prevention. The figure shows the learner's actions and the system's responses to it. This lesson stresses the prevention of accidents by presenting a number of situations and asking learners to identify the potentially dangerous conditions that these situations present. Is this lesson teaching about potential accidents or merely focusing learners' attention on dangers that may exist around them? Is this lesson helping learners recall situations from their own experience? Is this lesson helping students activate those mental models that provide context for the first skills to be taught?

FIGURE 2-3 Lesson 2—Accident Prevention—Activation

First Aid Lesson 2—Accident Prevention			
#	Learner Reaction	System Response	Graphic
1	Click on Lesson 2 on main menu.	**Audio:** Please click on items that represent a potential danger.	
2	Learner clicks on a potential danger in the photograph.	[Similar interaction for each of the potential dangers. If learners do not find them all, a message reminds them that there are more dangers.]	**Text:** Sharp knives lying around loose are a temptation for children and a potential hazard for adults. Make sure that they are kept in a drawer or purpose-made holder.
3	[Similar to above]	[Similar to above]	**Graphic:** Shop with dangerous items lying around.
4	[Similar to above]	[Similar to above]	**Graphic:** Pool area with dangerous situations present.

Australian First Aid, Version 1.5, Copyright 1995, St. John Ambulance Australia. Used with permission.

My comments: The accident prevention lesson illustrates situations that are likely to be similar to those in the learners' own homes. The lesson seems to have two goals: increase the learners' awareness of potential dangerous situations and also activate learners' previous experience with potentially dangerous situations.

This activation of their own mental models will be especially relevant when they study the danger step of the DRABC tutorial.

Guided Case Study

The case studies are designed as a type of simulation known as microworlds, which place learners in a simulated real-world situation and ask them to make appropriate first aid decisions in response to the emergency presented. The format is a *Simon-says* type of demonstration; the instruction indicates the step that is next and directs learners to take that step. If learners perform some other action, the instruction indicates that the step was incorrect and again directs learners on which step to take.

Figure 2-4 illustrates the interface for the guided and application case studies. A menu on the right side of the screen represents the first aid actions that learners can take. Clicking a button on this menu causes the system to display a pop-up list of specific actions learners can select. For example, clicking the button *Position Casualty* causes the system to display a pop-up with the following list of actions: *lie in stable side position, lie in alternate side position, lie flat on back, sit down, sit (head between legs), bend over the back of a chair.* In the guided case study, only the button that is appropriate is active; in the application case studies, all of the buttons are active. Figure 2-5 presents the design of the first guided case study.

FIGURE 2-4 Case Study Simulation Interface

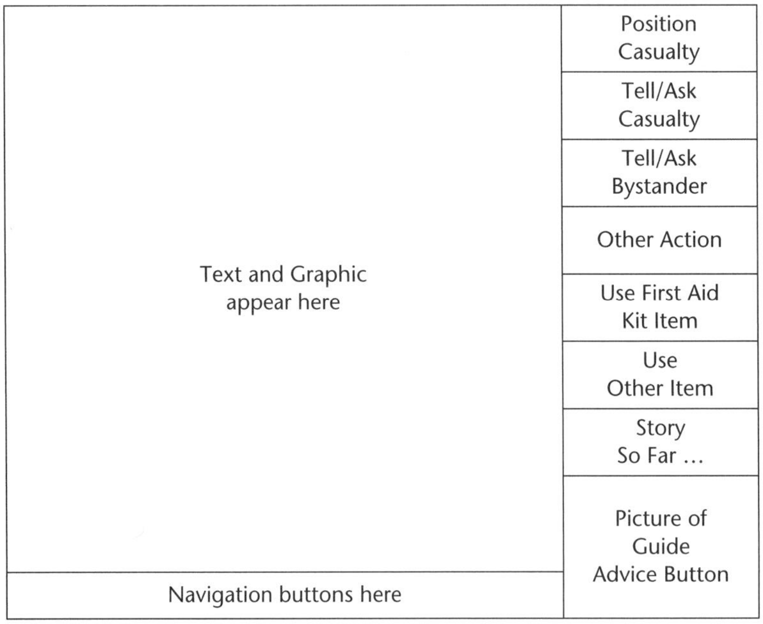

FIGURE 2-5 Guided Case Study—Demonstrate Problem

First Aid Case Study Demonstration			
#	Learner Action	System Response	Graphic
1	Select guided case study from the menu.	**Audio:** At the beginning of each case study, you will be given a list of the tutorials that cover the material you need to know to complete the case study. It is a good idea to view the tutorials before beginning the case study. You can view the tutorials at any time by clicking the Tutor button at the bottom of the screen and then selecting the tutorial you want to view.	**Text:** This case study deals with materials covered in the following tutorials: • DRABC action plan • Side position • EAR • CPR
2	Click Next.	**Audio:** You are working in your office when you hear one of your colleagues call out and then collapse. There is one other person around and you have a first aid kit and a telephone available. The first thing you must do is check to see whether there is any danger to yourself, to anyone else nearby, or to the casualty. Click on the Other Action button, then select Check for danger.	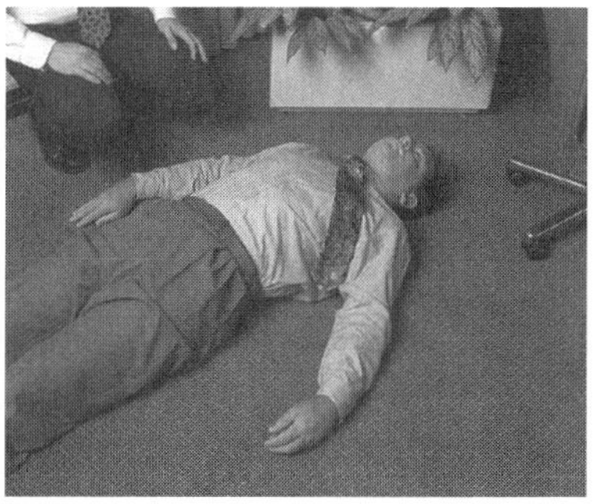
3	Click button. Other Action . . . check for danger	**Audio:** When you think it is safe to assist the casualty, you must then check to see whether the person is conscious. Click on either the Tell/Ask Casualty or Other Action button and select a way to check for a response.	**Text** [overlays graphic]: You do not see anything that could be dangerous to yourself, to others, or to the casualty. Select the next step.
4	Click button. Other Action . . . gently shake casualty	**Audio:** The casualty did not respond, so you must move him into the correct position for an unconscious person. Click on the Position Casualty button, then select a position from the list.	**Text** [overlays graphic]: You gently shake the casualty, but he does not respond. Select the next step.
5	Click button. Position Casualty . . . stable side position	**Audio:** The next step of the DRABC action plan is to clear and open the casualty's airways. However, before doing this, you should put on a pair of gloves from the first aid kit. Check on the Use First Aid Kit Item, then select gloves from the list.	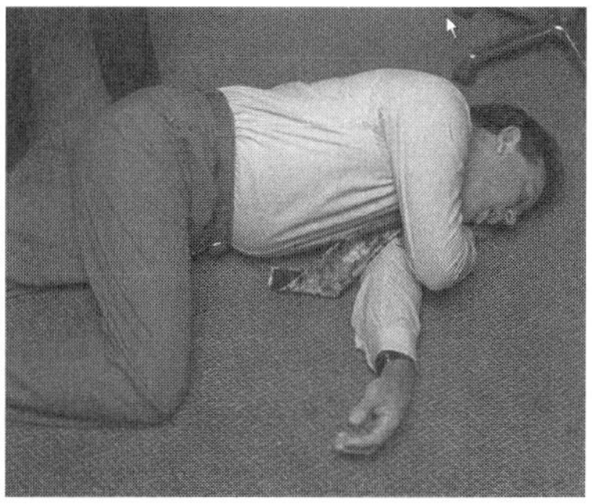 **Text** [overlays graphic]: Correct. You roll the casualty into a stable side position. Select the next step.

(continued)

FIGURE 2-5 *Continued*

6	The guided case study continues by having learners engage in additional required first aid actions, each followed by text and an audio message. When appropriate, the graphic is changed to reflect the situation. * * *		
7	After the last step is completed:	**Audio:** You check the casualty's pulse and breathing after one minute, then every two minutes. A siren is heard, indicating the arrival of the ambulance. When the ambulance arrives, the ambulance officers take over the resuscitation. At this point, you should wash your hands thoroughly with soap and water.	**Summary** * Check for danger and response. * Roll casualty into side position, clear and open airway, and check for breathing. * Roll casualty onto back, and give five full breaths in ten seconds. * Check circulation, and have someone telephone for medical aid. * Begin CPR, and continue until ambulance arrives.

What are the problems that this course will teach learners to solve? Does this case study demonstration show learners an example of this type of problem? Does this demonstration teach by showing rather than merely telling? This demonstration shows two things: first, it shows the first aid actions to take when someone collapses (see the summary); second, it shows how to use the navigation commands of the simulation interface. Were the graphics used relevant? Did they implement an instructional event rather than merely providing an irrelevant graphic?

My comments: The designers chose a problem-centered approach by designing a series of simulations representing potential real-world first aid situations. They then demonstrated an example of one of these situations while at the same time helping learners learn to use the simulation interface. Learners are both told and shown what to do in this real-world first aid situation. The photographs used in the instructional sequence were not superfluous pictures but actually carried instructional information. For example, the illustration of the stable side position shows how the patient should appear when positioned in this way. Audio directions guided learners not only in the steps to take next but also in how to execute these steps using the buttons of the simulation interface.

DRABC and Facial Injury Tutorials

The next place learners go in the course is to the application case studies. Once there, they might select a case for a bleeding nose from the main menu. When advised to complete tutorials first, learners go to the tutorials, whose design is presented in Figure 2-6. As you review the tutorials, consider how the designers apply some of the principles of e^3 learning. Do the two tutorials implement the demonstration principle? Are learners shown what to do rather than merely being told the action to take? Do the demonstrations include relevant graphics that actually carry part of the instructional load? Could this demonstration be improved to more adequately teach the skill being taught? How?

FIGURE 2-6 Tutorials—DRABC and Facial Injuries—Demonstration Application for Component Skills

<table>
<tr><th colspan="4">First Aid DRABC and Facial Injuries Tutorials</th></tr>
<tr><th>#</th><th>Learner Action</th><th colspan="2">System Response</th></tr>
<tr><td>1</td><td>Select Bleeding Nose from the practice case study menu.</td><td colspan="2">Text: You should complete the following tutorials before undertaking this case study:
• DRABC Action Plan
• Facial Injuries</td></tr>
<tr><td>2</td><td colspan="3">[The learner decides to complete the tutorials before completing the practice case study.]</td></tr>
<tr><td colspan="4">DRABC Tutorial</td></tr>
<tr><td>3</td><td>Click on DRABC Action Plan from tutorials menu.</td><td colspan="2">Text: DRABC Action Plan Tutorial
This tutorial covers the following topic areas:
• Introduction to the principles of DRABC
• The DRABC Procedure</td></tr>
<tr><td>4</td><td>Click Next.</td><td colspan="2">Text: From time to time, you may hear people say that they have done a first aid course but are not sure they remember what to do. This is not unusual, because some people don't get much opportunity to practice, and because first aid covers so many different situations and possibilities.
There is, however, a simple plan of action that provides an easy to remember, five-step, "must do" procedure known as the DRABC Action Plan.</td></tr>
<tr><td>5</td><td>Click Next.</td><td colspan="2">Text: The initials DRABC stand for (items in list appear one by one) Danger, Response, Airway, Breathing, Circulation</td></tr>
<tr><td>6</td><td>Click Next.</td><td colspan="2">Text: [The list moves to the left of the screen and each item is highlighted in turn.] Place the cursor over the title highlighted in blue and click the mouse button.</td></tr>
<tr><td>7</td><td>Click on Danger.</td><td colspan="2">Text: [Color of the word Danger changes to red.] As soon as you become aware that a first aid situation exists and before you do anything, you must immediately look at the whole scene to see whether there is any danger: to yourself, to any bystanders, or to the casualty.</td></tr>
<tr><td>8</td><td>Click Next.</td><td colspan="2">Text: Always check for danger . . .
To yourself—You can be of no help to anyone if you become a casualty yourself.
To any bystanders—Your task will become much more difficult if the people watching become casualties as well.
To the casualty—There is no point working on an injury if the casualty is still at risk from passing cars or falling rocks, etc.</td></tr>
<tr><td>9</td><td>Click Next.</td><td>Graphic: Photograph of a person lying on the floor of what looks like a shop. There is an electric drill lying next to the person, still plugged into an electrical outlet. On the workbench above the person is an object hanging partially off the workbench.</td><td>Text [next to the graphic]: You hear someone cry out and then a thump, so you go to see what has happened. You see a person lying unmoving on the floor, and you can smell hot electrical wiring.
Click on anything you think might be dangerous to yourself, to other people, or to the casualty.</td></tr>
</table>

(continued)

FIGURE 2-6 *Continued*

10	Click on electric drill in photograph.	**Graphic:** [same as previous]. **Text:** Correct. The casualty may have suffered an electric shock from the power drill, so before approaching him you should make sure the switch is off and the plug is disconnected.
11	Click Next.	**Graphic:** [same as previous] **Text:** You turn off the power and move the drill away from the casualty. However, there is something else that could be dangerous that should be removed.
12	Click on object on the workbench.	**Graphic:** [same as previous] **Text:** Well done. Very often people are so intent on what is happening on the ground that they miss the hazards above them. Remember, **always look up**.
13	Click Next.	**Graphic:** [same as previous] **Text:** You remove the overhead hazard. It will now be safe for you to approach the casualty and check for a response.
14	A similar presentation is used for the other four terms of the DRABC Action Plan: response, airway, breathing, circulation. After the learner has completed the DRABC tutorial, he or she goes to the tutorial on facial injuries.	
Facial Injuries Tutorial		
15	Click on Facial Injuries	**Text:** Facial injuries are those involving the facial features listed below: • The eye • The ear • The nose • The jaw • The teeth Click on a facial feature.
16	Click on the nose from tutorials listed on the main menu.	**Text:** Injuries to the Nose The three most common injuries to the nose are: Objects in the nose [explanation here omitted] Bleeding nose Some people, particularly children, have a tendency for their noses to bleed frequently and for no apparent reason. Others will receive bleeding noses from blows in fights or sports. Broken nose [explanation here omitted]
17	Click on Bleeding Nose Click Next	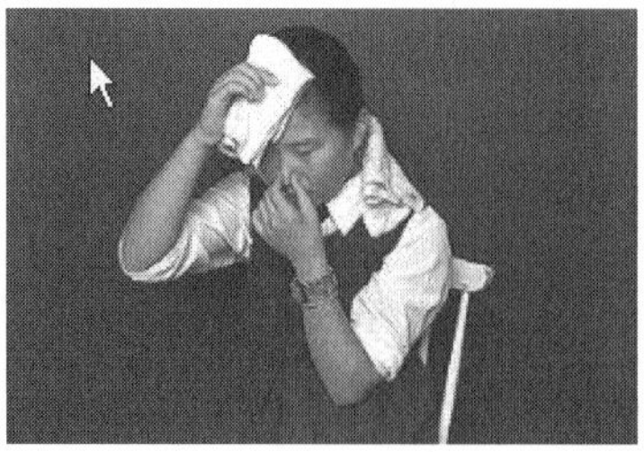 **Text:** A bleeding nose is one of the most common first aid problems and yet is one most often incorrectly managed. The correct procedure is for the casualty to: • Pinch the soft part of the nose and breathe through the mouth. • Tilt head slightly forward. It also helps to apply cold, wet towels or an ice pack to the back of the casualty's neck and forehead in order to reduce circulation in surface blood vessels.

Australian First Aid, Version 1.5, Copyright 1995, St. John Ambulance Australia. Used with permission.

Do the two tutorials implement the application principle? Are learners given the opportunity to apply the skill that they were just taught? Which tutorial lacks adequate application? What could be done to provide more adequate application for this tutorial? Do the tutorials provide intrinsic feedback? Intrinsic feedback allows learners to see the consequences of their actions. Could learners see the consequences of their actions in the application that is provided by these tutorials? Do the tutorials provide corrective feedback? Corrective feedback informs learners of the quality of their performance and shows them how they did or should have performed the procedure. Is there corrective feedback provided for these tutorials? How could more effective corrective feedback be employed? Is there any coaching available for the skills being taught? How could more effective coaching be included in these tutorials?

My Comments: In Figure 2-6, Rows 3 through 5 of the DRABC tutorial tell the five preliminary steps to take in any first aid situation. In Rows 7 and 8, the instruction elaborates the danger step. In Rows 9 through 13, there is then a brief application of the step. There is a *Tell* and a *Do* instructional event, but the instruction could be improved if there were also a *Show* instructional event including appropriate guidance. There are so many different ways that there may be danger in a given accident situation. Seeing this variety of situations will help learners recognize such dangers in the cases they will complete as part of this course and in the situations they are likely to encounter in the real world. The application does include coaching to be sure that the learner has identified all of the potential danger in the situation. There is also corrective feedback for the learner's responses.

The nosebleed tutorial also includes *Tell* and *Show*, but no *Do* is included. The graphic does illustrate the step described in the information. But there is very little additional guidance. The demonstration could be improved by illustrating the steps in sequence of graphics rather than with a single picture. Because there is no application for this component skill, there is also no feedback nor coaching. Some possible application exercises might include a series of pictures showing various ways to pinch the nose and asking which the best procedure is. Another application might show the victim in various positions, including lying down, sitting with head back, sitting with head between the knees, and so forth. Learners would then be asked to rank the pictures from the best to the least-best position. Corrective feedback could then be provided, explaining the consequence on the nosebleed for each of the positions.

Practice Case Studies

The practice case study in the course consists of the presentation of a variety of specific emergency situations. There are twenty individual application case studies, including ones on scalded arms, sprained ankles, an insect in the ear, drowning infants, and splinters in eye.

Each of these case studies is a simulation that places learners in a simulated real-world situation and asks them to respond to the emergency situations by making the appropriate decisions regarding first aid. The format of the cases is a semi-open simulation that presents learners with several alternative actions on any given screen. As in the guided case studies, a menu appears at the right of the screen presenting the actions to be taken. Each of the buttons causes the system to display a pop-up with a list of actions that learners can select. Unlike the guided case studies, in the practice case studies, all of the buttons are active and learners can take any of the actions listed. The feedback provided is appropriate for the action taken. Often this feedback includes advice about what learners should have done or may want to do next. Usually, the appropriate actions can be taken in any order. Figure 2-7 shows the interaction in the practice case study about handling an emergency with a bleeding nose. This illustration shows only one of many possible routes through this simulation.

FIGURE 2-7 Case Study—Bleeding Nose—Problem Application

First Aid Interactive Case—Bloody Nose	
Learner Action	**System Response**
[After completing the tutorials, the learner goes back to the exercise case study.]	
Select Bleeding Nose from the course menu.	**Text:** You should complete the following tutorials before undertaking this case study: Facial Injuries Communicable Diseases
Click Next button	**Audio:** You are walking near a high school when you see a teenage boy who looks as if he has been in a fight. There is no one else nearby and no telephone, but you have a small first aid kit with you. Select your first action.
[The learner is unsure of how to start interacting with the tutorial, so he clicks on the Expert Advice button.]	
Click on Expert Advice	**Audio:** The first thing you must do is check to see if there is any danger to yourself, to others nearby, or to the casualty. Click the Other Action button and then click Check for Danger.
Click button Other Action—check for danger.	**Text:** You do not see anything that could be dangerous to yourself, to others, or to the casualty. Select your next step.
Click Position Casualty button	**Text:** Yes, the casualty should sit with his head slightly forward.
Click on Tell/Ask Casualty . . . To apply pressure to his nose.	**Text:** He asks you what part of his nose he should hold. Click on the part of the casualty's nose to which he should apply pressure.
Click on the soft part of the boy's nose in the picture.	**Text:** Correct, the casualty should pinch the soft part of his nose.
Click button Tell/Ask Casualty. . . Not to blow his nose.	**Text:** Correct. You tell casualty that he should not blow his nose. Select your next step.

FIGURE 2-7 *Continued*

Click button Tell/Ask Casualty . . . To breathe through his mouth.	**Text:** Correct. You tell casualty to breathe through his mouth rather than his nose. Select your next step.
[Note that there are many different paths through the simulation, many of which are alternate correct paths.]	
Click button Other Action . . . Wait to see if the bleeding stops.	**Text:** You can do more to try and control the bleeding before waiting to see if it stops. Try again. Select your next step.
Click button Other Action . . . Look closely at casualty's face	**Text:** The casualty's nose is bleeding, but it is not swollen or bruised. A bruise is forming around his eye, but the eye itself does not look as if it is damaged. Select your next step.
Click button Use Other Item . . . Water	**Text:** Question. What do you want to use water for? Wash blood off casualty Wash your hands Dampen towel Click on your answer.
Click . . . Wash your hands	**Text:** Correct. When possible, you should wash your hands before and after managing a casualty. Select your next step.
Click button Use Other Item . . . Towel	**Text:** Yes. You could place a cold wet towel on the back of the casualty's neck to try to control the bleeding nose. Select your next step.
Click button Other Action . . . Take casualty to doctor.	**Text:** Medical aid may not be necessary. It may be possible for you to control the bleeding nose simply by using first aid. Try again. Select your next step.
Click button Other Action . . . Wait to see if bleeding stops.	**Text:** Wait. You have not treated the bruised eye. What should you do to manage this injury? Select your next step.
Click button Use First Aid Kit Item . . . Ice pack.	**Text:** Correct. You get an ice pack and wrap it in a cloth. For example, you could wrap it in a triangular bandage. Click and drag the ice pack to the area where you would use it.
Click and drag ice pack to the black eye.	**Text:** Correct. The casualty must hold the ice pack against his forehead and over the bruise near his eye. It should stay for about 20 minutes. Select your next step.
Click button Other Action . . . Wait to see if bleeding stops.	**Text:** Question. After a minute the casualty tells you he thinks the bleeding has stopped. Should he release the pressure from his nose? YES NO Click your answer.

(continued)

FIGURE 2-7 *Continued*

Click NO	**Audio:** Tell casualty that if his nose starts bleeding again after he lets go to apply pressure for another 10 minutes. If it starts again he should see a doctor. He should also apply ice to the bruise for 20 minutes every 2 hours for 24 hours. Remember to wash your hands after you have completed your first aid.
Click Next	**Text:** Summary Check for danger. Have casualty sit with head slightly forward, applying pressure on the soft part of his nostrils. He should not blow his nose. Place a cold, wet towel or ice pack wrapped in a cloth on back of casualty's neck. Apply an ice pack (wrapped in cloth) to the bruised area around the casualty's eye.

Does this case study require learners to solve a problem? Do the case studies represent a progression of problems? What are some of the component skills required for the solution of this problem? Which of these component skills are likely to be required for the other cases in the course? How is coaching provided? How could intrinsic feedback be provided? How is corrective feedback provided?

My Comments: In the tutorials recommended for the nosebleed case study, learners should have learned how to treat a nosebleed and other facial injuries. The case study allowed them to apply their knowledge in a simulated real-world situation. The learner in this example did not perform perfectly, but the system provided intrinsic feedback when appropriate. The feedback shows learners what happens as a result of certain actions. When appropriate, the instruction provides corrective feedback by showing or having learners take the correct action. In this course, the level of coaching remains constant across the case studies because learners are allowed to complete these case studies in any order. A more effective coaching strategy might be to suggest a progression of cases from simple to more complex and then decrease the amount of coaching with each subsequent case study.

As a course, first aid is relatively unique. Rather than being topic-centered, teaching one topic after another, it consists of a large set of first aid problems to be solved. This set of problems does not follow an easy-to-hard progression as suggested by First Principles, but it does provide a rich variety of practice situations for learners. Rather than teaching each of the component skills in turn, as in a typical topic-centered course, there is a large set of tutorials teaching the component skill needed to solve the first aid problems contained in the cases. Learners are advised to study the relevant tutorials before undertaking a given application problem or case. Although the course is problem-centered, it does use more conventional tutorial instruction to teach the component skills just in time as they are needed for a given problem.

During the course, learners' performance is recorded on a disk to be sent to St. John's, where learners are registered for the course. The CD-ROM course is followed up by a day-long, on-site practicum, during which learners have an opportunity to engage in a series of role-playing case studies treating various types of injuries. Upon completion of both the CD-ROM course and the practicum experience, learners are certified in first aid.

Knowing that at the end of their study they will have to demonstrate their skill in first aid through an all-day on-site experience adds significant motivation to learners to acquire the skills being taught. When learners know that they will be required to actually demonstrate their newly acquired skills, the instruction becomes more important to them. As a result, learners are more likely to be actively engaged in the learning. This practicum implements the Integration Principle.

Summary for First Aid Demonstration Course

While it could be improved, the first aid course does implement all of the First Principles of Instruction. The activation principle is implemented via the opening scenario and Lesson 2, which helps learners recall previous experience that can serve as a mental model on which the remainder of the course can be built. The problem-centered principle is implemented by the organization of the course around a series of cases, including demonstration cases, application cases, and test cases used to certify a learner's skill. The component skills required for the solution of these problems is implemented by a series of tutorials. Learners are directed to study these component skills just as they are needed for a given problem case. The demonstration principle is implemented at the course level by describing and illustrating the first aid procedures required for a couple of cases that are carefully guided to help learners see how such simulated problems can be solved. The demonstration principle is implemented at the component skill or tutorial level by telling and showing learners the procedures they will need to know how to do to solve the problems. The application principle is implemented at the course level by providing learners with a wide variety of simulated first aid problems to solve. These problem cases include coaching and both intrinsic and corrective feedback. The application principle is implemented at the component skill level within the tutorials. Not all of the tutorials include appropriate application, but many do. Where this application of individual skills is provided, there is usually appropriate coaching and feedback as well. The integration principle was implemented by a live experience at the end of the course where learners were required to apply the skills they have acquired in an all-day, live emergency mock-up experience with coaches and instructors present to evaluate their performance.

SUMMARY

This chapter is the foundation for the remainder of this book. The remainder of the book further elaborates each of the principles, demonstrates the application of these principles in a wide variety of different instructional examples, and provides tools for critiquing existing instruction and for designing new instruction. At this point you have been introduced to these principles, but as you proceed through the remaining chapters your understanding and ability to apply these principles to identifying e^3 instruction and designing e^3 instruction will be significantly increased. First Principles of Instruction are deceptively simple. In response to my workshops and talks, I'm sometimes told, "Oh good, I'm already doing these things." However, after a little more intensive study of the application of these principles, these students usually come to the realization, "Oh, I see how my instruction could be much more effective, efficient, and engaging." I hope you will have the same insight as a result of your study of this material.

PRINCIPLES AND PRESCRIPTIONS

- **Demonstration:** Learning is promoted when learners observe a demonstration of the knowledge and skill to be learned.
  - **Consistent:** Learning is promoted when learners observe a demonstration of the skills to be learned that is consistent with the type of content being taught.
  - **Guidance:** Learning from demonstrations is enhanced when learners are guided to relate general information or an organizing structure to specific instances.
  - **Multimedia:** Learning is promoted when multimedia implements prescribed instructional events and functions.
- **Application:** Learning is promoted when learners apply their newly acquired knowledge and skill.
  - **Consistent:** Learning is promoted when learners engage in application of their newly acquired knowledge and skill that is consistent with the type of content being taught.
  - **Feedback:** Learning from an application is effective only when learners receive intrinsic or corrective feedback.
  - **Coaching:** Learning from an application is enhanced when learners are coached and when this coaching is gradually withdrawn for each subsequent problem.
- **Problem-Centered:** Learning is promoted when learners acquire knowledge and skill in the context of real-world problems or tasks.
  - **Problem-Centered:** Learning is promoted when learners engage in a problem-centered instructional strategy in which component skills are taught in the context of a simple-to-complex progression of whole real-world problems.
- **Activation:** Learning is promoted when learners activate a mental model of their prior knowledge and skill as a foundation for new skills.
  - **Structure:** Learning is promoted when learners recall or acquire a framework or structure for organizing the new knowledge, when the structure is the basis for guidance during demonstration, is the basis for coaching during application, and is the basis for reflection during integration.
- **Integration:** Learning is promoted when learners reflect on, discuss, and defend their newly acquired knowledge and skill.
  - **Peer-Collaboration and Peer-Critique:** Learning is promoted when learners integrate their new knowledge into their everyday lives by being required to reflect on, discuss, or defend their new knowledge or skill via peer-collaboration and peer-critique.

APPLICATION

Select a course in which you are or have been a student. Or select a course that you are teaching. Examine the course to see whether it implements the First Principles of Instruction as they have been described and illustrated in this chapter. What level of instructional strategy is used in this course? How could this course be improved to move to a higher level of instructional strategy? Keep your description of the course and your analysis so that as you gain more skill in the application of First Principles of Instruction from your study of this book you can reexamine your analysis.

TO LEARN MORE

First Principles of Instruction were introduced and elaborated in the following papers. The material in this book updates the presentation from these original sources. See my website at www.mdavidmerrill.com for copies of these papers and additional information on First Principles of Instruction.

Merrill, M. D. (2002a). First principles of instruction. *Educational Technology Research and Development*, 50(3), 43–59.

Merrill, M. D. (2006). Levels of instructional strategy. *Educational Technology*, 46(4), 5–10.

Merrill, M. D. (2007a). First principles of instruction: a synthesis. In R. A. Reiser & J. V. Dempsey (Eds.), *Trends and issues in instructional design and technology* (2nd ed.) (Vol. 2, pp. 62–71). Upper Saddle River, NJ: Merrill/Prentice Hall.

Merrill, M. D. (2009b). First principles of instruction. In C. M. Reigeluth & A. Carr (Eds.), *Instructional design theories and models: Building a common knowledge base* (Vol. 3). New York: Routledge/Taylor and Francis Group.

COMING NEXT

Chapter 2 described First Principles of Instruction that form the foundation for the rest of this book. The next chapter, Chapter 3, begins to elaborate these principles by introducing a vocabulary that enables you, as an instructional designer, to more precisely describe the subject-matter content to be learned. Chapter 3 illustrates the five types of component skill that are involved in almost every problem. The chapter will also illustrate the content elements required to teach each of these types of component skill.

CHAPTER 3

INSTRUCTIONAL CONTENT

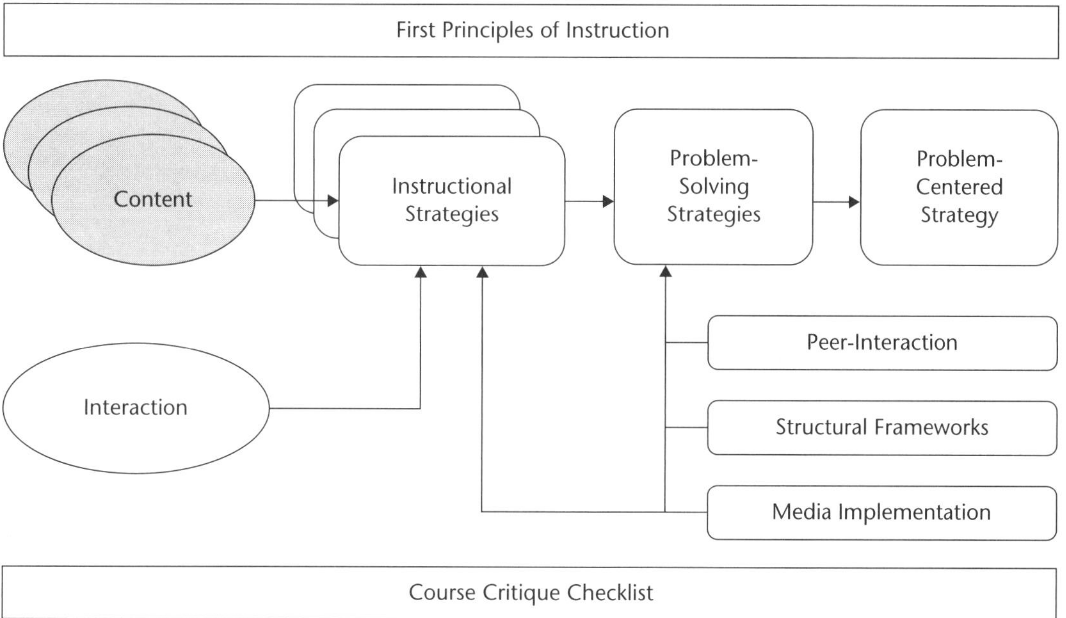

Quick Look

A primary component of an instructional strategy is the content to be taught. This chapter introduces five different types of skill required to solve problems. Each of these skills is composed of different content elements. This chapter describes and demonstrates these different types of skill and the content elements required for each. It answers the following questions: How can we, as instructional designers, describe different kinds of subject-matter content in a way that will enable us to carefully define instructional strategies? Why do we need a technical vocabulary to describe subject-matter content? What are the different types of skill required to solve a problem? What are the content elements required for each type of skill?

Key Words

Subject-Matter Content: what is taught; component skills from some area of interest.
Component Skill: a combination of knowledge and skill required to solve a complex problem or do a complex task.
Content Element: individual parts of subject-matter content that are involved in instructional events.

Instructional Event: the combination of an instructional mode with a content element.
Instructional Interaction: the action component of an instructional event, including *Tell, Ask, Show,* and *Do.*
Information-About: a component skill that requires learners to remember content associated with a specific entity, activity, or process.
Part-of: a component skill that requires learners to locate, name, or describe a piece of some object, event, or process.
Kind-of: a component skill that requires learners to identify instances of a class of objects, events, or processes that are characterized by a set of common properties; also called a concept.
How-to: a component skill that requires learners to perform a sequence of steps to bring about some consequence; also called a procedure.
What-Happens: a component skill that requires learners to predict a consequence from a set of conditions or to find inadequate or missing conditions for an unexpected consequence.

INTRODUCTION

Precision in communication depends on an agreed-upon vocabulary that is as unambiguous as possible. This chapter first explains why we need a precise vocabulary. It then identifies and provides labels for five types of skill that are required to solve problems. For each of these skills, this chapter identifies and labels the content elements that are important to identify if we are to be able to prescribe instructional strategies for acquiring the skill.

WHY DO WE NEED A TECHNICAL VOCABULARY?

Instruction consists of two major components: what to teach, or subject-matter content, and how to teach, or instructional strategies. This chapter is about subject-matter content. Not all subject-matter content is the same. Of course you are familiar with different subject-matter content areas like science, humanities, and music, but these categories are not very useful if we, as instructional designers, want to be able to critique instruction in a wide variety of areas. We need a way to describe content that applies to all different subject-matter areas. We need a vocabulary that will allow us to describe the details of the content of the instruction we wish to critique or design. This chapter provides a vocabulary that we can use to describe different types of skill that are components of all complex problems or tasks. This chapter describes and illustrates the content and content elements for five different types of component skill.

In this chapter we introduce key terms that this book uses to describe instructional content. As in any field, clear communication depends on the consistent use of technical vocabulary. The terms in this book are familiar words that already have considerable meaning. In this chapter we will try to define and illustrate a more specific meaning that should be associated with these terms as they are used throughout this book. It is important that you, the reader, remember that these particular terms have a specific and often more precise meaning when applied to effective, efficient, and engaging instruction. You should be careful to try to understand the meaning given to these terms in this chapter so that you won't misunderstand the prescriptions given later in this volume. For reference, these key terms are listed and defined at the beginning of the chapter and in the Glossary at the back of this book.

WHAT ARE THE DIFFERENT TYPES OF SKILL REQUIRED TO SOLVE A PROBLEM?

There is a difference between *knowledge*, what we know, and *skill*, what we do with what we know. Most subject-matter content can be described as a combination of some basic types of knowledge and skill. This volume uses the word *skill* to refer to a combination of both knowledge and skill. A *component skill* is a combination of knowledge and skill that is required to solve a complex problem or do a complex task. Table 3-1 identifies five primary types of component skill: *information-about, part-of, kind-of, how-to,* and *what-happens*. Each of these types of component skill requires different content elements. The following paragraphs briefly describe and illustrate the content elements that are required for each of these types of component skill.

Table 3-1 Content Information and Portrayal Elements

	Information	Portrayal
Information-about	Facts, associations	NA
Part-of	Name, description	Location of parts with regard to a specific whole
Kind-of	Definition—list of defining property values	Instances—specific examples and non-examples that illustrate property values
How-to	Steps and sequence	Portrayal of a specific example of the procedure
What-happens	Conditions and consequence	Portrayal of a specific example of the process

The instructional design literature uses a variety of terms for these different types of component skill. Information-about and part-of are sometimes called *verbal information*; kind-of is usually called a *concept*; how-to is usually called a *procedure*; and what-happens is sometimes called a *process*. Why did I choose to use different words? Over the years I have worked with many subject-matter experts in the design of instructional materials. I found that they often found words like concept, procedure, and process ambiguous and confusing. Therefore my colleagues and I began to use the words chosen for this chapter in an attempt to communicate more clearly. In our experience, practitioners in a variety of subject-matter areas found that these everyday terms were easier for them to understand in describing their content area. I hope you will also find that these terms more clearly communicate the nature of a given component skill.

Information-About

Remembering information is part of every component skill, but the nature of this content differs for each type of component skill. The content information required for an information-about component skill has the following property: the information is associated with a specific single entity, activity, or process and cannot be generalized. An *information-about component skill* is usually not the primary goal of a course but may play a supportive role. For a kind-of component skill, knowing information-about a specific entity, activity, or process may be necessary for identification. For a how-to component skill, knowing information-about a step may be necessary to be able to execute the step in a specific procedure. For a what-happens component skill, knowing information-about a condition may be necessary to identify the adequacy of the condition in a specific process. Figure 3-1 is an example of the content required for an information-about component skill.

FIGURE 3-1 Content for Information-About Component Skill—Famous Presidents

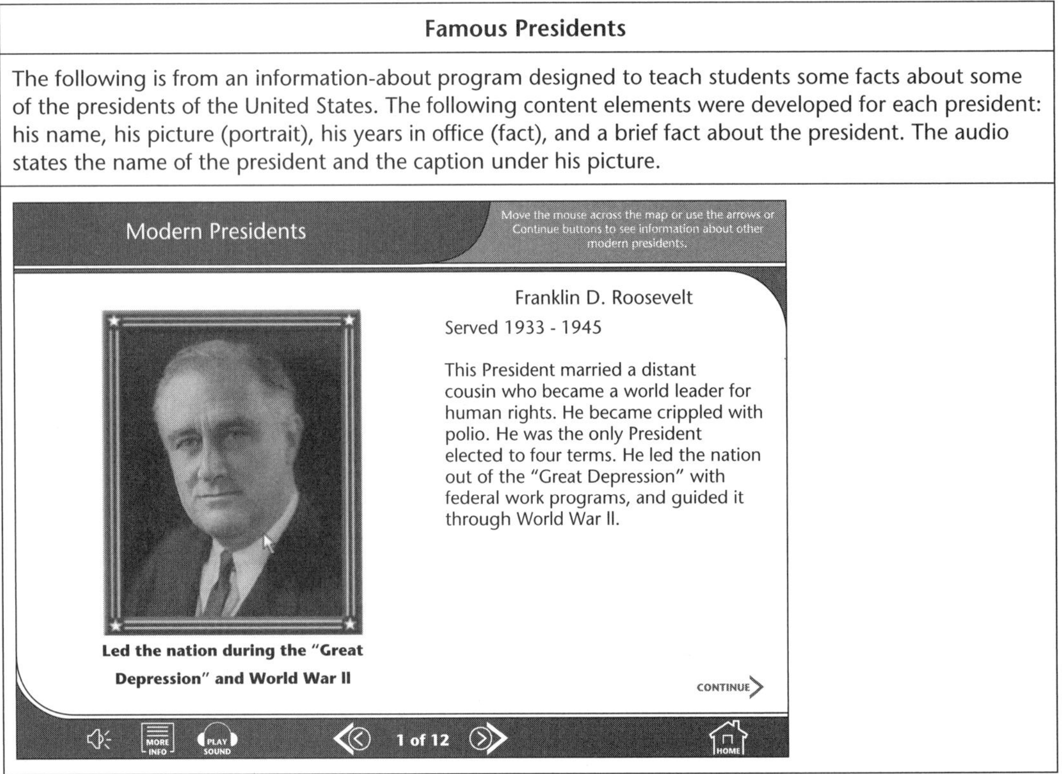

Copyright: Down Load Learning, Inc. Used with permission.

Part-of

Most entities, activities, or processes can be divided into parts. A *part-of component skill* is associated with almost any entity, activity, or process. The content required for a part-of component skill has the following property: the name, location, and description of the parts to be remembered are associated with a single specific entity, activity, or process and cannot be generalized. Like an information-about component skill, a part-of component skill is usually not the primary goal of a course but may also play a supportive role. For a kind-of component skill, knowing the parts may be an essential property of a specific entity, activity, or process. For a how-to component skill, knowing the parts may be necessary to execute a step in a specific procedure. For a what-happens component skill, knowing the parts may be necessary to identify the adequacy of a condition in a specific process. Figure 3-2 is an example of content required for a part-of component skill.

FIGURE 3-2 Content for Part-of Component Skill—Utah Counties

Utah Counties
The following is from a *part-of* program designed to teach students the counties of the state of Utah. The content consisted of a map of the state of Utah showing the relative location of each county to the whole. The content elements for each county consisted of its location, the name, the county seat, the population, and a brief fact about the county.

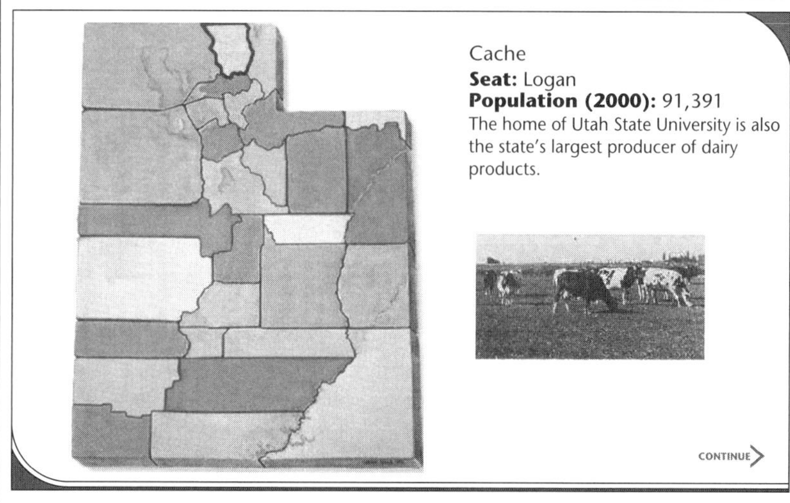

Cache
Seat: Logan
Population (2000): 91,391
The home of Utah State University is also the state's largest producer of dairy products.
CONTINUE

Kind-of

Almost all words in any language, except proper nouns, are category words called *concepts*. These concepts are the fundamental building blocks for complex problem solving. Acquiring a *kind-of component skill* by learning to recognize instances from a class of objects or events is very important to be able solve complex problems. The subject-matter content for kind-of component skill consists of classes or categories of objects, symbols, or events that share common properties. The content for kind-of component skill has the following property: examples of the class of the objects, symbols, or events to be identified are characterized by a set of common properties. Examples within the class are distinguishable from one another while still sharing these common properties. Figure 3-3 is an example of the content required for a kind-of component skill.

How-to

Remembering information, identifying parts, and classifying instances into classes are all ways to describe our environment. A *how-to component skill*, often called a *procedure*, provides ways for learners to act on their environment. A how-to component skill is appropriate when the content to be learned has the following property: The content specifies a sequence of activities for the learner to do to accomplish some goal or bring about some consequence. A how-to component skill is often the primary goal of instruction. Figure 3-4 is an example of the content required for a how-to component skill.

FIGURE 3-3 Content for Kind-of Component Skill—Elements of Art

Elements of Art

The following is from a *kind-of* course module designed to help learners recognize various elements of art including line, shape, color, and texture. The content consists of a definition listing the properties of *contour*. The property that defines contour is "*the outer edges of a shape*" or "*outline.*" The illustration is a portrayal of this kind of art element. The kind-of in this situation is an object or drawing. Note that the properties can apply to a wide variety of situations but that the portrayal is the application of these properties to a specific drawing.

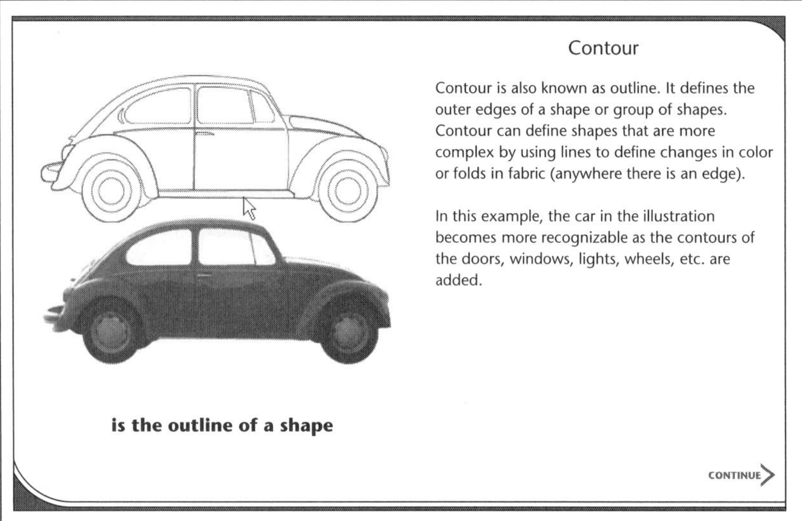

Contour
Contour is also known as outline. It defines the outer edges of a shape or group of shapes. Contour can define shapes that are more complex by using lines to define changes in color or folds in fabric (anywhere there is an edge).
In this example, the car in the illustration becomes more recognizable as the contours of the doors, windows, lights, wheels, etc. are added.
is the outline of a shape
CONTINUE

FIGURE 3-4 Content for How-to Component Skill—Spreadsheets

Using a Spreadsheet

Multiplying Cells

Summing Cells

Task:				
Determine weekly pay for each employee.				
Determine the total pay for the week.				
	A	B	C	D
1	Wages			
2		Per Hour	Hours	Total
3	John	$ 7.50	15	
4	David	$ 9.80	17	
5	Mark	$ 15.60	12	
6	Larry	$ 23.45	38	
7				

FIGURE 3-4 *Continued*

Step 1: Multiply each employee's per hour rate by the number of hours worked. 1.1 Select the cell. 1.2 Type = 1.3 Click on per hour to select cell 1.4 Click on * to multiply 1.5 Click on hours to select cell 1.6 Click on Enter ...	• Select cell D3 • Enter = • Click on cell B3 • Enter * • Click on Cell C3 The formula =B3*C3 should appear in the formula line. • Click on Enter The total of $112.50 should appear in Cell D3. • Repeat for Cells D4, D5, and D6
Step 2: Add the totals for each employee 2.1 Select the total cell 2.2 Type = sum (2.3 Click on first cell in column 2.4 Hold and drag to last cell in column 2.5 Type) 2.6 Click on Enter	• Select cell D7 • Type = sum (• Click on cell D3 • Hold and drag to cell D6 to select all totals • Type) The formula = sum (D3:D6) should appear in the formula line. • Click on Enter The total of $1,357.40 should appear in Cell D7.

Original lesson by the author.

What-Happens

The content for information-about, part-of, and kind-of component skills all describe the environment; the content for a how-to component skill provides ways for learners to act on their environment. A *what-happens component skill* enables learners to modify their environment or to comprehend their environment. The content for a what-happens component skill is often represented by an if-then proposition: If the conditions are true, then a consequence follows. A *condition* is a property of a situation that can assume different values. A *consequence* is a property of a situation that changes when there is change in the conditions. A change in a consequence as a result of changes in the conditions of a situation is called a *process.* A what-happens component skill is most appropriate when the content involves a process to be learned that has the following properties: (1) a set of conditions leads to some consequence; when the conditions change, the consequence changes, and (2) a change in a condition can be a naturally occurring event or an event caused by some action on the part of the learner. Figure 3-5 is an example of the content required for a what-happens component skill.

WHAT ARE THE CONTENT ELEMENTS REQUIRED FOR EACH TYPE OF SKILL?

Content elements are the individual parts of subject matter that are involved in instructional events. An instructional event is a combination of a content element with an instructional interaction (See Chapter 4). The content elements for one type of component skill differ from the content elements for another type of skill. The consistency corollary from First Principles states that the demonstration and presentation for a given type of component skill must be consistent with the goals of that skill. To be consistent, it is important that the content elements for a given component skill are those that are most appropriate for that type of skill.

FIGURE 3-5 Content for What-Happens Component Skill—Gantt Charts

Gantt Charts

This short how-to segment is from a course on Gantt Charts. The task is estimating the length of a project. The step being illustrated is shortening a task on the chart. The consequence is the change in the length of the project. The charts are a portrayal of the changes resulting from each of the steps indicated.

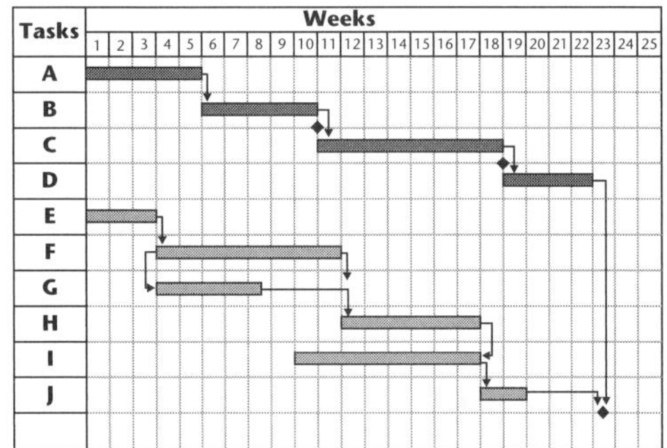

Gantt charts help us predict the effect of changes on the overall schedule. For example, let's see what happens when we shorten a task on the critical path. (Screen 1)

Suppose we could complete Task B in two weeks less time. What would be the effect on the overall project?

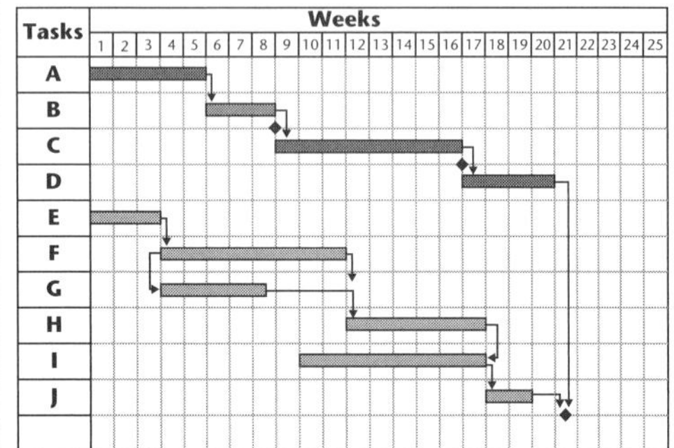

As you can see, the project is completed two weeks early. (Screen 2)

It is also tempting to believe that if we continue shortening the critical path, we shorten the project by an equivalent amount.

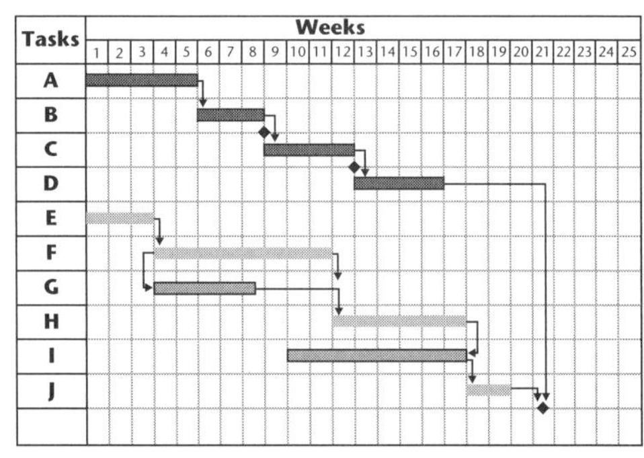

But let's see what happens as we shorten Task C by four weeks. After we shorten it by one week, a new critical path appears through tasks E, F, H, and J. This new critical path determines the length of the project. Shortening Task C by four weeks only shortened the project by two weeks. (Screen 3)

Though you can easily predict the effects of a single change in a simple example, estimating the effect of multiple changes in a complex project will require project-management software.

Content to be learned can be represented in two ways: general and specific. In this book, a general content element is called *information.* While the word *information* has many meanings, in this book it refers to a content element consisting of a description of the parts, properties, steps, conditions, or consequences for a class of objects, events, or processes. Information applies to many cases or situations. A specific content element is called a *portrayal.* A portrayal is an illustration, representation, vivid description, or graphic image of a specific event, person, or thing. A portrayal is limited and refers to one case or a single situation.

Let me illustrate: My wife and I write letters to our grown children. She is very good at summarizing lots of activities on a single page.

> "Mardi had a baby boy, Mark got a new job. Shaw finished school and will graduate next month. We saw big moose in the canyon. Love, Mom."

In other words, she is providing general information with very little specific detail. I, on the other hand, might write as follows:

> "As we were driving up the canyon to the cabin on Saturday you will never guess what we saw. Right there at the beaver ponds was a giant moose grazing in the water. He must have had a rack that was 8 or 9 feet across. He is the largest bull I've ever seen. I was anxious to get a picture but my camera was in the trunk. I pulled off the road, jumped out of the car, ran around and opened the trunk, and finally got my camera out of the case. I scrambled down the embankment to get a closer picture but by the time I got to the bottom the moose had decided he was finished with his lunch and started up the other side. I hurried and snapped a picture and got a great shot of the back end of a moose headed up the hill. You can barely see the antlers in the picture. I was disappointed. Love, Dad."

What is the difference? My wife's letter states general information, "We saw a big moose." On the other hand, my letter provides a vivid description or portrayal of this event.

Effective instruction content must have both types of content elements—general information and portrayal of specific events or objects. Too often instruction is limited to the general information. As a result, learners have insufficient content to really understand what is being taught.

Figure 3-6 illustrates information and portrayal content elements for three different kinds of component skill. In the first row the information column provides a *definition* content element for the rule of thirds. This is general information that can apply to any picture. In the right column a photograph and graph provide a *portrayal* content element for how the rule of thirds was applied to a specific photograph. It is a single specific portrayal content element for the definition.

FIGURE 3-6 Information and Portrayal Compared

Photography	
Information	Portrayal
The rule of thirds is a principle used to divide a photograph into thirds vertically and horizontally. Putting the object of interest into one of the crossing points makes the photo more interesting and professional. 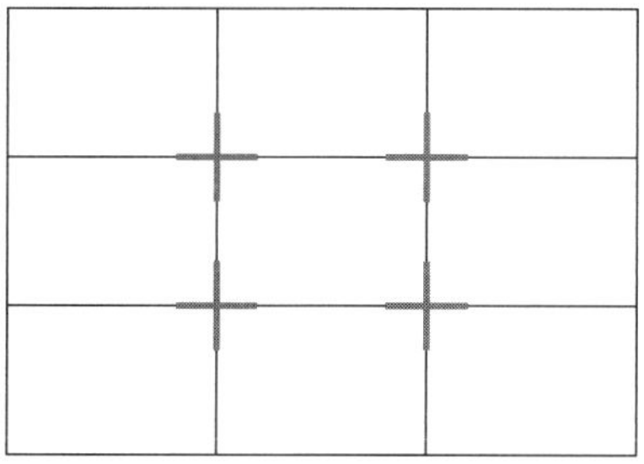	
• Insert a picture from a file. • Click location to insert picture. • Click picture icon on insert tab illustrations group. • Locate the picture you want to insert. • Resize picture to fit.	**Video:** A video animation shows the procedure. The cursor clicks on a location in a word document. The cursor then clicks on the insert tab, and then clicks on the picture icon in the illustrations group. *My pictures* file opens. The animation scrolls to a photograph and clicks. The picture appears in the word document. The cursor then grabs the lower right corner to reduce the size of the picture. An accompanying audio narration describes each step as it is completed.

(continued)

FIGURE 3-6 *Continued*

Pixels are measured in the form of ppi (pixels per inch). Remember, the more pixels per inch, the clearer the photo.	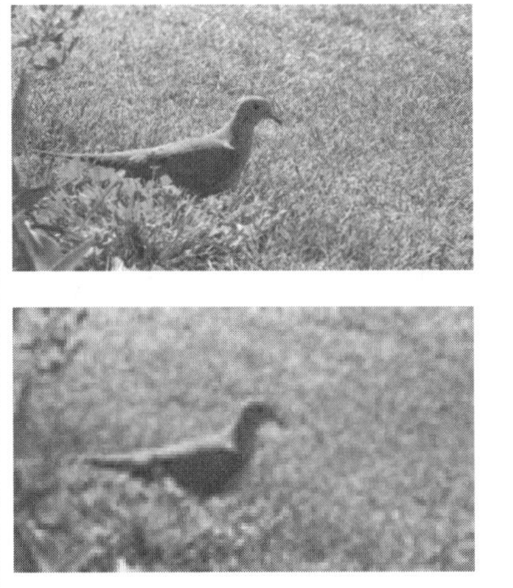

The second row in Figure 3-6 lists a series of steps in the procedure for inserting a picture in a Word document. The content elements in the information column are the steps and the sequence for applying these steps. This procedure can be used for any word document and any picture. The animation that is described in the right column represents a portrayal content element for this procedure. Of course, the actual video animation is the portrayal, not the description that is given here. The portrayal demonstrates the execution of each step in the procedure for a specific word document and a specific picture.

In the third row in Figure 3-6, the first column is a condition information content element—the number of pixels per inch (ppi), and the resulting consequence information content element—the clarity of a digital image. The number of pixels per inch is the condition; the resulting clarity of the photograph is the consequence. The illustration in the right column is a portrayal content element—a photograph with a large ppi and a photograph with a smaller ppi. The photographs are two specific portrayals of the process—if condition (ppi), then consequence (picture clarity). The information applies to all digital photographs; the portrayals are only a single example of this process.

Information-About

An *information-about* component skill requires the following content elements: the *name* of the information, the *facts* associated with the name, and any *graphic information* associated with the name. See Figure 3-1 for an example of information-about content. The name is Franklin D. Roosevelt, the facts are the paragraph and the information under the picture, the graphic information is the picture of FDR. It should be noted in this case that graphic information is not the same as a portrayal; a portrayal illustrates the application of information to a specific instance. The graphic information in this example is an arbitrary association of a name and information with a picture. It is arbitrary since one's name is usually assigned by parents and is unique to each individual.

Part-of

A *part-of* component skill requires the following content elements: (1) an *illustration* of the whole object or system, (2) a *location indicator* for each part, (3) a *name* for each part, and (4) *information* associated with each part. See Figure 3-2 for an example of part-of content. The illustration is a map of the state of Utah with the counties outlined; the location indicator highlights the outline of the county (part) in color; the name is given in the panel to the right when the part is identified by the location indicator; the information is also given in the panel to the right and includes the name of the county seat, the population, and a brief fact about the county.

Kind-of

A *kind-of* component skill has the following content elements: (1) the *name* of the category; (2) a *definition*, which is a list of discriminating properties and their values that determine class membership; and (3) a set of *examples* from the class of objects, symbols, or events being taught, including a portrayal or description showing the values on the discriminating properties. A *property* is a characteristic or attribute of a given class of objects, events, or process that is shared by members of the class. A given characteristic may have different values. If size is a property, then its values might be large or small; if color is a property, then its values might be red or green. It is the value on one or more properties that determines whether or not a given instance belongs to the class. Kind-of content can be concrete objects, as illustrated in Figure 3-3, or they can be symbolic objects, as illustrated in Figure 3-7, or they can be social activities, as illustrated in Figure 3-8.

In Figure 3-3 the name is *contour*, a characteristic of an art object. *Outline* is an alternative name. The definition is stated in the first paragraph and includes the following defining property: the outer edges of an object. The car with its contours drawn is an example and is described in the second paragraph.

Figure 3-7 illustrates the content elements of a symbolic kind-of, in this case English grammar. The name of the grammar concept is *adverb*. The definition of an adverb is given in the panel to the left and includes this key property: "a word that modifies a verb, adjective, or another adverb." The property *modifies* is also defined with these properties: describing, limiting, and qualifying and by providing questions that adverbs may answer. The panel also presents additional information about the definition by explicitly indicating that the –ly ending is a property that is not a defining property and by indicating that adverbs never modify nouns. The panel to the right provides examples of adverbs that modify in some of the different ways indicated in the definition of *modifies*. Guidance following each example indicates how the example relates to the definition.

FIGURE 3-7 Content for Kind-of Component Skill—Grammar Adverbs

<table>
<tr><th colspan="2">English Grammar</th></tr>
<tr><td colspan="2">The following is a kind-of segment from a course on English grammar. The kind-of is the part of speech "adverb." The properties are "modifies by describing, limiting, or qualifying." Note that the definition applies to all English communication but that examples are specific adverbs in the context of specific sentences.</td></tr>
<tr><td>An adverb is a part of speech that modifies verbs, adjectives, and other adverbs by describing, limiting, or in some way qualifying them. Adverbs usually answer questions like: When? How much? Where? How? and To what extent?

Adverbs never modify nouns or noun substitutes.

The most common adverbial ending is the suffix –ly. But a word need not end in –ly to be considered an adverb.

Here are some hints that will help you find adverbs:
1. Many, but not all, adverbs have an –ly ending.
2. An adverb can move around in a sentence without changing the meaning of the sentence.</td><td>The adverbs in the sentences below are shown in bold.

That test was really hard.

The adverb really, modifies hard, which is an adjective. It answers the question how much?

He is usually my sharpest student.

The adverb usually modifies is which is a verb. It answers the question when?

Phil was sound asleep but awoke quickly.

The adverb sound modifies asleep, which is an adjective.

The adverb quickly modifies awoke, which is an adverb. Both answer the question how much?</td></tr>
</table>

Based on a course from Brigham Young University.

FIGURE 3-8 Content for Kind-of Component Skill—Interview

<table>
<tr><th colspan="2">Job Counseling Skills</th></tr>
<tr><td colspan="2">The following is kind-of content from a course designed to train job counselors. The kind-of is "paraphrase," a communication skill of the counselor. The defining properties are "to restate in different words." The audio demonstrates this kind-of communication. The definition is general and can apply to many situations. The audio is a specific portrayal of this kind-of communication in a specific situation.</td></tr>
<tr><td>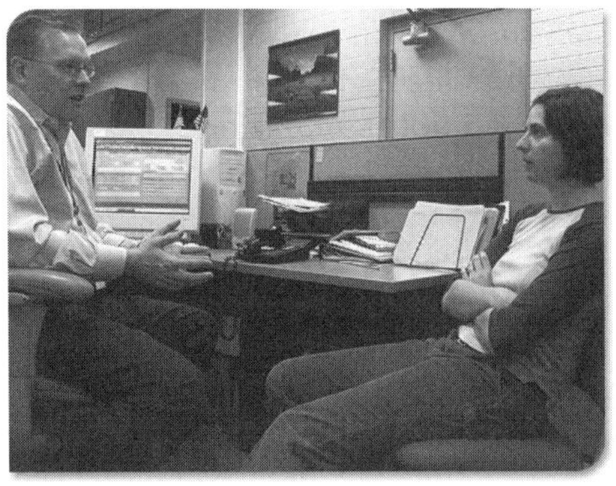</td><td>To paraphrase means to restate what the client said in different words to allow the client the chance to confirm that the intended message was understood.</td></tr>
<tr><td colspan="2">Audio:

Listen to this counselor paraphrase what the client has just said:

Client: I just don't know what hit me. I lost my job. My husband of ten years left me for another woman. And now my children have gone to live with him. I've had a horrible time lately.

Counselor: You've really been through a lot. You lost your job, your husband, and now the kids too.

Client: Ya, it's been tough. I don't know what I should do to keep my life moving.

Counselor: Life is getting pretty discouraging and you're not sure you have the strength to continue.</td></tr>
</table>

FIGURE 3-8 *Continued*

Client: I'm just not sure what I can do to support myself since I lost my job and my husband too.
Counselor: You're feeling the need to get back to work somewhere to support yourself.
Client: Ya, without a child-support check, money is going to get a lot tighter quickly.

Coordinate Concepts Kind-of content often involves a coordinate set of concept classes rather than a single kind-of. Each coordinate class shares the same properties, but the values on these properties are different for each class to determine different class membership. Figure 3-9 illustrates a set of coordinate categories for kinds of sailboats. The properties that determine the type of sailboat include: number of masts (a property with values of 1 or 2), location of masts (a property with values aft or mid ship), tallest mast (a property with values #1 or #2), number of sails (a property with values of 1 or >1), and tiller location (a property with values aft #2 mast or fwd #2 mast). The kinds of boats are listed at the top of each column in Figure 3-9. The properties are in the first column of Figure 3-9, and the property values are entered in the cells opposite the property and in the column for each kind-of sailboat. It is the combination of values on each of these properties that determines the category for the sailboat.

FIGURE 3-9 Content for Coordinate Kind-of Component Skill—Sailboats

Sailboats						
	Catboat	Sloop	Cutter	Ketch	Yawl	Schooner
# Masts	1	1	1	>1	>1	>1
Mast Loc		forward	midship			
Tallest Mast	--	--	--	#1	#1	#2
# sails	1	>1	>1	>1	>1	>1
Tiller loc	--	--	--	aft #2	fwd #2	--

Original material by author.

When teaching coordinate concepts, the challenge for learners is to discriminate one of the coordinate categories from another. In the example, a ketch and a yawl are very similar. As can be seen from the table of property values, the difference between these two categories of sailboat is only the location of the tiller.

Unencountered Examples *Unencountered examples* are new examples that are different from the examples used during the demonstration. Unencountered does not mean that the learner has never seen the example before but only that it was not encountered as part of the demonstration of the kind-of being taught. If the same examples are used for application and demonstration, then rather than practicing the ability to apply the defining properties, learners are merely required to remember the example. Using encountered examples reduces kind-of learning to information-about or part-of learning. The goal of kind-of instruction is transfer to new situations or new instances. Therefore, it is necessary to provide learners an opportunity to use their newly acquired skill to classify new examples during the application.

For kind-of content it is often necessary to identify a *non-example,* that is, an instance from a category of objects, events, or symbols that is similar to the target concept and that may be easily confused with examples of the target concept. The examples of one class of a coordinate concept may be easily confused with examples of another class of the coordinate concept, as is the case with a ketch and a yawl sailboat. So a ketch is a non-example of a yawl, and a yawl is a non-example of a ketch.

Incomplete Examples Another type of non-example is an instance that is incomplete or whose value for a defining property is missing or inadequate. Figure 3-10 illustrates two examples with a corresponding incorrect or non-example for which a property value is incorrect or missing. The leaf weaving example in Row 1 contrasts an incorrect step with a correct step. In both instances the property is the loop, but the critical value is the size of the loop. Both instances show making a loop, but the instance in the non-example fails to make the loop large enough. The photography example in Row 2 contrasts a correct position of the subject with respect to the edge of the photograph. The property is the position of the subject; the value is the location of this position with respect to the rule-of-thirds grid.

FIGURE 3-10 Example and Non-Example Comparison

Coconut Leaf Weaving and Photography	
The left column shows a non-example contrasted with a matched example in the right column. The first row is from a course on weaving with coconut leaves. The second row is from a basic course on photography.	
Portrayal of Incorrect Examples	**Portrayal of Correct Examples**
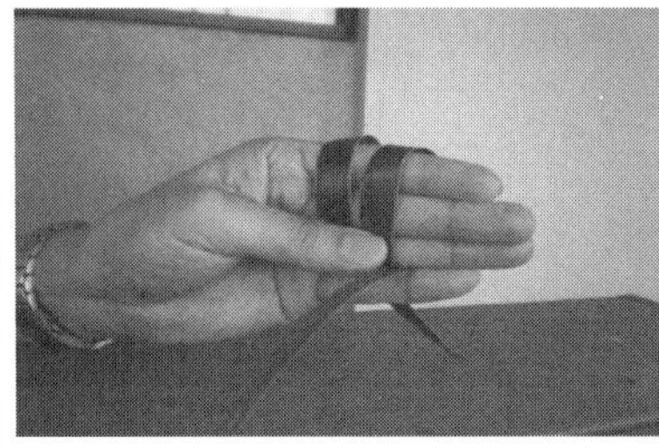 *Incorrect.* There is no space on top of the index finger in order to start the fish weaving.	 *Correct.* You need to leave roughly 2 inches of space on top of your index finger before weaving starts.

FIGURE 3-10 *Continued*

Incorrect. Point of interest should be at the intersection of the lines for the rule of thirds.	*Correct.* Point of interest is at the intersection of the lines for the rule of thirds.

Coconut Leaf Weaving, student project, BYU Hawaii, Garren Venzon and Jonathan Seng. Creating a Professional Photo, student project, BYU Hawaii, Jessica Judy and Derek Williams.

Pseudo Examples An example must actually show the property values that determine class membership for the instance being portrayed. Often what is presented as an example is really a *pseudo example:* It is an instance of the class under consideration, but the portrayal of the example is not sufficient to show the presence of the property values that determine class membership. If an example fails to show the discriminating properties that determine class membership, then it really conveys little or no information. Too often the instructor or designer of the instruction assumes that the learners are familiar with the examples being used and fails to provide sufficient detail for the learner to be able to observe the defining characteristics.

Consider Figure 3-11, which provides examples and pseudo examples of the concept *helping relationship.* The middle column identifies the person as either an example or a non-example of a helping relationship and restates the definition, but does not actually show an example of helping, cooperation, or trust. The third column includes a very brief scenario of a specific situation in which the properties of trust, collaboration, and faith in the recipient are demonstrated.

FIGURE 3-11 Example and Pseudo Example Comparison

Job Counseling
The following is kind-of content from a course designed to train job counselors. It teaches a kind of relationship, a *helping relationship*. The pseudo examples state but do not show the critical properties. The examples illustrate the property values that determine whether the instance is a helping relationship or not a helping relationship.
Definition:
The Helping Relationship is a constructive relationship that is collaborative in nature, grounded in trust and respect, and based on the belief that the customer has the capacity for personal growth and change.

(continued)

FIGURE 3-11 *Continued*

Example:	Pseudo example and non-example	Better example and non-example
	Maybe you have a mentor who helps you professionally. This is usually a helping relationship in that it is generally supportive, grounded in trust, collaborative, and based on the belief that persons have the capacity for change.	**Audio:** Consider this mentor helping a business student. Is this a helping relationship? *Mentor:* What is the evidence that this idea will really work? Did you consider these cost projections? *Client:* I forgot. It is so helpful that you have this business background to help me. Do you think I'll ever get it? *Mentor:* You'll get it! You just need to always consider all the data before you decide that an idea is a good one.
Non-Example:	A military officer is not an example of a helping relationship. Military officers do not collaborate with troops; they give orders. They are often perceived as nonsupportive, even if their personnel trust them.	**Audio:** Consider this officer drilliing his troops. Is this a helping relationship? *Officer:* Attention! Today I want 50 pushups. Ready, Go! *Officer:* Private. Are you a sissy? Keep that belly off the ground! Move it!

How-to

A *how-to* or procedure component skill has the following content elements: (1) an object or situation to be modified by the procedure (the *task*); (2) the *name* of the procedure; (3) a list of the *steps* or activities for executing the procedure; (4) the *sequence* for executing the steps; (5) a *demonstration* of the task illustrating the individual activities or steps required; (6) the *consequence* of each step; and (7) the *consequence* of the completing the whole procedure. How-to content can involve a symbol manipulation task, as illustrated in Figure 3-4, or a social task, as illustrated in Figure 3-12.

Figure 3-4 illustrates a couple of instructional events from a course teaching how to use spreadsheets. The task is to use the spreadsheet to determine the amount of weekly pay for each of several employees, given their hourly wage and number of hours worked, and to determine the total wages paid for the week. The names of the procedures are multiplying cells and summing cells. The primary steps and substeps for each procedure are listed in the first column. The second column is a demonstration of the execution of each step and substep in the task. The bullets indicate the action to take for each substep, and the note following indicates the consequence of each set of substeps. The consequence is a spreadsheet with the totals shown. In practice this task would be done using the actual spreadsheet software.

Figure 3-12 illustrates a brief instructional event from a course on selling furniture. The name of the procedure, which is really just a step in the larger whole task of making a sales presentation, is indicated in the left panel of the second row. The steps or activities for executing this procedure are indicated in each of the remaining cells of the left column of Figure 3-12. The sequence for these steps is indicated by their order and also by a number for each step. The right column is a demonstration of the procedure. The complete demonstration is a video plus the audio track. Only a still picture and audio track are included here so some of the portrayal is missing from this representation. Note that each row in the figure states the activity for each step (left column) and demonstrates the corresponding execution of this step (video described in the right column) and the response of the customer (the consequence of each step). The consequence for this whole brief procedure is illustrated in the final row of the figure; the customer is ready for the sales presentation.

FIGURE 3-12 Content for How-to Component Skill—Sales

Selling with Service	
The following is a short *how-to* segment from a course on selling furniture. The first major activity is a *friendly approach.* The steps and hoped-for consequence for each step are listed in the left column. The pictures and audio represent a video portrayal demonstrating these steps and the consequence of each step.	
Friendly Approach	 **Audio Accompanying Video**
(1) Warm greeting. **Audio:** A warm and friendly greeting sets the customer at ease and helps her feel comfortable.	**David:** Hi, how are you today? **Maria:** Fine, thank you.
(2) Open-ended question. **Audio:** Open-ended questions encourage conversation, while yes-and-no questions don't!	**D:** How do you like all this sunshine we are having? **M:** It's a nice change.
(3) Sincere response.	**D:** Looks like spring is finally here. **M:** Finally!
Audio: After a friendly approach, customers are more likely to share the purpose of their visit and tell you what their needs are.	**D:** What brings you into our store on such a beautiful day? **M:** I think my sofa is starting to get worn. I think that it needs to be replaced. **D:** I'd love to show you some sofas. Do you want to come with me? **M:** Okay.

What-Happens

A *what-happens* component skill has the following content elements: (1) a specific situation to which a *process* applies (the *problem*); (2) the *name* of the process; (3) a set of *conditions* that should lead to the consequence; and (4) a *consequence* resulting from the conditions. The relationship among the conditions and the consequence are often represented by *if-then* propositions or rules.

Figure 3-5 illustrates a planning tool for project management. The problem is estimating the time required to complete a project. The conditions are the length of each task and the dependencies of one task on other tasks and the resulting critical path. When a condition is changed and there is not a change in the critical path, then the consequence is a shortened time for the whole project (Screen 2). When a condition is changed and there is a change in the critical path, then there is a new critical path and the consequence is no change in the time required for the whole project (Screen 3).

Figure 3-13 illustrates what-happens content for a naturally occurring event, dissolving salt in water. The specific problem is what happens when water forms a solution with salt. The conditions are the polarity of the water molecule and the positive or negative charge on the salt atoms or ions. Because of this polarity of the water molecule, there is an attraction of the positive end of the water molecules to the negative chloride ions (consequence) and an attraction of the negative end of the water molecule to the positive sodium ions (consequence) of the salt crystals. This attraction allows the atoms to form a solution. This process cannot be observed without special equipment, but it can be described and portrayed with diagrams.

FIGURE 3-13 Content for What-Happens Component Skill—Properties of Water

<table>
<tr><th colspan="2">Physical Properties of Water</th></tr>
<tr><td colspan="2">The following what-happens segment is from a biology course in a module on the Chemical and Physical Properties of Solutions. The specific situation is salt dissolving in water. The process is chemical bonding of molecules. The condition is the polarity of water molecules that allows them to bond to the sodium and chloride molecules of salt.</td></tr>
<tr><td>Water Is Polar
Region of high electron density</td><td>Audio
Most of water's chemical and physical properties can be traced to its polar structure. This means that it has an uneven distribution of electron density [condition].</td></tr>
<tr><td>Polarity Enables Compounds to Dissolve
</td><td>One important implication of the polarity of water is its ability to dissolve ionic compounds and small polar molecules [problem].</td></tr>
</table>

FIGURE 3-13 *Continued*

<table>
<tr><td>Polarity Enables Compounds to Dissolve</td><td>Water molecules surround the ions or molecules as they break free from the crystal [condition].</td></tr>
<tr><td>Polarity Enables Compounds to Dissolve</td><td>In this example, the more positive end of the water molecule is oriented toward the negative chloride ion [consequence] and the more negative end of the water molecule is oriented toward the positive sodium ion [consequence]. The consequence is a solution in which the atoms or ions of the salt are attracted to water molecules, i.e., dissolved.</td></tr>
</table>

Figure 3-14 illustrates a counseling event for a job counseling course. The conditions are the actions and comments of the counselor. In this course counselors are taught to paraphrase, to show empathy, and to be helpful (conditions required for a positive consequence). In this situation, the body language of the counselor conveys annoyance (faulted condition) and her comments show she is not listening to the applicant (faulted condition). The unintended consequence is that the applicant is discouraged and will probably not come back to find the help she needs. The goal of the course is to show that if the counselor uses appropriate counseling techniques the consequence will be more positive and she will be able to help the applicant.

FIGURE 3-14 Content for What-Happens Component Skill—Interview

<table>
<tr><th colspan="2">Job Counselors</th></tr>
<tr><td colspan="2">This what-happens segment is from a course training job counselors. The situation is an interview to try to get help to find a job. The conditions are the actions and comments by the counselor. The consequence is the feelings in the applicant.</td></tr>
<tr><td></td><td>Animation with Audio
Applicant: Hi, I was told I should speak with you.
Counselor: Go ahead and sit down (does not stop typing).
A: I'm sorry to interrupt you.
C: That's okay, you get used to it in this job.</td></tr>
<tr><td></td><td>C: Do you have your registration form for services with you?
A: Here it is. I did the best I could with it. I've always been able to hold a job. I don't know what happened.
C: Let me take a look at it.</td></tr>
</table>

(continued)

FIGURE 3-14 *Continued*

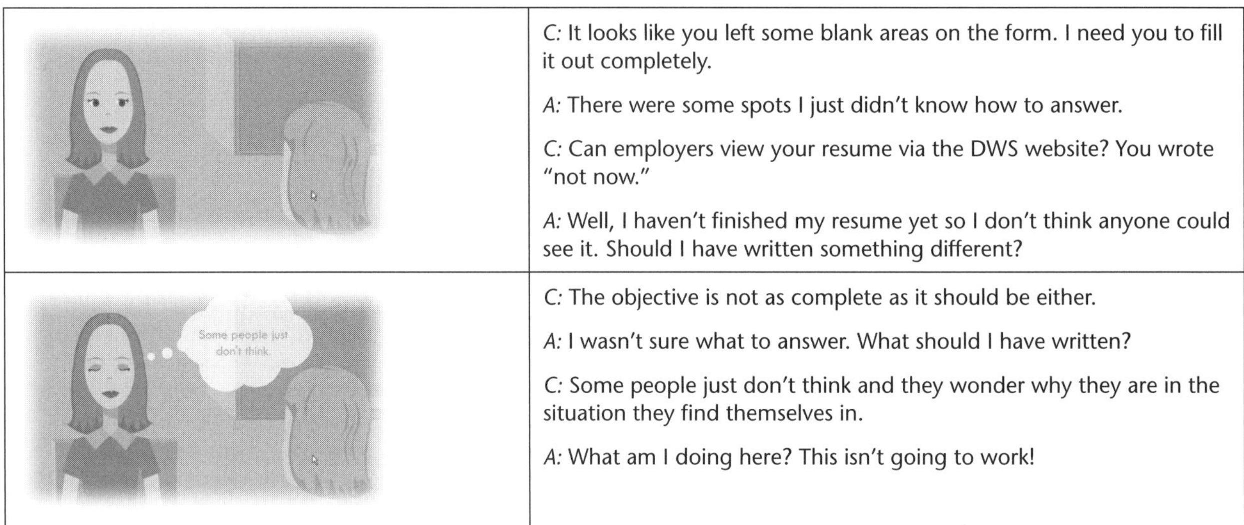

	C: It looks like you left some blank areas on the form. I need you to fill it out completely. *A:* There were some spots I just didn't know how to answer. *C:* Can employers view your resume via the DWS website? You wrote "not now." *A:* Well, I haven't finished my resume yet so I don't think anyone could see it. Should I have written something different?
	C: The objective is not as complete as it should be either. *A:* I wasn't sure what to answer. What should I have written? *C:* Some people just don't think and they wonder why they are in the situation they find themselves in. *A:* What am I doing here? This isn't going to work!

PRINCIPLES AND PRESCRIPTIONS

- To facilitate communication about instructional content, First Principles of Instruction defines five types of component skill—information-about, part-of, kind-of, how-to, and what-happens.
- Content elements for information-about include a name, facts associated with the name, and graphics associated with the name or facts.
- Content elements for part-of include a name, an illustration of the whole object, a location indicator for each part, a name for each part, and facts associated with each part.
- Content elements for kind-of include a name, a definition, and a set of examples.
- Content elements for how-to include a name, an object or situation to be modified, the required steps, the sequence for the steps, a demonstration of the task, and the consequence of performing the task.
- Content elements for what-happens include a name, a problem, a set of conditions, and a consequence that results from the conditions.

APPLICATION

It will help you remember and identify examples of the technical terms for describing instructional content if you will look for the different types of content and content elements described in this chapter. Choose a textbook or online course with which you are familiar. See whether this instructional material contains each of the different types of component skill described in this chapter. Select types of component skill in your chosen material and see whether you can find the content elements described in this chapter. You may find that some of these content elements are missing. See whether you can suggest content elements that could be added to the instructional materials you examine.

TO LEARN MORE

Clark, R. C. (2008a). *Developing technical training: A structured approach for developing classroom and computer-based instructional materials* (3rd ed.). San Francisco: Pfeiffer. Ruth Clark elaborated on my work by further describing and illustrating facts, concepts, procedures, processes, and principles.

Foshay, W. R. R., Silber, K. H., & Stelnicki, M. B. (2003). *Writing training materials that work: How to train anyone to do anything.* San Francisco: Pfeiffer. These authors also elaborate teaching facts, concepts, principles, and problem solving.

Gagné, R. M. (1985). *The conditions of learning and theory of instruction* (4th ed.). New York: Holt, Rinehart and Winston.

Gagné, R. M., Wager, W. W., Golas, K., & Keller, J. M. (2005). *Principles of instructional design* (5th ed.). Belmont, CA: Thompson Wadsworth. Robert Gagné identified five varieties of learned capabilities: intellectual skills, verbal information, cognitive strategies, motor skills, and attitudes. He further subdivided intellectual skills into discriminations, concepts, higher-order rules, and procedures. His premise was that each variety required different internal and external conditions (instructional events) for learning to occur. While there are significant differences, Gagné's verbal information is similar to *information-about* and *part-of*; his concepts are similar to *kind-of*; his procedures are similar to *how-to*; and his higher-order rules are similar to *what-happens*

Merrill, M. D. (1994). *Instructional design theory* (Section 3: Component display theory). Englewood Cliffs, NJ: Educational Technology Publications. I have elaborated on the work of Gagné by describing four types of intellectual skill: facts, concepts, procedures, and principles. The five types of content described in this chapter correspond to facts (information-about and part-of), concepts (kind-of), procedures (how-to) and principles (what-happens).

COMING NEXT

This chapter illustrated five types of component skill, the content required by each, and the content elements included in this content. Chapter 4 will demonstrate the four types of instructional interaction—*Tell, Show, Ask,* and *Do.* These instructional interactions will then be combined with content elements to describe instructional events. Chapter 5 will then illustrate the instructional strategies comprised of the prescribed instructional events for each of the five types of component skill.

CHAPTER 4

INSTRUCTIONAL INTERACTION

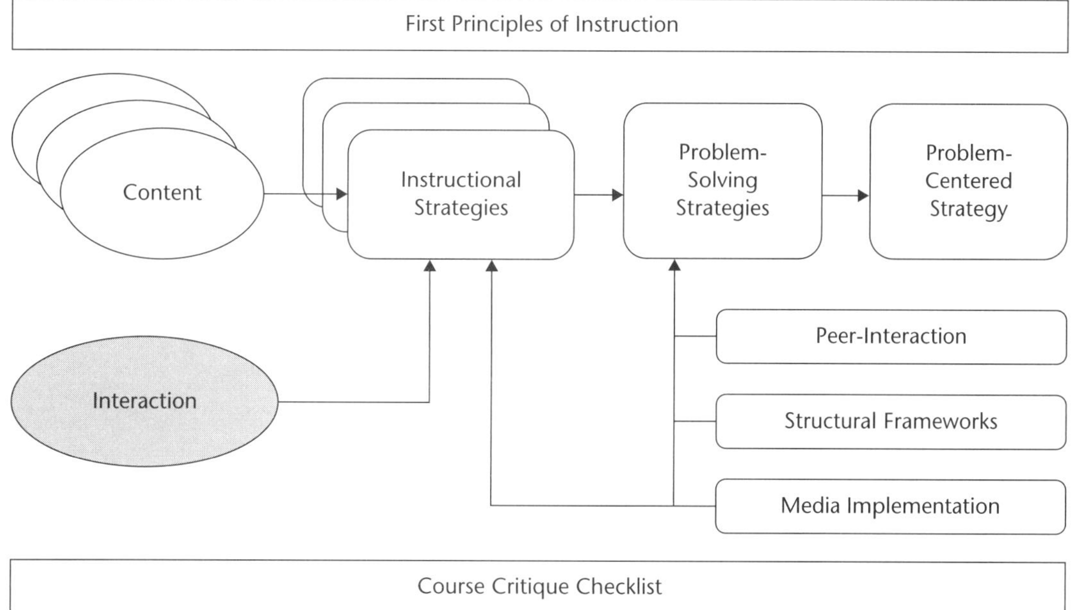

Quick Look

In Chapter 3 I introduced a technical vocabulary for describing subject-matter content and the elements of this content for five types of component skills. In this chapter I introduce a technical vocabulary for describing learner interaction with these content elements. This chapter answers the following questions: How can we, as instructional designers, describe the different components of an instructional interaction in a way that will enable us to carefully define e^3 instructional strategies? Why do we need a technical vocabulary to describe instructional interaction? What are the primary forms of instructional interaction? What are other essential features of an e^3 demonstration interaction? What are other essential features of an e^3 application interaction?

Key Words

Instructional Mode: the four primary instructional interactions—*Tell, Show, Ask,* and *Do.*
Tell: an instructional interaction that provides information to the learner.
Show: an instructional interaction that provides portrayals to the learner.

Ask: an instructional interaction that requests learners to recall or recognize information.

Do: an instructional interaction that requires learners to apply information to a portrayal.

Simon-Says: a form of a *Tell-and-Show* instructional interaction in which learners interact with a representation of a real-world device. They are told a step to take; they execute the step; and, if they are correct, the device responds to their action. If they execute the wrong step, they are told that their response is wrong; the correct part of the device is highlighted; and they are directed to try the step again.

Attention-Focusing Guidance: an instructional interaction that helps learners relate information to the details of a portrayal.

Matching Guidance: an instructional interaction that pairs examples from two or more kinds of objects, events, or processes that are similar on many of their non-discriminating properties but differ only on their discriminating properties.

Divergent Guidance: an instructional interaction that provides a sequence of portrayals that are all examples of a component skill but which differ from each other in significant ways that reflect the range of difference that occurs in the real world.

Range-of-Difficulty Guidance: an instructional interaction that provides learners with a sequence of examples that vary from those that are easy to solve to those that are difficult to solve.

Corrective Feedback: information following a response indicating the correct response and why it is the correct response.

Intrinsic Feedback: an instructional interaction that shows the learner the consequence of his or her response.

Coaching: an instructional interaction that provides help to learners during *Do* instructional events.

INTRODUCTION

During a visit to an instructional development company, I saw the following maxim on the wall: "If a product does not teach, it has no value!" I couldn't agree more. Why are we spending billions of dollars for training unless we expect this training to lead to quality performance, quality products, and more efficient and effective performance on the part of our students or our employees? Yet I frequently have the opportunity to review instructional products that do not teach. Why? Because too much instruction does not involve instructional interactions that are appropriate for learning the desired skills.

Today's headlines often contain the word *information*. We are told that this is the "information age." We are encouraged to jump onto the information highway. There seems to be an assumption that if we have sufficient information, then people will learn. The Internet is a wonderful new medium for the exchange of information. However, dare I suggest that information is not instruction?

Much of what is called *instruction* is merely providing information. Instruction involves much more. In addition to information, e^3 instruction involves several other very important activities, including *demonstration* with *guidance* to help the learner connect the information with the portrayals and *application*, which includes appropriate feedback and coaching that requires learners to use the information they have acquired to solve a problem or complete a complex task.

WHY DO WE NEED A TECHNICAL VOCABULARY FOR INSTRUCTIONAL INTERACTION?

Instructional interactions are procedures designed to promote learning; they prescribe how the instruction and the learner work together to promote learning. You are familiar with many forms of instructional interaction, including lectures, discussions, role playing, assignments, projects, and many more. However, these broad categories are not useful in trying to describe and critique a wide variety of different approaches to instruction. As instructional designers we need a more precise and more detailed set of terms that allows us to dissect these broader categories to identify the instructional events from which they are constructed. This chapter provides terms for describing different types of instructional interaction.

WHAT ARE THE PRIMARY FORMS OF INSTRUCTIONAL INTERACTION?

This book describes primary instructional interactions on two dimensions: (1) providing the content to the learner and (2) having the learner respond to the content. These primary instructional interactions are called *instructional modes.* This book describes and illustrates two instructional modes to provide content to the learner: *Tell* (*present*) and *Show* (*demonstrate*). It also describes and illustrates two instructional modes to have a learner respond: *Ask (recall)* and *Do (apply*). The four *instructional modes* of *Tell, Ask, Show,* and *Do* are the primary interactions for any instructional strategy. The combination of an instructional mode and a content element is an *instructional event.*

As in earlier chapters, I have chosen common terms to describe these modes to facilitate communication. There is a danger, however, that because these terms are so common, readers often assume they know their meaning. So be careful. Even though I have used very common words—*Tell, Show, Ask,* and *Do*—these words have a more limited meaning when describing instructional interactions than their everyday use. It is important as you study the instructional interactions described and illustrated in this chapter that you pay close attention to the limited meaning of these words as they are used in this book.

Tell

Tell provides information to the learner. *Tell* is always used in conjunction with information content elements rather than portrayal content elements. *Tell* provides information to the learner by the voice of the instructor, an audio message, a video message, a text message, or in a variety of other ways. *Tell* is not limited to audio or voice; it is not limited to instructor-led. *Tell* should be more than the passive dispensing of information. *Tell* can also be accomplished in an interrogatory mode by asking rhetorical questions rather than merely making declarative statements. A rhetorical question is one that is designed to cause the learner to think about the content, but not one for which the instructor expects an answer. *Tell* is most effective when required information is given just as it is needed to solve the problem. See Figures 4-2 and 4-3 for examples of *Tell.*

Show

Show provides portrayals to the learner. *Show* is always used in conjunction with portrayal content elements rather than information content elements. *Show* can be accomplished with graphics, video, animation, diagrams, and a variety of other ways. A demonstration is most effective when *Tell* is interwoven with *Show* in a *Tell-and-Show* instructional interaction. See Figures 4-2 and 4-3 for examples of *Show*.

Ask

Ask requests learners to recall or recognize information. Many typical test formats such as multiple-choice, true-false, short-answer, and matching often require learners to recall or recognize information rather than portrayals. In this book, *Ask* is always used in conjunction with information content elements rather than portrayal content elements. Please note that, while these test formats are frequently used to ask learners to recall or recognize information, it is not the test format that determines whether an item is *Ask* but whether the item requires learners to recall or recognize information content elements or whether it requires them to apply information to portrayal content elements. See Figure 4-1 for an example of *Ask*.

Tell-and-Ask

Figure 4-1 illustrates a very common form of *Tell-and-Ask* instruction. This is far and away the most common form of instructional interaction currently available. The example is based on a course that is basically a textbook online. The instructional events in Figure 4-1 are obviously only a tiny fraction of the course. The actual course includes many pages of information and direction. *Tell-and-Ask* is one of the least effective instructional interactions.

FIGURE 4-1 Often Used *Tell-and-Ask* Instructional Interaction

Acute Pain Management in Adults

The following abbreviated segment is based on an online course for nurses. The first panel is a brief snippet from the presentation, which is primarily expository text describing the procedures involved. The second panels are a couple of questions from the quiz that followed this segment of instruction. The actual content of this course is many pages of instruction, and the quiz included many additional questions. The actual course included other forms of instruction as well.

Pain Management and Reassessment

The process of managing postoperative pain, including patient education, begins prior to the operation.

Pain is a complex subjective response with several quantifiable features, including intensity, time course, quality, impact, and personal meaning. Studies suggest that providing a patient with information preoperatively may reduce the required analgesics postoperatively and shorten the length of stay.

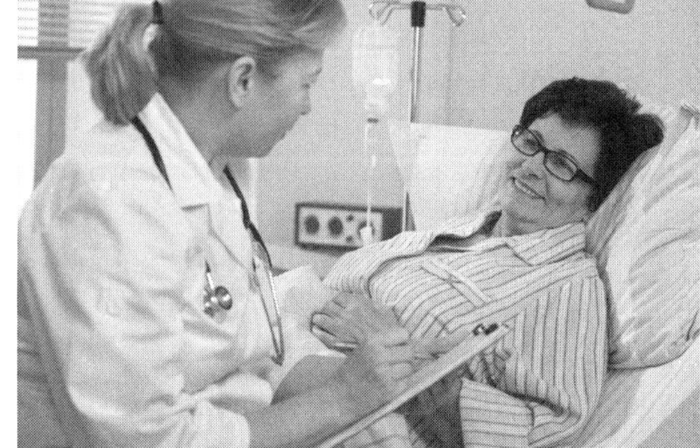

Obtaining a Pain History

One of the first steps in planning pain control strategies with the patient is obtaining a pain history. An anesthesiologist or nurse anesthetist should obtain the history during the preoperative visit. Taking steps to establish good communication between the patient and clinicians can result in accurate assessment of the pain and better control of the pain.

FIGURE 4-1 *Continued*

1. Unrelieved pain may: • Promote the breakdown of body tissues • Increase water retention • Impair immune function • All of the above	2. True or False? An individualized pain management plan is developed preoperatively because pain is easier to control when it is prevented from becoming established. • True • False

Original material modeled after an online course.

Tell-and-Show

Tell is often most effective when interwoven with *Show* in a combination of presentation and demonstration instructional events. Figure 4-2 illustrates a *Tell-and-Show* demonstration for a motor skill. The illustration is only two instructional events from the original instruction but is sufficient to show the simultaneous presentation of information and its portrayal.

FIGURE 4-2 *Tell-and-Show* Instructional Interaction—Skateboard Ollie

The Ollie and Newton's Laws	
The following instructional event is from a student course designed to teach some principles of skateboarding. The *Show* here are pictures but *Show* could just as easily be represented by video.	
Tell In skateboard terms, Newton's second law basically says that if your front foot slides up and forward, then the board will follow and also go up and forward. This is the key to the Ollie. In order to get off the ground, you must apply an upward and forward motion by sliding your foot forward up the board and jump up into the air.	*Show* 
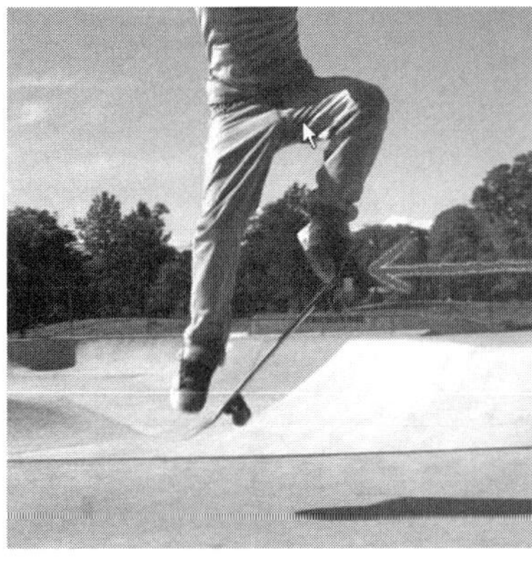	Notice how the board is following the direction of the front foot, forward and up.

Student project, BYU-Hawaii, Michael Shoneman and Christopher Gardner.

Figure 4-3 is a *Tell-and-Show* demonstration for a physics principle using a simulation to show the portrayal. The advantage of the simulation is that learners can see the consequence or what happens (the location of the focal point) when the condition (the curvature of the lens) changes.

FIGURE 4-3 *Tell-and-Show* or Demonstration Instructional Events Involving Simulation—Focal Length

Refraction of Light	
This instructional event is from a short course on the microscope. This segment deals with refraction of light. This is a *Tell-and-Show* strategy using a dynamic demonstration that can be manipulated by the learners.	
Tell	*Show*
The *principal plane* of a lens is an imaginary slice from edge to edge through the center of the lens. The *principal axis* of a lens is an imaginary line through the center of the lens perpendicular to the principal plane of the lens. A light ray passing through the lens on the principal axis is not bent. Light rays that are parallel to the principal axis are bent when passing through the lens. Light rays bend toward the thicker part of the lens. The *focal point* of a convex lens is that point on the principal axis where all the light rays passing through the lens parallel to the principal axis converge or meet.	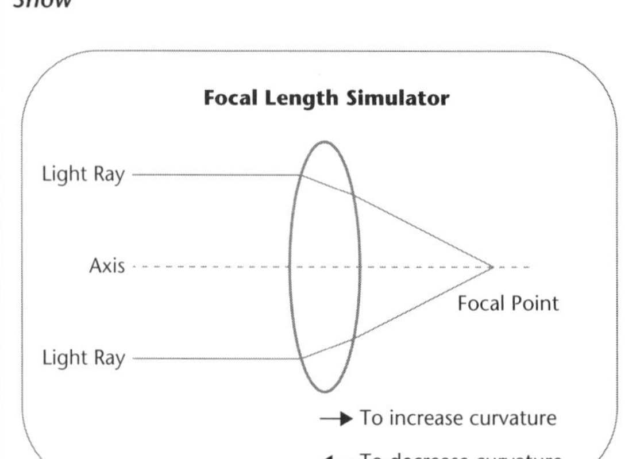 Experiment with the curvature of the lens using the arrow keys. As the curvature is increased, the focal point moves closer to the lens and the focal length gets shorter. Try it.

Original design by the author.

Simon-Says

Simon-Says is a form of a *Tell-and-Show* instructional interaction in which learners interact with a representation of a real-world device. They are told a step to take; they execute the step; and, if they are correct, the device responds to their action. If they execute the wrong step, they are told that their response is wrong; the correct part of the device is highlighted; and they are directed to try the step again. Figure 4-4 illustrates a *Simon-says* instructional interaction. This instructional interaction is often called *simulation* or *practice* by the vendors of these programs. However, this strategy is primarily a *Tell-and-Show* strategy for how-to type of subject-matter content. The text message is a *Tell* instructional event and the learner's interaction with the portrayal of the spreadsheet is a *Show* instructional event. This demonstration helps learners locate the part and demonstrates the consequence of the student's action with the part. A *Simon-says* interaction is more effective than a passive interaction in which the instruction merely shows learners what to do. The interactive demonstration helps ensure that the learner has attended to the step told by the text message and is able to locate the part in question by having to actually click on it.

FIGURE 4-4 *Simon-says* Instructional Interaction—Excel

Microsoft Excel

The following snippet of instruction is from an online course teaching learners how to use Excel spreadsheets. This course uses a "Simon-says" type of demonstration, where each command necessary to carry out some procedure in using the sheet is stated and the learner then follows the direction given to carry out the step.

Instructional Events	Text Messages
[Note this is only one event in a series of events this course tells and shows to the student. The learner has already been working with this specific spreadsheet for earlier commands.] Tell text message 1. The learner clicks on the display. If the location of the click is correct, the message for the next command is displayed. **OR ELSE** If the location of the click is not correct, message 2 is displayed. If the location of the click is still incorrect, the green arrow and message 3 are displayed. This interactive demonstration is continued for all of the commands that are part of the instructional segment.	(1) To copy the selected data, use the Copy tool on the Standard toolbar. When selected, the Copy tool copies the data to the Windows clipboard. Click on the Copy tool. (2) That is not the Copy tool. Try again. (3) The green arrow shows the Copy tool. Click on the Copy tool.

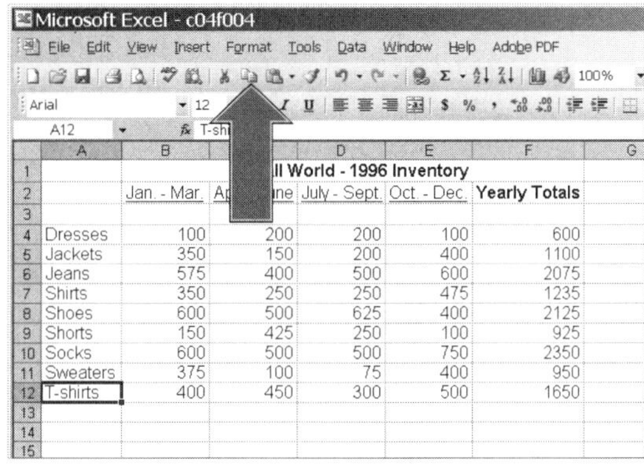

	A	B	C	D	E	F	G
1				ll World - 1996 Inventory			
2		Jan. - Mar.	Ap ne	July - Sept.	Oct. - Dec.	Yearly Totals	
3							
4	Dresses	100	200	200	100	600	
5	Jackets	350	150	200	400	1100	
6	Jeans	575	400	500	600	2075	
7	Shirts	350	250	250	475	1235	
8	Shoes	600	500	625	400	2125	
9	Shorts	150	425	250	100	925	
10	Socks	600	500	500	750	2350	
11	Sweaters	375	100	75	400	950	
12	T-shirts	400	450	300	500	1650	
13							
14							
15							

Original design by the author modeled on commercial course.

Do

A *Do* interaction requires learners to apply information to a portrayal to solve a specific problem. *Do* is always used in conjunction with portrayals of specific problems. A *Do* interaction can be implemented with a wide variety of activities that engage learners with specific content situations. *Do* interactions are required for learners to acquire component skills. Learners learn by doing when this doing is accompanied by appropriate feedback, as described in subsequent paragraphs in this chapter. Multiple-choice, short-answer, and matching-item formats can be used to have learners solve a specific problem or do a specific task. In these situations, the items are asking questions about the portrayal rather than about the information. In these situations, these item formats involve application or *Do* interactions rather than *Ask*.

Figure 4-5 illustrates a *Do* interaction for kind-of content. The application simultaneously assesses several properties of a good photograph—pixels per inch, rule of thirds, appropriate lighting, correct shutter speed, and white balance. The picture illustrates an example or non-example of each of these properties. Learners must examine the photograph to determine whether it includes an example or non-example of each of these characteristics of a good photograph. This application assesses a whole problem of taking a good photograph.

FIGURE 4-5 *Do* Instructional Interaction, Kind-of Component Skill—Photography

Creating a Professional Photo	
This instructional event requires the learners to apply what they have learned about taking professional photos to the specific photograph shown here.	
Look at the following photo. Click on the factors that the photographer did not use correctly in taking this photo. PPI Rule of Thirds Lighting Shutter Speed White Balance	

Student project 2009, BYU–Hawaii, Jessica Judy and Derek Williams.

Figure 4-6 illustrates a *Do* interaction for how-to content. The application requires learners to execute a set of individual Excel commands in order to produce the required spreadsheet. The application assesses a whole problem of building a simple spreadsheet.

FIGURE 4-6 *Do* Instructional Interaction, How-to Component Skill—Spreadsheet

Spreadsheet
Martha has opened a small restaurant. She has been very successful and wants to expand her business. To finance this project, Martha needs a bank loan. She knows that an accurate and well-designed presentation will help her obtain the loan. You have agreed to prepare the last month's sales figures for Martha. Your job is to create and format a spreadsheet to present Martha's sales figures. Your spreadsheet should be formatted like the sample on the right.

FIGURE 4-6 *Continued*

She gives you the following data:

Lunch Items	Units Sold	Unit Price
Sandwiches	6000	$3.25
Mini Pizzas	5600	$1.75
Salad Bar	3900	$3.25
Soup	4100	$1.25
Desserts	3200	$1.25
Beverages	6100	$0.75

	A	B	C	D
1	Total Lunch Earnings			
2				
3	Lunch Items	Units Sold	Unit Price	Gross Sales
4	*Sandwiches*	6000	$3.25	
5	*Salad Bar*			
6	*Mini Pizzas*			
7	*Soup*			
8	*Beverages*			
9	*Desserts*			
10				
11	Total Sales			
12				

Original design by the author modeled on commercial course.

Figure 4-7 illustrates *Do* interaction for what-happens content. The application requires learners to make a prediction based on a law of physics. After learners respond with a predicted value for θ, the simulation becomes available and provides animated feedback. If the prediction is correct, the box slides off the truck.

FIGURE 4-7 *Do* Instructional Interaction, What-Happens Component Skill—Newton's Laws

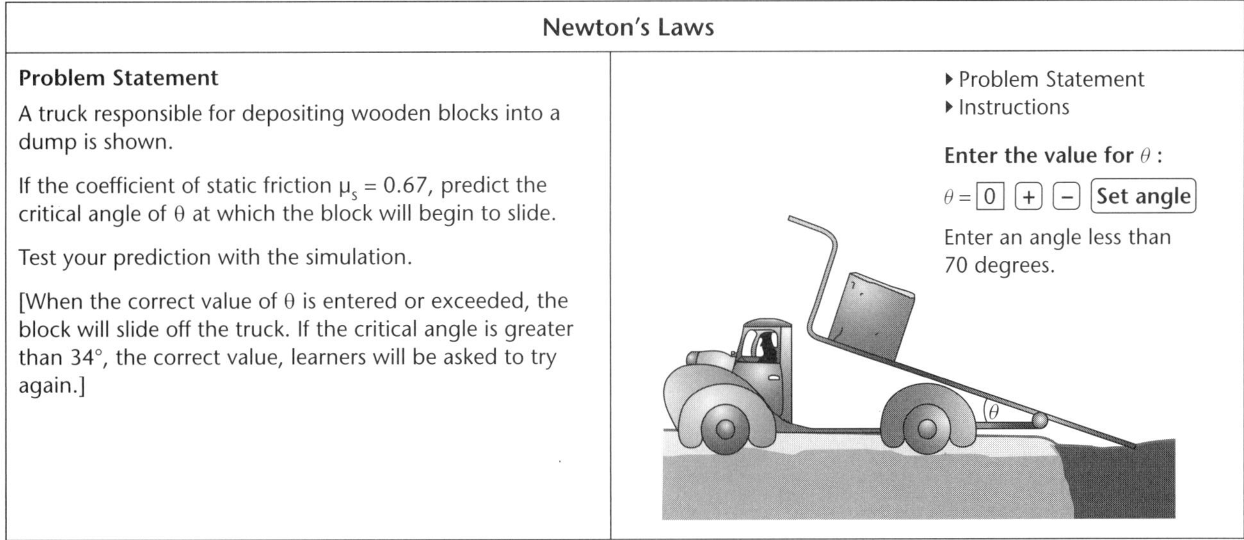

Newton's Laws
Problem Statement
A truck responsible for depositing wooden blocks into a dump is shown.
If the coefficient of static friction $\mu_s = 0.67$, predict the critical angle of θ at which the block will begin to slide.
Test your prediction with the simulation.
[When the correct value of θ is entered or exceeded, the block will slide off the truck. If the critical angle is greater than 34°, the correct value, learners will be asked to try again.]
▸ Problem Statement
▸ Instructions
Enter the value for θ :
θ = 0 + − Set angle
Enter an angle less than 70 degrees.
θ

Original design by the author modeled on commercial course.

WHAT ARE OTHER ESSENTIAL FEATURES OF AN E³ DEMONSTRATION?

One of the primary functions of instruction is to promote active mental processing by the learner. There is ample evidence that the amount and quality of the resultant learning is a direct function of the learner's appropriate cognitive processing of the information presented and the portrayals demonstrated. What must be added to the primary instructional modes to help promote this active mental processing? An important instructional interaction during demonstration is to provide *guidance* to the student. Guidance helps learners relate information to the portrayal of this information. This guidance can take many forms including: attention-focusing, matched examples, divergent examples, and a range-of-difficulty for portrayals. Another important feature of an effective demonstration is multimedia that implements the instructional interaction rather than merely providing graphics that carry no instructional function. Finally, providing learners with a single portrayal for any component skill is insufficient for them to form an adequate mental model. The interactive features of guidance, multimedia, and multiple examples are described and illustrated in the following paragraphs.

Guidance

The demonstration guidance principle states:

> *Learning from demonstrations is enhanced when learners are guided to relate general information to specific instances.*

The following paragraphs describe a variety of different forms of guidance.

Attention-Focusing Guidance This interaction shows learners how to relate the details of a portrayal to the information related to the portrayal. This guidance highlights the properties that enable learners to discriminate instances of one class from instances of a related class. Merely presenting an example is often insufficient. Even if the discriminating property values are present and included in the portrayal, it may be difficult for the learner to discriminate these property values in the specific instance being shown. Guidance during a demonstration will isolate the portrayal of these critical property values so that they can be easily discerned by learners. This can be done with explanatory text, graphics, animation, highlighting, audio overlay, or other attention-focusing devices. While such devices facilitate early demonstration, learners should be encouraged to identify the portrayal of discriminating property values for themselves in later demonstrations.

Figure 4-8 is an instructional event from a short course on Gantt charts. As each part of the Gantt chart is described by the audio, the part being described remains prominent (while other parts are dimmed) and a call-out label appears on the display. This clearly shows learners the part that is being described by the narration. This is a very good use of attention-focusing guidance.

FIGURE 4-8 Attention-Focusing Guidance—Gantt Charts

Gantt Charts
As each part is described in the audio, the call-out appears and the part of the chart being described remains prominent while the rest of the chart is faded. The example only shows representative instructional events.

FIGURE 4-8 *Continued*

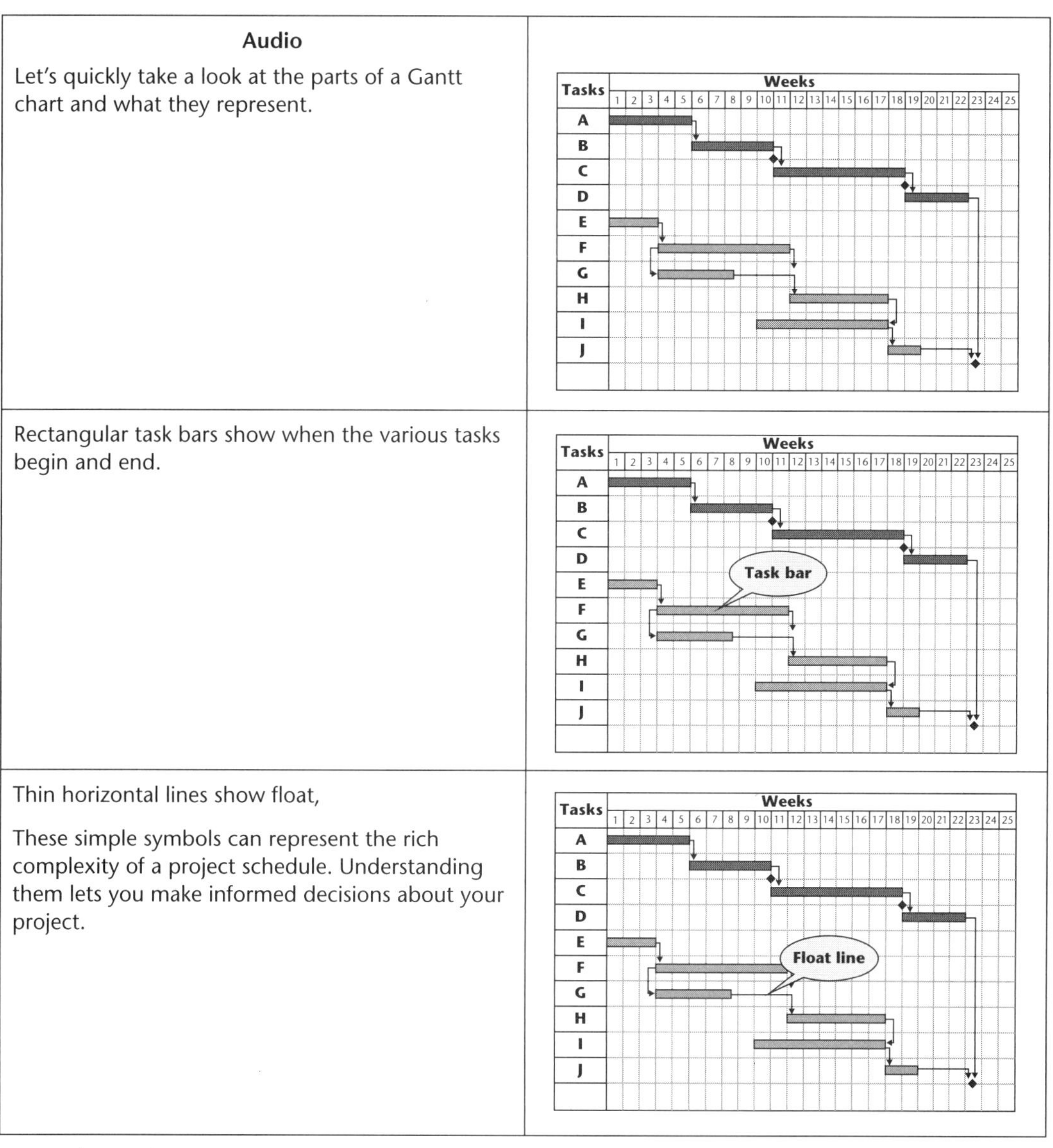

Audio
Let's quickly take a look at the parts of a Gantt chart and what they represent.
Rectangular task bars show when the various tasks begin and end.
Thin horizontal lines show float,
These simple symbols can represent the rich complexity of a project schedule. Understanding them lets you make informed decisions about your project.
Tasks
Weeks
A
B
C
D
E
F
G
H
I
J
Task bar
Float line

Matching Guidance This guidance pairs examples from two or more kinds of objects, events, or processes that are similar on many of their non-discriminating properties but differ only on their discriminating properties. Kind-of component skill enables learners to discriminate instances that belong to a category from those that don't belong or that belong to another category. To discriminate instances from one another requires learners to focus on those properties that enable this discrimination and to ignore those properties that are not used for this discrimination. Matching is one form of guidance that promotes this focus. This form of guidance pairs an example with a non-example such that the two instances share properties that are not used for discrimination and differ only on those properties that enable the discrimination. Acquiring kind-of component skill is enhanced when examples are matched with non-examples for demonstration instructional events early in the sequence. Except for coaching, matched examples should not be used during application instructional events because they provide too much help to learners, making it difficult to assess their classification skill.

In Figure 4-9 the properties that are not used for discrimination include subject of the sentence, the stem word (*easy*), and the message of the sentence. These things are all the same or very similar. The discriminating property is the word that is modified by the word based on *easy*. In the first sentence *easily* modifies *understood,* a verb. In the second sentence *easy* modifies *book,* a noun.

FIGURE 4-9 Matching Guidance—Grammar Adverbs

Grammar—Adverbs	
The kind-of component skill being taught is the part of speech, adverb. One sentence contains an adverb, whereas the second sentence contains an adjective.	
Example of Adverb The book was easily understood.	**Matched Non-Example of Adverb** It was an easy book to understand.

Original design by the author.

Divergent Guidance A *divergent relationship* demonstrates a sequence of portrayals that are all examples of the component skill but which differ from each other in significant ways that reflect the range of difference that occurs in the real world. Component skills require learners to generalize to all examples of a class, even if these examples differ significantly from one another except on their discriminating properties. Each time learners encounter a different portrayal, it expands the boundaries of their mental model of the skill being taught. Learners then learn to generalize their understanding to a variety of portrayals. Acquiring component skill is enhanced when examples are as divergent as possible. Divergent examples should be used both during demonstration and during application instructional events.

In Figure 4-10 the divergent examples illustrate three different kinds of adverbs. These examples are divergent on the basis of the kind of word modified. The adverbs answer different questions—When? To what extent? How? *Yesterday* appears after the word it modifies while *not* and *very* appear before the word they modify. Only one adverb ends in *–ly*. The convergent examples all end in *–ly*. The *–ly* ending is not a discriminating property of adverbs, but based on these examples learners are likely to assume it is a necessary property. All three adverbs answer the question *how*? All three adverbs follow the words they modify.

Range-of-Difficulty Guidance This type of instructional interaction provides learners with a sequence of examples that vary from the easy to solve to the difficult to solve. For any class, some examples are obvious members of the class, while others more closely resemble members of a coordinate class and are more difficult to identify as class members. Multiple examples that cover a wide range of discrimination difficulty help learners generalize to all members of a given class. If possible, it is advisable to test out the difficulty of examples and non-examples with a sample of students because it is often not easy to estimate the difficulty of individual examples and non-examples. Acquiring a component skill is enhanced when examples include a range of discrimination difficulty.

FIGURE 4-10 Divergent Guidance Contrasted with Convergent Examples—Grammar Adverbs

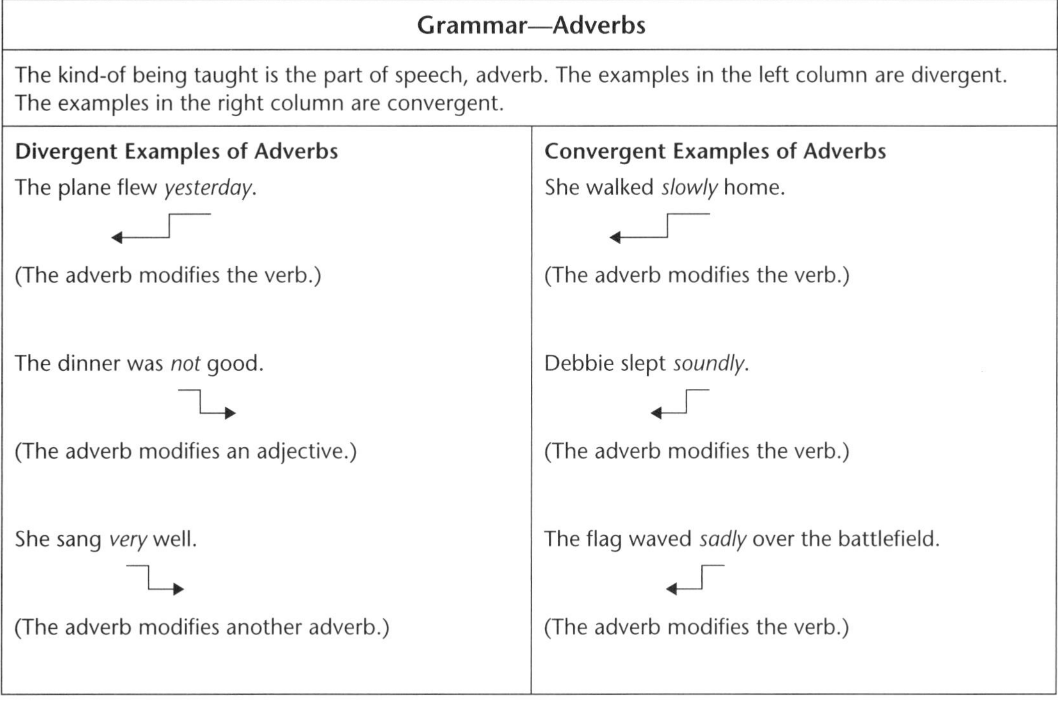

Grammar—Adverbs	
The kind-of being taught is the part of speech, adverb. The examples in the left column are divergent. The examples in the right column are convergent.	
Divergent Examples of Adverbs	**Convergent Examples of Adverbs**
The plane flew *yesterday*. (The adverb modifies the verb.)	She walked *slowly* home. (The adverb modifies the verb.)
The dinner was *not* good. (The adverb modifies an adjective.)	Debbie slept *soundly*. (The adverb modifies the verb.)
She sang *very* well. (The adverb modifies another adverb.)	The flag waved *sadly* over the battlefield. (The adverb modifies the verb.)

Original design by Bob Tennyson and the author.

The instances in Figure 4-11 were given to a sample of 110 seventh-grade students after they had studied the definition. For each instance in the figure, the percent of students correctly identifying it as an example or non-example is given in parentheses after the item. Learners are much more likely to be able to identify new examples and non-examples of adverbs if they have studied this wide range of instances.

FIGURE 4-11 Range-of-Difficulty—Grammar Adverbs

Grammar—Adverbs
The kind-of component skill being taught is the part of speech, *adverb.* Given only a definition, 70 percent or more of the students were able to correctly classify examples and non-examples in the first row; less than 30 percent were able to correctly classify examples and non-examples in the last row; the middle row were between 30 and 70 percent correct. (A few of the non-examples—as noted—ranked higher than their row would otherwise indicate.)
Definition: An adverb is a word that modifies a verb, an adjective, or another adverb and answers one of these questions: When? How? Where? or To what extent?

(continued)

FIGURE 4-11 *Continued*

	Examples	Matched Non-Examples
Easy	*Slowly*, she walked home. (84%)	She is *slow*. (75%)
	Are you *fighting* mad? (70%)	Do you *fight*? (90%)
Medium	You are *so* happy. (68%)	*Sewing* makes you happy. (88%) **(Easy)**
	The train chugged *loudly*. (66%)	The *loud* train chugged. (60%)
	She has been absent *lately*. (64%)	She has been *late*. (89%) **(Easy)**
	Clouds gathered *threateningly*. (56%)	The *threatening* clouds gathered. (50%)
	The book had *three* color pictures. (44%)	The book had *three* pictures. (55%)
	Cats are my *No. 1* favorite pet. (40%)	*One* special cat is my favorite pet. (40%)
Hard	He wants the *dark* purple bicycle. (28%)	He wants the *dark* trim to match. (30%)
	The *small* floral print looked pretty. (22%)	The *small* print looked pretty. (10%)
	It was *not* difficult to explain. (14%)	It is difficult to explain that *not* is a negative word. (43%) **(Medium)**

Original design by Bob Tennyson and the author.

Multimedia

New tools for creating audio, graphics, video, and animations have significantly reduced the effort to use multimedia in instructional materials. However, far too much of this media is added to make the instruction more appealing in an effort to motivate learners, even when much of this media is irrelevant to the instructional interactions and may, in fact, interfere with learning. It is critical that, when multimedia is used, it has a specific instructional purpose to implement the required instructional interaction or to represent the required content elements. Chapter 9 describes and illustrates the use of multimedia to implement instructional events.

The demonstration multimedia principle states:

Learning is promoted when multimedia implements prescribed instructional events and function.

The graphics in Figure 4-2 illustrate the skateboard move called the Ollie. These graphics provide the *Show* interaction for this procedure. The visualization graphic in Figure 4-3 enables learners to see the what-happens to the focal point when the curvature of the lens is changed. This is the *Show* interaction for this physical phenomenon. On the other hand, the photograph in Figure 4-1 does not really illustrate the information. We assume that the nurse is taking a pain history, but learners are not shown sufficient detail for them to know how to take a history.

Multiple Examples

A major factor in the acquisition of component skill is the amount of interaction learners have with the content material. Too often, information is illustrated with a single portrayal, or learners have only a single opportunity to apply their component skills to a problem. A single *Show* instructional event is seldom sufficient for acquisition of component skill. An e[3] instructional strategy includes multiple *Show* and *Do* instructional events to provide sufficient interaction with the content. The number of *Show* and *Do* instructional events required for a given component skill depends on the complexity of the skill and the experience of the learners. This book uses the symbol *>3* to represent the need for more than a single *Show* or *Do* instructional event.

WHAT ARE OTHER ESSENTIAL FEATURES OF AN E[3] APPLICATION?

There are three essential features of application that promote e[3] learning: (1) *coaching* early in the application, (2) corrective or intrinsic *feedback* following a response, and (3) multiple *opportunities for application. Coaching* is direction that accompanies a *Do* instructional event to help learners apply information to a portrayal. *Feedback* is information following a learner's response to indicate the correct responses or to show the consequence of an action.

Coaching

Coaching provides processing direction to learners during *Do* instructional events. Coaching helps learners apply information to a portrayal. The function of coaching is to help learners recall relevant informational elements as they are trying to apply these elements to a given portrayal. Coaching is most effective for the first one or two *Do* instructional events for a given component skill. However, if coaching is continued, then learners do not learn to apply the information to a portrayal on their own. Effective coaching is gradually withdrawn over a sequence of *Do* application events. Too much coaching can interfere with learning. Like guidance, coaching can also be accomplished in a number of different ways.

Figure 4-12 is a segment of an application of the concept *adverb.* The learner is asked to underline the adverbs in a set of sentences. The learner is reminded by a question to remember that the modified word must be a verb, adjective, or another adverb. In the first few sentences, the word being modified is bold-faced, but the learner must still determine its part of speech. In the last few sentences, the learner must determine which word is being modified and which word is doing the modifying. In the actual application, there would be more instances.

FIGURE 4-12 Coaching and Corrective Feedback—Grammar Adverbs

Grammar—Adverbs	
The following is an application of the concept *adverb*. See Figures 4-9 and 4-10 for a demonstration of this kind-of content.	
Application	**Feedback**
Underline the adverbs in the following sentences. Is the word being modified a verb, adjective, or another adverb?	You are *so* **happy**. The word *happy* is an adjective modifying *you*. The word *so* is an adverb.

(continued)

FIGURE 4-12 *Continued*

In the first two sentences, the word being modified is in bold font to help you.	The threatening **clouds** gathered.
You are so **happy**.	The word *clouds* is a noun.
The threatening **clouds** gathered.	The word *threatening* is an adjective modifying *clouds*.
The book had three color pictures.	The book had *three* **color** pictures.
He wanted the dark trim to match.	The word *color* is an adjective modifying *pictures*.
	The word *three* is an adverb.
	He wanted the dark **trim** to match.
	The word *trim* is a noun.
	The word *dark* is an adjective modifying *trim*.

Original design by Bob Tennyson and the author.

Feedback

Corrective feedback is information following a response indicating the correct response and why it is the corrective response. Right/wrong information is helpful but not sufficient for e^3 instructional events; better feedback is to provide information that shows learners the correct response after both right and wrong responses. Corrective feedback is often sufficient for information-about, part-of, and kind-of skill, but is not sufficient for how-to and what-happens. The second column in Figure 4-12 shows the corrective feedback for each of the sentences in the application.

Intrinsic feedback is a portrayal that shows the consequence of learners' actions. Intrinsic feedback, because it is a naturally occurring event, is the best feedback for how-to and what-happens skills. Figure 4-13 is one application problem from an introductory course on spreadsheets. Learners are directed to complete the spreadsheet and then they are given a key sum in the fifth bullet item that will allow them to determine whether they completed the spreadsheet correctly. If they did not, then their sum will be different from the key given and they will have to check and redo their work in order to arrive at the correct sum.

FIGURE 4-13 Intrinsic Feedback—Spreadsheets

Spreadsheets

Problem 5—Project Costs and Wages

The client wants to know how many hours and how much each project costs. Employees work on more than one project, so their time and wages have to be divided against the projects.

- In Row 9, determine the total wage paid to each employee.
- In Column F, determine the total hours for each project.
- In Column G, determine the cost per project. For each employee who worked on the project, multiply the hours worked by the hourly rate, and then add these amounts in the cells of Column G.
- In Cell G9, indicate the total wages paid to all employees for all projects.
- In Cell G10, check your work by summing the Total Wage Paid in Row 9. The amount in Cell G9 and G10 should be the same. This amount should equal $7,189.90. Did it work?
- After you have submitted your work, you may obtain a copy of the completed spreadsheet.

FIGURE 4-13 *Continued*

	A	B	C	D	E	F	G
1				Project Costs and Wages			
2		Jake	Sally	Deon	Chan	Hrs	Cost
3	Hourly wage	$ 23.45	$ 26.87	$ 53.40	$ 62.98		
4	Project 1	10.3		24			
5	Project 2	5.1	6.4		31		
6	Project 3		15.2		29		
7	Project 4	4.6	8.4	16			
8	Total hours						
9	Total Wage Paid						
10							

Original design by the author.

PRINCIPLES AND PRESCRIPTIONS

- To facilitate communication about instructional interactions, First Principles of Instruction defines four primary presentation modes: *Tell, Ask, Show,* and *Do.*
- First Principles of Instruction also defines other essential features of demonstration, including *guidance* and effective *multimedia* implementation.
- First Principles of Instruction defines other essential features of application, including *coaching* and *feedback.*

Table 4-1 summarizes the instructional interactions identified in this chapter.

Table 4-1 Instructional Interactions

Demonstration	**Tell**	**Show**	**Multimedia**	**Guidance**
	Provides information	Provides portrayal	Implements instructional events	Directs attention to relevant properties
Application	**Ask**	**Do**	**Feedback**	**Coaching**
	Requires recall or recognition of information	Requires using information to solve a problem	Provides corrective or consequence information	Provides processing directions

APPLICATION

You will come to understand the instructional interactions illustrated in this chapter if you try to identify these interactions in existing instructional materials. Select several courses that you are taking, designing, or that you can find on the Internet. Examine these courses to see whether you can identify the primary instructional interactions—*Tell, Ask, Show,* and *Do*. See whether you can find examples of the various kinds of guidance, coaching, corrective feedback, and intrinsic feedback. If some of the instructional interactions are missing from the material you examine, attempt to design some of the missing interactions.

TO LEARN MORE

The material in this chapter is a simplification of my earlier work on Component Display Theory. You can learn more about Component Display Theory from the following:

Merrill, M. D. (1983). Chapter 9: Component display theory. In C. M. Reigeluth (Ed.), *Instructional design theories and models: An overview of their current status* (pp. 279–333). Hillsdale, NJ: Lawrence Erlbaum Associates.

Merrill, M. D. (1987a). Chapter 7: A lesson based on component display theory. In C. M. Reigeluth (Ed.), *Instructional design theories in action* (pp. 201–244). Hillsdale, NJ: Lawrence Erlbaum Associates.

Merrill, M. D. (1987b). The new component display theory: Instructional design for courseware authoring. *Instructional Science, 16*, 19–34.

Merrill, M. D. (1994). *Instructional design theory* (Section 3: Component display theory). Englewood Cliffs, NJ: Educational Technology Publications.

COMING NEXT

Chapter 3 illustrated content elements. This chapter described and illustrated instructional interactions that, when combined with content elements, create instructional events. The next chapter, Chapter 5, illustrates instructional strategies, which are prescribed sets of instructional events, for each type of component skill.

CHAPTER 5

INSTRUCTIONAL STRATEGIES

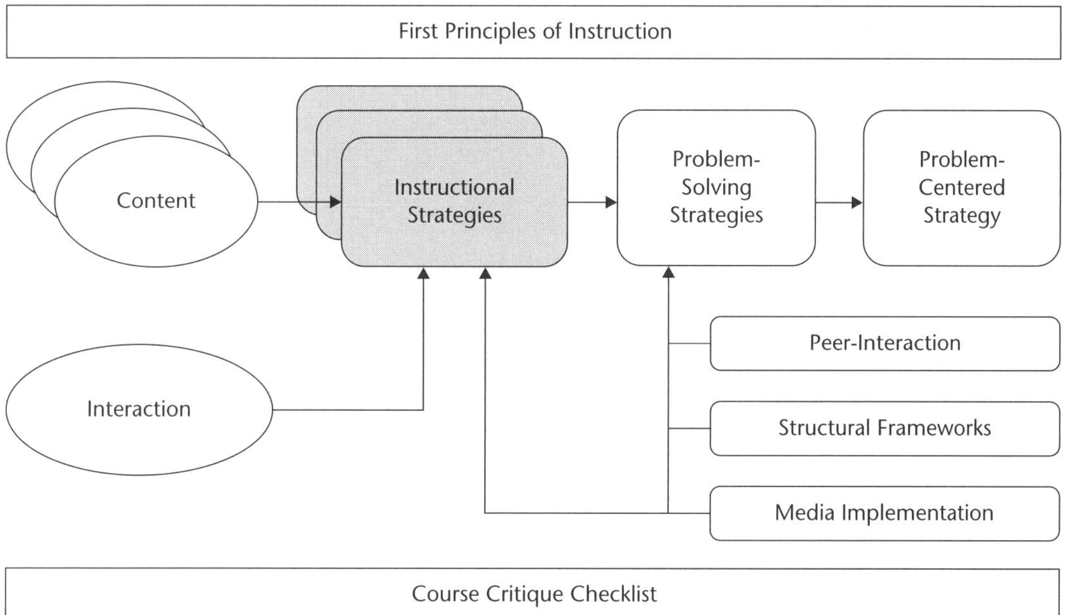

Quick Look

In Chapter 4 I introduced a technical vocabulary for describing learner interaction with content elements. In this chapter I combine Instructional Modes—*Tell, Show, Ask,* and *Do*—with content elements to prescribe instructional strategies for each of the five types of component skill identified in Chapter 3. This chapter answers the following question: What are the prescribed instructional events that comprise an e^3 strategy for each of the five types of component skill?

Key Words

Instructional Event: the combination of an instructional interaction with a content element.
Instructional Strategy: a set of instructional events that is appropriate for, and consistent with, a given type of component skill.
Presentation: *Tell* instructional events.
Practice: *Ask* instructional events with corrective feedback.

Demonstration: *Show* instructional events with guidance.
Application: *Do* instructional events with coaching and corrective or intrinsic feedback.
Mnemonic: a memory aid that helps learners remember information.
Sequence Cue: presenting items in the same order when sequence is not the goal of the instruction.

INTRODUCTION

Chapter 3 illustrated five different types of component knowledge and skill: information-about, part-of, kind-of, how-to, and what-happens. It also illustrated the appropriate information and portrayal content elements for each type of component skill. Chapter 4 illustrated four instructional interaction modes: *Tell, Ask, Show,* and *Do.* It also illustrated other essential features of demonstration and application interactions. This chapter illustrates instructional events. An *instructional event* is a combination of an instructional interaction with a content element. This chapter also illustrates instructional strategies. An *instructional strategy* is a prescribed set of instructional events appropriate for a given type of component skill.

This chapter is based on the premise that there are different types of component skill and that e^3 instruction requires different instructional strategies for each type of skill (Gagné, 1985; Gagné, Wager, Golas, & Keller, 2005). If the instructional experience does not include the instructional strategy that is most appropriate for the acquisition of the desired skill, then effective, efficient, and engaging learning is less likely to occur (Merrill, Drake, Lacy, & Pratt, 1996). The fundamental architecture of an instructional strategy is a set of instructional events that is appropriate for, and consistent with, a given instructional goal. The demonstration consistency principle states:

> *Learning is promoted when learners observe a demonstration of the skill to be learned and engage in application of their newly acquired skill that is consistent with the type of content being taught.*

Table 5-1 summarizes the primary instructional strategies for each type of component skill. The instructional modes—*Tell, Ask, Show,* and *Do*—combined with the content modes—*information* and *portrayal*—are listed across the columns. In this book, *Tell*-information is called *presentation*; *Ask*-information is called *practice*; *Show*-portrayals is called *demonstration*; and *Do* is called *application.* The types of component skills are listed in the first column for each row. The entries in the cells of the table are the primary content elements for a given component skill that are combined with the instructional modes to provide instructional strategy events. An instructional strategy is a sequence of instructional events as indicated by each row in the table. The strategies summarized in Table 5-1 will be elaborated and illustrated in the following paragraphs.

Table 5-1 Instructional Strategies for Component Skills

	Tell-Information PRESENTATION	*Ask* (Remember) Information PRACTICE	*Show* (Portrayal) DEMONSTRATION	*Do* (Apply) Info to Portrayal APPLICATION
Information about	name—information	name—information	----------------	----------------
Parts-of	name—information	name—information	name—location	name—location
Kinds-of	definition	definition	examples, non-examples	classify examples
How-to	steps—sequence	steps—sequence	demonstrate task	perform task
What-happens	if . . . then statement of conditions and consequence	if . . . then statement of conditions and consequence	demonstrate process	predict consequences or find conditions

INFORMATION-ABOUT INSTRUCTIONAL STRATEGY

Goal: Identify information about a set of objects, activities, or processes.

Prescribed instructional events:

Presentation: Tell name, information, and portrayal item-by-item; focus attention; explore; repetition.

Practice: Ask for the name given the description or portrayal. Ask for the description or portrayal given the name. Immediate response; avoid sequence cues; corrective feedback; scoring goal: 100 percent mastery.

Information-about component skill is sometimes prerequisite for other component skills.

Presentation

Learners are given a name for the information, shown some portrayal of the information if required, and provided the description of the information. This portrayal and description together provide information that the student is expected to remember about some object, activity, or process. The presentation should allow the student to *explore* the items by allowing control over which items to observe and should allow the student to *repeat* the presentation.

A presentation may also include *nice-to-know* information that the student will not be required to remember or later identify. When nice-to-know information is presented, learners should be told that this is for interest only and they will not be required to remember this information.

During the presentation, distinctive characteristics of the information are pointed out to the student (*attention-focusing guidance*). If appropriate, the student is provided with a *mnemonic* to assist in remembering the information. A mnemonic is a memory aid that helps learners remember information. The presentation should also make the context of the information clear to the student.

Information-about should be available on learner demand in other types of instructional strategies such as *part-of, kind-of, how-to,* and *what-happens* strategies.

Practice

Given the description or portrayal, learners are able to recognize or provide the name associated with the information. Or given the name, the learners are able to recognize the portrayal or description or to paraphrase the description. This is often accomplished with multiple-choice, matching, or short-answer questions. The practice should provide for repetition until mastery is reached.

Effective *information-about* practice requires an *immediate response* with little or no delay. Mastery of memorized information should not require the learner to try and figure out the answer. Students will be more motivated to practice until mastery if they compete with themselves to acquire a higher score each time they practice. Keeping track of the learner's score can facilitate this repetition. Repetition should *avoid sequence cues* by using a random order when the items are repeated. For many learners it is easier to remember paired items when they always appear in the same order. They remember which items are first, which are last, which are in the middle. A *sequence cue* is always presenting items in the same order when sequence is not the goal of the instruction. Games are often effective in learning *information-about* if they encourage repetition, improved performance, and competition with self. Learners should be provided immediate *correct answer feedback* for both correct and incorrect responses.

Strategy Demonstration—Famous Presidents

The *information-about* instruction illustrated in Figure 5-1 consists of information about twelve famous U.S. presidents. For each of the twelve presidents, there are four instructional events: *Tell* and three forms of *Ask*, which occur in random order throughout the lesson. The presentation (*Tell*) was called *exploration* in the program and allowed learners to examine the information about each president as long as they wanted and to return to any of the information if they wished. The program also included several more detailed paragraphs about each president (*nice-to-know*), but this information was not included in the practice. There were three different types of practice (*Ask*): (1) *Who's Who* (given name, recognize picture), (2) *What's My Line* (shown picture, recognize primary accomplishment), and *(3) Who Did What* (given facts, recognize name). Learners were shown the correct response after they responded (*correct answer feedback*). Avoid *sequence cue*s: the items in each practice appeared in random order so if the learner repeated one kind of practice, the items were in a different order each time. *Mastery:* the program reported the learner's score after each practice session and encouraged learners with the following admonition: "Check your knowledge. Try to score 100 percent on each."

FIGURE 5-1 Information-About Instructional Strategy—Famous Presidents

<table>
<tr><th colspan="3">Famous Presidents</th></tr>
<tr><td colspan="3">The following is from an information-about program designed to teach students some facts about some of the presidents of the United States. The presentation shows a picture of the president and tells his term of office, the primary thing he is noted for, and some facts about the president. There are three types of practice: given the name match the picture, given the name match what he is noted for, and given facts about the president match his name.</td></tr>
<tr><td>PRESENTATION</td><td colspan="2">
George Washington
Was elected unanimously as America's first President
Served 1789 to 1797
This president turned down an offer to be king, and was instead elected unanimously as America's first President. He formed the first presidential cabinet, passed the Bill of Rights, and was the commanding general of the Revolutionary War.</td></tr>
<tr><td>PRACTICE</td><td colspan="2">Which picture is James Monroe?
  </td></tr>
<tr><td>PRACTICE</td><td colspan="2">
Which of these is President James Monroe known for?
A. was elected unanimously as America's first President
B. established a doctrine of non-interference
C. was President when the stock market crashed
D. was the first American awarded the Nobel Peace Prize</td></tr>
<tr><td>PRACTICE</td><td>This statement describes which president?
An inventor, philosopher, naturalist, and musician, this President spoke six languages and wrote the Declaration of Independence. His election as President was the first to end up being decided in the House of Representatives. He sent Lewis and Clark on their expedition and was responsible for the Louisiana Purchase.</td><td>A. George Washington
B. James Monroe
C. Woodrow Wilson
D. Thomas Jefferson</td></tr>
</table>

This short course is a very good example of an effective information-about instructional strategy. This course is a stand-alone example of information-about instruction. In most cases information-about instruction is a component skill for a more complex problem or task.

PART-OF INSTRUCTIONAL STRATEGY

Goal: Identify the name and location of a given part with respect to the whole of some object or system.

Prescribed instructional events:

Presentation/demonstration: *Show* its location in the whole and *Tell* the part name and information about the part. Avoid location cues; use chunking; provide for repetition.

Practice/application: (*Do*) point to location of the part given its name or information; recall or recognize its name and information shown the location of the part. Use random order; avoid location cues; require an immediate response; scoring goal: 100 percent; corrective feedback.

Part-of component skill is often prerequisite for other component skills.

Presentation/Demonstration

It is important to ensure that learners are associating the location of the part with the information about the part. If the presentation is passive, where a part is highlighted for the student and the information presented, then learners may not attend to the location. A better procedure is to ask learners to click on each part in the whole. *Tell* learners the name and information associated with the part only after they click on the part. An effective technique is to have the name and description pop up when students point to or click on a part. When learners are required to locate and click on a part, it is more likely that they are attending to the location of the part and associating the label and information with the location.

Learners often prefer *explore* type presentations where they can click on the parts in any order to be given the name, description, and other information. This allows the student to go back to a given part as many times as necessary to learn the necessary information. Learners should be allowed to explore the parts until they feel that they can locate each part.

It is important in part-of practice to prevent learners from associating the label with the location of the label rather than with the location of the part under consideration. If the label is located near the part, then the learner may learn that Label 1 is located in the upper left of the diagram, Label 2 in the lower right of the diagram, etc., rather than associating the label with the part. When this happens, if a new diagram is shown where the parts are located in a different place, then learners may not be able to locate the parts. A solution is to present all of the labels in the same location on the display while highlighting the part under consideration.

Acquisition of this skill will be more effective if learners are required to learn *chunks* of parts where each chunk contains seven or fewer parts. It is important that after a chunk is learned that items in this chunk are then included in later chunks. We have described presentation/demonstration separately, but in effective instruction learners should be presented a chunk of the parts and then allowed to practice.

Then there should be another round of presentation and practice for a second chunk, which includes items from the first chunk, and so forth.

Practice/Application

Ask learners to point to the location of the part given the name or information (*location practice*). *Ask* learners to remember or recall the name or description given the location of the part (*naming practice*).

When the learning has been mastered, learners should be able to provide an *immediate response* without having to think about it. The practice should provide *correct answer feedback* after each response whether correct or incorrect. Practice is more effective when it requires both naming and location practice and when the parts are shown in *random order* to help prevent learners from merely memorizing a sequence.

If the label is located next to the part then the learner may learn which name belongs in which location rather than which name is associated with each part. Learning is more effective if the parts are practiced in random order to prevent the learner from merely memorizing the labels in sequence. Each of these recommended practice conditions improve the quality of the learning.

If it is important to learn the parts of some device or event, then it is important to learn them all. It is not sufficient to know only 80 percent of the parts of a device if all of the parts are necessary for operating the device. Therefore the criterion for acceptable performance should be 100 percent. If it is unnecessary to know some of the parts, then is it necessary to know any of the parts? Perhaps the practice should require only those parts that are necessary to know.

An effective practice technique is to use *sampling with replacement.* That is, when a learner misses a particular part, this part is put back into the queue for another try. A good criterion for practice is to have learners practice until they can name each part or locate each part at least twice.

Strategy Demonstration—Utah Counties

The part-of instructional strategy illustrated in Figure 5-2 is about the twenty-nine counties in the state of Utah. The presentation consists of a map of the state (the whole) with each of the counties outlined and shown in a different color, shown in shades of gray in the illustration (the parts). For each of the twenty-nine counties, there are five instructional events: *Tell/Show,* and four types of *Do.*

Tell/Show. Learners explore each county by placing the mouse over the county on the map (*show location*). Learners are then told the name of the county, the county seat, the population, and a brief fact about the county (name and information). Learners could *explore* the counties as many times as they wanted in this presentation mode. *Nice-to-know:* This short course also included two or three paragraphs about the county, but learners are not required to remember this information. *Avoid location cues:* When a learner points to a county, it is highlighted on the map, but the information about the county always appears in the panel next to the map in the same location for each county. *Chunking:* There are twenty-nine counties and the instruction might have been more effective if learners were asked to learn only groups of counties at a time rather than all counties at once. The parts were not chunked in this particular short course.

FIGURE 5-2 Part-of Instructional Strategy—Utah Counties

<table>
<tr><td colspan="2">Utah Counties
The following is designed to teach students the counties of the state of Utah.</td></tr>
<tr><td>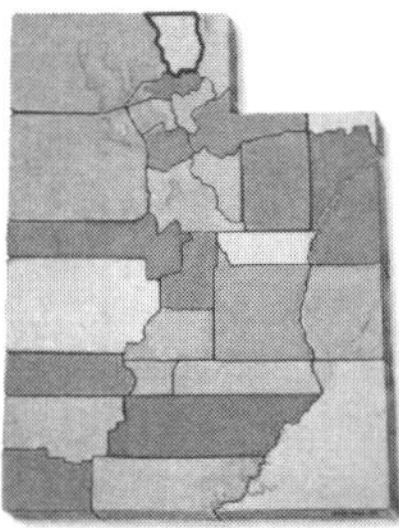</td><td>Cache
Seat: Logan
Population (2000): 91,391

The home of Utah State University is also the state's largest producer of dairy products.</td></tr>
<tr><td>What county is highlighted?
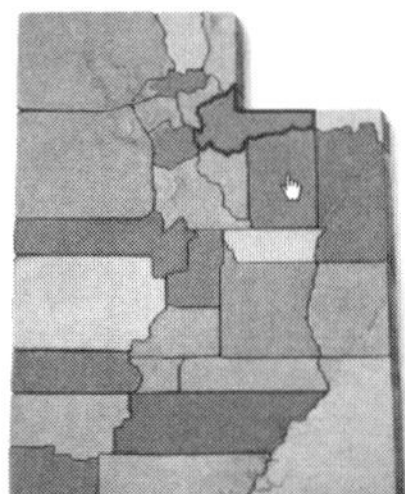
A. Piute
B. Summit
C. Morgan
D. Daggett
E. Garfield

Feedback when the learner clicks on a county other than the target: Incorrect! Summit County is highlighted on the map.</td><td>Point to the county that is described below.
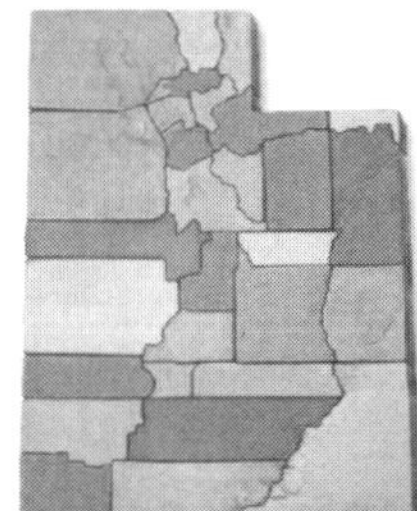
Park City (a city in this county) was on the verge of becoming a ghost town for several decades. The area's rugged terrain and deep snow has led to its rebirth as a winter sports center.

Feedback when the learner clicks on the target county: Correct! Summit County is correct.</td></tr>
<tr><td>Point to Rich County.
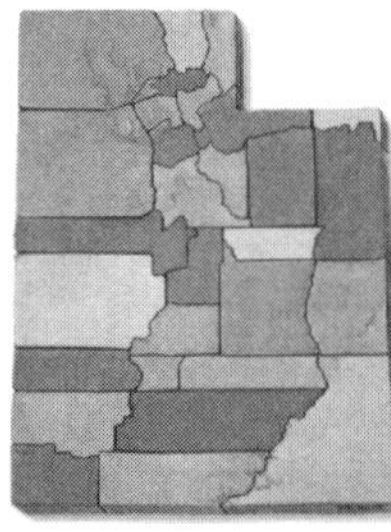

Feedback when learner clicks on a county other than the target: Incorrect. Rich County is now highlighted on the map.</td><td>What is the county seat of this county?
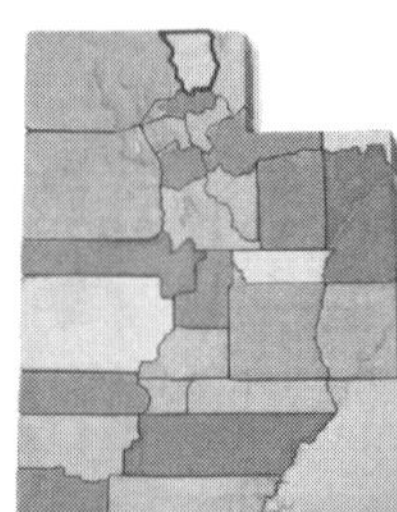
A. Manti
B. Logan
C. Moab
D. Kanab
E. Junction

Feedback when learner clicks on the correct county name: Correct! Logan is the county seat of Cache County.</td></tr>
</table>

There were four different types of application or *Do,* as illustrated in Rows 2 and 3 of Figure 5-2: (1) Identify the name of the county that is highlighted (shown the location recognize the name); (2) Point to the county that matches the description (given the information about the part, find its location); (3) Point to a county given its name (given a name of a part, find its location with respect to the whole); and (4) Recognize the county seat given the location of the county (given the location of a part, recognize some information about the part). It should be pointed out that these types of application could have been combined by having the student recognize the name and county seat given the location of a county, etc. *Feedback:* learners were shown the correct location or information if they were incorrect. *Repetition:* learners could also practice any of the different practice modes as many times as they wanted. *Random order:* the order of items was different each time the learner practiced. *Scoring goal:* learners were encouraged to get 100 percent on each of the quizzes.

KIND-OF INSTRUCTIONAL STRATEGY

Goal: Classify unencountered instances—objects, devices, procedures, actions, or symbols—as belonging to a particular class.

Prescribed instructional events:

Presentation: *Tell* the name of the class and the values on the discriminating properties (definition) that determine class membership.
Demonstration: *Show* examples and non-examples of the class. Provide attention focusing guidance; a divergent set of examples; matched examples and non-examples; increasingly difficult examples and non-examples.
Application: *Do* require learners to classify unencountered examples and non-examples of the class. Provide coaching on early items and corrective feedback.

Kind-of component skills are the building blocks for how-to and what-happens component skills.

Presentation

Tell learners the name of the class(es) being taught. *Tell* learners "X is a kind of ____" to indicate the superordinate class name. A *superordinate class* is a concept whose meaning encompasses the meaning of more specific concepts. Boat is a superordinate class of the class sloop (see coordinate concepts, Chapter 3). *Tell* learners the definition of the class or classes. A definition is a list of discriminating properties and the values they must assume that identifies members of the class or classes under consideration. Be sure that the definition does not include properties that are not used for discrimination. It is okay to describe other properties, but the presentation should make it very clear which properties and values are required to define members of the class and which are not.

Demonstration

Show learners a sequence of several divergent examples matched with non-examples of the class under consideration. Be sure the examples illustrate each of the defining properties of the class; be careful not to use pseudo examples. Learning is enhanced when the presentation of the definition and the demonstration of the instances simultaneous rather than sequential.

Application

Give learners unencountered examples and non-examples and ask them to identify those that belong to a given class and those that do not (*Do*). Ask learners to explain why. Explaining why requires learners to point out the presence or absence of discriminating properties. *Coach* early instances in the application by focusing learners' attention on the defining properties; gradually reduce this coaching for later instances in the application. Provide *corrective feedback* that focuses learners' attention on the discriminating properties that determine class membership.

I have included three different examples for kind-of instructional strategies because a kind-of strategy is fundamental to learning to solve problems. Each of these kind-of strategies demonstrates some subtle but important characteristics of a kind-of instructional strategy.

Strategy Demonstration—Helping Relationships

The Helping Relationships demonstration shows what appears to be a good implementation of a kind-of strategy but with some potential problems, as identified in the following paragraphs.

Figure 5-3 is a segment for teaching the concept *Helping Relationship* from a course on job counseling. The instructional events are: *Tell*-definition (Row 1), *Show*-examples (Row 2), *Show*-non-examples (Row 3), and require learners to classify (*Do*) unencountered examples (Row 4). The definition includes three properties: *collaborative, trust,* and *personal growth.* These are all relevant attributes for discriminating among different kinds of personal relationships. The examples are divergent, but the examples are not matched with non-examples; there is no attention-focusing guidance; and the difficulty of the instances is unknown.

FIGURE 5-3 Kind-of Instructional Strategy—Job Counseling

Helping Relationship		
The following is kind-of content from a course designed to train workforce counselors. It teaches a kind-of relationship, *a helping relationship.*		
Definition	**Helping Relationship** The helping relationship is a constructive support relationship that is collaborative in nature, grounded in trust and respect, and based on the belief that the client has the capacity for personal growth and change.	

FIGURE 5-3 *Continued*

Demonstration—Examples	**Helping Relationship** Think about the people you interact with in your daily routine. Do you have relationships with others that could be classified as helping relationships? Maybe you have a mentor who helps you professionally. Both the teacher-student and doctor-patient relationship could be classified as helping relationships. Students usually trust their teachers or mentors and patients trust their doctors. Teachers, doctors, and mentors believe that their students or patients can change. And in all cases there is collaboration among the participants in the relationship.	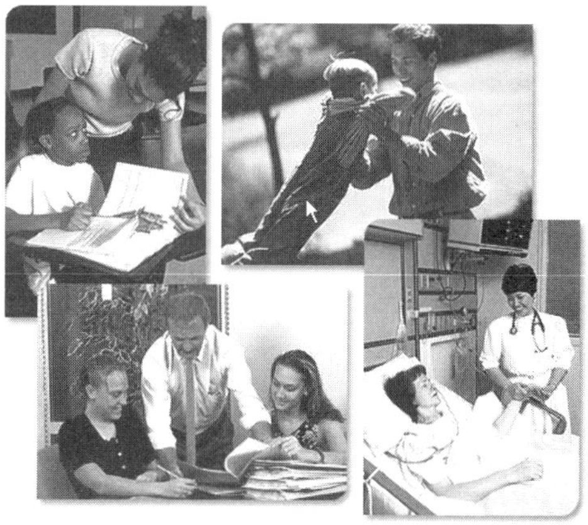
Demonstration—Non-Examples	Most relationships probably aren't true helping relationships because they lack one or more of the characteristics that define a helping relationship. For example, criminal prosecutors are adversaries rather than supporters of defendants. Military officers do not collaborate with troops; they give orders. Telemarketers are not always trusted by their customers. Landlords do not need to believe in the growth potential of their renters.	
Application	**Feedback:** *Incorrect:* this relationship does not contain all four key characteristics of a helping relationship. *Correct:* this relationship is a helping relationship.	Which of the following is the best example of a helping relationship? Counselor/client * Grocery clerk/customer Bus driver/passenger Judge/defendant Click on your answer for feedback.

The application requires learners to classify four instances. However, the instruction assumes that the learners are familiar with the relationships used as instances. If learners are not familiar with these relationships, then these instances border on being pseudo examples. Why? They do not actually show or fail to show the collaboration, trust, or confidence in personal growth. To actually show these properties would require a short audio dialog or video to observe the interaction among the participants in the interaction. The designers probably felt that because it was a reasonable assumption that most learners would be sufficiently familiar with these situations that the instructional time required and the expense of developing more extensive instances was not justified. There is no coaching provided. Feedback is right/wrong feedback rather than intrinsic or corrective feedback. If corrective feedback were included, it might show and explain specific illustrations of each of the four key characteristics for the instances shown. If intrinsic feedback were included, it might even show the reaction of a client that demonstrates that the example of the relationship was not helping.

This example illustrates the primary instructional events for kind-of instruction, but has a number of areas for improvement including: (1) avoid pseudo examples by providing more complete illustration of the instances showing sufficient details of the interaction that learners can observe examples of each of the key characteristics; (2) include attention-focusing guidance to direct learners' attention to the illustration of these key characteristics; (3) more carefully match examples with non-examples; (4) provide coaching for at least one of the instances in the application; and (5) use at least corrective feedback for the application.

Strategy Demonstration—Rule of Thirds

The Rule of Thirds demonstration is an attempt to show a complete kind-of instructional strategy. My intent is for this demonstration to serve as a model to help you identify and design kind-of instructional strategies.

Figure 5-4 is a segment of a course on professional photography. This segment teaches the composition principle called the *rule of thirds*. The instructional strategy for this segment includes the following instructional events:

Tell-definition (Row 1); show matched example/non-example pairs (Rows 2, 3, and 4); require learners to classify unencountered photographs as to whether or not they implement the rule of thirds (Rows 5 and 6). In Rows 2 and 3, attention-focusing guidance in the form of a graph is used to focus the learners' attention on the location of the key point of interest in the picture with relation to the border of the picture. Row 4 is a set of divergent example/non-example pairs using scenery instead of people. Applying the rule of thirds to scenery is more difficult than applying it with people. The attention-focusing guidance is less obvious, providing some explanation first and then suggesting that learners click to see the grid lines.

FIGURE 5-4 Kind-of Instructional Strategy—Photography Rule of Thirds

Creating a Professional Photo—Rule of Thirds	
The following is a kind-of segment from a course on photography. The kind-of being taught is a composition principle called the rule of thirds. The segment includes a definition, examples and non-examples, and an application that requires learners to identify photographs that use this principle.	
1. Definition	**Rule of Thirds** The rule of thirds is a principle used to divide a photograph into thirds vertically and horizontally. Putting the object of interest of the photo onto one of the crossing lines makes the photo look more interesting and professional.

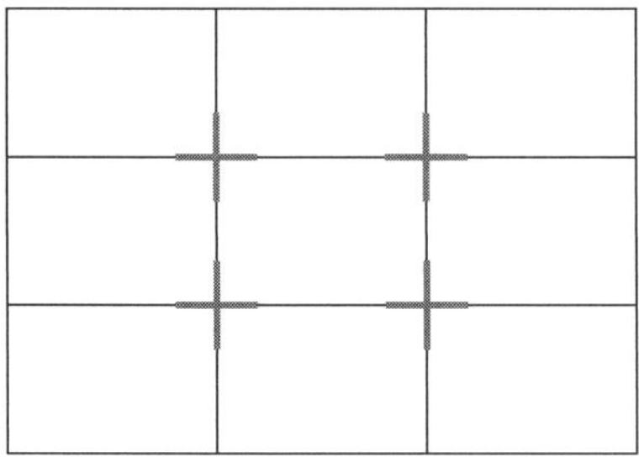

FIGURE 5-4 *Continued*

<table>
<tr><td>2. Example/Non-Example</td><td colspan="2">Using Rule of Thirds
In portraits, the object of interest is the person's eyes.
When the rule of thirds isn't applied, the picture looks awkward. The viewer's eyes can't easily determine what to focus on while looking at the picture.
The bottom picture shows a correct application of the rule of thirds. Notice the lines cross on the girls' eyes.
</td></tr>
<tr><td>3. Example/Non-Example</td><td colspan="2">Click on pictures to see grid lines.
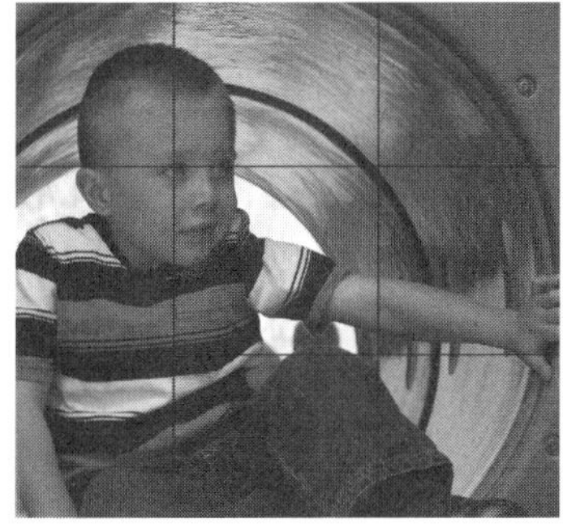 </td></tr>
<tr><td rowspan="2">4. Example/Non-Example</td><td colspan="2">In each pair of pictures, which is the most interesting? Why?</td></tr>
<tr><td>Does not use rule of thirds, there is no point of interest where the lines cross.

</td><td>Uses rule of thirds. The rock and large tree add a point of interest and help focus the viewer's attention.

</td></tr>
<tr><td></td><td colspan="2">Click on picture to see grid lines.</td></tr>
</table>

(continued)

FIGURE 5-4 *Continued*

5. Application	Which of the following pictures correctly use the rule of thirds? Explain. If you need help, click on the picture to see the grid lines.    
6. Application	Which of the following pictures use the rule of thirds? Explain.     **Feedback:** After you respond, click on the picture to see grid lines.

Original lesson by the author.

Rows 5 and 6 provide new unencountered photographs that are also divergent in content, including people, scenery with people, and scenery without people. Learners are asked to respond by selecting photographs that implement the principle and then to explain their choice. After they respond, they can overlay the grid to provide feedback to their response. The directions in Row 5 coach learners, if they feel they need help, by suggesting they click on the picture to see the grid lines before they respond. This coaching is not available in the remaining application problems. For the photographs in Row 6, the grid is used to provide extrinsic feedback after learners have responded. Figure 5-4 implements most of the suggestions for an e^3 kind-of instructional strategy.

Strategy Demonstration—Poetic Meter

The Poetic Meter demonstration is a more complex instructional strategy. I debated about including such a long example but decided that it was valuable to you for a number of reasons. First, it is a demonstration of teaching coordinate concepts, which is perhaps the most common type of kind-of content you will encounter or design. Second, it demonstrates some subtle aspects of a kind-of instructional strategy. You should note the use of an alternative representation of the definition of the different types of poetic meter. It also demonstrates the careful use of matched examples; it demonstrates an effective demonstration of gradually reducing the amount of guidance; and it demonstrates gradually increasing the level of difficulty of the examples used.

Figure 5-5 illustrates an instructional strategy for teaching the coordinate concepts for kinds of poetic meter—trochaic, iambic, dactylic, and anapestic. In this case there are ten instructional events: two *Tell/Show* events, four *Show* events, and four *Do* events. Note that in this case each instructional event deals simultaneously with all four kinds of poetic foot. The first *Tell/Show* presents a definition for three of the properties used to define a poetic foot: stressed syllables, rhythm, and a poetic foot. The second *Tell/Show* presents a definition and an example of each of the four stress patterns for each kind of poetic foot.

Alternative representation: this presentation uses both a chart and definition statements of the stress patterns. The chart is designed to help the student remember the patterns and relate them to one another. An alternative representation of information is a good guidance technique. *Attention-focusing guidance:* Each of the instances shown with the definitions uses several techniques to help learners discriminate the defining properties. Dots separate words into syllables; bold font indicates the stressed syllables; vertical lines divide the lines into poetic feet of two or three syllables. Following the definitions is some procedural guidance to help learners apply the definitions to the examples that follow and to future instances so that they can determine the stress pattern of instances of poetry. I included this lengthy demonstration to help you see a demonstration of these nuances of an effective kind-of instructional strategy.

FIGURE 5-5 Kind-of Instructional Strategy—Coordinate Concept Poetic Meter

Types of Poetic Meter

Purpose:

The purpose of this lesson is to teach you how to determine the different types of rhythmic patterns that distinguish poetry from ordinary prose. You will learn to recognize and name four different rhythmic patterns.

Definitions of properties:

Stressed Syllable: A stressed syllable is louder or higher in pitch than an unstressed syllable.

Rhythm: Rhythm in poetry results from a recurring pattern of stressed and unstressed syllables.

Poetic Foot: It is possible to break a poem into rhythmic sections called feet. Each poetic foot consists of one stressed syllable plus one or two unstressed syllables.

Definitions of kinds-of poetic feet:

The four kinds-of stress patterns can be represented by the following table. The stressed syllable is in bold.

	First syllable stressed	Last syllable stressed
Two syllables	**dai**.ly Trochaic	her **glance** Iambic
Three syllables	**Praise** to the Dactylic	In.ter.**vene** Anapestic

A **trochaic foot** consists of a stressed syllable followed by an unstressed syllable. A single foot is called a *trochee.*

An **iambic foot** consists of an unstressed syllable followed by a stressed syllable. A single foot is called an *iamb.*

A **dactylic foot** consists of a stressed syllable followed by two unstressed syllables. A single foot is called a *dactyl.*

An **anapestic foot** consists of two unstressed syllables followed by a stressed syllable. A single foot is called an *anapest.*

Guidance: The following procedure will help you detect the stress pattern in poetic verse.

1. Read the poem out loud. Emphasize the stressed syllables. It is helpful to mark those that are stressed.

2. Divide each line into feet. This can be done by drawing a line before or after each foot. If the first syllable is stressed, draw a line before each stressed syllable. If the second or third syllable is stressed, draw a line after each stressed syllable. To produce a regular pattern, it is sometimes necessary to group the natural stresses in a forced way. Each line starts with a foot. Sometimes a partial foot with only one syllable will occur, particularly at the end of a line.

Go and | **catch** a | **fall**.ing | **star**

The **fall** | ing **flow** | er

3. Decide which pattern is used for each foot.

1. Demonstration:

The following verses illustrate each of the four types of meter. Bold font is used to help you see which syllable is stressed. Syllables are separated by dots. Feet are separated by vertical lines

Trochaic: stressed – unstressed **Pan**.sies, | **lil**.ies, | **king**.cups, | **dais**.ies.	**Iambic**: unstressed – stressed A.**long**, | a.**lone**, | a.**las** | he **sat**.
Dactylic: stressed – unstressed – unstressed **Moth**.er.ly, | **fath**.er.ly, | **sis**.ter.ly, | **broth**.er.ly.	**Anapestic**: unstressed – unstressed – stressed As he **spoke**, | in.di.**rect** | in.dis.**creet**, | im.ma.**ture**

FIGURE 5-5 *Continued*

2. Demonstration:

In this demonstration you will need to remember the definition for each type of meter.

Trochaic:	Iambic:
Out of | **friend**.ship | **came** the | **red** man **Teach**.ing | **set**.tlers | **where** the | **deer** ran. (Longfellow)	The **sun** | that **brief** | Dec.**em** | ber **day** Rose **cheer** | less **ov** |er **hills** | of **gray**. (Whittier)
Dactylic:	**Anapestic:**
Come to the | **crag** where the | **b**.con is | **blaz**.ing **Come** with the | **buck**.ler the | **lance** and the |**bow**. (Scott) [The final foot in each line is incomplete. Don't let this confuse you.]	The **pop** | lars are **felled** | fare.**well** | to the **shade** And the **whis** | per.ing **sound** |of the **cool** | col.on.**ade**. (Cowper) [In the first line, the first and third feet are incomplete. Don't let this confuse you. Poets often use incomplete feet.]

3. Demonstration:

In the following examples the divisions between feet have been removed. You may want to add these divisions to more clearly see the stress pattern.

Trochaic:	Iambic:
As near **por**.te **bel**.lo **ly**.ing **On** the **gen**.tly **swell**.ing **flood**,. **At** mid **night** with **stream**.ers **fly**.ing **Our** tri **umph**.ant **na**.vy **rode**. [Lines 2 and 4 both end on the stressed syllable.]	Good **mor** row **to** the **day** so **fair**, Good **morrow** **sir** to **you**: Good **morrow** **to** mine **own** torn **hair** Be**dab**bled **with** the **dew**. (Herrick) [Lines 1 and 3 each have four feet, whereas lines 2 and 4 have only 3 feet.]
Dactylic:	**Anapestic:**
Moth.er, dear **Moth**.er! the **years** have been **long** **Since** last I **list**.ened. your **lul**.la.by **song**; **Sing**, then, and **un**.to my **soul** it shall **seem** **Wo**.man.hood's **years** have been **on**.ly a **dream**. (Allen)	I am **mon**.arch of **ail** I sur.**vey**; My **right** there is **none** to dis.**pute**: From the **cen**.tre all **round** to the **sea** I am **lord** of the **fowl** and the **brute**. (Cowper) [Line 2 starts with an incomplete foot.]

4. Demonstration:

Poets sometimes use mixed meter to produce a particular effect. One line uses one meter while the next line uses a different meter. They may also shift meter within a given line. Note these variations in the following stanzas. You may want to identify the stressed syllables and divide these lines into poetic feet.

If the heart of man is de.pressed with cares,

The mist is dis.pelled when a wo.man ap.pears. (Gay)

(continued)

FIGURE 5-5 *Continued*

[This stanza is primarily anapestic; however, in Line 1 the second and fourth feet are iambic and in Line 2 the first foot is iambic.]

That the low.est boughs and the brush wood sheaf
Round the elm tree bole are in tin.y leaf,
While the chaf finch sings on the orch.ard bough
In Eng.land – now! (Browning)

[A common pattern is to alternate iambic and anapestic. The last foot uses a pause instead of an unstressed syllable.]

Beau.ti.ful Ev.e.lyn hope is dead.
(Browning)

[This is a blend of dactylic and trochaic. The last foot ends on a stressed syllable, a masculine ending.]

Two roads di.verged in a yel.low wood,
And sor.ry I could not trav.el both
And be one trav.eller, long I stood
And looked down one as far I could
To where it bent in the und.er growth.
(Frost)

[As variations become extreme, the poetry tends toward free verse. Frost here uses iambic and anapestic.]

1. Application:
For each of the following words or phrases, underline the letter that corresponds to the type of meter involved.

[There were seventeen instances for this application. The course provides feedback (right column) after learners enter their response for each item.]

T I D A 0 return	T **I** D A 0 re **turn**
T I D A 0 yesterday	T I **D** A 0 **yes** ter day
T I D A 0 reproduce	T I D **A** 0 re pro **duce**
T I D A 0 resurrection	**T** I D A 0 **res** ur| **rec** tion

2. Application:
For each of the following stanzas circle the letter that corresponds to the type of meter involved. There were eight instances for this application. The course provides feedback (right column) after learners enter their response for each item.

Out of the dusk and the glittering	**Out** of the | **dusk** and the | **glit**.ter.ing
Splendor of stars and of nebulae,	**Splend**.or of | stars and of | neb. u.lae,
Out of the night with its magical	**Out** of the | **night** with its | **mag**.i.cal
Breath of the wind from the galaxy.	**Breath** of the | **wind** from the | **gal**.ax.y.
(Wood)	(Wood)
T I D A 0	T I **D** A 0

FIGURE 5-5 *Continued*

Now the day is over Night is drawing nigh; Shadows of the evening Steal across the sky. (Gould) T I D A 0	**Now** the | **day** is | **o**.ver **Night** is | **draw**.ing | **nigh**; **Shad**.ows | **of** the |**even**.ing **Steal** a | **cross** the | **sky**. (Gould) <u>T</u> I D A 0 [Lines 2 and 4 end on stressed syllables and have incomplete feet. This should not confuse you by now.]
3. Application: For each of the following stanzas circle the letter that corresponds to the type of meter involved. [There are eight instances for this more challenging application. The course provides feedback (right column) after learners enter their response for each item.]	
The poplars are felled farewell to the shade And the whispering sound of the cool colonnade The winds play no longer and sing in the leaves Nor Ouse of his bosom their image receives. (Cowper) T I D A 0	The **pop** | lars are **felled** | fare.**well** | to the **shade** And the **whis** | per.ing **sound** | of the **cool** | col.on.**nade** The **winds** | play no **lon** | ger and **sing** | in the **leaves** Nor **Ouse** | of his **bos** | om their **im** | age re.**ceives**. (Cowper) T I D <u>A</u> 0 [This one is more difficult. Lines 2, 3, and 4 each leave off the first unstressed syllable. Also the third foot in Line 1 is iambic. Do you see how this is basically anapestic with some iambic substitutions?]
As a sloop with a sweep of inoculate15 wing on her delicate spine And a keel as steel as a root that holds in the sea as she leans. (Shapiro)	As a **sloop** | with a **sweep** | of in.**ac** | cu.late **wing** on her **del** | i.cate **spine** And a **keel** | as **steel** | as a **root** | that **holds** in the **sea** | as she **leans**. (Shapiro) [This is a very long line for anapestic meter – 6 feet per line. Note feet 2 and 4 in the second line both use iambic. Did this confuse you?]

Original lesson by Robert D. Tennyson and the author. Originally published in Merrill & Tennyson, 1977.

The four *Show* events each present a set of matched examples representing the four kinds of poetic feet. The first set provides considerable attention-focusing guidance to learners: It states the definition of each kind of poetic foot with its name; it separates the syllables with dots; it indicates the stressed syllable by bold font; and it separates each poetic foot by vertical lines. The amount of guidance is gradually reduced. The second set of instances does not give the definition with the name. The third set does not separate the lines into the poetic feet, leaving this for learners to do. The fourth set does separate the syllables, but does not indicate which syllable is stressed or where to divide the line into poetic feet. This procedure gradually reduces the amount of guidance provided to learners, requiring them to do more and more of the analysis of the poetry themselves.

Divergent and Range of Difficulty: Each succeeding set of demonstrations increases in difficulty of the items and thereby increases the effort required to identify the stress pattern involved. The fourth set introduces exceptions to the use of consistent use of poetic meter which further increases the challenge of determining the poetic meter involved. The three applications each increase in difficulty. The first application only requires learners to determine the poetic foot for a single word or very short phrase consisting of only a single poetic foot. The second application presents short verses where the poetic feet are regular and consistent. The third application introduces exceptions where there are incomplete feet. Corrective feedback is provided by dividing the lines into poetic feet and by using boldface type to show the stress pattern.

HOW-TO INSTRUCTIONAL STRATEGY

Goal: perform a series of actions that lead to some desired consequence for unencountered instances of the task.

Prescribed instructional events:

Presentation: *Tell* the name of the procedure and the steps and their sequence required to complete the procedure.

Demonstration: *Show* the execution of each of the steps in instances of the procedure. Provide attention-focusing guidance; a divergent set of instances of the task; and increasingly difficult instances of the procedure.

Application: *Do* require learners to execute each of the steps for a set of increasingly difficult unencountered instances of the task. Provide coaching on early items and intrinsic feedback.

How-to component skills are often the primary goal of the instruction.

Presentation/Demonstration

For a how-to component skill it is best to *Show* a representation of the task to be accomplished before listing the steps. *Show* a specific instance of the task to be accomplished; list the steps required to complete the task (*Tell*); demonstrate the execution of each step, and show the consequence of executing each step. Learning is best promoted if, when a given step is described, the instruction simultaneously shows the execution of this step and the consequence of this execution in the specific portrayal of the task. One approach is for the instructor to perform each step for the learner while directing the learner's attention to what action is taking place and the consequence of this action. *Guidance* is used to direct the learner's attention to the name of the step being executed, the relevant part of the task on which to act, the action that is taking place, and the consequence of this action. However, when possible, the best demonstration is to have learners actually do each step as it is described in the real task or a simulation of the real task—a *Simon-says* type of demonstration. This has the advantage of focusing the learner's attention on the relevant part of the task by having to actually do something with or to this part. If this hands-on demonstration takes place for a real instance of the task or a simulation of the task, then it has the advantage of immediately showing learners the consequence of their action. It also has the advantage of allowing learners to play with the task to explore what happens when they don't do the correct step. If the task is complex, repeat the presentation/demonstration for several new instances of the task.

Application

Require learners to execute each step in an unencountered real or simulated portrayal of the task (*Do*). Adequate application consists of performing the complete task. For complex tasks, those with many steps or difficult steps, the application should move from coached practice to an opportunity to perform the whole task without any coaching. If the task cannot be performed using the actual device or system, then the student should have the opportunity to practice with an exploratory environment or simulation of the device or system. The simulation should allow the student to perform the task in a way that is similar to doing the procedure with the actual device or system. Functional fidelity, meaning it acts like the real thing, is more important than appearance fidelity, meaning it looks like the real thing. *Intrinsic feedback*, when learners see the consequence of their actions, is most effective, but extrinsic feedback, informing the student about the appropriateness of a given action or set of actions, should also be available.

Strategy Demonstration—Spreadsheets

Figure 5-6 presents a few instructional events from an early lesson in an introductory course on spreadsheets. The portrayals in these instructional events use a generic spreadsheet and teach fundamental formulas, rather than introducing the complexity of an actual spreadsheet such as Excel. Row 1 is the first instance of the task—a sales spreadsheet. Each row introduces a new slightly more complex instance of the task: Row 2 a check register spreadsheet; Row 3 a percent rainfall spreadsheet; Row 4 a wages paid spreadsheet; and Row 5 a project costs and wages spreadsheet. The instructional events for the first problem include: *Tell* problem; *Tell* step 1 and provide the individual key strokes to guide learners to accomplish the step; *Do* step 1 using Simon-Says; *Tell* step 2 and provide individual key strokes to guide learners; *Do* step 2 using Simon-Says; provide intrinsic *feedback* in the form of the consequence of the total amount ($157.05) and encourage learners to check their work (Did it work?). The first problem demonstrates the steps using the arithmetic operators plus and sum, including guidance for the individual key strokes, but allows learners to actually do the steps.

FIGURE 5-6 How-to Instructional Strategy—Spreadsheets

Using a Spreadsheet

Following are a few instructional events from an early lesson in using a spreadsheet. In this lesson the basic functions of a spreadsheet are taught rather than the specialized functions and shortcuts of a commercial spreadsheet like Excel. In the course the spreadsheet would be active and the directions enable learners to actually carry out the calculations.

Problem 1: Total Sales

Determine the total sales amount for each item and then add up the total sales amount.

Step 1 Multiply item # sold by its cost ($).

Click in D3. Enter = B3 * C3

Click in D4. Enter = B4 * C4

Repeat for Rows 5 and 6

Don't forget the = sign. The = sign indicates that you are entering a formula in the cell rather than a number or alphabetic character. The address of a cell (B3) enters the number in that cell into the formula. This enables the same spreadsheet to be used the next day by merely changing the numbers in the cells but not changing the formulas.

Step 2 Add up the total for all items sold.

Click on D7. Enter =sum(D3:D6)

The function *sum* indicates that you want to add the cells indicated in the parentheses. The colon between D3 and D6 indicates that you wish to add all the numbers between the two cells. Don't forget the parentheses.

Your total should be $157.05. Did it work?

	A	B	C	D
1	Sales			
2	**Item**	**# sold**	**$**	**Total**
3	Sandwich	23	$ 3.75	
4	Drink	32	$ 1.25	
5	Chips	17	$ 0.75	
6	Cookie	19	$ 0.95	
7			Total	

Problem 2: Check Register

Balance your checkbook for each check written by showing the remaining balance in your account.

Step 1 Subtract the amount of the check from the balance and enter the remaining balance.

Click in D4 Enter =D3 – C4

You can enter a cell address by merely clicking on the cell rather than typing the address.

Click in D5 Enter the = sign; click on D4; enter the – sign; click on C5. This enters the formula = D4 – C5 in cell D5

Enter = D5 – C6 in cell D6

Enter the appropriate formula in cells D7 and D8.

Your final balance in cell D8 should be $2,712.39. Did it work?

	A	B	C	D
1	Check Register			
2	**Payee**	**#**	**Amt**	**Balance**
3	Deposit			$ 3,650.00
4	Electricity	231	$ 32.63	
5	Telephone	232	$ 57.21	
6	Cable	233	$ 48.12	
7	Groceries	234	$ 49.65	
8	Rent	235	$ 750.00	

FIGURE 5-6 *Continued*

Problem 3: Percent Rainfall Per Month

Determine the percent of the annual rainfall that falls for each two-month period.

Step 1 Determine the total annual rainfall.

In G3 sum the amounts for each two month period.

Step 2 Determine the percent for each month. Divide the total rainfall into the amount for each month.

Click in A4 enter = A3/G3

Click in B4 enter = B3/G3

Repeat for cells C4 through F4

Step 3 Check your work by adding the percentages for each period to be sure they equal 100%

Click in cell G4. Sum the percentages across cells A4 through F4

Did your percentages add up to 100%?

	A	B	C	D	E	F	G
1	Rainfall						
2	Jan/Feb	Mar/Apr	May/Jun	Jul/Aug	Sep/Oct	Nov/Dec	Total
3	4.3	6.2	5.1	1.2	2.8	4.1	
4							

Problem 4: Wages Paid

- In column D, determine the wage to be paid to each employee.
- In row 8, determine the total wages paid to employees, the total hours worked, and the total amount of wages paid to everyone.
- In row 9, determine the average wage, the average number of hours worked, and the average amount of wages paid. Divide the totals by the number of employees.
- The average amount paid per employee in cell D9 should be $303.59. Did it work?
- After you submit your work, you may obtain a copy of the completed spread sheet.

	A	B	C	D
1	Name	Wage	Hrs	Amount
2	Jose	$ 7.35	23.0	
3	Albert	$ 7.65	19.0	
4	JoAnne	$ 8.95	31.0	
5	Hiroshi	$ 9.12	19.0	
6	Alicia	$ 15.34	40.0	
7	Kim	$ 12.30	36.0	
8	Totals			
9	Averages			

(continued)

FIGURE 5-6 *Continued*

Problem 5: Project Costs and Wages

The client wants to know how many hours and how much each project costs. Employees work on more than one project, so their time and wages have to be divided across the projects.

- In row 9, determine the total wage paid to each employee.
- In column F, determine the total hours for each project.
- In column G, determine the cost per project. For each employee who worked on the project, multiply the hours worked by the hourly rate, and then add these amounts in the cells of column G.
- In cell G9, indicate the total wages paid to all employees for all projects.
- In cell G10, check your work by summing the Total Wage Paid in row 9. The amount in cell G9 and G10 should be the same. This amount should equal $7,189.90. Did it work?
- After you have submitted your work, you may obtain a copy of the completed spreadsheet.

	A	B	C	D	E	F	G
1				Project Costs and Wages			
2		Jake	Sally	Deon	Chan	Hours	Cost
3	Hourly wage	$ 23.45	$ 26.87	$ 53.40	$ 62.98		
4	Project 1	10.3		24			
5	Project 2	5.1	6.4		31		
6	Project 3		15.2		29		
7	Project 4	4.6	8.4	16			
8	Total hours						
9	Total Wage Paid						
10							

Original lesson by the author.

The instructional events for the second problem include: *Tell* problem; *Tell* step 1 with key stroke guidance; *Tell* alternative approach to entering formula; provide intrinsic *feedback* in the form of a final balance for learners to check their work. The second problem also demonstrates the similar steps using the arithmetic operator minus and a running balance.

The instructional events for the third problem include: *Tell* problem; *Tell* step 1 but do not provide individual key strokes; *Do* step 1; *Tell* step 2 with individual key strokes using the arithmetic operator divide with the same cell; *Do* step 2; provide intrinsic feedback by indicating that the percentages should sum to 100 percent. The third problem is a combination demonstration application that provides different kinds of formulas but requires learners to apply what they have already learned.

The instructional events for the fourth problem include: *Tell* the problem and information needed; *Do* the problem; provide intrinsic feedback by giving the amount in cell D9; provide extrinsic feedback by providing a completed spreadsheet after they have completed their own work. The fourth problem is application with intrinsic and extrinsic feedback.

The instructional events for the fifth problem include: *Tell* the problem and information needed; *Do* the problem; provide intrinsic and extrinsic feedback. The fifth problem is the application for what has been taught in this short module.

You should note how guidance and coaching were gradually withdrawn through the five problems and that intrinsic feedback was provided by giving one piece of information that allowed learners to check their own work if there was a disagreement. This is a good example of e^3 how-to instruction.

WHAT-HAPPENS INSTRUCTIONAL STRATEGY

Goal: given a set of conditions, predict the consequence for unencountered instances of the process. Given an unexpected consequence, identify the missing or flawed conditions responsible for the consequence.

Prescribed instructional events:

Presentation: *Tell* the name of the process and the conditions for each event in the process.

Demonstration: *Show* the process in real or simulated instances. Provide attention-focusing guidance; a divergent set of increasingly difficult instances of the process.

Application: *Do* require learners to predict the consequence or find missing or flawed conditions for a set of increasingly difficult unencountered instances of the process. Provide coaching on early items. Provide for intrinsic feedback.

What-happens component skills are often the primary goal of instruction.

Presentation/Demonstration

Identify an instance of the process for the learners. *Tell* the conditions necessary for each event while simultaneously *Show*ing the execution of each event in an actual or simulated portrayal of the process. A process can be demonstrated for the learner by carefully stating the conditions involved for each event as it occurs and directing the learner's attention to the conditions and the consequence of each event in the process. However, passive demonstrations of a process are less effective than having learners trigger the events by setting a parameter for a condition or executing an action that is a condition for the event to occur. Allowing learners to manipulate the conditions for an event and see the consequence enable them to explore what happens for various values of the conditions. An effective form of guidance is to allow learners to ask for an explanation of an unexpected consequence during this exploration of the process. This explanation identifies conditions that resulted in the consequence. Demonstrate the process in increasingly complex scenarios.

Application

Present a specific unencountered situation to the learners. Based on the conditions of the device or system, require learners to predict the consequence (*Do*). Provide *intrinsic feedback* by allowing learners to confirm their prediction by triggering the process and observing the consequence of the execution.

In an alternative application, present learners a consequence (correct or flawed) for a specific unencountered situation and ask them to identify the condition or conditions that were met or not met that resulted in the observed consequence (*Do*). In complex systems, learners may have to trace the execution back through several events to find the condition(s) that caused the observed consequence. Learners should have an opportunity to make predictions or find flawed conditions in several specific situations where the conditions vary. Coaching on early instances could involve focusing the learners' attention on the critical conditions that may lead to the consequence.

Strategy Demonstration—Momentum

Figure 5-7 demonstrates a what-happens experiential environment for a guided discovery lesson on momentum in physics. The introduction to the lesson, which is not shown, tells the name of the process, *momentum*, and explains the operation of the experiential environment. The system asks learners a number of questions related to the description, conditions, and consequence of the process. The system presents a situation and asks learners to make predictions by selecting hypotheses about the outcome of the situation. The directions suggest that learners do some experiments [*Show-portrayal*] in order to make the necessary predictions. Following the experiments, the system asks learners to reflect on the experience by giving the description and identifying the relationships among the conditions or variables that lead to the consequence [*Ask-information*]. Finally the system provides information by telling learners the description, condition(s), and their relationships to the consequence [*Tell-information*].

An introduction introduces the principle of momentum and provides directions for interacting with the experiential environment. The lesson provides the following directions to learners: (1) it suggest that learners conduct experiments; this provides an opportunity to see the process several times; (2) it discourages learners from guessing at the hypotheses or making predictions from memory; the system will not allow learners to make a prediction until they have conducted the experiments required to verify the hypotheses; and (3) it encourages learners to repeat the experiments using different kinds of freight cars. It is not necessary to use different kinds of freight cars, but it is hoped that learners will be curious enough to repeat the experiments.

How do learners interact with this environment? Learners link to this experiential environment from a menu page. When the experiential environment shown in Figure 5-7 first appears, the *Control Panel, Problem, and Hypothesis* windows do not appear. Instead, the goal statement shown in Figure 5-8 is displayed below the picture. When learners click the NEXT button, the system then displays the *Control Panel, Problem,* and *Hypotheses* windows and plays the audio message in Figure 5-9.

FIGURE 5-7 What-Happens Instructional Strategy—Experiential Environment for Momentum

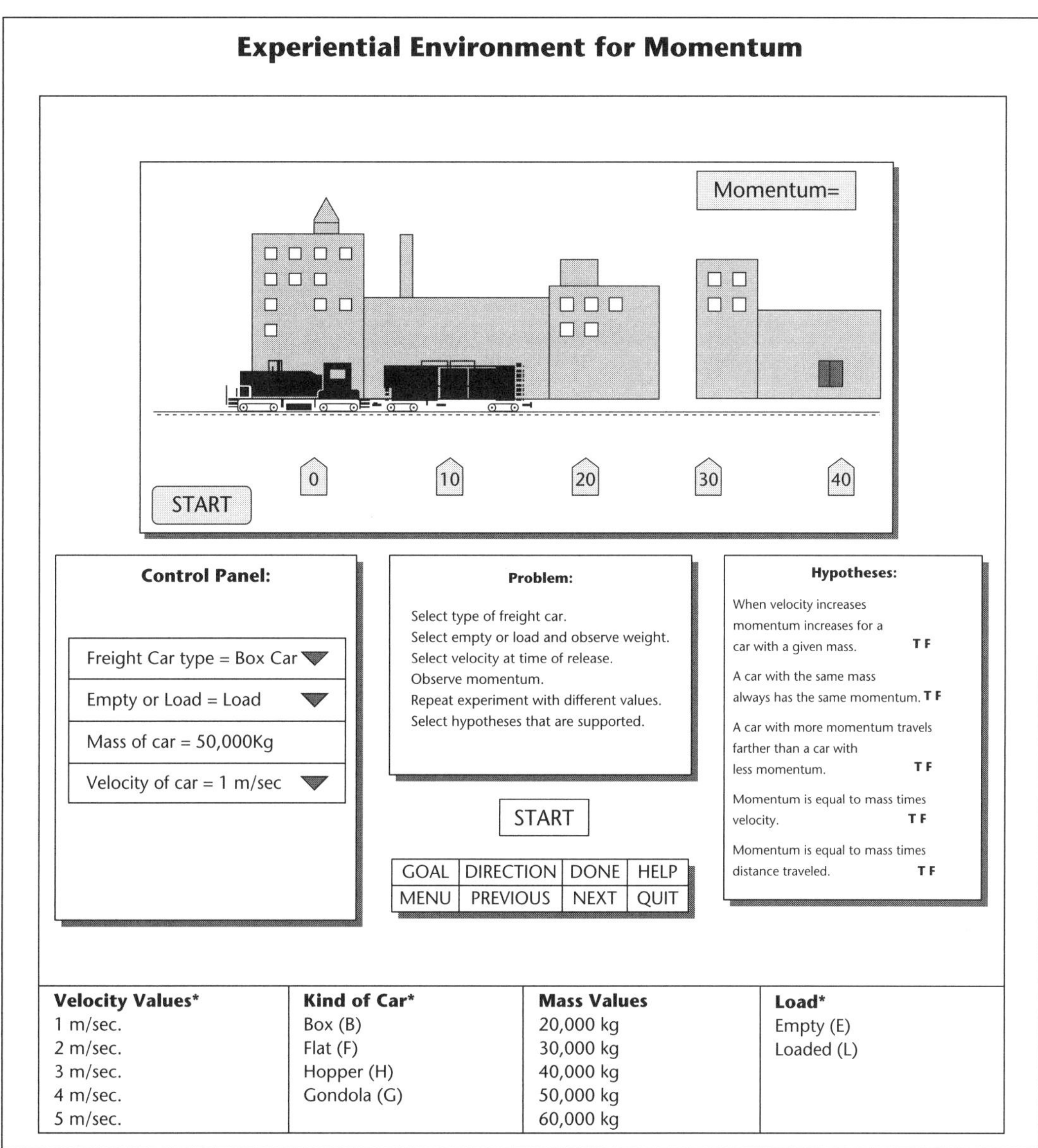

Velocity Values*	Kind of Car*	Mass Values	Load*
1 m/sec.	Box (B)	20,000 kg	Empty (E)
2 m/sec.	Flat (F)	30,000 kg	Loaded (L)
3 m/sec.	Hopper (H)	40,000 kg	
4 m/sec.	Gondola (G)	50,000 kg	
5 m/sec.		60,000 kg	

Original lesson by the author. Originally published in Merrill, 2001.

FIGURE 5-8 Goal for Problem 1 Momentum Experiential Environment

Momentum Goal
In this lesson, you will do some experiments to learn about momentum.
You should ask yourself these questions:
What is momentum?
How is momentum related to velocity?
How is momentum related to mass?
Click NEXT for the next problem.

FIGURE 5-9 Audio Directions for Problem 1 Momentum Experiential Environment

Audio Directions

The situation is a rail yard where a switcher locomotive is sorting freight cars. The switcher pushes the car to a given velocity and then stops. The railroad car continues to roll until its brakes stop it or it collides with other cars. While there is some friction in the wheels and axles, it is very small and for this problem you may consider this a frictionless environment. In this simulation the car will eventually disappear off the screen. Don't worry; even though you won't see it happen, a brakeman will apply the brakes and stop the car.

Your task is to conduct a series of experiments that will enable you to determine whether the hypotheses that are stated in the hypothesis box [highlight *Hypotheses* box] are either true or false. When you have done an experiment that tests a given hypothesis, click either the T or F to indicate whether the hypothesis is supported. Your choice will be highlighted in green. The computer will monitor your experiments. It will not allow you to indicate whether a given hypothesis is true or false until you have conducted the experiment that is necessary to test the hypothesis. You may change your mind and change the answer for a given hypothesis at any time.

To run an experiment, select a value for each of the variables listed in the control panel [highlight *Control Panel* box]. You select a value by clicking on the down arrow in the variable box and selecting a value from the drop-down menu. When you have selected each of the required variables, click the Start button [highlight START button] to run the experiment.

The switch engine will push a freight car in from the left of the screen and will release the freight car at the meter post marked 0. The car will continue to roll past the buildings for several seconds before disappearing off the screen. You should observe the momentum of the freight car in the indicator box in the upper right corner of the screen.

Click the DIRECTIONS button to replay this message.

When you have tested all of the hypotheses, click the DONE button.

To do an experiment, learners select three values: *velocity*, *kind of car*, and *load (Show-conditions)*. The mass of the car is determined automatically by the type of car and its load. When the values have been selected for a given experiment, learners click START.

The animation works as follows [*Show-portrayal*]: First, the switch engine moves from the left at the velocity selected. At meter post 0, the switch engine stops but the car continues to roll. The value of its momentum is displayed in the box on the upper right of the display [*Show-consequence*]. As the car reaches the center of the screen, the car stops moving, but the buildings in the background and the mileposts begin to scroll to the left, giving the appearance that the freight car is still rolling. The switch engine will also scroll off the screen to the left with the buildings since it is now stationary. After several seconds, the buildings stop scrolling and the car scrolls off the screen to the right. For the student, the locomotive and car are not shown until the START button is clicked.

The program monitors the student's experiments. For the first problem, learners must conduct the following experiments in order to test the hypotheses [*Do-application*].

Experiment 1: Select a given mass, select a given velocity.

Experiment 2: Select the same mass as a previous experiment but select a different velocity.

Experiment 3: Select a different mass than a previous experiment but select the same velocity.

If the student has not conducted the experiments required for a given hypothesis, the following message is played [coaching]: "You have not conducted the experiments that adequately test this hypothesis. Do some more experiments. Click the HELP button if you need a suggestion."

Clicking the HELP button causes the program to check which experiments the student has done and to suggest the next experiment that the student has not done. For example, if the student had conducted Experiment 1, but not Experiment 2, then clicking HELP would provide the following audio message [coaching]: "Select the same mass as a previous experiment but select a different velocity."

After learners have conducted their experiments and pressed the DONE button on the navigation panel, they will be given the questions in Figure 5-10 for reflection [*Ask*-conditions and consequence].

FIGURE 5-10 Reflection Questions for Problem 1 Momentum Experiential Environment

Reflection Questions

Please type an answer to the following questions:

1. What is momentum? Please describe in your own words.
2. How is momentum related to velocity? To mass? To distance?

Type your answer here. [ ]

Click DONE when you are finished.

After learners finish their reflection and click the DONE button, they are presented this audio message: "*The answers to hypotheses you may have missed are indicated in red.*" The summary in Figure 5-11 is shown to the student in the same area of the screen [*Tell-conditions and consequence*].

FIGURE 5-11 Summary for Problem 1 Momentum Experiential Environment

What is momentum?

It is a characteristic of a moving object. It requires a force equal to its momentum, applied in opposition to its direction of movement, to stop a moving object.

How is momentum related to velocity?

Momentum (p) = mass (m) times velocity (v).

How is momentum related to mass?

p = mv

How is momentum related to distance?

It is not.

Click NEXT for the next problem.

After they have completed the first problem, learners are given a second problem [*divergent instance*]. When learners click NEXT PROBLEM, they are shown the simulation graphic in Figure 5-12. The *Control Panel, Problem,* and *Hypotheses* boxes are hidden and the information in Figure 5-13 is displayed below the picture. When the DIRECTIONS button is clicked, the goal message in Figure 5-13 is hidden and the *Control Panel, Problem,* and *Hypotheses* boxes are shown. The audio message shown in Figure 5-14 is played and provides additional explanation of the problem.

FIGURE 5-12 Problem 2 for Momentum Experiential Environment

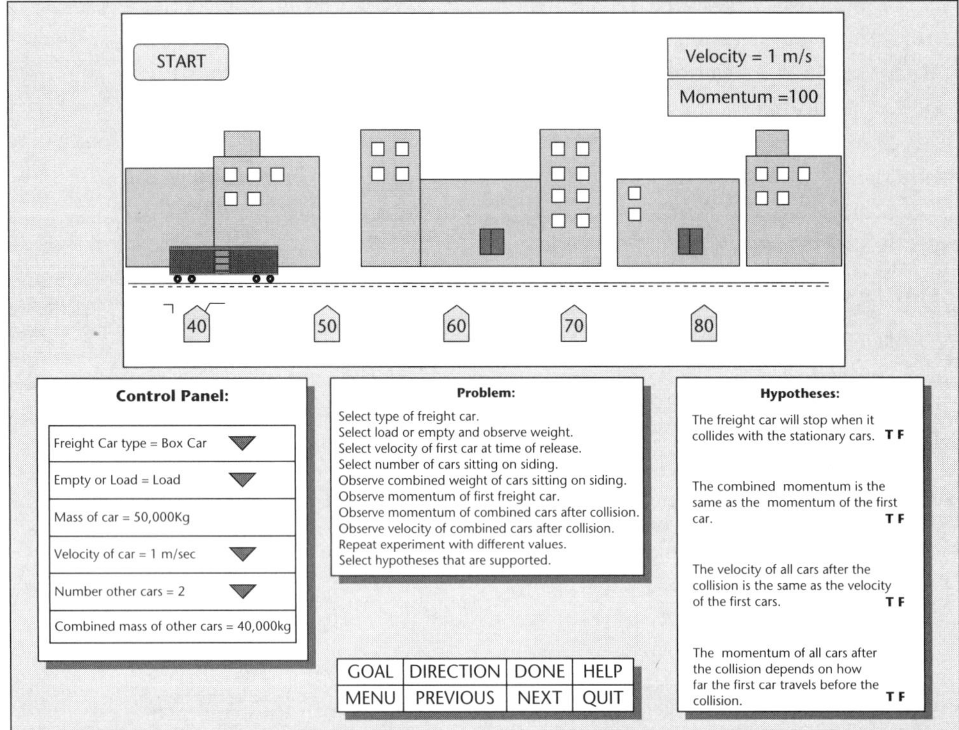

FIGURE 5-13 Goal for Problem 2 Momentum Experiential Environment

Goal

In this lesson, you will learn about the conservation of momentum.

The total momentum after a collision will be the same as the total momentum just before the collision.

You should ask yourself this question:

What happens to the momentum of an object when it collides with another object?

Click DIRECTIONS button to continue.

FIGURE 5-14 Audio Explanation for Problem 2 Momentum Experiential Environment

Audio Explanation

"In this problem, the switch engine will push a freight car in from the left of the screen and will release the freight car at the meter post marked 0. The car will continue to roll past the buildings until it collides and couples with the freight cars already sitting stationary on the siding. These cars do not have their brakes set, so they may also roll when the freight car collides with them. In the real world there is some friction in the wheels and axles of the cars, but for the purpose of this problem you should consider this a frictionless environment. You should observe the momentum of the freight car in the indicator box in the upper right corner of the screen [*guidance*]. You should also observe the velocity shown in the box in the upper right corner of the screen [*guidance*]. After the car collides with the stationary cars, the indicator boxes will give the momentum and velocity of all of the cars combined [*consequence*]. After a few seconds the cars will roll off the screen. Don't worry; even though you won't see it happen, a brakeman will set the brakes and stop the cars."

At this point, the audio instructions about the task and procedures to use in responding are similar to those presented for Problem 1. As with the first problem, if the student has not performed the experiments necessary to test a given hypothesis, the system provides a message indicating that the student needs to conduct more experiments. The HELP button provides a suggestion about what kind of experiment to conduct.

When the student clicks the DONE button, he or she is given the suggestions/questions shown in Figure 5-15 for reflection [*Ask-information*]. The *Control Panel* and *Problem* boxes are hidden and the questions in Figure 5-15 appear in the lower left quadrant of the screen.

FIGURE 5-15 Reflection Questions for Problem 2 Momentum Experiential Environment

Reflection Questions

Please type an answer to the following questions:

How is velocity related to conservation of momentum?

How is mass related to conservation of momentum?

Type your response here. [ ]

Click DONE when you are finished.

After learners finish their reflection and have clicked the DONE button, they are presented this audio message: *"The correct answers to hypotheses you may have missed are indicated in red."*

The summary in Figure 5-16 is shown to the student in the lower left quadrant of the screen [*Tell-information*].

FIGURE 5-16 Summary for Problem 2 Momentum Experiential Environment

Summary

This problem should have helped you answer the questions posed earlier.

What is conservation of momentum? Conservation of momentum means that the total momentum is the same after a collision as just before the collision.

How is conservation of momentum related to velocity? Momentum is the product of mass times velocity (p = mv). The momentum of the single car in motion is its mass x its velocity. The momentum of all of the cars after the collision is their combined mass x their combined velocity. Since the mass of the combined cars is larger than the mass of the single car, and since the total momentum must remain the same, then the velocity of the combined cars must be less than the velocity of the single car before the collision.

How is conservation of momentum related to mass? The mass of the objects involved in the collision is added to the mass of the original object in motion. The total mass has increased, but the momentum remains the same because of the decrease in the velocity of the combined objects.

Click on NEXT PROBLEM to continue.

An experiential environment provides a dynamic demonstration of the conditions and consequence of the process. Note that this is an inductive approach where *Show-portrayal* is done first and *Tell-information* is used as a summary to be sure that learners inferred the correct relationship among conditions and consequence.

Learners set different values into the conditions and observe the effect on the consequence. Requiring learners to apply what they observe to test different hypotheses enables learners to see a progression of variations on the problem. Problem 2 provides a second somewhat divergent problem. The experiential environment combines demonstration and application into an integrated activity. At the same time the system is demonstrating the effect of different values on the conditions, learners are asked to make predictions about the consequence that will occur and are asked to set the values on the conditions so that they can confirm their hypothesis. In this environment, demonstration also provides the feedback for learners on their predictions.

PRINCIPLES AND PRESCRIPTIONS

Demonstration: Learning is promoted when learners observe a demonstration of the knowledge and skill to be learned.

Application: Learning is promoted when learners apply their newly acquired knowledge and skill.

Information-About Instructional Strategy

Goal: Identify information about a set of object, activities, or processes.

Prescribed instructional events:

> **Presentation:** *Tell* name, information and portrayal item-by-item; focus attention; explore; repetition.
>
> **Practice:** *Ask* for the name given the description or portrayal. *Ask* for the description or portrayal given the name. Immediate response; avoid sequence cues; corrective feedback.

Information component skill is sometimes prerequisite for other component skills.

Part-of Instructional Strategy

Goal: Identify the name and location of a given part with respect to the whole of some object or system.

Prescribed instructional events:

> **Presentation/demonstration:** *Show* its location in the whole and *Tell* the part name and information about the part. Avoid location cues; use chunking; provide for repetition.
>
> **Practice/application:** (*Do*) point to location of the part given its name or information; recall or recognize its name and information shown the location of the part. Use random order; avoid location cues; require an immediate response; 100 percent; corrective feedback.

Part-of component skill is often prerequisite for other component skill.

Kind-of Instructional Strategy

Goal: Classify unencountered instances—objects, devices, procedures, actions, or symbols—as belonging to a particular class.

Prescribed instructional events:

> **Presentation:** *Tell* the name of the class and the values on the discriminating properties (definition) that determine class membership.

Demonstration: *Show* examples and non-examples of the class. Provide attention-focusing guidance; a divergent set of examples; matched examples and non-examples; increasingly difficult examples and non-examples.

Application: *Do* require learners to classify unencountered examples and non-examples of the class. Provide coaching on early items and corrective feedback.

Kind-of component skills are the building blocks for how-to and what-happens component skills.

How-to Instructional Strategy

Goal: perform a series of actions that lead to some desired consequence for unencountered instances of the task.

Prescribed instructional events:

Presentation: *Tell* the name of the procedure and the steps and their sequence required to complete the procedure.

Demonstration: *Show* the execution of each of the steps in instances of the procedure. Provide attention-focusing guidance; a divergent set of instances of the task; and increasingly difficult instances of the procedure.

Application: *Do* require learners to execute each of the steps for a set of increasingly difficult unencountered instances of the task. Provide coaching on early items and intrinsic feedback.

How-to component skills are often the primary goal of the instruction.

What-Happens Instructional Strategy

Goal: given a set of conditions, predict the consequence for unencountered instances of the process. Given an unexpected consequence identify the missing or flawed conditions responsible for the consequence.

Prescribed instructional events:

Presentation: *Tell* the name of the process and the conditions for each event in the process.

Demonstration: *Show* the process in real or simulated instances. Provide attention-focusing guidance; a divergent set of increasingly difficult instances of the process.

Application: *Do* require learners to predict the consequence or find missing or flawed conditions for a set of increasingly difficult unencountered instances of the process. Provide coaching on early items. Provide for intrinsic feedback.

What-happens skills are often the primary goal of instruction.

APPLICATION

You will come to understand the instructional strategies illustrated in this chapter if you try to identify these strategies in existing instructional material. Select several courses that you are taking, designing, or that you can find on the Internet (it might be wise to use the courses you selected for the application for Chapter 4). Examine these courses to see whether you can identify each of the instructional strategies—information-about, part-of, kind-of, how-to, and what-happens. Did these instructional strategies include the prescribed instructional events? If some of the prescribed instructional events are missing, you can design some of these missing instructional events.

TO LEARN MORE

The material in this chapter is an update on my earlier work on Component Display Theory. You can learn more about Component Display Theory from the references listed in the *To Learn More* section for Chapter 4.

Clark, R. C. (2008b). *Developing technical training: A structured approach for developing classroom and computer-based instructional materials* (3rd ed.). San Francisco: Pfeiffer. Ruth Clark has presented the instructional prescriptions from Component Display Theory in a much more readable form than the formal papers cited in the To Learn More section of Chapter 4. This source is a very readable presentation of instructional strategies for different kinds of component skills.

Gagné, R. M. (1985). *The conditions of learning and theory of instruction* (4th ed.). New York: Holt, Rinehart and Winston. Much of my work on instructional strategies was inspired by this seminal work.

Gagné, R. M., Wager, W. W., Golas, K., & Keller, J. M. (2005). *Principles of instructional design* (5th ed.). Belmont, CA: Thompson Wadsworth.

COMING NEXT

Chapter 3 illustrated content elements. Chapter 4 illustrated instructional interactions. This chapter describes instructional strategies composed of prescribed instructional events for each of the five types of component skill. The next chapter, Chapter 6, illustrates how these five types of component skill are combined to form an instructional strategy for teaching learners how to solve a whole problem.

CHAPTER 6

INSTRUCTIONAL STRATEGIES FOR PROBLEM SOLVING

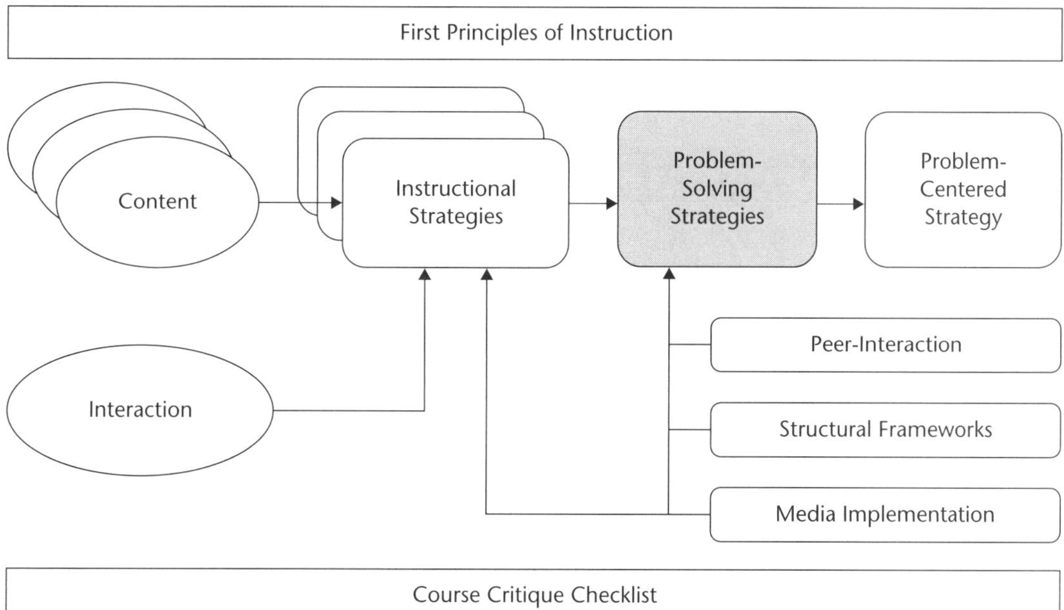

Quick Look

In Chapter 5 I demonstrated instructional strategies for five types of component skill. In this chapter I demonstrate how all these strategies are combined to form an integrated strategy for problem solving. This chapter answers the following questions: How are the content elements for different component skills combined to provide an integrated set of content elements for a whole problem? How are the instructional strategies for different component skills combined to provide a problem solving instructional strategy? What is a problem-solving event? What are the content elements of a problem-solving event? What is the instructional strategy for teaching a problem-solving event?

Key Word

Problem-Solving Event: one of a series of activities involved in solving a problem; consists of a step and the condition it brings about.

INTRODUCTION

Chapter 3 illustrated five types of component skills: information-about, part-of, kind-of, how-to, and what-happens. The chapter also illustrated the content elements for each of these types of component skill. Chapter 4 illustrated four primary instructional interactions and other instructional interactions that promote learning. Chapter 5 illustrated instructional strategies for teaching each of these types of component skill. Because these skills seldom occur in isolation, they are labeled *component skills* to indicate that they work together as components of a whole problem. It is important when teaching problem solving that the content elements and strategies for each of these types of skill are included and taught in an integrated way. This chapter illustrates how the content elements for these individual component skills are integrated into problem-solving events. The chapter then illustrates instructional strategies, which are comprised of these problem-solving events, for teaching these integrated component skills.

CONTENT ELEMENTS FOR A PROBLEM-SOLVING EVENT

All problems involve at least one what-happens component skill. The content elements for a what-happens component skill are a set of conditions that lead to some consequence. Figure 6-1 shows three conditions, represented by rectangular boxes connected by plus signs, which lead to a consequence. Most problems also involve at least one how-to component skill. The content for many problems is often represented as a set of steps that leads to some consequence, as shown in Figure 6-2; such a representation is incomplete. The steps executed by the learner do not in and of themselves cause the consequence. In real-world problems, every step is a trigger that changes some condition, and it is the set of changed conditions that bring about the consequence, as shown in Figure 6-3. The steps, rather than leading directly to the consequence, each bring about a condition that, together with the other conditions in the set, brings about the consequence.

FIGURE 6-1 Content Elements for What-Happens Component Skill

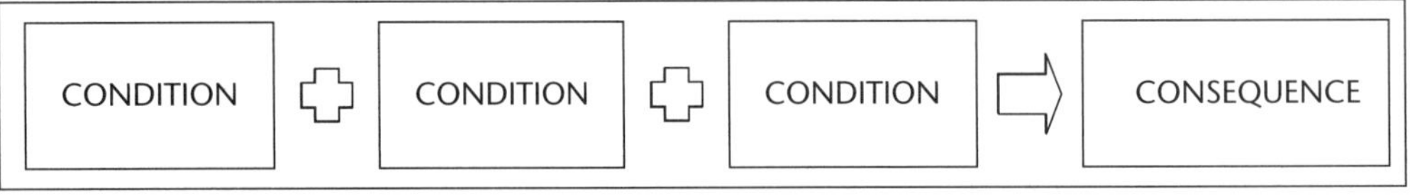

FIGURE 6-2 Typical Content Elements for How-to Component Skill

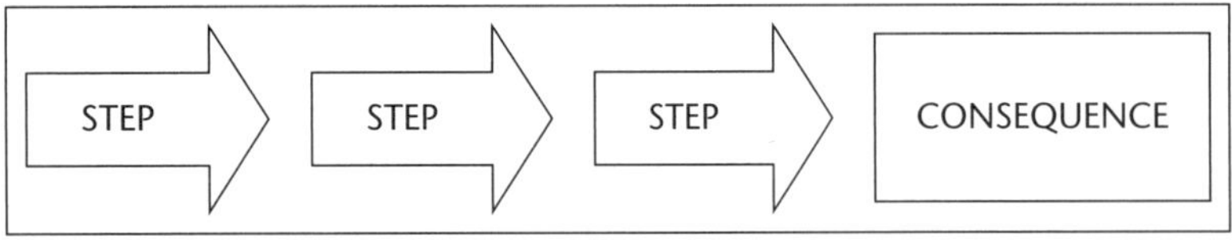

FIGURE 6-3 Steps Bring About Conditions That Lead to the Consequence

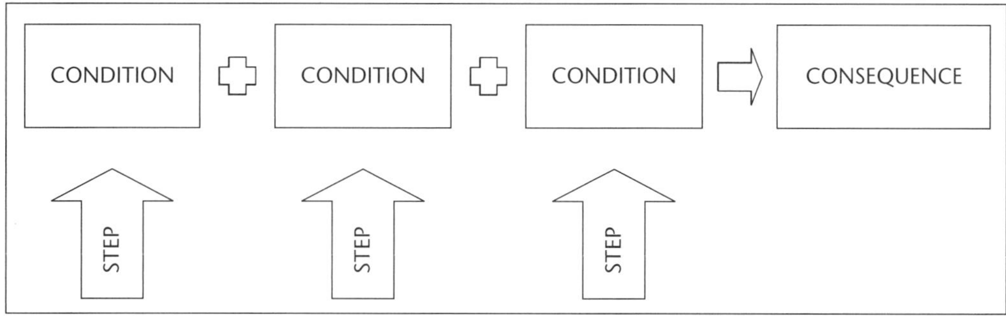

A step and the condition it changes are called a *problem-solving event.* Figure 6-4 illustrates the content elements of a problem-solving event. A problem-solving event includes content elements for at least three types of component-skill. These include a step (*how-to*), which changes the properties of a condition (*what-happens*). A *condition* is often an object or act that is an instance of a class or kind-of. Kind-of content is a class of objects, activities, or processes characterized by a set of common properties. Figure 6-4 includes a box labeled *properties* that represents these property content elements associated with the condition. A condition may also consist of information that cannot be generalized and therefore must be remembered. Therefore, the property for such a condition may be content elements from an information-about or part-of component skill.

The activities associated with a step also require kind-of component skill. Important content elements for a kind-of component skill are the properties that define a given instance. Figure 6-4 includes a box below the step representing the properties associated with the step. Learning to execute a step requires two types of acquired skill: first, learners must use these properties to identify a correct execution of a step when they observe it; and second, they must acquire the skill to execute the step themselves. The properties of a step are those features of the action that learners must be able to identify to determine if others correctly execute the step. When they attempt to do the step, they must also be able to identify their own correct execution of the step.

INSTRUCTIONAL STRATEGY FOR A PROBLEM-SOLVING EVENT

Instruction for a problem-solving event involves three major activities: (1) demonstrate the first portrayal of the problem-solving event, (2) identify the step and condition for a second portrayal, and (3) execute the step and identify the resultant condition for a third portrayal. Table 6-1 lists the prescribed instructional events for a problem-solving event. Note that there are two levels of *Do*—Do_{id} is identify an instance for a kind-of component skill; Do_{ex} is execute a step for a how-to component skill. Before learners can execute a step, they must first be able to identify an effective execution of the step when they see it (Do_{id}-S). This identification may take several forms, including distinguishing a correct execution of the step from an incorrect execution or identifying which of two executions of the step is the most effective. Learners must also be able to execute the step (Do_{ex}-S). The purpose of executing a step is to change a condition. To know whether the step accomplished its purpose, the learner must be able to identify an effective portrayal of the condition after the step has been executed (Do_{id}-C).

FIGURE 6-4 Content Elements for a Problem-Solving Event

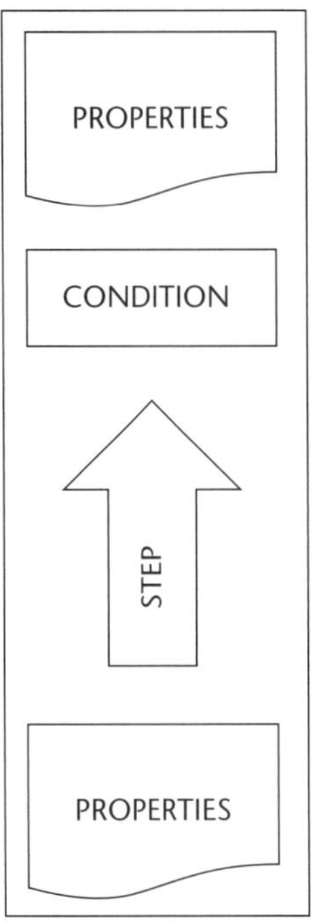

Table 6-1 Prescribed Instructional Events for a Problem-Solving Event

Demonstrate the Problem-Solving Event (Portrayal 1)		
Tell-C	Describe the condition (C).	kind-of
Show-C	Show an instance of the condition (C).	kind-of
Tell-S	Describe the step (S).	kind-of ; how-to
Show-S	Show the execution of instances of the step (S).	kind-of ; how-to
DO_{id} the Problem-Solving Event (Portrayal 2)		
Do_{id} –S	Identify instances of the step (S).	kind-of
Do_{id} –C	Identify instances of the condition (C).	kind-of
DO_{id} and DO_{ex} the Problem-Solving Event (Portrayal 3)		
Do_{ex} –S	Execute instances of the step (S).	how-to
Do_{id} –C	Identify the resulting condition (C).	kind-of
Key: C = Condition; S = Step; Do_{id} = identify an instance; Do_{ex} = execute a step The abbreviations in Column 1 facilitate communication about instructional events, making it unnecessary to explain a given instructional event each time it is referenced. A given instructional strategy can be described more succinctly and with fewer words using these abbreviations.		

STRATEGY DEMONSTRATION FOR PROBLEM-SOLVING EVENT

Figure 6-5 illustrates the first four instructional events of an instructional strategy for one small problem-solving event from a course on selling. Figure 6-6 illustrates the component skills involved in this problem-solving event. This problem-solving event shows how even a simple act like giving a warm greeting includes three types of component skill. The step, a warm greeting, is a kind-of greeting. It has three defining properties: like a friend, a smile, and a simple greeting. A warm greeting involves a resultant condition—the reaction of the customer. The condition has two defining properties—the customer is at ease and he or she feels comfortable.

In Row 2 the narrator describes the step (*Tell*-S) and the video illustrates the execution of the step (*Show*-S). In Row 3 the narrator describes the properties of the condition (*Tell*-C) and the video shows the reaction of the customer (*Show*-C). All four of these instructional events take place in just a few seconds.

This illustration involves only a single portrayal of this problem-solving event. To be more complete the instruction should, at some point, show another salesperson giving a warm greeting and the resultant reaction of the customer and have the learner identify whether the greeting step was done effectively and whether the reaction of the customer indicated that he or she was at ease and comfortable.

This illustration does not involve any response from the learner. To be more complete the instruction should, at some point, have the learner actually perform a warm greeting with a real or role-playing customer, and observe the reaction of the customer.

FIGURE 6-5 A Problem-Solving Event—A Warm Greeting

Selling with Service				
		Information	Audio Portrayal	Video Portrayal
1	**Kind-of**	**Defining properties:** Like a friend Warm smile Simple greeting		
2	**How-to**	**Step:** Think of greeting a customer in the same way as you would a friend coming to your home. Share a warm, sincere smile and a simple greeting. For example, you could say "Hello," "Good evening," or "Welcome to our store." Use greetings that are familiar and commonly used in the area where you live.	Hi, how are you today?	
3	**What-happens** **Kind-of**	**Condition (consequence):** Research, as well as our own experience, tells us that the first impression is the most lasting one. A warm and friendly greeting sets people at ease and makes them feel comfortable.	Well, fine, thank you.	

FIGURE 6-6 Content Elements for the Problem-Solving Event—A Warm Greeting

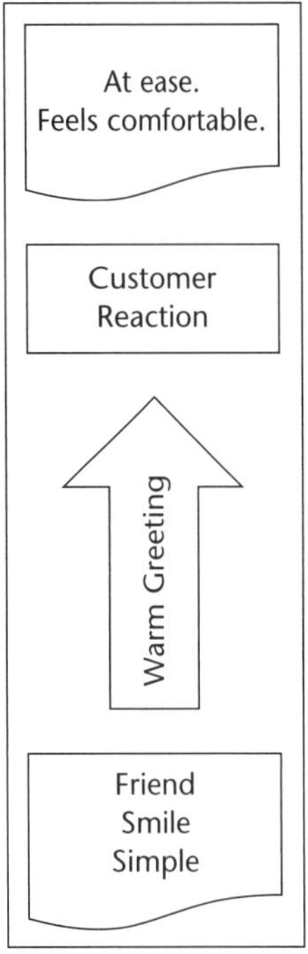

CONTENT ELEMENTS FOR A WHOLE PROBLEM

Figure 6-7 identifies the content elements for a whole problem. Note that this diagram indicates that this whole problem consists of three problem-solving events. These problem-solving events include content elements from at least three different component skills—what-happens, how-to, and kind-of. The content elements for what-happens are represented by three conditions (boxes connected by plus signs) leading to a consequence. The content elements for how-to are represented by the steps pointing to the conditions. The content elements for kind-of are represented by the properties associated with each of the conditions, the consequence, and each of the steps.

Figure 6-8 is a diagram showing all of the *content elements* required for the whole problem of selling furniture. This diagram includes four *problem-solving events* consisting of a major step and the condition it changes that leads to the sale. In the diagram, the conditions, problems, and properties have been represented by a word or short phrase. Note that the consequence of this sales process is that the customer agrees to the sale. The conditions leading up to this sale are the following responses from the customer: accepts help, shares needs, and likes a solution. There are four major steps in this sales process: a friendly approach, the discovery process, present solution, and close. Each of the conditions, brought about by each of the steps, is a reaction of the customer that is characterized by the properties indicated in the boxes above each condition. Recognizing these properties is critical if learners are to acquire the skill to identify the reaction conditions in the customer when they occur. Furthermore, each of the steps in the selling process is also characterized by certain properties that learners must be able to identify if they are to identify these steps when they are executed by others or if they are to identify when they execute these steps correctly. In addition, the learner must also learn to execute each of these steps in the sales process.

FIGURE 6-7 Content Elements for a Whole Problem

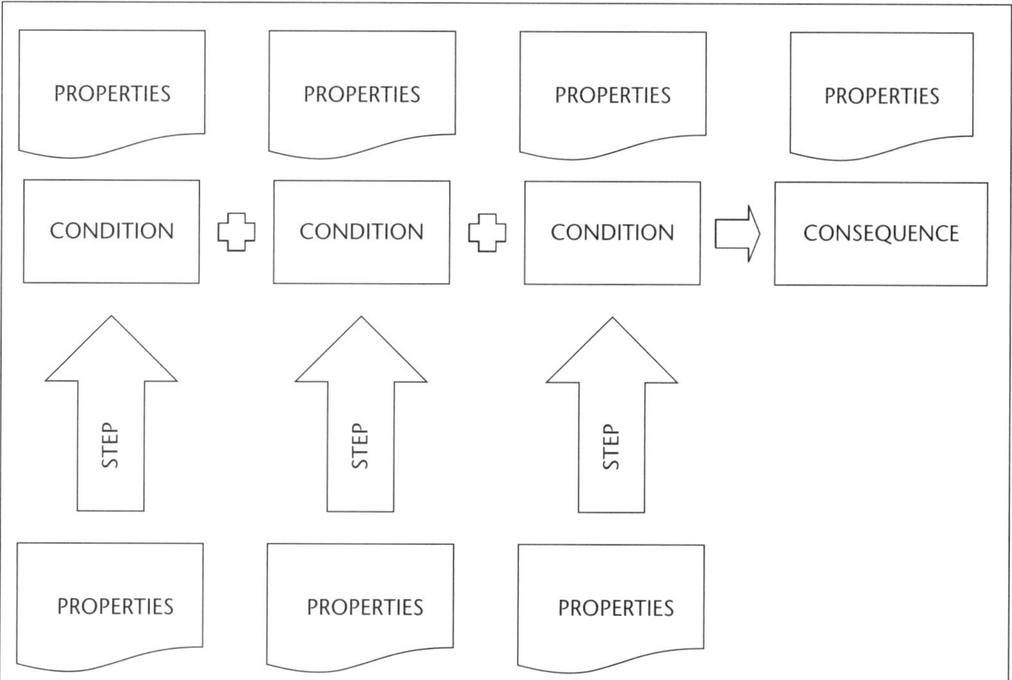

Consider the first step in the selling process, A Friendly Approach. Note that this component skill includes three discrete properties for this step: (1) a warm greeting, (2) an open-ended question, and (3) a sincere response. Earlier in this chapter a warm greeting was illustrated as a problem-solving event. In this illustration a warm greeting is shown as a property of a larger problem-solving event. Problem-solving events may be nested within one another. Figure 6-9 illustrates the content elements for the three problem-solving events that are included in the larger problem-solving event, a friendly approach. The content elements for the whole problem may be represented as one set of problem-solving events, as in Figure 6-8. Then each of the problem-solving event steps in this whole problem may be represented by a more detailed set of problem-solving events, as illustrated in Figure 6-9.

INSTRUCTIONAL STRATEGY FOR A WHOLE PROBLEM

Figure 6-8 shows that a whole problem is typically a sequence of problem-solving events that lead to the desired consequence. Table 6-2 lists the prescribed instructional events for a whole problem. The major instructional activities for teaching a whole problem include: (1) demonstrate the whole problem, (2) teach each of the component skills or problem-solving events that comprise the problem, and (3) do the whole problem.

FIGURE 6-8 Content Elements for the Whole Problem of Selling Furniture

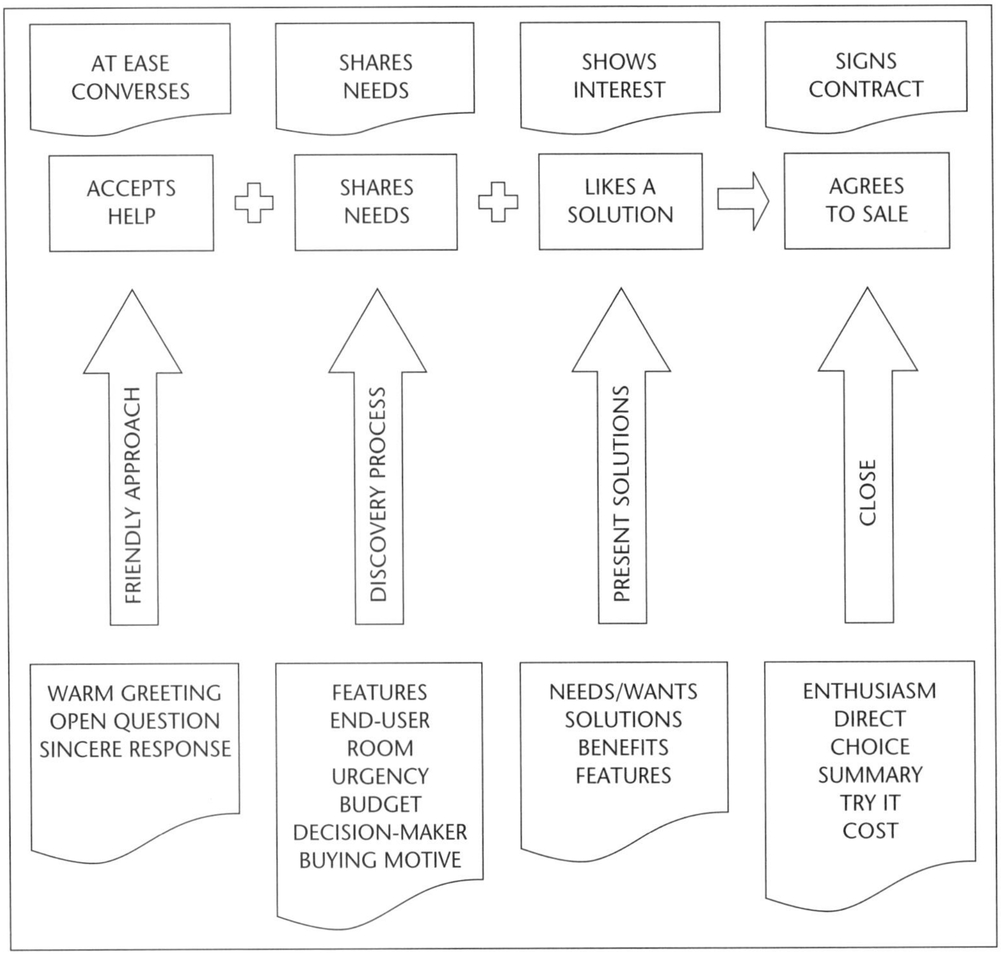

AT EASE CONVERSES | SHARES NEEDS | SHOWS INTEREST | SIGNS CONTRACT

ACCEPTS HELP + SHARES NEEDS + LIKES A SOLUTION ⇒ AGREES TO SALE

FRIENDLY APPROACH | DISCOVERY PROCESS | PRESENT SOLUTIONS | CLOSE

WARM GREETING OPEN QUESTION SINCERE RESPONSE	FEATURES END-USER ROOM URGENCY BUDGET DECISION-MAKER BUYING MOTIVE	NEEDS/WANTS SOLUTIONS BENEFITS FEATURES	ENTHUSIASM DIRECT CHOICE SUMMARY TRY IT COST

In simple terms, the first instructional activity for teaching a whole problem is to demonstrate a specific instance of the whole problem. To be sure that this demonstration is complete, it should include all of the following instructional events: describe and show the consequence or desired solution to the problem (*Show*-Q); describe and show portrayals of the conditions that lead to the consequence (*Show*-C); and describe and show the steps that result in the conditions that lead to the consequence (*Show*-S).

The next instructional activities are to teach each of the component skills that are necessary to do the whole problem. Too often instructional products fail to include all of the instructional events prescribed for instruction for these component skills. Most component skills are comprised of a combination of kind-of, how-to, and what-happens skills of a problem-solving event. Too often the condition elements of these problem-solving events are not explicitly taught, leaving the resulting instruction incomplete. The prescribed instructional events for a problem-solving event are listed in Table 6-1. These instructional events for each problem-solving event are also included as the second major instructional activity in teaching a whole problem, as illustrated in Table 6-2.

FIGURE 6-9 Problem-Solving Events Nested in the Larger Problem-Solving Event—A Friendly Approach

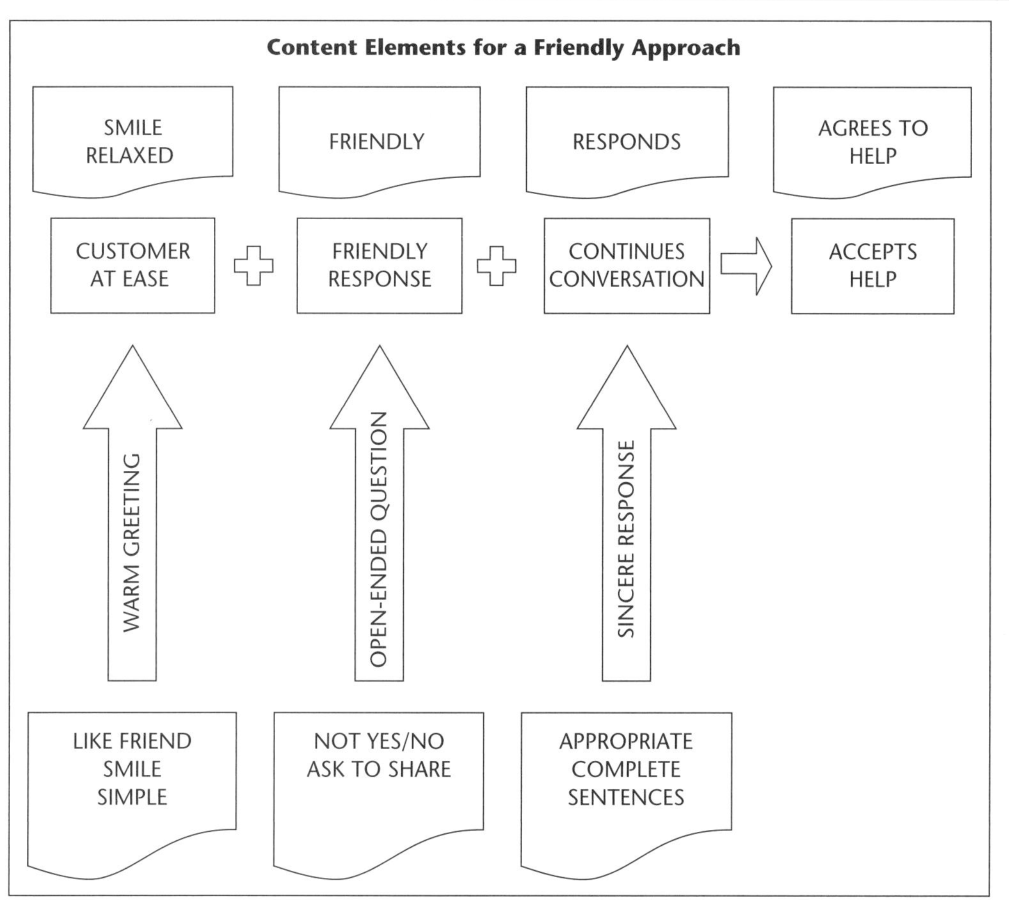

Table 6-2 Prescribed Instructional Events for a Whole Problem

Demonstrate the Whole Problem		
Show-Q	Show an instance of the consequence (Q) for the whole problem.	kind-of
Show-C	Show instances of conditions (C) that lead to the consequence.	what-happens
Show-S	Show instances of the steps (S) that lead to each of the conditions.	how-to
▼Teach the Component Skills (Problem-Solving Events of the Whole Problem)▼		
Demonstrate Each Problem-Solving Event (Portrayal 1)		
Tell-C	Describe the condition (C).	kind-of
Show-C	Show instances of the condition (C).	kind-of
Tell-S	Describe the step (S).	kind-of how-to
Show-S	Show the execution of instances of the step (S).	kind-of how-to
***Do_{id}* the Problem-Solving Event (Portrayal 2)**		
Do_{id} -S	Identify instances of the step.	kind-of

(continued)

Table 6-2 *Continued*

Do$_{id}$ -C	Identify instances of the condition.	kind-of
Do$_{ex}$ the Problem-Solving Event (Portrayal 3)		
Do$_{ex}$-S	Execute instances of the step (S).	how-to
Do$_{id}$ -C	Identify instances of the condition (C).	kind-of
▲Repeat for each problem-solving event in the whole problem.▲		
Do the Whole Problem		
Do$_{ex}$-Q	Predict a consequence from a set of conditions for instances of the problem.	what-happens
Do$_{ex}$-C	Find faulted conditions or steps for an unanticipated consequence for instances of the problem.	what-happens
Do$_{ex}$-S	Execute all of the steps for instances of the whole problem.	how-to

Key: C = Condition; S = Step; Q = Consequence; *Do*$_{id}$ = identify an instance; *Do*$_{ex}$ = predict consequence (*Do*$_{ex}$-Q); find faulted conditions (*Do*$_{ex}$-C); execute steps (Do$_{ex}$ -S).

After each component skill or problem-solving event has been taught, the final major instructional activity in teaching a whole problem is to have learners do the whole problem. However, just as there is more than one level of *Do* for the individual problem-solving events, there are also several levels of *Do* for the whole problem. Learners will be much more effective in their execution of the steps leading to a consequence if they first clearly understand the relationship of the conditions to the consequence in the problem. They can demonstrate this understanding in one of two ways: given a specific set of conditions, predict the consequence that will result (*Do*$_{ex}$ -Q) or, given an unexpected consequence, critique the conditions that led to this unanticipated consequence to find faulted or missing conditions (*Do*$_{ex}$ -C).

The final activity in teaching a whole problem is to have learners do the whole problem using a different specific situation than that used to teach the whole problem in the first place. This doing should involve executing each of the steps, observing the resulting condition, redoing or modifying the step if the expected condition does not occur from a given step, and finally, observing the consequence to determine whether the desired outcome was achieved.

STRATEGY DEMONSTRATION FOR A WHOLE PROBLEM

The following paragraphs will illustrate these relationships and demonstrate instructional strategies for teaching component skills in the context of a whole problem. Figure 6-10 is a storyboard for a video portrayal for the whole problem of selling furniture to a customer. The video demonstration is divided into segments representing each of the major problem-solving events in the selling process. The video can be shown as a whole, or each segment could be shown separately.

FIGURE 6-10 Example of a Whole Problem—Selling Furniture

SalesForce: Selling with Service **Example of Whole Problem** The narrator's comments can be turned on or off for different instructional purposes.	
Video	**Audio Accompanying Video**
Problem-solving event 1: **Friendly Approach** 	**Narrator:** Watch as David uses a friendly approach with this customer. Pay attention to what he says and how the customer reacts. Does the customer agree to look? **David**: Hi, how are you today? **Maria:** Fine, thank you. **D:** How do you like all this sunshine we are having? **M:** It's a nice change. **D:** Looks like spring is finally here. **M:** Finally! **D:** What brings you into our store on such a beautiful day? **M:** I think my sofa is starting to get worn. I think that it needs to be replaced. **D:** I'd love to show you some sofas. Do you want to come with me? And while you are looking, let me ask you a few questions about the room you are going to put this in. **M:** Okay. **D:** By the way, my name is David Miller. **M:** Hi, Maria Sanchez.
Problem-solving event 2: **The Discovery Process** 	**Narrator:** Watch as David uses the discovery process with this customer. Did the customer share her needs? What did he learn about the furniture she may want to purchase? **D:** While you are looking, let me ask you a few questions about the room you are going to put the sofa in. **M:** It's decorated mainly in earth tones and I have some antique pieces on display in it. **D:** That sounds really nice. **M:** Thank you. **D:** Is it a room that you use to entertain guests? **M:** No, not really, I like to go in there to unwind, and sometimes when my daughter comes home from college she likes to sit in there and read, too. **D:** Oh wow, where is she going to school? **M:** She goes to the State University. **D:** Oh, that's a really good school. My sister went there. **M:** Really! It is a good school.

(continued)

FIGURE 6-10 *Continued*

Video	Audio Accompanying Video
	**D:** About your sofa, what do you like most about your current sofa? **M:** It's very comfortable. I like to stretch out on it. And there is enough room for my dog to curl up next to me. **D:** That sounds really comfortable. **M:** Very comfortable! **D:** Are there other pieces in the room that you are planning to replace soon? **M:** Not really; I like things that last for a long time. **D:** I understand; you want something of quality. **M:** Yes. **D:** Are you planning on replacing your sofa soon? **M:** I'd like to, but I'd like to make sure that I find something I really like. **D:** Okay, let's look at some sofas. **M:** Lead the way.
Problem-solving event 3: Present Solutions   	**Narrator:** Watch as David presents possible solutions to Maria. Note how he considers her needs and tries to present an option that meets those needs. How did Maria indicate that she probably liked the solution? **D:** So Maria, based on what you told me, it sounds like you want a large, comfortable classic sofa that will last a long time and take whatever abuse your dog might give it. Is that right? **M:** Oh, ya, I hadn't even thought about the dog. But that sounds like something I'm looking for. **D:** Then I think that we should look at this sofa—it's got a very classic, comfortable style to it and it will last a long time. Go ahead and try it out. **M:** Ya, okay. Oh, this is comfortable! **D:** Go ahead and relax. As you can see, this sofa is the perfect size for stretching out on and it's got plenty of room for your dog, too. And it will last for years because it is made of kiln-dried hard wood, which is a good sign of high-quality furniture. Besides, the corner blocks are double doweled and glued for extra support. The leather has a classic look and will last longer than fabric. And leather is a good choice for dog owners because it is so strong and cleans up easily. The low rolled arms on this sofa make it very comfortable for curling up with a good book or even taking a nap. **M:** Ya, I can see that. You know, when my daughter comes home, she sleeps on the sofa, since her old bed is pretty much worn out. **D:** This sofa would be nice to sleep on, but we can look at some beds if you like later. **M:** Okay. I'm not sure about this leather. I think it might be too dark for my room. Does this couch come with that fabric [pointing]?

Video	Audio Accompanying Video
	D: Actually, that fabric over there is a cotton polyester blend, which really isn't that durable. This sofa does come in some microfiber fabrics, which are also a good choice for pet owners. If you choose the microfiber option, then I can give you a discount on the fabric protection plan as part of the sale that we have going on right now. And we have free delivery and removal of your old sofa going on this week, too. **M:** Oh, well that sounds interesting. Uh, I'd like to see what the microfiber looks like. **D:** Okay, great. But please don't get up. I've got some microfiber samples right over here. Now don't fall asleep. **M:** I'll try not to.
Problem-solving event 4: Close with Confidence 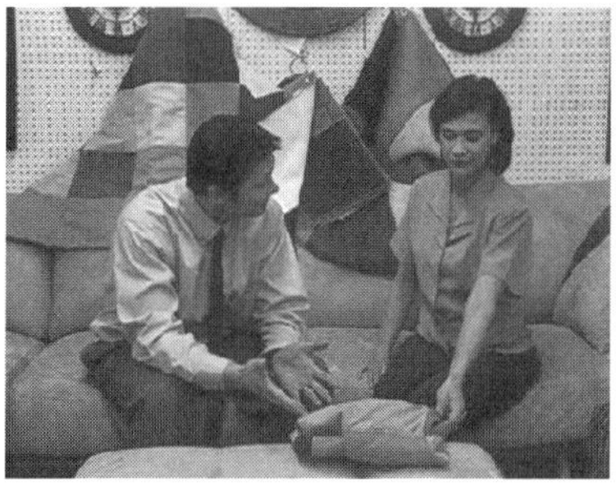  	**Narrator:** Finally, watch how David closes the sale. How does he help Maria make her decision to buy? **D:** This sofa will be perfect for your room with that microfiber that you picked out; don't you think so, Maria? **M:** Oh, it's so beautiful and the fabric is so soft. **D:** This sofa is beautiful and the high-quality workmanship means that you will be able to enjoy it for many years. Why don't I go ahead and write up the sofa for delivery and have our certified application take care of the fabric protection before we send it out to your home? **M:** Well, I love the sofa, and this fabric is beautiful, but won't it wear out quickly? **D:** That's a good question. I know you want this gorgeous sofa to last many years and the microfiber seems pretty luxurious to stand up to lots of abuse, is that right? **M:** Well, exactly! I'd hate to have to reupholster in just a few years. **D:** I wouldn't want that either, so let me explain. Not only will this sofa's fabric resist dirt, stains, and spills, especially after we add the fabric protection, but microfiber is such a strong fabric that it's used on sofas because it is so durable. Of course, it might fade in direct sunlight, but that's why we add the UV protection as part of our fabric protection. It also solves that problem, too. Pretty reassuring isn't it? **M:** Hmm. Certainly is! **D:** What day would you like the sofa delivered to your home? **M:** Ah, can you delivery it by next Friday? **D:** Absolutely, just let me take a minute to fill out the order and make arrangements. **M:** Okay, great! **D:** I'll be right back. **M:** Thank you!

(continued)

FIGURE 6-10 *Continued*

Video	Audio Accompanying Video
Consequence: 	**Narrator:** David has made a successful sale by applying the four steps in the SalesForce approach. How does Maria indicate that she is a happy customer? Is it likely that Maria will return for another purchase in the future? Do you think that she will seek out David as her sales associate when she returns? **D:** Here is your receipt, Maria. Delivery will be next Friday. And I look forward to working with you again soon. **M:** Thank you. I am so excited about my new sofa. I love it. And I promise when my daughter comes home from college I'll bring her in. I want you to show me those beds we talked about. **D:** Great. I'd love to help with that. **M:** Okay, thank you. **D:** Okay. **M:** Bye-bye. **D:** Good bye.

The video describes the goal or consequence of engaging in the selling process as follows:

> "This program will give you the skills necessary to sell more furniture to more customers through genuine personal service. Your income will increase, and your customers will benefit by getting the furniture products that are right for them."

An appropriate instructional strategy for a whole problem involves three major instructional activities: show the whole problem, teach the component skills or problem-solving events, and do the whole problem. Each of these major instructional activities includes a number of prescribed instructional events. Table 6-2 lists the prescribed instructional events for teaching a whole problem. The following paragraphs illustrate these instructional events for teaching a whole problem.

Figure 6-11 illustrates an instructional strategy for demonstrating the whole problem of selling furniture. Each of the instructional events in this demonstration is numbered to facilitate comparison with the prescribed instructional events listed in Table 6-2. To catch the attention of the learner, the first instructional event shows an undesirable consequence—there is no sale. This is a non-example of the prescribed instructional event *Show-Q*. Instructional event 2 is an introduction that states the goal of the instruction. Instructional event 3 shows the whole sales procedure (as illustrated in Figure 6-10) without interruption and without the commentary of the narrator (*Show-S, Show-C, Show-Q*). The question, "What was the result of his sales presentation?" focuses the learner's attention on the positive consequence of the procedure (*Show-Q*).

FIGURE 6-11 Instructional Strategy for Demonstrating the Whole Problem—Selling Furniture

Selling with Service Demonstrate the Whole Problem		
	Audio	**Video and Display**
1	**David:** Are you sure I can't put this sofa on a sales slip for you? These great prices won't last long. **Maria:** No thanks! I really want to keep shopping around. Okay? **David:** Okay. Well come back again soon, okay? **Maria:** Okay. **Narrator:** There goes a lost opportunity. Every visitor to your store who doesn't accept your assistance represents one less chance to make a sale, to increase your income, and most importantly, to build a lasting relationship with a customer.	
2	**Narrator:** Welcome to SalesForce: Selling with Service. This course will give you the skills necessary to sell more furniture to more customers through genuine personal service. Your income will increase and your customers will benefit by getting the furniture products that are right for them. During this training, you will be watching and learning with David, a sales associate, who, like you, wants to be more successful at selling furniture.	TITLE PAGE APPEARS HERE Sell more furniture Your income will increase Your customers will benefit
3	**Narrator:** So is there anything David, and you, can do about all those lost chances? Of course there is. Let's see how the results change when David demonstrates how he uses the skills he learned in the SalesForce training program. What was the result of his sales presentation?	The video of the whole sales presentation that appears in Figure 6-10 is presented at this point in the training. The narrator's commentary is turned off for this demonstration.
4	**Narrator:** In this training, you will learn the four steps of the SalesForce program. These steps are: 1. A friendly approach. 2. Discover the customer's needs. 3. Present solutions. 4. Close with confidence.	1. A friendly approach. 2. Discover the customer's needs. 3. Present solutions. 4. Close with confidence.

(continued)

FIGURE 6-11 *Continued*

5	**Narrator:** Why are these steps important? 1. A friendly approach helps customers be at ease and agree to let you help them. 2. Discovery helps customers share their needs and wants. 3. Customer is pleased with a solution. 4. Customer makes the purchase. **Narrator:** Not only will you learn to do the steps in the SalesForce approach but you will also learn to observe the reaction of your customers. It is important that each step lead the customer toward a decision to make the purchase.	What is the result of these steps? 1. Customer agrees to look. 2. Customer shares his or her needs. 3. Customer likes the solution. 4. Customer makes the purchase.
6	**Narrator:** Watch the video again. This time I will direct your attention to each of the steps in the SalesForce program. I will also direct your attention to the reaction of the customer to each of these steps.	The video in Figure 6-10 is repeated with the narrator's commentary enabled.
7	**Narrator:** Remember the steps: A friendly approach so customers will agree to your help, discover needs so customers will share why they came into the store, present solutions so customers have options that meet their needs, and close with confidence so customers will complete the transaction. Learning and mastering these four steps and your customers' reactions will increase your sales and enable you to provide expert professional assistance to your customers. As you use the SalesForce program to learn how to sell furniture through genuine personal service, you will see an increase in the number of sales you are able to make. Even if you have had years of experience selling furniture and have achieved a certain level of success, it's still true: the more you know the more you sell.	The more you know, the more you sell.

The remaining *instructional events* in this demonstration provide guidance to direct the learner's attention to the portrayal of the steps and condition of each problem-solving event. Event 4 tells the four major steps in the SalesForce approach (*Tell*-S). Event 5 tells the reaction of the customer or conditions that should result from the execution of these steps (*Tell*-C). Event 6 shows the video demonstration of the whole process again, but this time with narrator guidance to focus the learner's attention on the four problem-solving steps in the sales process (*Show*-S), the reaction of the customer to each of these steps (*Show*-C), and the final consequence of the customer purchasing the furniture (*Show*-Q). Instructional event 7 summarizes the demonstration by again telling each of the steps (*Tell*-S) and the reaction of the customer to each step (*Tell*-C). This summary also reminds the learner of the goal of the instruction.

The demonstration of the whole problem included all of the steps, their conditions, and the consequence of the whole problem, but it did not provide the learner with sufficient instruction to acquire all of the component skills as represented by the problem-solving events. The next steps in an integrated strategy are to help learners acquire each of the component skills that comprise the whole problem. Each of these component skills is a small problem nested within the whole problem.

Figure 6-12 illustrates an instructional segment for teaching the component skill, *A Friendly Approach.* As with a whole problem, when teaching a nested problem-solving event, the first instructional event is to demonstrate the whole event. Instructional events 1 and 2 replay a portion of the whole problem that illustrates a friendly approach. Event 1 shows the steps (*Show*-S) and Maria's reactions (*Show*-C). In event 2, the narrator focuses the learner's attention on Maria's reaction, the condition of this first step, *a warm greeting.*

FIGURE 6-12 Instructional Strategy for Problem-Solving Event—A Friendly Approach

Instructional Strategy for the Problem-Solving Event: The Friendly Approach		
	Narration and Video Audio	**Display and Video**
1	**Narrator:** To begin, let's watch how David approaches Maria. Audio for video: **David:** Hi, how are you today? **Maria:** Fine, thank you. **D:** How do you like all this sunshine we are having? **M:** It's a nice change. **D:** Looks like spring is finally here. **M:** Finally! **D:** What brings you into our store on such a beautiful day? **M:** I think my sofa is starting to get worn. I think that it needs to be replaced. **D:** I'd love to show you some sofas. Do you want to come with me? And while you are looking, let me ask you a few questions about the room you are going to put this in. **M:** Okay.	
2	**Narrator:** There are four goals of a friendly approach: First, to put the customer at ease; second, to encourage conversation; third to get the customer to share his or her needs and wants; and finally to accept your help in making a decision. Listen again to David's friendly approach. Was Maria at ease? Did she engage in conversation? Was she willing to state her need? Was she willing to accept David's help in making a decision?	

(continued)

FIGURE 6-12 *Continued*

<table>
<tr><th colspan="3">A Warm Greeting</th></tr>
<tr><td>3</td><td> Narrator: How did David approach Maria? What did he say? Narrator: A friendly approach involves three steps: (1) a warm greeting, (2) an open-ended question, and (3) a sincere response. (Numbered items appear on display as they are stated by narrator.) Listen again to David's friendly approach. What was his greeting? What open-ended question did he ask? How did he respond to Maria? Let's examine each step of the approach. </td><td> The Friendly Approach 1. A warm greeting 2. An open-ended question 3. A sincere response </td></tr>
<tr><td>4</td><td> Narrator: The approach begins with a warm greeting. A warm and friendly greeting sets people at ease and makes them feel comfortable. In David's approach, he smiled and said, "Hi, how are you today?" Think of greeting a customer in the same way you would greet a friend coming to your home. Share a warm, sincere smile and a simple greeting. For example, you could say, "Hello!" "Good evening!" or "Welcome to our store." (Phrases pop up as they are spoken.) Use greetings that are familiar and commonly used in the area where you live. </td><td> 1. A warm greeting  "Hello!" "Good evening!" "Welcome to our store." </td></tr>
<tr><td>5</td><td> Narrator: How did Maria respond to David's warm greeting? Do you think her response, "Fine, thank you," indicated that she was at ease with David? </td><td></td></tr>
</table>

<table>
<tr><th colspan="3">A Warm Greeting</th></tr>
<tr><td>6</td><td> Jared: Hi, my name is Jared. I've been a sales associate for many years. I've learned a few things about selling furniture, which I will share with you from time to time. Sometimes I shake hands when greeting a customer. When I do I make sure my hands are clean and dry. I use a firm grip, not a dead fish . . . ugh. On the other hand, I don't overpower them either. No, their first contact shouldn't be painful. Shake hands if that's your thing, but do it in the right way. </td><td> TIPS FROM THE PRO:

CLEAN AND DRY FIRM GRIP </td></tr>
<tr><td>7</td><td>Jared: Remember first impressions! You only get one. If you blow it, there is no second chance. So I be sure to dress appropriately and keep myself clean and neat. Deodorant is good stuff, mouthwash, too, but I never chew gum. It's well—unprofessional. Save it for the baseball game.</td><td>

DRESS APPROPRIATELY BE CLEAN AND NEAT NEVER CHEW GUM </td></tr>
<tr><th colspan="3">A Poor Greeting</th></tr>
<tr><th colspan="2">Audio</th><th>Video</th></tr>
<tr><td>8</td><td> Narrator: Observe David giving a different greeting to Maria. Watch for her reaction. David: Hi, can I help you? (David is obviously eating something as he greets Maria.) Maria: No, I'm just looking. David: Well, let me know if I can help you. My name is David. (As he speaks, David wipes his mouth and then cleans his hand under his arm before extending his hand to Maria for a handshake.) </td><td>

</td></tr>
</table>

(continued)

FIGURE 6-12 *Continued*

	Maria: Okay, uh, thanks. (Maria frowns, does not take his hand, and walks past him into the store as quickly as possible.)	 
9	**Narrator:** Did David's greeting put Maria at ease? What was her reaction? Did David make a good first impression? List the errors David made in his greeting to Maria.	
10	**Narrator:** Consider the following greeting. **Salesperson:** (Trying to be humorous) Hi! Did you bring your checkbook or credit card with you today? **Narrator:** What is the reaction of the customer likely to be? Does this attempt at humor put the customer at ease? List the errors that this salesperson made in his greeting.	
	An Open-Ended Question	
	Narration and Video Audio:	**Display and Video:**
11	**Narrator:** After greeting the customer, ask an open-ended question like David did. Do you remember his question? Let's listen to it again. **David:** Hi, how are you today? **Maria:** Fine, thank you. **David:** Well great! How do like all this sunshine we are having? **Maria:** It's a nice change. **Narrator:** How did Maria respond? Did David's question encourage her to engage in the conversation? **Narrator:** The question, "How do like all this sunshine?" encourages conversation, which is the purpose of an open-ended question. Questions that can be simply answered with yes or no don't give customers a chance to open up and talk. The best questions encourage customers to share something with you: feelings, experiences, and so forth.	 **Encourage conversation.** **Avoid yes/no questions.** **Share feelings or experiences.**
12	**Narrator:** Open-ended questions encourage conversation, while yes or no questions don't. Select each of the questions that cannot be answered with a simple yes or no.	Are you having a good day today? What did you think about the game last night? Do you like this warm weather? That's a beautiful broach; tell me about it. Did you do anything fun over the weekend? What fun do you have planned for this weekend?

	An Open-Ended Question	
13	**Narrator:** Select the question that is most likely to encourage conversation.	A. Can I help you find anything? B. Are you having a good day today? C. How do you plan to enjoy your holiday weekend? D. Hi, my name's Sarah. And you are?
14	**Narrator:** Which of the following questions is open-ended and therefore likely to encourage conversation?	A. Did you see that game last night? B. How did you manage to navigate the road construction? C. Have you been to the Music Festival this summer? D. Can I help you find anything?
	A Sincere Response	
	Narration and Video Audio:	**Display and Video:**
15	**Narrator:** Let's go back and listen to David again. **David:** Well great! How do you like all this sunshine we are having? **Maria:** Well, it's a nice change. **David:** It certainly is. It looks like spring's finally here. **Narrator:** How did Maria respond to David's response? Did she seem to be involved in the conversation with David? **Narrator:** David listened to what she said and then responded sincerely. Listen to what the customer says, then encourage conversation by following up with an appropriate and sincere response. It's important to respond using complete sentences like David did. Complete sentences encourage customers to share and to be more involved in the conversation.	**Listen to what the customer says.** **Respond appropriately.** **Use complete sentences.**
16	**Narrator:** Let's listen to another example. **Associate:** Hi, how are you today? **Customer:** Fine, thanks. **Associate:** Good. . . What do you think of this weather? **Customer:** I'm really enjoying the sunshine. **Associate:** Great. **Narrator:** This greeting started off warmly, but the response "great" indicates a lack of interest and sincerity. Remember to use complete sentences.	Sales Associate says: Hi, how are you today? Customer says: Fine, thanks. Sales Associate says: Good . . . What do you think of this weather? Customer says: I'm really enjoying the sunshine. Sales Associate says: Great.

(continued)

FIGURE 6-12 *Continued*

17	**Narrator:** Here is another example. **Associate:** Hi, how are you today? **Customer:** Fine, thanks. **Associate:** Good, what do you think of this weather? **Customer:** I really like the sunshine. **Associate:** Me too! It's a nice change. What plans do you have to take advantage of it? **Customer:** I hope to go for a walk this afternoon. **Associate:** That sounds like fun. **Narrator:** This sales associate has engaged the customer in a meaningful conversation. Her question, "What plans do you have to take advantage of it?" and the response "That sounds like fun" show that she listened to what the customer was saying. This customer will probably feel comfortable enough to share the purpose of her visit to your store.	Sales Associate says: Hi, how are you today? Customer says: Fine, thanks. Sales Associate says: Good, what do you think of this weather? Customer says: I really like the sunshine. Associate says: Me too! It's a nice change. What plans do you have to take advantage of it? Customer says: I hope to get out in the garden this afternoon. Associate says: That sounds like fun.
18	**Narrator:** Which of the following responses shows that you are listening to the customer's comment about gardening?	A. Yeah, I need to do some yard work myself. B. Oh, fun! C. Well great. How can I help you today? D. What are you growing?
19	**Narrator:** In summary, the three steps to a friendly approach are (1) a warm greeting, (2) an open-ended question, and (3) a sincere response. The way you greet customers sets the tone for their experience in your store. A warm and friendly greeting helps the customer feel comfortable and willing to talk to you. It forms the basis for gaining his or her confidence so you can help with his or her furniture needs.	The Friendly Approach **1. A warm greeting** **2. An open-ended question** **3. A sincere response**

<table>
<tr><th colspan="3">Application</th></tr>
<tr><td colspan="3">Directions: The first impression is the most lasting one and it's not always easy. It is important to use words and phrases that are comfortable to you. Use this worksheet to brainstorm approaches you can use. On the left, write (1) a warm greeting, (2) an open-ended question, and (3) a possible response. On the right side, write what you think the typical reaction would be. The first entry is from our instruction to give you an example of what is required for this exercise.</td></tr>
<tr><td>20</td><td>Approaches
1. Hi, how are you today?
2. What do you think of this weather?
3. Me too. It's a nice change.

1. ____
2. ____
3. ____

1. ____
2. ____
3. ____</td><td>Reaction
____
____
____

____
____
____

____
____
____</td></tr>
<tr><th colspan="3">Application</th></tr>
<tr><td>21</td><td>Narrator: Look at this lost opportunity for David. This is not the outcome he hoped for.
David: Are you sure I can't put that sofa on the sales ticket for you? These great prices won't last long.
Maria: No thanks! I really want to keep shopping around. Okay?
David: Okay. Well come back again soon. Okay?
Maria: Okay. (As she leaves the store)
(David looks disappointed, as he lost the sale.)</td><td>
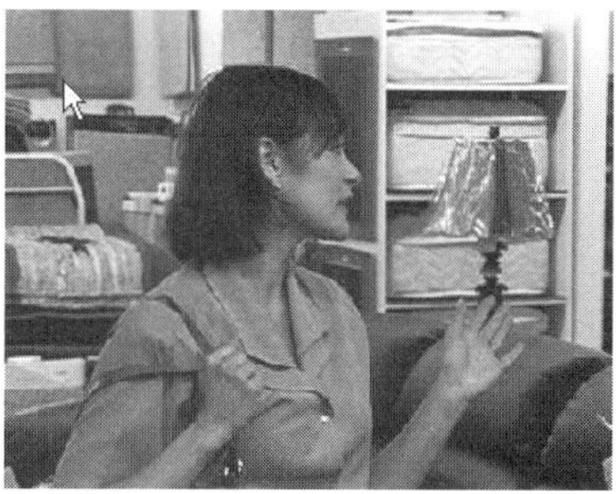</td></tr>
</table>

(continued)

FIGURE 6-12 *Continued*

Application		
22	**Narrator**: What happened? Why did David lose this sale? Let's go back and examine this sales event. As Maria enters the store. **David:** Hello, how can I help you? **Maria:** I'm just looking! **David:** Feel free to look around. What kind of furniture are you looking for? **Maria:** Where are your sofas? **David:** Let me show you (leading the way). Did you see the game last night? **Maria:** Yes. **David:** Wasn't Jack's final shot at the bell amazing? **Maria:** It was pretty spectacular. Rest of Demonstration Continues Here	
23	**Narrator:** Now that you have watched this demonstraiton, please do the following: Identify each of the steps in Selling with Service that David used. Did he include all the steps? For each step, consider the details of that step. Did David omit some of the details or perform the step incorrectly? Following each step, what was Maria's reaction? At each step, was she progressing toward a successful sale? At what point did David lose this customer? Where David did not execute a step in sales procedure adequately, indicate what he should have done to assist Maria so she would have been more likely to purchase.	

In Figure 6-12 the instruction is divided into three instructional segments, each corresponding to one of the problem-solving events nested in the problem-solving event, *A Friendly Approach*. Instructional event 3 tells the properties of a warm greeting; event 4 shows a portrayal of a warm greeting (*Show*-S) and gives a couple of additional examples of the words to use for a warm greetings (*Show*-S); and event 5 shows Maria's reaction (*Show*-C). Events 6 and 7 further elaborate this warm greeting of a friendly approach by telling and showing additional properties. Events 8 and 9 show a negative example of a greeting that David might have used (S*how*-S). The narrator guides the learner's attention to Maria's negative reaction, which is an unanticipated consequence (*Show*-C). Event 10 provides another inappropriate greeting and asks learners to identify the mistakes made by the sales associate (Do_{id}-S).

Both the open-ended question and sincere-response *problem-solving events* are taught in a similar manner. Event 11 is the *Tell*-S, *Show*-S, *Tell*-C, *and Show*-C for the next problem-solving event, *An Open-Ended Question.* Instructional events 12, 13, and 14 provide application for the problem-solving event, *ask an open-ended question* (Do_{id}-S). Event 15 is *Show*-S and *Show*-C events for the problem-solving event, *a sincere response.* Instructional events 16 and 17 use a matched example/non-example pair to illustrate another portrayal of a friendly approach (*Show*-S and *Show*-C).

Instructional event 20 attempts to have learners find additional examples of each of the properties of a friendly approach (Do_{id}-S). *Instructional-events* 21 through 23 are instances of the final activity for teaching a whole problem—find faulted conditions in a whole problem (Do_{ex}-C). This instruction would not take place until after all of the component skills or problem-solving events had been taught.

A careful comparison of all of the instructional events of this instruction with the prescribed instructional events will indicate that not every prescribed instructional event was used for every problem-solving event in the sales procedure. Very rich and complete instruction would implement every prescribed instructional event for every problem-solving event in the problem. However, such rich instruction may be counterproductive. When a condition is already familiar to learners, then having learners identify unencountered instances of the condition would probably be perceived as unnecessary and may be seen as boring by learners. For example, the condition for a warm greeting is that the customer feels at ease. Very rich instruction could provide several examples of customer reactions and have learners identify customers who appeared to be at ease and those who did not. But such additional instruction would probably be seen as unnecessary and therefore boring by learners. A similar argument follows for steps that learners already have in their repertoire. On the other hand, when it is likely that learners have not already attained a given concept (such as how to ask an open-ended question), then if the prescribed instructional events are not implemented, learners may not acquire the concept and therefore be unable to execute the step that requires them to use this concept.

One of the most important prescribed instructional events is Do_{ex}-S—execute all the steps. The instruction provides good demonstrations of each of the problem-solving events in the problem and also provides opportunity for learners to identify steps, properties of steps, and the consequence of these steps. An opportunity to perform the whole sales procedure with a customer would complete this integrated instruction. Providing such an opportunity in the instructional setting is often difficult. In this case the designers provided the learners with a checklist and instructions to have a colleague observe and critique their performance in the real world (Figure 6-13). Ideally, the instructor would be the observer and provide feedback to learners on their performance. But when this is not possible, having a colleague do so is perhaps the next-best approach. If no colleague is available, then the student is encouraged to do a self-appraisal of his or her own performance.

FIGURE 6-13 Final Application for Selling Furniture

Sales: Selling with Service

Application

You have completed this course on Selling with Service and should now have studied the skills that will allow you to sell more furniture and better provide for your customers' needs. But you won't really have acquired these skills until you have an opportunity to apply them with real customers in your store.

If possible, work with a colleague who has also completed this course. During a sales event, have your colleague work with you as you serve a customer. Your colleague should be friendly but let you handle all aspects of the sale.

Following the sale, have your colleague use the checklist below to evaluate your performance. For each step, have your colleague rate how well you executed the step on a 1 to 5 scale, with 1 being poorly and 5 being very well.

Don't use the checklist while working with the customer. Discuss your performance later in detail with your colleague. Identify areas where you can improve and study this material again in the course.

If another sales associate is not available to observe, you can rate yourself using the checklist.

When completed, add up the six scores; the result will be a number between 6 and 30. If you score:

25 to 30	You are an outstanding sales associate.
20 to 24	You need to improve in those areas where you scored less than 4.
Less than 20	You should study the course again, especially in those areas where you scored low.

Rate your colleague on these steps in the furniture sales process:

1. Building a relationship with the customer	1 2 3 4 5
2. Sharing your purpose statement	1 2 3 4 5
3. Discovering the customer's needs	1 2 3 4 5
4. Presenting appropriate solutions	1 2 3 4 5
5. Handling all customer objections	1 2 3 4 5
6. Asking for the order with confidence	1 2 3 4 5

Regular evaluation will help you to continue to improve your skills at selling with service and enjoy greater success and job satisfaction.

Best wishes for a very successful furniture sales career.

PRINCIPLES AND PRESCRIPTIONS

Problem-centered: Learning is promoted when learners acquire knowledge and skill in the context of real-world problems. Implementation of this principle requires two instructional design activities: identifying the content elements of the problem and designing the instructional strategy to teach these content components.

The content elements for a whole problem consist of a sequence of problem-solving events, each of which is comprised of a step leading to a condition and where the conditions are necessary to bring about the consequence (see Figure 6-7).

The instructional strategy to teach a whole problem consists of (1) a demonstration of the whole problem, including showing the consequence, conditions, and steps; (2) for each problem-solving event a *Tell/Show* demonstration, a Do_{id}, and a Do_{ex} for the step and condition; (3) a Do_{ex} for predicting the consequence, a Do_{ex} for finding faulted conditions, and/or a Do_{ex} for executing all of the steps of the whole problem (see Table 6-2).

APPLICATION

The analysis of whole problems presented in this book is more complex than some other recommendations for teaching problems. You will learn to identify the content elements of complex problems best by trying to identify them in existing instructional materials. Select several courses that you are taking, designing, or that you can find on the Internet. Examine these courses to see whether they involve problem solving. If they do, try to identify the content elements of the problem and the prescribed instructional events for teaching problem solving. If content elements are not included, see whether you can find content elements that could be added to the instruction. If some of the prescribed instructional events are missing, see whether you can design instructional events that could be added to the instruction.

TO LEARN MORE

van Merriënboer, J. J. G., & Kirschner, P. A. (2007). *Ten steps to complex learning.* Hillsdale, NJ: Lawrence Erlbaum Associates. These authors present a detailed approach to teaching complex tasks that is similar to the approach presented here.

COMING NEXT

Chapter 3 provided vocabulary for the content elements necessary to provide demonstration and application. Chapters 4 and 5 provided instructional interactions and strategies that could be used to teach component skill. This chapter combined these content elements and instructional strategies into an integrated instructional strategy for teaching whole problems. The next chapter extends the strategy for teaching problem solving by introducing problem-centered instructional strategy involving a progression of increasingly difficult problems. In this problem-centered approach, the teaching of component skills is distributed across the problem progression.

CHAPTER 7

PROBLEM-CENTERED INSTRUCTIONAL STRATEGY

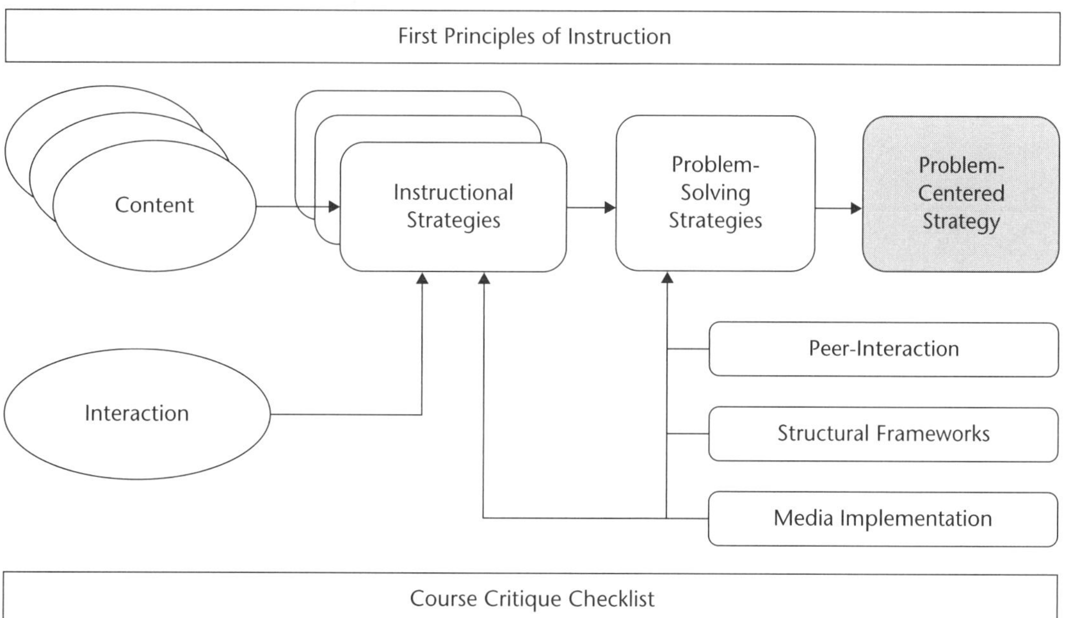

Quick Look

In Chapter 6 I demonstrated a problem-centered instructional strategy that integrates the instructional strategies for individual component skills. In this chapter I demonstrate a problem-centered instructional strategy that consists of a progression of increasingly complex problem portrayals. This chapter answers the following questions: What is a problem-centered instructional strategy and how does it differ from a traditional curriculum strategy? How are the instructional events distributed across each of the problems in a problem-progression?

Key Words

Topic-Centered Instructional Strategy: an approach that teaches each component skill in turn, often without reference to a final problem.

Problem-Centered Instructional Strategy: an approach that teaches component skills in the context of progression of problem portrayals. Instructional events for each component skill are distributed across the problem portrayals in the progression; teach all of the component skills required for the first problem portrayal, and then revisit these component skills, adding additional component skills or elements as required, for each subsequent problem portrayal in the progression.

Problem-Progression: a series of problem portrayals of the same type from a given content area; a straightforward version of the problem is presented first and each successive problem portrayal increases in complexity.

Distributed Instructional Events: instructional events are distributed when the demonstration of a given skill occurs in the early problem portrayals in a progression, and the application of this skill occurs in subsequent problem portrayals in the progression.

INTRODUCTION

This chapter elaborates the Problem-Centered Principle of instruction. Previous chapters have described and illustrated content elements and strategy modes, e^3 instructional strategies for helping learners acquire component skills, and how these component skills combine in a whole problem. This chapter describes and illustrates how all these ideas come together in a problem-centered instructional strategy.

PROBLEM-CENTERED INSTRUCTIONAL STRATEGY

Research has demonstrated that when learners acquire knowledge in the context of real-world problems they are more motivated to learn, the information they learn is easier to retrieve, and the information is easier to apply following the course (R.E. Mayer, 1998). However, a traditional instructional strategy (see Figure 7-1) is often topic-centered. A *topic-centered instructional strategy* teaches each component skill in turn. Too often the individual skills are taught without reference to the final problem. The arrows represent presentation of information and demonstration of portrayals for the topic. The cubes represent a quiz or application of the information. Typically, all the information related to the given topic or component skill is taught before going on to the next topic. After learners have completed every topic, they are often required to apply what they have learned in some form of final project, which may be a whole problem.

FIGURE 7-1 A Topic-Centered Instructional Strategy

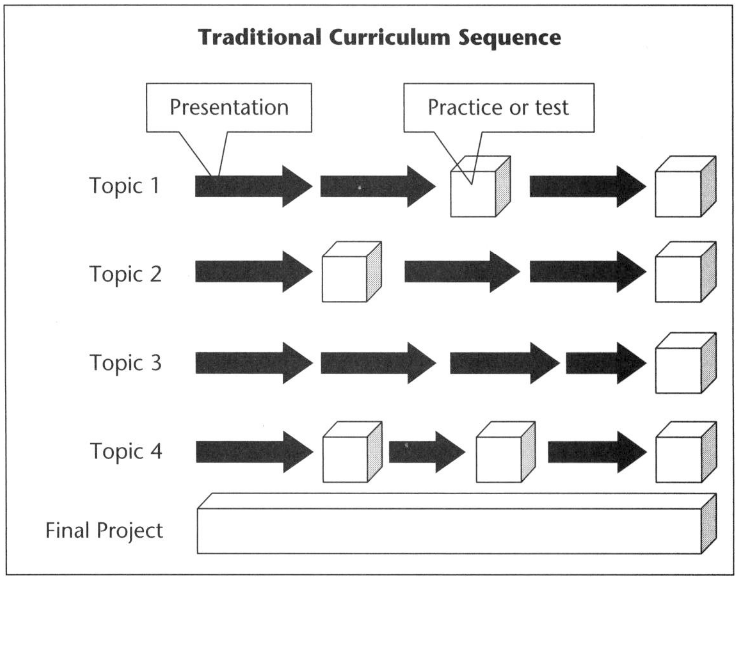

One of the limitations with this topic-centered strategy is that learners may have partially forgotten information presented and demonstrated in early topics before they have an opportunity to apply this information in the context of a whole problem. Another limitation is that learners may not see the relevance of a given skill because they are not familiar with the whole problem for which the skill is required. We have all heard the admonition, "You won't understand this now, but later it will be very important to you!" How many times did *later* never come and we never arrived at the time when it was *really important* or how many times have we forgotten the information before it became important? An e^3 sequence finds a way to help learners see the relevance of each skill they must acquire and have the opportunity to apply this skill to a whole problem as they progress through the instruction. The traditional curriculum sequence most often has a single opportunity to apply what has been learned. Too often this single opportunity is at the end of the instructional period, so there is often no time for adequate feedback on learners' performance, no time for learners to learn from their misunderstandings, and no time to revise their work. An e^3 sequence provides an opportunity to receive performance feedback early and often, an opportunity for learners to learn from their mistakes, and an opportunity for learners to revise their work.

Figure 7-2 illustrates a problem-centered instructional strategy. A *problem-centered instructional strategy* teaches component skills in the context of a progression of problems; instructional events for each component skill are distributed across the problems in the progression. A *problem-progression* is a series of problems of the same type from a given content area. The problems in the progression increase in complexity; the simplest version of the problem is presented first and each successive problem is more complex than the previous problem. This approach involves learners in the whole problem early in the instructional sequence.

FIGURE 7-2 A Problem-Centered Instructional Strategy

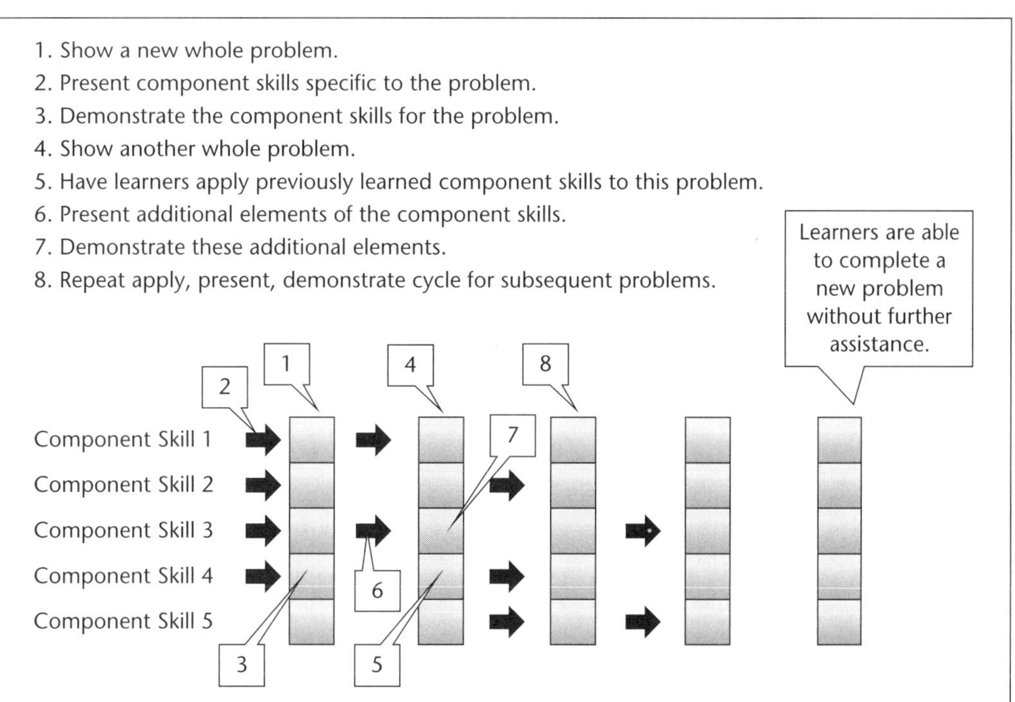
1. Show a new whole problem.
2. Present component skills specific to the problem.
3. Demonstrate the component skills for the problem.
4. Show another whole problem.
5. Have learners apply previously learned component skills to this problem.
6. Present additional elements of the component skills.
7. Demonstrate these additional elements.
8. Repeat apply, present, demonstrate cycle for subsequent problems.
Learners are able to complete a new problem without further assistance.
1
2
4
8
7
6
3
5
Component Skill 1
Component Skill 2
Component Skill 3
Component Skill 4
Component Skill 5

The sequence of instructional events is outlined in Figure 7-2. The instruction first demonstrates [1] the first whole problem in the progression. This demonstration provides the context for learners, shows learners what they will be able to do following the instruction, and forms the objective for the module or course. Too often formally stated objectives are not comprehensible by learners because they are abstractions of the content. On the other hand, learners can more easily grasp a demonstration of the whole problem.

This first demonstration should be a complete problem, but it should be the least complex version of the whole problem in the progression. While this demonstration should include all of the components of the whole problem, it should do so at a high level so as to not overwhelm the learners with details during this initial demonstration.

The second step [2] presents (*Tell*) those elements of each component skill that are required for the first problem. The third step [3] demonstrates (*Show*) these elements as they apply to this first problem. The fourth step [4] presents a second problem. The next step [5] requires learners to apply (*Do*) their previously acquired skill from Steps 2 and 3 to this new problem. The sequence then [6] presents (*Tell*) additional elements of the component skills and [7] demonstrates (*Show*) how to apply these elements to this new problem. The sequence repeats the *apply, present, demonstrate* series of events [8] for additional problems until learners have acquired all of the elements of each component skill and have demonstrated their application to a new problem.

INSTRUCTIONAL EVENTS DISTRIBUTED ACROSS A PROBLEM PROGRESSION

In more traditional instruction, all of the instructional events required to teach a given component skill are implemented for each topic in turn. In a problem-centered instructional strategy, the instructional events for a given component skill are distributed across the several problems in the progression. *Distributed instructional events* occur when the demonstration of a given skill occurs in the early problems in a progression and the application of this skill occurs in subsequent problems in the sequence.

Table 7-1 illustrates a possible sequence of *Tell, Show,* and *Do* that might be used for the instructional events required to teach each of the problems. Component 1 is easily understood and a single presentation/demonstration may be sufficient. Component 2 may be more difficult to understand, and an additional demonstration in a subsequent whole problem may be necessary for comprehension. Component 3 may require additional information for subsequent problems, so an additional *Tell* and *Show* are required for this component. Component 4 may not be required for problems early in the sequence, so it is introduced (*Tell/Show*) for the subsequent problems for which it is relevant. Component 5 may be sufficiently complex that the instances included in the whole problems are not sufficient to enable learners to grasp the concept or procedure. In this situation, additional examples, which are not included in the progression of whole problems, are provided for demonstration or application.

Table 7-1 Distribution of Instructional Events Across Problems

	Problem 1	Problem 2	Problem 3	Problem 4	Problem 5
Component 1	*Tell/Show*	*Do*	*Do*	*Do*	*Do*
Component 2	*Tell/Show*	*Show*	*Do*	*Do*	*Do*
Component 3	*Tell/Show*	*Tell/Show*	*Show*	*Do*	*Do*
Component 4		*Tell/Show*	*Tell/Show*	*Show*	*Do*
Component 5		*Tell/Show*	*Do*	*Do*	*Do*

Table 7-1 also illustrates how *Tell, Show,* and *Do* instructional events are distributed across the problems in the progression. Component 1 is demonstrated for the first problem, and then learners are asked to apply this skill for the remaining problems in the progression. Component 2 is demonstrated for Problem 1 and again for Problem 2; learners are then required to apply this skill for the remaining problems. Component 3 is apparently more complex; there is a *Tell/Show* demonstration for Problem 1, and there is a *Tell/Show* demonstration of additional element of the skill for problem 2.

There are two primary sequences that could be applied to this distribution of instructional events. The more traditional topic-centered strategy teaches each of the component skills in turn across the progression of problems. The *problem-centered strategy* is to teach all of component skills required for the first problem and then to revisit these component skills, adding additional component skills or elements as required, for each subsequent problem in the progression.

This problem-centered instructional strategy has several advantages over a more traditional sequence. It (1) allows learners to see the relationship of the skills to one another; (2) demonstrates the component skills several times in the context of different problems; (3) provides multiple opportunities for learners to apply the component skills they acquire; (4) provides multiple opportunities for learners to receive feedback on their application of the component skills; and (5) provides an opportunity for learners to revise their work.

PROBLEM-CENTERED STRATEGY EXAMPLE: ENTREPRENEUR COURSE

Brigham Young University–Hawaii developed an online problem-centered entrepreneur course designed to help third-world students start their own businesses when they returned home (Mendenhall, Buhanan, Suhaka, Mills, Gibson, & Merrill, 2006). This problem-centered approach puts the emphasis on real world examples (*Show-me*) instead of on the abstract concepts (*Tell-me*). The abstract concepts are still taught, but in the context of whole, real-world problems. Each concept is demonstrated multiple times in different contexts for each of the problems in the course. Learners thus form a whole schema for how to start a business and have several cases that illustrate the entire process.

For the entrepreneurship course, there were six topics or skills thought to be appropriate for starting and running a business: (1) identify a business opportunity, (2) define the idea that best fits the opportunity, (3) identify resources, (4) acquire resources, (5) start the business, and (6) manage the business. The whole problems chosen were simple businesses developed by former students: (1) a product business—Veasna's Pig Farm, (2) a service business—Tseegii and Tsogto's Instant Carpet Cleaning Service, (3) a retail business—Da Kine Wireless Mobile Phone, and (4) a restaurant business—Fiesta Mexican Restaurant. These businesses were selected because they are similar to the type of businesses that the students might be expected to form in the future. Some subset of each of the six skills is illustrated or applied for each of the businesses in turn.

Entrepreneurship is an online course developed specifically to implement the problem-centered instructional strategy illustrated in Figure 7-2. Real-world problems are the focus of the instruction. Up front, the course introduces learners to the first business—Veasna's pig farm product business. The course then teaches the portion of each of the six component skills that apply to a product business. It demonstrates how each of these skills is applied to the product business. It then introduces a second whole problem—Tseegii and Tsogto's carpet cleaning service business. This lesson requires learners to apply the skills they were taught for the pig farm to the service business. It also demonstrates additional elements for each of the component skills that apply to this new business. The course repeats this same sequence of events for a third and fourth business. Subsequent lessons teach additional information for each component skill as it is relevant for each new problem. With each successive problem in this progression, learners do more and more of the problem, and the course demonstrates less and less so that, by the end of the course, with coaching, learners are able to select, plan, and organize their own business.

Figure 7-3 shows a problem-solving event diagram showing the top-level content elements involved in entrepreneurship—starting a new business. There are six major problem-solving events corresponding to the six major steps in forming a business and the consequent condition that results from the execution of each of these steps. The conditions that lead to operating a successful business include developing an opportunity statement, an idea statement, a proforma income statement, a business plan, and a final (adjusted) business plan. It should be obvious to the reader that within these major problem-solving events are nested *additional problem-solving events.* The problem-centered strategy in this course includes instruction for each of these problem-solving event*s* for each business.

As noted in Table 7-1, in a problem-centered approach, the instructional events associated with a given problem-solving event may be distributed across several of the problems. For your convenience, Table 7-2 lists the prescribed instructional events for teaching a problem-solving event. Table 7-3 shows how the instructional events for the first component skill are distributed across the five problems in this course. The following paragraphs will illustrate examples of these instructional events in the context of each of the problems in this course.

For the pig farm, an opportunity statement is introduced and the defining properties are stated (*Tell*-C) and illustrated (*Show*-C). For the carpet cleaning problem, a new property for the opportunity statement is described (*Tell*-C). Learners are asked to identify the properties of a second statement of business opportunity (Do_{id}-C). For the cell phone problem, the steps required to find a business opportunity are described (*Tell*-S) and an example shown (*Show*-S). Learners are also required to identify the properties of a third statement of business opportunity (Do_{id}-C).

The restaurant problem requires learners to remember the properties of a business opportunity statement (*Ask*-C) and the steps required to find a business opportunity (*Ask*-S). *Ask* instructional events are not prescribed but can be useful in helping learners remember as long as they are accompanied by *Do* instructional events. The lesson requires learners to identify the properties of a new statement of business opportunity (Do_{id}-C) and shows an expanded statement of business opportunity (*Show*-C) and the steps required to find this information (*Show*-S). The last problem reminds learners again of the steps to find a business opportunity (*Tell*-S) and then coaches them in carrying out the steps required to find their own business opportunities (Do_{ex}-S).

FIGURE 7-3 Problem-Solving Event Diagram Showing Major Content Elements for Entrepreneurship

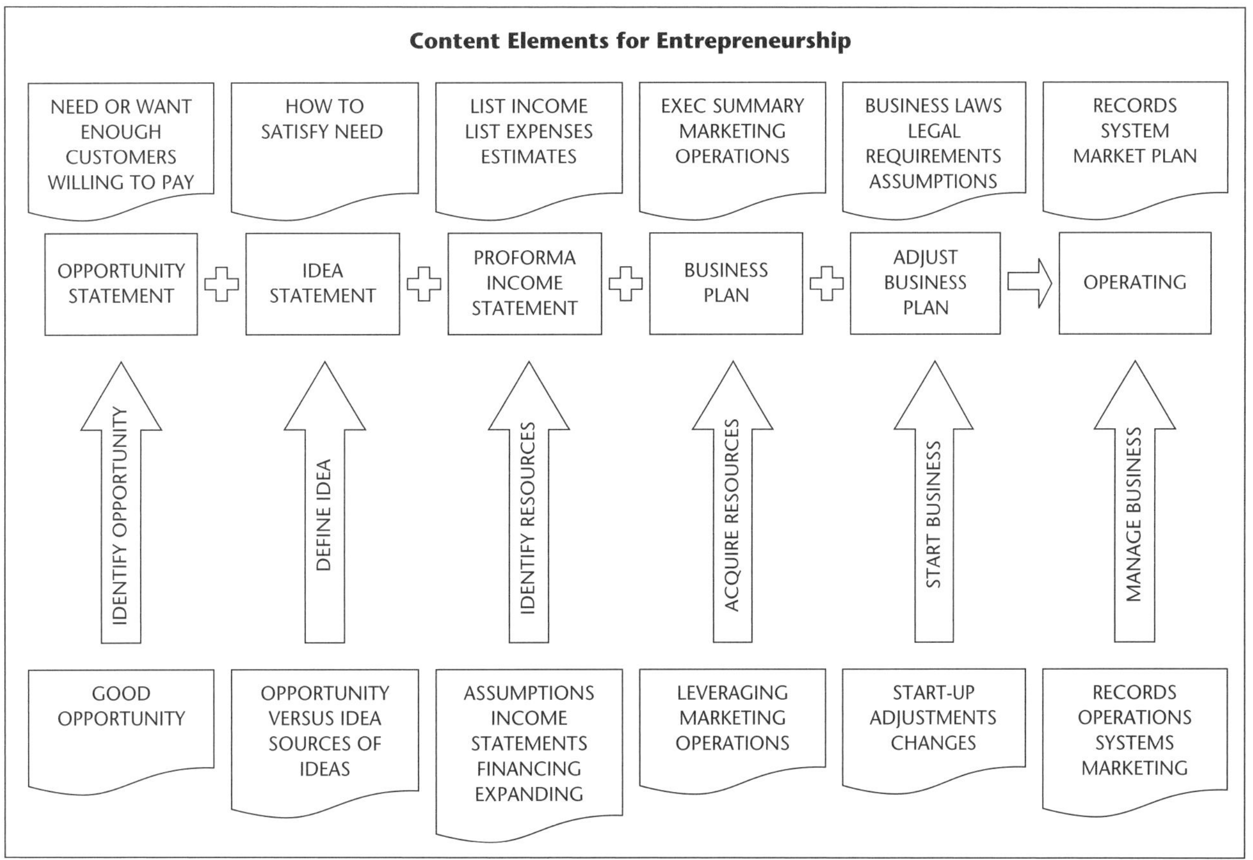

Table 7-2 Prescribed Instructional Events for a Problem-Solving Event

Demonstrate the Problem-Solving Event (Portrayal 1)		
Tell-C	Describe the condition (C).	kind-of
Show-C	Show an instance of the condition (C).	kind-of
Tell-S	Describe the step (S).	kind-of; how-to
Show-S	Show the execution of instances of the step (S).	kind-of; how-to

(continued)

Table 7-2 *Continued*

Do_{id} the Problem-Solving Event (Portrayal 2)		
Do_{id} -S	Identify instances of the step (S).	kind-of
Do_{id} -C	Identify the instances of the condition (C).	kind-of
Do_{id} and Do_{ex} the Problem-Solving Event (Portrayal 3)		
Do_{ex} -S	Execute instance of the step (S).	how-to
Do_{id} -C	Identify the resulting condition (C).	kind-of

Key: C = Condition; S = Step; *Do_{id}* = identify an instance; *Do_{ex}* = execute a step

Table 7-3 Entrepreneur Instructional Events Distributed Across Different Problems

	Pig Farm	Carpet Cleaning	Cell Phone	Restaurant	Own Business
Identify Opportunity	*Tell-C* *Show-C*	*Tell-C* *Do_{id} -C*	*Tell-S* *Show-S* *Do_{id} -C*	*Ask-C* *Show-S* *Do_{id} -C* *Ask-S* *Show-C*	*Tell-S* *Do_{ex} -S*

The course leads learners through all of the instructional events for all of the problem-solving events (component skills) in the first problem before going on to the second problem. Each of these component skills is visited again for each new business in the problem progression. As illustrated above, the first business may only demonstrate the conditions or steps involved in the skill; the second business may illustrate the conditions or steps for a second portrayal; the third business may ask learners to identify the condition or the steps involved in third portrayal; and later businesses may require learners to actually do the steps and identify the resulting condition from their actions. Thus the instructional events for the content elements of a given component skill may be distributed across the progression of problems as illustrated in Table 7-1. In this example I illustrated only the first component skill, as it was distributed across the businesses in the progression.

Figure 7-4 illustrates the format of the interface for the Entrepreneur course. The tabs across the top correspond to the five business problems in the course—product business, service business, retail business, restaurant business, and own business. The menu buttons on the left side correspond to the six component skills required for each of these businesses. The Introduction button provides an overview demonstration of each business. The panel on the left presents words or short phrases summarizing the information that is elaborated by the audio. The panel on the right presents portrayals of the information itemized on the left and elaborated by the audio.

FIGURE 7-4 Interface for Entrepreneur Course

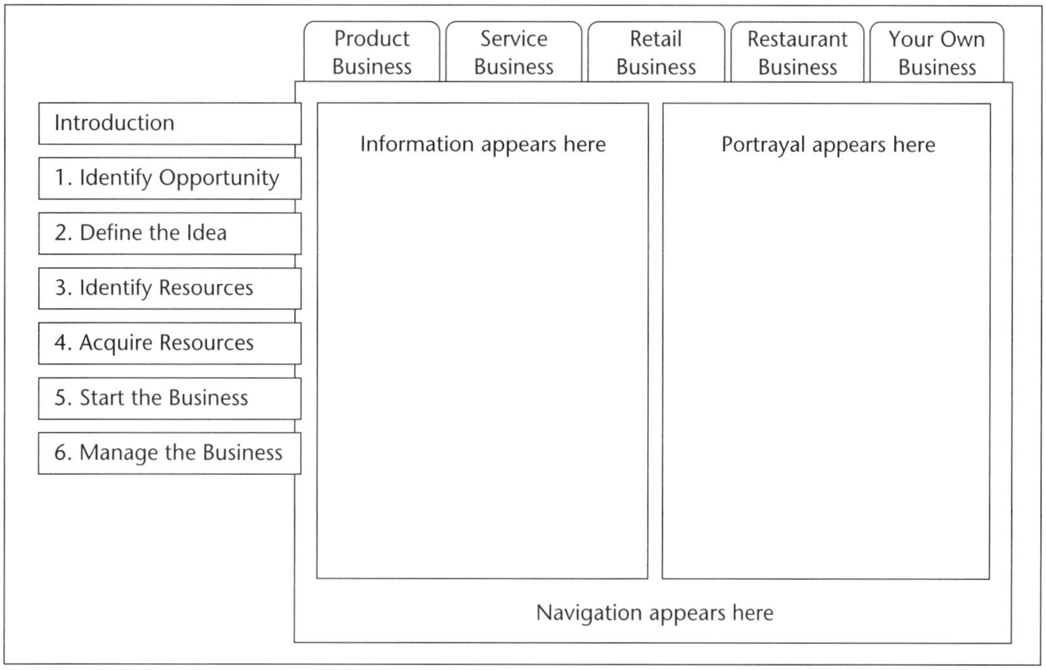

	Product Business	Service Business	Retail Business	Restaurant Business	Your Own Business
Introduction	Information appears here			Portrayal appears here	
1. Identify Opportunity					
2. Define the Idea					
3. Identify Resources					
4. Acquire Resources					
5. Start the Business					
6. Manage the Business					
	Navigation appears here				

Learners have control over the content in that they can select any business by clicking on its tab at the top. They can select the instruction for any of the component skills for that business by clicking on the menu buttons to the left. When clicked, the component skill buttons show pop-down menus for the problem-solving events within that skill. Learners are encouraged to systematically go through the instruction for each business before proceeding to the next business. The content control allows learners to return to any previous instruction with one or two clicks. While they are encouraged to study the material for each business in turn, learners have the option of reviewing a given component skill across businesses before going on to the next component skill. The original plan for this course was to provide a tool for research on the relative advantage of a problem-by-problem sequence compared with a component skill-by-skill sequence. To the author's knowledge, this research with this course has not yet been conducted.

Figure 7-5 shows excerpts from the introduction to the pig farm product business. Note that this brief introduction to the business references each of the steps. The figure identifies each of the steps in brackets, but this information is not shared with learners. Showing the whole problem is the first step in a problem-centered instructional strategy.

Figure 7-6 illustrates the instructional events for the first component skill, Identify an Opportunity, for the pig farm business. The audio and left panel are the *Tell*-C event and the right panel is the *Show*-C event. Figure 7-7 illustrates the instructional events for the first component skill for the carpet cleaning business. The audio and left panel are the *Tell*-C event and the right panel is the Do_{id}-C instructional event. Figure 7-8 illustrates the instructional events for the first component skill for the cell phone business. The first row is a *Tell*-S instructional event giving the steps in finding a business opportunity. The second row is a second application of the Do_{id}-C event for a new statement of business opportunity. The third instructional event is a *Show*-C instructional event illustrating how Devin improved his statement based on the feedback from the Do_{id}-C event.

FIGURE 7-5 Entrepreneur Pig Farm Introduction

Entrepreneur: Pig Farm Introduction	
Audio/Information	**Portrayal**
Narrator: Veasna Yen wanted to start his own business in his homeland of Cambodia, a poverty-stricken country. The economy is slow and mostly based on agriculture. One day, Veasna's brother tells him that two things are needed in Cambodia—construction and pigs [business opportunity]. After careful analysis and research, Veasna decided to start a pig farm [idea]. He was not an experienced businessman, so he first looked for mentors who could help him. Veasna introduced himself to a potential investor [identify resources]. He gave the man his business plan and proforma financial statements. Veasna explained to the man that his pig farm would give him a competitive edge in Cambodia based on the size of his farm. Most other pig farmers were small and raised pigs only for family use. With a bigger farm, he could respond to the high demand for pork and supply customers. The man invested $10,000 in Veasna's pig farm. Veasna also used his savings and a contribution from his family to start his business [acquire resources]. He leased land and hired workers to construct and run the farm [start the business].	 The portrayal was a series of still pictures showing Veasna, his brother, the investor, and various pictures of the farm.

FIGURE 7-6 Instructional Events for Business Opportunity—Pig Farm

Entrepreneur—Business Opportunity—Pig Farm		
Audio	Information	Portrayal
Narrator: There are two characteristics of a good business opportunity. First, there must be enough people with an unsatisfied need or want, and second, it must have the potential to make a profit.	**Identify a Good Opportunity** **1. Unsatisfied need or want** **2. Profit Potential**	
Narrator: Here is a beginning checklist for how to recognize a complete business opportunity statement: Is there an unsatisfied need or want? Are there enough people with this unsatisfied need or want? Are there enough of these people with this unsatisfied need or want who are willing to pay for a solution, and pay enough so that the business can make a profit?	**Business Opportunity Checklist** **1. Is there an unsatisfied need or want?** **What is the evidence?** **2. Are there enough people?** **What is the evidence?** **3. Are they willing to pay?** **What is the evidence?**	**Veasna's Business Opportunity Statement** My brother told me that one of the two most needed things in Cambodia is pigs. More than 50 percent of the meat consumed has been imported from the neighboring countries, mostly Thailand and Viet Nam. The cost of importing is high and the delivery time is long, and the pork quality is not consistent.

(continued)

Entrepreneur—Business Opportunity—Pig Farm		
Entrepreneurs are not wild risk-takers. In fact, they do all they can to reduce as many risks as possible. That is why you need to make sure that your opportunity is a real opportunity. With each item, what is the evidence this is a potentially successful business opportunity? Where did the information come from? How do we know it is true or accurate? Here is a statement of a business opportunity. Click on each paragraph to see how each part of the statement relates to the Business Opportunity Checklist. [Portrayal shown here.]	**NOTE:** Numbered items appear as mentioned in audio. For portrayal, when an above item is clicked, the corresponding paragraph in the statement of business opportunity is highlighted. When Item 1 is clicked, this message is shown: "This is a great need, but the evidence for it is weak. Only his brother is mentioned. Where did the information come from?" There are similar pop-up messages for each of the items.	Following recent outbreaks of the bird flu (which affects chickens and ducks) in Southeast Asia, many people have turned to eating other kinds of meat. There are also a lot of Chinese people in Cambodia, and Chinese people eat a lot of pork. I went to the marketplace to see if people were purchasing pigs. I observed lots of people purchasing pigs daily. I asked an employee how many pigs they sell every day. The employee said they usually sell most all of the pigs they bring to the market. A local butcher told me that if I could provide grown pigs every month, at a cheaper price than imported meat, he would buy from me.

FIGURE 7-7 Instructional Events for Business Opportunity—Carpet Cleaning

Entrepreneur—Business Opportunity—Carpet Cleaning		
Audio	Information	Portrayal
Narrator: A good business opportunity is the foundation on which any successful business is built. You have already seen this beginning checklist on how to recognize a complete statement of a business opportunity. In this lesson we will add one more item to the checklist. When researching a business idea, you will need to know whether potential customers are able to pay for the product or service. Many people are willing to pay, but they may not have the financial resources. The checklist can be summarized or combined into one question that you will need to ask yourself: "Are there enough people who need or want a product, and will buy it, for my business to be profitable?" **Narrator:** Look at this new business opportunity statement and decide whether Tseegii and Tsogto followed the business opportunity checklist and determine how complete their answers are. Now read the statement. Is this a complete business opportunity statement? Click on your answer.	**Business Opportunity Checklist** 1. Is there an unsatisfied need or want? What is the evidence? 2. Are there enough people? What is the evidence? 3. Are they willing to pay? What is the evidence? 4. Are they able to pay? What is the evidence?	**Tseegii and Tsogto's Business Opportunity Statement** We have lived for many years in the capital city of Mongolia, Ulaanbaatar. We have noticed that the cold Mongolian weather has led to having carpets everywhere: houses, buildings, offices, etc. We know from experience that one of the major problems people face here in the city is trying to keep their carpets clean. This is the case because there aren't a lot of paved streets or grassy areas in the city, so the streets tend to be muddy. Thus, carpets get dirty very rapidly. Unfortunately, there is no professional carpet cleaning service available in Mongolia, and any non-professional attempt to clean carpets shortens their useful life. As a result, people have to change their carpets frequently, costing them a lot of money and time. Is this a complete business opportunity statement? Yes No Not Sure
Feedback for all answers: The statement could be improved. More evidence is required. How often do people change their carpets and how much do replacement carpets cost? Tseegii and Tsogto have not stated whether their potential customers are able to pay for this service.		

FIGURE 7-8 Instructional Events for Business Opportunity—Cell Phone Business

Entrepreneur—Business Opportunity—Cell Phone		
Audio	**Information**	**Portrayal**
Narrator: You learned in the first two lessons about general sources of good opportunities. Problems to solve and changes in technology and society are usually good sources of business opportunities. There are several places or ways people could identify these problems and changes; for example, you could talk to your family and friends, read newspapers and magazines, or watch the news on TV. However, most entrepreneurs admit that they recognized opportunities through their previous work experiences. Over half of successful businesses are started from ideas based on previous jobs and skills obtained through those experiences.	Finding Business Opportunities 1. Look for problems to solve. 2. Look for changes in technology. 3. Look for changes in society. 4. Previous work experience.	
Narrator: Here is a statement of a business opportunity. Decide whether you think it is a complete business opportunity statement or not.	**Business Opportunity Checklist** 1. Is there an unsatisfied need or want? What is the evidence? 2. Are there enough people? What is the evidence? 3. Are they willing to pay? What is the evidence? 4. Are they able to pay? What is the evidence?	**Devin's Business Opportunity Statement** I was attending a university in La'ie, on the North Shore of Hawaii, when I realized that many students had needs that were not satisfied. At the beginning of every semester, a fair was organized for businesses to present their products to college students. I was looking for a way to make a little money so I asked a cell phone company if I could sell for them at the school fair. It was while selling phones at these fairs that I realized hundreds of new international students were coming every semester, and it seemed that one of the first things students wanted to have was a cell phone so they could keep in touch with all their new friends. The closest cell phone store was 45 minutes away by car, so it was very convenient for the students to have somebody on location to sell phones instead of them having to travel so far. I learned from first-hand experience that new students really had a need that hadn't been met yet. Is this a complete business opportunity statement? YES NO Not Sure
Feedback: Although it looks like Devin spotted a great need through his work, more evidence is needed. Most of the statements are not very specific. Instead of saying "hundreds" it would be better to have a specific number for how many new international students come every semester, an estimate of how many of these new students buy mobile phones, and an estimate of how much they typically pay. Additionally, what evidence is there to support this information? This is a great start, but it just needs more research to be complete.		

FIGURE 7-8 *Continued*

<table>
<tr>
<td>Narrator: Devin decided to do more research for his business opportunity. Compare his old statement to his new statement. What makes Statement 2 more complete than Statement 1?

Click on the checklist items to highlight corresponding sections of Devin's statement.

Click here to compare your answer.</td>
<td>Devin's First Business Opportunity Statement

I was attending a university in La'ie, on the North Shore of Hawaii, when I realized that many students had needs that were not satisfied. At the beginning of every semester, a fair was organized for businesses to present their products to college students. I was looking for a way to make a little money so I asked a cell phone company if I could sell for them at the school fair. It was while selling phones at these fairs that I realized hundreds of new international students were coming every semester, and it seemed that one of the first things students wanted to have was a cell phone so they could keep in touch with all their new friends. The closest cell phone store was 45 minutes away by car, so it was very convenient for the students to have somebody on location to sell phones instead of them having to travel so far. I learned from first-hand experience that new students really had a need that hadn't been met yet.

Business Opportunity Checklist

1. Is there an unsatisfied need or want?
What is the evidence?

2. Are there enough people?
What is the evidence?

3. Are they willing to pay?
What is the evidence?

4. Are they able to pay?
What is the evidence?</td>
<td>Devin's Revised Business Opportunity Statement

I was attending a university in La'ie, on the North Shore of Hawaii, when I realized that many students had needs that were not satisfied. At the beginning of every semester, a fair was organized for businesses to present their products to college students, faculty, staff, and community members. Last year there were approximately 2,200 people in attendance. This number is based upon a booth, from an insurance company, that handed out a gift to each person. They gave away approximately 2,200 small gifts to attendees.

I was looking for a way to make a little money so I asked a cell phone company if I could sell for them at the school fair. It was while selling phones at these fairs that I realized hundreds of new international students were coming every semester, and it seemed that one of the first things students wanted to have was a cell phone so they could keep in touch with all their new friends.

I asked the registrar how many new international students came to the university each semester. His data concluded that there were 376 new students in the fall, 154 new students for winter semester, and 109 new students for spring and summer semesters.

After reviewing the sales slips for the entire week, the company I worked for sold 264 cell phones; 189 of those sales were to international students. 177 out of 189 phones sold were the basic phone that was on special for $69.95.

The closest cell phone store was 45 minutes away by car and about an hour and a half by bus. So it was very convenient for the students to have somebody on location to sell phones instead of them having to travel so far. I learned from first-hand experience that new students really had a need that hadn't been met yet.</td>
</tr>
<tr>
<td colspan="3">Feedback: As you can see, Devin did more research. He found out about how many attendees there were at the fair. An exact number of international students visiting the mobile phone booth would be ideal, but that data was not collected by anyone. So the next-best information he found was the insurance company that kept a tally of how many individuals came to their booth for their free gift. He also gathered information from the registrar about how many potential new students came each year. His own experience as a salesperson also showed him the potential number of sales for new phones.</td>
</tr>
</table>

Figure 7-9 illustrates the instructional events for the first component skill for the restaurant business. The first row is an *Ask*-C instructional event—list properties of a good statement of business opportunity. The second row is a Do_{id}-C instructional event—identify examples of each property and the evidence for this information. The third row is an *Ask*-S instructional event—asking learners to list the steps to take to find a good business opportunity. The fourth row is a *Show*-C event showing the results of Heber's research to find evidence for his statement of business opportunity.

FIGURE 7-9 Instructional Events for Business Opportunity—Restaurant

Entrepreneur—Business Opportunity—Restaurant		
Audio	Information	Portrayal
Narrator: You have been through three businesses and recognized how Veasna, Tseegii and Tsogto, and Devin all identified their business opportunities. Now it is your turn to list the four questions asked in a beginning checklist for how to recognize a complete business opportunity statement.	List the four questions asked in a business opportunity checklist. 1. 2. 3. 4. SUBMIT	**Feedback:** [After they click SUBMIT, learners are shown the questions.]
Narrator: Olga and her husband Heber would like to start a business in Olga's hometown, Khabarovsk, in Far East Russia. Heber is from Texas, U.S.A., but lived in Russia for two years and he is familiar with local culture and practices. They are thinking about opening a Mexican restaurant in Khabarovsk, Russia. Heber conducted a lot of research on the Internet to help him determine whether there was a good opportunity for his business idea. He found a website called BISNIS, which stands for Business Information Service for the Newly Independent States. This organization provides information about the Eurasia market economy. Read the paragraphs and determine which one answers each of the questions to the right. Determine the evidence for each answer.	**Business Opportunity Checklist** 1. Is there an unsatisfied need or want? 2. Are there enough people? 3. Are they willing to pay? 4. Are they able to pay?	1. Heber is very good at cooking Mexican food. He researched the industry reports from BISNIS for Khabarovsk, Russia, where he would like to start a business. The report from BISNIS states that ethnic foods would be a good market prospect and that only two ethnic foods restaurants are found in the area and they are twelve hours away from Khabarovsk. 2. There are about 582,100 people in Khabarovsk. Furthermore, there is a steady increase in real income, causing a stronger demand for quality products and services. Furthermore, BISNIS states that a food new to the market, such as Mexican, would be the best prospect. 3. A foreign restaurant that opened recently in Vladivostok, a city twelve hours away from Khabarovsk, Country Fried Chicken, serves an average of three hundred customers a day and has a hard time meeting demand during peak hours. 4. The fast-food market is very poorly developed in the Russian Far East and has a shortage of cafes serving inexpensive, nutritious food quickly. Because of the lack of fast-food restaurants, BISNIS reports that people pay \$3 to \$4 from a \$100 monthly salary for a single course.

FIGURE 7-9 *Continued*

Narrator: What are four ways you can look for good business opportunities? Type in your answer and hit the SUBMIT button.	Four ways to look for good business opportunities. 1. 2. 3. 4. SUBMIT	**Feedback:** [After they click SUBMIT, learners are shown the questions.]
Narrator: Read about Heber's research through the BISNIS website. He found four articles that helped him answer the questions on the business opportunity checklist.	**Business Opportunity Checklist** 1. Is there an unsatisfied need or want? What is the evidence? 2. Are there enough people? What is the evidence? 3. Are they willing to pay? What is the evidence? 4. Are they able to pay? What is the evidence?	The first article, Franchising Opportunities in the Russian Far East, states that there is a steady increase in the incomes of consumers, causing a stronger demand for quality products and services. Also, the quality of service is very poor and the ability of any business to offer a Western style of management and customer service would instantly obtain a competitive advantage over competitors. Furthermore, few if any restaurants offer quick, affordable, quality dining experiences. [There are four additional articles cited with the evidence for each of the relevant questions highlighted.]

Figure 7-10 illustrates the instructional events for the first component skill for starting your own business. The instructional events are *Tell*-S and Do_{ex}-S where the steps are those necessary to find a new business opportunity. The learner is reminded of the steps to take and then encouraged to do them.

FIGURE 7-10 Instructional Events for Business Opportunity—Own Business

Entrepreneur—Business Opportunity—Your Own Business		
Audio	**Information**	**Portrayal**
Narrator: Go to the *CIA World Fact Book* online and study the living conditions in the country where you would like to start a business. Look in a recent newspaper and think about the situations and people around you. Talk to your family and friends about changes and problems around you that might be opportunities for starting a business.	Defining the business opportunity Click here for *CIA World Fact Book* Check newspaper Talk to family and friends	Answer the following questions: 1. List a problem that you have that other people are also likely to have. Can you think of a way to solve it? ________ 2. List new technology that can be used to solve existing problems faster or cheaper. ________ 3. List changes in society that have caused a problem. Can you think of a way to solve it? ________

(continued)

FIGURE 7-10 *Continued*

Based on your research, answer these questions: What problems do you or others have that you might solve? What new technologies might be used to solve existing problems faster or cheaper? What changes in society have caused problems? Can you think of a solution to one of these problems? List your thoughts in the panel to the right.		
Narrator: Think about your previous work experience. What skills and training did you acquire that might be helpful in starting your own business? Who were your customers? Who were your suppliers? Which customers from your previous job are likely to remain your customers if you start a new business?		Answer the following questions: 1. List your skills and training. ____________________ 2. Who were your customers? ____________________ 3. Are they likely to be your customers in a new business? ____________________
Narrator: Out of the ideas you have written, pick the best opportunity and research it further. Interview someone who runs a similar business. Study the community where your business will be located. Interview people who know the needs of the community. Now answer the questions about whether or not this is a good business opportunity.	Interview business owner Research community	Answer the following questions: 1. What is the need or want for your product or service? What is the evidence? ____________________ 2. Who are the potential customers for your product or service? What is the evidence? ____________________ 3. Can these customers pay for your product or service? What is the evidence? ____________________

The instructional strategies illustrated show an implementation of some of the prescribed instructional strategies listed in Table 7-2, Prescribed Instructional Events for a Problem-Solving Event. The Do_{ex}-S (execute all the steps for the whole problem) instructional events include considerable coaching. While learners are guided in the steps to start their own business, there is no opportunity within this course to receive intrinsic feedback on their performance. Of course, attempting to start a business in the real world does have built-in intrinsic feedback if it succeeds or does not succeed. It is difficult in the context of a course to monitor an open-ended Do_{ex}-S instructional event. Obviously, the ultimate goal of this instruction is for learners to successfully start their own business. A possible way to assess the ability of learners to do the whole problem is to implement a Do_{ex}-Q (predict a consequence from a set of conditions) or Do_{ex}-C (find faulted conditions or steps for an unanticipated consequence) instructional event for another business. The conditions—opportunity statement, idea statement, proforma income statement, and business plan—are all conditions for acquiring venture capital. An effective Do_{ex}-Q strategy might consist of providing learners with a business plan for yet another business and having them predict whether or not this plan is sufficient to obtain venture capital from an investor. This critique application requires learners to examine each of the conditions of the plan, using the following prompts: identify where and if the statement of business opportunity states instances of the properties need or want, enough customers, willing to pay, and able to pay; identify where and if the statement of business opportunity provides evidence for each of these properties; and indicate how the statement of business opportunity could be improved. A similar set of prompts would be provided for each of the conditions leading to the acquisition of resources.

A Do_{ex}-C variation of this application instructional event provides a business plan and the information that the plan was rejected for funding when submitted to an investor. The challenge for learners is to determine why the plan may have been rejected and how the plan could be improved so that the probability of obtaining funding is increased.

PROBLEM-CENTERED STRATEGY EXAMPLE: GENERAL EDUCATION COURSE

Many courses, including general education courses, involve more than a single type of problem or even a single subject area. How is a problem-centered approach implemented for this type of course? One such general education course, a traditional biology 100 course at Brigham Young University–Hawaii, was revised to implement a problem-centered approach (Francom, Bybee, Wolfersberger, Mendenhall, & Merrill, 2009; Francom, Wolfersberger, & Merrill, 2009).

The first challenge was to limit the scope of the course so that it could be taught using a problem-centered strategy. The instructor chose topics that were essential for learners to form a foundation in biology. He had to take into account departmental mandates, which require a certain breadth of topics, while still allowing learners sufficient time to engage in a progression of problems in each subject area. He chose six topic areas: the process of science, chemistry, cells, genetics, evolution, and ecology.

The second challenge was to identify a progression of problems within each subject area. The instructor selected three problems for each of the six topic areas. Figure 7-11 briefly summarizes the three problems selected for the process-of-science topic. The description of the problem and the data given to the learners is very much abbreviated here, but the problem learners were asked to solve is indicated by the questions.

The next challenge was how to get learners engaged with this progression of problems and how to get learners to interact effectively with each other (see Chapter 8 for more detail on peer-interaction). Figure 7-12 identifies the instructional-event sequence that was repeated for each major topic of the course.

Pre-Class Instructional Events

The instructor selected all of the reading assignments to help learners complete the course problems. Before class, learners read the case study and then read sections of the textbook and supplemental tutorials related to this problem. In the process-of-science section of the class, learners complete a case study concerning the fish kill mystery. The questions require learners to apply what they just learned about the process of science. The case study and questions are the first problem for the learners. The directions encourage learners to look for clues that would help them understand the case study problem and answer the questions. The strategy required learners to answer the questions before they came to the class meeting.

FIGURE 7-11 Problem Progression for Biology 100—Process of Science

Biology 100—The Process of Science	
Problem 1. The Fish Kill Mystery A detailed case study is presented: Dead fish are discovered in an estuary. Participants in the story, along with a scientist, begin to speculate about the cause. The process of dissolved oxygen and its effect on fish is explained by a participant in the story. Dissolved oxygen maps are provided for the river. As the story unfolds, more hypotheses are suggested and more data are provided by participants in the story. At the end of the scenario, learners are challenged to answer the questions shown in the panel to the right.	Use the scientific method to figure out how the fish died. What observations were made? What hypotheses were developed? What predictions could be made based on those hypotheses? How would you test those hypotheses? What results would support your hypothesis and what results would not?
Problem 2. The Ivory-Billed Woodpecker Supposed discovery of a thought-to-be-extinct ivory-billed woodpecker. *Data:* Video supposedly showing woodpecker. Email exchange where Brad's friend Mary is challenging his evidence from the video.	*Question:* What evidence would convince you that the ivory-billed woodpecker is not extinct? *Question:* Evaluate the merit of the video scientific evidence. *Questions:* 1. What is the major conflict between Brad and Mary in terms of the scientific process? Make a list of Brad's arguments and valid pieces of evidence and Mary's response to each. 2. What do you think about Brad's concern that by waiting with the announcement they could miss their chance to save the birds? 3. Imagine you are the owner of a company that owns the logging rights adjacent to the area of the woodpecker sightings, or a biologist trying to protect the habitat of another endangered species in another part of the state. Do you think that you would be satisfied with the same amount of evidence in this case as Brad? Why/Why not? 4. What is the right amount of evidence? How can you determine the answer to that question?

FIGURE 7-11 *Continued*

Problem 3. Nanobacteria: Are They or Aren't They Alive? Biomineralization is explained. In this problem, we will be considering the evidence for the existence of nanobacteria and their role in the process of biomineralization. The fundamental issue is whether nanobacteria are alive. Properties of life. *Experiment 1.* Transferability (description of experiment follows). *Experiment 2.* Gamma Radiation *Experiment 3.* Kidney Stones Corroborating Evidence. Conflicting Evidence from two experiments.	Decide whether you think nanobacteria are alive or not and explain your answer based on information given.

FIGURE 7-12 Instructional-Event Sequence for Biology 100

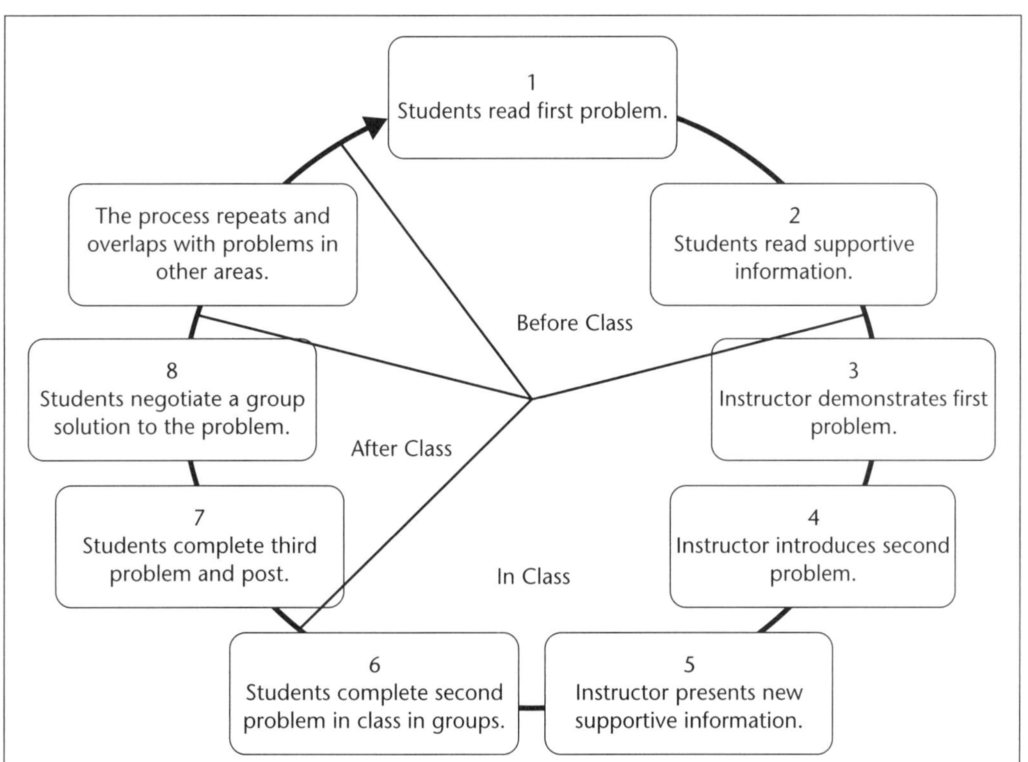

In-Class Instructional Events

The first instructional event in a problem-centered strategy demonstrates how the problem is to be completed. In the class session, the instructor demonstrates how the information learners read is applied to the first case study and shows learners how to complete the problem they are given represented by the questions they were to answer. The instructor then presents a second problem, demonstrates a partial solution, and conducts a class discussion to help learners see how information from the textbook and supplemental materials are applied to complete the problem.

After-Class Instructional Events

After the class, learners work on a third problem with little guidance. These problems are real-world cases that learners first solve individually and then in groups. Learners are introduced to the problem by reading it and then answering questions that require application of the skills they have acquired from the first two cases.

Each of the sections of the course followed a similar instructional strategy. Learners read a problem and study the text and supplemental materials relevant to the problem. Then they come to class and are shown how the information can be used to complete the problem. Next, they are presented with a second problem and asked to solve it in class group discussion. For homework, learners post their individual solutions to a third problem and then work with a collaboration group to post an agreed-on group solution to the problem.

How does this sequence of instructional events implement the prescribed instructional events for teaching problem solving? The two instructional events that are clearly identified in the above strategy are the *Show*-Q (show the consequence for the whole problem) and Do_{ex}-C (find faulted conditions for the observed consequence) instructional events. It is presumed that the course included *Show*-C and *Show*-S *instructional events* as part of the text, supplemental materials, and in-class demonstrations. There is no indication in the description that the course included Do_{id}-C, Do_{id}-S, or Do_{ex}-S events. Using a more traditional approach, the instructor selected reading and supplemental materials that he thought included the concepts and principles related to a given biological problem. His emphasis was on the content included rather than the instructional events involved. A careful problem-solving event analysis of the material included in the case studies, reading materials, and supplemental materials would reveal the problem-solving event structure of the problems and would indicate additional identify (Do_{id}) and execute (Do_{ex}) *instructional events* that could contribute to e^3 instruction. As is often the case, however, time and content coverage requirements limit the number of additional instructional events that could be added to the instruction. Nevertheless, the problem-centered approach in this biology course represents a significant improvement over its original *Tell-Ask* approach.

PRINCIPLES AND PRESCRIPTIONS

Problem-Centered: Learning is promoted when learners engage in a problem-centered instructional strategy in which component skills are taught in the context of a simple-to-complex progression of whole real-world problems.

The steps in a problem-centered strategy are as follows:

1. Identify a progression of increasingly complex problem portrayals.
2. Present first problem portrayal.
3. *Tell/Show* component skills for the first problem portrayal.

4. Present a second problem portrayal.
5. Have learners apply (*Do*) component skills to second problem portrayal.
6. *Tell/Show* new elements of component skills for the second problem portrayal.
7. Repeat 4, 5, and 6 for subsequent problems until all elements of all component skills have been demonstrated and applied.
8. Have learners apply (*Do*) all component skills to a final problem portrayal.

APPLICATION

Select several courses that you are taking, designing, or that you can find on the Internet. Examine these courses to find one that uses a problem-centered instructional strategy. See whether you can identify each of the problem-centered strategy components in this course. Courses that use a problem-centered instructional strategy are not common so you may not be able to find a good example. In this case select a course that involves a problem and identify a problem progression for the course; see whether you can design each of the steps in a problem-centered strategy for this course.

TO LEARN MORE

Francom, G., Bybee, D., Wolfersberger, M., Mendenhall, A., & Merrill, M. D. (2009). A task-centered approach to freshman-level general biology. *Bioscene, Journal of College Biology Teaching, 35*(1), 66–73. Introduction to Biology is described in this paper.

Francom, G., Wolfersberger, M., & Merrill, M. D. (2009). Biology 100: A task-centered, peer-interactive redesign. *TechTrends, 53*(3), 35–100. Introduction to Biology is also described in this paper.

Mendenhall, A., Buhanan, C. W., Suhaka, M., Mills, G., Gibson, G. V., & Merrill, M. D. (2006). A task-centered approach to entrepreneurship. *TechTrends, 50*(4), 84–89. Introduction to entrepreneurship: how to start your own business is described in this paper.

Merrill, M. D. (2007c). A task-centered instructional strategy. *Journal of Research on Technology in Education, 40*(1), 33–50. The ideas presented in this chapter were originally published in this paper.

COMING NEXT

Chapter 5 elaborated the Demonstration Principle and the Application Principle for individual component skills. Chapters 6 and 7 elaborated the Problem-Centered Principle. Chapter 8 will elaborate the Activation and Integration Principles and illustrate how structural frameworks and learner interaction can be integrated with the instructional strategies for component skills and whole problems.

CHAPTER 8

ENHANCING INSTRUCTIONAL STRATEGIES WITH STRUCTURAL FRAMEWORKS AND LEARNER INTERACTION

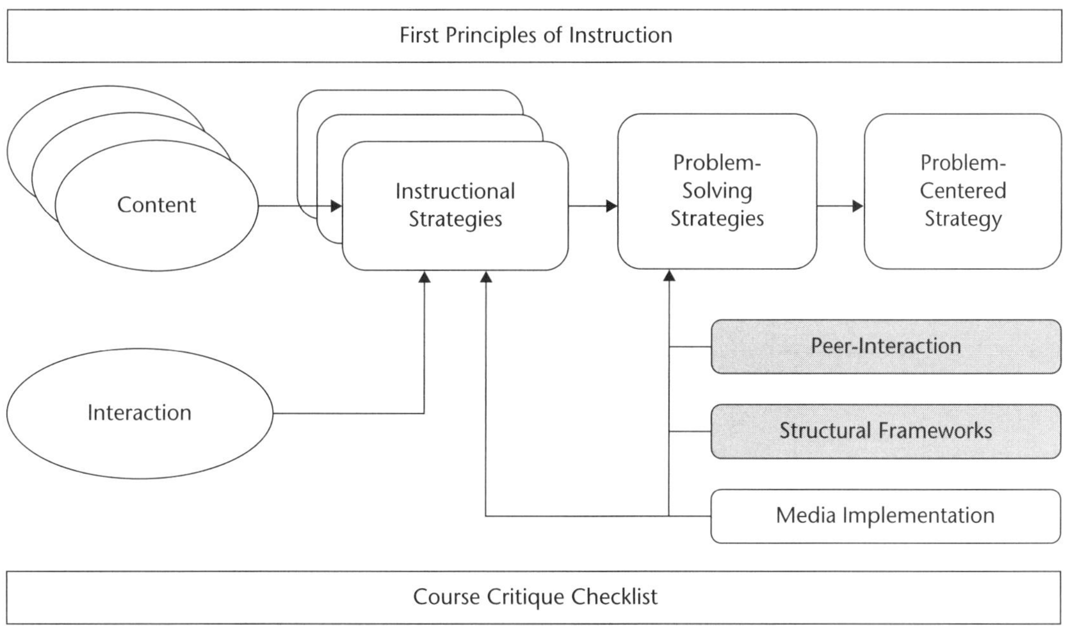

Quick Look

In Chapters 6 and 7 I demonstrated instructional strategies for teaching whole problems. In this chapter I demonstrate two enhancements to problem-solving strategies that implement the Activation and Integration Principles. This chapter answers the following questions: What are effective activation activities and how are they integrated with e^3 instructional strategies? What can be done to help learners integrate the problem-solving skills they develop into their everyday lives following instruction? How can learners help one another learn?

Key Words

Structural Framework: an organization of previously learned information that learners can use to adapt an existing mental model or to build a new mental model for new content.

Structure-Guidance-Coaching-Reflection Cycle: presenting a structural framework early in instruction and using this framework for guidance during demonstration, for coaching during application, and for reflection during integration.

Peer-Telling: an ineffective form of learner-interaction in which learners review and present information to other students.

Peer-Sharing: an instructional event in which learners share with each other prior relevant experience with the subject-matter content under consideration.

Peer-Discussion: a form of learner-interaction in which learners deliberate the proposed solution of example problems.

Peer-Collaboration: a form of learner-interaction in which learners work together in small groups to solve problems.

Peer-Critique: a form of learner-interaction in which learners evaluate the problem-solving activities of fellow learners and provide constructive suggestions for improvement.

INTRODUCTION

Previous chapters have introduced instructional strategies for teaching component skills and instructional strategies for teaching whole problems. These chapters elaborated the Demonstration Principle, the Application Principle, and the Problem-Centered Principle. First Principles of Instruction also include the Activation Principle and the Integration Principle. How are these principles implemented in instructional materials and combined with instructional strategies to further promote e^3 learning?

Activation is accomplished when instruction stimulates mental models that can be modified to enable learners to incorporate the new knowledge into their existing knowledge. How can these existing mental models be stimulated and related to instructional strategies? The first section of this chapter suggests that helping students use their existing experience to form structural frameworks and using these structural frameworks as the basis for guidance during demonstration and coaching during application facilitates e^3 learning.

Integration is accomplished when instruction provides an opportunity for learners to explain their new skill to others and to defend what they know when it is challenged. What can be done to provide an opportunity for learners to reflect on, discuss, and defend their newly acquired skill? The second section of this chapter demonstrates how learner-interaction can be incorporated into each phase of an e^3 activation, demonstration, application, integration cycle.

EFFECTIVE ACTIVATION THROUGH STRUCTURAL FRAMEWORKS

Based on a meta-analysis of research on instruction Marzano, Pickering, and Pollock (2001) cite research that demonstrates that making students aware of specific structures in information enables them to use this information more effectively. Rosenshine (1997) indicates that, when students organize information, summarize information, and compare old material to new material, these activities require processing that strengthens cognitive structures and helps students develop more appropriate mental models. These findings suggest that during activation students should be helped to develop a structural framework for organizing the to-be-learned information. A *structural framework* is an organization of previously learned information that learners can use to adapt an existing mental model or to build a new mental model for the new content. During the demonstration phase, guidance should help the students relate the new information to this framework. During the application phase, coaching should help students use this framework to complete the task. During the integration phase, reflection helps learners incorporate this framework into their mental model for subsequent application.

Chapter 2 suggests that learners are often not efficient in adapting existing mental models or in constructing frameworks that they can use to organize their newly acquired skills. Left on their own, they often use inefficient or even inappropriate organizational schemes. If the learner's mental model is insufficient to adequately organize the new knowledge, then learning can only be facilitated if the instruction provides a structural framework that learners can use to build the required organizational mental model for the new knowledge. Providing learners with an appropriate structural framework and helping them relate this framework to their existing knowledge and to the new content being taught can help them modify their existing mental models to form an appropriate structural framework to facilitate learning the new material.

Various forms of structural frameworks have been used in instruction. Some of the most common forms of structural frameworks include mnemonics, metaphor and analogy, and checklist summary frames. A *mnemonic* is a form of structural framework that provides a memory aid that helps learners remember information, parts, a definition, the steps in a procedure, or the conditions for a process. A *metaphor* or *analogy* is a form of structural framework that helps learners relate the relationships in a familiar entity, activity, or process to similar relationships in the entity, activity, or process to be learned. A *checklist summary frame* is a form of structural framework that presents an outline and a set of questions to help learners see the structure in new content material.

These structural frameworks are all forms of advanced organizers. An *advance organizer* is information presented prior to learning new material that can be used to help learners organize and interpret the new content. An advance organizer's contribution to learning is most apparent when the new content involves problem-solving rather than merely recall of information (see R. E. Mayer, 2003a).

Mnemonics

A mnemonic is a form of memory aid. This form of a structural framework is most appropriate for information-about and part-of component skills but can also be useful in helping learners remember definitions for kind-of, the steps in a procedure for how-to, and the conditions leading to a consequence for what-happens. A mnemonic can be an acronym, rhyme, diagram, or other forms of information that are easily remembered and that can be associated with the new information to be remembered.

There are many different forms of mnemonics. Many children learn the ABC song to learn the alphabet. Funny names are used to remember a set of terms. For example, ROY G. BIV is often used for the colors of the spectrum—red, orange, yellow, green, blue, indigo, and violet. Sometimes a funny phrase is used. For example, "Please Excuse My Dear Aunt Sally" for the order of operations in math—Parentheses, Exponents, Multiply, Divide, Add, and Subtract. And many mnemonics are rhymes. For example, "*I* before *e* except after *c*, or when sounding like *a* as in neighbor and weigh."

Mnemonics Example—Sportsmanship

A common form of a mnemonic is an acronym. An *acronym* is a word formed from the initials of several other words. Remembering the acronym facilitates learners' ability to recall the words represented by each of the letters. Figure 8-1 illustrates a few instructional events from an animated character development program that teaches what sportsmanship means using the STAR—stop, think, act, replay—approach to dealing with situations in sports. The program uses the idea of a STAR player as a mnemonic to help young people remember the steps they need to take to show good sportsmanship or, as the program emphasizes, to be a star player.

FIGURE 8-1 Mnemonic as a Structural Framework—Sportsmanship

STAR Sportsmanship		
1	**Coach:** "Someone who is a good sport is what I call a STAR player." [Discussion about why sportsmanship is important.] "You can't be a star in life if you are not a good sport."	
2	**Student:** "No one ever told me *how* to be a good sport." **Coach:** "Well, to be a good sport you need to know the Star Player Guidelines. These four guidelines help you make smart decisions in sports and in life. The STAR player guidelines are easy. Just think of the type of athlete you want to be—a STAR. Here is what you need to know: Stop, Think, Act, Replay."	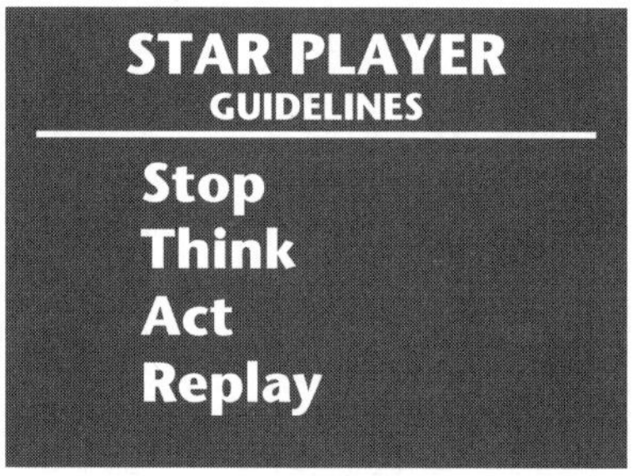 STAR PLAYER GUIDELINES Stop Think Act Replay
3	"To be a STAR player you first need to know about Stop. When you are in a situation that requires a sportsmanship-like decision, you need to Stop before you do something you might regret." **Student:** "How do I know when to stop? "Let's check some examples." [Several examples are shown here.]	 STAR PLAYER GUIDELINES Stop
4	"Young Jake is a prime example of how poor sportsmanship can affect you. First Jake scored a nice touchdown, but then he missed an easy catch because he was too busy boasting. . . . You've got to have your mind in the game. Great receivers are smart receivers, so Stop and Think."	 Stop 32

FIGURE 8-1 *Continued*

5	"Time for you to decide when to Stop. For each situation, choose whether to Stop or Keep Playing." [Students are shown situations and then asked to push a Stop or a Keep Playing button.] ***Feedback:*** "That's right; Ray needs to Stop before he starts yelling at the ump."	
6	"What about the STAR player guidelines. Let's see what you remember." **Student:** Oh ya, I need to Stop and make a sportsmanship decision; then I Think I should shake hands because that will help everyone feel good; and to Act, I should shake everyone's hand; and Replay, that is what I'm doing now."	

Earlier instructional events in this short course introduce the idea of sportsmanship using a coach-like animated character and a group of animated students. He discusses poor sportsmanship and shows examples of poor sportsmanship. In the first instructional event shown here, the mnemonic for this course is introduced (2). In the second instructional event the letters of the word *star* are used to introduce the four guidelines for showing good sportsmanship—**S**top, **T**hink, **A**ct, and **R**eplay. The rest of this short course is organized around these guidelines. Each of the guidelines is introduced one by one (instructional event 3), examples and non-examples are shown (instructional event 4), and the young learners are asked to recognize situations when it is appropriate apply one or more of these guidelines (instructional event 5). Instructional event 5 asks the young learners to indicate whether the situation shown requires the player to stop or keep playing. When a response is made, the corrective feedback uses the mnemonic to explain why the learner made a correct (as shown) or incorrect response to the situation. Instructional event 6 is part of a discussion the coach has with the students after they have been taught all of the guidelines. In this event a student is asked to use the star player guidelines to replay or reflect on her actions that were shown in a brief video clip.

Metaphor or Analogy

A metaphor or analogy is a form of structural framework that helps learners relate the relationships in a familiar entity, activity, or process to similar relationships in the entity, activity, or process to be learned. A metaphor and analogy differ from one another; some have suggested that an analogy is an elaborated metaphor. For our purposes the distinction is not critical. To be effective in instruction, it is important that guidance and coaching elaborate the structural framework whether it is a metaphor or an analogy. If learners already know the attributes of one entity, called the *source*, then they have a framework for understanding the attributes of a new entity, called the *target*. The challenge of metaphors or analogies, as structural frameworks, is to help learners determine which characteristics of the source are relevant to the target and which are not; in other words, to what extent do the characteristics of the source apply to the target? Learners vary in their ability to understand abstractions, and the challenge of using metaphors or analogies is to help learners identify the abstract characteristics of the source and the target to see their similarity.

The use of metaphor in computing is ubiquitous. A personal computer is an office; the computer screen is a desktop; a deletion comment is a trash can; and an electronic meta-file is a folder. The Internet is an ocean; to explore the web is to surf; to access a site is to navigate. The use of analogies, especially in science, is so prevalent that we often fail to recognize that an analogy is being used: likening an atom to the solar system; likening the brain to a computer; liking the body to a machine; and likening electricity to water flow.

Metaphor/Analogy Example—Transistors

Figure 8-2 demonstrates a straightforward lesson teaching the operation of a transistor. This fundamental instruction on the operation of a transistor was modeled on several different Internet lessons I found describing this electrical device. This instruction includes the following instructional events: (1) description of transistor; (2) circuit diagram symbol for a transistor; (3) an example of transistor in a simple circuit; (4) a what-happens application asking learners to make a prediction based on the conditions represented by the circuit diagram; and (5) corrective feedback that learners can use to compare to their own prediction.

FIGURE 8-2 Straightforward Lesson on Transistors

Transistors Without Analogy		
1	**Description** A transistor is a type of electronic switch. Transistors have three leads: The **base** activates the transistor. The **collector** is the positive lead. The **emitter** is the negative lead.	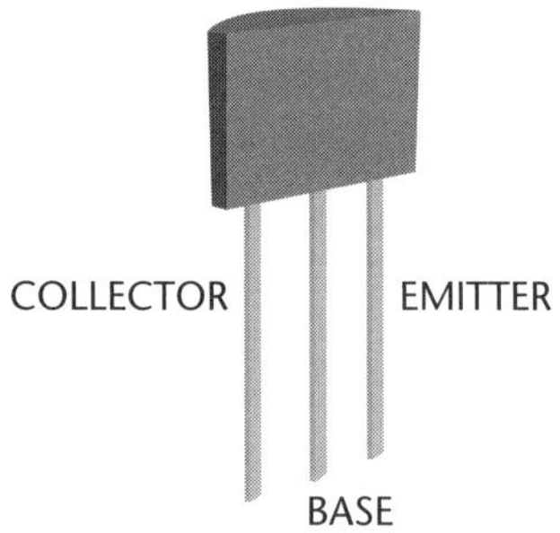 COLLECTOR EMITTER BASE
2	**Circuit Symbol** The figure at the right is a circuit diagram symbol for an NPN transistor. A small current applied to the base allows current to flow through the other two leads from the collector to the emitter. If there is no current on the base, then no current will flow through the transistor. The amount of current flowing from the collector to the emitter increases proportional to the amount of current applied to the base.	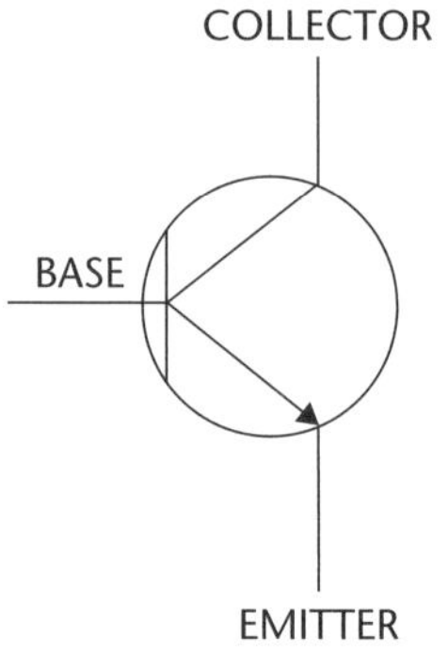 COLLECTOR BASE EMITTER

FIGURE 8-2 *Continued*

3	**Example** In the circuit shown here, when the switch is pressed the light-emitting diode comes on. When the switch is released the light goes out. What happens? When the switch is pressed a current passes through the resistor into the base of the transistor. When there is current on its base, the transistor allows the current to flow from the + terminal of the battery through the transistor and the light comes on. When the switch is released there is no current on the base of the transistor, the current stops flowing, and the light goes out. The resistors in the circuit limit the voltage to protect the transistor and diode.	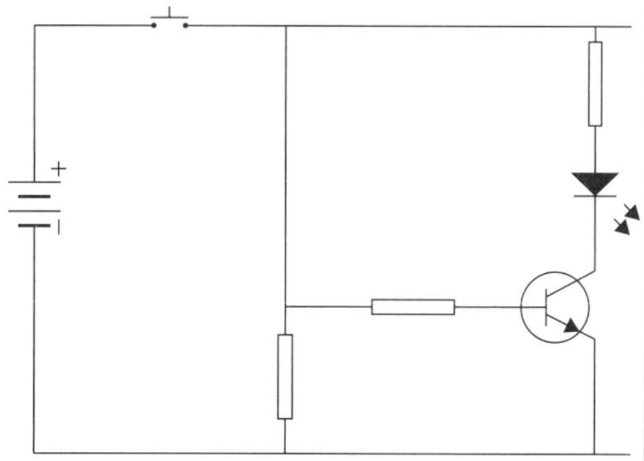
4	**Application** You have learned about resistors and transistors. Study this circuit diagram and predict what happens to the light-emitting diode in the circuit.	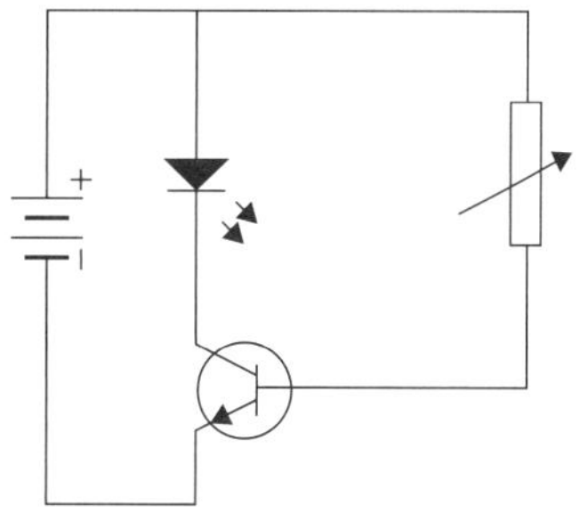
5	**Corrective Feedback** When the variable resister reduces the current, then at some point the amount of current to the base of the transistor is insufficient to allow current to flow through the transistor and the light-emitting diode goes out. As the current through the variable resistor increases, the amount of current to the base of the transister increases with a corresponding increase in the amount of current flowing through the transistor and to the diode, thereby increasing the brightness of the light-emitting diode.	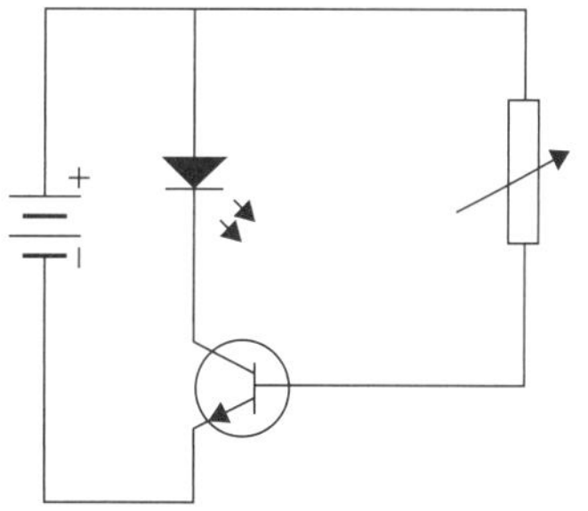

Figure 8-3 demonstrates the same lesson enhanced by the addition of a water flow analogy to explain the operation of a transistor. You are familiar with the fundamental analogy of water for electricity as illustrated in the first instructional event (1). You are likely not familiar with the water flow example for a transistor as shown in the fourth instructional event (4). The following instructional events were modified or added to the straightforward lesson: (1) an analogy for water flow was added; (2 and 3) these events remained the same; (4) the water flow analogy for the operation of a transistor was added; (5) guidance using the analogy was added to the example; (6) coaching via the analogy was added to the application; and (7) the use of the analogy was included in the corrective feedback.

FIGURE 8-3 Analogy as a Structural Framework—Transistors

Transistors with Analogy		
1	**Analogy** A simple analogy may help you understand how electricity works. A battery is like a resovoir. The reservoir causes pressure on the water line; the battery causes voltage (electrical force) in the circuit. The pipe conducts water flow; the wire conducts electron flow. A narrow pipe restricts the amount of water that flows; a resistor restricts the amount of current. A valve varies the amount of water flow; a variable resistor varies the amount of current.	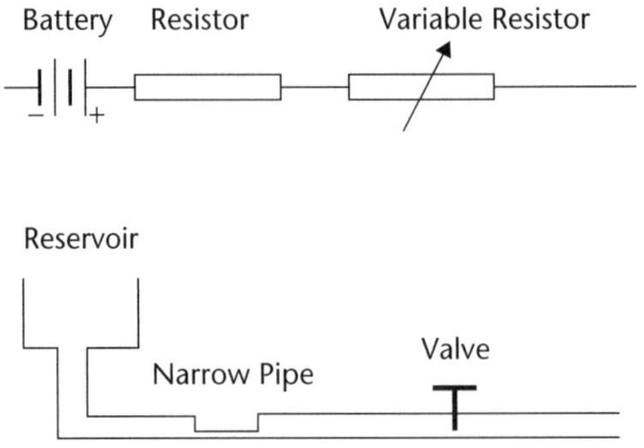 Battery Resistor Variable Resistor Reservoir Narrow Pipe Valve
2	**Description** A transistor is a type of electronic switch. Transistors have three leads: The **base** activates the transistor. The **collector** is the positive lead. The **emitter** is the negative lead.	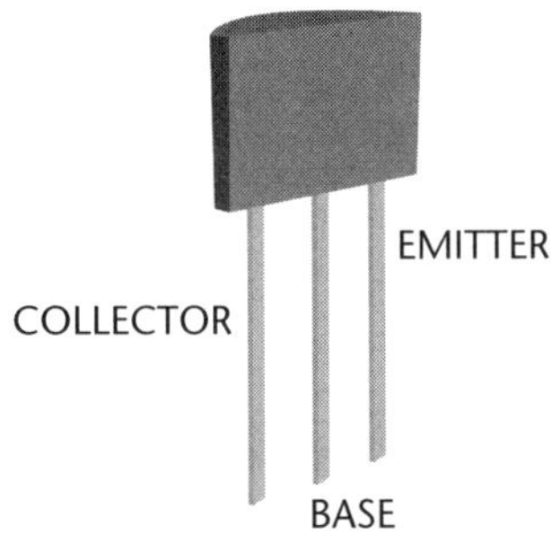 EMITTER COLLECTOR BASE
3	**Circuit Symbol** The figure at the right is a circuit diagram symbol for an NPN transistor. A small current applied to the base allows current to flow through the other two leads from the collector to the emitter. If there is no current on the base, then no current will flow through the transistor. The amount of current flowing from the collector to the emitter increases proportional to the amount of current applied to the base.	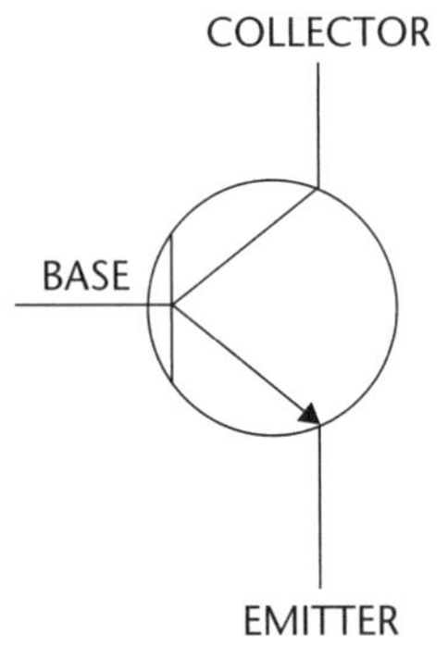 COLLECTOR BASE EMITTER
4	**Water Flow Analogy** A simple water flow analogy may help you understand how a transistor works. Consider the plumbing at the right. Water under pressure enters the valve chamber through the collector pipe. If there is no water flowing in from the base pipe, the pressure of the water coming in pushes the diaphram down, preventing water from flowing into the emitter and the pipe beyond. When water is allowed to flow into the base pipe, it pushes the diaphram up, allowing water to flow past the diaphram into the emitter pipe.	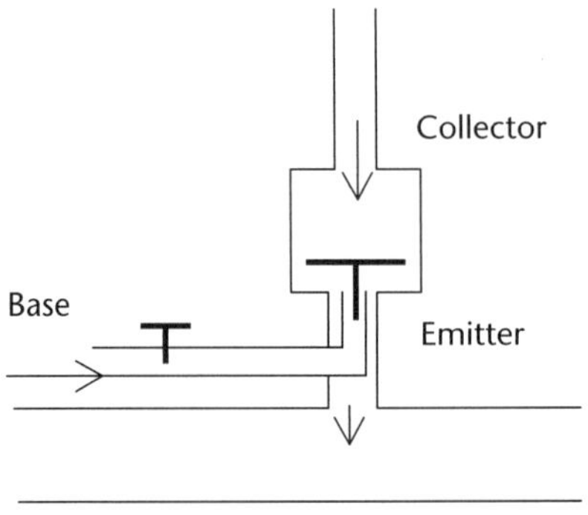 Collector Base Emitter

FIGURE 8-3 *Continued*

	If the water pressure in the base pipe is very small, the diaphram will lift only a small amount, letting only a small amount of water through to the emitter. As the water pressure in the base pipe increases, the diaphram is opened more and more until it reaches its maximum opening. This allows more and more water to flow past the diaphram.	
5	**Example with Analogy Guidance** In the circuit shown here, when the switch is pressed the light-emitting diode comes on. When the switch is released the light goes out. Pressing the switch is like opening the tap in the water analogy. This allows current to flow through the resister to the base of the transistor. Current to the base of the transistor is like water flowing into our valve and lifting the diaphram. This allows current to also flow through the transister and therefore through the light-emitting diode, causing the diode to light. The diode in this situation is acting as a switch. When the switch is released there is no current on the base of the transistor, the current stops flowing through the transister, and the light goes out. The resistors in the circuit limit the voltage to protect the transistor and diode.	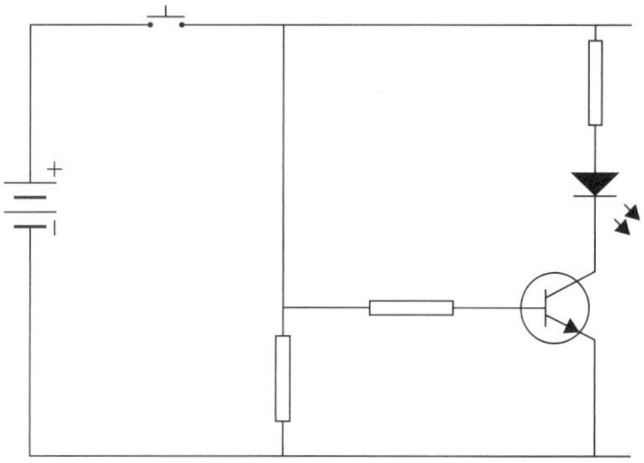
6	**Application** You have learned about resistors and transistors. Study this circuit diagram and predict what-happens to the light-emitting diode in the circuit. **Coaching:** Apply what you know about how water flow is affected by opening or closing a valve. What happens to the current when the variable resistor increases or decreases the resistance? Apply what you know about how a transistor works. In our analogy. What happens when the water pressure is increased in the base pipe? In the transistor, what happens when the current to the base is increased? What happens to the light-emitting diode when the current changes?	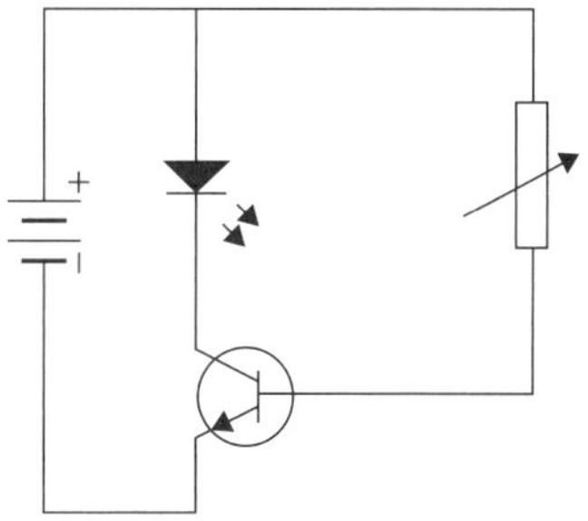

(continued)

FIGURE 8-3 *Continued*

7	**Corrective Feedback via the Analogy** When the variable resister (like our valve in a water line) reduces the current (like the amount of water flowing), then at some point the amount of current to the base of the transistor is insufficient (like not enough water pressure to raise the diaphram in the water system) to allow current to flow through the transistor and the light-emitting diode goes out (because no current is flowing through the diode). As the current through the variable resistor increases, the amount of current to the base of the transister increases, with a corresponding increase in the amount of current flowing through the transistor and to the diode (like the diaphram in our analogy being raised higher and higher, allowing more and more water to flow) thereby increasing the brightness of the light-emitting diode.	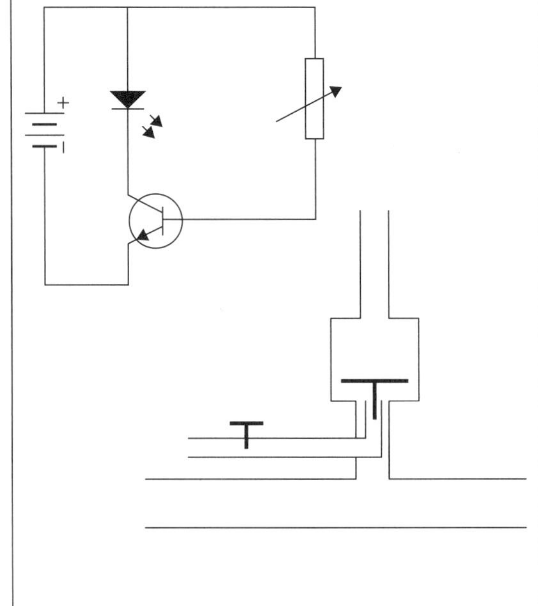

Water analogy for transistor described on www.satcure-focus.com.

Did you find the operation of the transistor easier to follow with the addition of the analogy? Did you find your ability to make a prediction of what happened in the simple circuit was easier after studying the analogy? I hope your answer to these questions is yes! A well-chosen structural framework added to a straightforward lesson enhances the effectiveness of the instructional events included.

Checklist

The presentation of information almost always has some form of organization. Learners will acquire the information more easily if they are made aware of the explicit organization of the information. Marzano, Pickering, and Pollock (2001) call such checklists *summary frames.* These summary frames have two parts: an outline of the structure and a set of questions to guide learners in observing this structure. Like other forms of structural frameworks, checklists are most effective when they are involved in all of the phases of e^3 instruction: present the checklist outline and questions; use the checklist for guidance during the demonstration; use the checklist to coach performance; and use the checklist to provide corrective feedback.

Checklist Example—Persuasive Essay

Figure 8-4 illustrates a segment of a lesson on writing a persuasive essay. This demonstration illustrates the use of a checklist or summary frame to help learners recognize the organization of an effective persuasive argument. (1) The first instructional event presents the controversy and briefly describes the purpose of persuasive communication. (2) The next instructional event presents the organization of persuasive communication and poses a set of questions corresponding to this organizational outline. (3) Event three demonstrates the statement of the controversy. (4) Event four demonstrates the second part of the outline—stating an opinion. (5) Event five illustrates the first of the several paragraphs needed to present evidence or experience in support of the reasons. (6) Event six demonstrates the final paragraph in a persuasive essay—presenting the conclusion. (7) This event demonstrates a Do_{ex} application for which learners are asked to critique a sample persuasive essay to identify each of the parts of the outline for an effective persuasive essay as they occur in this new example. (8) Finally, the last line of the chart provides an evaluation guide for the instructor to use in checking a learner's response to the application. Here again, the teacher is encouraged to use the checklist outline and questions to structure his or her evaluation of the learner's response.

FIGURE 8-4 Checklist Summary Frame as a Structural Framework—Persuasive Essay

Persuasive Essay		
	Audio	**Display**
1	There are many controversies all around us. Folks present arguments to persuade others to their points of view. One such controversy might be about the lunch period in your school. One way to present such an argument is to write a persuasive essay. A persuasive essay is designed to convince others that your opinion about the controversy is the right one. You could write a persuasive essay for your principal about the lunch period controversy.	**The Controversy** Here is an example of a controversy you might experience in your school. Your principal would like to shorten your lunch period from 35 minutes down to 25 minutes. She has asked the students at her school to provide feedback about this topic before she makes a decision.
2	Most effective writers or speakers use an obvious organization to present their ideas. When trying to convince or persuade someone to agree with you, the organization of your essay should include the four ideas shown: State the controversy. Choose a side and state your opinion and reasons. Provide data or experience to explain your reasons. Restate the controversy with a strong conclusion. When writing a persuasive essay you should ask yourself the following questions: 1. What is the controversy? What are the two sides of the argument? 2. Did you clearly state your opinion? Did you clearly state the reasons for your opinion? 3. Did you present evidence for your opinion? Did you describe your own experience supporting your opinion? 4. Did you restate the argument and your opinion? Did you clearly state a strong conclusion?	**Structure for Persuasive Essay** State controversy. State your opinion and reasons. Provide evidence or experience. Strong conclusion. **Questions to Ask** 1. Two sides of the argument? 2. Your opinion? Your reasons? 3. Your evidence? 4. Your conclusion?

(continued)

FIGURE 8-4 *Continued*

3	**What is the controversy?** What are the two sides of the argument? Here is an example of a statement of the controversy.	**Two sides of the argument?** The principal would like to shorten the lunch hour from 35 minutes to 25 minutes. Many students think that is not a good idea.
4	**Did you clearly state your opinion?** After creating your outline, begin writing your first paragraph with a strong heading that is going to grab your reader's attention. Did you clearly state the reasons for your opinion? You will then need to identify what your position is and why you have chosen this particular side. Without explaining your reasons, state them in this paragraph.	**Your opinion?** I barely have enough time to eat my sandwich, let alone my fruit and dessert! Cutting back our lunch time from 35 minutes to 25 minutes is a horrible idea. I do not agree with this and that's why I am writing you this letter. **Your reasons?** First of all, if you shorten lunch, students won't have enough time to eat. Second, there won't be enough time to get healthy exercise. And third, students will create more waste.
5	**Did you present evidence for your opinion? Did you describe your own experience supporting your opinion?** Paragraphs 2, 3, and 4 will be used to explain the three reasons you just stated in your opening paragraph. Keep in mind that you are trying to convince the readers to agree with you. Using detailed examples and personal experiences will help them relate to you, and you will get your point across much easier.	**Your evidence?** The first reason you should not shorten lunch time is because you will be sending students back to class hungry. After lining up for lunch, walking to the cafeteria, and waiting in line for my meal, I barely have enough time to eat. There are some days that I only finish my main course, which leaves my fruit, chips, and dessert on my tray. I'm still hungry, but I can't eat because the lunch aide is asking us to leave to make room for the next grade. [Paragraphs 3 and 4 would follow here.]
6	**Did you restate the argument and your opinion? Did you clearly state a strong conclusion?** Writing a conclusion is your last chance to convince your reader! Use your last paragraph to restate the side you've chosen and the three reasons why. Be sure to restructure your words so you're not repeating your first paragraph. Finish your essay with a great closing line similar to the way you started your first paragraph.	**Your conclusion?** In conclusion, I feel strongly that you should not take away 10 minutes of our lunch time. We don't have enough time to eat as it is, more food will be wasted, and students will have less time to get the physical activity they need to stay healthy. Remember, the last thing parents want to see is two large dumpsters filled up with uneaten food! [The complete essay is available here.]
7	**Written Directions for Application** **Problem:** Critique this persuasive essay concerning the following controversy. Your school district is hosting a city council meeting to discuss the option of extending the school day by two hours each day. By doing this, students will not have to go to school on Fridays. The extended hours will be from 7:30 a.m. to 4:00 p.m., Monday through Thursday, and there will not be a short day.	**Student Essay** Permanent three-day weekends sounds like the best idea that the government has thought of in years. I feel that taking our five school days and turning them into four days is a great idea because it will allow more time with our families, and we will get more schoolwork done during the weekends.

FIGURE 8-4 *Continued*

	Remember the following questions: 1. What is the controversy? What are the two sides of the argument? 2. Did the essay clearly state the author's opinion? Did it clearly state the reasons for this opinion? 3. Did the author present evidence for his or her opinion? Did he or she describe his or her own experience supporting this opinion? 4. Did the author restate the argument and his or her opinion? Did he or she clearly state a strong conclusion?	The first and most important reason we should cut school down to four days is because it will give us more time to be at home with our families. Many government buildings have gone to a four-day week so we will have the same schedule as our parents. I guess other kids with parents at work can find a babysitter. Another reason we should shorten the school week is so we can have more time to finish homework and big projects that are done at home. Having Friday off would allow students to finish homework that they didn't get done during the week. They can also go to the city library and do research and use the computers there. In conclusion, I believe that changing the school week to four days a week will improve test scores at school, students will be happy to do their homework, and everyone will get to spend more time with their families.
8	The following would be used to evaluate the student's response to this application: 1. *Controversy?* The controversy was not stated nor the two sides of the argument clearly identified. 2. *Opinion and reasons?* Paragraph 1 is a good example. 3. *Evidence?* Paragraph 2 elaborates the first reason but also contains a counterargument in the last sentence. Paragraph 3 elaborates the second reason but may not be convincing since it seems unlikely that students will take the time to do more homework unless teachers make a point to assign homework for this extended weekend. 4. *Conclusion?* The conclusion adds a third reason that was not introduced in the beginning and not discussed in the evidence section.	

Based on student project. Dallin Miller, Utah State University.

PROBLEM-SOLVING INTEGRATION THROUGH LEARNER-TO-LEARNER INTERACTION

The previous section of this chapter demonstrated how to implement the Activation Principle by introducing a structural framework and integrating this framework in to demonstration through guidance, into application through coaching, and into integration through reflection. This last section of this chapter demonstrates a way to implement the Integration Principle through peer-interaction.

For the past decade, there has been a strong emphasis in the instructional technology field on learner-centered instruction. A colleague recently asked me, "Which is best, problem-centered instruction or learner-centered instruction?" The question suggests that these two approaches are somehow competitive. There appears to be some debate, both in research and in practice, as to which strategy is more effective. But must we choose one or the other?

The question is misdirected. Peer-interaction is most effective when thoughtfully orchestrated around a progression of problems to be solved. On the other hand, the best problem-centered learning is enhanced by carefully structured peer-interaction. Both problem-based learning and peer-instruction are forms of learner-centered instruction. And while the former is content-focused and the latter is process-focused, both require active engagement on the part of the learners and, when effectively combined, the resulting learning is more effective than when either approach is used in isolation.

In the past two decades, there has been an increasing emphasis on peer-interaction (Crouch & Mazur, 2001; King, 1992; Mazur, 1997; Slavin, 1995). This pedagogical approach can be summarized as a teaching method where instructors design experiences that allow learners to learn from each other. Contrary to common perceptions, this definition implies that instructors are not only involved in the process of enabling peers to learn from each other, but that instructors design a reasonable degree of direction and structure in the peer-learning process itself. For example, the literature suggests that peer-interaction is most effective when there is some form of peer scaffolding, which can take the form of worked problems, structured questions, and even evaluation rubrics (King, Staffieri, & Douglas, 1998; van Merriënboer & Kirschner, 2007).

Instruction consisting of activation, demonstration, and application enables a learner to form an appropriate mental model; integration, via interaction with peers, enables the learner to tune this model, to help stabilize the mental model, and to make it more flexible and adaptable to new situations. Mental models are most appropriate for complex phenomena where there is not a single solution or a single path to a solution. When a learner is required to collaborate with a fellow learner or to critique the work of a fellow learner, then he or she is required to test his or her mental model of the phenomena against the process or product resulting from the mental model of a fellow learner. When there is a discrepancy, learners have to examine their own models more carefully and either make accommodation to the variations they observe or defend their own interpretation as a more adequate interpretation of the phenomena under consideration. Both of these activities require them to adjust or tune their mental models.

Most students are motivated by the reaction of their peers. Peer-collaboration requires deeper processing for students to make their intent clear to their collaborators. Collaboration encourages deeper processing of the information and a more careful examination of their assumptions. Furthermore, more and more real-world problems are solved by teams of people rather than by individuals working in isolation. Peer-interaction in a problem-solving situation replicates more closely the environment learners are likely to encounter in their world following instruction.

Peer-Telling

When one thinks of learners teaching each other, it is too often equated with the dissemination of information. *Peer-telling* is an ineffective form of learner-interaction in which learners review and present information to other students. We see this form of peer-telling when learners are asked to read papers and present them to the rest of the class or learners are asked to each select a chapter and present the information to a study group. Having peers present information is perhaps the least effective form of peer-interaction, much as having a teacher dispense information is perhaps the most ineffective form of teaching. The learning involved in peer-telling often requires only associative memory rather than the activation of mental models. Peer-telling may help learners who make the presentation remember the information but does little to help them and their fellow learners learn to solve problem or complete complex tasks.

Not only do problems help prevent peer-telling, they provide needed structure and guidance for effective peer-interaction (Kirschner et al., 2006) . The effective use of a well-structured problem in the context of peer-interaction directs that discussion toward a specific learning objective and forces the tuning of mental models described earlier. They also provide a way of measuring learning outcomes as they emerge from a peer-interaction. For example, peer-instruction in physics teaching uses concept tests, which are conceptual problems that are initially presented to students prior to a process of peer-discussion where they are then allowed to try to convince fellow students why they have the right solutions (Crouch & Mazur, 2001; Hake, 1998). What is interesting about this example is that, even though the approach is described in the literature as peer instruction, the empirical data supporting this effective learning always demonstrates the use of a problem in the context of the peer-interaction.

While this chapter stresses peer-collaboration and critique, there are other forms of learner-interaction that can enhance instruction for each of the First Principles of Instruction. The following paragraphs briefly describe each of these variations.

Peer-Sharing

Peer-sharing is a form of learner-interaction in which learners relate prior relevant experience to other learners. The Activation Principle states that learning is promoted when learners recall, describe, or demonstrate relevant prior knowledge and skill. Having learners share relevant experience with one another early in the instruction is an appropriate way to provide this activation experience. The learners who are relating their experience are activating their previously acquired mental models. Learners who are listening to these experiences are being provided new vicarious experience, which in turn activates their previous experience and the associated mental models.

Peer-Discussion

Peer-discussion is a form of learner-interaction in which learners deliberate the proposed solution of example problems. The Demonstration Principle states that learning is promoted when learners are shown a demonstration of the skill they are expected to acquire. The best forms of a problem for this demonstration are worked examples that show an appropriate solution and the process used to solve the problem (van Merriënboer & Kirschner, 2007). For complex problems, a set of carefully constructed questions that require learners to examine the example in considerable detail and that challenge their understanding significantly improves the value of the problem. Having learners discuss these questions with one another is an effective form of peer-interaction that requires those involved in the discussion to tune their mental models for representing the problem. After seeing a demonstration of the task to be learned, having learners find and demonstrate another worked example of the problem is also an effective peer-interaction activity. Finding another worked example of the problem expands the number and variety of instances for both those finding the new examples and those seeing the demonstration of the new examples.

Peer-Collaboration

Peer-collaboration is a form of learner-interaction in which learners work together in small groups to solve problems. The Application Principle states that learning is promoted when learners apply their newly acquired skill to new problems. After observing the demonstration of sample problem solutions, learners should then have the opportunity to solve additional problems. Assigning learners to work in small groups and to collaborate in the solution of these problems is perhaps one of the most effective forms of peer-interaction. This is similar to the type of peer-collaboration that occurs in more open problem-based learning, but in problem-centered learning learners have had an opportunity to acquire the required component skill and to interact with demonstrations of cases illustrating the whole task before they are asked to work together to engage in the solution of additional problems.

Peer-Critique

Peer-critique is a form of learner-interaction in which learners evaluate the problem-solving activities of fellow learners and provide constructive suggestions for improvement. The Integration Principle states that learning is promoted when learners reflect on, discuss, or defend their new skills. Having engaged in collaborative problem solving, the appropriate form of peer-interaction in this final stage of a problem-centered strategy is to engage in peer-critique. An effective rule for this type of interaction is constructive criticism, that is, any criticism must be accompanied by recommendations for improving the solution or problem-solving process.

While I have presented each of these principles in turn, it is important to realize that in an actual instructional situation there is a flow among the various stages in the learning cycle described by First Principles. Peer-sharing during the activation phase should flow smoothly and perhaps overlap peer-discussion in the demonstration phase. Peer-discussion should also overlap peer-collaboration. And peer-critique, from the integration phase, should take place simultaneously with peer-collaboration in the application phase. From the learners' point of view, the phases should be a seamless flow of activities leading to mastery of the problem-solving skills that are the focus of the instruction.

Figure 8-5 illustrates one procedure for effective peer-collaboration and -critique. This procedure emphasizes individual work as well as collaboration and critique. Too often in group work one or two individuals do the work and other members of the group coast on their coattails. Another disadvantage of group work is that students often divide up the task and thereby are involved in only part of the problem-solving process. The proposed procedure attempts to compensate for these potential challenges.

The procedure is to present learners with a problem to be solved or a task to be completed. Each learner then completes the task or solves the problem and posts his or her work to a site available to other learners. Once the individual solutions are submitted, a small group of students collaborate to strive for consensus in the solution to the problem or execution of the task. Learners outside of the collaboration group then critique the solution and post their critique to a site available to other learners. The collaboration group then reviews the critique and revises its solution to accommodate the recommendations. The advantage of this procedure is that learners are engaged in the problem at least three times. The following paragraphs will describe some applications of this basic collaboration and critique procedure.

FIGURE 8-5 Effective Peer-Interaction

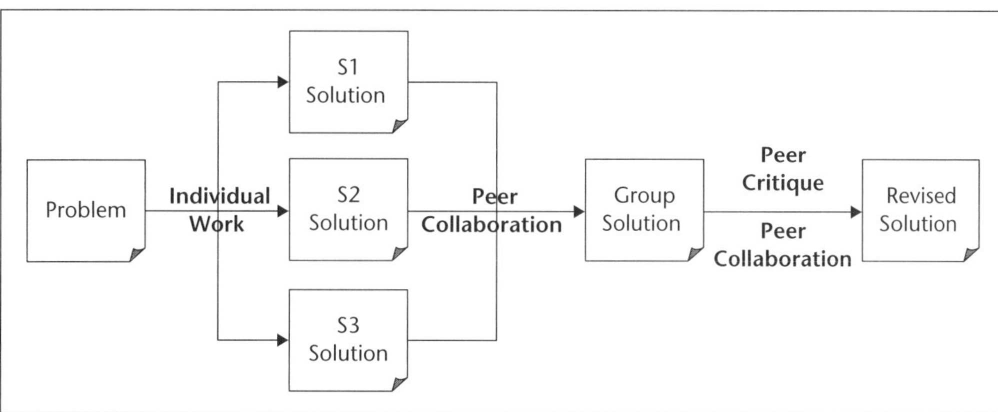

Learner-Interaction Example—Biology 100

Chapter 7 described a task-centered approach to a Biology 100 course. For each of the six content areas that comprised the course, students used the following procedure: Before class, students (1) read the first problem and (2) read supportive information for the first problem. In class, (3) the instructor demonstrates how the information they studied could be used to solve the first problem; (4) the instructor introduces a second problem within the same subject area; (5) the instructor presents new supportive information for the second problem; and (6) students complete the second task in groups in class. After class, students (7) complete a third task and post their individual task solution online and (8) negotiate a group solution to the third task and post it to their instructor. The procedure repeats and overlaps with tasks in other subject areas.

A survey of learner reaction to this course found that 70 percent indicated that the course gave them an opportunity to apply their knowledge in a meaningful way; 53 percent indicated that their interest in biology has increased; 69 percent indicated that the class helped them to improve their critical thinking and analysis skills; and 51 percent indicated that the class helped them improve their reading and writing skills (Francom, Bybee, Wolfersberger, Mendenhall, & Merrill, 2009). One student, in a question to the university president's monthly Q&A session, indicated that she learned more from this class than any class previously taken at the university and wondered why all classes were not taught this way. She indicated that students tended to struggle for the first couple of problems in the class, but once they got the idea of the peer-interactive procedure, they really got involved and liked the procedure.

Learner-Interaction Example—Instructional Design Classes

I have explored several variations of this procedure in my instructional design classes at both the graduate and undergraduate level. My classes are taught online using a studio approach, where students complete a project that is then critiqued by other students and by their instructor. Each class involves a progression of such projects. (1) In my undergraduate class, students are assigned to a collaboration group of three students. In my graduate class, students are allowed to self-select their collaboration partners. I have found that a group of three is ideal for collaboration. A group of three tends to encourage everyone to participate, whereas when there are four or five some students let the others do the collaboration. Each collaboration group is assigned a wiki where members can post their work and collaborate together. (2) After studying appropriate resource materials, including examples of previous work by other students, each student posts his or her preliminary design for each project to the wiki. The collaboration group then develops a group consensus for the design. I have used two approaches to collaboration. In the first approach, the collaboration group members agree on a topic for their instructional development and then all members of the group work on the same content area. In the second approach, each student may use a different topic and each student develops his or her own design. The collaboration group members then critique one another to make sure that each student's design is the best that it can be. In the second approach there seems to be more commitment to the project, whereas when there is a group project, some students seem to have less commitment to the final product. (3) When the collaboration group members feel their design(s) are ready for review, they post a notice to a discussion board. (4) Each student is assigned as a critic for a student in a different collaboration group. When the designs are ready for review, the critic uses a checklist (see Chapter 10) to critique the design and then posts the critique to the discussion board. Other students are encouraged to critique their fellow students, even if they are not the assigned critic. (5) There is an online discussion each week in which the instructor selects projects to discuss with the whole class either as good examples or as examples that could be improved. In these discussions, the critic is first asked to comment, other students are invited to comment, and finally the instructor comments, usually to emphasize what has already been suggested or to point out areas of improvement that the critic or other students may have missed or misinterpreted. (6) Based on the critiques, students then revise their designs in collaboration with their collaboration group and post their revised designs to their wiki. In these classes, some designs are subjected to this process for a second round and students are allowed to revise their designs until the end of the semester. An informal comparison with projects from previous classes, in which peer-collaboration and -critique were not used, shows that the quality of the designs produced by the students using peer-interaction is much higher.

PRINCIPLES AND PRESCRIPTIONS

Activation—Structure: Learning is promoted when learners recall or acquire a framework or structure for organizing the new knowledge and when the structure is the basis for guidance during demonstration, coaching during application, and reflection during integration.

Mnemonics, metaphor and analogy, and checklist summary frames are all effective structural frameworks when presented during activation, used for guidance during demonstration, used for coaching during application, and used for reflection during integration.

Integration—Peer-Collaboration: Learning is promoted when learners integrate their new knowledge into their everyday life by being required to reflect on, discuss, or defend their new knowledge or skill via peer-collaboration and peer-critique.

Use peer-sharing for activation; peer-discussion for demonstration; peer-collaboration for application; and peer-critique for integration.

APPLICATION

Select several courses that you are taking, designing, or that you can find on the Internet. You may want to use classes that you have analyzed for previous applications. Do these classes include the use of a structural framework? Is this framework used for guidance, coaching, or reflection? If not, can you find an appropriate structural framework that could be used with one of these classes? How could the framework you identify be used for guidance, coaching, and reflection?

Describe the peer-interaction used in the courses you selected. If no peer-interaction is used, can you design appropriate peer-sharing, peer-discussion, peer-collaboration, and peer-critique for one or more of these courses?

TO LEARN MORE

Marzano, R. J., Pickering, D. J., & Pollock, J. E. (2001). *Classroom instruction that works: Research-based strategies for increasing student achievement.* Alexandria, VA: Association for Supervision and Curriculum Development. Marzano and his associates did an exhaustive study of what works in classroom instruction. Their research is summarized along with prescriptions for how to implement the findings in this book. The following chapters are of particular interest to the content of this chapter:

Chapter 3, *Summarizing and Note Taking,* and Chapter 10, *Cues, Questions, and Advance Organizers*; these chapters provide good examples of the use of structural frameworks.

Chapter 7, *Cooperative Learning*; this chapter provides guidance for peer-cooperation and peer-critique.

COMING NEXT

This chapter demonstrated how to implement the Activation Principle by the addition of a structural framework incorporated into the application, demonstration, and integration phases of an e^3 instructional strategy. It also demonstrated how to implement the Integration Principle by enhancing problem-solving strategies by effective learner-interaction. Chapter 9 demonstrates how instructional strategies can be implemented through the appropriate use of multimedia.

CHAPTER 9

MULTIMEDIA IMPLEMENTATION OF INSTRUCTIONAL STRATEGIES

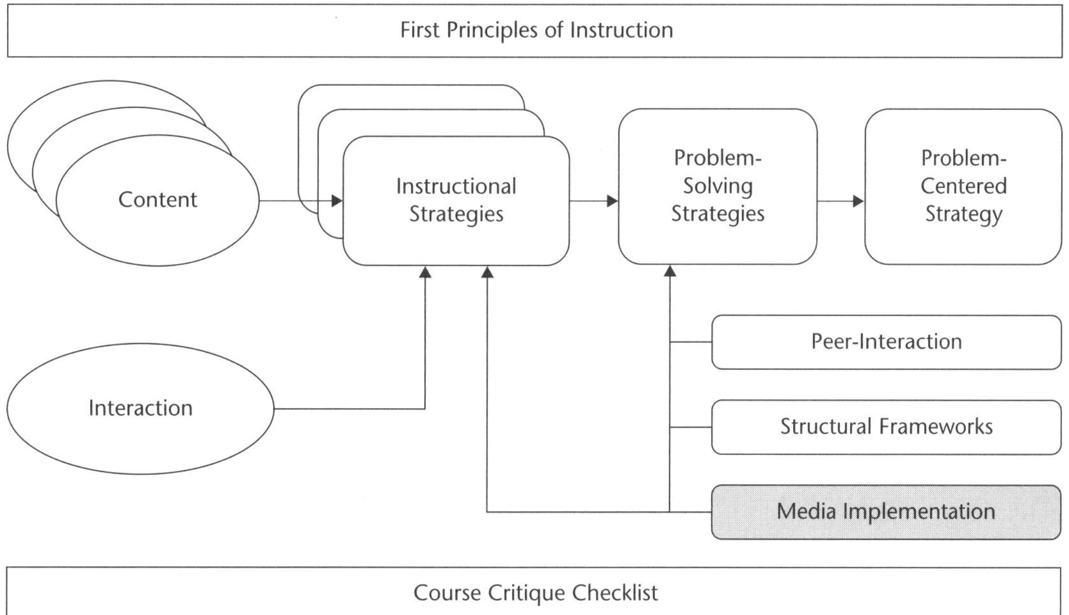

Quick Look

The previous chapters in this part of the book demonstrated instructional strategies for individual component skills and for problem solving. They also demonstrated the use of structural frameworks and peer-interaction. This chapter demonstrates some ways to implement the instructional events of these strategies with multimedia. This chapter answers the following questions: How is multimedia used to implement the instructional strategies demonstrated in this book? How is multimedia effectively used to implement the instructional events prescribed for different instructional strategies? How is multimedia used to help learners understand the format of the instructional materials? What constitutes effective navigation? What constitutes effective learner interaction with the instruction? What makes some multimedia irrelevant or even disruptive to effective instruction?

Key Words

Concurrent *Tell-and-Show*: information and portrayal appearing together to facilitate comparison.
Content Menus: navigation buttons related to next content that require learners to make a decision about what to preview, study, or review next.
Distracting Multimedia: media included for interest but that has no instructional function and that may interfere with e^3 learning.
Distracting Animation: animation included to increase interest that has no other instructional function.
Irrelevant Color: colored text, backgrounds, and decorations included to increase interest that has no other instructional function.
Learner Control: buttons that enable learners to select the next content to study; to control audio, video, and animation; and to control learning events.
Successive Disclosure: showing text or graphic items synchronized with their audio elaboration.

INTRODUCTION

Previous chapters described and illustrated instructional strategies for teaching component skills and for teaching whole tasks. These strategies cannot be implemented without some vehicle to carry the content to the student; some means to represent the content elements; and some controls to enable learner interaction with the instructional events of the course. These vehicles, forms of representation, and controls for interaction are called *multimedia,* meaning that they are a combination of text, audio, graphics, video, animation, and control. *Audio,* in the form of voice, is as old as the human race, and for instructor-led instruction, is often the primary vehicle for representing content and carrying it to the student. Audio in the context of this chapter refers to recorded audio. *Text* has also been available for centuries and consequently is the most used media to represent content. The term *graphics* includes a whole variety of media forms, including drawings, photographs, charts, diagrams, and graphs. This book also uses the term *dynamic graphics* to include video and animation. For many years recorded audio and graphics were expensive and time-consuming to produce, so their use was often limited to a supporting role. With the advent of digital technology, however, recorded audio, graphics, video, and animation have become readily available and much less time-consuming and expensive to produce—to the point where anyone can have these many forms of multimedia available to them literally at the touch of button. The programming capabilities of electronic devices have also made possible *control* at the touch of a button. Control is the most recent addition to the multimedia arsenal.

MULTIMEDIA FOR INSTRUCTIONAL EVENTS

Learning is promoted when multimedia implements prescribed instructional events.

Chapter 3 defined an instructional event as a combination of a strategy mode (*Tell, Show, Ask, Do*) with a content element (*definition, step, condition,* etc.). Chapters 4 and 5 described and illustrated instructional strategies, consisting of prescribed instructional events, for different types of component skills and whole problems. A primary purpose of multimedia is to enable the implementation of these prescribed instructional events. If multimedia is not used appropriately to implement these events, then learning may not be promoted and may, in fact, be hindered.

In this chapter, multimedia is also used to implement other instructional functions, including the structure of the course (*format*), learners' progress within and among instructional events (*navigation*), and learner control of instructional events (*interaction*). Appropriate implementation of format facilitates the learning process by making the structure of the course more apparent to learners. Appropriate implementation of navigation also facilitates the learning process by enabling learners to more easily go from one instructional event to the next without confusion. Appropriate interaction facilitates learning by enabling learners to control their learning experience.

The word *facilitates* is used for format, navigation, and interaction, in contrast to the word *promotes*, which is used for the implementation of instructional events. Format, navigation, and interaction control make learning easier but do not necessarily promote the learning of the content, whereas appropriate implementation of instructional events is necessary to enable efficient and effective learning of the component skills to occur.

Digital multimedia is readily available whether the instruction is online or instructor-led. The multimedia implementations described in this chapter are just as appropriate for instructor-led teaching as for online instruction. It is my position that all instructors should use the multimedia implementations described whether they are teaching live or online, synchronous or asynchronous, in a classroom or at a distance.

The following paragraphs illustrate the e^3 implementation of instructional events including presentation, demonstration, application, and guidance.

Use Abbreviated Text Elaborated with Audio to Present Information

Text is involved in almost every instructional product. It is a fundamental element. How can it be used most effectively? How can we avoid some of the misuses of text? A fundamental role of text is to *tell-information*. This information can be a definition for kind-of, a statement of steps for how-to, a statement of the conditions and consequence for what-happens. The presentation of information often has two parts—a name or phrase identifying the information and an elaboration of the information. In electronic media, wall-to-wall text is intimidating and not an effective way to present the information. This section prescribes the use of abbreviated text. The term *abbreviated text* indicates that the best presentations include a short phrase or bullet point identifying the key points of the information. The detail for the information is then presented via audio elaboration. This keeps the display simple and well organized while still providing learners with the information they need to learn the content.

Instruction is not a textbook. Instruction should promote learning and interaction and should facilitate information processing. Margin-to-margin text may be appropriate for a textbook or reference manual, but instruction is active learning and should be more than a textbook. During a presentation, the text should bullet the key points and the audio should elaborate these points. Short-term memory can only hold a few items at a time. Learners get the big picture better if they have four or five main points to remember and when each of these points is elaborated by audio explanation.

If *tell-information* is represented by abbreviated text, then an important role for audio is to elaborate this information. This is especially important if the *tell-information* is simultaneous with *show-portrayal.* Learners can then attend to the portrayal while they listen to the elaboration of the information. This elaboration of the information can also be combined with audio guidance to focus the learner's attention on the relevant parts of the portrayal.

Figure 9-1 illustrates a short segment from a course on copyright and fair use. (1) Instructional event 1 lists the title of this segment while the audio introduces the topic on common myths. (2) Instructional event 2 identifies the first myth, the myth is identified on the display, and the audio elaborates this idea. The use of abbreviated text elaborated by audio is also a very good rule when making a presentation in an instructor-led class as well as for online instruction.

FIGURE 9-1 Abbreviated Text with Audio Elaboration

Copyright—Fair Use

Audio	Display
There are common myths about copyright that can act as a barrier to people learning about copyright because they think that they already know what the rules are. In this brief presentation we are going to take a quick look at these myths, dispel them, and find out why the answer to a copyright question is usually not obvious.	**Copyright Myths**
The first common myth is the myth of 30 seconds. This myth is usually applied to audio or video clips. People think that if they only use a fragment of what the original source is—30 seconds of song, 30 seconds of a video—they should be fine and they will not be found to have violated copyright. This is not true.	**Copyright Myths** **1. The Myth of "30 Seconds."**

Student project, University of Hawaii, Ariana Eichelberger and Susan Jaworowski.

Use Audio to Elaborate Graphics Rather Than On-Screen Text

Learners have a visual channel and an auditory channel. Learners can look at a graphic (visual channel) and listen to an explanation (auditory channel) at the same time. However, they cannot look at a graphic (visual channel) and look at printed text (visual channel) at the same time. Looking back and forth from text to graphic causes learners to lose their focus in the graphic and their place in the text, thus making learning the material more difficult (see Clark & Mayer, 2003, 2008; R.E. Mayer, 2001).

Figure 9-2 illustrates two instructional events from a course on copyright and fair use. The first graphic provides an alternative representation of the information. The audio provides descriptions of two situations that fall at different places on this illustrated spectrum. The second event provides a portrayal of a commercial use of copyrighted material. The audio explains the poster and calls attention to the properties that cause it to fall on the commercial end of the fair use spectrum.

FIGURE 9-2 Use of Audio to Elaborate Graphics Rather Than On-Screen Text

<table>
<tr><th colspan="3">Copyright—Fair Use</th></tr>
<tr><td rowspan="2">1</td><td colspan="2">Audio:
Let's place the purpose of the use on the spectrum. When it comes to this, there are two opposite ends of the spectrum. On the one end is non-profit, educational use, and this end of the spectrum favors your use. On the other end is for-profit, non-educational use, and that favors the content owner's use. The more the copyrighted material is being used to benefit you commercially, the less likely it will be that the fair use exception will apply. Copies that are made for commercial or profit-making activities are presumed to be unfair. Someone wanting to use the material for part of a course at a non-profit educational institution, like the University of Hawaii, would fall close to the fair use end of the spectrum. Someone teaching in a for-profit educational institution, such as the University of Phoenix, would be a little more toward the center.</td></tr>
<tr><td colspan="2">Display:
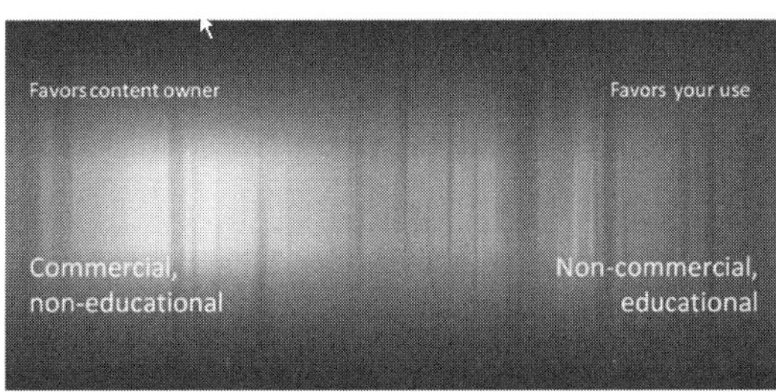
</td></tr>
<tr><td>2</td><td>Audio:
And here is an example of something that would be way over on the commercial use side of the spectrum. Let's say you have a restaurant owner who wants to use the famous poster from The Godfather with its tag line, "I'm gonna' make him an offer he can't refuse," to advertise his new restaurant. So it says "Italian Night at Robert's" and "make him a dinner he can't refuse." This is a purely commercial use and falls all the way on the side that favors the copyright owner.</td><td>Display:

</td></tr>
</table>

Student project, University of Hawaii, Ariana Eichelberger and Susan Jaworowski.

Allow Learners to Control the Pace of Text Presentation

Some presentations display a segment of text for a fixed time and then automatically remove the text from the screen. For slow readers this causes the text to be removed before learners have finished reading; for fast readers this causes frustration when they have finished reading the text and are ready to move on to the next segment. Do not automatically remove a text or graphic presentation from the screen. All text messages and graphics should provide control buttons to enable learners to change the display when they are ready. When there are multiple segments of a presentation, learners also need a way to return to a previous segment. Dynamic displays should provide navigation buttons to enable learners to replay the display. Exceptions to this rule may be when there is a time limit for the reading text or observing a graphic such as timed reading or perception applications.

Use Graphics to Provide an Alternative Representation of the Information

Some learners are more visual, and some learners are more verbal. Some learners may have a difficult time grasping a verbal presentation of the information, but they may be able to comprehend the information better if it is also represented visually. An effective use of graphics—picture, chart, diagram, animation—is to provide a visual representation of the information. This is not the same as a portrayal. The graphic is merely another way to present the information, whether it is a definition, a set of steps, or a relationship among conditions and their consequence. Figure 9-3 uses a spectrum of colors (in the actual course the spectrum was in full color) to convey the idea that there are degrees of agreement about what constitutes fair use for copyright. Figure 9-4 defines depth of field, a principle important to photography. The verbal statement is the information that defines this principle, but the graphic presents this same information in visual form, providing an alternative representation of the definition.

FIGURE 9-3 Relevant Use of Color to Emphasize a Property

Copyright—Fair Use		
	Audio	**Display**
1	The answers to each question are evaluated on a sliding scale like the spectrum on the screen. The answers are usually not pure red or pure violet, pure yes or pure no; they will most often fall somewhere in-between, somewhere along the spectrum—more green, more orange, or more yellow. After you determine where on the spectrum each answer lies, you can sum up the total and make an overall determination of your ability to use the material.	**The four questions are** (1) What is the purpose and character of the use? (2) What is the nature of the content to be used? (3) What is the amount of the content to be used? (4) What is the impact of your use on the value of the content to be used?

Student project, University of Hawaii, Ariana Eichelberger and Susan Jaworowski.

FIGURE 9-4 Alternative Representation of Information

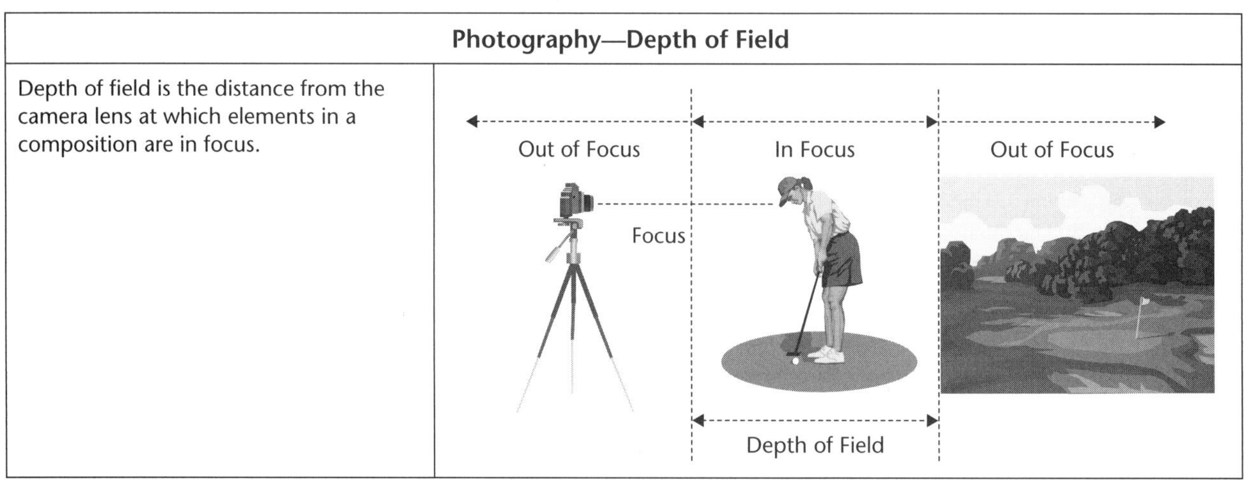

Original material based on a student project, Brigham Young University–Hawaii, Michael Cheney, Justin Smith, and Russ Jung.

USE THE FORM OF MULTIMEDIA THAT MOST CLEARLY REPRESENTS THE PROPERTIES OF A PORTRAYAL

The following paragraphs illustrate how text, audio, graphics, and video can be effectively used to show the properties of a portrayal.

Use Text When Words Are a Defining or Ordering Property

Some portrayals are text. The defining property is in the text itself. In these situations it is important to help learners discriminate the text that is the portrayal from text that may elaborate or describe the portrayal.

Figure 9-5 is a short excerpt from a short course for young students on organizing and writing a persuasive essay. The left panel briefly provides how-to information for writing a first paragraph in a persuasive essay. The right panel provides a sample first paragraph. Obviously, since the portrayal is an essay it is represented by text. The portrayal should provide a positive answer to the following questions: Does it illustrate the defining properties of a persuasive first paragraph? Does it contain a strong beginning statement? Does it state the author's position? Does it give reasons why the author has taken this position?

FIGURE 9-5 Text for Showing Defining Properties

Organizing and Writing a Persuasive Essay	
Step 2: After creating your outline, begin writing your first paragraph with a strong statement that is going to grab your reader's attention. You will then need to identify what your position is and why you have chosen this particular side. Without explaining your reasons, state them in this paragraph. The explanations will follow.	Here is an example of a strong first paragraph. I barely have enough time to eat my sandwich, let alone my fruit and dessert! Cutting back our lunch time from 35 minutes to 25 minutes is a horrible idea. I do not agree with this and that's why I am writing you this letter. First of all, if you shorten lunch, students won't have enough time to eat. Second, there won't be enough time to get healthy exercise. And third, students will create more waste.

Student project, Utah State University, Dallin Miller.

The grammar lesson on adverbs (see Figures 4-9 and 4-10) and the poetry lesson (see Figure 5-5) both include portrayals that are represented by words. These portrayals must provide a positive answer to the following questions: Do these portrayals show the relevant properties? Do these portrayals contain irrelevant text that may confuse learners?

Use Audio When Sound Is a Defining or Ordering Property

The defining attribute of some portrayals is sound; it is not possible to represent these portrayals without audio. For an obvious example, a lesson on the instruments of the orchestra might show a picture of each of the instruments, provide a brief description of the instrument, and then play a brief audio clip so that learners can hear how this instrument sounds. It is not possible to teach the sound of an instrument of the orchestra without allowing learners to hear this sound. A lesson on birds might include not only a picture of the bird, its habitat, and its nest, but also an audio of the bird's song.

As previously described, audio that is there only to increase interest, such as sound effects, background noise, music, and other sounds that are not properties of the portrayal, may actually make learning more difficult. This is especially true when some audio represents discriminating properties and some audio for a given portrayal is extraneous, increasing the challenge for students to distinguish the relevant audio from the extraneous audio. You have no doubt observed that illustrating these examples in a book is not feasible, so these examples, which really require sound to illustrate their properties, are merely described using words. I'm counting on your previous experience to understand these examples.

Use Graphics When Properties Can Be Visualized

Whenever the properties of a portrayal can be visualized, it is advantageous to represent these properties with an appropriate graphic. These graphics can take many forms depending on the content being taught. Previous chapters illustrated a number of different types of graphic representation of portrayals, including Gantt charts (see Figure 4-8), pictures of presidents (see Figure 5-1), a map of the counties of Utah (see Figure 5-2), photographs (see Figure 5-4), and spreadsheets (see Figure 5-6). These portrayals must provide a positive answer to the following questions: Did each of these graphic representations show the properties of the portrayals in each case? Were these graphic representations used to implement instructional events?

It is important that the demonstration instructional events for a given module contain only graphics that implement these instructional events—graphics that clearly show the relevant properties of the portrayals. If a module contains both irrelevant graphics and relevant graphics, learners are faced with the task of distinguishing those that are relevant and show properties of the portrayal from those that are merely for interest that carry no instructional function. Learners may try to find properties in the irrelevant graphics that they then confuse with relevant properties, often resulting in misconceptions and misunderstanding of the component skill being taught.

Use Video or Animation When Properties Require Dynamic Visualization

Some properties are difficult to describe in words and difficult to visualize with still graphics. When properties involve subtle cues demonstrated only by dynamic action of the objects or persons being portrayed, then video or animation is the appropriate representation of these properties.

The furniture selling lesson illustrated in Chapter 6 (see Figure 6-5) is a good example of a dynamic representation of subtle properties. The use of text and static graphics in this book to represent this dynamic graphic illustrates why these subtle cues cannot be demonstrated in still graphics and text. The video for this sales demonstration contains numerous cues that are important for learners to observe. The lesson required learners to view the video demonstration several times, focusing their attention on different properties of the sales presentation. Chapter 6 emphasized observing the condition that resulted from each step in the sales process. These conditions are the response of the customer to the sales step. The critical properties of these conditions are the tone of voice of the customer, the facial expressions of the customer, and other cues from her body language, rather than what she actually said. It is very difficult to show these subtle properties via descriptions, still pictures, or printed text. It is unlikely that you can observe these subtle properties from the demonstration in Figure 6-10.

Physical phenomena that are difficult to observe are often best represented by animation that can allow learners to observe dynamic properties that would not be easy to observe without special equipment or inference. Animations of many devices and physical phenomena are available on the Internet. Many of these animations are excellent and effectively show the defining properties of the phenomena being illustrated. But not all animations are adequate. In reviewing an animation, always ask the following question: Does the animation effectively show the defining properties of the desired portrayal?

I like steam locomotives but was puzzled about how they work. Figure 9-6 is a static graphic of an animation for a Walschaert valve gear on a steam locomotive. The animation shows how the valve above the cylinder allows steam to flow into the cylinder behind the piston, pushing it forward and then ahead of the piston, pushing it backward. The gears are arranged so that when the piston pushes backward the crank is below the axle, causing the wheel to turn clockwise, and when the piston pushes forward the crank is above the axle, causing the wheel to continue to turn clockwise. To reverse the locomotive the engineer reverses this relationship so the wheel turns counterclockwise. It is very difficult to explain, and this is why the animation helps a viewer understand the operation of this complex mechanism.

FIGURE 9-6 Animation to Show Operation of Locomotive Walschaert Valve Gear

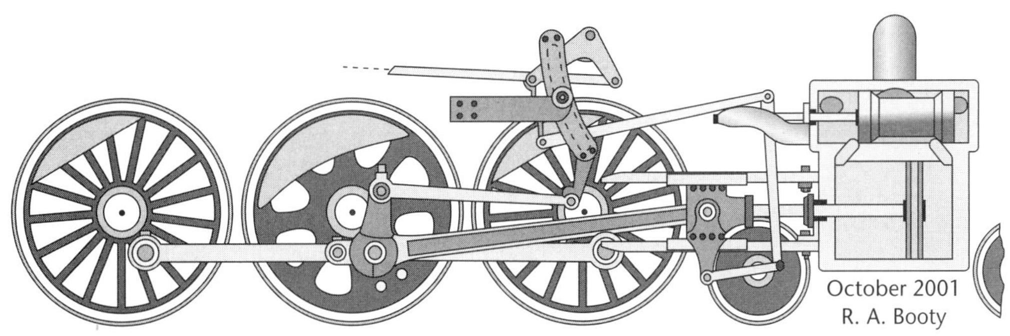

Online animation, Robert A. Booty. used with permission. www.roadrunner.com/~trumpetb/loco.

Use Graphic Devices to Focus Attention on the Properties of a Portrayal

Graphic devices are an excellent way to provide learner guidance during demonstration or coaching during application. Such devices include synchronizing the successive disclosure of text with the audio that elaborates this text; synchronizing audio with the demonstration of a graphic; and using callouts, arrows, color, and animation to focus attention on the properties of a portrayal or the activities of an event. The following paragraphs elaborate these uses of multimedia to provide guidance and coaching.

Use Successive Disclosure of Text Synchronized with Audio to Focus Attention When using abbreviated text items with audio elaboration, the learner's attention can be focused on each item if the items are presented one-by-one and elaborated as they occur. As previously discussed, it is important when text is successively disclosed and elaborated by audio that there is a way for learners to replay the display, especially if the test items are removed after they are elaborated. Figure 9-4 illustrates this prescription for a brief course on copyright.

Use Synchronized Graphic Devices with Audio to Focus Attention When graphics are successively disclosed or dynamic, then synchronizing the audio with these actions serves to focus the learner's attention on the element of the graphic that is under discussion. The Gantt chart course provides an excellent example of the synchronization of the audio with the graphic devices to identify the parts of the chart (see Figure 4-8). The table format attempts to provide a storyboard for this synchronization, even though it is difficult to illustrate in a book.

Use Callouts, Arrows, Color, Highlighting, and Animation to Focus Attention Irrelevant colored text is usually distracting and may interfere with learning. However, colored text can also be used as a way to focus learners' attention. Figure 9-7 is an instructional event from an online course on English grammar. Colored text is used to help learners identify the noun referent and the corresponding pronoun in the sentence portrayal. Because this text is gray scale, the nouns are shown as white letters on a black background and the pronouns are shown with black letters on a gray background. In the actual course, the nouns were red and the pronouns were blue.

FIGURE 9-7 Use of Color to Focus Attention

English Grammar	
A pronoun can refer to or take the place of a noun. The nouns pronouns refer to or replace are called referents.	Dick laughed when he saw the ghost.

Based on English Grammar Webclips.byu.edu.

The Gantt chart demonstration in Chapter 4 (see Figure 4-8) is an excellent example of using graphic devices to focus the learner's attention. In this example the chart is faded and then, as each part of the Gantt chart is introduced and described, the part is bolded and a callout labels the part. It is difficult to show the power of these animated graphic devices in a book without the accompanying animation, but the availability of digital multimedia makes this type of attention-focusing guidance relatively easy.

Another frequently used type of attention focusing is an animated demonstration where the actions required by the learner are shown. This type of guidance is frequently employed for teaching computer applications where the computer screen is shown, the cursor moves slowly to the next button or object to click, the object is clicked, and the consequence of the action is shown. A more interactive version of this type of guidance is a Simon-says demonstration where, instead of a passive demonstration of the actions to take, the learner is directed to take the action on a live or simulated version of the application. If the learner follows the directions and selects the correct object on the screen, then the consequence follows; if the learner fails to select the correct object, then the guidance uses some graphic object to highlight the object to select and directs the learner to try again. The spreadsheet example in Chapter 4 illustrated this Simon-says guidance (see Figure 4-4).

MULTIMEDIA FOR FORMAT

Learning is facilitated when format clearly indicates the structure of the course.

Learners are not always very good at seeing the organization of a course. What seems logical to the author may not be to learners. This can easily be demonstrated by having students read a section of almost any textbook with instructions to underline the key idea of the material, an exercise often advocated by how to-study courses. When you have students share what they have underlined, you will often find that there is a surprising lack of agreement. On the other hand, if the key idea is clearly identified for the student, then this ambiguity goes away. But, some instructors object, isn't an important part of learning to be able to identify key ideas, to dissect prose to find the real meaning? So true! Understanding communication is an important skill and as such should be taught as a skill rather than being subtly included in almost every course without explicit instruction for acquiring this interpretive skill. If the goal of instruction is to learn to solve some other type of problem, then e^3 instruction uses graphic format devices to facilitate the acquisition of this skill. If the problem it to interpret text, then that becomes the problem and the e^3 principles in this book can be used to design instruction for this skill.

The following paragraphs prescribe two uses of multimedia for format. First, use multimedia to show how the content is organized, and second, use multimedia to clearly identify the different types of instructional events.

Use Format to Indicate the Organization of the Content

It is important for learners to know how the content of a course is organized and how they can access different parts of the course. The format of the interface can be used to show this organization. Figure 9-8 is the organization of the Entrepreneur course that was described in Chapter 7. The tabs across the top correspond to the five problem portrayals that form the progression of problems for the course. It shows learners that there is a progression of businesses that will be used to demonstrate these component skills. The buttons down the left side correspond to the component skills that are required for each of the business portrayals in the progression. These buttons serve to remind learners of the component skills involved. This graphic organization helps learners see that the same component skills are present in each type of business. Learners are encouraged to study all of the component skills for each business in turn, but this format also provides a content menu for the students that allows them to access any of the component skills for each business or to access any of the businesses in the progression. This format shows learners how many problems are in the course and the component skills involved with each problem.

FIGURE 9-8 Format for Course Organization—Entrepreneur Course

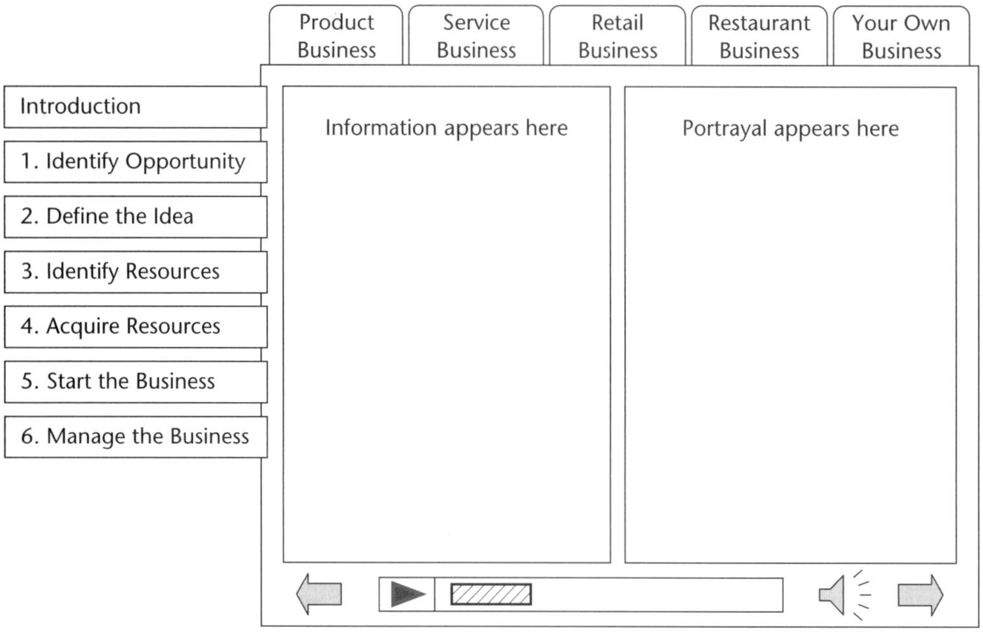

Product Business | Service Business | Retail Business | Restaurant Business | Your Own Business

Introduction
1. Identify Opportunity
2. Define the Idea
3. Identify Resources
4. Acquire Resources
5. Start the Business
6. Manage the Business

Information appears here

Portrayal appears here

Use Format to Differentiate Instructional Events

Textbook publishers typically use a single font for the text in a book. However, using a different style of font can also be a useful device for helping learners differentiate among the elements of an instructional event. In a book on teaching concepts (Merrill & Tennyson, 1977), we used three different fonts to differentiate a definition from its elaboration from an example illustrating this concept. Figure 9-9 illustrates a small segment from this book. Note in the figure that the concept name and its definition are bold Times New Roman font, the elaboration of the definition is in regular Times New Roman font, and the example is in Ariel font.

FIGURE 9-9 Using Font to Differentiate Elements of an Instructional Event

Clouds	
Name and Definition	**Classification Behavior: A student has learned a concept when he or she can correctly identify the class membership of a specific symbol, object, or event.**
Elaboration of the Definition	Classification behavior occurs when, given a specific symbol, object, or event, the student can name or point to the general word that refers to a class to which the specific instance belongs or, when given the general name of the class and shown representations of specific instances of this and other classes, the student will be able to identify those symbols, objects, or events that are members of the class and those symbols, objects, or events that are not members of the class.
Example	The following test question requires classification behavior. Below are pictures of clouds. Under each picture write the word cirrus, cumulus, or nimbus to indicate the type of cloud pictured. 

From Merrill and Tennyson, 1977. Used with permission.

Books often try to assist the reader by using headings, bold type, italics, figures, and other format devices to make the message more apparent to the reader. These devices are most often related to the content that is presented but may also be used to differentiate different instructional events. This author has also attempted to use format to differentiate different instructional events. The examples are shown in separate figures and tables, while the explanation appears in the body of the text. Key principles in this chapter are in italics at the beginning of each section. Italics are used to identify technical vocabulary.

Use Format to Keep *Tell-and-Show* Concurrent

Learning is facilitated if the information for a portrayal, guidance focusing attention on the portrayal, and the portrayal itself are all available without requiring learners to turn the page or open another display. This allows learners to compare the information to its implementation in a portrayal. When the information or guidance is audio rather than text, then this simultaneous presentation is easily accomplished. When the information or guidance is text, then this text should be simultaneously available on the same display with the portrayal. One way to accomplish this concurrent presentation of information and portrayal is to use pop-up messages, especially for guidance related to the portrayal. Another technique is to use bullet points for the information with elaboration of these bullets available as pop-up messages or audio.

In the Entrepreneur course (Figure 9-8) the large panel at the left displays the information for the component skill under consideration; the panel on the right displays the portrayal of this information. This format helps learners identify which is the information and which is the portrayal of this information. The main panels adjacent to each other and on a single display keep the information and its portrayal concurrent so that learners can easily compare the questions of the checklist with the portrayal of these items.

MULTIMEDIA FOR NAVIGATION

Learning is facilitated when navigation is unambiguous.

This book uses the term *navigation* for two distinct instructional functions. The most obvious is a control for moving learners from one instructional event to the next. The second is to move learners among multiple displays that may be included within an instructional event.

Use Conventional Buttons for Navigation

A *conventional* button is one that is commonly used. Figure 9-10 illustrates some commonly used navigation buttons. It is usually best to keep it simple. Many users will be familiar with these commonly used buttons. However, it is important that you not assume that these buttons are obvious to all users. Always provide navigation directions that explain all the buttons used either prior to the module or on the first one or two screens that use the navigation buttons.

FIGURE 9-10 Examples of Conventional Navigation Buttons

▶	Go to next page or display.	◀	Go to previous page or display.
▶❙	Go to last page or display.	❙◀	Go to first page or display.
	Go to home page or menu.		Return to last page or display.
	Play audio.		Play video.
	Show document.	?	Show directions or help.
	Media Control Bar		

It is better to avoid unique navigation buttons that may represent objects related to the content of the module but which have no other function except navigation. When instruction uses icons that may reflect the theme of the presentation, but which are not commonly used for navigation, you increase the cognitive load for learners, requiring them to learn the function of these new icons. For example, a short course for travel agents used airplanes for the Next and Previous buttons. These airplanes, flying either to the right or to the left, are not difficult to use for navigation, but do they really contribute to learning?

Use Content Menus to Navigate Among Instructional Events

The too frequent use of Next and Previous buttons often results in page-turner instruction. Learning is promoted when learners are required to interact with the content in meaningful ways. Clicking a Next button does little to promote learning and encourages learners to merely sit back and flip through the displays. Requiring learners to make a decision related to the content or to the instructional event that is about to occur requires them to focus their attention on what is coming next. Navigation with *content menus* requires this relevant mental effort. Such menus can be embedded in the content of a display or may appear as separate content or interaction menus. In either case, it is extremely important to provide clear and unambiguous directions to learners about how to use these embedded content menus to navigate the course. These directions should be given to learners as an introduction to the course, the first few displays that use these embedded content menus should include directions on the display, and subsequent displays should have an easy way for learners to review these directions.

For the Entrepreneur course the different business tabs across the top and the component skill menus down the left side are embedded content menus (see Figure 9-8). Clicking on a tab allows the learner to navigate to any of the businesses in order to preview the content to come, to study the content, or to review the content already studied. This component skill menu enables learners to preview, study, or review any of the component skills within a given business. These navigation menus are always present for the student to use to navigate to the various parts of the course. The navigation directions at the beginning of the course indicate this navigation function to learners and a Help button on each display enables learners to review these directions. Learners are encouraged to study the course in a sequential order, but these problem and component skill navigation menus enable learners to overview the entire course, to study the content of the course, and to later return to any business for review.

Use Next and Previous Buttons to Navigate Within Instructional Events

Many courses use Next, Previous, First, and Last buttons for navigation between the instructional events of the course. As already mentioned, there is a temptation for learners to merely use these buttons to skim through the course. A better use of Next and Previous buttons is to navigate *within* an instructional event.

The Entrepreneur course includes navigation buttons below the information and portrayal panels. The Previous and Next arrows are conventional buttons allowing the learner to navigate within the instructional events for a given component skill. There is a successive disclosure of information and the corresponding portrayal in the information and portrayal panels of Figure 9-8. The Next and Previous buttons enable learners to control the pace of this demonstration. After each statement and its portrayal are shown, learners are directed to click the Next button to continue. Clicking on the Previous button repeats the previous part of the demonstration. Clicking on the Next button displays the bullet information, displays the portrayal of this information, and plays the elaboration of this information and its portrayal. At the beginning of this instructional event, the Previous button is not available; at the end of this instructional event, the Next button is not available. The audio reminds learners to use the content menus to navigate to the next instructional event.

MULTIMEDIA FOR INTERACTION

Learning is promoted when instructional events are interactive.

Previous to the introduction of digital technology, learner interaction with instructional events was passive. Learners were presented information in either text or audio format and were shown static and dynamic graphics, but their interaction with these instructional events was primarily limited to observation. Overt learner interaction was limited to input in the form of exercises, projects, papers, and tests that were completed, submitted, and reviewed by instructors, who then hopefully provided feedback on the students' work, typically with some period of delay between submission and feedback.

Computer technology makes it possible for learners to have some control of the media. This control makes possible a much more dynamic interaction of learners with instructional events. Control enables learners to start, pause, and replay audio, video, and animations. Learner input to digital devices makes it possible for learners to receive immediate right/wrong or corrective feedback to their inputs to the instructional event. Media control also enables animated devices and microworlds with which learners can interact in a way that simulate to some degree their interactions with the real world. Media control also introduces the capability of the students to direct their own learning. The following paragraphs describe and illustrate each of these types of media control.

Use Media Control of Audio, Video, and Animation

Text messages are easy to review, since they are typically fixed. Audio and video messages are transient and disappear when they have finished playing. It is important to provide a way for learners to pause, review, and replay these dynamic messages. Figure 9-10 illustrates a typical control bar for dynamic multimedia. The dynamic media is controlled with the conventional start ▶, pause | |, and stop ■symbols along with a progress bar and a moving symbol to indicate the length of the audio. Learners can also drag the marker on the progress bar to skip part of the audio or video or to replay part of the audio or video. Clicking on the speaker symbol at the end of the bar allows learners to adjust the volume or to mute the audio.

Use Media Control to Input Learner Response and Provide Corrective Feedback

Following are a few ways to implement media control of learner response for different types of instructional strategies.

Kind-of Response Kind-of strategies require learners to identify instances that belong to a given class. Just as for demonstration, the portrayal of instances for kind-of application must also adequately represent the defining or ordering properties. There are a wide variety of appropriate response patterns for kind-of strategies. Following are some possibilities: Instances are presented one-by-one and learners directed to select a label from a list or to type a label for each instance. Learners can also sort instances by dragging each instance to a location designated for each concept. Learners are directed to select a reason for their classification from a list of specific but unlabeled properties for the instance. For some concepts it may be possible to have learners click on a graphic to identify the defining properties.

Learners need to not only identify examples and non-examples, but they also need to determine when one example is better than another example. An effective type of response is to provide a set of examples that vary in the degree to which they exemplify the concept being taught. The system directs learners to rank the instances. For example, in the Entrepreneur course, learners could be given several statements of business opportunity and asked to indicate which is best, next best, and so forth.

When learners select their responses from a list, immediate corrective feedback is easily provided by a pop-up message or a new display triggered by the learner's selection. When learners input text, the media must provide some form of answer-processing software that enables the program to identify the learner's input and compare it to the anticipated response. Such software should provide allowance for typos, misspelling, and even synonyms when they exist. Corrective feedback is guidance provided after a response and is similar to guidance provided during the demonstration. Such feedback focuses the learner's attention on the portrayal of the defining or ordering properties as they are exhibited in each specific instance.

How-to Response Identification of the steps in a procedure is very similar to kind-of described in the previous paragraphs. The step is portrayed for the learner in a way that clearly exemplifies all of the critical characteristics of the step. When presented with one or more steps in the procedure, learners are able to correctly label the instances of each step and identify the critical characteristics of each step. Several instances of a given step could be provided and learners asked to rank these as to which is the best example, next best example, and so forth. Corrective feedback for how-to is also guidance presented after the learner's classification response.

Another frequently used form of response for procedures is to have learners order the names of the steps in the procedure. This form of response for a procedure is merely memory and does not allow the student or the instructor to know whether learners are able to execute the procedure. A variation that is somewhat better is to present a dynamic representation of each step of a previously unencountered instance of the procedure and have learners order these brief scenarios. This combines two skills: the ability to recognize the execution of a previously unencountered instance of each step (kind-of) and the ability to order the steps once they are identified.

Having learners execute the steps in a procedure often poses a challenge for mediated instruction. If the instruction involves the manipulation of symbols—using a word processer or spreadsheet, writing a poem, solving a math problem, editing a document—then either simulating the electronic application or having learners perform the procedure using the actual application are relatively easy to accomplish. However, when procedures involve social interaction—furniture sales, interview skills—then providing a way to use media to enable learners to input their responses is much more challenging. It is possible to approximate some behaviors by using simulations. It is also becoming more possible to input psychomotor performance using devices such as the Nintendo Wii.

Using media to provide corrective feedback for complex procedures is also a considerable challenge. While it is relatively easy to input the responses for component skills, it is much more difficult to assess the performance of a complex task as a whole. If a whole task is carefully analyzed, as previously described in Chapter 6, and if the component skills of the whole task are carefully input according to the type of component skill involved, then it is possible to assess these individual component skills. Ways to assess whole tasks will be described and illustrated in the second part of this book.

What-Happens Response Perhaps the most neglected type of response in much of the available mediated instruction is what-happens. As indicated in Chapter 5, an appropriate response for what-happens is to predict a consequence given a set of conditions or to find a faulted or missing condition given an unexpected consequence. The last few instructional events in Figure 6-12 briefly describe a possible what-happens set of responses for the furniture sales lesson. In this situation, the customer does not buy. Learners are asked to watch the video and identify where Maria's response to each of the steps may not have been the desired consequence for the step and hence not the appropriate condition to lead to a sale. Capturing learners' responses and providing corrective feedback is challenging in this situation. Perhaps an application such as Camtasia or Captivate could be used to enable learners to edit a copy of the video to identify the steps and resulting conditions, identify steps that are missing or inadequate and conditions that are unexpected or inadequate, and to indicate how inadequate steps might be improved to result in the desired conditions that would lead to the desired consequence of a sale.

In a course on photography, after being taught several component skills for photographic exposure, learners are shown a set of pictures and asked to identify the conditions that led to the photo or, in the case where a picture was not well exposed, what conditions were faulted or missing that let to this undesired exposure. Figure 9-11 indicates a possible way that media control could be used to enable learners to make a what-happens response. Using the up and down arrows, learners can adjust the shutter speed, the aperture, the white balance, and the ISO that were used to take the picture (in the actual instruction the picture is in color). As they make these adjustments, the picture changes to show the consequence of each of these changed conditions. Learners receive immediate feedback by seeing the result of their adjustments. While learners can continue to respond until they get the desired consequence, the learners who are able to make the best adjustments in these conditions in the fewest trials receive the highest scores. This response control requires learners to both diagnose the faulted conditions and to adjust these conditions to predict a better consequence.

FIGURE 9-11 What-Happens Response Control

<table>
<tr><th colspan="2">Photographic Exposure</th></tr>
<tr><td colspan="2">For the situation and photo below, make the adjustments in shutter speed, aperture, ISO, and white balance that will help Jill accomplish her goal.</td></tr>
<tr><td>Jill has a vase of flowers on her nightstand. She wants to take a picture of them before they die so she will never forget the wonderful way in which her husband surprised her. She would love to frame this picture to a 16 x 20 poster size but is frustrated with her poor exposure. What adjustments could she make to correct the exposure and show all the pretty colors of her flowers?</td><td></td></tr>
<tr><td>Shutter speed 30 ▼▲
Aperture f 8.0 ▼▲
White Balance Tungsten ▼▲
ISO 100 ▼▲
SUBMIT SCORE</td><td>When you click SUBMIT, the picture will change to show the result of your change. If you are not satisfied with the result, you can try again. The fewer tries to get a quality picture, the higher your score.</td></tr>
</table>

Modified from a student project, Utah State University, Micah Murdock.

Use Learner Control to Interact with Simulations and Microworlds

Use multimedia to visualize devices or situations in the real world and provide controls so that learners can adjust conditions in the device to see the consequence. Figure 9-12 illustrates a simulation of a simple circuit demonstrating Ohm's law. The sliders enable learners to adjust the voltage and/or the resistance to see the effect on the current flow in the circuit.

FIGURE 9-12 Simple Circuit Simulation—Ohm's Law

The circuit below demonstrates these relationships.

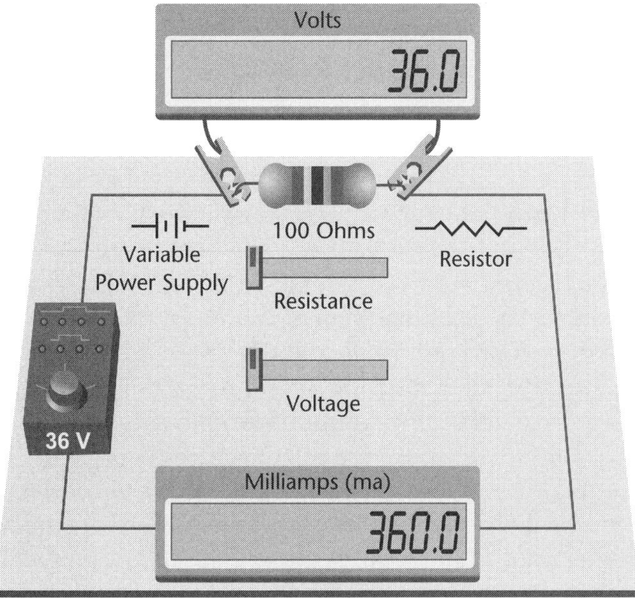

- Click on the resistance slider to change resistors.
- Click on the voltage slider to adjust voltage of the variable power supply.

A microworld enables learners to interact with a representation of items that might appear in a particular environment. The term *microworld* was coined at the MIT Media Lab. We have broadened the term to refer to all simulations of complex environments that enable learners to manipulate different items in these environments. Learners can click on these objects to obtain information, provide information, make decisions, and see the consequences of their actions.

One popular type of microworld is an in-basket simulation. These exercises simulate the problems and decisions required of a typical manager. The participant is given background information on a fictitious organization and assumes the role of a manager in this organization. As a new manager, he or she must respond to letters, memos, reports, phone calls, emails, and other information indicating problems that require his or her attention. With digital technology, in-basket simulations can graphically represent the manager's office, complete with file cabinets, fax, phone, and other communication equipment. Individuals can also be simulated through animation or short video clips. There is no space in this book to describe the many variations of simulations in detail, but even a quick search for various types of simulation on the Internet will provide many possibilities.

Use Learner Control of Instructional Events

This chapter previously suggested the use of content menus for navigation among instructional events, as opposed to merely selecting a Next button. If learners have to deliberately select the content for their next instructional event, it is hoped that this mental effort will help focus their attention on the task at hand and prevent mindless page turning. Obviously, such learner control of the content also provides the mechanism for learners to preview material yet to be studied and to review material already studied. For much instruction even when learners are given content control, the navigation within instructional events is linear—the same path for all students. This approach suffers from the individual difference challenge. In any group of learners, there are a wide range of different abilities, experience, and learning preferences. How can we address these differences? Creating multiple paths for learners with different levels of experience or ability is usually not feasible. Most training budgets are limited and don't provide for multiple versions of a course. Even if the budget is sufficient, how many different paths are enough? Trying to anticipate the needs of different students is challenging at best. Who knows best what an individual student needs at any given moment during instruction?

Learning may be facilitated when learners are given some control over instructional events. Such learner control of instructional strategy has not been widely used, but holds the promise of greater ability for learners to adapt the instruction to their own needs. After studying a definition, how many examples does a given learner need to feel secure about identifying the properties of a yet-to-be-encountered example? The complexity of the concept is one variable that determines the number of instances required, but learner experience, aptitude, and preference also play a significant role. Many learners can decide at any point in a kind of instructional strategy whether they would like to see another example or non-example. Do all learners need attention-focusing guidance? Some learners may immediately be able to see the portrayal of the properties in an instant, whereas others may need considerable help to identify the presence of these property portrayals. Many learners can decide whether or not they need to see guidance for a given instance. How many practice items does a given learner need to be able to identify future unencountered instances? How many times does a given learner need to execute a procedure before being comfortable enough to do the procedure in the real world? Making these decisions for students by trying to create multiple strategies for different students is not feasible. However, giving learners control over these parameters within instructional strategies enables them to adapt the strategies to their own needs and will facilitate e^3 learning.

Figure 9-13 illustrates a possible display for the lesson on photography's rule of thirds. The buttons on the left enable learners to control this instructional event. Clicking the ? button while in demonstration (*Show*) mode provides the following audio directions: "Click the TELL button to learn more about the rule." Clicking the TELL button plays an audio elaboration of the rule. "Click the SHOW button to see another example." Clicking the SHOW button presents another example/non-example pair. "Click the HELP button for an explanation of why a photograph illustrates the rule of thirds." Clicking the HELP button displays the grid lines over the photographs and plays an audio explanation. "Click the DO button to test your skill in recognizing the rule of thirds." Clicking the DO button displays another photograph with three additional buttons labeled: RULE OF THIRDS, NOT RULE OF THIRDS, and FEEDBACK.

FIGURE 9-13 Learner Control of Instructional Events

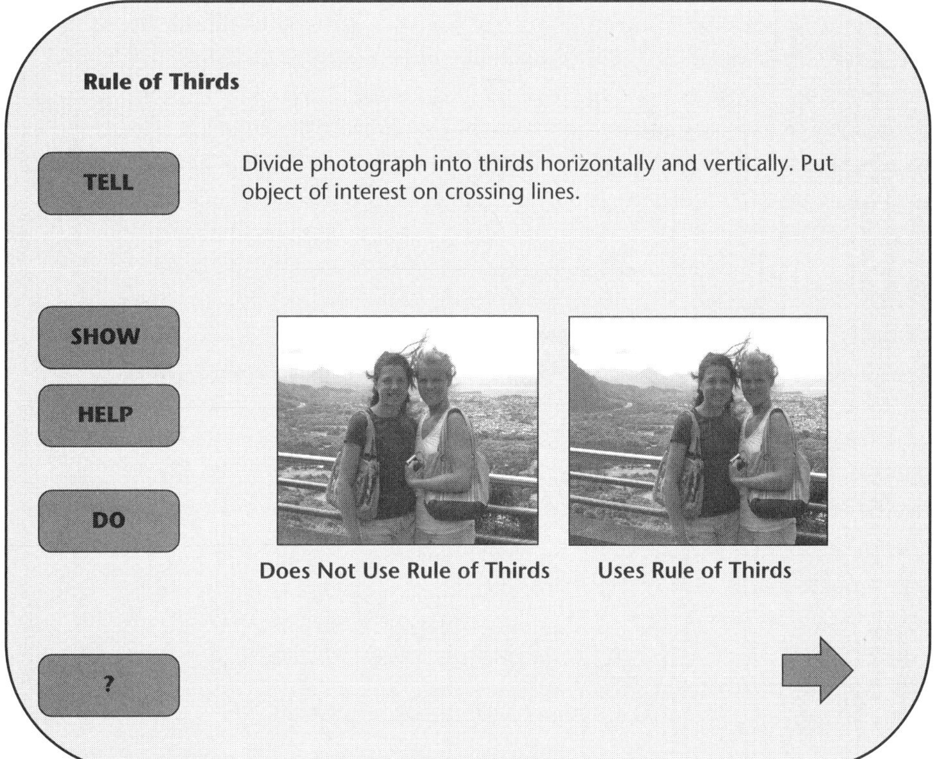

Original material by author.

Clicking the ? button while in application (*Do*) mode provides the following audio directions: "Click the button that correctly identifies the use of rule of thirds in the photograph. Click the FEEDBACK button for an explanation of the correct response." Clicking the FEEDBACK button after a response displays the grid lines with audio elaboration.

Clicking the forward arrow goes to the next instructional event in the module. A bit of intelligence within this display could also provide the following learner guidance: If when a learner clicks the DO button and he or she has not viewed at least two additional examples using the SHOW button, the following audio message plays: "You may want to look at more examples before you try to apply your skill." If when a learner clicks the forward arrow he or she has not tried at least three application items, the following audio message plays: "You should try to apply your ability to recognize photographs that use the rule of thirds before you continue." Neither of these messages forces the learner to see more examples or to try more application items. Clicking the DO button a second time goes to the application; clicking the forward arrow a second time goes to the next instructional event.

MISUSE OF MULTIMEDIA

This chapter describes and illustrates effective use of multimedia to carry the instruction to the student. Unfortunately e^3 instructional strategies can be rendered ineffective by misuse of the multimedia used to represent the content elements and implement these instructional strategies. In the concluding paragraphs of this chapter I will identify some common misuses of media in instruction.

Irrelevant Media

Relevance is the most important property of multimedia. Relevance is a positive answer to the question, "Does it have an instructional function?" If the multimedia does not have an instructional function, then it will not contribute to learning and may actually interfere with learning. For every piece of multimedia included in an instructional product, ask, "What instructional content does this media represent or what instructional event does this media enable?"

The inclusion of graphics that have no instructional function is so common that almost any instructional product you examine will have an example of a picture that is related to the content but that neither adequately represents a content element nor enables an instructional event. Textbooks seem to have a rule that a picture must appear on every two or three pages. Online instruction seems to have a rule that every display needs to include a graphic. Many online courses are merely illustrated lectures—lots of text with a picture that is somehow related to the text. An examination of these graphics shows that they do not implement any instructional event, they do not show the properties of a portrayal, and more often than not they are merely included to make the presentation more interesting.

Distracting Media

Another common practice for e-learning is to provide media that is thought to make the material more interesting. These media may be sound effects, background music, entertaining graphics, and decorative graphics. Does this extraneous multimedia contribute to learning? The evidence seems to indicate that, rather than increasing interest, such media actually interfere with learning (Clark & Mayer, 2003, 2008; R.E. Mayer, 2001). One form of distracting media is a sound that accompanies every page turn. Does this sound contribute to learning? A really annoying form of distracting media is a sound such as clapping or a cheer whenever learners have a correct response or a buzzer or other negative sound whenever learners have an incorrect response to practice or application. Do these sound effects contribute to the corrective feedback? Such repetitive sound effects should be avoided.

Even sound effects related to the content have been demonstrated to be distracting if the sound is not a discriminating or ordering property of the portrayal being demonstrated (see Clark & Mayer, 2007; R.E. Mayer, 2001). For instruction on how lightning works, Mayer found that thunder sound effects actually caused a decrement in learning. Include sound effects only if they are a necessary discriminating property of a portrayal.

Background music, especially at the beginning of an instructional program, is almost universal. If this music is unrelated to the content of the instruction, does it contribute to learning or distract? If this music is familiar to learners, does it activate mental models unrelated to the content, thereby increasing cognitive load and making learning more difficult? What instructional purpose does such background music have? Background music has been used in the movies and video to carry the audience from one scene to another. For entertainment it probably serves an important function. But does merely including background music in instruction contribute to or distract from learning? The data is not in on these important questions, but if we extrapolate from Mayer's research about extraneous sounds, it is likely that this almost universal use of background music may actually interfere with learning.

Excessive Text

Many online courses are merely textbooks with too much text. Previous paragraphs suggested that abbreviated text accompanied by audio elaboration is more effective than too much text.

Reading On-Screen Text

A common practice for online instruction is to use audio to read on-screen text. As previously described, reading the text to learners often interferes with their learning process, especially if there is a graphic.

Distracting Animation

Presentation software provides an extensive array of special animation effects. The temptation is to include a variety of these effects in an effort to make a presentation more interesting. It may make a presentation more entertaining, but the result is almost always a distraction from the content being presented. I recently viewed a short course in which every display used a different clever way to animate the bullet items. These clever animations may be entertaining to the viewer, but they significantly distract attention from the message of the course.

Irrelevant Color

A previous prescription indicated that irrelevant color may interfere with learning. Irrelevant color distracts from the instructional use of color. For example, if color is used as a guidance technique to focus the learner's attention, then using additional color that has no instructional purpose causes confusion for the learner. If some text is in color to focus attention and some text is in color merely to increase interest, then it is likely that learners may try to determine the instructional relevance of the irrelevant color or fail to recognize the instructional function of the relevant color.

Good design may include colored background to give a course an attractive appearance. The text of a given course may appear in an attractive color rather than merely black on white. Consistency is the most important principle here. If the course uses a certain color for the background and a distinctive color for the text, then it is important that this color scheme stay consistent throughout the course. Readability is also a critical consideration when using colored backgrounds and colored text. Some color combinations are very difficult to read. There is not space in this book to provide a sufficient discussion of color theory. A quick Internet search for *color + readability* will give you a number of sites that provide guidance for effective color combinations.

Some courses make use of a color background to help learners know their location in the course or to discriminate instructional events. The color scheme may change to indicate new content, or information may have one background color while portrayals may have a different color to discriminate portrayals from related information. If color is used for these instructional purposes, then this use of color should be clear to learners; course directions should carefully explain this use of color for instructional purposes and the color scheme should be consistent throughout the course.

EXAMPLE OF E^3 MULTIMEDIA IMPLEMENTATION—ENTREPRENEUR

Table 9-1 is a multimedia checklist that provides a checkbox for the prescriptions included in this chapter. The upper section of this table is the checklist and the lower key indicates the prescription corresponding with each checkbox. How does the use of multimedia in the Entrepreneur course stack up on the multimedia checklist? The multimedia implementation for the Entrepreneur course is shown checked in the table.

Table 9-1 Multimedia Checklist

Course:	Evaluator:	Date:	
Misuse: ☐ Irrelevant ☐ distracting ☐ > text ☐ - animation ☐ - color ☐ - read			
Instructional events	Format	Navigation	Interaction
☒ Text/Audio	☒ Organization	☒ Buttons	☒ Control Video/Audio
☒ Portrayal	☒ Inst. Events	☒ Content Menus	☐ Response and Feedback
☒ Guidance	☒ Tell/Show	☒ Next/Last	☐ Simulation/Microworld
			☐ Control Inst. Events
Key to Checklist:			
Misuse:			
Avoid irrelevant multimedia (irrelevant)		Avoid irrelevant animation (–animation)	
Avoid distracting multimedia (distracting)		Avoid irrelevant color (–color)	
Avoid excessive text (>text)		Avoid reading online text (–read)	
Instructional events, use:		**Navigation, use:**	
Abbreviated text with audio elaboration		Conventional buttons	
Text, audio, or graphics to show properties		Content menus among instructional events	
Graphics and audio to focus attention		Next/last within instructional events	
Use Format:		**Interaction, use:**	
To indicate organization of content		Audio, video, animation control	
To differentiate instructional events		Learner response and feedback	
To keep *Tell* and *Show* concurrent		Simulation or microworld	
		Control of instructional events	

Figure 9-14 uses callouts to indicate the multimedia implementation for the Entrepreneur course. The captions in the callouts correspond to the check boxes on the multimedia checklist. This display implements many of the multimedia prescriptions illustrated in this chapter. The multimedia implementation for this course is summarized in the following paragraphs.

FIGURE 9-14 Multimedia Implementation for Entrepreneur Course

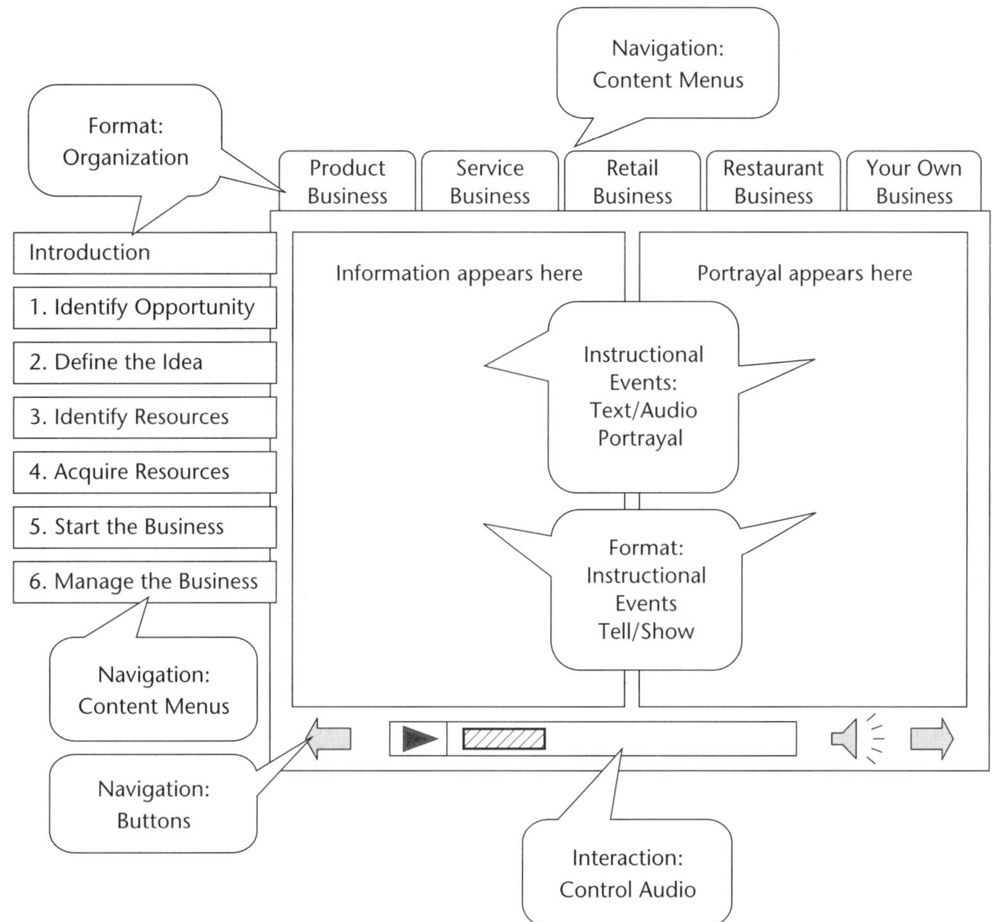

Instructional Events

Text/audio. The left main panel displays a checklist elaborated by audio.

Portrayal. The right main panel shows a statement of good business opportunity. Veasna's business opportunity statement is a text portrayal of the checklist information. Since the artifact in the real world is a written statement, text is the appropriate media to portray the properties of this specific object. The statement does contain an instance of each of the items in the checklist.

Guidance. This display uses successive disclosure of the items in the checklist as they were elaborated by audio. The abbreviated text in the information presentation is displayed to correspond with the audio elaboration of the item. Following the presentation of each of the items in the checklist, the portrayal of the corresponding property in the statement of business opportunity is displayed, giving learners a chance to compare the checklist to the portrayal of each item. When the idea of evidence is introduced, the part of each statement that shows evidence is highlighted for the student.

Format

Organization. The Entrepreneur course uses a format where tabs represent the progression of businesses that will be used in the course and where the menu on the left side of the screen represents the component skills. This format serves as a structure for the organization and content of the course.

Instructional Events. The large panel at the left displays the information for the component skill under consideration; the panel at the right displays the portrayal of this information. This format helps learners identify which is the information and which is the portrayal of this information.

Tell/Show. The main panels adjacent to each other and on a single display keep the information and its portrayal concurrent so that learners can easily compare the questions on the checklist with the portrayal of these items.

Navigation

Buttons. The Next and Previous buttons and the audio control bar are all conventional buttons.

Content menus. The tabs and component skill menu are embedded content menus. Clicking on a tab allows the learner to navigate to any of the businesses either to preview the content to come, to study the content, or to review the content already studied. This component skill menu enables learners to preview, study, or review any of the component skills within a given business. These navigation menus are always present for the student to use to navigate to the various parts of the course.

Next/Last. The Entrepreneur course includes navigation buttons below the information and portrayal panels. The Previous and Next arrows are conventional buttons allowing the learner to navigate within the instructional events for a given component skill. The Entrepreneur course uses successive disclosure of the information on the display for one component skill. The Next and Previous buttons enable learners to control the pace of this demonstration. After each statement and its portrayal are shown, learners are directed to click the Next button to continue. Clicking on the Previous button repeats the previous part of the demonstration. Clicking on the Next button displays the bullet information, displays the portrayal of this information, and plays the elaboration of this information and its portrayal. At the beginning of this instructional event, the Previous button is not available; at the end of this instructional event, the Next button is not available. The audio reminds learners to use the content menus to navigate to the next instructional event.

Interaction

Control Audio. The entrepreneur display includes a media control bar that enables learners to start, pause, replay, and select any part of the audio messages. The illustration of the Entrepreneur course included here does not include *Response & Feedback, Simulation/Microworld,* or *Control of Instructional Events.*

PRINCIPLES AND PRESCRIPTIONS

Multimedia. Learning is promoted when multimedia implements prescribed instructional events and functions.

Multimedia for Instructional Events

Use abbreviated text elaborated with audio to present information.

- Use audio to elaborate graphics rather than on-screen text.
- Allow learners to control the pace of text presentation.

Use graphics to provide an alternative representation of the information.

Use the multimedia that most clearly represents the properties of a portrayal.

- Use text when words are a defining or ordering property.
- Use audio when sound is a defining or ordering property.
- Use graphics when properties can be visualized.
- Use animation or video when properties require dynamic visualization.

Use graphic devices and audio to focus attention on the properties of a portrayal.

- Use successive disclosure of text synchronized with audio to focus attention.
- Synchronize graphic devices with audio to focus attention.
- Use callouts, arrows, color, highlighting, and animation to focus attention.

Multimedia for Format

Learning is facilitated when format clearly indicates the structure of the course.

- Use format to indicate the organization of the content.
- Use format to differentiate instructional events.
- Use format to keep *Tell-and-Show* concurrent.

Multimedia for Navigation

Learning is facilitated when navigation is unambiguous.

- Use conventional buttons for navigation.
- Use content menus to navigate among instructional events.
- Use Next and Previous buttons to navigate within instructional events.

Multimedia for Interaction

Learning is promoted when instructional events are interactive.

- Use learner control of audio, video, and animation.
- Use media control to input learner's response and provide corrective feedback.
- Use learner control to interact with device simulation and microworlds.
- Use learner control of instructional events.

Avoid Misuse of Multimedia

Avoid irrelevant media.

Avoid distracting media.

Avoid excessive text.

Avoid reading on-screen text.

Avoid irrelevant animation.

Avoid irrelevant color.

APPLICATION

You will come to recognize the effective use of multimedia only if you apply the principles and prescriptions of this chapter to many examples of existing instruction. Select several courses that you are taking, designing, or that you can find on the Internet. Examine these courses to see how they used multimedia to implement their instructional strategies. Did these courses use multimedia to effectively implement instructional events? Did these courses use multimedia to indicate the format of the materials; to provide efficient navigation; and to provide for learner interaction with the content and instructional events? Did these courses avoid irrelevant multimedia?

TO LEARN MORE

Multimedia in Instruction

Clark, R. C., & Lyons, C. (2004). *Graphics for learning.* San Francisco: Pfeiffer. This book shows how to select and develop graphic materials that are appropriate for different instructional strategies.

Clark, R. C., & Mayer, R. E. (2008). *e-Learning and the science of instruction* (2nd ed.). San Francisco: Pfeiffer. This book takes the research of Dr. Mayer and others and applies this research to the design of instruction.

Mayer, R. E. (2001). *Multimedia learning.* Cambridge: Cambridge University Press. This book describes some of the seminal research conducted by Dr. Mayer on the use of multimedia in instruction.

Using Color

See www.hgrebdes.com for a website that allows you to experiment with different colors of text on different colors of background. This site also contains a number of good recommendations about color and readability.

COMING NEXT

The previous chapters in this section demonstrated instructional strategies for component skills, instructional strategies for problem solving, strategy enhancements, and the multimedia implementation of instructional strategies. Chapter 10, the last chapter in Part I, brings all of the previous prescriptions for implementing First Principles of Instruction together into a single Course Critique Checklist to facilitate your evaluation of existing instruction.

CHAPTER 10

CRITIQUING INSTRUCTIONAL STRATEGIES IN EXISTING INSTRUCTION

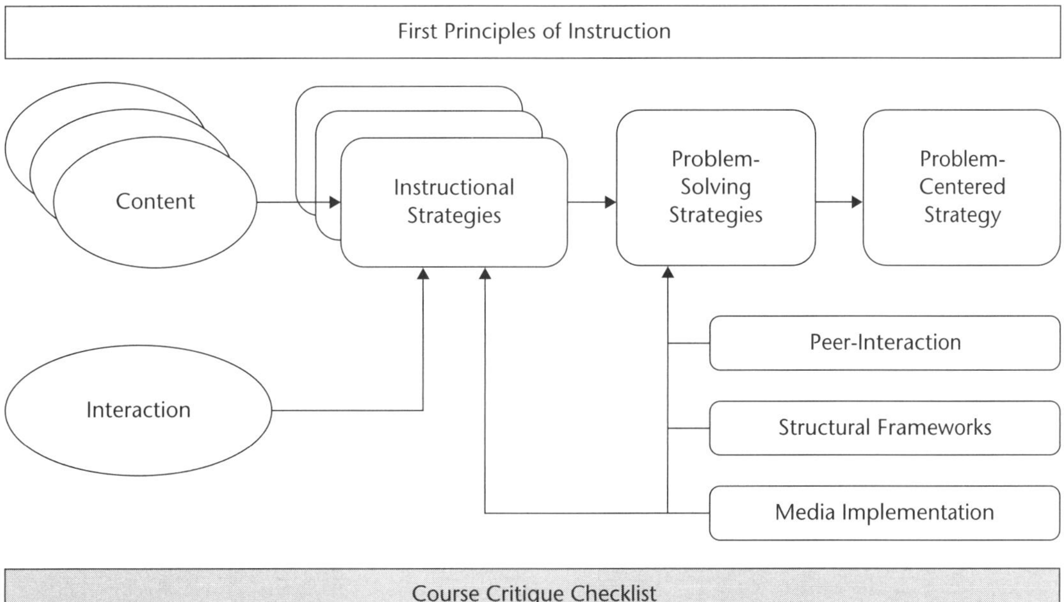

Quick Look

The previous chapters in Part I of this book presented principles and prescriptions that you can use to evaluate the e^3 quality of existing instruction. This chapter brings all of these prescriptions together into a checklist that you can use to evaluate your own courses or the courses of others. This chapter answers the following questions: When you encounter a new instructional product how do you know if it is likely to result in e^3 learning? Can you determine in advance the degree to which a given instructional product implements First Principles of Instruction? How do you evaluate the e^3 potential of instructional strategies for individual component skills? How do you evaluate the e^3 potential of instructional strategies for whole problems?

Key Words

Course Critique Checklist: questions to evaluate the presence and adequacy of prescribed instructional events for teaching individual component skills and whole problems.

Summary Critique: a chart indicating the presence or absence of prescribed instructional events in a given instructional module.
Kind-of Strategy Checklist: a set of questions to evaluate the instructional events for teaching concepts.
How-to Strategy Checklist: a set of questions to evaluate the instructional events for teaching procedures.
What-Happens Strategy Checklist: a set of questions to evaluate the instructional events for teaching processes.

INTRODUCTION

When you encounter a new instructional product, how do you know if it is likely to result in e^3 learning? Of course, one way is to try it out with a sample of prospective learners from the target audience. But this requires acquiring and implementing the product at considerable expense and effort. Can we critique a given product before it is implemented to predict its potential for effectiveness, efficiency, and engagement? Can we determine in advance the degree to which a given instructional product implements First Principles of Instruction? A primary purpose of this book is to enable you to use First Principles of Instruction to evaluate existing instruction to determine the extent to which it implements these principles and to estimate its potential for producing e^3 learning of the desired goals. This chapter brings together the concepts and strategies previously presented into tools for critiquing existing instruction. These tools, the *Course Critique Checklists,* consist of questions to evaluate the presence and adequacy of prescribed instructional events for teaching individual component skills and whole problems.

COMPONENT SKILL CHECKLISTS

Chapter 5 described different strategies for teaching different types of component skills. The first tools presented in this chapter are a series of checklists that are used to critique the component skills of a course as to their implementation of these primary instructional strategies.

Questions in the checklists are organized in a matrix (See Tables 10-1 through 10-12). The demonstration row (*Tell, Show, Multimedia, Guidance, >3*) corresponds to the Demonstration Principle. The application row (Do_{id}, Do_{ex}, *Feedback, Coaching, >3*) corresponds to the Application Principle. A Do_{id} application requires learners to recognize a new correct instance; a Do_{ex} application requires learners to carry out a step, make a prediction, or solve a problem. An information-about strategy does not involve showing an instance so the demonstration row is labeled presentation and the *Do* requires only remembering rather than application so the application row is labeled practice. For the part-of strategy there is only one level of *Do* that requires learners to locate the part on the whole. For a kind-of strategy there is also only one level of *Do*; a Do_{id} interaction requires learners to identify a new instance. For a how-to strategy a Do_{id} interaction requires learners to identify a new instance of a step and a Do_{ex} interaction requires learners to actually execute the step. For a what-happens strategy a Do_{id} interaction requires learners to identify a new instance of a condition and the consequence and a Do_{ex} interaction requires learners to predict a consequence or find faulted conditions.

The questions corresponding to each of the cells in this course critique matrix differ for each of the different types of component skill. Tables 10-1, 10-3, 10-5, 10-8, and 10-11 are the checklist questions for evaluating the prescribed instructional events for each type of component skill: information-about, part-of, kind-of, how-to, and what-happens.

Information-About: Famous Presidents

Table 10-1 Information-About Strategy Checklist

	Tell	*Show*	**Multimedia**	**Guide**	**>3**
Presentation	Does the presentation tell learners the name and information?	No show is required.	Does the presentation use effective Multimedia Principles?	Does the presentation focus attention?	Does the presentation provide repetition?
	Do		**Feedback**	**Coach**	**>3**
Practice	Does the practice require learners to immediately remember the name and information with complete mastery?		Does the practice provide corrective feedback?	Does the practice avoid sequence cues?	Does the practice require learners to practice several times?

Consider the Famous Presidents course shown in Figure 5-1. Table 10-2 is a summary critique that corresponds to the questions in Table 10-1. A summary critique is a chart that indicates the presence or absence of prescribed instructional events in a given instructional module. The plus (+) sign represents a positive response and the minus (–) sign represents a negative response to the questions in the Information-About Checklist. Let's consider each question. *Tell* is positive; Row 2 of Table 5-1 presents a name (George Washington), information ("elected unanimously," served, a fact about his presidency), and a picture (information). The picture is merely another form of information. Multimedia is positive since the information is presented adjacent to the name. Guidance is positive since there is little or no distracting information and in the actual course only the information in Row 1 is shown to the learner. And >3 is positive since learners were encouraged to repeat the presentations until they could name all the presidents shown.

Do is positive, as shown in Rows 3, 4, and 5 of Figure 5-1 that required learners to identify one piece of the information given the name or another piece. Feedback is positive since learners were told the correct answer after they responded. Coaching is positive since each president was presented one by one without sequence cues. Repeated practice is encouraged so >3 is marked positive. This is a very good example of information-about instruction.

Table 10-2 Summary Critique for Figure 5-1—Famous Presidents

	T	S	M	G	>	
Presentation	+		+	+	+	**4 of 4**
	D		**F**	**C**	>	
Practice	+		+	+	+	**4 of 4**

Part-of: Utah Counties

Table 10-3 Part-of Strategy Checklist

	Tell	*Show*	**Multimedia**	**Guide**	>3
Demonstration	Does the demonstration tell learners the name and information for each part?	Does the demonstration show learners the location of each part?	Does the demonstration use effective Multimedia Principles?	Does the demonstration use chunking and avoid location cues?	Does the demonstration provide for repetition?
	Do		**Feedback**	**Coach**	>3
Application	Does the application require learners immediately remember the name, information, and location associated with each part with complete mastery?		Does the application provide corrective feedback?	Does the application use random order and avoid location cues?	Does the application require learners to identify each part several times?

Consider the module on Utah Counties in Figure 5-2. Table 10-4 is my critique of this module. Let's consider each question. Row 1 is the presentation, so *Tell* is positive. The location of the county under consideration is shown, so *Show* is positive. The map of the state with the counties shown is a good representation of the whole and the picture illustrates one of the key characteristics of the county so Multimedia is positive. The module does avoid location clues but it does not use chunking so Guidance is negative. Learners are encouraged to repeat the presentation until they can remember every county so >3 is positive.

Table 10-4 Summary Critique for Figure 5-2—Utah Counties

	T	**S**	**M**	**G**	>	
Demonstration	+	+	+	–	+	**4 of 5**
	Do		**F**	**C**	>	
Application	+		+	+	+	**4 of 4**

Rows 2 and 3 illustrate four different kinds of practice for each combination of information with the name and/or location of the county. So *Do* is positive. There is corrective feedback providing learners with the correct information after they respond, so Feedback is positive. The counties appear in random order during practice and there are no location cues, so Coaching is positive. And learners are encouraged to practice until their performance has no errors so >3 is positive. This is a very good example of effective part-of instruction.

Kind-of: Rule of Thirds

Table 10-5 is the Kind-of Strategy Checklist—a set of questions to evaluate the instructional events for teaching concepts. The following paragraphs will demonstrate the use of this checklist to evaluate kind-of instructional strategies.

Table 10-5 Kind-of Strategy Checklist

	Tell	*Show*	Multimedia	Guide	>3
Demonstration	Does the demonstration tell learners the name and properties of each category?	Does the demonstration show learners examples of each category?	Does the demonstration use effective Multimedia Principles?	Does the demonstration provide guidance by highlighting discriminating properties or by showing matched examples among categories?	Does the demonstration include at least three examples from each category?
	Do_{id}		Feedback	Coach	>3
Application	Does the application require learners to classify new examples and non-examples?		Does the application provide corrective feedback that focuses learners' attention on discriminating properties?	Does the application provide coaching early in the sequence and gradually withdraw this coaching as the application continues?	Does the application require learners to classify a series of three or more divergent examples?

Consider the Rule of Thirds photography lesson previously shown in Figure 5-4. Table 10-6 is a summary critique that corresponds to the questions in Table 10-5. Let's consider each question. *Tell* is positive; Row 1 of Figure 5-4 provides a definition of the *rule of thirds.* The key property is the location of the focal point of the photograph on one of the cross points of the lines that divide the photograph into thirds. *Show* is positive; the second, third, and fourth rows in Figure 5-4 present examples and matched non-examples. Multimedia is positive since the photographs are all clearly relevant to illustrate the property being taught. Guidance is positive since there are several forms of guidance, including the grid to show the focal point; a divergent set of examples, including individual people, groups of people, and scenery; each example matched with a non-example; and photographs for which determining the focal point is increasingly difficult. >3 is positive since there are four examples each matched to a non-example. An e^3 score can be determined by counting the number of yes answers (+) to the questions in each cell. The demonstration score is 5 out of 5.

Table 10-6 Summary Critique for Figure 5-4—Rule of Thirds

	T	S	M	G	>	
Demonstration	+	+	+	+	+	5 of 5
	D_{id}		F	C	>	
Application	+		+	+	+	4 of 4

Consider the application row of the Summary Critique in Table 10-6. Do_{id} is positive since there are multiple opportunities to identify the presence or absence of the rule of thirds in a number of different photographs (Rows 5 and 6 in Figure 5-4). Feedback is positive since learners can apply the grid to their responses, which provides corrective feedback showing why a response was correct or incorrect. Coaching is positive since learners could use the grid to help them on early examples in the practice. >3 is positive since there are eight opportunities for learners to apply their skill with a divergent set of instances including individuals, groups, and scenery (Rows 5 and 6 in Figure 5-4). The application score is 4 out of 4. This short segment receives a 9 of 9 rating for an e^3 rating of 100 percent. (I may have been a bit biased since I created this lesson ☺.)

Kind-of: Helping Relationship

Consider the *Helping Relationship* example in Figure 5-3. Table 10-7 is a summary critique for the module in Figure 5-3. A plus (+) represents a positive response and minus (–) represents a negative response to the questions in Table 10-5. Let's consider each question: The first row of Figure 5-3 states the definition and lists three properties: collaborative, trust, and potential for growth, so *Tell* is marked positive. The second and third rows in Figure 5-3 identify examples and non-examples of helping relationships, so *Show* is marked positive. However, the pictures don't really illustrate the properties, so Multimedia is marked negative. A video where the properties of the relationship could be observed would be a better representation of the examples. There is an attempt to provide both examples and non-examples, which is a form of guidance, so the guidance cell is marked positive. Even though the portrayal of the examples is weak, there are several examples so the >3 cell is marked positive.

Table 10-7 Summary Critique for Figure 5-3—Helping Relationship

	T	S	M	G	>	
Demonstration	+	+	–	+	+	4 of 5
	D_{id}		F	C	>	
Application	+		–	–	+	2 of 4

There is an attempt at application with several examples. However, there is no portrayal of these examples and observing the properties depends on the experience of the student. Nevertheless, we gave the designers the benefit of the doubt and marked Do_{id} positive. There is right/wrong feedback but this is not sufficient for e^3 instruction, which requires corrective feedback that provides an explanation of why a given response is correct or incorrect, so we marked feedback negative. There is no coaching provided, so a negative mark. There are four divergent examples, so we were generous and marked >3 positive. The total score for this instructional segment is 4 for demonstration and 2 for application for a total score of 6 of 9 for a 67 percent e^3 rating. As you can observe from this example, rating an existing course is far from an exact science. Different raters may differ in their judgment as to whether a given question should be answered yes or no. Nevertheless, the questions do provide the opportunity for a discussion about the properties of the course.

How-to: Spreadsheets

Table 10-8 is a How-to Strategy Checklist—a set of questions to evaluate the instructional events for teaching procedures. The following paragraphs will demonstrate how to apply this checklist to evaluate existing instruction.

Table 10-8 How-to Strategy Checklist

	Tell	*Show*	**Multimedia**	**Guide**	>3
Demonstration	Are the defining and ordering properties of each step described?	Is the execution of each step illustrated for a specific task?	Does the demonstration use effective Multimedia Principles?	Does the demonstration provide guidance by focusing attention on the execution of each step?	Is the procedure demonstrated in a progression of at least three increasingly difficult situations?
	Do_{id}	*Do_{ex}*	**Feedback**	**Coach**	>3
Application	Are learners required to identify new instances of each step?	Are learners required to execute each step?	Does the application provide intrinsic feedback?	Are tasks early in the progression coached and is this coaching gradually withdrawn for successive tasks in the progression?	Does the application require learners to do a simple to complex progression of at least three tasks?

Consider the spreadsheet example in Figure 5-6. Table 10-9 is a summary critique where a plus (+) represents a positive response and minus (–) represents a negative response to the questions in the How-to Checklist of Table 10-8. This short module uses a problem-centered approach where the spreadsheet commands are introduced in the context of a progression of increasingly difficult problems. A unique feature of this module is the amount of application required of the student. The first problem is primarily an interactive demonstration in which learners are given directions and then must carry out these directions in a live spreadsheet. There is also intrinsic feedback provided to enable learners to check if they executed the commands as they were directed. In the second problem, learners use the commands they have been taught and are taught some new commands. Each problem provides less guidance or coaching and allows learners to do more of the problem. In Problems 1, 2, and 3, learners are told the commands (steps) required and are also allowed to do these steps and see the consequence. *Tell, Show,* and Guidance are all marked positive. Multimedia is also marked positive since learners are actually using a live spreadsheet to execute the commands. Greater-than-3 is marked positive since learners are guided or coached through four of the five problems. The demonstration score is 5 of 5.

Table 10-9 Summary Critique for Figure 5-6—Spreadsheets

	T	S	M	G	>	SCORE
Demonstration	+	+	+	+	+	5 of 5
	D_{id}	D_{ex}	F	C	>	
Application	–	+	+	+	+	4 of 5

Learners are carefully guided or coached to do more and more of the each problem as they work their way through the progression of problems. Do_{ex} is marked positive since learners are executing the commands in an actual spreadsheet. Do_{id} is marked negative since learners are not asked to correct an existing spreadsheet. This might be a useful addition to this module, although the module is very effective without this addition. Each of the problems includes intrinsic feedback by providing a value for a cell to enable learners to check their work. If their value does not agree, then they know that there is a problem in one or more of their commands. Guidance and coaching are smoothly integrated so that guidance is provided for early problems and it morphs into coaching for the later problems in the sequence. Again there are a total of five problems. The first problem is clearly demonstration and the fifth problem is clearly application. The middle problems are a blend of demonstration and application. Hence we scored >3 positive for both demonstration and application. The total score for this module is a strong 9 of 10 for a 90 percent e^3 rating.

How-to: Coconut Leaf Weaving

Figure 10-1 is a section of a course on how to weave using coconut leaves. Table 10-10 is a summary critique that corresponds to the checklist for a how-to instructional strategy in Table 10-8. The plus (+) indicates a positive response to the checklist questions; the minus (–) indicates a negative response to the checklist questions. Let's consider each of these questions with regard to these instructional events. The text in each cell describes each of the eleven steps in the procedure; we marked *Tell* plus. The illustration in each of the cells shows the condition that should result from the completion of each step; we marked *Show* plus. The lesson makes effective use of relevant multimedia; we marked Multimedia plus. The text is adjacent to the illustration and the outcome for each step is illustrated. The course also included a short video demonstrating the procedure with commentary.

This video is not included in the figure. It provides another *Tell/Show* demonstration that allows learners to concentrate on the actions involved in the step as it is performed. That is better than having to read the description of these actions and then see the illustration of the outcome. The commentary in the video (not shown) provided guidance helping learners relate the steps to the action they needed to take to accomplish the step. With the video, the procedure is shown twice, once with still pictures and text and once with a video demonstration. An additional trial would increase the probability that learners would acquire the skill, so we did not give a positive response to the >3 question. The demonstration scored 4 out of 5.

FIGURE 10-1 How-to Skill—Coconut Leaf Weaving

Coconut Leaf Weaving
Instructions for fish weaving by coconut leaves

 **Step 1.** Find mature coconut leaves that are ready.	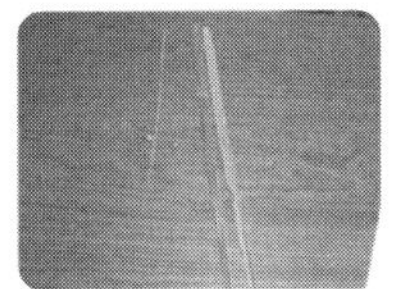 **Step 2.** Tear off the leaves along the line in the center of the coconut leaf into two strips. Then fold the strips in half.	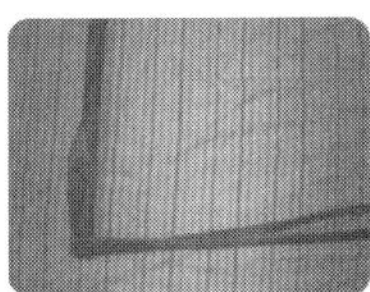 **Step 3.** Interlace the two strips of leaves so they are like the letter "L."	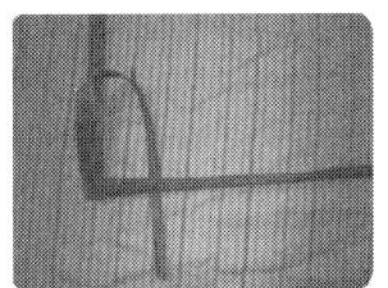 **Step 4.** Fold downward to form a loop.	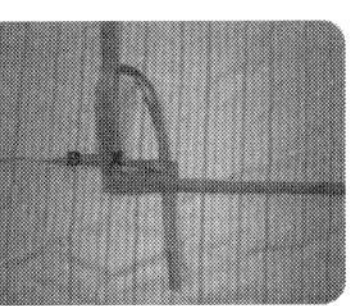 **Step 5.** Weave B across toward the left. Note that B goes over X and then under X (the usual over-and-under pattern).
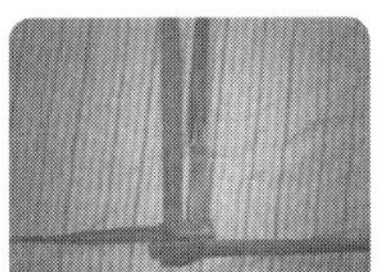 **Step 6.** Weave upwards by going over first leaf and under second leaf.	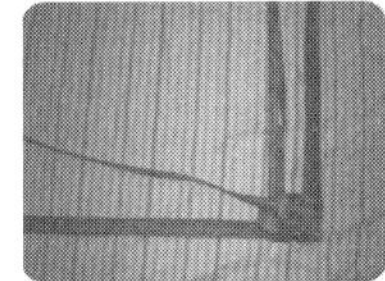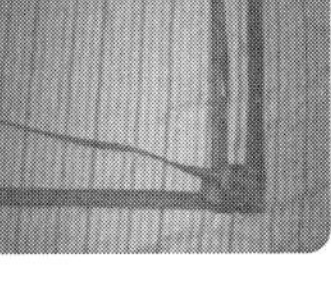 **Step 7.** Tighten the weave by pulling on each tail/edge of the leaves. **Step 8.** Turn over.	**Step 9.** Weave the incomplete left-sided leaf toward the right by going over first vertical leaf and under second vertical leaf. Notice again that this is the typical over-and-under pattern. Note also the checkboard pattern.	 **Step 10.** Tighten the weave by pulling on each side of the leaves.	 **Step 11.** Trim the tail and fins with scissors and you are done! You can string it up and use it as a decoration or make it into a mobile.
Play this video and pay attention to what was wrong. Select all that apply: a. 90-degree fold across b. Overlapping c. Separation of stem and leaves d. 90-degree fold up		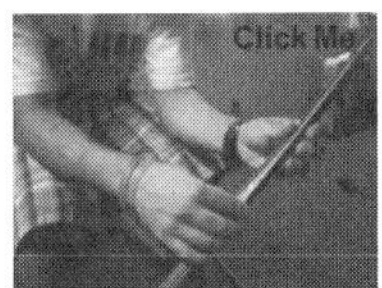	**Feedback:** After submitting their responses, learners could play a corrected demonstration video.	

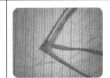

Student project, Brigham Young University–Hawaii, Garren Venzon and Jonathan Seng.

Table 10-10 Summary Critique for Figure 10-1—Leaf Weaving

	T	S	M	G	>	
Demonstration	+	+	+	+	–	4 of 5
	D_{id}	D_{ex}	F	C	>	
Application	+	–	–	–	–	1 of 5

Having learners watch someone perform the task and check to be sure that all of the steps are included and performed correctly is a D_{id} application and a prerequisite for having learners actually do the task. This instructional module included a Do_{id} application; we marked Do_{id} positive. This module does not include a Do_{ex} application. Learners will not acquire this skill unless they actually perform the steps using a Do_{ex} application. Can you think of a way to have learners perform this task even if the course is taught online? Playing a second corrected version of the procedure provides extrinsic correct-answer feedback to the student. Intrinsic feedback would follow from actually having learners perform the steps and observe to see whether their weaving matched the pictures shown, but this is not included in this module; Feedback is marked negative. The module does not include coaching; Coaching is marked negative. Reminding learners of each step as they attempt to perform the task with real leaves would be an appropriate type of coaching. This coaching could prompt every step during the first trial. During the second trial, this coaching would be reduced to help when the learner got stuck and didn't remember what to do next. During the third trial, learners would be left on their own to perform the task. This should be sufficient for most learners to acquire the coconut weaving skill. If some learners had more difficulty, the second level of coaching could be repeated for a third trial and the students then left on their own for a fourth trial. There is only a single Do_{id} application so >3 is marked negative. The application instructional events score 1 out of 5. This short course scored a total 5/10 for an e^3 percentage of 50 percent.

How could these how-to instructional events be improved? The following additions would increase the e^3 quality of this short course: (1) add a third demonstration of the procedure in addition to the step-by-step and video. (2) Find a way to have learners actually perform the task by trying to do the coconut leaf weaving demonstrated. This would also provide intrinsic feedback as they compared their efforts with the pictures of the outcome of each step. (3) Find a way to have learners perform the task at least three times with different leaves. (4) Find a way to provide coaching to learners as they perform the task the first time and then gradually reduce this help on subsequent trials.

What-Happens: Focal Length

Table 10-11 is a What-Happens Strategy Checklist—a set of questions to evaluate the instructional events for teaching processes. The following paragraphs will demonstrate the application of this checklist.

Table 10-11 What-Happens Strategy Checklist

	Tell	*Show*	Multimedia	Guide	>3
Demonstration	Does the demonstration tell learners the conditions and consequence of the process?	Does the demonstration show the process in a specific real or simulated situation?	Does the demonstration use effective Multimedia Principles?	Are the conditions and consequence clearly identified in the demonstration?	Is the demonstration of the process demonstrated in a progression of at least three increasingly complex scenarios?
	Do_{id}	*Do_{ex}*	Feedback	Coach	>3
Application	Are learners required to predict the consequence in a specific situation?	Are learners required to diagnose an unexpected consequence in a specific situation?	Are learners able to receive intrinsic feedback by being able to test their predictions or test their diagnosis?	Is coaching provided for problems early in the progression and gradually withdrawn as the progression continues?	Are learners required to predict or diagnose a series of at least three increasingly complex problems?

Figure 10-2 is a segment of a course on photography. The content for these instructional events is focal length in photography dealing with the condition of aperture and its effect on the consequence of focal length. Table 10-12 is a summary critique that corresponds to the What-Happens Checklist in Table 10-11. For the demonstration, the diagram illustrates the condition and the photograph illustrates the consequence for both a wide aperture and a small aperture. The *Tell, Show,* and Multimedia questions were answered positively. However, there is very little guidance; Guidance is marked negative. Guidance could be provided to highlight the properties of a given photograph that illustrates the effect of the aperture. There is only a single example so the >3 cell is negative.

Table 10-12 Summary Critique for Figure 10-2—Focal Length

	T	S	M	G	>	SCORE
Demonstration	+	+	+	–	–	3 of 5
	D_{id}	D_{ex}	F	C	>	
Application	–	+	+	–	-	2 of 5

FIGURE 10-2 What-Happens Skill—Focal Length

Photography: Focal Length—Aperture

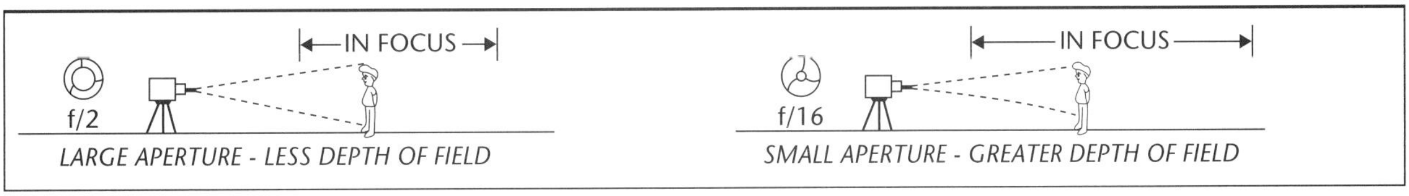

IN FOCUS
f/2
LARGE APERTURE - LESS DEPTH OF FIELD

IN FOCUS
f/16
SMALL APERTURE - GREATER DEPTH OF FIELD

(continued)

FIGURE 10-2 *Continued*

wide aperture

small aperture

Depth of field increases as you decrease aperture.

When making aperture smaller, your subject and background get sharper.

Choose the best f-stop to bring more of the train into focus.

f-16 f-5 f-2,0

Click on the best alternative.

The picture will change to show you the result.

What is the most likely f-stop used for this photograph?

f-2.0 f- 5.0 f-8 f-22

Click on your choice.

The picture will change to show you the result.

The first photograph in the application requires learners to predict an aperture to make a specified change in the photograph (Do_{ex}). The second photograph requires learners to identify the probable aperture (condition) that resulted in the photograph (Do_{ex}). Intrinsic feedback is provided in each of these Do_{ex} applications by allowing learners to see the consequence of each of the alternative conditions or change in conditions listed; Feedback is marked positive. There is little guidance or coaching in this module. The instruction could be improved by adding guidance to the presentation and coaching to the application and by including additional examples for both presentation and application. The total score for these instructional events is 5/10 or 50 percent.

WHOLE PROBLEM CRITIQUE

The demonstration of the course critique checklists thus far has illustrated their application to the critique of a single component skill or simple problem that involves only one type of skill. This section will apply the checklists to the evaluation of a course or module that attempts to teach a whole problem that consists of a number of different component skills.

Figure 10-3 is a design for a module in photographic exposure. The author states the purpose of this module is "developing a better understanding of how four specific variables [conditions] affect exposure and how they play a part in creating a beautiful image [consequence] under a variety of lighting conditions." The final task for the learners it to examine a series of photographs and determine what conditions contributed to the image or what conditions should have been modified to create a better image.

FIGURE 10-3 Whole Problem Module—Photographic Exposure

Photographic Exposure

1	**Definition:** Exposure is the total amount of light that passes through the lens and onto the medium of a camera. It is responsible for determining many of the characteristics of an image. The following slides give examples of some of the most important elements of controlling an image's exposure	
2	First, let's find out what you already know about exposure. Here is an example of an image many would consider well exposed. Using what you already know, what are some of the reasons this could be considered true? **Suggested Answer** The colors are bright and vivid. There is good contrast between the bright and dark portions of the image. The main subject is in focus, while the background is less so. This provides additional interest for the viewer. The butterfly seems to be stopped in mid-motion.	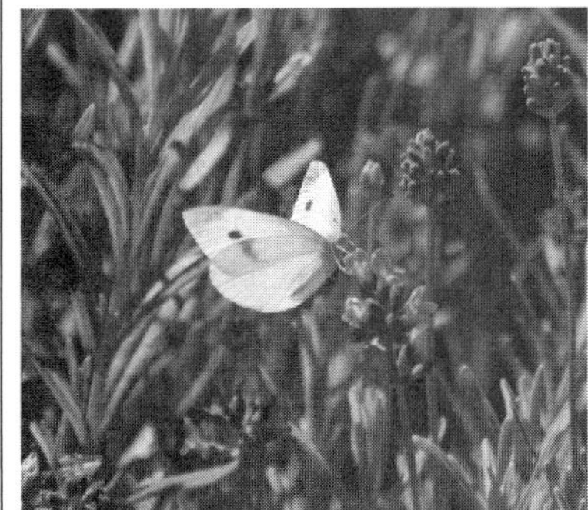
3	**The Four Elements of Exposure** When taking a picture of someone or something, there are many elements that combine to determine the quality of that picture. One of the most significant elements is the exposure. We will start first by developing a better understanding of how four specific variables affect the exposure and how they play a part in creating a beautiful image under a variety of lighting situations. They are 1. Aperture 2. Shutter Speed 3. ISO 4. White Balance	

(continued)

FIGURE 10-3 *Continued*

4	**Exposure Defined** **Aperture:** The opening in the lens that slows light to enter the camera. **Shutter Speed:** The mechanism in the camera that controls the amount of light allowed to reach the camera's sensor/film. **ISO:** A measurement of the relative light sensitivity of the camera's sensor. **White Balance:** The color of the light source as it will appear in the picture relative to pure white.
5	**Aperture** The aperture setting controls the amount of light that is able to strike the sensor by restricting or enlarging the size of an opening in the lens. The aperture also has an impact of what is called the depth of field in your photo. The depth of field is the range of distance in which the subject being photographed is focused sharply. In general, the smaller the aperture the more shallow your depth of field.
6	**The Effects of Aperture** Although the overall exposure between the two pictures of this gumball machine looks the same, there is one major difference between them. The picture on the left has a much larger aperture. This impacts the picture in the following ways: When the aperture is small it means the opening of the camera is small; therefore, it takes a longer time for the same amount of light to correctly expose the image (the larger the f-stop, the smaller the aperture). The background in the picture on the left is blurry compared to the one on the right. This is referred to as a shallow depth of field. A large aperture (the picture on the left) creates a more shallow depth of field. In this case the photos both look correctly exposed because I compensated for the larger aperture by slowing down the shutter speed.  **Aperture: f 5.6** **Shutter Speed: 1/16** **ISO: 100** **White Balance: Auto**  **Aperture: f 25** **Shutter Speed: 1.3 sec** **ISO: 100** **White Balance: Auto**
7	**Shutter Speed** Shutter speed adjusts the speed at which the shutter exposes the sensor. It can be adjusted to manipulate the amount of time that light is allowed to reach the sensor/film. In the example at the right, a fast shutter speed was used to create a stop action effect. The medium was only exposed to the image for a very brief amount of time, allowing the photographer to catch the movement of the surfer in a clear and focused moment, seemingly stopping him in mid-air. 

<table>
<tr><td></td><td colspan="2">In the example on the right, the shutter was left open for a longer amount of time, allowing the movement of the train to blur as it moved. This can be used to create a feeling of motion or time.</td><td></td></tr>
<tr><td>8</td><td>The Effects of Shutter Speed

In this example the picture on the left has the correct shutter speed for a correct exposure, showing all the color and detail of the plant.

With all else remaining constant, the picture on the right has a faster shutter speed. This results in a picture that is underexposed. To compensate for this, we could slow down the shutter speed or decrease the aperture.

However, remember that if we decreased the aperture, it would also affect our depth of field.</td><td>
Aperture: f 13
Shutter Speed: 1/40 sec
ISO: 100
White Balance: Auto</td><td>
Aperture: f 13
Shutter Speed: 1/250 sec
ISO: 100
White Balance: Auto</td></tr>
<tr><td>9</td><td colspan="3">ISO

Remember, ISO is the setting that adjusts the camera's sensitivity to light. In film cameras this was determined exclusively by the film being used. If you wanted to change the ISO of your pictures, you would have to change your film. Luckily, in digital cameras today, the ISO can be changed with a simple adjustment of the setting on your camera.

The main reason one would adjust the ISO is to increase the camera's ability to properly expose a photo in low-light situations.

A drawback to this is the effect it has on the quality of the image. Increasing the ISO too high can create "noise" or grain in your photo. This also makes pictures more difficult to enlarge, as this will only emphasize the grainy look.</td></tr>
<tr><td>10</td><td>The Effects of ISO

In this example, all things remaining equal, we see that the picture on the right is severely underexposed. However, this is not due to either shutter speed or aperture.

In this case you can see the ISO of the picture on the left was set to the maximum, while the one on the right is at the minimum.

Adjusting the ISO is easy enough, but there can be a price paid in the quality of the picture.</td><td>
Aperture: f 5.0
Shutter Speed: 1/10 sec
ISO: 1600
White Balance: Auto</td><td>
Aperture: f 5.0
Shutter Speed: 1/10 sec
ISO: 100
White Balance: Auto</td></tr>
</table>

(continued)

FIGURE 10-3 *Continued*

11	**White Balance** Believe it or not, there are many shades of white. At least that is how your camera will see it. Right is a powerful example of how many shades of white there are. Adjusting your white balance can help your exposure to reflect the mood or feel of your picture in many ways.	 Automatic White Balance Daylight Shady Cloudy Fluorescent Incandescent Tungsten  
12	**The Effects of White Balance** The color white can change dramatically, depending in large measure on the color of the light illuminating it. Here we see a good example of this variation. In order to compensate for this variation, most digital cameras have a white balance setting. In this case we see a white phone that changes color four times as a result of four different settings. The only factor that truly changed was the way I told the camera to see the white. The setting for each photograph is indicated. These pictures were taken in a room lit mostly by natural sunlight, so the first picture (auto) and fourth picture (natural light) are the most correctly exposed. All other settings Aperture – f 5.0 Shutter speed – 1/12 sec ISO – 400	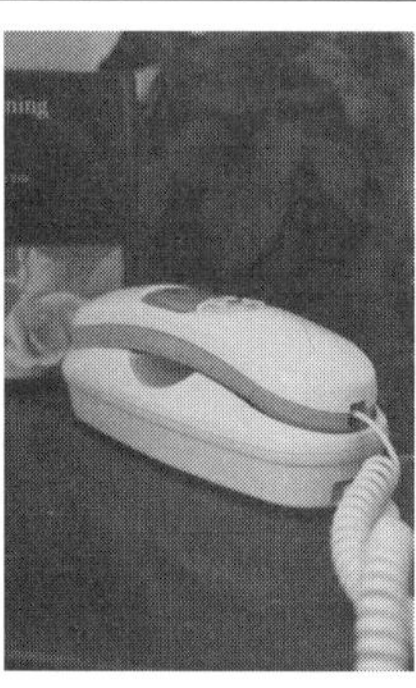  Auto 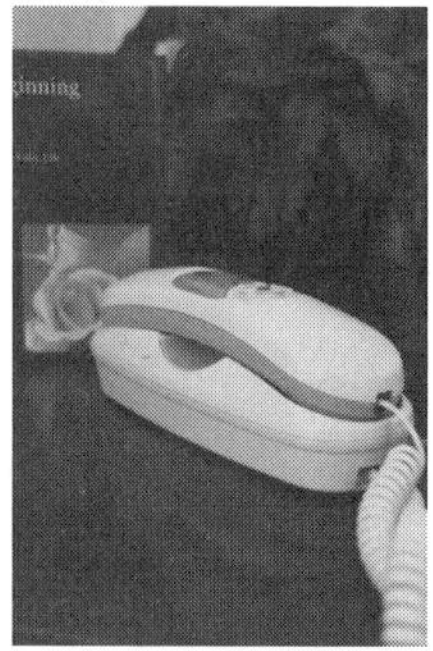 Fluorescent 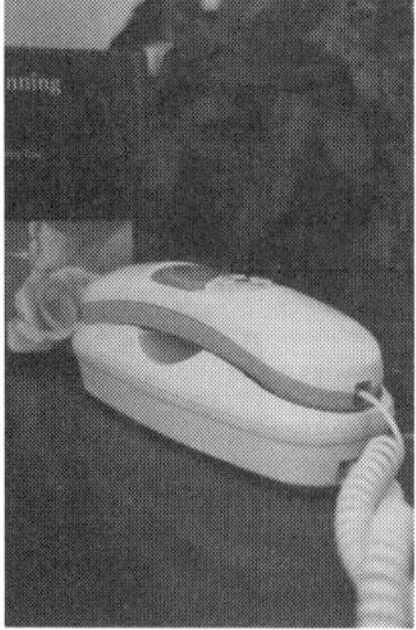 Tungsten 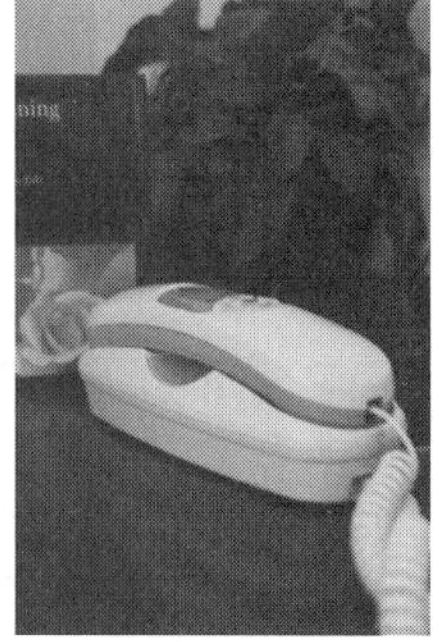 Natural light

Unfortunately, white balance affects color, so the above gray-scale photographs fail to show the difference in color produced by different white balance settings. In the actual course, these images are in color and clearly show the effect of adjustments to white balance.

<table>
<tr><td>13</td><td>Practice

Now that you have been given the specifics on the four elements of exposure, let's do some practice.

In the following slides you will be presented a series of photographs. Read the scenario and then either suggest what setting adjustments would improve the exposure or determine which setting could have been used to create the effect shown.

First read the description of what the photographer did or was trying to do, then write your answers. Once you have written your answers, you can check them by clicking on the button to view our answers.</td></tr>
<tr><td>14</td><td>This picture was taken in the middle of the day with plenty of sunshine and gives a good example of a "stop motion" technique. What exposure settings would you use to replicate this picture and eliminate blurring when the subject is moving quickly?

Suggested Answer

With lots of light in the middle of the day, the stop action technique is not hard to achieve; just increase your shutter speed to something above 1/250 sec.

Adjust the ISO to the lowest possible setting (around 100). This allows the quality of the picture to be as high as possible.

Aperture may need to be slightly larger than normal to compensate for the fast shutter speed.

White balance can almost always be left on auto when outdoors.</td></tr>
<tr><td>15</td><td>Jill has a vase of flowers on her nightstand. She wants to take a picture of them before they die so she will never forget the wonderful way in which her husband surprised her. She would love to frame this picture to a 16x20 poster size but is frustrated with her poor exposure. What adjustments could she make to correct the exposure and show all the pretty colors of her flowers?

Suggested Answer

Jill could move her vase of flowers to a place where there is more light.

She could slow down the shutter speed to allow the camera's sensor more time to pick up more light; however, she may need a tripod to ensure she doesn't take a blurry picture.

She could increase the aperture, allowing more light to come through the lenses. This would reduce her depth of field, leaving some of the flowers at the back of the vase more out of focus (this may or may not be a desired effect).

It would not be a good idea to increase the ISO, as this would reduce the quality of her photo and thwart her plans to enlarge and frame the picture.</td></tr>
</table>

(continued)

FIGURE 10-3 *Continued*

<table>
<tr><td>16</td><td>While I was hiking I came across this beautiful stream and wanted to capture the flowing water in a way that gave life to the motion of the stream. When I looked at my picture I was thrilled to see that, while the branches that framed my photo were clear and sharply focused, I was able to show this soft, silky effect on the waves of the water. What settings would you use to achieve this? (Hint: you will need a tripod).

Suggested Answer
Put your ISO on the lowest available setting (normally 100).
Aperture should be set high to allow the depth of field to keep both the river and the branches in focus.
Slow your shutter speed WAY down. (This is where the tripod comes in.) I would recommend taking several shots at 1, 5, and 10 sec. It's hard to tell which setting will give you the best results, as all streams flow differently.
White balance would remain on Auto.</td></tr>
<tr><td>17</td><td>I was trying to take a stunning picture of this beautiful sunset scene. I wanted to ensure I could see the mountains and the green field, but I found that if I exposed the sun correctly the foreground was too dark and if I exposed the foreground correctly the sun was overexposed. What can I do here?

Suggested Answer
This is a very tricky scenario because of the problem described above. One thing many photographers will do is make a choice. Which do I want to see more, the beautiful red sky or the way it affects the foreground, and then sacrifice one or the other.
Another consideration for this picture could have been to wait until the sun was completely behind the mountain. This reduces the chance of overexposing significantly.
Last, you could adjust your white balance to a cloudy or shady preset (if available). This helps your camera expose the sunlight more accurately</td></tr>
<tr><td>18</td><td>Congratulations
You have finished the exposure tutorial.
Great job and may you always have great light.</td></tr>
</table>

Student project, Utah State University, Micah Murdock.

Remember from Chapter 6 (see Figure 6-7) that a whole problem consists of a series of problem-solving-events, each consisting of a step that leads to a condition. The conditions lead to a consequence, which is the solution to the problem. The condition in each problem-solving event is characterized by a set of properties, and the step in each problem-solving event is also characterized by a set of properties. The analysis of instruction for teaching problem solving is easier if you first identify the content elements for the problem-solving events involved. The drawing in Figure 6-7 is useful to show the relationships, but for analysis it is more convenient to merely use a table to represent these content elements of a whole problem. Table 10-13 is a process event analysis of the photographic exposure module in Figure 10-3.

Table 10-13 Content Elements for Whole Problem—Photographic Exposure

Condition properties	Aperture f-stop	Shutter speed	ISO film speed	White balance	Depth of field Good contrast Clear picture Vivid color
Conditions	Depth of field	Blur Contrast	Picture grain	Picture color	WELL-EXPOSED PHOTOGRAPH
Steps	Adjust aperture	Adjust shutter speed	Adjust ISO	Adjust white balance	
Step properties					

The shaded cells represent the four conditions, called variables, in the module that lead to the consequence of a well-exposed photograph. The properties for each of these conditions are identified in the top row of the table. The steps necessary to modify these properties to create an appropriate condition are identified in the third row of the table. I have inferred these steps from the module because the instruction does not explicitly state these steps. Since there is no instruction as to how to adjust aperture, shutter speed, ISO, or white balance, I have left the step properties row blank. I will make some suggestions for what might have been included to make this instruction more complete at the conclusion of my analysis of this module.

Having identified the content elements included in the course, the next step in my whole problem analysis is to identify the instructional events that implement the prescribed instructional events for a whole problem instructional strategy. Table 6-2 listed the prescribed instructional events for teaching a whole problem. Table 10-14 represents these prescribed instructional events in a matrix form. The first set of instructional events in teaching a whole problem is to demonstrate an instance of the problem for the learners. This demonstration consists of showing the execution of each of the steps, showing the condition resulting from each step, and showing the consequence that follows from the conditions. These instructional events are represented by the *Show-Steps*, *Show-Conditions*, and *Show-Consequence* cells in the matrix. To critique an instructional module, I will first write the number of each instructional event in the cell that corresponds to a prescribed instructional event. If there is no implementation for one or more of the prescribed instructional events, then the cell is left blank. The next four columns (G, M, >, S) are for indicating whether these *Show* events include Guidance (G), relevant Multimedia (M), several portrayals of the problem (>), and the use of a structural framework (S). If the Guidance and Multimedia for an instructional event are appropriate, I will put a plus (+) in the cell; if either is missing or inappropriate I will leave the cell blank. For the >3 attribute I will write the number of portrayals that have been demonstrated in the > cell.

Table 10-14 Course Critique Checklist for Whole Problem

	Tell	*Show*	G	M	>	S	*Do*$_{id}$	*Do*$_{ex}$	C	F	>	P	Score
Problem:													
Steps (S)													
Conditions (C)													
Consequence (Q)													
Component Skill 1 =													
Condition													
Step													
Component Skill 2 =													
Condition													
Step													
Component Skill 3 =													
Condition													
Step													
Component Skill 4 =													
Condition													
Step													
Component Skill 5 =													
Condition													
Step													
Total Score													
Comments:													

After an instance of the problem has been demonstrated for the learner, the next phase of problem-solving instruction is to teach each of the component skills. Each component skill or problem-solving event has two primary components: a step and a condition that results from the execution of the step. The prescribed instructional events for teaching each component skill are represented by the cells in the matrix following each component skill. There is a *Tell-and-Show* event for the component and a *Tell-and-Show* event for the step. I will write the identification number for instructional events that implement these prescribed instructional events in the corresponding cell in the matrix. I will indicate appropriate Guidance and Multimedia with a plus in the corresponding cells. I will write the number of portrayals used in the >3 cell. The structural framework cell (S) is appropriate only for the whole problem.

There are two levels of *Do* for these component skill instructional events. Do_{id} indicates that learners are required to identify a previously unencountered instance of either a step or a condition. Do_{ex} indicates that learners are required to execute a step. There is no Do_{ex} prescribed event for conditions, as indicated by the shaded cell. The peer-interaction cell (P) is shaded to indicate that this applies only to the solution of the whole problem.

After the component skills have been taught, learners are expected to execute the steps to solve the problem. The Do_{id} and Do_{ex} cells for this application are on the right side of the first section of the table under the Problem heading. For solving a whole problem, there are two levels of *Do:* Do_{id} is when learners are able to identify the steps, the conditions, and the consequence in a new instance of the problem; Do_{ex} is when learners are able to execute the steps, identify an appropriate condition resulting from each step, and identify an appropriate consequence resulting from the conditions. The next four columns (C, F, >, P) are for indicating if these *Do* events include coaching (C), appropriate feedback (F), several instances of the problem for learners to solve (>), and whether the problem-solving activity involves learners in peer-collaboration or peer-critique (P).

For whole problems, the use of a structural framework facilitates the learning. The S column is used to indicate whether a structural framework was provided and if it was related to the steps, conditions, and consequence of the problem. The acquisition of problem-solving skills is facilitated if learners have an opportunity to interact with one another through peer-collaboration and peer-critique. The P column is used to indicate whether peer-interaction was provided. Structural frameworks and peer-interaction are appropriate for instruction related to the whole problem, so there is only one cell for each of these instructional activities. In the following paragraphs I will demonstrate how these columns are used for the photographic exposure module.

Table 10-15 is my critique of the photographic exposure module. You should carefully study the program and my analysis. Did you associate the instructional events in the program with the same prescribed instructional events that I did, as indicated by the instructional event numbers entered into the Course Critique Form? Note the many blank cells. What does this indicate?

What does my critique of this module show? If you study the critique form you will immediately notice that many of the cells are empty, meaning that there were no instructional events in the module that implemented these prescribed instructional events. What are my recommendations for a revision of this module?

First consider the instructional events for the whole problem. Instructional event 2 does show an example of a well-exposed photograph, which is the consequence of solving this problem. The accompanying suggested answer to the question does list some of the properties of this photograph that make it a good example of a well-exposed photograph. However, the demonstration of the whole problem stops with this one portrayal. The following recommendations would significantly improve this problem demonstration: (1) Show several examples of well-exposed photographs. (2) For each, isolate and show the individual conditions that make each a good example. How could this be done? Include multiple examples of each portrayal. Match examples with different apertures to the final photo to show why the aperture chosen is the best for this composition. Match examples with different ISO setting to the final photo to show why the ISO setting is the best for this composition. Match examples with different shutter speeds to the final photo to show why the shutter speed is the best for this composition. Each of these matched examples would isolate and show the individual conditions that make up the final photograph.

Table 10-15 Course Critique Checklist for Photographic Exposure

Program: Photograph Exposure
Author: Micah Murdock
Evaluator: Dave Merrill
Date: 3/25/2011

	Tell	*Show*	G	M	>	S	Do_{id}	Do_{ex}	C	F	>	P	**Score**
Problem = Well-Exposed Photograph													
Steps (S)													
Conditions (C)								14–17		+	4		3/11
Consequence (Q)		2	+	+	1								3/11
Component Skill 1 = Aperture													
Condition	4 5	6	+	+	1								4/9
Step													
Component Skill 2 = Shutter Speed													
Condition	4 7	8	+	+	3								5/9
Step													
Component Skill 3 = ISO													
Condition	4 9	10	+	+	1								4/9
Step													
Component Skill 4 = White Balance													
Condition	4 11	12	+	+	2								4/9
Step													
Total Score													
Comments:													

(3) Appropriate Do_{id} application would also improve the course. After having seen several examples with the conditions leading to the consequence clearly indicated, then it might be well to show learners sets of photographs and have them identify those that are well exposed and those that are not. This is not the same as having them execute a Do_{ex} application, as is done in events 14 through 17, where they are actually trying to identify which conditions were not met. A Do_{id} application would merely have them identify well-exposed photographs, whereas a Do_{ex} application would have them identify the conditions that contributed to or failed to contribute to the quality of the photograph.

(4) The author of this module did not intend to teach the steps necessary to take a well-exposed photograph; this decision is certainly acceptable. However, if the whole problem is to teach how to take such a well-exposed photograph, then the module would need to have instruction about how to set a camera to obtain the settings described. A complete demonstration would show a location for a photograph; have the photographer explain the effect he wanted to achieve; show how to set aperture, shutter speed, ISO, and white balance; take the photo; and then show the consequence.

(5) The demonstration for each of the condition elements of the component skills is well done. As indicated by the Course Critique Checklist, except for shutter speed, each could benefit from more examples. However, the instruction for these individual component skills does not include application. The *Do* columns are conspicuously blank. What would comprise effective application for these component skills? For aperture, learners could be shown a set of photographs and indicate what likely aperture setting was used. The answers would not be exact predications of the f-stop used but rather broader categories such as small, medium, and large aperture. This could also be a place where learners can be taught that a large f-stop number, f-22, means a small aperture, whereas a small f-stop number, f-2.2, means a large aperture. A similar type of application could be designed for each of the component skills.

(6) If the problem was expanded to include taking a well-exposed photograph rather than merely identifying a well-exposed photograph, then the appropriate *Tell*, *Show*, Do_{id}, and Do_{ex} instruction for these steps could be added to the module.

What if I wanted a score for this instruction? How do I score a module for a whole problem? Since our designer did not intend to teach the steps, I will score only the instruction for identifying the conditions that lead to a well-exposed photograph. Scoring is a matter of counting the cells that are marked positive. For the whole problem demonstration, there is only one example of a well-exposed photograph (consequence); including some guidance (I was generous here) and a relevant graphic. There is no application for recognizing well-exposed photographs. There are eleven cells corresponding to consequence, not counting the structure and peer cells. Counting our entries gives three out of eleven possible for whole problem consequence. For *conditions*, there is good Do_{ex} application requiring learners to find which conditions contributed to the consequence in each of a set of four photographs. However, there is no demonstration of this activity in the *Show*, G, M, and > columns. Counting Do_{ex} with feedback and four instances gives a score of 3 of 11 for conditions. For this score we are not counting the steps row since the designer did not intend to include instruction for the steps. There is no use of a structural framework or any peer-interaction for this problem-solving activity. Excluding the steps row, there are 22 points possible. Combining the scores gives us 6 of 22 or a percentage score of 27 percent for the whole problem.

Next I will score the instruction for the component skills. For aperture, ISO, and white balance, since there is only one or two demonstration examples for each, the score for each is 4 of 9; for shutter speed, since there are three examples, the score is 5 of 9. Again ignoring steps, the average score for components is 17 of 36 or a percentage score of 47 percent. Combining the two averages, 27 percent + 40 percent divided by 2, gives us a percentage of 33.5 percent. This procedure for scoring weights the problem-solving component of the instruction as half of the score.

You will recognize that much instruction falls short of the ideal. You should also realize that instruction that includes all of the prescribed instructional strategies identified in this book would be very rich instruction and may be overkill, especially for very bright students. The purpose of these prescriptions is to show what is possible. Just as the designer of the photographic module decided for his purposes it was not necessary to teach the steps required for setting aperture, shutter speed, ISO, and white balance, in any given situation there may be good reasons not to include all of the prescribed instructional strategies.

PRINCIPLES AND PRESCRIPTIONS

This chapter provides checklists for each of five types of component skills and for critiquing a whole module or course. These checklists assume that you understand the material presented in Part I of this book and are merely a quick reminder of the prescriptions presented. These checklists provide rubrics for evaluating existing instruction or for evaluating your own instruction to determine how well it implements First Principles of Instruction.

Information-About Strategy Checklist

	Tell	*Show*	**Multimedia**	**Guide**	>3
Presentation	Does the presentation tell learners the name and information?	No show is required.	Does the presentation use effective Multimedia Principles?	Does the presentation focus attention?	Does the presentation provide repetition?
	Do		**Feedback**	**Coach**	>3
Practice	Does the practice require learners to immediately remember the name and information with complete mastery?		Does the practice provide right corrective feedback?	Does the practice avoid sequence cues?	Does the practice require learners to practice several times?

Part-of Strategy Checklist

	Tell	*Show*	Multimedia	Guide	>3
Demonstration	Does the demonstration tell learners the name and information for each part?	Does the demonstration show learners the location of each part?	Does the demonstration use effective Multimedia Principles?	Does the demonstration use chunking and avoid location cues?	Does the demonstration provide for repetition?
	Do		Feedback	Coach	>3
Application	Does the application require learners immediately remember the name, information and location associated with each part with complete mastery?		Does the application provide corrective feedback?	Does the application use random order and avoid location cues.	Does the application require learners to identify each part several times?

Kind-of Strategy Checklist

	Tell	*Show*	Multimedia	Guide	>3
Demonstration	Does the demonstration tell learners the name and properties of each category?	Does the demonstration show learners examples of each category?	Does the demonstration use effective Multimedia Principles?	Does the demonstration provide guidance by highlighting discriminating properties or by showing matched examples among categories?	Does the demonstration include at least three examples from each category?
	Do_{id}	*Do_{ex}*	Feedback	Coach	>3
Application	Does the application require learners to classify new examples and non-examples?	Are learners required to classify a divergent set of examples?	Does the application provide corrective feedback that focuses learners' attention on discriminating properties?	Does the application provide coaching early in the sequence and gradually withdraw this coaching as the application continues?	Does the application require learners to classify a series of three or more divergent examples?

How-to Strategy Checklist

	Tell	*Show*	Multimedia	Guide	>3
Demonstration	Are the defining and ordering properties of each step described?	Is the execution of each step illustrated for a specific task?	Does the demonstration use effective Multimedia Principles?	Does the demonstration provide guidance by focusing attention on the execution of each step?	Is the procedure demonstrated in a progression of at least three increasingly difficult situations?

	Do_{id}	Do_{ex}	Feedback	Coach	>3
Application	Are learners required to identify new instances of each step?	Are learners required to execute each step?	Does the application provide intrinsic feedback?	Are tasks early in the progression coached and is this coaching gradually withdrawn as for successive tasks in the progression?	Does the application require learners to do a simple to complex progression of at least three tasks?

What-Happens Strategy Checklist

	Tell	*Show*	Multimedia	Guide	>3
Demonstration	Does the demonstration tell learners the conditions and consequence of the process?	Does the demonstration show the process in a specific real or simulated situation?	Does the demonstration use effective Multimedia Principles?	Are the conditions and consequence clearly identified in the demonstration?	Is the demonstration of the process demonstrated in a progression of at least three increasingly complex scenarios?
	Do_{id}	Do_{ex}	Feedback	Coach	>3
Application	Are learners required to predict the consequence in a specific situation?	Are learners required to diagnose an unexpected consequence in a specific situation?	Are learners able to receive intrinsic feedback by being able to test their predictions or test their diagnosis?	Is coaching provided for problems early in the progression and gradually withdrawn as the progression continues?	Are learners required to predict or diagnose a series of at least three increasingly complex problems?

Course Critique Checklist for Whole Problem

	Tell	*Show*	G	M	>	S	Do_{id}	Do_{ex}	C	F	>	P	Score
Problem:													
Steps (S)													
Conditions (C)													
Consequence (Q)													
Component Skill 1 =													
Condition													
Step													
Component Skill 2 =													
Condition													
Step													
Component Skill 3 =													
Condition													
Step													
Component Skill 4 =													
Condition													
Step													
Component Skill 5 =													
Condition													
Step													
Total Score													
Comments:													

APPLICATION

Select several courses that you are taking, designing, or that you find on the Internet. Select several component skills from these courses. Apply the appropriate Component Skill Checklist to evaluate each course. Write up a set of recommendations for improving the instruction for each component skill.

Select a whole course. Determine whether it teaches problem solving. Determine the content elements for the problem-solving events in the course. Apply the Course Critique Checklist to identify the use of prescribed instructional events in the course. Write a set of recommendations for improving the course.

TO LEARN MORE

There are many available examples of criteria, rubrics, and standards for effective instruction. However, most are very high level and do not provide the detail that enables you to examine your instructional strategies in depth. For example, one site lists the following standard under instructional strategies: "A teacher understands and uses a variety of instructional strategies to encourage student development of critical thinking, problem solving, and performance skills" (Minneapolis Standards of Effective Instruction). Another site lists the following under instructional design: "Uses sound instructional design . . . uses logical presentation of material including: instructor guidance, demonstrations, feedback. . . ." (University of California, San Francisco). The e^3 Course Critique Checklist provides details for how to actually implement these standards. It is a good idea for you to look at some of these standards and compare them with the Course Critique Checklists provided in this chapter. I have not listed individual websites because they come and go so frequently that by the time you read this a given site may no longer be available. I have been most successful in locating relevant sites using the following search words: standards for online courses; standards for effective instruction.

An early version of the Course Critique Checklist was published in Merrill (2009a).

COMING NEXT

Part I of this book has demonstrated prescribed instructional strategies for teaching component skills and whole problems. Part II of this book demonstrates the Pebble-in-the-Pond model for instructional design. This model is designed to facilitate the design of modules and courses that implement First Principles of Instruction. Chapter 11 provides background for this new model by reviewing The Systematic Design of Instruction, perhaps the most popular model for designing instruction.

PART

II

DESIGNING E^3 INSTRUCTION

Part II describes the Pebble-in-the-Pond model for instructional design. This model facilitates the design of instruction that implements First Principles of Instruction. Figure II-1 illustrates the organization of the content for Part II of this book. Each ripple in this diagram represents an instructional design activity in this model and is elaborated in each chapter: Chapter 13 problem, Chapter 14 progression, Chapter 15 component skills, Chapter 16 enhance strategies, Chapter 17 finalize design, and Chapter 18 evaluation.

FIGURE II-1 The Pebble-in-the-Pond Model for Instructional Design

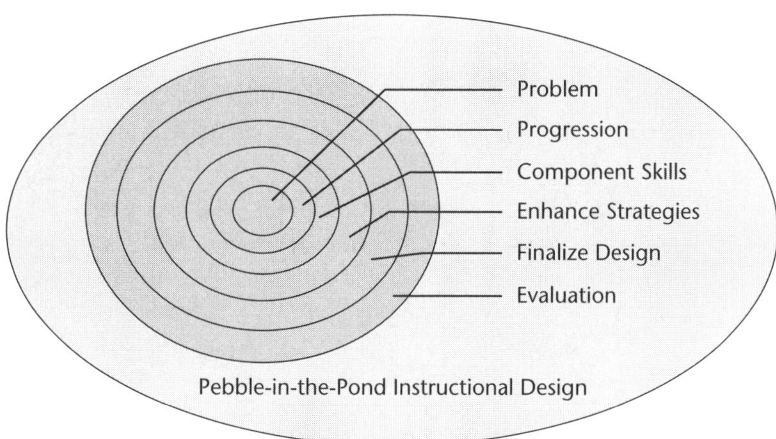

Chapter 11, A Pebble-in-the-Pond Model for Instructional Design. This chapter is an overview of the instructional design model that comprises Part II of this book. This chapter compares the Pebble model with a more traditional model of instructional systems design (ISD).

Chapter 12, Designing Functional Prototypes. (This chapter is not represented in the model). This chapter recommends that, instead of a design document, instructional design is more easily communicated by preparing a functional prototype. This chapter provides guidance for designing a functional prototype.

Chapter 13, Design a Problem Prototype. This chapter demonstrates how to start the design process by identifying a specific problem to be solved (the pebble) and designing a demonstration and application prototype for a portrayal of this problem.

Chapter 14, Design a Problem Progression. This chapter demonstrates how to identify the component skills required for a series of problem portrayals and how to arrange them in an increasingly complex progression.

Chapter 15, Design Strategies for Component Skills. This chapter demonstrates how to design instructional strategies for each of the component skills required to solve the portrayals of the problem and how to distribute the instructional events of these strategies across the progression of problem portrayals.

Chapter 16, Design Structural Framework and Peer-Interaction Strategy Enhancements. This chapter demonstrates how to add a structural framework and how to incorporate peer-interaction into your problem-solving instructional strategy.

Chapter 17, Finalize the Functional Prototype. This chapter demonstrates how to improve navigation within your prototype and how to add other features like a title page, menu, summary, and additional materials to enhance your instructional design.

Chapter 18, Design Assessment and Evaluation. This chapter demonstrates how to modify your functional prototype to enable you to collect and save learner performance data and how to use your functional prototype for formative evaluation of your course with a sample of learners from your target population.

Chapter 19, Pebble-in-the-Pond Instructional Design Checklist. This chapter is the culminating chapter for Part II and provides a checklist that you can use to guide and critique your instructional design efforts.

CHAPTER 11

A PEBBLE-IN-THE-POND MODEL FOR INSTRUCTIONAL DESIGN

Quick Look

This chapter begins with a brief overview of a common instructional systems development (ISD) model. It then provides an overview of the Pebble-in-the-Pond model for instructional design. It answers the following questions: What is the pebble that initiates the instructional design process? What are the phases or ripples of this model of instructional design? How do the instructional design activities of the Pebble model compare to similar activities in the common ISD model? What are the unique characteristics of the Pebble-in-the-Pond model?

Key Words

Principle-Oriented: instructional design that emphasizes the instructional design products (conditions) that lead to an e^3 learning consequence rather than the steps that bring about these conditions.

Content-First: instructional design that uses the actual content materials (portrayals) as the primary vehicles for design rather than descriptions of these materials (information).

Problem-Centered: instructional design that demonstrates and applies component skills in the context of problems to be solved rather than as a set of skills that will eventually be used to solve a problem toward the end of the instruction.

Prototyping: instructional design that develops a functional prototype as the primary design product rather than an abstract design specification.

INTRODUCTION

This chapter introduces the Pebble-in-the-Pond model for instructional design. In order to provide a context for the Pebble model, I first briefly review a popular model of instructional systems design (ISD). Pebble-in-the-Pond is not a substitute for ISD, but rather a modification that facilitates incorporating First Principles of Instruction into an instructional product.

The second section of this chapter provides an overview of the Pebble-in-the-Pond model of instructional design. As illustrated in Figure 11-2, the model involves the following design phases: (1) design a problem, (2) design a progression of problems, (3) design instruction for component skills, (4) design instructional strategy enhancements, (5) finalize the instructional design, and (6) design assessment and evaluation.

The final section of this chapter describes some unique properties of the Pebble-in-the-Pond model. (1) It is *principle-oriented*, that is, it emphasizes the instructional design products (conditions) that lead to an e^3 learning consequence rather than the steps that bring about these conditions. (2) It is a *content-first* approach, that is, the actual content materials are the primary vehicles for instructional design rather than descriptions of these materials. (3) It is *problem-centered*, that is, the instruction is demonstrated and applied in the context of problems to be solved rather than as a set of skills that will eventually be used to solve a problem toward the end of the instruction. (4) And finally, it is a *prototyping approach*, that is, a functional prototype of the instruction is the primary design product rather than an abstract design specification.

INSTRUCTIONAL SYSTEMS DESIGN (ISD)

Designing instruction is a problem solving task. Figure 11-1 uses the problem-solving event diagram from Chapter 6 to illustrate a popular model for the systematic design of instruction (Dick, Carey, & Carey, 2009). The boxes with the up-arrow point represent the steps in the instructional systems design procedure as identified by this model. Figure 11-1 separates the instructional product shown by the page symbols ▭ from the instructional design step that creates this product. The words listed above each instructional product are the primary properties of this instructional product. The arrows connecting the instructional products show that each is a condition for the following instructional product in the model, for example, a goal statement is a condition required to conduct an instructional analysis, which in turn is a condition for writing performance objectives. The large arrows show how the problem-solving events (step-condition-properties) relate to the major design phases of this **a**nalysis, **d**esign, **d**evelopment, **i**mplementation, and **e**valuation model (ADDIE). This ISD model presumes that, if an instructional designer executes each of the steps in the model, then the final instructional product will be a course that results in effective, efficient, and engaging learning. The summative evaluation report, which is the last instructional product in the model, should provide evidence for this e^3 consequence.

Formal instructional design has come under criticism for being too rigid, too time-consuming and too linear and for failing to produce instructional products that lead to the desired learning outcomes (Gordon & Zemke, 2000). There are many examples of when instructional designers seem to have followed the steps in the ISD process only to have the resulting instructional product fail to enable learners to perform the desired performance specified by the instructional goal. What accounts for this unexpected outcome? What really leads to the consequence of e^3 learning, the steps in the process or the conditions that result from these steps?

Perhaps one contribution to less than effective outcomes from ISD is a failure of many instructional design models to emphasize all of the elements of the problem-solving events required for effective problem solving. ISD is too often seen as a set of steps to be executed, with the assumption that the consequence will follow. However, in too many cases, executing the step does not necessarily result in an instructional product that is characterized by all of the necessary critical properties. Both instructional designers in training and instructors teaching ISD may fail to recognize this relationship. They teach the steps, but fail to teach novice instructional designers to identify whether or not the instructional product resulting from the step is adequate, that is, it has all of the necessary defining properties required if it is to lead to the desired learning consequence. Where appropriate, I will contrast the principles and prescriptions of the First Principles Pebble-in-the-Pond approach with this model of ISD.

FIGURE 11-1 Instructional Systems Design

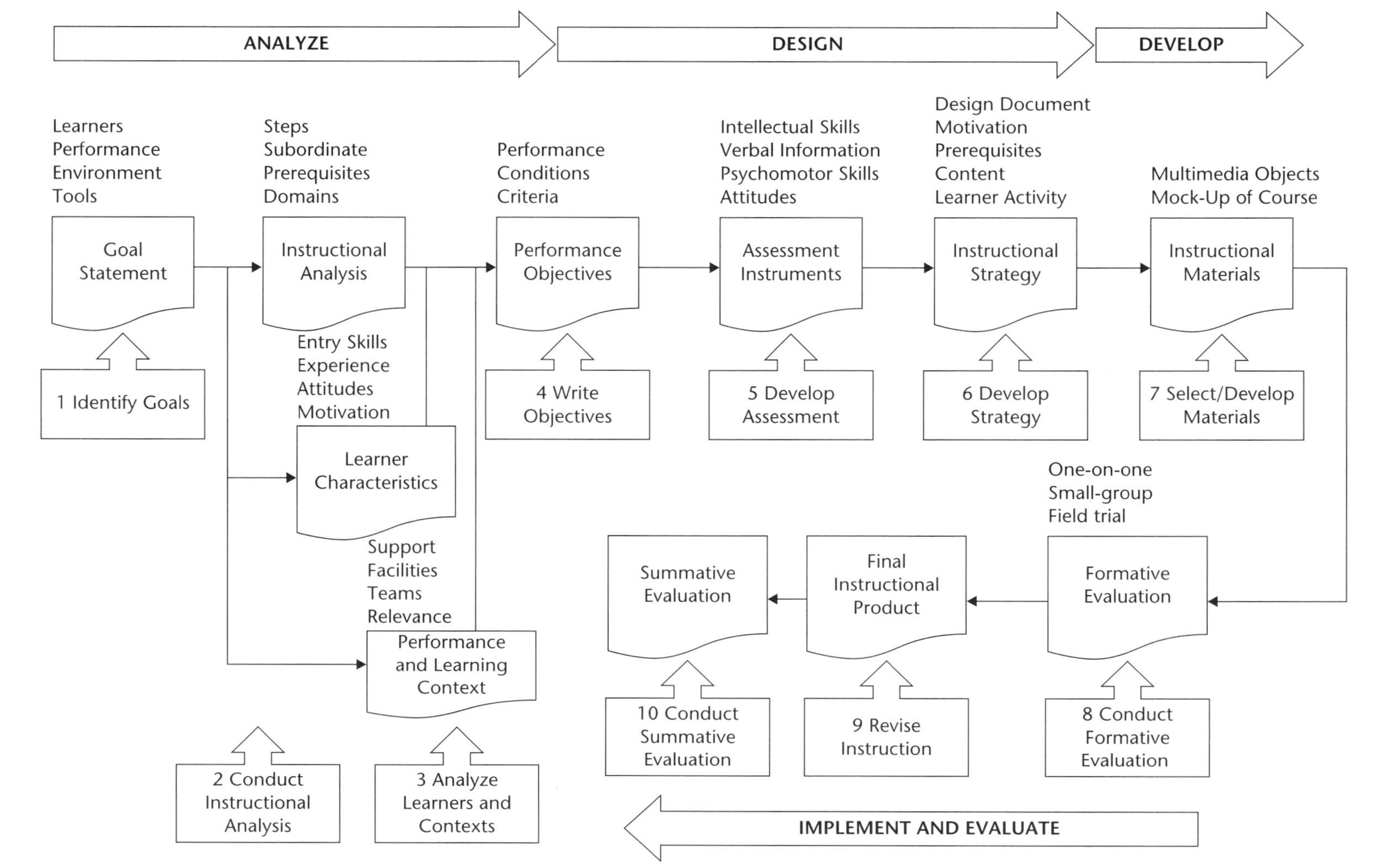

PEBBLE-IN-THE-POND

Figure 11-2 illustrates the primary products in the Pebble-in-the-Pond model for instructional design. The metaphor is an environmental pond in which instruction is to occur. The pebble is an instance of a problem that learners need to be able to solve in the context of the pond. The problem pebble thrown into the instructional pond is the trigger for the instructional design process. The instructional products comprising the first ripple are a prototype demonstration and application of this *problem.* The second ripple is a *progression* of problems of the same type. The instructional products comprising this second ripple are demonstrations or applications for each problem in the progression. The third ripple is the *component skills* required to solve this class of problems. The instructional products comprising this third ripple are demonstrations or applications for each of the component skills as they are taught in the context of the problems in the progression. The fourth ripple is *enhance strategies* and consists of structural framework and peer-interaction added to the problem demonstrations and applications. The fifth ripple is *finalize design* and includes the *final design* for the interface, navigation, and supplemental instructional materials. The sixth ripple is *evaluation* and contains data collection, formative *evaluation,* and prototype revision.

FIGURE 11-2 A Pebble-in-the-Pond Model for Instructional Design

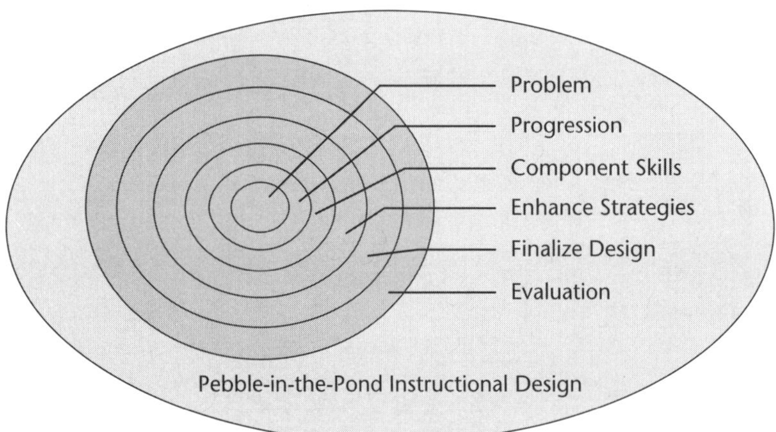

The Pebble-in-the-Pond model, as demonstrated in this book, is somewhat more constrained than the ISD procedure illustrated in Figure 11-1. The model as presented in this book focuses primarily on the instructional design phase of the whole instructional development process and emphasizes self-contained courses. Instructional development, as illustrated in Figure 11-1, includes some steps that are not included in the Pebble model as it is presented here. This does not imply that these steps are not important. The procedures for completing these steps are taught in other sources and the Pebble model has little to add to these already well-established procedures. The pond of the Pebble model assumes that some front-end analysis has already determined that there is a problem that can be solved by instruction rather than by some other means. It assumes that the content area and some form of instructional goal have been previously identified through front-end analysis or some other appropriate methodology. The procedures for making this determination are important, but beyond the scope of this book.

The Pebble model is a design rather than a development model. This means that the important steps of production, implementation, and summative evaluation are not considered in this book. The model does involve the development of a functional prototype, but does not include the final production of multimedia objects, packaging, and other production concerns. Other sources deal with these procedures, which are beyond the scope of this book. The Pebble model results in a functional prototype that can be used as the model on which the final production is based. Finally, implementation of a course in an organization is a complex process in its own right. The involvement of stakeholders and organizations in the implementation of a course is also beyond the scope of the present work. Summative evaluation of the course after it has been implemented involves concerns that have also been treated in other sources and are therefore not considered here. In short, the Pebble model starts with the existence of an instructional pond consisting of a problem that learners in this context need to learn to solve. The model starts with a previous identification of the context, the subject matter, the learning population, and some idea of the instructional goal. The model concludes with a functional prototype that serves as a specification for the production, implementation, and summative evaluation of the final version of the course.

A self-contained course is one that is not dependent on a live synchronous instructor. The examples in this book and the application exercises recommended suggest that the principles presented here be applied to self-contained courses. Why? Live instruction often hides considerable instructional design in the mind of the instructor. If you are designing a course for live presentation, it is possible and even desirable to leave some aspects of the course for extemporaneous design-on-the-fly. But it is difficult to examine strategy that is not public, that is contained in the personality of an instruction, and that is not explicitly specified. However, in spite of my reliance primarily on self-contained technology-based instruction as examples, the prescriptions of the Pebble model are just as applicable to live, instructor-led instruction as they are to self-contained, asynchronous instruction delivered via some mediated delivery system.

In the following sections I will elaborate each of the phases of the Pebble model: problem, progression, component skills, strategy enhancement, strategy finalization, and evaluation. For each of these phases I will identify the steps and conditions involved. The remaining chapters of Part II of this book will elaborate and illustrate these phases and the steps and conditions included in each phase of the model.

Design a Problem

Traditional ISD advocates the early specification of instructional objectives. The problem with this approach is that instructional objectives are abstract representations of the knowledge to be taught rather than the knowledge itself. Often the specification of the actual content is delayed until the development phase of ISD. Many designers have experienced the difficulty of writing meaningful objectives early in the design process. Often, after the development starts, the objectives written early in the process are abandoned or revised to more closely correspond with the content that is finally developed.

Pebble-in-the-Pond avoids this problem by starting with the content to be taught (the whole problem to be solved) rather than some abstract representation of this content (objectives). Pebble-in-the-Pond assumes that the designer has already identified an instructional goal (not detailed objectives) and a learner population. The first step, the pebble, is to specify an instance that represents the whole problem that learners will be able to solve following the instruction. The word, *specify*, indicates that a complete instance of the problem should be identified, not just some information about the problem. A complete instance of a problem includes the information that the learner is given and the transformation of this information that will result when the problem is solved. The best way to specify this instance of the problem is to design a demonstration showing in detail every step required to solve the problem. It is also desirable at this point to design an application that requires learners to solve the problem.

The example in the following pages is based on a design task completed by me and some of my former students in collaboration with a commercial training company. The design challenge was to revise their commercial course for teaching Excel. The existing approach was Simon-Says, in which every command in Excel was systematically taught one-by-one. The learning activities directed learners to execute each command in a simulated Excel spread sheet. The assessment was a large pool of questions, each asking learners how to execute a single or small combination of commands. Learners were never shown or asked to use these commands in the context of a whole Excel problem. Our challenge was to revise this course to more closely represent First Principles of Instruction and design a problem-centered approach. The first task was to find instances of the type of spreadsheet problems learners should be able to solve following instruction. Figure 11-3 illustrates a typical problem that we identified. We identified the information to be given to learners and the solution of the problem.

FIGURE 11-3 Identify the Problem

Excel Course

Susan has opened a small restaurant. She has been very successful and wants to expand her business. To finance this project, Susan needs a bank loan. She knows that an accurate and well-designed presentation will help her get the loan. You have agreed to prepare the last month's sales figures for Susan.

The first spreadsheet shows the information that Susan has recorded.

Microsoft Excel - Lunch Restaurant

File Edit View Insert Format Tools Data Window Help

Arial 10 B I U $ %

H14

	A	B	C	D
1	Total Lunch Earnings			
2				
3	Lunch Items	Units Sold	Unit Price	Gross Sales
4	Sandwiches	6000	3.25	
5	Mini Pizzas	5600	1.75	
6	Salad Bar	3900	3.25	
7	Soup	4100	1.25	
8	Desserts	3200	1.25	
9	Beverages	6100	0.75	
10	Total Sales			
11				
12				

The second spreadsheet shows the spreadsheet after you have organized it for Susan.

Microsoft Excel - Susan

File Edit View Insert Format Tools Data Window Hel

Arial 10 B I U $

H17

	A	B	C	D	E
1	**Total Lunch Earnings**				
2					
3	**Lunch Items**	**Units Sold**	**Unit Price**	**Gross Sales**	
4	*Sandwiches*	7200	$3.25	$23,400	
5	*Healthfood Salad Bar*	3900	$3.25	$12,675	
6	*Mini Pizzas*	5600	$1.75	$9,800	
7	*Soup*	4100	$1.25	$5,125	
8	*Beverages*	6100	$0.75	$4,575	
9	*Desserts*	3200	$1.25	$4,000	
10					
11	**Total Sales**			**$59,575**	
12					

Having identified the givens and the solution for the problem, the third part of specifying the problem is to design a demonstration showing how to solve this instance of the problem. Figure 11-4 is a portion of our demonstration of the problem solution. We implemented this using a Simon-says approach. The final step in problem specification was to use the same instance of the problem to design an application. Figure 11-5 illustrates this same instance of the problem as an application exercise.

FIGURE 11-4 Demonstrate the Problem Solution

Excel Spreadsheets

Step 1: Create the Gross Sales formulas.

1. Click Cell D6.
2. Type = B6*C6. Press Enter.
3. Click D6.
4. Copy the formula using Fill Handle from D6 to D7 through D11.

Step 2: Create the Total Sales formula.

1. Click D12.
2. Click the AutoSum button on the Standard toolbar.
3. Press Enter to accept the formula =SUM(D6:D11).

Etc.

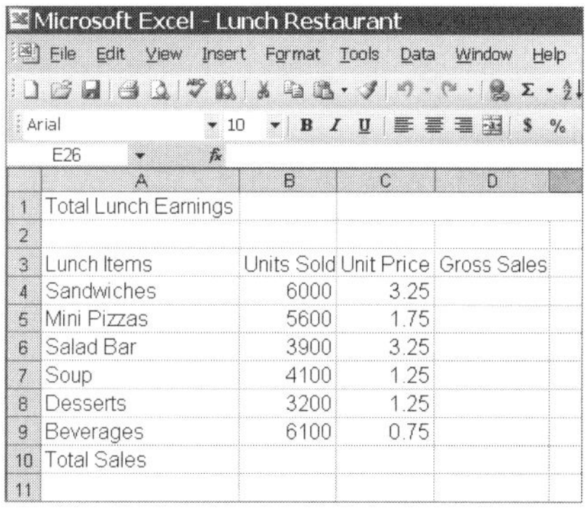

Microsoft Excel - Lunch Restaurant

File Edit View Insert Format Tools Data Window Help

Arial 10 B I U $ %

E26

	A	B	C	D
1	Total Lunch Earnings			
2				
3	Lunch Items	Units Sold	Unit Price	Gross Sales
4	Sandwiches	6000	3.25	
5	Mini Pizzas	5600	1.75	
6	Salad Bar	3900	3.25	
7	Soup	4100	1.25	
8	Desserts	3200	1.25	
9	Beverages	6100	0.75	
10	Total Sales			
11				

FIGURE 11-5 Problem Application

Excel Spreadsheets

Susan has opened a small restaurant. She has been very successful and wants to expand her business. To finance this project, Susan needs a bank loan. She knows that an accurate and well-designed presentation will help her get the loan. You have agreed to prepare the last month's sales figures for Susan.

Susan gives you the spreadsheet shown here. Revise this spreadsheet to make it a more informative and attractive presentation.

Do the following:

- Make key headings bold.
- Multiply each row under Gross Sales.
- Sum the Gross Sales to show Total Sales.
- Make Total Sales heading and total figure bold.

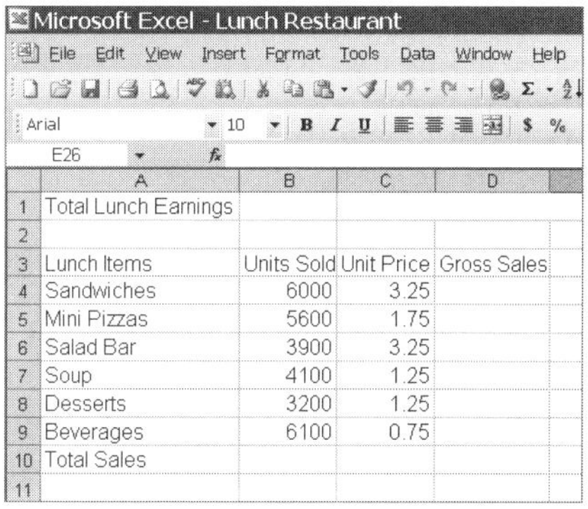

Microsoft Excel - Lunch Restaurant

File Edit View Insert Format Tools Data Window Help

Arial 10 B I U $ %

E26

	A	B	C	D
1	Total Lunch Earnings			
2				
3	Lunch Items	Units Sold	Unit Price	Gross Sales
4	Sandwiches	6000	3.25	
5	Mini Pizzas	5600	1.75	
6	Salad Bar	3900	3.25	
7	Soup	4100	1.25	
8	Desserts	3200	1.25	
9	Beverages	6100	0.75	
10	Total Sales			
11				

In summary, designing a problem includes the following instructional design activities:

- Identify the content area and primary goal of the instruction.
- Identify the learner population for the instruction.
- Identify a class of problems that, when solved, accomplish the learning goal.
- Design a prototype demonstration of the problem.
- Design a prototype application for the problem.

Design a Progression of Problems

Having specified a typical problem for the goals of the instruction, the next ripple in the pond is to specify a progression of problems that gradually increase in complexity, difficulty, or the number of component skills required to complete the task. Each problem in the progression should be completely specified including the givens, the solution, and the steps necessary to solve the problem. The component skills for each problem should then be identified. These component skills should be reviewed to be sure that, by solving each problem in the progression, learners will acquire all the intended knowledge and skill required by the instructional goals. If the problem progression does not include all the required knowledge and skill, additional problems should be added to the progression or the problems in the progression should be modified to require the necessary knowledge and skill.

In a problem-centered approach, the early problems in the progression should be demonstrated to learners. As the learner progresses from one problem to the next, the learner should be required to solve more and more of each problem in the sequence. The specification of the problems in the sequence is accomplished by designing a demonstration or application for each of the problems in the sequence. Design a demonstration for the first one or two problems; design a combination demonstration application for the next one or two problems; and design application for the remaining problems in the sequence.

Figure 11-6 indicates the first three problems for the Excel course. Each problem in this sequence is a bit more difficult than the previous problem. We considered a large number of possible problems, but finally settled on a progression of eight problems. We made a chart that listed under each problem those Excel commands that were required to complete the spreadsheet. These commands are the component skills. We reviewed these component skills to be sure that each was required at least three times. This enables it to be demonstrated when it is first required and then applied when required for later problems. We also reviewed these component skills to be sure that they represented a significant set of Excel commands.

FIGURE 11-6 Progression of Problems

Excel

Problem 1

Susan has opened a small restaurant. She has been very successful and wants to expand her business. To finance this project, Susan needs a bank loan. She knows that an accurate and well-designed presentation will help her get the loan. You have agreed to prepare the last month's sales figures for Susan.

Problem 2

Susan has given the Total Lunch Earnings worksheet to Isaac, one of her main suppliers, who has been successful in getting bank loans for his business. He is impressed with your work and offers three improvements. First, include a column that calculates percentage of sales. Second, add some nice borders and shading formats. Finally, set up the page to give the printout a professional appearance.

Problem 3

Susan expanded her business. Her restaurant is busier and she needs more staff. To judge her new staffing requirements accurately, Susan conducted a count of customers before and after the renovations. Each survey was taken over a four-week period. You have agreed to help Susan determine her new staffing levels by calculating statistics from her second survey.

We designed demonstrations for the first two problems in the sequence; we designed prompted applications for Problems 3 and 4 in the sequence; and we designed an unprompted application for the fifth problem in the sequence. Problems 6, 7, and 8 were used to assess learning. We designed unprompted application for each of these problems. Figure 11-7 shows the directions and some of the demonstration for Problems 1 and 2. In the instruction we called these demonstrations *worked examples.* Describing an interactive prototype of a course in the pages of a book necessitates a considerable abbreviation of the actual instruction. I hope the descriptions in the figures are sufficient for you to visualize the instructional events involved. Figure 11-8 shows the directions and some of the prompted application for Problems 3 and 4. We called these applications *prompted examples.* In this situation, the prompting consisted of a worked example of the problem that was available to learners after they had completed one try at completing the problem. If their final spreadsheet varied from the sample given after their response, then they could compare their response to the worked version of the problem. They were encouraged to modify their previous entries in the spreadsheet. Figure 11-9 illustrates the directions for the fifth application problem. Figure 11-10 illustrates the directions for the final three application problems, Problems 6, 7, and 8. We called these *authentic problems.*

FIGURE 11-7 Demonstration for Problems 1 and 2 in the Progression

<table>
<tr><th colspan="3">Excel Worked Examples—Problems 1 and 2</th></tr>
<tr><td>1</td><td>In this scenario, we will guide you through the process of steps to complete the worksheet.

Please follow the directions carefully.

Step 1: Create the Gross Sales formulas.
1. Click cell D6.
2. Type = B6*C6. Press Enter.
3. Click D6.
4. Copy the formula using Fill Handle from D6 to D7 through D11.
Step 2: Create the Total Sales formula.
1. Click D12.
2. Click the AutoSum button on the Standard toolbar.
3. Press Enter to accept the formula =SUM(D6:D11).
Etc.</td><td>Worked Example 1

Susan has opened a small restaurant. She has been very successful and wants to expand her business. To finance this project, Susan needs a bank loan. She knows that an accurate and well-designed presentation will help her get the loan. You have agreed to prepare the last month's sales figures for Susan. 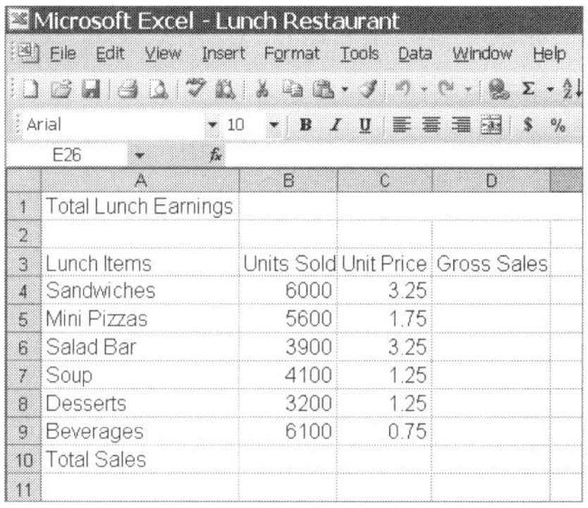

Microsoft Excel - Lunch Restaurant
File Edit View Insert Format Tools Data Window Help
Arial 10 B I U $ %
E26
<table><tr><th></th><th>A</th><th>B</th><th>C</th><th>D</th></tr><tr><td>1</td><td>Total Lunch Earnings</td><td></td><td></td><td></td></tr><tr><td>2</td><td></td><td></td><td></td><td></td></tr><tr><td>3</td><td>Lunch Items</td><td>Units Sold</td><td>Unit Price</td><td>Gross Sales</td></tr><tr><td>4</td><td>Sandwiches</td><td>6000</td><td>3.25</td><td></td></tr><tr><td>5</td><td>Mini Pizzas</td><td>5600</td><td>1.75</td><td></td></tr><tr><td>6</td><td>Salad Bar</td><td>3900</td><td>3.25</td><td></td></tr><tr><td>7</td><td>Soup</td><td>4100</td><td>1.25</td><td></td></tr><tr><td>8</td><td>Desserts</td><td>3200</td><td>1.25</td><td></td></tr><tr><td>9</td><td>Beverages</td><td>6100</td><td>0.75</td><td></td></tr><tr><td>10</td><td>Total Sales</td><td></td><td></td><td></td></tr><tr><td>11</td><td></td><td></td><td></td><td></td></tr></table></td></tr>
<tr><td>2</td><td>In this scenario we will guide you through the process of steps to complete the worksheet.

Please follow the directions carefully.

Step 1: Create percentage labels and formulas.
1. Type =D6/$D$13 in cell E6 and press Enter.
2. Etc.</td><td>Worked Example 2

Susan has given the Total Lunch Earnings worksheet to Isaac, one of her main suppliers, who has been successful in getting bank loans for his business. He is impressed with your work and offers three improvements. First, include a column that calculates percentage of sales. Second, add some nice borders and shading formats. Finally, set up the page to give the printout a professional appearance.

[Interactive Spreadsheet is included here.]</td></tr>
</table>

FIGURE 11-8 Prompted Applications for Problems 3 and 4 in the Progression

<table>
<tr><th colspan="3">Excel Prompted Examples—Problems 3 and 4</th></tr>
<tr><td>1</td><td colspan="2">In the previous scenarios, you were guided step-by-step in the application of the commands to complete the scenario. In this scenario, you will not be given this step-by-step guidance. You should first review the modules teaching the commands that you will need to complete this scenario. Then, you should try to complete each task in the scenarios on your own. If you need help, there is learner guidance provided at the end of the exercise for each of the tasks. You will learn more if you try to do the task before you look at this guidance material and use this guidance only when you are unable to perform the required commands. After each task, you will be shown an interim spreadsheet that you can use to compare with your own work. In this scenario, you will design a new worksheet.</td></tr>
<tr><td>2</td><td>Step 1:
• Enter your User ID in Cell D1.
• Create Income formulas in Cells B9, C9, and D9.
• Create Cost formulas in Cells B15, C15, and D15.
• Create Profit/Loss formulas in Cells B17, C17, and D17 for the Theater Final worksheet.</td><td>Prompted Example 4
[The scenario for the example is presented here.]
[The spreadsheet to be modified or the data to be used is presented here.]
[An interactive spreadsheet is provided for learners to modify.]</td></tr>
<tr><td>3</td><td>If you have completed Scenarios 1 and 2, you are familiar with creating formulas, since this information was covered. The detailed guidance for creating formulas in this exercise is provided at the end of the scenario in a section called Learner Guidance.
You should not simply type in the values. You need to apply the appropriate formulas. You have successfully created Income, Cost, and Profit/Loss formulas for the Theater Final worksheet. At this point, your worksheet should contain the following data.
If your worksheet does not look like the following worksheet, you may want to try again or go to the Learner Guidance section.</td><td>[Final worksheet is shown here.]</td></tr>
</table>

FIGURE 11-9 Unprompted Application for Problem 5 in the Progression

<table>
<tr><th colspan="3">Excel Unprompted Problem</th></tr>
<tr><td>1</td><td colspan="2">In this exercise, there is no Learner Guidance section. If your screens do not match the sample screens provided, you should return to the Excel course and review the appropriate modules.</td></tr>
<tr><td>2</td><td>Step 1: Enter your User ID in Cell D1. Add formulas to compute the totals in Column G and generate the expenses (with no decimals) in Row 18.
Step 2: Format the data. Use 12 pt bold for table headings. Add months as column headings.
Etc.</td><td>Unprompted Example
[Description of the problem appears here.]
[Data to be used appears here.]
[Interactive spreadsheet appears here.]
[After learners submit their spreadsheets, the correct form of the spreadsheet is shown for comparison.]</td></tr>
</table>

FIGURE 11-10 Application for Problems 6, 7, and 8 in the Progression

<table>
<tr><th colspan="2">Excel Authentic Problems</th></tr>
<tr><td>1</td><td>In this authentic task, you apply your knowledge of Microsoft Excel to redesigning a worksheet.</td></tr>
</table>

FIGURE 11-10 *Continued*

2	**Authentic Problem 6** Jake has returned from a holiday in France. He had set a budget for the vacation and wants to compare his actual and planned expenses. He is unsure of the correct exchange rate. You have agreed to work this out for Jake in return for a bottle of vintage French Chardonnay. Jake has given you the basic information on the following worksheet named **Holiday**. [Jake's data appears here.]	
3	You must create formulas and redesign the worksheet to make it look like the following example. Refer to the target screen on the previous page to ensure that the columns and rows in that example and your final screen are identical. • Insert a new row under Row 1. • Calculate the value of goods purchased in $ terms. • Calculate the variance of goods purchased in $ terms compared to the budget. • Calculate the totals for each of the four columns of numeric data. • Center and bold the title across the five main data columns and change the font size to 12 point. • Italicize the Items row labels. • Bold the Total row. • Bold all column labels, except for the Exchange Rate column label. • Right-align column labels over numeric data. • Format the numbers, except for the Exchange Rate value, with thousand separators, two decimal places, and red negative. • Create a double line border around all the data, except for the Exchange Rate data. • Shade the column labels—except for the exchange rate—with dark green background and white font. • Change the exchange rate to 6.685. Is the total variance better or worse? • Save the file with the name Finance Final.	[Interactive Worksheet appears here.]

In summary, designing a problem progression includes the following activities:

- Determine the component skills required to solve each of the problems in the sequence.
- Arrange a progression of problems from simple to complex such that all of the desired component skills are required to solve the problems in the sequence.
- Design prototype demonstration or application for each problem in the progression.

Design Instruction for Component Skills

The third ripple in the pond is to design prototype instruction for the component skills required to complete each of the tasks in the progression. In designing a progression of problems, it is necessary to consider the component skills that are required by each of the problems in the progression to be certain that all of these component skills are taught. One advantage of a progression of problems is that the component skills required for one problem in the progression are also required for subsequent problems. In this situation, it is possible to demonstrate the skill the first time it is taught and then to provide application for this skill on subsequent occasions. In this phase of the Pebble model, each of the component skills is carefully identified for each of the problems in the progression. This chart of skills is then examined to determine when a given skill is first taught. This occasion is then tagged for a demonstration of the skill. When the skill is required for a second instance of the problem, then the skill is tagged for application. The next activity in this ripple is to prepare a prototype demonstration and applications for each of the component skills, as determined by this analysis of their occurrence during the progression of problems.

In our Excel example, one component skill required for the first problem is to enter a formula into a cell to multiply the number in one cell with a number in another cell. Figure 11-11 again illustrates the demonstration of the first problem in the progression, but in this expanded demonstration, learners are branched to instruction that teaches the component skill for how to enter a formula into a spreadsheet and how to copy this formula to a series of cells. Figure 11-12 illustrates the instruction in this first component skill. The procedure for entering formulas into the spreadsheet is then demonstrated using a Simon-Says approach directing the learner in each step. A similar branch would be included for each new component skill learners encounter in this first problem.

FIGURE 11-11 Branching to Component Skill Instruction

Excel Spreadsheets

Step 1: Create the Gross Sales formulas.

To complete this step. it is necessary to enter a formula in the cells of Column D so that the spreadsheet will multiply the amount in Column B by the amount in Column C for each item on the list.

Click here to learn how to enter formulas for basic arithmetic operations into a spreadsheet.

[The learner is branched to the component skill instruction shown in Figure 11-12.]

Now that you have learned how to enter a formula to determine a sum for a row or column of numbers, let's modify the spreadsheet for Susan.

1. Click Cell D6.
2. Type = B6*C6. Press Enter.
3. Click D6.
4. Copy the formula using Fill Handle from D6 to D7 through D11.

Step 2: Create the Total Sales formula.

1. Click D12.
2. Click the AutoSum button on the standard toolbar.
3. Press Enter to accept the formula =SUM(D6:D11).

Etc.

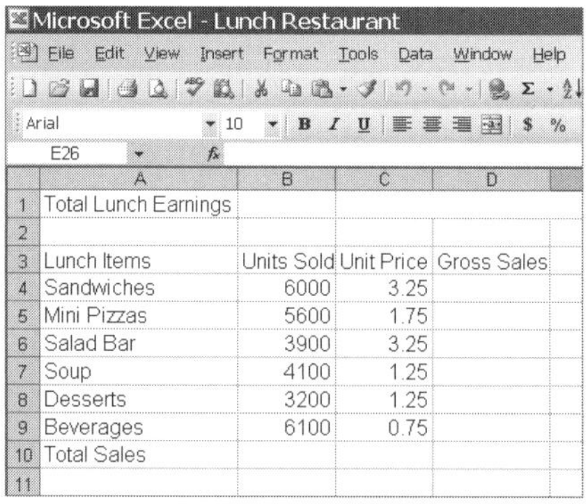

Microsoft Excel - Lunch Restaurant

File Edit View Insert Format Tools Data Window Help

Arial 10 B I U $ %

E26

	A	B	C	D
1	Total Lunch Earnings			
2				
3	Lunch Items	Units Sold	Unit Price	Gross Sales
4	Sandwiches	6000	3.25	
5	Mini Pizzas	5600	1.75	
6	Salad Bar	3900	3.25	
7	Soup	4100	1.25	
8	Desserts	3200	1.25	
9	Beverages	6100	0.75	
10	Total Sales			
11				

FIGURE 11-12 Component Skill Instruction for Entering Formulas

<table>
<tr><th colspan="3">Entering Formulas for Arithmetic Operations</th></tr>
<tr><td>1</td><td>One way to enter formulas in your worksheet is to manually type the actual formula in the cell. How do we add the number in A1 to the number in B1? Click on Cell C1. Type an = sign. Then click on Cell A1. Type a + sign. Then click on Cell B1. Then press Enter. Try it. The number in A1 will be added to the number in B1 and the sum will appear in C1. Did the number 77 appear in C1? If not, try again.

What happens? You have told the spreadsheet to add whatever number appears in A1 to whatever number appears in B1. Once you have entered the formula, if you change the number in A1, the sum in C1 will change as well. Try it.</td><td><table><tr><th></th><th>A</th><th>B</th><th>C</th></tr><tr><td>1</td><td>45</td><td>32</td><td></td></tr><tr><td>2</td><td></td><td></td><td></td></tr></table></td></tr>
<tr><td>2</td><td>Another way to sum numbers is to use a predefined mathematical function, in this case the word sum. Click in C2. Type sum(. Don't forget the parenthesis. Then click on A2; then click on B2. Then type) after the formula. Don't forget the parentheses. Press Enter. Did it work? Did the number 32 appear in C1? If not, try again.</td><td><table><tr><th></th><th>A</th><th>B</th><th>C</th></tr><tr><td>1</td><td>45</td><td>32</td><td>77</td></tr><tr><td>2</td><td>23</td><td>9</td><td></td></tr></table></td></tr>
<tr><td>3</td><td>You can add a column or row of several numbers the same way. Let's add the numbers in Column C with the total appearing in C5. Click in C5. Type the = sign. Then type sum(. Then click on A1 and drag the cursor across all the cells in Column C. Type the closing parenthesis. Press enter. Did it work? Did the number 167 appear in C5? If not, try again.</td><td><table><tr><th></th><th>A</th><th>B</th><th>C</th></tr><tr><td>1</td><td>45</td><td>32</td><td>77</td></tr><tr><td>2</td><td>23</td><td>9</td><td>32</td></tr><tr><td>3</td><td>12</td><td>14</td><td>26</td></tr><tr><td>4</td><td>21</td><td>11</td><td>32</td></tr><tr><td>5</td><td></td><td></td><td></td></tr></table></td></tr>
<tr><td>4</td><td>Now it is your turn. Add the numbers in each column and then add the sums in Row 5 with the total appearing in C5. Did it work? Your total in C5 should have been 237. Did it work? If not, press Reset and try again.</td><td><table><tr><th></th><th>A</th><th>B</th><th>C</th></tr><tr><td>1</td><td>10</td><td>20</td><td></td></tr><tr><td>2</td><td>35</td><td>15</td><td></td></tr><tr><td>3</td><td>57</td><td>40</td><td></td></tr><tr><td>4</td><td>35</td><td>25</td><td></td></tr><tr><td>5</td><td></td><td></td><td></td></tr></table></td></tr>
<tr><td>5</td><td>Entering formulas for other arithmetic operations is similar. The operators are as follows: add +, multiply *, divide /, and subtract –. A formula to multiply the numbers in two cells is =A1*B1; to subtract is =A1-B1; to multiply is =A1*B1; to divide is = A1/B1.

You try. First subtract the numbers in Column B from the numbers in Column A; then multiply the numbers in Column A by the numbers in Column B; and finally, divide the numbers in Column A by the numbers in Column B.</td><td><table><tr><th></th><th>A</th><th>B</th><th>C</th></tr><tr><td>1</td><td>10</td><td>7</td><td></td></tr><tr><td>2</td><td>35</td><td>15</td><td></td></tr><tr><td>3</td><td>57</td><td>40</td><td></td></tr><tr><td>4</td><td>35</td><td>25</td><td></td></tr><tr><td>5</td><td></td><td></td><td></td></tr></table></td></tr>
<tr><td>6</td><td colspan="2">The instruction continues here.</td></tr>
</table>

The second problem also requires learners to enter formulas into the spreadsheet. But in this problem there would not be a branch to the component skill instruction. Instead, learners would be expected to apply this component skill.

Demonstration and application instruction is designed in a similar manner for each of the skills in the component skill chart associated with the problems in the progression. The skill would be taught the first time it is encountered, but then learners would be expected to apply this skill when it is encountered for subsequent problems.

In summary, designing instruction for component skills includes the following activities:

- Based on the chart of component skills, design a demonstration for each component skill the first time it is required by a problem.
- Check to be sure that application of the component skill is required by at least two additional problems.

Design Instructional Strategy Enhancements

The result of the first three ripples in the Pebble model is a functional prototype of your course that includes a demonstration or application strategy for each of the problems in the progression and a demonstration or application strategy for each of the component skills required to solve these problems. The remaining ripples in the instructional design pond fine-tune these instructional strategies by enhancing their potential e^3 quality.

Structural Framework One form of enhancement is to provide a structural framework that can provide guidance during the problem demonstrations and coaching during the problem applications. A spreadsheet computer program is built on a structural framework. It is an electronic implementation of a paper-and-pencil device that has been used for centuries for keeping track of accounts and other forms of data. If students are familiar with paper spreadsheets, then this built-in structural framework already provides guidance for their efforts. But what about those learners who are not already familiar with paper spreadsheets? How can we provide a structural framework for them? One way is to take a problem with which they are probably familiar and demonstrate to them how a spreadsheet would facilitate their solution to this problem.

Figure 11-13 illustrates a presentation of a structural framework for the Excel course. This presentation introduces what is hoped is a familiar situation for the learner and describes how a spreadsheet can facilitate this situation. Figure 11-14 demonstrates how this structural framework, introduced at the beginning of the course, can be used for guidance for the demonstration of the first component skill of inserting formulas into the spreadsheet. Figure 11-15 demonstrates how this structural framework can be used for guidance in the solution of the first whole problem in the progression. Figure 11-16 demonstrates the same problem as an application and shows how the same structural framework information can be used to coach performance on a whole problem.

FIGURE 11-13 Structural Framework for Excel Course

<table>
<tr><th colspan="3">Spreadsheet Structural Framework</th></tr>
<tr><td>1</td><td>Are you familiar with a spreadsheet? A spreadsheet is a piece of graph paper that can be used to organize numbers such as expenses.</td><td></td></tr>
<tr><td>2</td><td>Suppose you are a college student. Your parents have agreed to help you with your expenses, but they have requested that you keep track of how much you spend. Your father requests an accounting at the end of every month. He suggests that you use the spreadsheet to the right to keep track of your expenses. He instructs you to put the date of expenditure in the left column and then write the amount in the column representing the category of the expense.

At the end of the month, he asks you to calculate the total of each category and then to put the total amount you spent in the lower right cell of the spreadsheet.</td><td><table>
<tr><th></th><th>Rent</th><th>Food</th><th>Car</th><th>Fun</th><th>Books</th><th>Misc.</th></tr>
<tr><td>2/4</td><td></td><td></td><td></td><td></td><td></td><td></td></tr>
<tr><td>2/7</td><td></td><td></td><td></td><td></td><td></td><td></td></tr>
<tr><td>2/14</td><td></td><td></td><td></td><td></td><td></td><td></td></tr>
<tr><td>Total</td><td></td><td></td><td></td><td></td><td></td><td></td></tr>
</table></td></tr>
<tr><td>3</td><td colspan="2">Excel is merely an electronic version of such a spreadsheet. Just like a paper spreadsheet, you can write words or numbers in the cells. But an electronic spreadsheet has an advantage. Instead of having to add up each column and write the total in the cell, you can put a formula in the cell for the total and it will automatically add up the numbers in the column. Then when you change an amount, the total automatically changes as well. With an electronic spreadsheet, you can use the same spreadsheet for each month. You merely save a copy, clear the numbers—but not the formulas—and use the sheet for the next month.</td></tr>
</table>

FIGURE 11-14 Guided Demonstration Using Structural Framework for Component Skills

<table>
<tr><th colspan="3">Entering Formulas for Arithmetic Operations</th></tr>
<tr><td>1</td><td>Remember the spreadsheet your father asked you to keep for your college expenses? The next few displays will show you how to enter a formula in an electronic version of this spreadsheet. But how do I tell the computer which number to enter into my formula? The electronic version of your college expenses has a row at the top identified by letters and a column to the left identified by numbers. The address or name of each cell in the spreadsheet is a combination of the letter and the number. Thus, the word "rent" is in Cell B1, the date 2/4 is in Cell A2, etc.</td><td><table>
<tr><th></th><th>A</th><th>B</th><th>C</th><th>D</th><th>E</th><th>F</th><th>G</th></tr>
<tr><td>1</td><td></td><td>Rent</td><td>Food</td><td>Car</td><td>Fun</td><td>Books</td><td>Misc</td></tr>
<tr><td>2</td><td>2/4</td><td></td><td></td><td></td><td></td><td></td><td></td></tr>
<tr><td>3</td><td>2/7</td><td></td><td></td><td></td><td></td><td></td><td></td></tr>
<tr><td>4</td><td>2/14</td><td></td><td></td><td></td><td></td><td></td><td></td></tr>
<tr><td>5</td><td>Total</td><td></td><td></td><td></td><td></td><td></td><td></td></tr>
</table></td></tr>
<tr><td>2</td><td>One way to enter formulas in your worksheet is to manually type the actual formula in the cell. Or you can learn a shortcut. How do we add the number in A1 to the number in B1? Click on Cell C1. Type an = sign. Then click on Cell A1. Type a + sign. Then click on Cell B1. Then press Enter. Try it. The number in A1 will be added to the number in B1 and the sum will appear in C1. Did the number 77 appear in C1? If not, try again.

What happens? You have told the spreadsheet to add whatever number appears in A1 to whatever number appears in B1. Once you have entered the formula, if you change the number in A1, the sum in C1 will change as well. Try it.</td><td><table>
<tr><th></th><th>A</th><th>B</th><th>C</th></tr>
<tr><td>1</td><td>45</td><td>32</td><td></td></tr>
<tr><td>2</td><td></td><td></td><td></td></tr>
</table></td></tr>
<tr><td colspan="3">[The demonstration and application for the first component skill continues here.]</td></tr>
</table>

FIGURE 11-15 Guided Demonstration Using Structural Framework for Problem

Excel Worked Examples—Problems 1 and 2

1

Remember your college spreadsheet. Does Susan's problem look familiar? In your college spreadsheet, you had to add numbers in each column and determine a total. In Susan's problem, you have to multiply the number of items sold by the price and then add up the total.

Susan has opened a small restaurant. She has been very successful and wants to expand her business. To finance this project, Susan needs a bank loan. She knows that an accurate and well-designed presentation will help her get the loan. You have agreed to prepare the last month's sales figures for Susan.

Microsoft Excel - Lunch Restaurant

File Edit View Insert Format Tools Data Window Help

Arial 10

E26

	A	B	C	D
1	Total Lunch Earnings			
2				
3	Lunch Items	Units Sold	Unit Price	Gross Sales
4	Sandwiches	6000	3.25	
5	Mini Pizzas	5600	1.75	
6	Salad Bar	3900	3.25	
7	Soup	4100	1.25	
8	Desserts	3200	1.25	
9	Beverages	6100	0.75	
10	Total Sales			
11				

2

In this scenario, we will guide you through the process of completing the worksheet.

Please follow the directions carefully.

Step 1: Create the Gross Sales formulas.

1. Click Cell D6.
2. Type = B6*C6. Press Enter.
3. Click D6.
4. Copy the formula using Fill Handle from D6 to D7 through D11.

Step 2: Create the Total Sales formula.

1. Click D12.
2. Click the AutoSum button on the Standard toolbar.
3. Press Enter to accept the formula =SUM(D6:D11).

Etc.

Worked Example 1

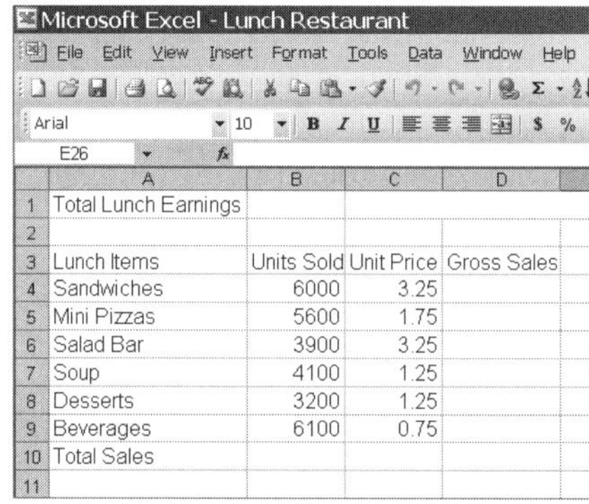

Microsoft Excel - Lunch Restaurant

File Edit View Insert Format Tools Data Window Help

Arial 10

E26

	A	B	C	D
1	Total Lunch Earnings			
2				
3	Lunch Items	Units Sold	Unit Price	Gross Sales
4	Sandwiches	6000	3.25	
5	Mini Pizzas	5600	1.75	
6	Salad Bar	3900	3.25	
7	Soup	4100	1.25	
8	Desserts	3200	1.25	
9	Beverages	6100	0.75	
10	Total Sales			
11				

FIGURE 11-16 Coached Problem Application Using Structural Framework

<table>
<tr><th colspan="3">Excel Spreadsheets</th></tr>
<tr><td>1</td><td>Remember your college spreadsheet. Does Susan's problem look familiar? In your college spreadsheet, you had to add numbers in each column and determine a total. In Susan's problem, you have to multiply the number of items sold by the price and then add up the total.</td><td>Susan has opened a small restaurant. She has been very successful and wants to expand her business. To finance this project, Susan needs a bank loan. She knows that an accurate and well-designed presentation will help her get the loan. You have agreed to prepare the last month's sales figures for Susan. 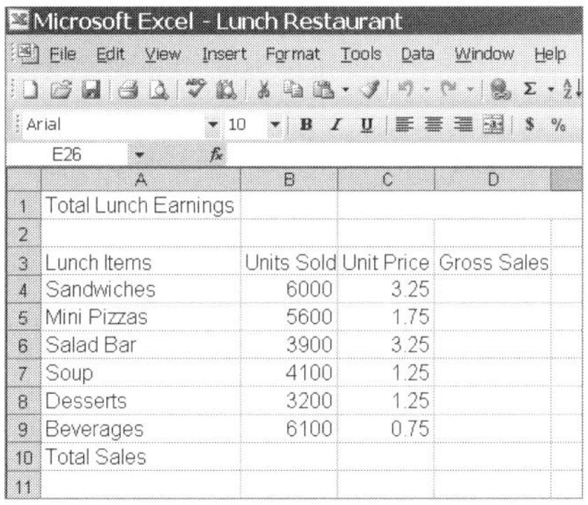
Microsoft Excel - Lunch Restaurant
File Edit View Insert Format Tools Data Window Help
Arial 10 B I U $ %
E26
<table>
<tr><th></th><th>A</th><th>B</th><th>C</th><th>D</th></tr>
<tr><td>1</td><td>Total Lunch Earnings</td><td></td><td></td><td></td></tr>
<tr><td>2</td><td></td><td></td><td></td><td></td></tr>
<tr><td>3</td><td>Lunch Items</td><td>Units Sold</td><td>Unit Price</td><td>Gross Sales</td></tr>
<tr><td>4</td><td>Sandwiches</td><td>6000</td><td>3.25</td><td></td></tr>
<tr><td>5</td><td>Mini Pizzas</td><td>5600</td><td>1.75</td><td></td></tr>
<tr><td>6</td><td>Salad Bar</td><td>3900</td><td>3.25</td><td></td></tr>
<tr><td>7</td><td>Soup</td><td>4100</td><td>1.25</td><td></td></tr>
<tr><td>8</td><td>Desserts</td><td>3200</td><td>1.25</td><td></td></tr>
<tr><td>9</td><td>Beverages</td><td>6100</td><td>0.75</td><td></td></tr>
<tr><td>10</td><td>Total Sales</td><td></td><td></td><td></td></tr>
<tr><td>11</td><td></td><td></td><td></td><td></td></tr>
</table>
</td></tr>
<tr><td>2</td><td>Susan gives you the spreadsheet shown here. Revise this spreadsheet to make it a more informative and attractive presentation.
Do the following:
• Make key headings bold.
• Multiply each row under Gross Sales.
• Sum the Gross Sales to show Total Sales.
• Make Total Sales heading and total figure bold.</td><td>Microsoft Excel - Lunch Restaurant
File Edit View Insert Format Tools Data Window Help
Arial 10 B I U $ %
E26
<table>
<tr><th></th><th>A</th><th>B</th><th>C</th><th>D</th></tr>
<tr><td>1</td><td>Total Lunch Earnings</td><td></td><td></td><td></td></tr>
<tr><td>2</td><td></td><td></td><td></td><td></td></tr>
<tr><td>3</td><td>Lunch Items</td><td>Units Sold</td><td>Unit Price</td><td>Gross Sales</td></tr>
<tr><td>4</td><td>Sandwiches</td><td>6000</td><td>3.25</td><td></td></tr>
<tr><td>5</td><td>Mini Pizzas</td><td>5600</td><td>1.75</td><td></td></tr>
<tr><td>6</td><td>Salad Bar</td><td>3900</td><td>3.25</td><td></td></tr>
<tr><td>7</td><td>Soup</td><td>4100</td><td>1.25</td><td></td></tr>
<tr><td>8</td><td>Desserts</td><td>3200</td><td>1.25</td><td></td></tr>
<tr><td>9</td><td>Beverages</td><td>6100</td><td>0.75</td><td></td></tr>
<tr><td>10</td><td>Total Sales</td><td></td><td></td><td></td></tr>
<tr><td>11</td><td></td><td></td><td></td><td></td></tr>
</table>
</td></tr>
</table>

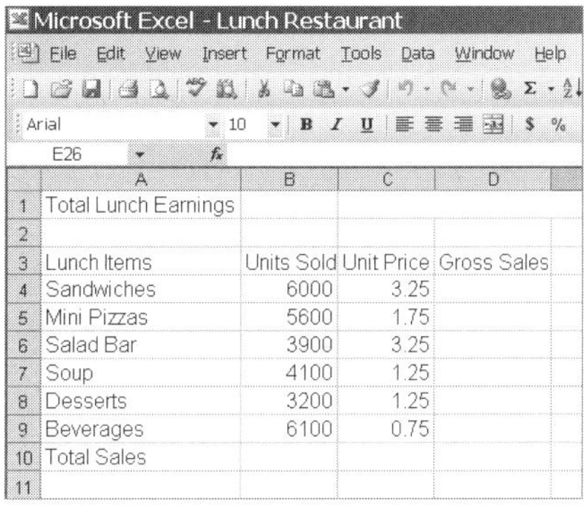

Peer-Interaction In the course we designed, learners worked alone to acquire the Excel skills taught in the course. Perhaps the instruction could be enhanced by providing an opportunity for learners to work together. In the course we designed, learners worked in a live version of Excel but, because the spreadsheets were scored by machine, it was necessary to provide considerable directions to ensure that learners were entering their formulas into the correct cells. A peer-collaboration situation might provide a better opportunity for learners to demonstrate their acquisition of the desired skills. For this collaboration, a small group of students would be given a set of data and directions for creating a spreadsheet to analyze and present this data. The problems would be less structured than those used in our course and perhaps a bit more challenging. Learners would still study the instruction in the progression of the first five problems, but would then be given the unprompted problems to solve as a group. In this situation, leaving the format more open would give learners a chance to provide different correct solutions to the problem. There are several possibilities for this collaboration. One alternative is to have a group of three students work together to come up with a single solution. A second form of collaboration would be for each student in a collaboration group to come up with his or her own solution and then present the solution to members of the collaboration group for critique. In this situation, there could be more than one correct solution to the problem because there are different ways to enter formulas that result in the same spreadsheet. A further enhancement might be to have another one or two students evaluate the solutions for accuracy and correct use of formulas, format, and so forth. This situation would likely require a live instructor to monitor the solutions and the work of the student critics.

In summary, designing structural framework enhancement includes the following instructional design activities:

- Design a structural framework.
- Design guidance based on this structural framework.
- Design coaching based on this structural framework.

Designing peer-interaction enhancement includes the following instructional design activities:

- Modify applications to facilitate peer-collaboration.
- Assign collaboration groups to collaborate and critique one another as they solve application problems.

Finalize Instructional Design

The next ripple in the Pebble model is to bring your prototype to a final form ready for evaluation, production, and implementation. Perhaps the first consideration at this point is to troubleshoot and bulletproof your navigation. Navigation includes the devices that enable a learner to move from one place in the instruction to another. Even with a great instructional strategy, nothing can kill motivation and interfere with learning more than ineffective navigation. Learners should be able to easily determine where they are in a course. They should be able to quickly return to an overall menu of the course. The navigation should be as clear as possible, with clear identification of what happens.

Depending on your artistic inclinations, you may have been working on an interface while developing strategies for problem and component skill demonstration and application. If your artistic inclinations are as limited as mine, you may have developed a utilitarian prototype that shows the strategy but leaves something to be desired for its aesthetic appeal. You have a functional prototype at this point; now is the time to consult with a graphic designer to develop an appealing interface for the product. You may want to encourage the graphic designer to add a mock-up of the graphic design to the prototype. Like the cover of a book, the interface of your product is what makes the first impression. If the interface is unappealing, then learners may undertake learning with less than a positive attitude about what's next. For the Excel course, the company had its own color scheme, layout for screen design, and previously established navigation procedure. This predesigned interface was then overlaid on our instructional strategies to provide the final course.

If you have developed a technology-based instructional product, it may be desirable to accompany it with supplemental material. This might include a user's guide; it might include off-line materials to supplement what is in the online course. For the Excel course, there were two major supplemental components. First, online mentors were provided for learners 24/7. When learners had a problem, either with the logistics of the course or with the content, they could phone a mentor. It was necessary to develop training materials for the mentors, not in the content area where they were already expert, but in procedures, to encourage learning so that they didn't just work the problems for the student. Second, based on our formative evaluation, we also developed a set of frequently asked questions that dealt with both the functioning of the course and some content questions. A link at the beginning of the course enabled learners to access this information whenever they felt it was necessary.

In summary, finalizing the instructional design includes the following activities:

- Finalize navigation.
- Finalize interface.
- Design supplemental materials.

Design Assessment and Evaluation

The final ripple in the Pebble model is to design appropriate data collection procedures, conduct a formative evaluation, and revise the prototype. Examine the application strategies to identify where learner responses actually demonstrate competency in a component skill or in problem solution. Adapt the prototype to enable you to collect this data. Conduct a tryout of your prototype. Use the data to revise your prototype and make it ready for production.

In our development effort, we were conducting research on the effectiveness of this problem-centered approach, so we were interested in a considerable amount of data. Consider Figure 11-12, Row 4. This instructional event requires learners to apply what they just learned to a new example of a spreadsheet. We collected two types of data from this exercise. When the learner exited the page or pressed the Reset button to try again, the system recorded the formula the learner placed in each cell in the C column. We were then able to compare what the learner placed in the column with the correct formula. The system also recorded how many times a learner tried to solve the problem before going on to the next display.

Consider Figure 11-8. The spreadsheet is not shown in our example, but we recorded the spreadsheet created by each student and were able to compare the formatting changes they made, the formulas they used, and other commands they were to have made to solve the problem with an acceptable version (or versions) of these items. We also recorded the time required to solve each problem.

This is also the ripple where questionnaires, interview forms, and other instruments should be designed to gather information to help you revise the prototype of the course. For course revision, these items may include questions about format, navigation, and interface. You may also want learners to identify areas where they felt confused either by the content or by the operation of the learning system. If you plan a one-on-one formative evaluation of your prototype, this is the time to begin to consider the questions you will ask as learners participate in your instruction. You may want to consider embedding some of these questions into the course itself.

Once you have adapted your prototype to enable you to collect performance data and have developed appropriate questionnaires soliciting learner attitudes about the course, you are ready to conduct a tryout of the prototype. The data from these individual and small group tryouts give you information about where there are problems in the course. The final step is to revise your prototype to overcome the problems you discover from this formative evaluation.

In summary, designing assessment and evaluation includes the following activities:

- Identify data sources.
- Modify the prototype to enable data collection.
- Design other evaluation instruments.
- Conduct formative evaluation.
- Revise prototype.

UNIQUE PROPERTIES OF PEBBLE-IN-THE-POND

In the following paragraphs I will briefly elaborate on the unique properties of the Pebble-in-the-Pond model, including principle-oriented, content-first, problem-centered, and designing a functional prototype.

Principle-Oriented

The instructional design approach illustrated in Figure 11-1, and most of the modifications of this approach, emphasize a series of steps that are supposed to result in an instructional product that is effective and efficient in accomplishing the goal of the instruction. The problem is not that the steps are the wrong steps, but rather that the emphasis is on the procedure rather than on the instructional design product that results from carrying out a step in the procedure. Designers must be taught not only to carry out the prescribed steps, but to observe the consequence of each step to be sure that it is characterized by the properties that define an effective instructional product. If a designer specifies a performance goal for a given step in the instructional analysis and this goal fails to adequately specify performance that is appropriate for that kind of learning or the conditions under which this performance should occur, then when using this objective to specify presentation or practice instructional events, it is likely that these events will also fail to implement all of the required properties for an effective or efficient demonstration, practice, or assessment. The steps in the instructional design procedure are not what lead to an e^3 learning consequence; rather, it is the products that these steps produce that are the conditions for the desired learning outcomes.

The Pebble-in-the-Pond model attempts to implement First Principles of Instruction. This book suggests recommended or prescribed steps that are thought to implement these principles and that have been found to lead to instructional products (conditions) that result in an e^3 learning consequence. In the pebble model these instructional products are a mock-up of the actual instruction, using multimedia or placeholders to create a functional prototype of the instruction rather than an abstract description. The Pebble approach is based on the properties for e^3 demonstrations and application prescribed in the first part of this book. If a demonstration instructional event fails to implement the prescribed properties for the type of learning involved, then the designer is encouraged to revise the prototype demonstration until it does implement the prescribed properties.

Content-First

The ISD model illustrated in Figure 11-1 commences with a number of steps that describe or specify the content to be presented. In Chapter 3 I differentiated information from a portrayal of that information. The early steps in the traditional ISD model are information-oriented rather than portrayal-oriented; they describe what is to be done rather than showing what is to be done. For example, a goal statement is information; it describes the problem that learners will be able to solve as a result of the instruction. A goal analysis is information; it describes the steps learners will have to execute and the subordinate skills learners must have in order to accomplish the goal. The performance objectives are information; they describe the performance associated with each step or subordinate skill. Even the instructional strategies are often represented as information; they are often merely descriptions of how learners will interact with the content.

A content-first approach designs with the portrayals of the content rather than with information about the content. The Pebble-in-the-Pond approach begins the design process with a portrayal of an instance of the problem learners will learn to solve. This problem is a portrayal of the goal to be accomplished, rather than an abstract description of the problem and its solution. An actual portrayal of the problem to be solved and a demonstration of its solution are far less ambiguous than an abstract description of the problem. The Pebble approach compresses steps in the ISD process by moving directly to the development of a functional prototype of the actual instructional strategy, subsuming goal analysis, performance objectives, and media selection into a combined instructional design activity. This prototyping approach leads to an interim instructional product that can be formatively evaluated and revised as the design proceeds, thus resulting in a more efficient design process.

Problem-Centered

The ISD model illustrated in Figure 11-1 prescribes a *cumulative content sequence.* A cumulative content sequence first teaches the subordinate skills for the first step in the goal analysis, and then the step that depends on these subordinate skills is taught. The sequence then proceeds to the next step in the goal analysis sequence until all of the subordinate skills and steps in the process have been presented. Finally, after all the steps required to accomplish the instructional goal have been taught, learners are required to use the skills in an integrated way to solve a problem or accomplish a complex task. This cumulative content sequence often suffers from several limitations. First, if the content is complex and there are a large number of subordinate skills or steps in the sequence, then it is possible that by the time learners are required to apply the skills, they may have already forgotten some of the skills acquired early in the sequence. Second, without a context for where a given skill will be used, its relevance may not be apparent to learners. Without an assurance of relevance, the motivation for learning the skill is reduced and effective learning hindered. Acquiring skills in a cumulative fashion brings to mind the teacher phrase we all learned to dread, "You won't understand this now, but later it will be really important to you!" This often is processed by the student to mean, "This is not important to me now because later I'll have to learn it again anyway."

The Pebble-in-the-Pond approach overcomes this problem by demonstrating an instance of the problem to be solved as one of the first learning activities in the sequence. Seeing a portrayal of an actual problem and a demonstration of its solution is far more easily understood by learners than an abstract statement describing the problem. The Pebble approach then demonstrates the component skills specifically required for this problem and demonstrates how each of these specific instances of each skill was used to solve the problem. Rather than an abstract objective stating what the learner will be able to do, learners are shown what they will be able to do with a concrete demonstration of an actual instance of the problem.

The content sequence in the Pebble model is not cumulative; it is problem-centered. The component skills are taught in the context of a progression of problems. After the first problem and its component skills are demonstrated, a second problem of the same type is shown to the learners. Learners are then required to apply the skills they learned for the first problem to this problem. If there are new component skills required for this problem, they are demonstrated to the learner in the context of this problem. This sequence of demonstrating and applying component skills is repeated until all of the component skills have been demonstrated multiple times and learners have had multiple opportunities to apply these skills to new instances of the problem.

In the Pebble design process therefore, rather than describing the goal and describing the problem, an actual instance of the problem to be solved is identified; a demonstration of this problem is designed and prototyped; and an application for this problem is designed and prototyped. In other words, in the Pebble approach the actual content to be learned is identified, demonstrated, and designed for application early in the instructional design process. The Pebble design approach is thus problem-centered.

Prototyping

The ISD model illustrated in Figure 11-1 produces a number of instructional design products as a result of carrying out the steps in the instructional design procedure described. As indicated, most of these instructional design products are abstract descriptions of the content and instructional strategy to be developed. The actual use of the content materials themselves or multimedia representations of this content do not take place until after the objectives, assessment, and instructional strategy have been described. Typically, this process produces an instructional design document. A significant problem with this approach is the number of translation errors that can occur when developing the actual instruction from the abstract design document. This is not so much a problem when a single designer carries out all of the steps of the process, but when a team of people is involved, it is frequently the case that the instructional strategies, as implemented, are often significantly different from the design envisioned by the designer who wrote the strategy specification. This translation problem results in misunderstandings and almost always delays the efficient development of the instruction. Critics have been quick to identify the long delays that result as a significant weakness of the ISD process.

The Pebble model attempts to overcome this problem by using actual materials or placeholders to develop a functional prototype of the strategies, interactions, and assessments. A *functional prototype* is a mock-up of the instructional strategy that includes actual content material, or placeholders for this material; that allows learner interaction with the instructional strategies and that approximates the learner interaction available in the final product. A functional prototype uses a development tool that allows rapid development, is easily modified, and can be used for formative evaluation with actual learners. Developing a functional prototype is incorporated as part of the Pebble-in-the-Pond model for instructional design (Allen, 2003).

PRINCIPLES AND PRESCRIPTIONS

Designing a problem includes the following activities:

- Identify the content area and primary goal of the instruction.
- Identify the learner population for the instruction.
- Identify a class of problems that, when solved, accomplish the learning goal.
- Design a prototype demonstration of the problem.
- Design a prototype application for the problem.

Designing a problem progression includes the following activities:

- Determine the component skills required to solve each of the problems in the sequence.
- Arrange a progression of problems from simple to complex such as all of the desired component skills required to solve the problems in the sequence.
- Design a prototype demonstration or application for each problem in the progression.

Designing strategies for component skills includes the following activities:

- Based on the chart of component skills, design demonstration and application for each component skill the first time it is required by a problem.
- Check to be sure that application of the component skill is required by at least two additional problems.

Designing structural framework enhancement includes the following activities:

- Design a structural framework.
- Design guidance based on this structural framework.
- Design coaching based on this structural framework.

Designing peer-interaction enhancement includes the following instructional design activities:

- Modify applications to facilitate peer-collaboration.
- Assign collaboration groups to collaborate and critique one another at they solve application problems.

Finalizing the instructional design includes the following activities:

- Finalize navigation.
- Finalize interface.
- Design supplemental materials.

Designing assessment and evaluation includes the following activities:

- Identify data sources.
- Modify the prototype to enable data collection.
- Design other evaluation instruments.
- Conduct formative evaluation.
- Revise prototype.

APPLICATION

The second part of this book has a primary goal of providing guidance in the use of the Pebble-in-the-Pond model of instructional design. Each of the following chapters in this part elaborates on the design products and steps in this model. At this point in the process, you may want to identify a content area, an instructional goal in this content area, and a learner population for your instruction. Subsequent chapters will guide you in developing instruction for this goal. You may want to revise one of the courses you evaluated for the application in Part I of this book.

TO LEARN MORE

Merrill, M. D. (2002b). A pebble-in-the-pond model for instructional design. *Performance Improvement, 41*(7), 39–44. Pebble-in-the-Pond was introduced in this paper.

van Merriënboer, J. J. G., & Kirschner, P. A. (2007). *Ten steps to complex learning.* Hillsdale, NJ: Lawrence Erlbaum Associates. Pebble-in-the-Pond is closely related to the whole problem 4C/ID instructional design model advocated by van Merriënboer and Kirschner.

COMING NEXT

Pebble-in-the-Pond advocates the development of a functional prototype as the design proceeds. Chapter 12 provides guidance in developing a functional prototype. It demonstrates easy-to-use procedures for building a functional prototype. The chapter also introduces the notion of instructional templates to facilitate the prototyping of instructional strategies for problem solving and for different types of component skills.

CHAPTER 12

DESIGNING FUNCTIONAL PROTOTYPES

Quick Look

One of the characteristics of the Pebble-in-the-Pond model of instructional design is the development of a prototype for the module or course rather than a design document. This chapter describes a functional prototype in more detail and uses the presentation software PowerPoint to illustrate how you might design such a prototype. This chapter answers the following questions: What is a design specification and what are its weaknesses? What is a functional prototype? How might a prototyping tool be used to design a functional prototype? What is an instructional strategy template? How can I design instructional strategy templates for different instructional strategies?

Key Words

Functional Prototype: a mock-up of the instructional strategy that includes actual content material or placeholders for this material; that allows learner interaction with the instructional strategies; and that approximates the learner interaction available in the final product.

Instructional Strategy Template: a tool for developing a functional prototype that contains placeholders for media objects and interaction that is appropriate for a given instructional strategy.

INTRODUCTION

This chapter suggests that a functional prototype provides a much better specification of an instructional product than a written design specification or traditional storyboard. It describes a functional prototype. It suggests reasons why a functional prototype is better than a design specification. It provides guidance for designing a functional prototype. I provide an example of how I might use presentation software such as PowerPoint as a design tool to build a functional prototype. The remaining chapters in Part II of this book will use a functional prototype to illustrate the design prescriptions that are demonstrated for each of the design activities in the Pebble-in-the-Pond model for instructional design. Because a functional prototype includes actual content and implements actual learner interaction and navigation, there is a possibility that you might think that the functional prototype is the final product of the design. It is important as you study the remainder of this book that you realize that a functional prototype is merely a form of a design specification for the final production of the instructional product.

WHAT IS A FUNCTIONAL PROTOTYPE?

A *functional prototype* is a mock-up of the instructional strategy that includes actual content material or placeholders for this material; that allows learner interaction with the instructional strategies; and that approximates the learner interaction available in the final product. A functional prototype replaces information with portrayals; it replaces descriptions with the actual content and learner interaction. A functional prototype speeds up the process by initiating a preliminary development of the instructional product early in the instructional design process. It replaces tell-me with show-me. It operates on the assumption of successive approximations; it assumes that the early versions will not be adequate and will be modified as the instructional design process unfolds. Each iteration enables reviewers to see a representation of the actual instruction and to make suggestions for its improvement. Each iteration usually improves the product by correcting weaknesses and problems as they occur. A functional prototype makes formative evaluation feasible from the very beginning of the process by enabling potential learners to interact with a mock-up of the actual instructional product rather than merely reviewing descriptions of a product yet to be born.

WHY A FUNCTIONAL PROTOTYPE?

The most common instructional design product is a design specification. This design spec is used to guide the production of the final product. Design specs can be very abstract, serving only as a guide for later development, or they can be very specific and be where the instruction is actually developed as the designer moves into the instructional strategy and instructional materials phase of the process.

A major weakness of a design spec is that it is primarily information rather than portrayal; it is a description of an instructional product rather than the instructional product itself. Language is replete with ambiguities. It is very difficult to write a description that is sufficiently complete that the resulting development is exactly as intended by the author of the description. In a design spec there are numerous places where this translation must occur, increasing the probability of miscommunication. The design spec raises the following concerns: Does the instructional analysis really identify all of the steps necessary to accomplish the goal? Do the performance objectives really identify the performance and conditions implied by a given step or subordinate skill? Does a given assessment instrument really measure the performance specified by the objective? It is likely at each of these junctures that the intended design is modified at every transition until the instructional product at the end only approximates the original intent.

Another weakness of a design specification is the long delay between the identification of the instructional goal and the actual development of the instructional product. This ISD procedure assumes that each phase is done well so that the next phase follows without difficulty. But here is the problem. Instructional design is seldom perfect. It is very likely that, as the design proceeds, it becomes clear that the goal was not adequately stated, that the instructional analysis was incomplete, that performance objectives don't adequately specify the performance required by a given step, and so forth. When the actual development finally gets underway during the instructional materials phases of the process, differences in interpretation of what is intended cause delays and often require rethinking the assumptions made early in the process. One of the major criticisms of ISD is the linear nature of its representations. Almost all designers find that the ideal process cannot be linear, that it is necessary to continually circle back to earlier phases as the development proceeds.

A functional prototype helps overcome some of the weaknesses of a design specification. First, it is a mock-up or portrayal of the instructional design, not merely a description, so that everyone involved in the project can see what the instruction looks like, how learners will interact with the instruction, and how learners will navigate through the instruction; it is a show-me specification, not merely a tell-me specification. Second, it facilitates rapid prototyping. Instead of describing desired changes in the design and the project progress, these changes can be immediately implemented in the prototype so that the prototype always represents the most recent version of the design. Finally, it facilitates ongoing evaluation of the design by enabling learners to interact with early versions of the prototype, providing valuable information for revision before the design is complete or implemented in its final form.

DESIGNING A FUNCTIONAL PROTOTYPE

A variety of computer-based tools enable building a functional prototype. It is important that the tool you choose enables you to build a prototype quickly with a minimum amount of effort. The tool chosen should allow you, as a designer, to spend your energy designing appropriate learning experiences rather than having to worry about programming details. The tool chosen should allow you to modify the prototype with a minimum of effort so that the prototype can evolve as fast as better ideas arise. It is important that each modification move the prototype closer to the final representation of the instructional course that accomplishes the instructional goal.

If you have access to a high-end authoring tool and are proficient in its use, then this tool makes an excellent candidate for building a functional prototype. For purposes of illustration in this book, I chose to use presentation software, such as PowerPoint, for building a functional prototype. Presentation software is economical, widely available, easy to use, and easy to modify. It supports a wide variety of multimedia, including text, audio, graphics, video, and animation. It enables you to emulate the interaction of learners with the instructional materials. It is easy to distribute. It is easy to use with learners for formative evaluation.

In the following paragraphs I will demonstration how I used presentation software to design a functional prototype. I will use the features available in PowerPoint for illustration, but similar functionality is available in other versions of presentation software. Because new versions of software occur on a regular basis, I have not given specific directions for enabling these features. To identify the controls that enable the functions described, you will need to study the help available for the version of the presentation software you are using. All of these features are available in the latest versions of PowerPoint, but they may not all be available in other presentation software. My purpose here is to illustrate the process of building a functional prototype. I am not advocating PowerPoint as a final development tool.

Control the Layout of Your Prototype

Presentation software enables you to select from a wide variety of screen layouts. Most default to a layout that has a title at the top of the screen and a box for bulleted or numbered text items. For purposes of instructional design, it is important that you, as the designer, have complete control of the screen. As you start to build a functional prototype, it is best to select a completely blank layout for your design. Later, after you have determined a layout that is appropriate for your instruction, you can use your custom layout for subsequent slides.

Provide a Way for Learners to Move from Slide to Slide

Presentation software usually displays the next slide when there is a mouse click on the background. For instructional design, you do not want learners to be able to merely turn the page by clicking the mouse. You don't want an accidental click to prematurely display the next slide, causing the learners to wonder where they are and what happened. You want to have learners make a deliberate decision and click on a specified object on the screen to interact with your learning events, including displaying the next slide. So turn off automatic slide transition.

To enable learners to move to the next screen, you will need to provide an alternative to merely clicking the mouse. For now, insert an object, perhaps a large arrow pointing right, on your blank screen. Next, select an action to be associated with this object. One option will be *go to next slide.* When learners interact with the slide show, they will be shown the next slide in the sequence only when they click on the arrow. You can also add an object to return to the previous slide. In many cases, you may not want this Next or Previous button to appear until after the learner has finished interacting with the other learning events on the slide. Later, I will discuss how to make the appearance of this button conditional on other interactions within the slide. Presentation software also allows you to have a slide master that can include objects that will appear on every slide. If you always want learners to be able to go to the next or previous slide, you may want to add these navigation objects to the slide master rather than to each slide individually. However, this limits your ability to make the appearance of this Next or Previous arrow conditional on other interactions.

Design Learner Interactions

Like most people, you have probably suffered through very boring presentations consisting of slide after slide, each with a list of bullet items. This is not a good presentation, and it is certainly not good instruction. Good instruction is interactive. You will want your learners to be involved with the instructional events. The key to effective interactive instructional events using presentation software is custom animation. *Custom animation* is simple programming that controls the display of objects on the screen, including appearance, disappearance, and the ability for a click on one object to cause an animation for another object. Custom animation allows you to display a set of examples one-by-one as requested by the learner; it allows learners to make a selection from among several objects on the screen to indicate their understanding; and it allows you to provide feedback on their choices.

Consider the instructional strategy for learning about famous presidents illustrated in Figure 5-1. Figure 12-1 shows a possible slide designed in presentation software for a functional prototype. When this slide first appears, the answers to the questions are not present. When the learner clicks on the question, *What is his name?,* the words "George Washington" appear and an audio message says his name. When the next question is clicked, the dates of his service appear. And so forth for each of the four questions. Why did I include this interactivity rather than merely presenting the information? The hope is that the learner is then encouraged to read the questions before clicking for the answer. This is a device to focus his or her attention and to associate the information with the question.

How can you design this functional prototype using presentation software? This is where custom animation comes to the rescue and why you need to start with a blank screen. Each of the questions was created as a separate text box. A text box is an object that can be associated with interaction. Each of the answers was also created as a separate text box. There are four question objects associated with four answer objects. To create the animation for the first answer, select the textbox for George Washington. Then click on the animations menu and select a type of animation; in this case I selected *appear.* Customize the animation by selecting it in the animation pane and selecting *timing.* Under timing, there is an option *Triggers.* Select this option and then select the text box object, *What is his name?* as the trigger. When the slide is shown in a slide show, the name George Washington is hidden. When the learner clicks on the question, Washington's name appears. Animation for each of the other questions was designed in the same way.

Figure 12-2 illustrates a functional prototype slide for the application in this information-about lesson on Famous Presidents. For this slide, learners are asked to click on the picture of the president described by the sentence above the pictures. When the learner clicks on the picture of Woodrow Wilson, the feedback message under the pictures pops up. If the learner clicks on one of the other two pictures, the feedback message reads *Incorrect!* and then describes the president shown in the picture.

This is accomplished using presentation software in a way very similar to the previous slide. In this case, select a feedback message, select an animation type, and select as a trigger the picture corresponding to the feedback. Repeat this process for each of the other two pictures and feedback messages.

When this slide was created, I positioned all of the feedback messages on top of each other. If the learner makes a mistake and then tries again, which is the desired interaction, then it is necessary for the previous message to disappear before the next feedback message is displayed. This requires additional animation for each message. Select a feedback message, select an animation type for *exit,* and select a picture that does not correspond to the message as a trigger. Repeat this for the other picture. When you are finished, each feedback message has three animations associated with it: an *appear* animation triggered by the correct picture and an *exit* message triggered by each of the two incorrect pictures.

FIGURE 12-1 Demonstration Animation for Functional Prototype

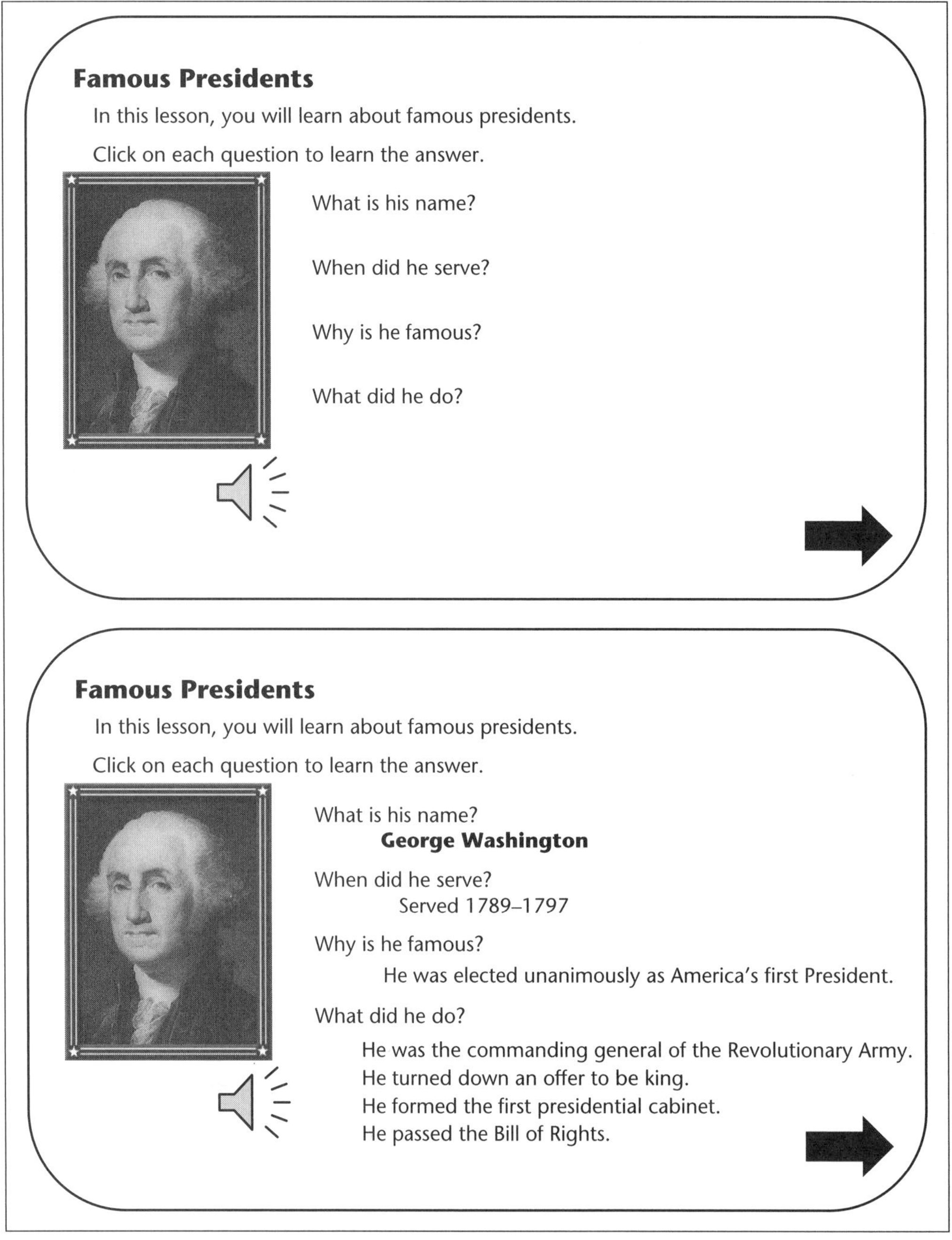

Based on Famous Presidents. Copyright Down Load Learning. Used with permission.

Finally, in each of the above you may not want the Next Slide arrow to appear until after the learner has responded to the screen. To accomplish this for the display in Figure 12-1, select the Next arrow; select an *appear* animation type; and select the final question as the trigger. When the learner clicks on the last question, the information will appear along with the Next Slide arrow. A similar animation will cause the Next Slide arrow to appear for the display in Figure 12-2. In this case, use clicking on the correct picture as the trigger to cause the Next Slide arrow to appear. This assures that the learner will see the correct answer before he or she can continue to the next slide.

FIGURE 12-2 Functional Prototype for Application for Famous Presidents

Famous Presidents

Click on the picture of the president who was famous for the following:

He tried to create the League of Nations after World War I.

Correct! Woodrow Wilson spent his childhood in the Civil War south. He was a lawyer, college professor, and then president of Princeton University. He kept the U.S. out of World War I until 1917. He tried to create the League of Nations, but the U.S. wouldn't join. He received the Nobel Peace Prize.

Based on Famous Presidents. Copyright Down Load Learning. Used with permission.

Much more complex animations are really just combinations of these simple animation procedures. As the animation becomes more complex, you have to be careful about the order of the animations. Remember the caution in Chapter 9 on using irrelevant sounds and animations. Rather than dissolve, fly-in, and other of the many animation effects available, it is usually better to stick with simple *appear* and *disappear*. It is usually not desirable to play sound effects when learners click on a choice; it is likewise usually unwise to play sound effects for a correct answer.

Simple graphics and text were used to demonstrate the above animations. It is possible to substitute video or audio messages for these simple messages. For example, in the Famous Presidents demonstration in Figure 12-1, the response to clicking on the question, *Why is he famous?* could trigger a short video clip about the president. Instead of a text message, the feedback messages in Figure 12-2 could be short audio clips playing the information.

In order to show the details of the interaction on this simple information-about instructional event, I described my use of PowerPoint is some detail. My purpose was to demonstrate some important characteristics of a functional prototype. Let me summarize the characteristics that I tried to illustrate. First, be in control of all interactions; don't rely on automatic bullet items, next slide on button click, or other functions of the software. Second, provide an action for learners to take to move to the next slide or the previous slide. Third, design interaction that requires learners to focus on the information that is being presented. Fourth, design interaction that requires learners to remember or apply what they have been taught. Fifth, design interaction that provides feedback on a learner's responses.

INSTRUCTIONAL STRATEGY TEMPLATES

An *instructional strategy template* is a tool for developing a functional prototype that contains placeholders for media objects and interaction that is appropriate for a given instructional strategy. The advantage of a strategy template is that the same interaction can be programmed once and used for demonstrating or applying different content. This allows for more efficient design, provides a way to keep your interactions parallel so that they are similar from slide to slide, and provides a tool for helping less experienced designers implement effective instructional strategies.

I will use PowerPoint to illustrate how you can design an instructional strategy template. PowerPoint allows the designer to develop a slide master. A *slide master* is a slide layout that can be used for multiple slides in a presentation. Instead of media objects, a slide master is constructed of placeholders. A *placeholder* is a location on a slide master that can be replaced with a media object, including text, picture, chart, table, video, audio, or clip art. The slide master retains the screen layout, format, and animation associated with the placeholders. Presentation software comes with a number of slide masters already available for different slide layouts. But you are not limited to the slide masters furnished with the software. PowerPoint allows you to create your own slide masters and then to use them to create your presentation. This capability allows you to create a slide master for different kinds of instructional events and for different kinds of instructional strategy.

In the Famous Presidents short course described in Chapter 5, there are a number of very similar slides describing the different presidents. There are also a number of different application slides asking learners to associate a given president with his primary accomplishment or his term of office. It is tedious to have to complete the animation for every object on every one of these slides. Fortunately, using instructional strategy templates (slide masters in PowerPoint) is a time-saving solution.

Figure 12-3 shows the instructional strategy template or slide master that I designed for the presentation in Figure 12-1. Most of the objects on this slide master are placeholders. Some placeholders are reserved for one kind of media object, but there is also a placeholder that will allow you to insert any kind of media. I inserted a text placeholder for the slide title. When inserted, the placeholder has the direction, *Click to insert text.* I changed this direction to *Click to insert slide title.* When you are using this template to design a new slide and you click on this placeholder, the cursor appears and you can either type or paste text. I used a text box for the next two sentences. These sentences are not placeholders and appear when the slide master is used for a new slide. The questions are also text that is part of the template. I then inserted a picture placeholder. When you click on the icon, the software opens your picture file where you can select a picture. The name, term of service, and primary accomplishment are text placeholders. The last placeholder allows any object to be used, including text, pictures, clip art, video, audio, a spreadsheet, or graph.

FIGURE 12-3 Slide Master for Famous Presidents Demonstration

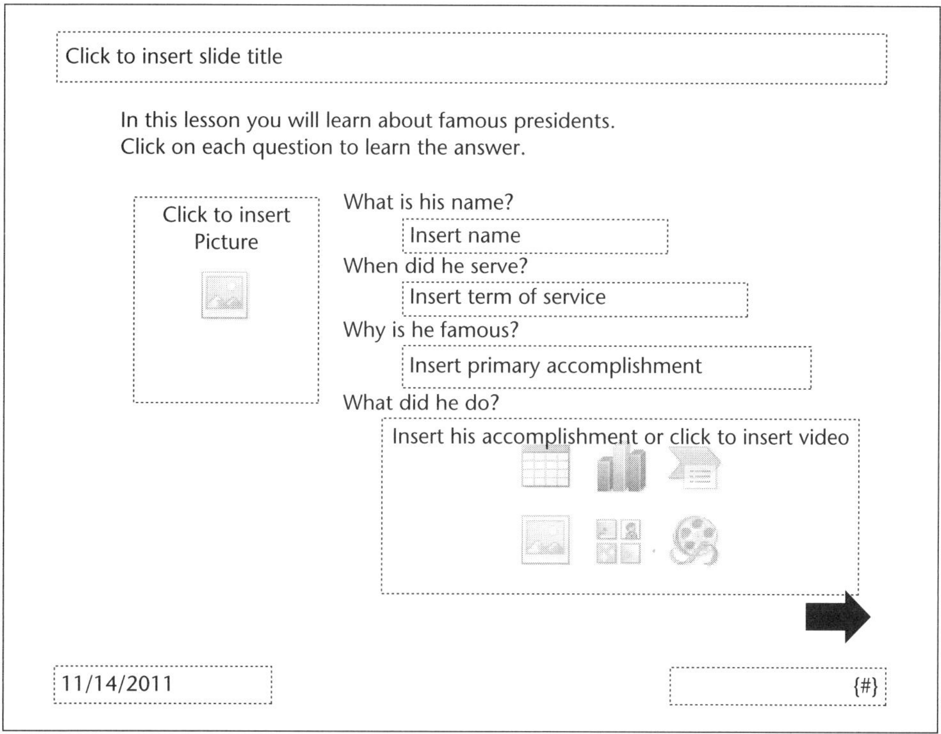

Once I had the placeholders and text in place for my slide master, I programmed animation for these placeholders. I selected the *Insert name* placeholder, selected *appear* animation, and then selected the first question as the trigger. This is the same procedure that was explained above, except in this case I was animating placeholders rather than specific objects. When the placeholders are replaced with media objects, these media objects are already programmed with the appropriate animation. I also programmed the animation for the Next Slide arrow so that it does not appear until the last question is clicked. Finally, I turned off the automatic next-slide-on-click option so that when this slide master is used only the Next Slide arrow will allow learners to move to the next slide. A big advantage of using slide master strategy templates is that I only have to do this animation programming once for each type of instructional interaction. I can then use the slide master over and over for different content without having to reprogram the animation. Be sure to name your file so that the slide master you created will be available the next time you open this file.

To create a new slide for your functional prototype, you select this slide master as your slide layout template. The slide format with its placeholders as it appears in Figure 12-3 is displayed for editing. Click on the title box and type or paste the title of the slide. Click on the picture placeholder and insert a picture of the president under consideration; click on the *Insert name* placeholder to insert his name; click on the *term of service* placeholder to insert his term of service; and click on the *Insert primary accomplishment* placeholder to insert his primary accomplishments. The last placeholder is for any type of media. You can insert his accomplishments as text or you can click on the video icon to insert a short video. The animation is already programmed for this slide master template, so you do not have to create any of the animation. Each of the answer boxes is already designed to be triggered when the learner clicks on the question. Remember to save your file as you are creating your new slide using the slide master so you won't lose any of your work.

Chapter 5 described instructional strategies for each of five different types of component skill. It is likely that in designing a functional prototype for a course you will have several different kind-of instructional events, several different how-to instructional events, and several different what-happens instructional events. The design of a functional prototype is much more efficient if you design an instructional strategy template or set of slide masters that can be used to design the instruction events for each of these strategies. In the following paragraphs I will describe a possible instructional strategy template or set of slide masters for each of the component skill instructional strategies and provide an example of each.

Information-About

The slide master instructional strategy template described for Famous Presidents in the preceding paragraphs in an example of an information-about strategy template. This particular template is specific to the Famous Presidents course. Figure 12-4 shows an information-about practice slide that requires learners to recognize the name of the president shown. When this slide appears, only the picture and the three names appear. When a learner clicks on a box next to a name of a president, the feedback message on the right is shown. For this example I have included all three feedback messages. Students are allowed to respond again if they do not get the correct answer on the first try.

Figure 12-5 illustrates the slide master instructional strategy template that was used to create this practice slide for Famous Presidents. This template is much more general than the previous template I described. This particular template could be used for almost any information-about practice. As you can see, any media object could be used in the placeholder at the left of the screen. Then any type of objects can be included for the choices presented to the student. The feedback text message and the picture next to each of the choices are used to provide feedback to the learner. These messages appear when the learner clicks in one of the boxes.

Figure 12-6 is another practice slide from Famous Presidents. In this case, the step was text and the choices were pictures. The feedback messages were text and the feedback pictures associated with each choice were not used. This same information-about practice template could be used for completely different subject matter. The picture could be a type of tree and the alternatives could be the name of the tree, with the feedback showing a picture of the incorrect choices. Or the reverse could be done. The placeholder on the left could describe the characteristics of a particular type of tree and the choices could be pictures of different trees. I hope you can see the flexibility of this information-about practice template. I purposely used a more specific template for the presentation and a much more general template for the practice to help you see that the templates you build can be specific to the course you are prototyping or they can be very general so that they can be used in a number of different situations for different courses.

FIGURE 12-4 Information-About Application for Famous Presidents

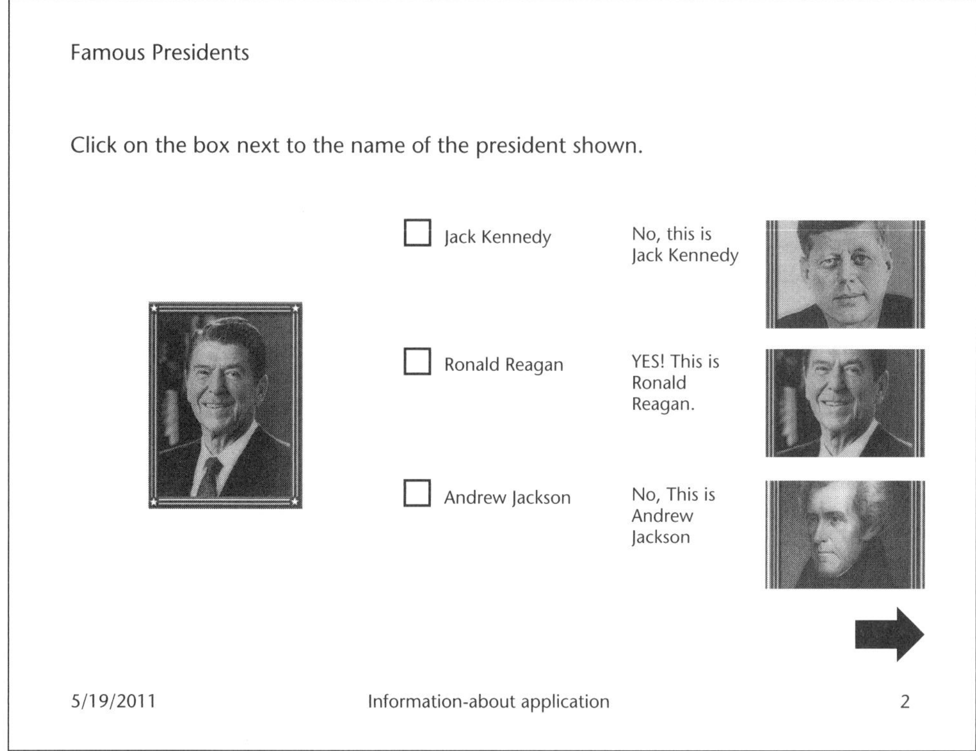

Based on Famous Presidents. Copyright Down Load Learning. Used with permission.

FIGURE 12-5 Slide Master for Information-About Application

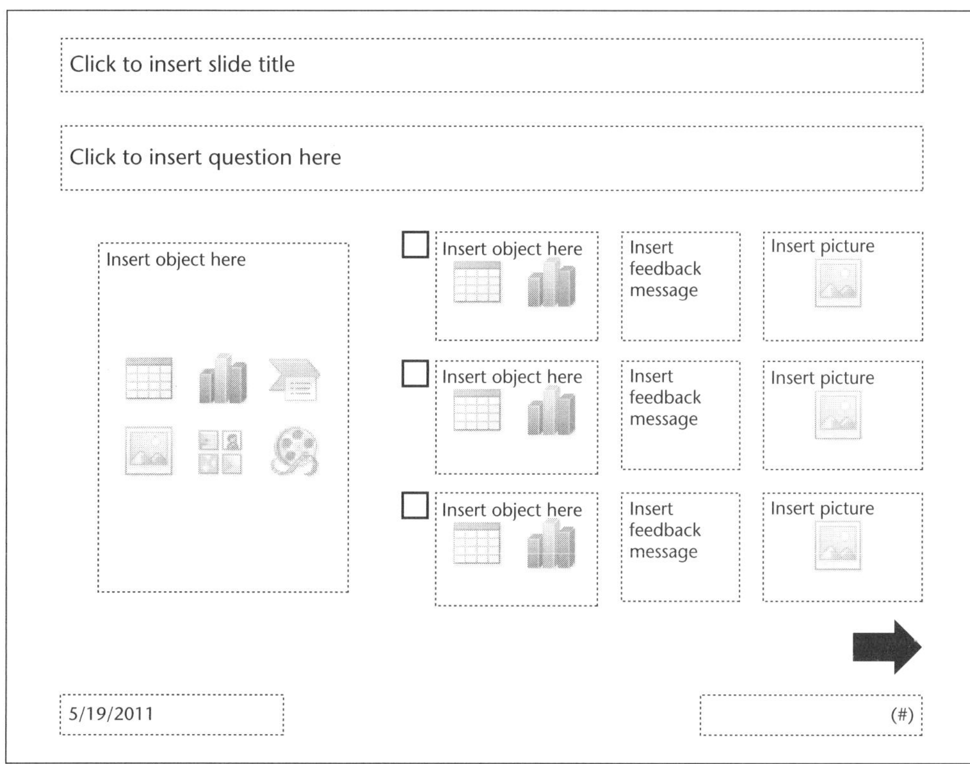

FIGURE 12-6 Another Information-About Application for Famous Presidents

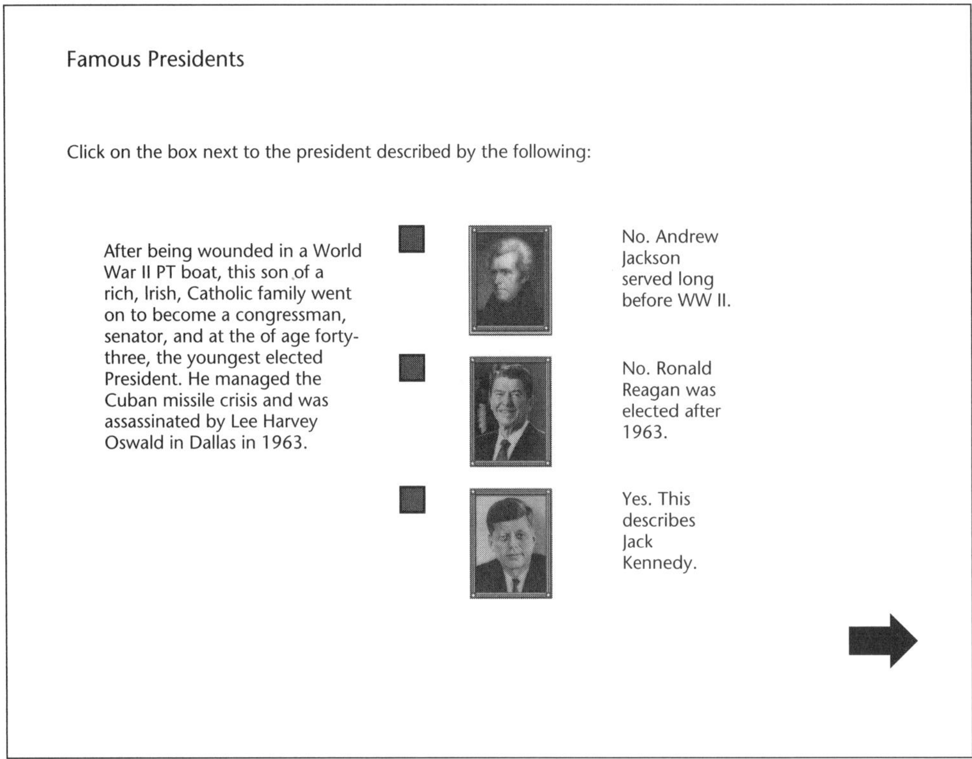

Based on Famous Presidents. Copyright Down Load Learning. Used with permission.

Kind-of

Figure 12-7 illustrates a kind-of demonstration instructional event for the photography principle Rule of Thirds. The paragraph at the top defines the principle. The two pictures show an example and a non-example. When this slide first appears, the bottom two pictures, which provide guidance, do not appear. When the learner clicks the *Click here for guidance* direction, the two guidance pictures appear, along with the Next Slide arrow.

Figure 12-8 illustrates the slide master instructional strategy template I used for this instructional event. There is a text placeholder for inserting the slide title; there is a text placeholder for inserting the definition. This is a very general strategy template that could be used for almost any concept. The placeholders for the example and non-example are object placeholders into which any type of media can be inserted by clicking on the appropriate icon in the placeholder. The placeholders for guidance are also object placeholders so that the guidance could be text, audio, a picture, or video. In the instance of the template in Figure 12-7, I used pictures with overlaid grid lines for this guidance. The animation for the guidance and Next Slide arrow to appear is already programmed into the slide master template. It occurs when the *Click here for guidance* direction is clicked.

FIGURE 12-7 Kind-of Demonstration Instructional Event for Rule of Thirds

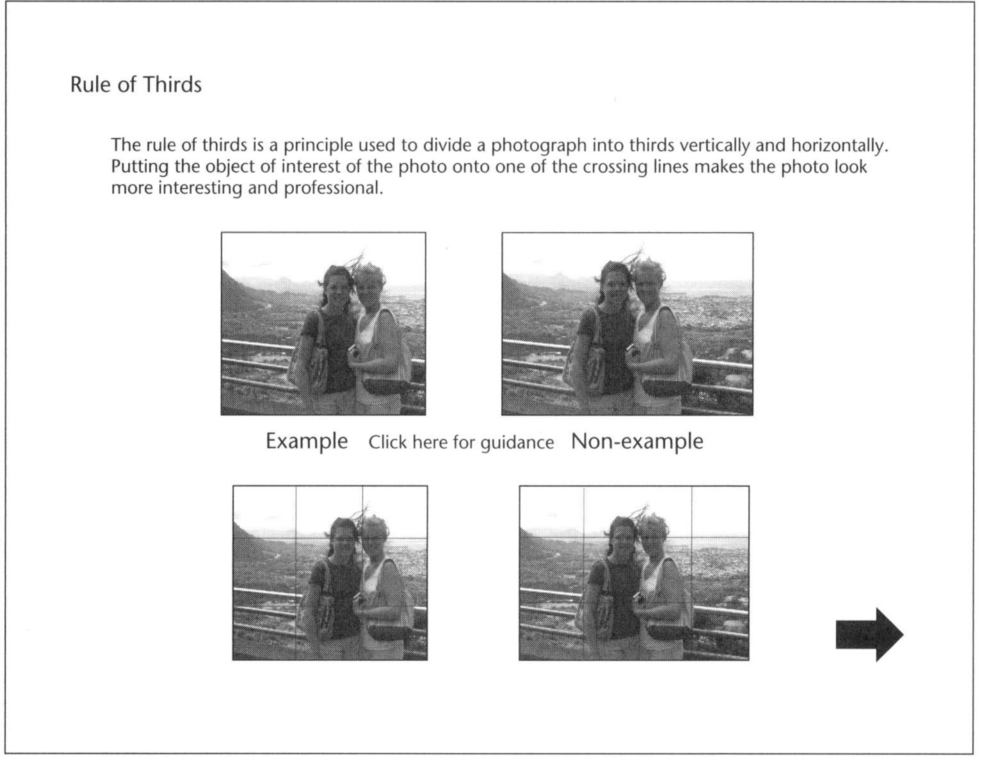

FIGURE 12-8 Slide Master for Kind-of Demonstration Instructional Event

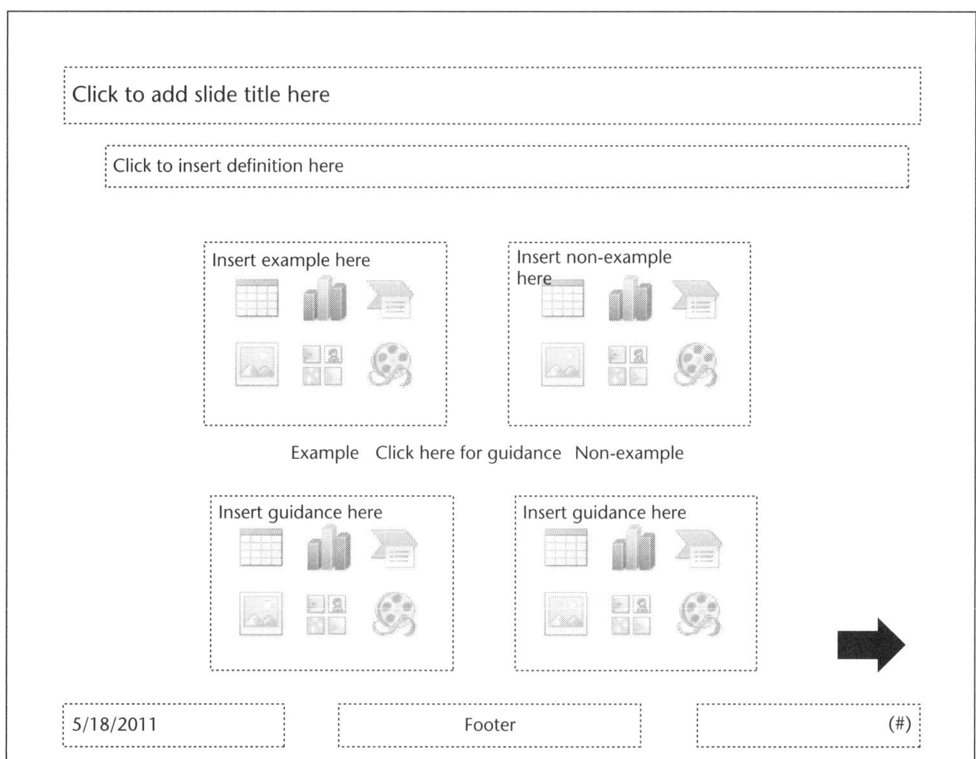

FIGURE 12-9 Kind-of Demonstration Instructional Event with Multiple Examples

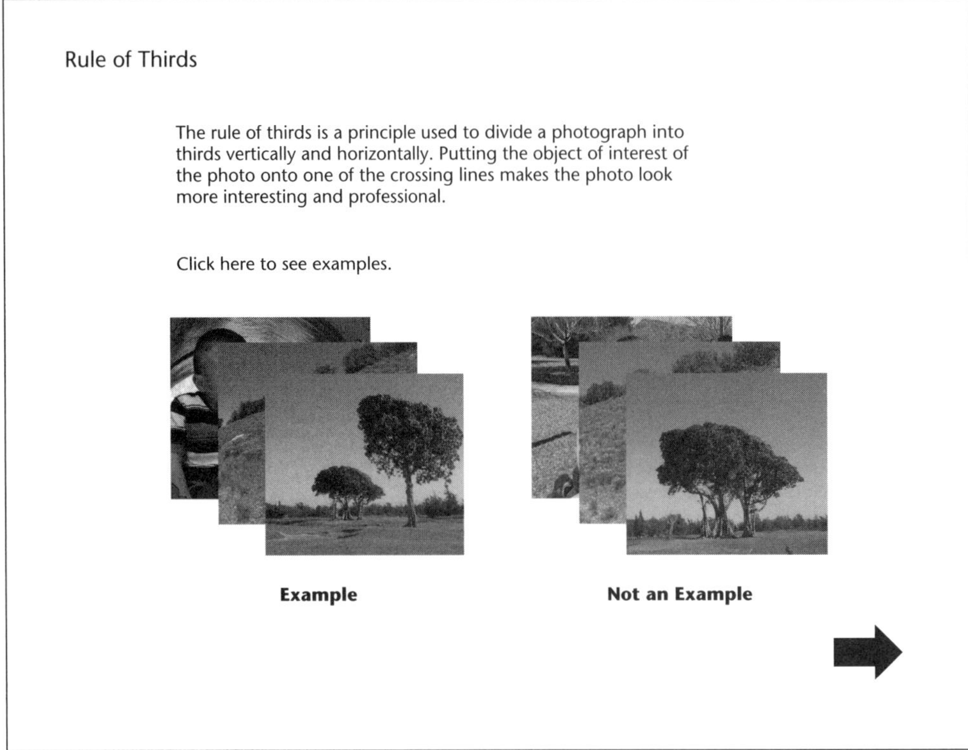

Figure 12-9 is a kind-of demonstration instructional event that presents a set of example/non-example pairs. In the figure, all three of the example/non-example pairs are overlaid on one another. In slide show mode, only one example/non-example pair shows at a time. When the *Click here to see examples* direction is clicked, the first pair disappears and the next pair appears. The Next Slide arrow appears when the last pair is displayed.

Figure 12-10 illustrates the slide master for this instructional event. Because the example/non-example pictures are overlaid, it is necessary to drag the top layer aside to insert the picture on the second and third layers. These pictures are then dragged back into position. Another approach with several objects that overlay one another is to select the top object, insert the picture, then move it to the back. Repeat this for the next object. When you finish, the objects will be overlaid in the same order as the template. These objects could be completely overlaid on one another. I find it a bit easier to find them when they are offset as shown. This slide master template could have been modified to use any objects as examples rather than just pictures. This modification would allow pairs of example/non-example audio messages or videos to be used.

Figure 12-11 is an application instructional event for the photography lesson on Rule of Thirds. When this slide is displayed to the learner, the feedback messages are all hidden. Clicking on the checkbox reveals the corrective feedback for each picture. The Next Slide arrow appears when the checkbox for the lower right photo is clicked.

FIGURE 12-10 Slide Master for Kind-of Multiple Examples Demonstration

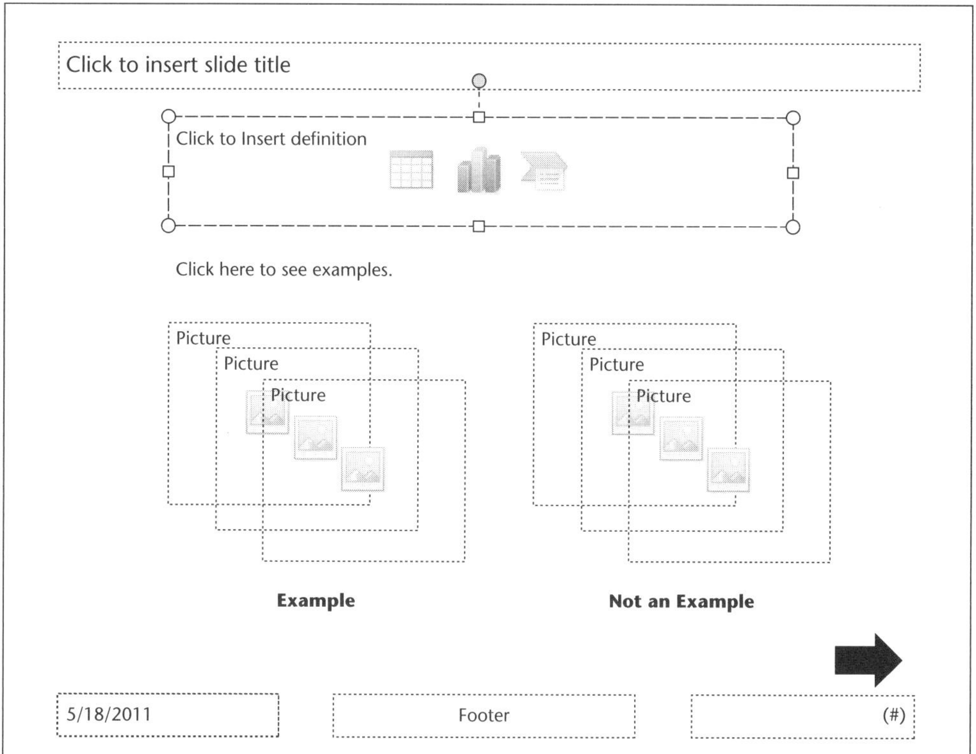

FIGURE 12-11 Kind-of Application Instructional Event for Rule of Thirds

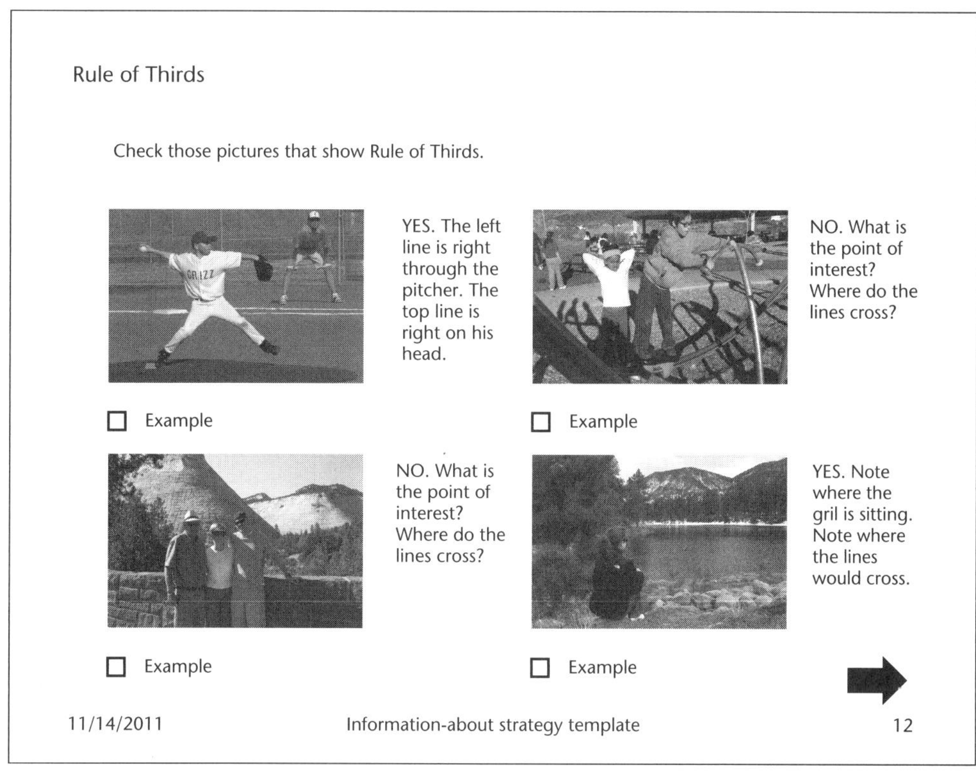

FIGURE 12-12 Slide Master for Kind-of Application

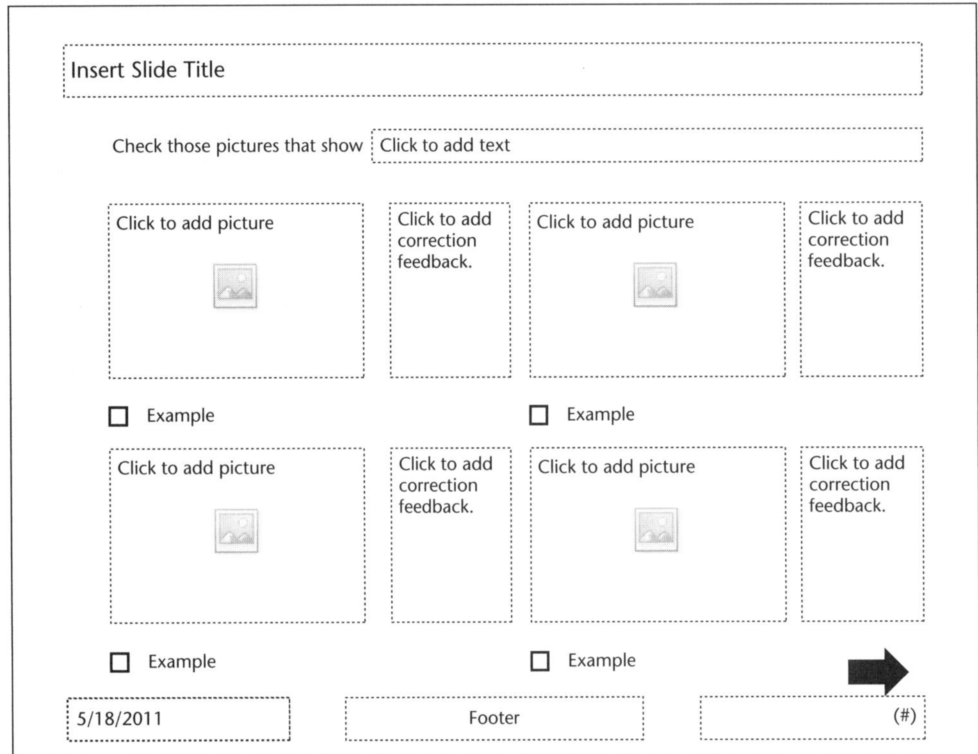

Figure 12-12 is the slide master template for this kind-of application instructional event. This template includes the usual slide title text placeholder. It also includes a placeholder to make the direction specific to the content of the slide. This template used picture placeholders for the instances and text placeholders for the feedback messages. The small checkbox is the trigger for the corresponding feedback message. In Chapter 18 I will demonstrate how to modify the slide master application template to record learner responses. By now you probably realize that I could have used object placeholders rather than limiting it to picture placeholders. In that situation, the instances being identified by learners could be video or audio as well as pictures.

How-to

Figure 12-13 is a slide from the SalesForce lesson described in Figure 6-10. This slide demonstrates one major step in the sales process—A Friendly Greeting. I included the video twice. The first showing, on the left, lists the name of the substeps of a friendly approach one-by-one as they occur in the video. The first two substep names are shown in Figure 12-13. The other two substeps are "a sincere response" and "asks purpose of visit." These words appear as David asks the corresponding question in the video. The second showing, on the right, lists words identifying Maria's reaction to each of the substeps in David's approach—the consequence for each step. Only the first two consequence names are shown in the figure.

FIGURE 12-13 A How-to One-Step Demonstration Instructional Event for Furniture Sales

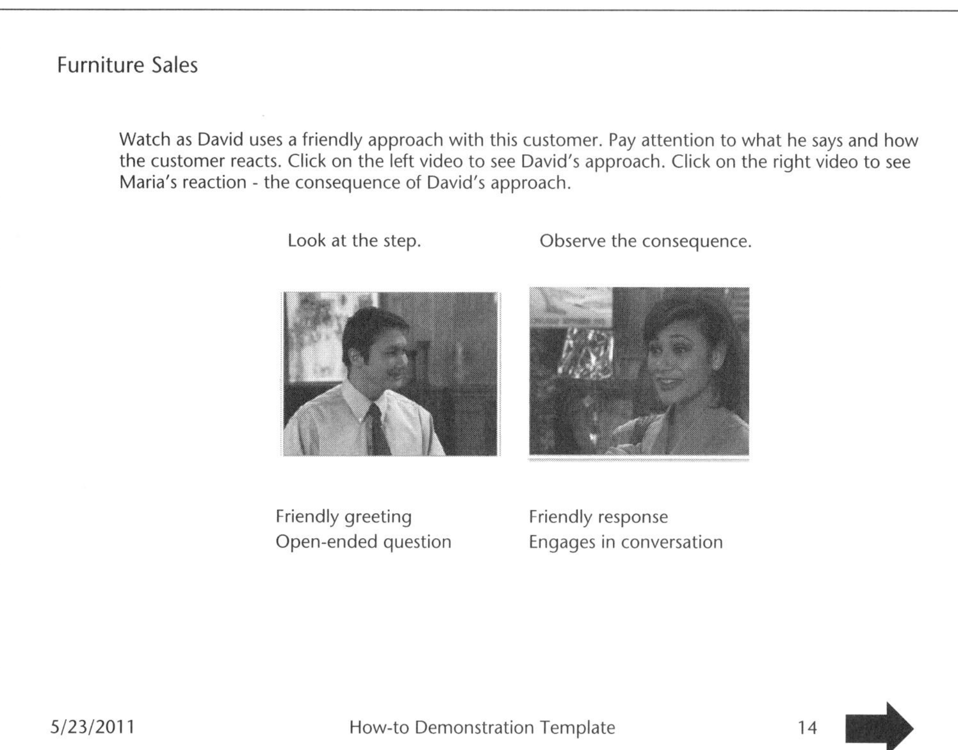

Furniture Sales
Watch as David uses a friendly approach with this customer. Pay attention to what he says and how the customer reacts. Click on the left video to see David's approach. Click on the right video to see Maria's reaction - the consequence of David's approach.
Look at the step.
Observe the consequence.
Friendly greeting
Open-ended question
Friendly response
Engages in conversation
5/23/2011
How-to Demonstration Template
14

Based on SalesForce: Selling with Service. Copyright The Furniture Training Company. Used with permission.

Figure 12-14 illustrates the slide master template I designed as a demonstration for a how-to component skill. I used media placeholders so I could use video to demonstrate both the step and the consequence of the step. The text items appear as the video plays, but this animation is not part of the template and must be programmed for the specific video that you use. This animation is easily programmed in PowerPoint. Insert a video in the placeholder and then, as the video plays, stop it when you want to insert a bookmark. You merely click on the "insert bookmark" command at appropriate points in the video. Then you select the first item, select animation to appear for this item, and select the first bookmark as the trigger. Repeat for each of the other items. I used the same video twice: for the left video I bookmarked and triggered the steps that David was taking. In the second video, on the right, I bookmarked and triggered the items identifying the consequences or Maria's response to each step.

Figure 12-15 is another version of a how-to demonstration. In this template the learner is required to click on a step number to see each step. When the learner clicks on the words *Step 1,* the video plays only that portion of the video that illustrates that particular step. As this video plays, the description or name of the consequence of the step is shown to the right of the video, similar to the successive disclosure of the consequence names in Figures 12-13 and 12-14. Like the template in Figure 12-14, this animation must also be programmed specific to a given piece of video. Play the video and insert bookmarks before and after each segment of the video you wish to use. Select the bookmark before the desired segment; select the animation tools for the video and select the *seek* command; select trigger with the text box *Step 1*; select the bookmark after the desired segment; select the *pause* command; and select trigger with the text box *Step 1.* In the slide show, when the learner clicks on the words Step 1, the video plays the selected segment. Repeat this animation programming for each step in the procedure. In this way the learner can play each step from the video individually. I also included a trigger to play the whole video without interruption.

FIGURE 12-14 Slide Master for How-to Demonstration

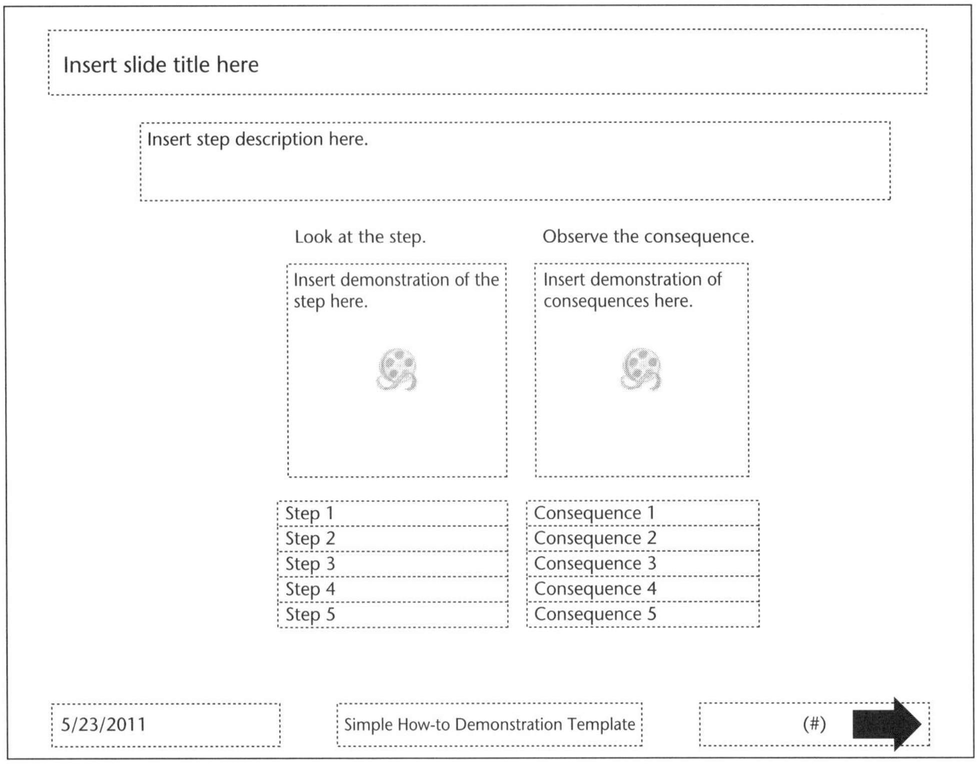

Insert slide title here

Insert step description here.

Look at the step.	Observe the consequence.
Insert demonstration of the step here.	Insert demonstration of consequences here.
Step 1	Consequence 1
Step 2	Consequence 2
Step 3	Consequence 3
Step 4	Consequence 4
Step 5	Consequence 5

5/23/2011	Simple How-to Demonstration Template	(#)

Figure 12-16 is a slide master template for a how-to application instructional event. An incorrect demonstration of the procedure is inserted in the left media placeholder. A correct demonstration of the procedure is inserted in the right placeholder. I again took advantage of the ability to use bookmarks in the video. In the incorrect video, I bookmarked the start and end of each step in the procedure. I then used the words *Step 1, Step 2,* etc., to trigger each of these steps in the video. I also bookmarked each of the steps in the correct video. I used the textboxes NO, ?, and YES to trigger each of these correct demonstrations of the procedure. I also animated each of the NO, ?, and YES boxes to turn green if it was the correct response and red if it was the incorrect response. The words, *Click here to see correct procedure,* do not appear until after learners have responded to Step 5. Clicking on these words plays the whole correct procedure without interruption.

How does this application work? The learner clicks on a step number; a version of the step is executed in the left video; the learner then evaluates the step and clicks the appropriate response box option; the box changes color to indicate correct or incorrect; and the correct execution of the step is demonstrated in the right video box. In Chapter 18, I will describe the procedure for recording student responses.

FIGURE 12-15 Slide Master for Active How-to Demonstration

Click to insert slide name
Click to Step number to see a demonstration of each step.
Insert how-to demonstration here
Step 1 Insert step name
Step 2 Insert step name
Step 3 Insert step name
Step 4 Insert step name
Step 5 Insert step name
Insert Consequence
Insert Consequence
Insert Consequence
Insert Consequence
Insert Consequence
Click here to see whole demonstration
5/24/2011
Active How-to Demonstration
(#)

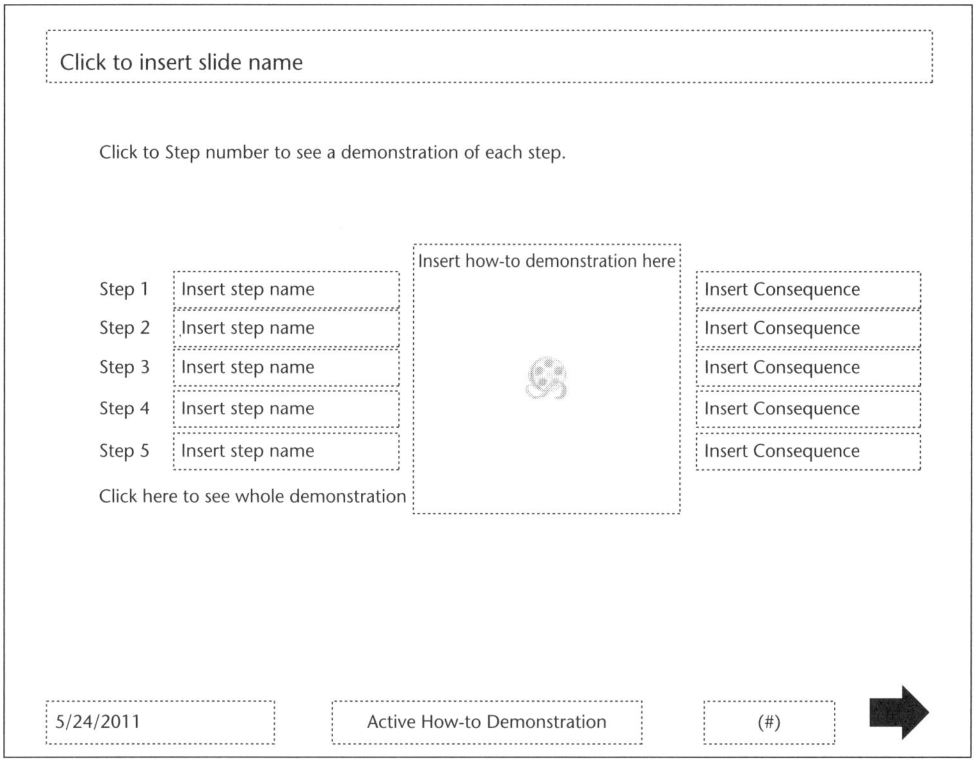

FIGURE 12-16 Slide Master for How-to Application

Click to insert slide title
Insert introduction here.
Click on step number to see step executed in left box. Click on your assessment of the execution of the step. The choice will appear green if it is correct; the choice will appear red if it is incorrect. The correct execution of the step will be shown in the right box.
Insert faulted how-to demonstration here.
Step 1 NO ? YES
Step 2 NO ? YES
Step 3 NO ? YES
Step 4 NO ? YES
Step 5 NO ? YES
Insert correct how-to demonstration here.
NO = not the correct step
? = correct step but poor execution
YES = correct step good execution
Click here to see correct procedure.
5/24/2011
How-to Demonstration
(#)

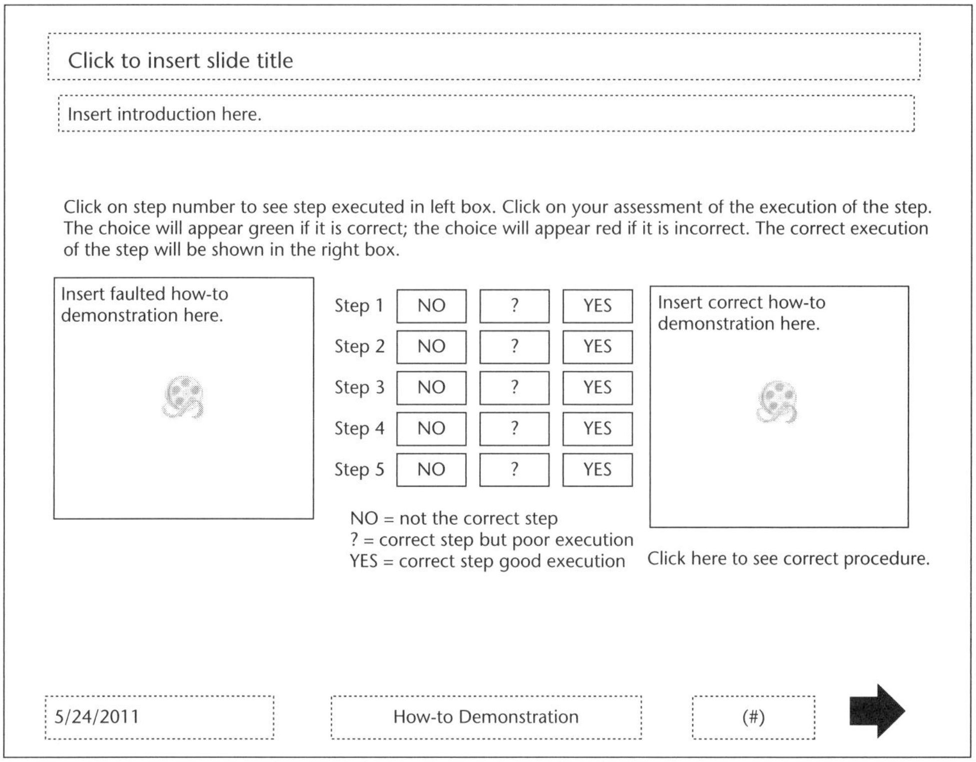

What-Happens

Figure 12-17 is a what-happens demonstration instructional event. The desired consequence is described using the photograph and explanation at the left of the slide. Several different conditions are identified in the middle panel of the screen. The learner is directed to click on one of the aperture settings and observe the consequence in the display on the right. The picture is changed to illustrate the effect of each of the aperture settings shown.

FIGURE 12-17 What-Happens Demonstration for Aperture and Focal Length

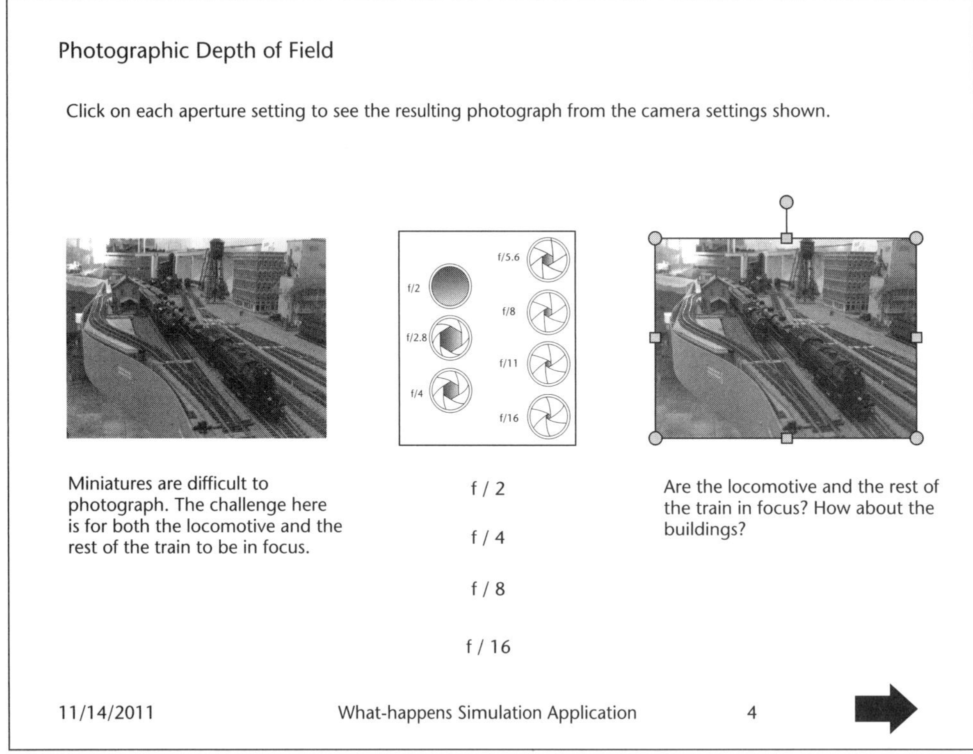

Figure 12-18 is the slide master template for this slide. This is a very general template that can be used in a number of different ways. In Figure 12-17, I inserted a photograph in the object placeholder on the left and inserted text below the photograph to explain the problem. In the center object placeholder, I inserted a photograph showing the aperture of different f-stop settings. In the right object panel, I used the technique described above; I made a video consisting of a series of photographs, each taken with a different f-stop. I then used the bookmark feature to mark the start and end of each photograph. I then used the option textbox placeholders that contained the different f-stop settings as triggers for the appropriate section of the video with the photograph corresponding to the f-stop selected. I also used the f-stop textboxes to trigger text guidance corresponding to each of the pictures in the video.

I could have also used a video in the first object placeholder to set up the problem. I also could have used a video and bookmarks in the conditions placeholder to show each of the options. This would be appropriate when the options involved motion or when they could be more adequately illustrated with video. Using bookmarks, the consequences could also have been short video clips as well. I hope that you can see that a given slide master strategy template can be very flexible. When you create a slide master template, be sure to use the Note function in the presentation software to document how you plan to use the template. I find that after a few weeks, I have forgotten what I did and how I planned to use a given template.

FIGURE 12-18 Slide Master for What-Happens Application

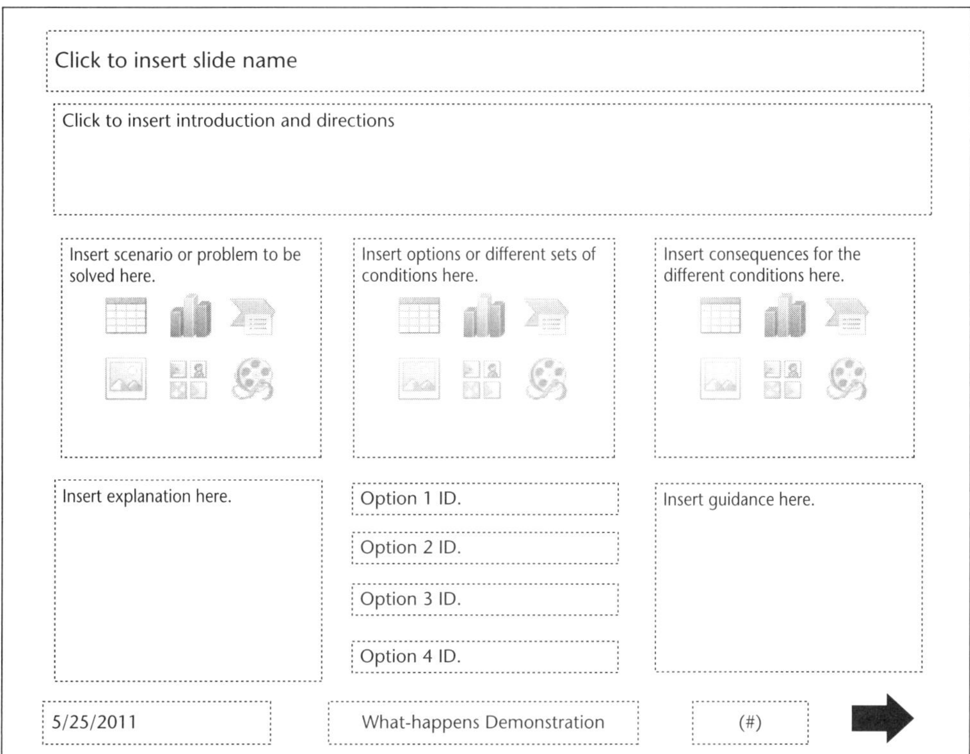

Finally, by changing the directions and the trigger animation, this same template can be used as a what-happens application. In the example in Figure 12-17, the directions would be changed as follows: "Click on the f-stop that would produce a picture with the greatest depth of field." The links would still be linked to the sections of the video in the last object placeholder, but I would add a text phrase in the guidance giving correct or incorrect feedback for the response.

Figure 12-19 is one slide from a what-happens dialog simulation application. This module taught car sales associates how to approach a customer. The purpose of this exercise is to provide an opportunity for the future sales associates to demonstrate what they have learned. The learner is presented a scenario, in this case represented by text and a picture. The learner must then select what to say to the customer from the options provided. Figure 12-20 is the slide that is displayed when the learner selects the first alternative, the statement, "What are you currently driving?" Selecting one of the other alternatives would link to another slide that indicates a possible reaction of the customer to the sales associate's response. This sequence of branching slides is repeated to provide a sufficient representation of the dialog. Some paths chosen by the learner lead to a sale; other paths lead to an unhappy customer. This is a successive what-happens series of events. The statement of the sales associate is the condition; the response of the customer is the consequence of this condition.

FIGURE 12-19 What-Happens Dialog Simulation for Car Sales

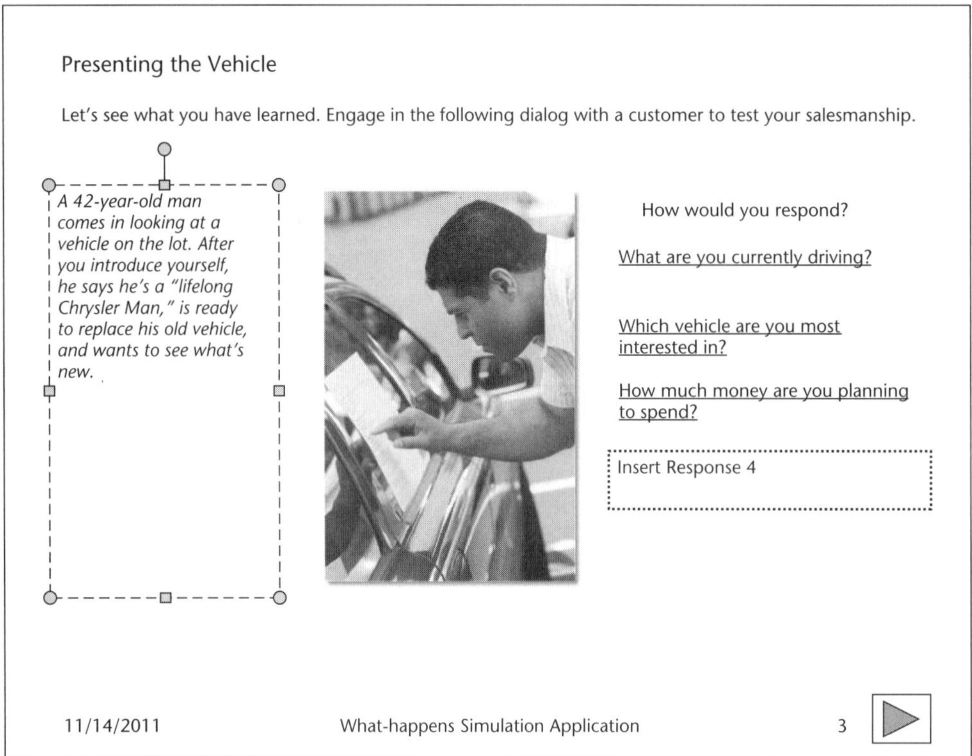

Student project, Utah State University, Dean Hammond.

Figure 12-21 is the slide master for this what-happens application. I inserted a text placeholder at the left of the screen to contain information about the problem. The center placeholder allows a picture or video representing a possible response of a customer to the alternative responses given. On the right I inserted text placeholders for each of the alternative responses that the learner could select based on the scenario presented in the other two placeholders. After the placeholders are populated and after the template is used to design a consequence slide for each of the response options, I hyperlinked each of the statements on the right to the appropriate consequence slide. This procedure is continued until there is sufficient dialog to represent the conversation.

I used an object placeholder for the scenario. In the example in Figure 12-19, the scenario was represented by a photograph and text. The scenario could be represented by a short video clip setting up the problem or situation to which the learner responds. While this is set up as a dialog, this same slide master template could be used by a variety of sequential what-happens problems. Instead of a verbal response, a response could be setting a dial or reading a meter on a piece of equipment. It could be selecting the next step in a complex procedure. Any sequence of events or actions that results in a consequence that serves as a condition for the next action or event can be represented in this template and provide an opportunity for a learner to make a series of sequential decisions.

FIGURE 12-20 What-Happens Dialog Simulation

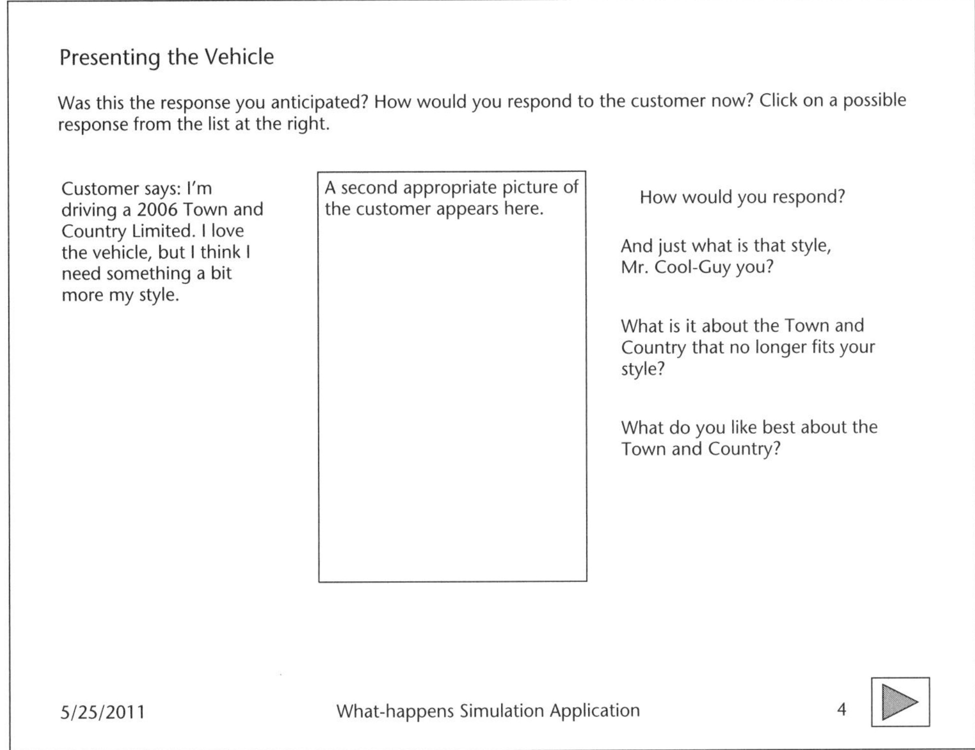

Presenting the Vehicle
Was this the response you anticipated? How would you respond to the customer now? Click on a possible response from the list at the right.
Customer says: I'm driving a 2006 Town and Country Limited. I love the vehicle, but I think I need something a bit more my style.
A second appropriate picture of the customer appears here.
How would you respond?
And just what is that style, Mr. Cool-Guy you?
What is it about the Town and Country that no longer fits your style?
What do you like best about the Town and Country?
5/25/2011
What-happens Simulation Application
4

FIGURE 12-21 Slide Master for What-Happens Dialog Simulation

Insert Slide Title

Insert introduction or directions here.

Insert description of the problem here.

0

Insert representation of scenario here.

How would you respond?

Insert Response 1

Insert Response 2

Insert Response 3

Insert Response 4

5/25/2011

What-happens Simulation Application

(#)

YOUR TEMPLATES

The preceding paragraphs have described and illustrated how presentation software can be used to design a variety of different functional prototype templates for instructional events. You should realize that these examples are only illustrative of what can be done. Each of the instructional strategies described in this book can be implemented in a wide variety of ways. It is my hope that the illustrations provided in this chapter help you become familiar with some of the capabilities of presentation software. I encourage you to experiment, to check out some of the many tutorials available on the Internet, to explore some of the other capabilities of these flexible tools. I encourage you to build your own library of slide master strategy templates that will enable you to rapidly prototype a wide variety of instructional strategies.

Let me reemphasize that I am not advocating doing your instructional design using presentation software. I'm only trying to illustrate how you might use this software to design a functional prototype. You could use a number of other computer tools for this design activity. You have probably observed that this book has at least three levels of abstraction: First Principles are at the highest level; they are abstract principles that apply in almost every instructional situation. In the subsequent chapters, I have introduced vocabulary and relationships that constitute a set of prescribed instructional strategies and their constituent instructional events for different kinds of component skills and for whole problems. These prescribed strategies are less abstract than First Principles. Nevertheless, these prescribed strategies are representative rather than exhaustive. My intent is to show you some sets of instructional events that are effective in implementing First Principles in a variety of different content areas. There are probably other strategies that also implement First Principles. Using the templates suggested in this chapter is even less abstract than the instructional strategies demonstrated in earlier chapters. My purpose here is to primarily show you some possibilities for designing a functional prototype with the expectation that you will explore and find many other ways that effectively implement instructional strategies and First Principles of Instruction.

PRINCIPLES AND PRESCRIPTIONS

Use a tool that allows you to rapidly design a functional prototype.

Turn off any automatic functions of the prototyping tool so that you have complete control of your presentation.

Use the functions of the prototyping software to design learner interaction with instructional events.

- Enable media to appear or disappear; to enable learners to make choices; to provide feedback on learner choices.
- Enable branching to different slides corresponding to learner choice.
- Use bookmarks to enable audio or video to display multiple media objects.
- Design reusable instructional strategy templates.

APPLICATION

Obtain a copy of software that can be used to design a functional prototype. Design some of the instructional interactions described in this chapter. Design a strategy template for some of the instructional interactions described in this chapter. Design a strategy template for one of your own instructional strategies you anticipate including in your course. Test your functional prototypes with content from the course you hope to design.

TO LEARN MORE

You are encouraged to go to the Internet, where you will find many tutorials on the use of presentation applications. This chapter assumes that you have some familiarity with how to use presentation software such as PowerPoint. If you have not had any previous experience, you may want to study some of the basic tutorials for this software. Then this chapter will be easier to understand. If you are already familiar with presentation software, you may want to study some of the advanced tutorials.

The Online Premium Content associated with this book contains the actual PowerPoint Slide Masters described in this chapter. You will understand this material better if you obtain and play with these PowerPoint Slide Masters. See "Slide Master Templates for PowerPoint Functional Prototypes."

COMING NEXT

I have introduced the Pebble-in-the-Pond approach to instructional design and have provided information and examples related to building a functional prototype. The next chapter will guide you in the selection of an appropriate problem for your content area and in designing a prototype demonstration and application for this problem.

CHAPTER 13

DESIGN A PROBLEM PROTOTYPE

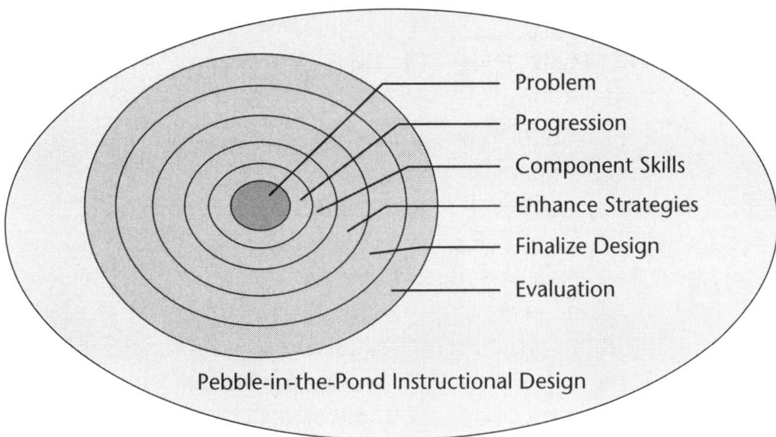

Quick Look

The splash in the pond portrays a problem. The first ripple is to design a problem prototype. This chapter will guide you in this design activity and addresses the following questions: How do I identify a content area, learner population, and instructional goal? How do I identify a class of problems? How do I identify the component skills for my class of problems? How do I design a prototype problem demonstration? How do I design a prototype problem application? How do I overcome some of the challenges in identifying a good class of problems?

Key Words

Problem-Solving Event Analysis: the instructional design process for identifying the consequence, conditions, and steps required by the class of problems to be taught.

Prototype Problem Demonstration: a functional mock-up of the instructional events that shows the learner the consequence, conditions, and steps required for an instance of the problem.

Prototype Problem Application: a functional mock-up of the instructional events that requires the learner to predict a consequence from a set of conditions, to find the faulted conditions for an unexpected consequence, or to execute the steps required to bring about the consequence.

INTRODUCTION

Traditional ISD and the Pebble-in-the-Pond model both have a similar beginning. Before you can design instruction, you need to identify the content area, the goal, and the learners. After this initial analysis, the Pebble approach differs significantly from more traditional instructional design. The first ripple is to identify a typical problem that, when solved, will accomplish the learning goal. This chapter guides you in (1) identifying a class of problems; (2) collecting a sample of problem portrayals; (3) identifying component skills for the problem portrayals; (4) designing a prototype problem demonstration; and (5) designing a prototype problem application.

IDENTIFY CONTENT, GOAL, AND LEARNER POPULATION

The Pebble model does not add anything unique to front-end analysis. As with traditional instructional design, you must first identify a need for instruction and determine that instruction is the best solution to satisfy this need. You must then determine the primary goal for the instruction: What change needs to be promoted in the skill set of the learner population? You must also determine the content area for this instruction: What is the domain of the skills that the learners need to require? And certainly not least, you need to identify the learner population. Who are the learners who will engage in your instruction? As with traditional instructional design, information about the learners, information about the learning environment, and information about the eventual performance environment are all useful data that informs and facilitates the subsequent instructional design process. This chapter assumes that these front-end analyses have been completed; that you know the content area of concern; that you have identified an instructional goal; and that you have identified the learners who will undertake the instruction you design.

Consider the following instructional goal, the learner population, and the learning environment for a short course on photographic composition:

> As a beginning photographer, using a single lens reflex camera, you will be able to take well-composed photographs of both people and scenery. The target audience is adult learners who have some experience with a digital camera and who have a desire to improve their photography of family, friends, and scenery. The facilities involve a digital camera, a tripod, and easy-to-use photographic editing software.

I'll continue to use this example throughout Part II of this book.

IDENTIFY A CLASS OF PROBLEMS

The first ripple in the Pebble model is to identify a class of problems that, when solved, will indicate that the learners have accomplished the learning goal. The following paragraphs specify some of the properties that should characterize these problems.

Good problems are typical of those the learner can expect to encounter in the real world following instruction. The problems are portrayals, not merely descriptions; they are specific instances of a class of problems for which there are multiple specific instances. The problems are complete. A complete problem includes at least three components: the givens of the problem; the identification of the solution or consequence that results from solving the problem; and a set of activities that transforms the givens into the solution.

Good problems are ill-structured and reflect real-world situations. They often do not have a single correct answer. They can be solved in several ways and the resulting solution can take several forms. The instruction allows learners to solve these problems in a real-world setting or in a simulation. A simulation is desirable if the real setting is dangerous, inaccessible, or potentially harmful when the solutions steps are not performed in an acceptable manner.

Taking well-composed photographs is an ill-structured task in that there are a wide variety of ways that any picture can be composed; there is not one correct answer. Taking photographs is a real-world activity. Using a camera is not dangerous and cameras are readily available, so a simulation is probably not warranted.

I have previously demonstrated portions of several courses that involved good problems. For the first aid course in Chapter 2, the problem was administering first aid in an emergency situation; for furniture sales in Chapter 6, the problem was providing help to a customer that resulted in a furniture sale; for the entrepreneur course in Chapter 7, the problem was developing a business plan and starting a small business; and for the Excel course in Chapter 11, the problem was designing a spreadsheet for a specific situation. All of these problems reflect real-world situations, they do not have a single correct answer, they can be solved in a variety of ways, and the resulting solution can take different forms.

COLLECT A SAMPLE OF PROBLEM PORTRAYALS

As a first step, you should collect a sample of problem portrayals. In this book we have previously distinguished between information and portrayal. This sample should represent a divergent set of portrayals. The portrayals should represent excellent examples, good examples, marginal examples, and poor examples of the solution to the problem. These problem portrayals should be typical of the types of problems you expect learners to be able to solve following instruction.

For photographic composition, I collected photographs of individuals, groups of people, buildings, and scenery. Some of these photographs were excellent examples, some were good but could be improved, some were marginal, and some were poor. Where possible, I tried to find good and poor photographs of the same subject or very similar subjects. Some photographs had been composed entirely in the viewfinder when the picture was taken; the composition of others could be improved by cropping and editing. The photographs were mostly of common everyday subjects typical of those available to the target audience of this module.

Each of the courses previously reviewed includes a sample of problem portrayals. For the first aid course in Chapter 2 the twenty practice case studies comprise the sample of problem portrayals; for the entrepreneur course in Chapter 7 the four businesses comprise the sample problem portrayals; for the Excel course in Chapter 11 there were five spreadsheets that comprise the sample of problem portrayals. For the furniture sales course in Chapter 6 only one problem portrayal is demonstrated. What would comprise a sample of problem portrayals for this course? While the original course only included this one sales portrayal, the course could have been improved by collecting four or five examples of sales representatives interacting with different customers and selling different types of furniture.

IDENTIFY COMPONENT SKILLS FOR THE PROBLEM PORTRAYALS

Once you have identified a sample of problem portrayals, the next activity in the Pebble approach is to do a problem-solving event analysis. *Problem-solving event analysis* is the instructional design process for identifying the consequence, conditions, and steps required by the class of problems to be taught. Chapter 6 introduced the idea that a problem is comprised of content elements from each of the types of component skill. In Chapter 6 we indicated that each problem-solving event consists of a step that leads to a condition; that each step is defined by both defining and ordering properties; and that the resulting condition is also defined by both defining and ordering properties. At this point in the Pebble procedure, you should use ideas from Chapter 6 to identify the content elements of your problems. The following paragraphs demonstrate this procedure.

Select one of the problem portrayals you have collected and identify the conditions that are present that contribute to the solution of the problem. Figure 13-1 includes the photograph I selected for this analysis. Three conditions are identified: simplicity, rule of thirds, and format. Simplicity is to compose your photo to eliminate elements that distract from the subject. Rule of thirds is to compose your photo so that the point of interest is located near the intersection of imaginary lines that divide your photograph in thirds horizontally and vertically. Format is to compose your photo using either a horizontal or vertical format that best frames your subject and allows any action to flow into the frame of the photograph.

FIGURE 13-1 Prototype Problem Demonstration for Photographic Composition

Photographic Composition

Does this picture attract your attention?
Does this picture hold your interest?
Does this picture tell a story?
Click the speaker for an explanation.

Simplicity

Rule of thirds

Format

FIGURE 13-1 *Continued*

Audio/Animation
This picture tells a story. The pitch is about to be delivered. Will it be a strike or will the batter be out?
Several things contribute to the composition of this photograph.
(1) The word *Simplicity* appears and the pitcher is highlighted. The pitcher is clearly the subject in the photograph. There is no distracting background except the coach, who contributes to the tension in the event. There is a clear and simple object of interest. [A Continue button is displayed beneath the picture.] Click Continue to go on.
(2) The words, *Rule of thirds*, appear and crossed lines that divide the picture into thirds are overlaid on the photograph. The primary point of interest in the photograph is the pitcher's windup. A composition is more interesting when the point of interest falls on one of the points where these imaginary dividing lines cross. Click Continue to go on.
(3) The word *Format* appears and an arrow is drawn on the picture to show the direction of the throw into the frame. Finally, the picture uses a landscape format with the pitcher at the left of the photograph so that he is throwing into the photograph. Go to the next slide to see the steps used to create this composition.

What were the steps required to create the composition in this photograph? There are two primary steps to create an excellent composition: compose in the viewfinder and adjust the composition through editing. The composition in Figure 13-1 relied primarily on editing. The photograph was composed through the viewfinder, but the subject was sufficiently far away that the original photograph included many distracting details. The final composition was created through two editing steps: cropping and removing unwanted elements.

Select a second portrayal of your problem divergent from the first. Do the same conditions apply to this instance of the problem? Are there any additional conditions that apply to this instance that did not apply to the first? Figure 13-2 includes the second portrayal of a well-composed photograph that I selected for my analysis. The conditions that contribute to this photograph also include simplicity and rule of thirds. Format is not as important in this photograph, but this photograph includes a new condition: framing. Framing is to use elements of the photograph to create a frame around your subject.

What were the steps required to create this composition? The subject had climbed on a rock in the landscaping behind the shrubs. I composed the photograph in the viewfinder to use the shrubs to frame the subject. The original photograph included too much of the shrubbery and this distracted from the child who is the subject of the photograph, so I cropped the photograph to eliminate unnecessary shrubbery.

Continue this process of analyzing the content elements of additional portrayals of the problem until you feel comfortable that you have identified the key conditions that contribute to the consequence. It may be advisable to complete a problem-solving-event chart as a guide to the analysis of additional instances of the problem. As you identify additional instances, you may find you need to add or modify the conditions, steps, and their properties. Figure 13-3 is the problem-solving-event chart that I prepared for the photographic composition course. As you can observe from the foregoing analysis, not all of the photographs that exemplify good composition involved all of the conditions.

FIGURE 13-2 Prototype Problem Application for Photographic Composition

Photographic Composition

How would you rate the composition of this photograph?

☐ Poor ☐ Marginal ☐ Good ☐ Excellent

What features most contribute to the composition of this photograph?

☐ Simplicity
☐ Rule of thirds
☐ Format
☐ Framing
☐ Line

Submit

Feedback Audio:

[If a learner's response is correct, the condition words turn green; if a learner's response is incorrect, the condition words turn red to provide right/wrong feedback on his or her response.]

[The word *Simplicity* changes color.] Is the subject of this photograph easily identified? Is the background simple and uncluttered with distracting elements? The simplicity of this photograph contributes to its composition.

[The words *Rule of thirds* changes color. Overlay the rule of thirds gridlines on the picture.] Is the point of interest in this photograph on the intersection of the imaginary lines that divide this photograph into thirds? Implementing the rule of thirds makes this a more pleasing composition.

[The word *Format* changes color.] Does the horizontal format allow the subject to look into the frame? Framing the subject so that he looks into the frame and out of the picture adds interest and makes this composition more dynamic.

[The word *Framing* changes color.] Is the subject framed by the shrubs in the picture? Does this framing help create interest and add depth to the photograph? The frame emphasizes the child and adds a bit of intrigue to the composition.

[The word *Line* changes color.] Is there a line leading into the frame? Is there a diagonal line emphasizing the subject? Is there an S-curve leading into the frame? This photograph does not use Line as a major contribution to its composition.

How does this problem-solving-event analysis compare with goal analysis of the more traditional approach to instructional design? The most significant difference is that traditional goal analysis emphasizes the steps that lead to the consequence, whereas the Pebble analysis emphasizes the conditions that lead to the desired consequence. Additionally, traditional instructional analysis emphasizes prerequisite relationships for the subordinate skills required by each step in the goal analysis, whereas the Pebble analysis emphasizes the interrelationships of the different types of component skill.

FIGURE 13-3 Problem-Solving-Event Chart for Photographic Composition

Photographic Composition

Properties	Simple No distractions	Point of interest at intersection	Frame subject	Frame subject	Leading line Diagonal S-curve	Attract attention Hold interest Tell a story
Conditions	Simplicity +	Rule of thirds +	Format +	Framing +	Line =	Good Composition
Steps	↑ Viewfinder Cropping Editing	↑ Viewfinder Cropping	↑ Viewfinder Cropping	↑ Viewfinder Cropping	↑ Viewfinder	
Properties	Simple background Remove distractions	Place point of interest at intersection of imaginary lines dividing into thirds.	Avoid mergers Move into picture	Frame subject with foreground objects	Draw viewer to subject Draw viewer into picture	

The problems described in previous chapters all involved a set of component skills that applied to most or all of the problem portrayals in the progression. For the first aid course in Chapter 2, the component skills were represented by the tutorials and the specific skills that applied to a given case study were indicated to learners in preparation for undertaking the solution of the case. For the furniture sales course, the component skills are identified in Figures 6-8 and 6-9. For the entrepreneur course, the component skills are represented in Figure 7-3. For the Excel course, the component skills are represented by the Simon-says instruction for the commands required for each portrayal in the problem progression and which were identified for learners to study prior to undertaking the solution to a give problem portrayal in the progression.

DESIGN A PROTOTYPE PROBLEM DEMONSTRATION

Having created a problem-solving-event diagram, the next activity in the Pebble approach is to design a prototype problem demonstration for the problem. A *prototype problem demonstration* is a functional mock-up of the instructional events that shows the learner the consequence, conditions, and steps required for an instance of the problem. Chapter 6 demonstrated the instructional events required to demonstrate a whole problem. Table 13-1 indicates that this demonstration should consist of three instructional events: (1) show an instance of the consequence (*Show*-Q) for the whole problem; (2) show instances of conditions (*Show*-C) that lead to the consequence; and (3) show instance of the steps (*Show*-S) that lead to each of the conditions.

Figure 13-1 illustrates a simple slide designed to demonstrate an instance of this problem. The text in the second row describes the audio and accompanying animation that plays when a learner clicks on the speaker. The numbers are the bookmarks that trigger the animation that is described in the brackets. Navigation would allow the learner to repeat the audio and the accompanying animation. Going to the next slide takes the learner to the slide shown in Figure 13-4. The audio and accompanying animation are shown in the second row of the figure below the slide. Figure 13-4 extends the demonstration of each of the steps required to create the composition shown in Figure 13-1.

Table 13-1 Prescribed Instructional Events to Demonstrate a Whole Problem

Show-Q	Show an instance of the consequence (Q) for the whole problem.	kind-of
Show-C	Show instances of conditions (C) that lead to the consequence.	what-happens
Show-S	Show instances of the steps (S) that lead to each of the conditions.	how-to

FIGURE 13-4 Prototype Demonstration of Steps for Photographic Composition

Photographic Composition

Click on the picture to see the steps used to create this composition.

Crop the original photograph to
Implement the rule of thirds
Enable the pitcher to throw into the frame

Edit the cropped photograph to
Remove distracting objects in the background

Audio/Animation

[The picture appears.] With considerable luck, the action was a split-second exposure at just the right moment. There was no time to carefully frame the photograph with the viewfinder. The original photo includes a broad view of the ballgame, and there are a number of elements that distract from the subject. Study the photograph and click the Continue button to go on. [A Continue button appears below the frame.]

FIGURE 13-4 *Continued*

The first step was to crop the picture as shown. [Crop box overlays the picture; the rest of the photograph is dimmed and eventually disappears, leaving only the cropped area.] This enabled me to adjust the rule of thirds by positioning the pitcher in my new frame and to position the pitcher to the left of the frame formed by the horizontal format, allowing him to throw into the picture. Study the cropped photograph. Click the Continue button to go on.

However, the cropped picture still contains some distracting elements. There are two ballplayers warming up behind the fence. There is a fireplug next to the coach. There is a large pole seeming to grow out of the fireplug. But editing software came to the rescue. I was able to remove the players behind the fence, the fireplug, and the pole. [The animation shows the editing process with the stamp tool slowly replacing the players with the background. The frame freezes with the final version of the edited photograph.]

A problem demonstration for the first aid course in Chapter 2 is illustrated in Figure 2-5; for the furniture sales course in Chapter 6 one is illustrated in Figure 6-10; for the entrepreneur course in Chapter 7 one is introduced in Figure 7-4; and for the Excel course one is illustrated in Figure 11-7. A good exercise is for you to see whether you can identify the *Show*-Q, *Show*-C, and *Show*-S instructional events in each of these problem demonstrations.

DESIGN A PROTOTYPE PROBLEM APPLICATION

The final activity for the first ripple of the Pebble model is to design a prototype problem application. A *prototype problem application* is a functional mock-up of the instructional events that requires the learner to predict the consequence from a set of conditions, to find the faulted conditions for an unexpected consequence, or to execute the steps required to bring about the consequence. Having designed a demonstration of my sample problem portrayal, I was ready to design application instructional events for a portrayal of the problem. Chapter 6 demonstrated the instructional events prescribed to enable learners to apply their new component skills to the solution of a new problem. Table 13-2 indicates that there are three prescribed application instructional events for a whole problem: predict a consequence from a set of conditions (Do_{ex}-Q); find faulted conditions or steps for an unanticipated consequence (Do_{ex}-C); and execute all of the steps for instances of the whole problem (Do_{ex}-S).

Table 13-2 Prescribed Instructional Events for Whole-Problem Application

Do_{ex}-Q	Predict a consequence (Q) from a set of conditions for instances of the problem.	what-happens
Do_{ex}-C	Find faulted conditions (C) or steps for an unanticipated consequence for instances of the problem.	what-happens
Do_{ex}-S	Execute all of the steps (S) for instances of the whole problem.	how-to

Figure 13-2 is a slide for an application requiring learners to recognize the quality of an example of the consequence (in this case poor, marginal, good, and excellent examples of a well-composed photograph) and to identify the conditions that contributed to the quality of this photograph (Do_{ex}-C). For formative evaluation this rating will be recorded. The procedure for identifying appropriate data source and recording student data will be described in Chapter 18. When the learner clicks the Submit button, he or she receives the corrective feedback.

Another Do_{ex}-C application would be similar to Figure 13-2. Rather than showing a well-composed picture, the photograph would exhibit composition problems. The question would be modified to read, "What features of composition are poorly used in this photograph?" Or "What features of composition could be improved by cropping or editing this photograph?"

A Do_{ex}-S application could provide learners with a photograph and ask them to use a simple editing tool to improve the composition.

A more advanced Do_{ex}-S application could require learners to use a camera to take a set of photographs and then edit them to improve their composition. Learners would be required to submit both their original composition and their edited version for review by an instructor. Learners may also be asked to identify the composition feature they used and why they felt it contributed to their composition.

How does designing an application for the problem differ from the *Develop Assessment Instruments* step of more traditional instructional design? The primary difference is that the Pebble approach is more holistic; you are designing an assessment for solving a whole problem rather than individual test items for the steps of the goal analysis and their subordinate skills. Another difference is that the Pebble approach prescribes a variety of appropriate application instructional events that assess different aspects of problem solving, that is, Do_{ex}-Q, Do_{ex}-C, and Do_{ex}-S.

A problem application for the first aid course is illustrated in Figure 2-7; for the furniture sales course in Figure 6-12 Rows 21 through 23; partially shown for the entrepreneur course in Figure 7-10; and for the Excel course in Figure 11-10. A good exercise for you is to see whether you can identify the Do_{ex}-Q, Do_{ex}-C, and Do_{ex}-S instructional events in each of these problem applications.

WHAT ARE SOME OF THE CHALLENGES IN IDENTIFYING A GOOD PROBLEM?

Perhaps the greatest challenge for a problem-centered approach is identifying a class of relevant problems. In many academic areas, especially survey courses, the goal seems to be the dispensing of a significant amount of information rather than learning to solve problems. Even in areas where solving problems or learning to perform complex tasks is the obvious goal of instruction, there remain some challenges in identifying appropriate problems for a problem-centered approach.

A common situation is to design a problem-centered approach for an existing course. I have worked with faculty members to help them try to identify a problem that represents the goal(s) of their course. In these situations the content is often dictated by some outline of the subject-matter content, often determined by a textbook or prescribed course of study. How can you select a problem from such a rich body of content?

The first challenge is that survey courses are not really about a single problem or set of problems. The solution is to consider the course not as a single entity, but rather as a series of mini courses. At BYU–Hawaii, my colleagues and I worked with a biology professor to redesign Biology 100. This course covered literally hundreds of ideas, almost every concept ever introduced into biology. To convert the course to a problem-centered one, the professor finally decided that there were six primary areas of interest. With our assistance, he then developed a short course around each area with a progression of three problems identified for each of these areas. This course is described in more detail in Chapter 7.

A second challenge is that many courses are topic outlines. These topics often comprise the component skills that can be used to solve problems, but too often no problems are included in the course materials or there is a single project (problem) at the conclusion of the course. The challenge is to find a progression of problems that require these component skills for their solution. My colleagues and I worked with a major software application training company to convert their Excel course to a problem-centered approach. Their approach was to teach each of the commands in Excel but with no opportunity to apply these commands in a holistic way to a complex problem. Our challenge was to help them find a progression of problems that could be used as the context within which to teach these commends. Our solution is described in some detail in Chapter 11.

Teaching a tool, such as Excel, that is in-and-of-itself not a problem, always requires two different content areas: the component skills of the tool and the component skills of the content area to which the tool is applied. As in the case of the initial Excel course, the content area to which the tool is applied is often represented by isolated bits of content from many areas chosen to illustrate a given command in the tool. One challenge with this approach is that the component skills of the tool are disassociated from a complete representation of the particular content for which the tool is applicable. Another problem with these isolated illustrations is that learners may not be familiar with the content used to illustrate the use of the tool so they have no mental model to which they can attach either the command of the tool or the disassociated piece of content to which the tool is applied.

A problem-centered approach suggests that teaching a tool should be turned inside-out from the way it is usually taught, that is, rather than teaching the commands of the tool illustrated with isolated bits of content for which the tool is relevant, it is better to make the area of application the primary focus of the instruction with the tool taught as a way to solve problems in this application area. In Excel, rather than teaching all of the commands, we chose simple real-world problems for which a spreadsheet was a tool to solve the problem Then we taught those commands of Excel that were relevant to the type of spreadsheet being designed. As previously indicated, the challenge is to find a progression of problems such that all of the desired commands are both demonstrated and applied by the learners.

Tool courses sometimes suffer the opposite challenge, that is, the course is about teaching a specific application of the tool rather than seeing the problem as only one instance of a more general class of problems. In a cooking class, the instructor had a lesson on making chocolate chip cookies. The lesson was basically following the recipe. In consultation with the instructor, I suggested that perhaps the chocolate chip cookie recipe being taught was only a specific instance or portrayal of a more general problem-solving skill: how to make cookies. The instructor accepted the challenge. The first step was to analyze the specific problem—the chocolate chip cookie recipe—to abstract the general component skills that apply to making any kind of cookie and the specific component skills that apply only to chocolate chip cookies. The second step was to find another cookie recipe and apply these generalized component skills to that recipe. Since much of the second recipe was a repeat of the same general skills from the first recipe, the challenge for the student was to recognize the unique steps required to make this new cookie. This process was repeated for several more different kinds of cookies. By now, students had acquired the skills necessary to make a wide variety of cookies. They began to recognize that most of each recipe was merely a reminder of the generalized cookie-making skill they had acquired. At this point, the instructor took the next step and suggested that the students create their own unique cookie recipe by merely adding some unique requirements to their generalized cookie-making skill.

There is a lesson in the cookie-making example for many areas of the curriculum. If the curriculum teaches a very specific procedure for a specific application, then you might be able to find a progression of problems by identifying the generalizable skills, identifying them for learners, and then having learners apply these skills to a new situation similar but different from the first. Learners eventually realize that their skills in this particular problem-solving area can be applied to many new previously unencountered situations. Thus, they have generalized from a very specific and limited skill to a more general problem-solving skill.

Do you recognize that this is the approach promoted by a problem-centered model of instructional design? In the Excel situation, as designers, we began with the component skills we wished to teach. But from the learner point of view, they were given a specific spreadsheet problem. After being shown how to solve the first problem, they were given a second problem and they realized that the skills they learned for the first problem applied to the second problem. By working through a progression of problems, learners come to realize that their component skills can be applied in a wide variety of new situations. The component skills are firmly anchored in their mental models of this particular problem-solving process tied to applications of these skills in a variety of specific situations. Learners retain tool skills better when they have an opportunity to see these skills applied to a variety of application situations.

Finding a problem in a tool course, such as Excel, was much easier than finding relevant problems in the biology course. Many academic courses are presentation rich but application poor; they provide much information but limited application. Too often they are merely *Tell-and-Ask* courses. How does one go about finding what problems may be appropriate in such courses? I usually ask the following questions of the instructor of the course: Why are you teaching this course? Why are learners taking this course? How do you hope that learners will use the skills they attain in your course in the future? What kind of problems are they likely to encounter for which they can apply the skills learned in the course? The answers to these questions are often unique to a given course or a given instructor, but on careful reflection often yield a problem that can be the pebble used in a problem-centered approach. Perhaps the following anecdotes will help you analyze the instructional situations you encounter where the problems to be solved are not obvious.

I was working with a conductor of a well-known choir who was serving as a volunteer instructor at BYU–Hawaii. He participated in my workshop on using a problem-centered approach. In the workshop I would work with each participant to help him or her identify a class of problems that he or she might consider in developing a problem-centered approach to instruction. When I asked what course he was teaching, he indicated that the course was music history. History is a one of those areas often characterized by an excess of information and a paucity of application. After some discussion, I asked him how he prepared his choir to sing a piece of period music. He indicated that he would analyze the piece to determine those particular properties that characterize music from that early period; then he would spend extra time rehearsing the choir on those unique dynamics of the music with which they may not be familiar. Together we realized that here was a problem he could use for his history class. For a given piece of music from the period under consideration, the problem is for learners to learn to analyze the piece to recognize unique characteristics that would affect its performance. In a problem-centered approach, the instructor would first demonstrate to the learners how he would analyze the piece for his rehearsal. The component skills require knowing the unique characteristics of music and performance from the period of time under consideration. Then have the learners acquire these component skills and apply these skills to additional pieces of music. He later told me that he used this problem-centered approach with his choir and that having them actually analyze the music, rather than merely rehearsing the unique dynamics, improved their performance.

An English instructor, teaching the novel, short story, and drama, indicated that he didn't see any problems for his courses. He explained that his approach was to have learners read the piece and remember the surface story; but he suggested that literature required critical thinking, which he explained required learners to go below the surface to find the real message in the story. He then illustrated his approach by describing *A Man for All Seasons*, about the conflict of Thomas More staying true to his values or loyal to the king. In answer to my query about why he taught this piece of literature, his reply was so that it would improve the quality of the students' lives. After some discussion, we identified the following problem for this particular unit in his class. At BYU–Hawaii, where there are mostly international students, one goal of the school is for students to return to their native lands after graduation. However, more than half remain in the United States, where opportunities for their family seem greater, even though as a condition of admission they have signed an agreement to return to their native lands. These students suffer a dilemma in their lives similar to that of Thomas More. We decided that, after acquiring the skills of looking beneath the surface of the story to identify the real message, students could be asked to apply these same component skills to an analysis of their own situations. The instructor decided to have students write a short essay on return-ability prior to studying the unit and a second essay after studying the unit. He could then compare the two essays to see whether learners were able to apply the meaning of the story to their own situation. He then began to look at the other stories he required to identify other real-world situations for which a deep analysis of the stories in literature could be applied to the life situations of his students.

An instructor in a biochemistry course indicated that his survey class was a required prerequisite for his later upper-division classes. The class consisted of memorizing a large number of concepts and principles without any real application. After some discussion, we determined that perhaps the curriculum was upside down. He admitted that students usually had to relearn most of this material as they undertook actual problem solving in the labs associated with his upper-division classes. In answer to my query about what problems were used in his later classes, he explained that his students learned to synthesize DNA. Being completely ignorant of biochemistry and especially how one might synthesize DNA in the lab, I asked if he could give me a ten-minute layman's description of the process. He did. I was able to follow his explanation without having learned any of the prerequisite concepts or principles. He did take a minute to introduce me to several concepts and a principle relevant to his explanation. After the demonstration, I suggested that he had at least one problem for his introductory class. The students would not be required to actually synthesize DNA, but they could certainly understand how it worked and be able to solve problems related to the process while learning the required component skills in the process. Perhaps one way to find relevant problems for an introductory course is to look to the problems that comprise advanced courses and see whether they couldn't be brought forward. The fundamental concepts and principles are much more relevant when learners can see how they are required to solve a real problem in the content area.

If you are developing a training course, one of the best ways to identify relevant problems is to observe and interview professionals who solve the problems in their workplace. Observe the type of problems they typically solve. Study documentation about the performance of the steps required to solve the problem. Study artifacts or consequences that result from performing the steps required to solve the problem. Capture the actual activity that results from a skilled performance that solves an instance of the problem. Identify specific tools and resources that are available when one is confronted with the problem or task. Develop criterion for acceptable and superior performance. Check your problem specification against the above properties for a real-world problem and a good real-world problem. Capture the actions of a skilled performer as he or she solves the problem. Capture the problem-solving process by having the performer "think out loud" as he or she solves the problem.

PRINCIPLES AND PRESCRIPTIONS

Demonstration: Learning is promoted when learners observe a demonstration of the knowledge and skill to be learned.

Application: Learning is promoted when learners apply their newly acquired knowledge and skill.

Designing a problem prototype includes the following activities:

- Identify the content area, primary goal, and learner population for the instruction.
- Identify a class of problems that, when solved, accomplish the learning goal.
- Collect a sample of problem portrayals.
- Identify the content elements—consequence, conditions, steps, and properties—of your problems.
- Design a prototype demonstration for a portrayal of the problem.
- Design a prototype application for a portrayal of the problem.

APPLICATION

Pick a class that you have taken as a student or one you have taught or designed. Was it problem-centered? If so, what was the problem? If not, what problem does this class prepare learners to solve? After you have identified the problem, collect a sample of problem portrayals for this problem. Identify the content elements required to solve portrayals of this problem. Design a prototype demonstration and a prototype application for portrayals of your problem.

TO LEARN MORE

van Merriënboer, J. J. G., & Kirschner, P. A. (2007). *Ten steps to complex learning.* Hillsdale, NJ: Lawrence Erlbaum Associates. These authors demonstrate a detailed set of procedures for identifying and designing problem demonstrations and applications

The Online Premium Content associated with this book contains the Photographic Composition functional prototype PowerPoint. See "Demonstration Functional Prototype for Photographic Composition" to see the implementation of the problem demonstration and application described in this chapter.

COMING NEXT

This chapter assisted you in identifying a problem, a set of portrayals of this problem, and designing a demonstration and application for each of the portrayals of this problem. Chapter 14 is the next ripple in the Pebble-in-the-Pond model. This activity is to design a progression of problem portrayals that serve as the context for teaching the component skills required to complete specific instances of the problem. Chapter 14 provides guidance in identifying the component skill required by each portrayal and using these component skills to design a simple to complex sequence of problem portrayals. Chapter 15 will then demonstrate how to design demonstrations and applications to teach each of these component skills.

CHAPTER 14

DESIGN A PROBLEM PROGRESSION

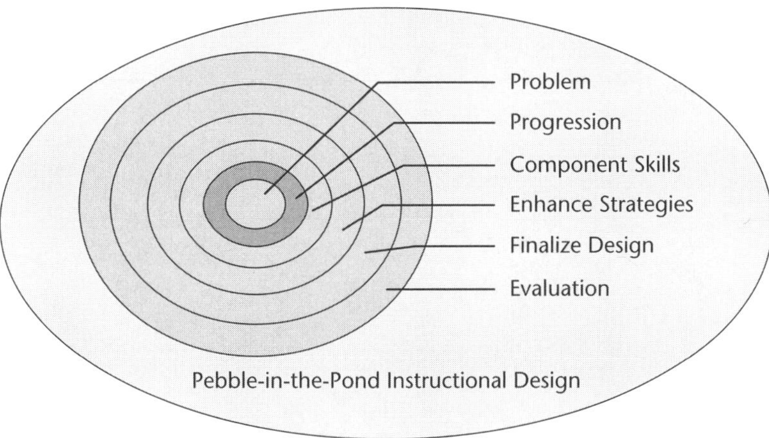

Quick Look

The second ripple in the Pebble-in-the-Pond model is to design a progression of problem prototypes. This chapter will guide you in these design activities and addresses the following questions: What is a problem progression? What are the design activities required to design a progression of problem prototypes? How can I be sure that the problem progression teaches all of the desired component skills?

Key Words

Problem Progression: a series of problem portrayals of the same type from a given content area; a straightforward version of the problem is presented first and each successive problem increases in complexity. A set of demonstrations or applications for problem prototypes is arranged in a sequence from the least complex to the most complex.

Problem Class: a set of problem portrayals that require the same set of component skills for their solution.

Component Skills Matrix: a chart that represents the consequences for a progression of portrayals across the top and the conditions and steps that lead to the consequences down the first column. The cells in the matrix indicate which steps and conditions are required for each consequence in the progression.

Skill Complexity Analysis: a procedure for sequencing a progression of portrayals from simple to complex determined by the number and type of conditions and steps required for each consequence in the progression.

INTRODUCTION

The previous chapter provided guidance for identifying a class of problems and for designing a demonstration and application for a sample problem. This chapter guides you in the design of a problem progression. A *problem progression* is a set of problem prototypes arranged in a sequence from the least complex to the most complex. This chapter identifies the properties that characterize a good progression and then guides you in the following activities required to design a good problem progression: acquire a sample of problem portrayals; identify the component skills required by each of the portrayals in your sample; adjust the sequence of portrayals to form a simple to complex sequence; and modify, delete, or add problem portrayals to ensure that all of the component skills are taught.

WHAT MAKES A GOOD PROGRESSION?

A good progression includes problem portrayals of increasing complexity. Increasing complexity means that each succeeding portrayal includes more detail for some component skills or more component skills than the preceding portrayal. Only one or two new components or revised components should be introduced for each succeeding problem portrayal. The first portrayal is the easiest version of the whole problem. The last portrayals are representative of the more complex versions of the problem to be performed in the real world. The portrayals in the progression, while from the same class of problems, should represent divergent problem portrayals that vary in those ways that instances of this problem differ in the real world. All of the component skills required by the final tasks are included in the progression.

ACQUIRE A SAMPLE OF PROBLEM PORTRAYALS

Before you can design a progression, you must have problem portrayals with which to form the progression sequence. The first activity in this design step is to select a sample of problem portrayals. A portrayal is a specific instance of the problem, not merely a description. The problem portrayals should be instances of the same class of problems. A *class of problems* is defined as those that require the same set of component skill for their solution. Each of the problem portrayals should represent a complete problem that can stand alone rather than merely being a component of a larger problem.

Figure 14-1 represents a very small sample of photographs selected as portrayals for photographic composition. I have included only a few representative photographs here to give you the idea; the actual sample included many more examples. As I looked at the photographs, I realized that there were many dimensions that contributed to the complexity of a photographic composition. My first concern was to represent a divergent set of subjects, so I included photographs of objects, individuals, groups, and scenery. I realized that a photographer has more control over the composition when the subject can be posed, so I included both posed and candid photographs. The most important step in composition is composing the picture in the viewfinder, so I included photographs that were already well-composed. However, it is not always possible for the photographer to position himself or herself for the best composition, so I included photographs that could be cropped or edited to improve the composition. Wherever possible I included the original photograph and the cropped or edited photograph. Where I had several photographs of the same or similar subjects, I included those that had the best composition and some that were poorly composed.

FIGURE 14-1 Sample Problem Portrayals for Photographic Composition

Photographic Composition—Sample Portrayals			
Objects	Individuals	Groups	Scenery

	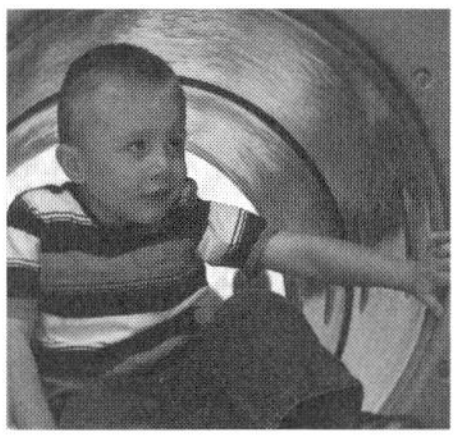		

For the courses described earlier, the sample of problem portrayals includes the practice cases for first aid; a series of different sales presentations for furniture sales (which were not included in the demonstration of the course); a series of increasingly more complex businesses for the entrepreneur course; and a series of increasingly difficult spreadsheets for the Excel course.

IDENTIFY THE COMPONENT SKILLS

Having collected a large sample of problem portrayals, how do you go about arranging them in a simple to complex sequence? An important dimension of complexity is the number of conditions required by the solution for a given portrayal. If the solution to one problem portrayal requires more conditions, then it is more complex. Another dimension of complexity is the number and type of steps required to bring about the desired conditions. If the solution for a given problem portrayal requires more, or more difficult to execute, steps, then it is more complex. *Component skill complexity analysis* is a procedure for sequencing a progression of portrayals from simple to complex.

As a first step in this design activity, arrange a set of the sample portrayals in what seems to be a good sequence. Figure 14-2 is a small set of the photographs of individuals. Except for the first instance, I included both the original photograph and the photograph after it was edited. I made a *Component Skills Matrix,* which represents the consequences for a progression of portrayals across the top and the conditions and steps that lead to the consequences down the first column. These conditions include simplicity, meaning that there are no distracting details in the photograph; rule of thirds, meaning that the subject of the photograph falls on the intersection of lines that divide the photograph into thirds horizontally and vertically; format, meaning that the photograph is oriented so that the action moves into the photograph rather than out of the photograph; frame, meaning that elements in the photograph form a frame around the subject, and line, meaning that there is a line in the photograph that leads the viewer into the photograph. The steps include pose, meaning that the subject was posed by the photographer rather than occurring naturally; viewfinder, meaning the that the photograph was composed primarily when the it was taken rather than altered by cropping or editing; crop, meaning that portions of the photograph were removed to improve the composition; and edit, meaning that some elements of the photograph were removed to improve the composition. The cells in the matrix indicate which steps and conditions are required for each of the photographs or consequence in the progression.

FIGURE 14-2 Component Skills Matrix for Photographic Composition

Photographic Composition—Partial Progression of Portrayals for Individuals					
	D	E	C	A	B

Simple		?	?	?	?
Rule of Thirds	X	X	?	X	?
Format	X	X	?	X	?
Frame			X		
Line					
Pose	X				
Viewfinder	X			X	
Crop		?	?		?
Edit				?	?

The first part of the matrix below the photographs represents the conditions for a good composition. I put an "X" in the cell corresponding to a condition for a given photograph if the original photograph already demonstrated the condition and a "?" if I thought I could improve the composition of the original photograph by cropping or editing.

The second part of the matrix below the darker line represents the steps that could be taken to produce the conditions of a good composition. I put an "X" in the cell to indicate the step had already been successful in producing a desired condition and a "?" to indicate that taking this step could improve one or more of the conditions.

For example, the first photograph of me working on my model railroad was posed so that it could be composed in the viewfinder and require no further cropping or editing to improve the composition. The second original photograph includes distracting detail in the foreground that distracts from the man operating the train. The simplicity condition of this photograph could be improved by eliminating these distracting details. This can be accomplished by cropping the picture. In the third photograph there is a nice frame around the child in the original, but the amount of shrubbery distracts from the subject, the subject is not located at the intersection of lines dividing the photograph into thirds, and the format could be improved so that the subject was looking into the picture. While there are several composition conditions to correct, they can all be corrected by carefully cropping the photograph to move the location of the subject in relation to the edges of the photograph, eliminating much of the shrubbery, and changing the format to allow the subject to look into the frame. The fourth photograph was well composed in the viewfinder, but the figures in the background of the original photograph distract from the mother and her child. This condition can be corrected by editing out the distracting figures in the background. The fifth photograph, taken during the action at a ball game, includes too much information. The photograph needs to be simplified by eliminating unnecessary elements and concentrating on the pitcher. This required both cropping the original photo and editing to eliminate the distracting figures and objects in the background. I made a note to myself that when I teach about the cropping step it is important to use a high-resolution photograph so that cropping a large part of a photograph does not result in excessive pixilation.

Figure 14-2 shows only a sample of the photographs involved in the planned problem progression. The actual progression included a number of photographs of objects, groups, and scenery as well. For each of these photographs, I indicated the conditions that were implemented by the photograph as it was composed in the viewfinder and the steps that could be taken to implement the other conditions of a good composition through cropping or editing.

ADJUST THE SEQUENCE IN THE PROGRESSION

Having determined the conditions and steps for each of the portrayals in the proposed progression, the next activity is to conduct a skills complexity analysis to be sure that the progression represents a smooth increase in complexity. A *skills complexity analysis* is a procedure for sequencing a progression of portrayals from simple to complex determined by the number and type of conditions and steps required for each consequence in the progression.

For my photographic composition module, I did not worry too much about the order of my photographs during the identification of the conditions and steps involved in the composition of each photograph. My original order is indicated by the letters in the first row of Figure 14-2. After I had determined the conditions, steps, and those photos that could be improved by cropping or editing, I reordered the photographs, as shown in Figure 14-2, to put the least complex photograph first and the most complex photograph last in the sequence. Photograph D is the least complex since no cropping or editing is required for a good composition. Photograph B is the most complex since it required extensive cropping and editing to create a good composition. Since I had a similar matrix of photographs in each of my other divergent categories—objects, groups, and scenery—I reordered the sequence in each of these to also form a simple to complex sequence based on the conditions that needed to be improved and the steps required to make this improvement.

The entrepreneur course described in Chapter 7 and the Excel course described in Chapter 11 both involved a carefully designed progression of problem portrayals. Figure 7-3 illustrates how the instructional events for demonstration and application were distributed across the different businesses in the entrepreneur course. The businesses were ordered from the least complex to the most complex business. The Excel course also involved a series of spreadsheet problems of increasing complexity. Each successive spreadsheet required additional commands to complete and required more advanced versions of the commands that had been demonstrated or applied for spreadsheets early in the sequence.

The first aid course described in Chapter 2 was designed independent of First Principles of Instruction. This course allows learners to undertake the application case studies in any order that they prefer. Learners are reminded just before undertaking any of the application cases of those tutorials (component skill instruction) that are particularly required for this case. However, this list does not include all of the tutorials that are relevant, but only those that are specific to the specific case. A careful analysis of the component skills involved indicates that there are some skills that apply to every one of the twenty application case studies, for example, the casualty assessment tutorial and the DRABC (check for danger, response, airways, breathing, and circulation) tutorial. Other component skill tutorials apply to several of the application cases; for example, the bleeding tutorial, the bandages and slings tutorial, and the communicable disease tutorial. And some component skill tutorials are specific to only one of the application cases, for example, the poisoning tutorial and the chest injuries tutorial. This course could be significantly improved by a careful sequencing of the cases based on a component skill matrix to form a better progression of cases and a more careful distribution of the demonstration and application learning events across these cases.

The furniture sales course included an extensive demonstration of a single sales presentation. The course does include some additional instruction for what to do when there is a resistant customer, how to engage a casual "just looking" customer, and how to overcome objections. Rather than merely including a brief tutorial on these problems, it would be possible to build a sequence of sales presentations where each presentation included more challenges and required more innovative application of the sales steps to get the conditions that are necessary for a sale.

MODIFY, DELETE, OR ADD PORTRAYALS

After ordering the sequence for the problem portrayals that I had collected, I studied the conditions and steps in the progression sequence to see whether there were conditions that were not represented or types of cropping or editing that were not represented. In the sample of photographs of individuals in Figure 14-2, I noted that the composition condition *line* was not represented. I then searched for another photograph that incorporated this condition—a diagonal line or an S curve line—in a photograph of an individual. I decided to include the photograph shown in Figure 14-3. Since this photograph required only cropping to improve the composition of the original photograph, I included it in the sequence just before photograph C in Figure 14-2. Figure 14-3 shows only the cropped final composition.

FIGURE 14-3 Modify the Progression by Adding a Photograph

Simple	X
Rule of Thirds	X
Format	?
Frame	X
Line	?
Pose	
Viewfinder	X
Crop	?

I examined each of the other divergent categories to see whether all of the conditions and steps that I wanted to teach were included. I also added some photographs to these sequences and eliminated some photographs that seemed to be redundant with those already included. After these adjustments, I felt that the progression sequence represented a good divergent set of problem portrayals for photograph composition for individuals.

PROBLEM PROGRESSION COMPARED WITH TRADITIONAL INSTRUCTIONAL DESIGN

Let us briefly compare designing a problem progression as demonstrated in this chapter with the more traditional approach to instructional design. Perhaps the most importance difference is that designing a problem progression is portrayal-based rather than information-based. Rather than gathering content at a later step, the problem portrayals and their multimedia representation are identified as an early activity in the process. A second important difference is that, rather than the problem being seen as a culminating activity, this approach stresses a progression of problems.

Goal analysis is the traditional design step that most closely parallels designing a problem progression. How does designing a problem progression compare to goal analysis? Both goal analysis and problem progression require the identification of steps that a learner must be able to execute to solve a problem or do a task. However, the Pebble model is more prescribed than goal analysis. Problem progression stresses the identification of conditions that lead to the consequence in addition to the steps that bring about these conditions. A number of different component skills are prescribed in this approach: the ability to identify a good consequence; the ability to identify an appropriate condition; the ability to identify an appropriate step; and the ability to execute an appropriate step. In Figure 14-2, identifying the conditions and steps for each problem portrayal is the analog for a goal analysis; however, these conditions and steps are in the context of specific problem portrayals rather than abstract.

PRINCIPLES AND PRESCRIPTIONS

Problem-Centered: Learning is promoted when learners engage in a problem-centered instructional strategy in which component skills are taught in the context of a simple-to-complex progression of whole real-world problems.

Take the following steps to design a problem progression:

- Design a progression of divergent problem portrayals from simple to complex.
- Identify the component skills required to solve each problem portrayal in the sequence.
- Adjust the progression to include sufficient opportunity for learners to acquire all of the desired component skills.

APPLICATION

You should have previously selected a content area and class of problems for your functional prototype. You should expand your project by selecting a sample of problem portrayals and applying the prescription of this chapter to determine a progression of these problem portrayals.

TO LEARN MORE

van Merriënboer, J. J. G., & Kirschner, P. A. (2007). *Ten steps to complex learning.* Hillsdale, NJ: Lawrence Erlbaum Associates. These authors present an alternative approach to selecting and sequencing a progression of problems.

See the Online Premium Content, "Demonstration Functional Prototype for Photographic Composition," to see the implementation of the problem progression described in this chapter.

TO LEARN MORE

The third activity in the Pebble-in-the-Pond model is to design demonstration and application for the component skills required by the portrayals in the problem progression. Chapter 15 provides guidance for identifying an appropriate sequence for the demonstration and application of the component skills involved and for designing a prototype demonstration or application for each of the problem portrayals in the progression.

CHAPTER 15

DESIGN STRATEGIES FOR COMPONENT SKILLS

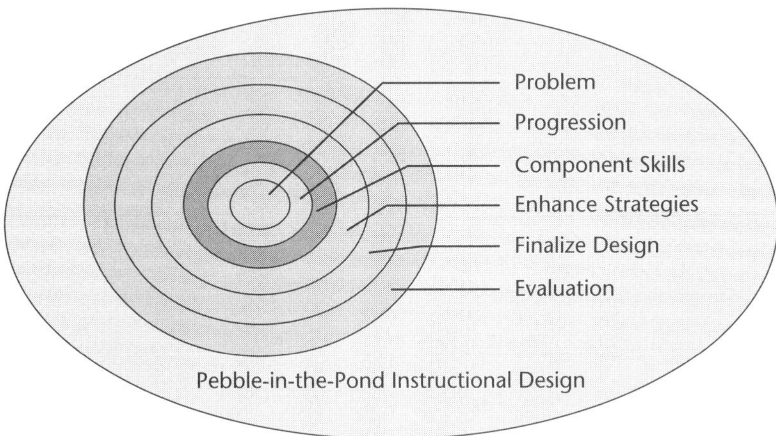

Quick Look

The third ripple in the Pebble-in-the-Pond model is to design instructional strategies for teaching the component skills (conditions and steps) for each of the prototypes in the problem progression. This chapter will guide you in the activities required to design demonstration and application for these component skills. It will answer the following question: How do I design demonstration or application for all of the conditions and steps of the portrayals in the progression?

Key Words

Problem-Centered Component Skill Instruction: demonstration and application for each of the conditions and steps distributed across the portrayals in a problem progression.
Instructional Event Table: a table that indicates when each condition or step should be demonstrated and when it should be applied.

INTRODUCTION

The previous chapter provided guidance for designing a problem progression. Once you are satisfied with the progression of problem portrayals, the next instructional design activity is to design problem-centered component skill instruction.

Problem-centered component skill instruction is a demonstration and application for each of the conditions and steps distributed across the portrayals in a problem progression. This chapter provides direction for determining an instructional event table that indicates when each condition or step should be demonstrated or applied and for using this instructional event table to design demonstrations or applications for these conditions or steps in the context of the portrayals of the problem progression.

DETERMINE AN INSTRUCTIONAL EVENT TABLE

An *instructional event table* indicates when each condition or step should be demonstrated and when it should be applied. First, examine each of the conditions and steps for each portrayal in the problem progression. The purpose of this examination is to determine whether the condition or step should be demonstrated for the portrayal or applied to the portrayal. It is best to demonstrate a condition or step when it is first introduced. When the condition or step is required for a subsequent portrayal, it may require additional demonstration if there are differences from the first demonstration. If not, then the learner should be required to apply the condition or step to the portrayal.

Table 15-1 is an instructional event table for photograph composition. The left column identifies each of the portrayals in the photographic composition progression, using the letter assigned to each picture in Figure 14-2. Photograph F was the photograph that included the condition of line shown in Figure 14-3. The second and third columns in Table 15-1 indicate the conditions and steps that should be demonstrated; the fourth and fifth columns indicate those conditions and steps that should be applied. This instructional event table becomes the strategy guide for designing appropriate demonstration or application instructional events for the conditions and steps for each portrayal in the progression.

Table 15-1 Instructional Event Table for Photographic Composition for Individuals

Photograph	Demo Condition	Demo Step	Apply Condition	Apply Step
D—Me working on railroad	Rule of Thirds, Format	Pose, Viewfinder		
E—Man running trains	Simplicity	Cropping	Rule of Thirds	
F—Woman next to building	Line		Rule of Thirds, Format	Crop
C—Child in bushes	Frame		Rule of Thirds, Format, Simplicity	Crop
A—Mother with child		Editing	Rule of Thirds, Simplicity	
B—Baseball pitcher			Rule of Thirds, Format, Simplicity	Crop, Edit

DESIGN DEMONSTRATIONS AND APPLICATIONS FOR CONDITIONS AND STEPS

Using the instructional event table, the next activity is to design demonstrations and applications as identified in this table. Table 15-2 identifies the prescribed instructional events for teaching the component skills required to solve each portrayal of the problem in the progression. Remember that a component skill or problem solving event includes step(s) that results in a condition. The combination of all the conditions leads to the consequence or solution to the problem. The following illustrations will demonstrate the implementation of these instructional events as they are distributed across the problem progression.

Table 15-2 Checklist for Prescribed Instructional Events for Component Skills

Demonstrate the Component Skill (Portrayal 1)		
Tell-C	Describe the condition (C).	kind-of
Show-C	*Show* instances of the condition (C).	kind-of
Tell-S	Describe the step (S).	kind-of, how-to
Show-S	*Show* the execution of instances of the step (S).	kind-of, how-to
Do_{id} the Component Skill (Portrayal 2)		
Do_{id} -S	Identify instances of the step.	kind-of
Do_{id} -C	Identify instances of the condition.	kind-of
Do_{ex} the Component Skill (Portrayal 3)		
Do_{ex} -S	Execute instances of the step (S).	how-to
Do_{id} -C	Identify instances of the condition (C).	kind-of
▲ Repeat for each component skill required by each portrayal in the progression. ▲		
Key: C = condition, S = step, Do_{id} = identify instance, Do_{ex} = execute step		

Figure 15-1 is a prototype demonstration for photograph D (portrayal 1) as prescribed in Tables 15-1 and 15-2. Since this is the first portrayal of these component skills, the learning events are only demonstrations as specified by Row 1 in Table 15-1 and the first section of Table 15-2. The slide as shown is displayed to the learner. The audio and animation associated with this slide are shown in the second panel of the figure. There are two *Tell*-C instructional events for rule of thirds and format; there are two *Tell*-S instructional events for pose and viewfinder; there are two *Show*-C instructional events for rule of thirds and format; and there is one *Show*-S instructional event for viewfinder. I did not include a *Show*-S instructional event for pose.

Figure 15-2 is an application/demonstration for photograph E (portrayal 2). The first response is an assessment of the learner's skill in recognizing the rule of thirds (Do_{id} -C rule of thirds). The simplicity demonstration is a *Show*-C learning event.

Figure 15-3 is an application/demonstration for photograph F (portrayal 3). There are two Do_{id} -C instructional events for rule of thirds and format; there is a *Show*-C instructional event for line; there is a Do_{ex} -S instructional event for cropping; and there is a *Show*-S instructional event for the cropping help.

Figure 15-4 is an application/demonstration for photograph C (portrayal 4) in the progression. There are three Do_{id}-C instructional events for rule of thirds, format, and simplicity; there is a *Show*-C instructional event for frame and a Do_{ex} -S instructional event for cropping.

FIGURE 15-1 Prototype Demonstration for Photograph D (Portrayal 1)

Photographic Composition

Rule of thirds. The primary point of interest should fall on the intersection of imaginary lines that divide the photograph into thirds horizontally and vertically. Click here for demonstration.

Format. Use either landscape or portrait format to best simplify the composition, position the subject and implement the rule of thirds. Click here for demonstration.

Pose. Posing the subject provides the most control over composition.

Viewfinder. Always compose the picture the best that is possible by using the viewfinder of the camera. Click here for demonstration.

Audio/Animation

[Clicking on Rule of Thirds displays grid lines over the picture and shows the following audio/animation.]

Notice that the lines cross right on the face of the subject, focusing the viewer's attention on his intense concentration on his project. This composition is a good illustration of the rule of thirds.

[Clicking on Format shows a landscape format of the photograph next to the portrait format and plays the following audio.]

The landscape format shows more of the model railroad, but in so doing distracts the viewer's attention away from the subject. The portrait format allows the viewer to concentrate on the subject with the model railroad scenery playing only a supporting role in the composition.

[Clicking on Viewfinder shows a wider view of the scene and then moves closer and back and forth to finally frame the picture as shown and plays the following audio.]

This view through the viewfinder illustrates how the photographer starts with a wide view and then moves closer to the subject and tries several compositions by moving from side to side, finally turning the camera for a portrait format and composing the subject using the rule of thirds.

FIGURE 15-2 Prototype Application/Demonstration for Photograph E (Portrayal 2)

Photographic Composition

Does the composition of this photograph demonstrate the rule of thirds?

☐ YES ☐ NO

Simplicity. An effective composition does not have a background or other elements that distract from the subject. Are there distracting elements in this photograph?
Click here for demonstration.

Feedback

[Clicking either of the response boxes records the learner's response, draws a grid over the photograph, and plays the following audio message.]

Does the composition demonstrate the rule of thirds? Yes, it does! Look at the lines drawn to divide the photograph into thirds. The subject's face is the point of interest. Does the intersection of these imaginary lines fall on his face?

[Clicking the Simplicity demonstration link plays the following audio/animation.]

Are there distracting elements in this photograph? Look at the bench work and wires beneath the train. Do these busy elements compete for the viewer's attention? [The bench work and wire section of the photograph are highlighted.] How can you simplify this photograph? Most photo programs enable you to crop a photograph. Cropping selects the portion of the photograph you want to retain and eliminates the parts of the picture that you don't want to retain. Watch as I crop this photograph. [The animation then draws a cropping line and slowly adjusts it to select the subject and the train but eliminate the bench work and the wiring. The cropped photograph remains when the animation concludes.] Does the photograph still use the rule of thirds? Note how the cropped photograph focuses the viewer's attention on the subject, the man and the train, by eliminating distracting elements.

FIGURE 15-3 Prototype Application/Demonstration for Photograph F (Portrayal 3)

Photographic Composition

Does the composition of this photograph illustrate the rule of thirds?

☐ YES ☐ NO

Does the composition of this photograph illustrate effective format?

☐ YES ☐ NO

Line is a type of composition that emphasizes a diagonal element that leads the viewer into the photograph. Click here for a demonstration.

Click here to crop the photograph to improve the rule of thirds and format of this composition.

Feedback

[Selecting a check box for the rule of thirds question records the learner's response and plays the following audio/animation.]

Does the composition illustrate the rule of thirds? As formatted, it does not. However, you could crop this photograph to move the woman into an intersection of the imaginary lines dividing the photograph into thirds. The last activity of this slide requires you to crop this picture to implement the rule of thirds.

[Selecting a check box for the format question records the learner's response and plays the following audio with the accompanying animation.]

The format could be improved by making it vertical to better emphasize the lines converging in the picture. The last activity of this slide requires you to crop this picture to implement a better format.

[Clicking the Line demonstration link plays the following audio/animation.]

Look carefully at this photograph. Notice how the sidewalk recedes into the distance. [A dark line is drawn up the sidewalk as it recedes into the picture.] Notice how the lines of the stone and the windows all converge with the sidewalk. [A couple of lines follow the mortar and window lines converging with the sidewalk line.] Diagonal lines that lead the viewer into the picture make a photograph composition interesting and engaging

[Clicking the Crop paragraph plays the following audio/animation.]

[A cropping tool is made available to the learner.] Use the cropping tool to crop this picture to improve the format and more clearly implement the rule of thirds. Click the Done button when you have finished cropping the picture. [The Done button appears under the photograph.] If you need detailed directions for using the cropping tool, click the Help button. [A Help button appears under the picture.]

[Clicking the Help button plays the following audio/animation.]

[Another picture is displayed with a portion of a picture-editing menu showing the Crop tool above the photograph.] First I select the Crop tool. [Cursor moves over the Crop tool menu item and a click is heard.] This places crop lines over the picture as shown [crop lines appear on the picture]. I then grab a handle, the small marks in the corners or sides of the crop lines, and adjust the crop lines to cover the area I want to include in my picture. [The cursor grabs a handle and drags the crop lines. This is repeated until the desired area of the picture is selected.] I then click the Enter key to accept the crop. The unwanted area of the picture is hidden. If I'm unhappy with my crop I can use the Undo button [show Undo button on menu above picture] to return to the original picture and try again. [The learner is returned to the slide under consideration.]

FIGURE 15-3 *Continued*

[Clicking the Done button saves the picture with the learner's crop lines and plays the following audio/animation.]

I placed my proposed crop lines over the photograph. [My crop lines appear in red.] Do we agree? I cropped the picture to produce a portrait format to emphasize the diagonal lines receding into the distance. By using a portrait format it was easier to place the woman, who is the subject of the photograph, closer to the intersection of the rule of thirds lines. The vertical format also eliminated some of the butterflies near the woman, which tended to distract attention from the subject of the photograph. [My cropped picture appears side-by-side with the learner's cropped picture.]

FIGURE 15-4 Prototype Application/Demonstration for Photograph C (Portrayal 4)

Photographic Composition

Does the composition of this photograph illustrate the rule of thirds?

☐ YES ☐ NO

Does the composition of this photograph illustrate effective format?

☐ YES ☐ NO

Does the composition of this photograph illustrate simplicity?

☐ YES ☐ NO

Frame is a type of composition that uses elements in the photograph to form a frame around the subject. Click here for demonstration.

Click here to crop the photograph to improve the simplicity, rule of thirds, format, and framing of this composition.

[Clicking a yes or no check box for the rule of thirds question records the learner's response and plays the following audio/animation.]

As it was composed through the viewfinder, this photograph does not illustrate the rule of thirds. [Grid lines appear over the photograph.] Notice that the child, who is the subject of the photograph, appears in the middle. However, this could be corrected by cropping. You will have an opportunity to crop this photograph.

[Clicking a yes or no check box for the format question records the response and plays the following audio with animation.]

The landscape format is okay, but it would be better when the picture is cropped to implement the rule of thirds. You will have an opportunity to crop this photograph.

[Clicking a yes or no check box for the simplicity question records the response and plays the following audio/animation.]

This photograph is very busy. There is too much foliage, and it distracts and almost hides the child. When you crop this picture, you can also correct this problem with the composition.

(continued)

FIGURE 15-4 *Continued*

[Clicking the frame demonstration plays the following audio/animation.]

Notice how the limbs of the shrubbery form a frame around the face of the child. Framing is a type of composition that focuses attention on the subject. When you crop this picture, you should try to enhance the effect of this natural frame around the child's face.

[Clicking the Crop link plays the following audio and enables the photograph for cropping.]

The photo is ready to be cropped. Use your mouse to outline the area of the photograph that you wish to retain. Try to enhance the composition features of rule of thirds, format, and framing. Click the Done button when you are satisfied with your cropping. [Done button appears below the photograph.]

[When the learner has finished cropping the photograph and clicked the Done button, the following audio with animation is played.]

[My crop lines in red overlay the photograph that still contains the learner's crop lines.] My crop lines are shown in red. Are they similar to your crop lines? When you have finished comparing your crop lines with mine, click the Done button again. [The area outside of my crop lines is removed and the cropped photograph remains.] Notice how the landscape format was retained but how it now implements the rule of thirds. [Grid lines are overlaid on the photograph for about 2 seconds.] Notice how the excess foliage was removed by the cropping and the foliage now frames the face of the child. Cropping significantly improved the composition of this photograph.

Figure 15-5 is a prototype application for rule of thirds and a demonstration for the composition principle of simplicity (portrayal 5). There are two Do_{id}-C instructional events for rule of thirds and simplicity and there is a *Show*-S instructional event for editing.

FIGURE 15-5 Prototype Application/Demonstration for Photograph A (Portrayal 5)

Photographic Composition

Does the composition of this photograph illustrate the rule of thirds?

☐ YES ☐ NO

Does the composition of this photograph illustrate simplicity?

☐ YES ☐ NO

When a photograph includes distracting elements **editing** can be used to remove these elements and simplify the photograph. Click here for a demonstration.

FIGURE 15-5 *Continued*

[Selecting a yes or no check box for rule of thirds records the learner's response and plays the following audio/animation.]

This photograph as composed through the viewfinder does implement the rule of thirds. Visualize the imaginary lines. Did you notice that the woman's face was on one intersection? The baby's face is in shadow, making the woman the primary point of interest in this photo.

[Selecting a yes or no check box for simplicity records the learner's response and plays the following audio/animation.]

Notice the woman and man in the background. These figures distract the viewer's attention from the woman and her child. The composition property of simplicity attempts to avoid or eliminate distracting elements in the photograph.

[Clicking the editing demonstration link plays the following audio/animation.]

This photograph is well composed, but the woman and the man in the background distract attention from the woman and her child. Here is where editing software comes to the rescue. Using the Clone stamp in Photoshop Elements, I can copy a bit of background and use it to replace these figures. Watch as the animation shows this process. [The animation shows the editing process in which a piece of background is selected and then used to replace a bit of the figure. This animation continues until both figures have been removed.] Notice the simplicity of the edited photograph. Note the viewer's attention can be focused on the woman and her child without distraction.

Figure 15-6 is the culminating application prototype for this section of the course, which teaches photographic composition using individuals (portrayal 6). There are three Do_{id}-C instructional events for rule of thirds, format and simplicity; there are two Do_{ex}-S instructional events for cropping and editing.

FIGURE 15-6 Culminating Prototype Application for Photograph B (Portrayal 6)

Photographic Composition

Does the composition of this photograph illustrate the rule of thirds?

☐ YES ☐ NO

Does the composition of this photograph illustrate effective format?

☐ YES ☐ NO

Does the composition of this photograph illustrate simplicity?

☐ YES ☐ NO

Click here to crop this photograph to improve its use of rule of thirds and format.

Click here to edit this photograph to improve the simplicity of the composition.

(continued)

FIGURE 15-6 *Continued*

[Selecting the yes or no check box for rule of thirds records the learner's response and plays the following audio/animation.]

As it was composed through the viewfinder, the composition of this photograph does not implement the rule of thirds. However, with appropriate cropping, the young man pitching the ball could be made the subject of the photograph and arranged in the remaining frame to implement the rule of thirds. You will have an opportunity to do this cropping.

[Selecting the yes or no check box for simplicity records the learner's response and plays the following audio/animation.]

The format of this photograph could be improved to emphasize the action of the pitcher about to throw the ball. A good landscape format would put the pitcher to the left of the frame so that he is throwing into the photograph. Here again, careful cropping can significantly improve the format of this picture. You will have an opportunity to do this cropping.

[The learner's response to the simplicity question is recorded and the following audio message is played.]

As composed through the viewfinder, this photograph has many distracting elements, including the fielder to the left of the photograph, other players warming up behind the fence, and houses in the background. As it stands, it is a very busy photograph. But, with appropriate cropping, the neighborhood houses can be eliminated and, with appropriate editing, the distracting players behind the fence can be eliminated. You will have an opportunity to make the appropriate cropping and editing improvements to this photograph.

[Clicking the crop link enables the photograph for cropping and plays the following audio directions.]

Crop this photograph to improve the rule of thirds, to improve the format, and to eliminate the distracting houses in the background. Click the Done button when you have finished cropping the photograph. [When the Done button is clicked, the learner's cropped photograph is saved and then cropped.] Now you will have an opportunity to edit the photograph.

[Clicking the Edit link enables the photograph for editing using the Clone stamp and plays the following audio directions.]

Use the Clone tool to eliminate distracting elements from this photograph. If you need detailed directions for using the Clone tool, please click the Help button. [A Help button appears below the picture. In the final version of the course, step-by-step instructions demonstrating the Clone tool used in this program will be added here. The appropriate editing tool will be available to the learner and the learner will be able to enlarge the photograph for editing.]

Click the Done button when you have finished editing the photograph.

[When the Done button is clicked, the learner's edited photograph will be saved and my version of the cropped and edited photograph will appear next to the learner's version.]

Compare your finished composition with mine. They will probably not be the same. Have you emphasized the rule of thirds? Have you used a format that emphasizes the young man pitching and shows him pitching into the frame? Have you eliminated distracting elements from the photograph?

Figure 2-6 is an example of component skill demonstration and application for the DRABC and facial injuries skills for first aid; Figure 6-12 is an example of the component skill demonstration and application for a friendly greeting for furniture sales; Figures 7-6 through 7-10 are an example of the component skill demonstration and application for identifying a business opportunity as it is distributed across the progression of portrayals for the entrepreneur course. A good exercise is to see whether each of these demonstration/application learning events implement the learning events as prescribed by Table 15-2.

CHECK YOUR INSTRUCTIONAL STRATEGY

In a problem progression, the instructional events for a given component skill are distributed across several different portrayals in the problem progression, as shown in Table 15-1. At this point in the instructional design, it is wise to take a close look to see whether the instruction for each of the component skills is complete. I wanted to be sure I had adequately taught each of the component skills. Table 15-3 is a section of the Course Critique Checklist for a Whole Problem (see Table 10-14 for the entire checklist), showing the component skills of rule of thirds, format, simplicity, line, and framing. The numbers in the cells refer to the figures in this chapter, Chapter 15, that include the instructional event—*Tell, Show,* G, M, > , S, Do_{id}, Do_{ex}, C, F, >, P—identified in Row 2 of the table.

Table 15-3 Checklist for Component Skills in Photograph Composition for Individuals

Component Skill 1 = Rule of Thirds													
	Tell	*Show*	G	M	>	S	Do_{id}	Do_{ex}	C	F	>	P	
Condition	1	1	X	X			2 3 4 5 6			X	X		
Step Viewfinder	1	1	X	X									
Step Crop	3	2	X	?			4 6	3 4 6		X	X		
Component Skill 2 = Format													
Condition	1	1	X	X			3 4 6			X	X		
Component Skill 3 = Simplicity													
Condition	2	2	X	X			4 5			X			
Step Edit		5		?				6		X			
Component Skill 4 = Line													
Condition	3	3	X	X									
Component Skill 5 = Framing													
Condition	4	4	X	X									

The instructional events for the component skill rule of thirds are distributed across six of the portrayals in the progression, as shown in Table 15-1 and Figure 15-3. The skill is defined and illustrated for photograph D (Figure 15-1). Learners are asked to identify whether or not the rule of thirds was implemented for each of the remaining photographs (Figures 15-2 through 15-6). The X in the G column indicates that guidance was provided to help learners see the application of this principle in the photograph. The X in the M column indicates that the use of multimedia was appropriate and did not include any of the multimedia errors identified in Chapter 9. The >3 column is left blank because there is only one demonstration of the rule of thirds principle. However, the Feedback for each of the Do_{id} learning events does provide another demonstration. In addition, when the instruction is designed for the other divergent categories in this course—objects, groups, and scenery—there will be at least one demonstration of rule of thirds for a photograph in each of these categories. The Coaching column was left blank since there is no explicit coaching provided. As photographs become more complex, especially for groups and scenery, it will become advantageous to provide this coaching.

The step of using the viewfinder was described and demonstrated for photograph D (Figure 15-1), but there was neither further demonstration nor opportunity for learners to practice this skill either by recognizing well-composed photographs that required no cropping nor by having learners actually compose photographs using a viewfinder or simulation of a viewfinder. This is a step that should be demonstrated and applied, especially in the section on scenery photography. There were several opportunities to apply the step of cropping.

Using the Course Critique Checklist is a good way to check the adequacy of your instructional design and to make revisions in your problem progression and prototype demonstration and application of the component skills required by the portrayals in this progression.

COMPONENT SKILL INSTRUCTION COMPARED WITH TRADITIONAL INSTRUCTIONAL DESIGN

Designing strategies for component skills in the Pebble model cuts across several instructional design steps in a more traditional ISD approach, including writing performance objectives, developing assessment instruments, developing an instructional strategy, and developing instructional materials. How does the approach in this chapter compare with these traditional ISD design activities?

How does designing prototype component skill instruction compare to writing performance objectives? Traditional instructional design leaves the form of performance objectives open. In the Pebble model, the instructional events required to teach a condition or a step are prescribed, and the task is to identify which instructional event is appropriate rather than writing a performance objective. Table 13-2 identifies the prescribed instructional events for application for a whole problem. Table 13-2 is an analog for performance objectives. Rather than writing performance objectives, these prescribed application instructional events are used to generate prototype applications.

How does designing prototype component skill instruction compare to developing assessment instruments? Component skill instruction includes the design of application prototypes for each of the conditions and steps of the problems in the progression. In component skill instruction, a given prototype slide often includes both demonstration and application (as was shown in Figures 15-2 through 15-6). These prototype applications are the analog to developing assessment instruments. As indicated above, an appropriate instructional event for these applications is prescribed (an analog to performance objectives) and this prescription is used to design a prototype application (an analog to assessment instruments). As indicated earlier, these instruments are not designed in the abstract but rather in the context of actual problem portrayals.

How does component skill instruction compare to developing an instructional strategy? Component skill instruction includes a decision about what to demonstrate and what to apply for each condition and step for each portrayal in the progression. Table 15-2 is an analog for an instructional strategy. This strategy is then implemented with prototype demonstration and application instructional events. This is the backbone of a problem-centered instructional strategy.

How does designing component skill instruction compare to developing instructional materials? A problem progression is a content-first approach. The first activity after determining the goal and learner population is to gather a sample of problem portrayals. This gathering of sample portrayals is the analog to developing instructional materials, but rather than occurring late in the process as a way to implement the design, it occurs at the beginning of the design. The rest of the component skill design effort occurs in the context of these actual content materials.

PRINCIPLES AND PRESCRIPTIONS

Demonstration: Learning is promoted when learners observe a demonstration of the knowledge and skill to be learned.
Application: Learning is promoted when learners apply their newly acquired knowledge and skill.

Use the following steps when preparing to design demonstration and application of component skills:

- Determine the distribution of demonstration and application for each condition and step required for the portrayals in the progression.
- Based on this strategy distribution, demonstration and application instructional events are determined for each condition and step of the portrayals in the problem progression.
- Use the Course Critique Checklist to check the adequacy of the instructional strategies you have designed.

APPLICATION

Using the portrayals in your problem progression that you previously identified (Chapter 14), use the prescriptions of this chapter to determine when each condition or step needs to be demonstrated and when it needs to be applied. As specified by the resulting instructional event table, design a demonstration or application for each condition and step for the portrayals in the progression.

TO LEARN MORE

van Merriënboer, J. J. G., & Kirschner, P. A. (2007). *Ten steps to complex learning.* Hillsdale, NJ: Lawrence Erlbaum Associates. These authors provide an alternative approach to designing demonstration and application for the component skill involved in solving complex problems or doing complex tasks.

See the Online Premium Content, "Demonstration Functional Prototype for Photographic Composition" to see the implementation of a structural framework and peer interaction described in this chapter.

COMING NEXT

The fourth ripple in the Pebble model is to enhance the problem-solving instruction by identifying a structural framework that can be used to provide a cognitive anchor for the component skills required to solve the problems in the progression. The problem-solving instruction can also be enhanced by providing opportunity for peer-collaboration and peer-critique. Chapter 16 provides guidance in adding these enhancements to the problem progression and component skill instruction.

CHAPTER 16

DESIGN STRUCTURAL FRAMEWORK AND PEER-INTERACTION STRATEGY ENHANCEMENTS

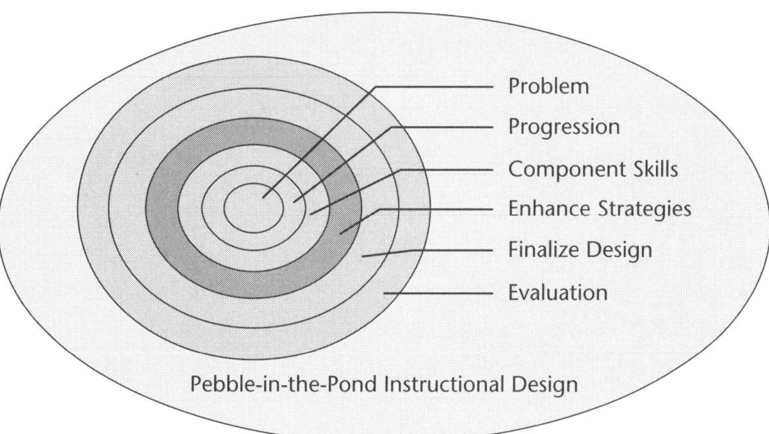

Quick Look

The fourth ripple in the Pebble-in-the-Pond model is to design enhancements that facilitate learning from the instructional strategies, including a structural framework and peer-interaction. The first part of this chapter will guide you in the activities required to design a structural framework and use it to facilitate guidance, coaching, and integration of the problem-solving skills being taught. It will answer the following questions: What are the properties of a good structural framework? How do you use this structural framework to provide guidance and coaching? How can this structural framework help learners transfer their problem-solving skill into their everyday life?

The second part of this chapter will guide you in the activities required to design effective peer-interaction. It will answer the following questions: What are the properties of effective peer-interaction? How do you integrate peer-interaction into activation, demonstration, application, and integration?

Key Words

Structural Framework: an organization of previously learned information that learners can use to adapt an existing mental model or to build a new mental model for new content.

Peer-Interaction: an instructional activity in which learners teach one another via sharing, discussion, collaboration, or critique.

Peer-Sharing: an instructional event in which learners share with each other prior relevant experience with the subject-matter content under consideration.

Peer-Discussion: a form of learner-interaction in which learners deliberate the proposed solution of example problems.
Peer-Collaboration: a form of learner-interaction in which learners work together in small groups to solve problems.
Peer-Critique: an instructional event in which learners evaluate the problem-solving activities of fellow learners and provide constructive suggestions for improvement.

INTRODUCTION

This chapter includes two types of instructional activity that can enhance the instructional strategies previously described: adding a structural framework and introducing peer-interaction. The first part of this chapter provides guidance in identifying an effective structural framework. It then guides you in the design of a demonstration of this structure and using this structure to provide guidance, coaching, and reflection instructional events. The second part of this chapter provides guidance in identifying effective peer-interaction activities. It then guides you in the design of peer-sharing, peer-discussion, peer-collaboration, and peer-critique learning events.

STRUCTURAL FRAMEWORKS

This chapter guides you in the design of a structural framework and the use of this framework for guidance, coaching, and reflection. A *structural framework* is an organization of previously learned information that learners can use to adapt an existing mental model or to build a new mental model for new content. This chapter identifies the properties that characterize a good structural framework and then guides you in the following activities: identify a structural framework, design a demonstration of this structural framework that helps learners recall what they already know about this structure, and design problem-solving guidance, coaching, and reflection based on this structural framework.

Chapter 8 identified several types of structural frameworks, including mnemonics, analogy or metaphor, and checklists. As an example of a structural framework, this chapter will demonstrate the use of metaphor. Adding other forms of structural frameworks would be similar. A *metaphor* is a form of structural framework that helps learners relate the relationships in a familiar entity, activity, or process to similar relationships in the entity, activity, or process to be learned. The content to be learned is called the *target content.*

What Makes an Effective Structural Framework?

An effective instructional framework is based on content that is already familiar to the learners. It must contain some elements that are similar to the elements of the target content; it must also contain relationships among its elements that are parallel to relationships among the elements in the target content. The structural framework must not be more complex than the target content. A structural framework requires significant guidance to facilitate a learner's ability to map the elements and relationships of the framework to the elements and relationships of the target content.

Identify an Appropriate Structural Framework

The first attempt to identify an appropriate structural framework should be a search to see whether there is a common metaphor or analogy that is often used with the content you are teaching. When such a commonly used structural framework is available, it is probably wise to use it.

If there is no commonly used structural framework, then the challenge is to create one. Some instructors encourage learners to identify their own structural frameworks. In fact, in the absence of guidance, many learners will try to find an existing mental model that they can use to understand the new content material. The danger in letting learners use their own structural frameworks is that they may think the framework they select has elements and relationships in common when it doesn't, leading to misconceptions. Learners often have a difficult time seeing the parallel elements and relationships resulting in a framework; the result is inefficient learning. It may even interfere with learning. When the instruction demonstrates a carefully constructed structural framework and uses it to guide and coach learners in acquiring the new content, it is more likely that this instruction can lead learners to see the parallel elements and relationships between the analogy and the target content. A carefully constructed structural framework added to an e^3 instructional strategy can enhance learning.

Identify the relevant features of the framework and the parallel features of the target concept. To create a new structural framework, study the conditions and steps of the whole problem; study the relationship among the conditions. Can you think of a common object or event that has some parallel to these relationships? For example, I looked at each of the conditions of an effective photographic composition to see what they had in common. It seemed to me that the purpose of a good composition is to focus the learner's attention by directing his or her line of site to the subject and action of the photograph.

Map similarities among the features of the metaphor and of the target concept. Indicate limitations of the metaphor, areas where the similarities are no longer parallel. Draw conclusions. To accomplish this I restated the conditions of a good composition to emphasize the effect that each has on the line of sight of the viewer:

- Simplicity is a photograph free of a complex background or other distracting elements that would pull the line of sight away from the subject;
- Format (either landscape or portrait) allows the viewer's line of sight to follow the action into the photograph;
- Rule of thirds is placing the point of interest in the area of a photograph where the viewer's line of sight tends to naturally look first;
- Line is a diagonal or S-curved line that leads the viewer's line of sight into the photograph;
- Frame is an arrangement secondary elements in the photograph that surrounds the subject and draws the viewer's line of sight to the subject of the photograph.

By restating each of these conditions in terms of the effect they have on the viewer's line of sight, I was able to see a relationship shared by all of these conditions, that is, that each was a device for directing the viewer's line of sight toward the subject or action represented in the photograph. I tried to think of an analogy or metaphor that would help a learner see the common purpose of these conditions. After some thought, it seemed to me that each of these composition conditions *funnels* the viewer's line of sight toward the subject or action of the photograph. Aha! Could a funnel be the metaphor I seek? Some substance, such as water, is poured through a funnel to direct the flow into a specific container or location; a photographic composition directs the viewer's line of sight into the specific subject or action of the photograph. I think that it may work.

Design a Demonstration of This Structural Framework

A structural framework is a form of activation; it activates a learner's previously acquired mental model of some phenomenon in the learner's experience. The first instructional event for a structural framework is to compare the target content with the previously acquired mental model represented by the metaphor. This comparison should show an example of the problem to be solved and a general introduction to the conditions involved in the solution, compared with a representation of the metaphor or mental model assumed to be previously acquired by the learner. Figure 16-1 provides a structural framework for the problem of identifying or creating an effective photographic composition. A well-composed photograph is presented. The eye/funnel diagram at the bottom of the slide is not presented at this time. The audio dialog first tries to engage the learner with the picture through some rhetorical questions. The audio then directly compares an element of the metaphor, material being directed to a specific location by the funnel, with element of the photograph, line of sight being directed to specific elements of the photograph.

FIGURE 16-1 Structural Framework for Photographic Composition

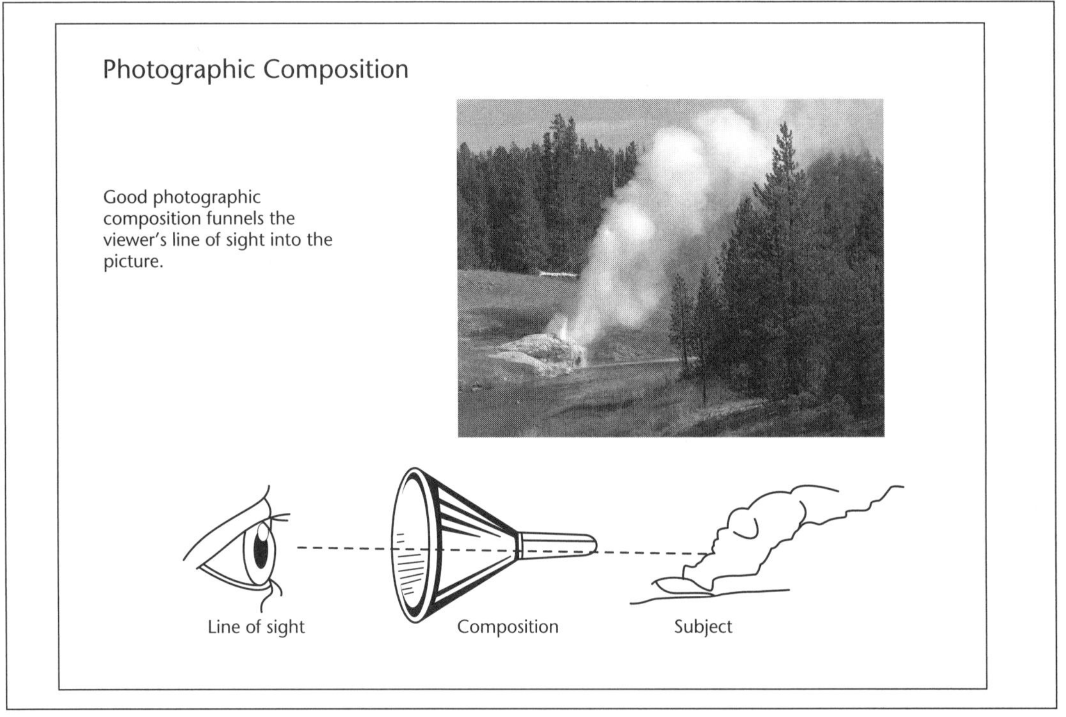

FIGURE 16-1 *Continued*

Audio: Look at this picture. What is the first thing you see?

What is happening in this photograph? Does this photograph tell a story?

Good composition is a funnel for the viewer's line of sight. Good composition funnels the viewer's line of sight into the picture. Did you notice how your eye tends to follow the river to the geyser? Good composition funnels the viewer's line of sight to the main subject of the picture. Did you notice how you are almost compelled to look at the geyser and notice the large volume of water gushing forth? Good composition funnels the viewer's line of sight to the action taking place in the picture. Did you notice how the volume of water is gushing higher than the tall pine trees in the foreground? Good composition draws the viewer's attention to the action in the photograph.

When I look at this photograph, my eye is drawn to the large volume of water gushing from the geyser near the river. My eye tends to follow the river into the picture and to the geyser. The trees emphasize the size of this geyser and the large volume of water gushing forth. This picture is an example of effective photographic composition.

[The eye/funnel diagram appears on the screen.]

It is useful to think of photographic composition as a funnel for the viewer's line of sight.

Design Guidance Based on This Framework

Guidance helps the learner relate the properties identified in the information with the portrayal of these properties in the example. Figure 16-2 is a presentation for the composition condition of *line*. The slide provides a written definition of *line*, and the photograph illustrates a composition whereby this condition is the primary property of the composition. The audio/animation provides guidance for this demonstration based on the metaphor of a funnel for the viewer's line of sight.

FIGURE 16-2 Presentation Guidance Based on Structural Framework

Photographic Composition

Line is a type of composition that leads the viewer into the photograph. Click here for a demonstration.

(continued)

FIGURE 16-2 *Continued*

Audio/Animation

What is the first thing you notice in this photograph? How does this composition funnel your line of sight? It is hard not to immediately focus on the small bridge wedged under the highway bridge by the rising flood waters. Notice how the diagonal line formed by the small bridge funnels your line of sight into the picture. [A dark diagonal line is drawn along the railing of the small bridge.] The opposing diagonal line formed by the highway bridge also funnels your line of sight to the action and story of the picture—the small bridge being wedged under the highway bridge by the flood waters. [Another dark line is drawn along the highway bridge.] This is a good example of the use of line in a photograph composition.

Design Coaching Based on This Framework

Coaching is an instructional interaction that provides help to learners during *Do* instructional events. When learners are provided with a structural framework, then this framework can serve as a basis for the coaching. Figure 16-3 is an application for my module on photographic composition. The problem for the learner is to edit this photograph to improve its composition. The learner is given a crop tool and an editing tool to use to modify this photograph. The learner is provided help based on the structural framework of a funnel. When the learner has finished cropping the picture and clicks the Submit button, a feedback message is played, as shown in Figure 16-4.

FIGURE 16-3 Application Coaching Based on Structural Framework

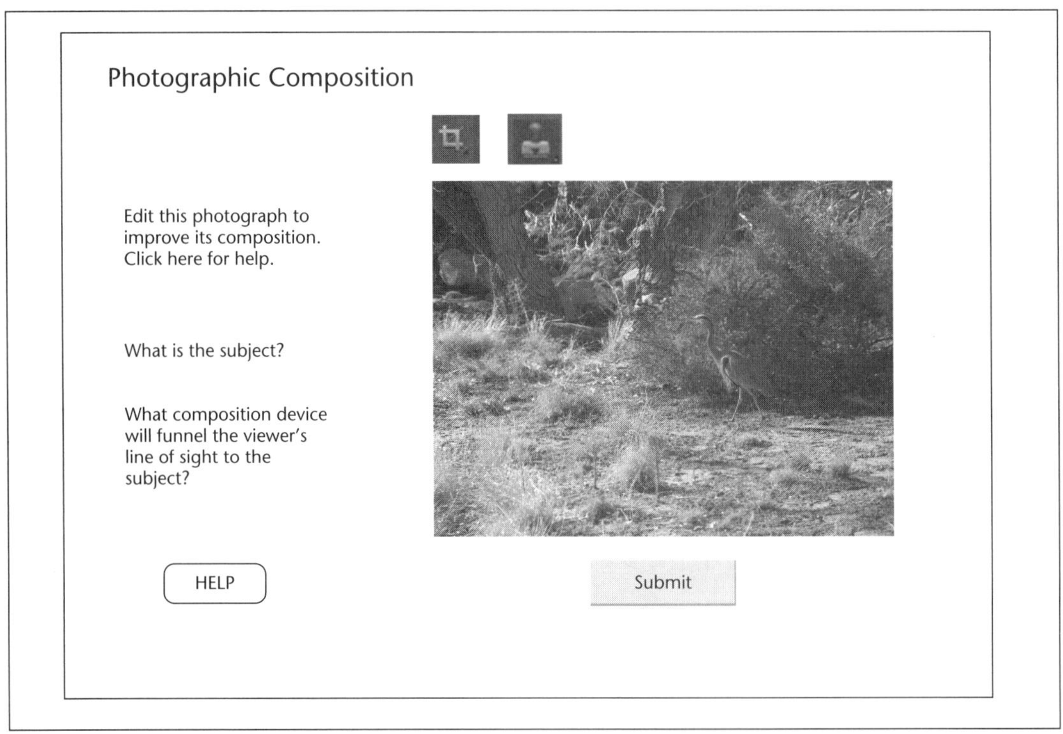

FIGURE 16-3 *Continued*

[Clicking the HELP button plays the following audio.]

This photograph is busy; the viewer's attention is distracted by a large foreground, dense shrubbery, and a busy background. There are so many elements in this photograph that the bird is almost obscured. The challenge is to funnel the viewer's line of sight to the point of interest in this photograph. What is the primary point of interest? For this photograph, what composition device can best direct the viewer's line of sight? Use the Cropping tool or the Editing tool to modify this photograph to improve its composition. Click the Submit button when you have finished.

FIGURE 16-4 Feedback for Photographic Composition Application

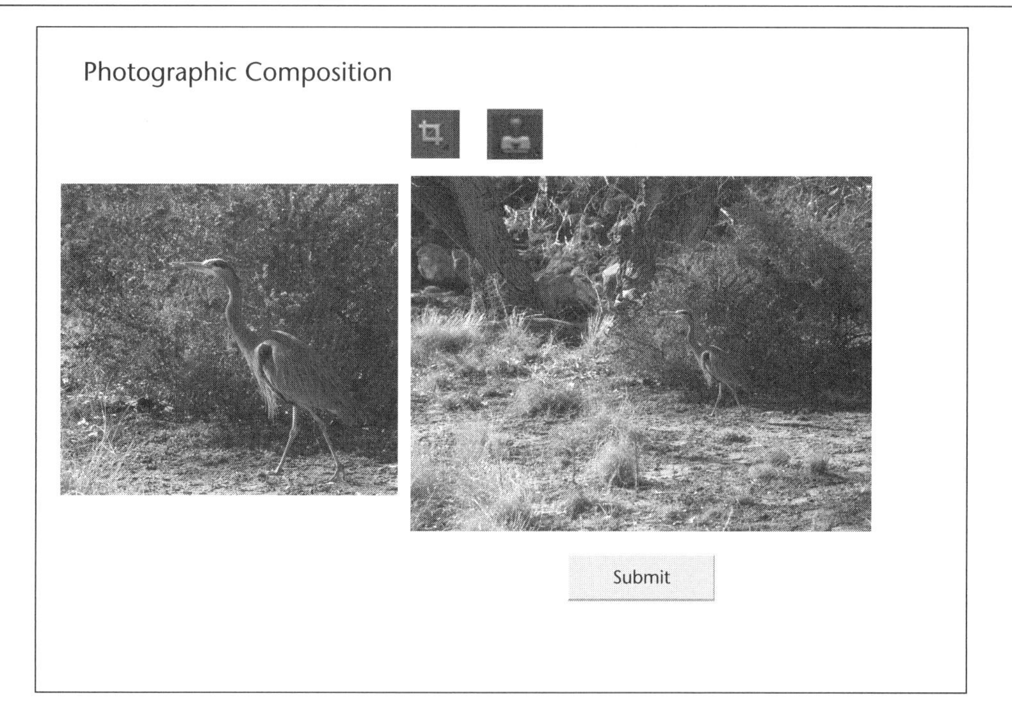

[Clicking the Submit button shows the modified photograph in Figure 16-4 next to the learner's modified photograph and plays the following audio.]

Here is my modified photograph. I felt that the bird was the subject of this photograph, and I wanted the viewer's line of sight to be funneled to the bird. Fortunately, this was a high-resolution photograph, so cropping a large portion of the photograph still left sufficient resolution in the part remaining. I know that the viewer's line of sight tends to be funneled to a location where imaginary lines dividing the photograph into thirds cross. I placed the bird about one-third of the way into the frame of the photograph to leave room for him to walk into the frame. The viewer's line of sight first falls on the bird and then on the action of the bird walking. After I cropped the photograph, I noticed some rocks showing in the upper left corner of the photograph that seemed to be an unnecessary element that would draw the viewer's attention so, using the Clone tool, I replaced the rocks with more shrubbery. This simplifies the background and allows the viewer to view the bird without having his or her line of sight drawn to distracting elements. How does your modified photograph compare with mine?

Design Reflection Based on This Framework

Reflection is an instructional event that requires learners to consider the skills they have acquired and attempt to extrapolate beyond these skills to other applications. Reflection helps learners to tune their mental models of the problem they have just learned to solve and to attempt to expand this model into new areas. Reflection is an attempt to encourage learners to go beyond what they have just learned. Figure 16-5 is a slide that encourages a learner to reflect on what he or she has learned about photograph composition. It presents three photographs that represent a different kind of composition than the conditions of composition taught in this module.

FIGURE 16-5 Reflection Based on Structural Framework

Photographic Composition

What contributes to the composition of these photographs?

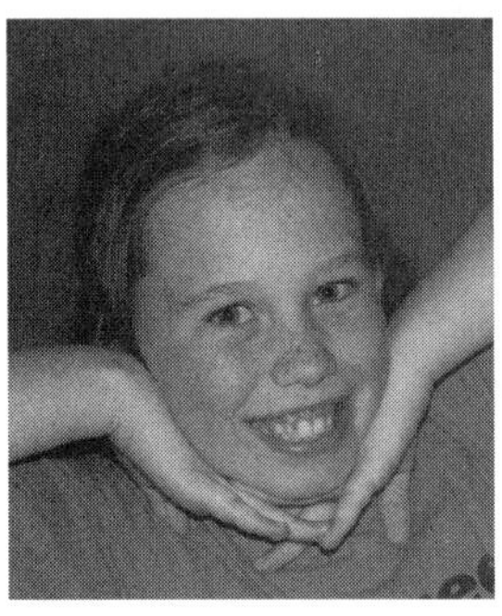

Click here for help.

Write your conclusions and submit to your instructor.

[Click here for help plays the following audio.]

You have learned some of the important properties of a good photographic composition, including frames, rule of thirds, line, and simplicity. This is not a comprehensive set of properties. There are other properties that may also contribute to an effective composition. The properties you have learned were likened to a funnel that directs the viewer's line of sight to particular locations in the photograph. Consider these three photographs of young women. Do you think that these photographs represent good composition? Some of the properties of a good composition that you have learned also apply to these photographs, but they also demonstrate some additional properties of effective composition. What new properties of good composition are used by these photographs to funnel the viewer's line of sight? Write your ideas and submit them to your instructor.

Structural Frameworks and Traditional Instructional Design

Traditional instructional design illustrated in Figure 11-1 does not include an explicit recommendation to include a structural framework to use for guidance, coaching, and reflection. However, the use of advance organizers in instructional design has been recommended for several decades. Recommending structural frameworks for activation, demonstration, application, and integration is a form of advance organizer, but adapted to First Principles of Instruction.

PEER-INTERACTION

Peer-interaction is an instructional activity in which learners teach one another via sharing, discussion, collaboration, or critique (described previously in Chapter 8). The next part of this chapter guides you in the design of peer-interaction in demonstration, application, and integration. Peer-interaction is promoted when learners are put in pairs or small groups and given specific assignments that require helping one another to acquire problem-solving skills.

What Makes for Effective Peer-Interaction?

Several properties contribute to effective peer-interaction. Without specific directions, the interaction among learners is often superficial and does little to contribute to learning. The most effective interactions are those that are carefully structured and where there is a specific assignment for each member of a group. Effective interactions are those that lead to collaboration among learners, where the assignments require this collaboration, and where each member of a group makes a contribution to the group outcome.

Small groups are more effective than large groups. Groups larger than five too often leave one or more members of the group out of the interaction. In some situations, pairs are the most effective form of interaction. Heterogeneous groups are more effective than homogeneous groups; mixing students with different backgrounds increases divergence of opinion and leads to broader considerations than in groups that share very similar ideas. Groups assigned by the instructor are often more effective than groups that self-select.

Peer-interaction is more effective when focused on producing a specific product rather than open-ended discussion. Guidance for group interaction results in more effective learning than unstructured interaction.

Assign Collaboration Groups

Following the guidelines above, assign learners into small groups. I have found that groups of three seem to be the ideal size. Have each group establish a wiki where they can collaborate together. At this writing, free wikis are available to anyone and more advanced wikis are available for little or no cost to educators. A wiki is a computer space where members can post documents, comment on documents, modify one another's documents, and enable others to view documents. The advantage of establishing a wiki is that it makes peer-interaction transparent and public. When small groups meet together in private, it is difficult or impossible to monitor their interaction, whereas when the interaction is via an electronic site, the discussion is public. A second advantage of a wiki is that it allows users of the wiki to post documents of various kinds to the wiki for editing, review, and modification by other members of the wiki. I prefer a wiki over a discussion board because of this capability.

A wiki can also have multiple levels of interaction: the two I find useful are (1) *public* where anyone can view or edit documents and (2) *protected* where anyone can view, but only members can modify one another's documents. More advanced wikis have several other levels of permissions.

For the photographic composition course, I assigned groups of three to work together. Each group has its own wiki where members can interact. Their interactions are available to view by other members of the class. The assignments for these interaction groups are described in the following paragraphs.

Design Peer-Sharing for Activation

Peer-sharing is an instructional event in which learners share with each other prior relevant experience with the subject-matter content under consideration. As a first type of peer-interaction, I decided to implement the following activity as an introduction to the course. Students were assigned to peer-interaction groups of three learners and helped to create a wiki for their group. Then they were given the directions in Table 16-1.

Table 16-1 Directions for Peer-Sharing for Photographic Composition

In this course we will explore photographic composition. Photographic composition is the arrangement of your subject and other elements of your picture within the area of your photograph. As an introduction to this course, please do the following:

Post three of your best photographs of individuals, groups, and objects or scenery to your group wiki. For each photograph, write a brief answer to the following questions: What features of this photograph contribute to its composition? What features distract from the composition of this photograph?

Study the photographs submitted by the other members of your group. For each photograph, write a brief answer to the following questions: What features contribute to the composition of this photograph? What features distract from the composition of this photograph?

This assignment attempts to implement the properties of good group interaction. The groups are small, the directions are specific, each learner has specific actions to complete, and each learner is required to review the work of the other members of the group.

Design Peer-Discussion for Demonstration

Peer-discussion is a form of learner-interaction for which learners deliberate the proposed solution of example problems. After engaging in the demonstrations and applications designed for this course in Chapter 15, as enhanced by a structural framework in the first part of this chapter, students are presented the rubric in Table 16-2 and asked to participate in the peer-discussion activity described in Table 16-3.

Table 16-2 Peer-Discussion and Peer-Critique Rubric for Photographic Composition

Discuss each photograph on the basis of the following statements and come to a group consensus on your rating.

Simplicity 1. The photograph is free from extraneous elements that distract from the subject.

Strongly Agree Agree No Opinion Disagree Strongly Disagree Not Applicable

Rule of Thirds 2. The photograph implements the rule of thirds.

Strongly Agree Agree No Opinion Disagree Strongly Disagree Not Applicable

Format 3. The format directs the action into the frame.

Strongly Agree Agree No Opinion Disagree Strongly Disagree Not Applicable

Frame 4. Elements of the photograph frame the subject.

Strongly Agree Agree No Opinion Disagree Strongly Disagree Not Applicable

Line 5. A diagonal or S-curve line leads the viewer into the photograph.

Strongly Agree Agree No Opinion Disagree Strongly Disagree Not Applicable

Table 16-3 Peer-Discussion Activity for Photographic Composition

Each group of students is given a set of photographs of individuals, groups, objects, and scenery. These photographs vary in their implementation of the principles of good composition. Each discussion group of three students is required to meet together, either face-to-face or via conference software, to review and discuss the photographs. They are given the following directions:

As a group, discuss each photograph. Use the peer-critique rubric (see Table 16-2) to guide your discussion. Try to reach consensus on the rating for each of the composition elements identified in the rubric. Write a brief explanation for your rating on each composition element for each photograph. Post your ratings and comments for each photograph to your wiki where it can be reviewed by other members of the class.

Design Peer-Collaboration for Application

Peer-collaboration is an instructional event in which learners work together in small groups to solve problems. As a concluding application, each group of learners is required to engage in the collaborative activity described in Table 16-4.

Table 16-4 Peer-Collaboration Activity for Photographic Composition

Take and edit a series of photographs that demonstrate effective composition. For each of the following categories, post two photographs to your group wiki: individuals, groups, objects, and scenery.

As a group, work together to critique and edit these photographs. Everyone in the group should agree that all of the photographs represent the best composition possible. Post your edited photographs to your group wiki for critique and evaluation. Your score for this activity will be the average score for all of the photographs of your group.

Design Peer-Critique for Integration

Peer-critique is an instructional event in which learners evaluate the problem-solving activities of fellow learners and provide constructive suggestions for improvement. As the final integration, each group of learners is required to engage in the peer-critique activity described in Table 16-5.

Table 16-5 Peer-Critique Activity for Photographic Composition

Working together as a group, you will be assigned to critique the photographs of two other groups. You should use the photograph composition rubric (see Table 16-2) to guide your critique. Write an explanation for each of your ratings. Select a first-place photograph, a second-place photograph, a third-place photograph, and an honorable-mention photograph for each group you critique. Strive for consensus among your group for your critique and awards.

Peer-Interaction and Traditional Instructional Design

Peer-interaction is not a formal part of the traditional instructional design model illustrated in Figure 11-1. However, forming learning communities and having learners participate in their own instruction have become very popular, especially with the availability of communication software and social networks that make learner-to-learner communication easily available, even from remote locations. A *learning community* is a group of people who are actively engaged in learning together and from each other. The Pebble model has combined three disparate instructional design movements—problem-based learning, learning communities, and online learning—into a coherent model of instruction that takes advantage of the best features from each of these areas. The Pebble model is more structured than many problem-based models and many learning communities. It combines these approaches with a more traditional tutorial model that is highly structured and includes significant guidance and coaching, as described in this book.

PRINCIPLES AND PRESCRIPTIONS

Structure: Learning is promoted when learners recall or acquire a framework or structure for organizing the new knowledge, when the structure is the basis for guidance during demonstration, is the basis for coaching during application, and is the basis for reflection during integration.

Designing structural framework enhancement includes the following activities:

- Design a structural framework.
- Design guidance based on this structural framework.
- Design coaching based on this structural framework.
- Design reflection based on this structural framework

Peer-Collaboration and Critique: Learning is promoted when learners integrate their new knowledge into their everyday lives by being required to reflect on, discuss, or defend their new knowledge or skill via peer-collaboration and peer-critique.

Designing peer-interaction enhancement includes the following activities:

- Assign peer-interaction groups.
- Design peer-sharing for activation.
- Design peer-discussion for demonstration.
- Design peer-collaboration for application.
- Design peer-critique for integration.

APPLICATION

Using the functional prototype you designed for Chapters 13, 14, and 15, identify a structural framework and use this framework to add or modify the guidance and coaching provided for the portrayals in your progression and add a reflection activity based on this framework.

Using the functional prototype you designed for Chapters 13, 14, and 15, determine peer-interaction groups and design peer-sharing, peer-discussion, peer-collaboration, and peer-critique to accompany your instruction.

TO LEARN MORE

Marzano, R. J., Pickering, D. J., & Pollock, J. E. (2001). *Classroom instruction that works: Research-based strategies for increasing student achievement.* Alexandria, VA: Association for Supervision and Curriculum Development. Marzano and his associates did an exhaustive study of what works in classroom instruction. Their research is summarized, along with prescriptions for how to implement the findings. The following chapters are of particular interest to the content of this chapter:

Chapter 3, Summarizing and Note Taking, and Chapter 10, Cues, Questions, and Advance Organizers; these chapters provides good examples of the use of structural frameworks.

Chapter 7, Cooperative Learning; this chapter provides guidance for peer-cooperation and peer-critique.

For more information-about peer-interaction, see:

Clark, R. C., & Mayer, R. E. (2008). Chapter 12: Learning together virtually. In *e-Learning and the science of instruction* (2nd ed.). San Francisco: Pfeiffer.

Merrill, M. D., & Gilbert, C. G. (2008). Effective peer-interaction in a problem-centered instructional strategy. *Distance Education, 29*(2), 199–207.

See the Online Premium Contents, "Demonstration Functional Prototype for Photographic Composition," to see the implementation of a structural framework and peer interaction described in this chapter.

COMING NEXT

The fifth ripple in the Pebble model is to bring all of the various components you have designed together. Chapter 17 will guide you in bringing these various design elements together into a coherent whole. This chapter will also guide you in designing and finalizing navigation both within and between slides in your course, designing and finalizing the interface—the look and feel—of your course, and designing supplemental materials for your course, including learner directions for using the course and takeaway materials to accompany your course.

CHAPTER 17

FINALIZE THE FUNCTIONAL PROTOTYPE

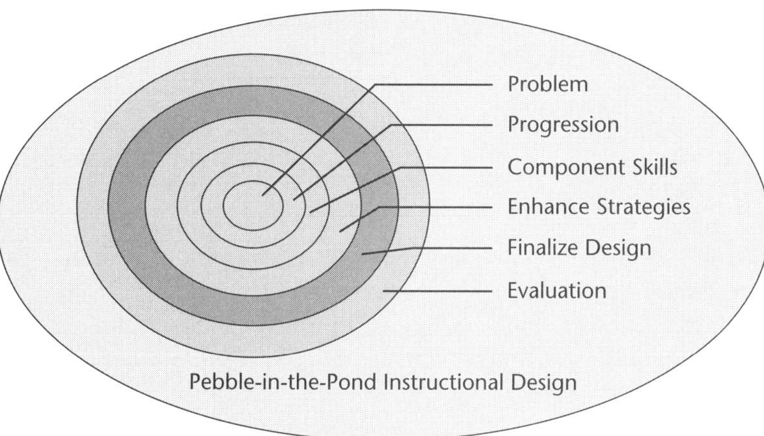

Quick Look

The fifth ripple in the Pebble-in-the-Pond model is to finalize the instructional design. This chapter will guide you in the activities required to bring the previously designed course components together into a coherent whole. It will answer the following questions: How do you organize your course into a coherent whole, including checking for and designing missing course components, such as a title page and introduction, incorporating a structural framework and peer-interaction? How do you improve the learner interface, including course appearance and location indicators? How do you design unambiguous navigation and directions? How do you identify and design appropriate supplemental materials for your course?

Key Words

Location Indicator: information that enables learners to know where they are in relation to the whole module or course.

Navigation: a set of controls that enable learners to interact with learning events within a slide and to move to the next slide or a previous slide; learners' progress within and among instructional events.

INTRODUCTION

Previous chapters have guided you in design of the demonstration and application for whole problems, a problem-centered progression of problems, instructional events to teach component skills, and enhancement of your design with a structural framework and peer-interaction. This chapter provides guidance in bringing all of these pieces together into a coherent whole. The first section suggests ways to be sure your course is complete, that it has a coherent organization including a title and introduction, that you have integrated a structural framework and peer-interaction into your course. The second section provides suggestions to for improving the appearance and appeal of your course and mechanisms for helping learners locate themselves within the structure of the course. The third section provides suggestions for effective and unambiguous learner navigation through the course. The final section provides suggestions for adding supplemental material to the course.

COURSE ORGANIZATION

Previous Design Activities

The previous chapters in this section have suggested the following steps in designing e^3 instruction based on *First Principles of Instruction*: Chapter 13, identify a class of problems to be solved and design a demonstration and application for a portrayal of this problem; Chapter 14, design a progression of problem portrayals; Chapter 15, design instructional strategies for the component skills involved in the portrayals in the progression; and Chapter 16, design strategy enhancements for structural frameworks and peer-interaction. This chapter brings all of these course components into a coherent whole and adds introductory, navigation, and supplemental material that may be required for the course.

For my sample course, Figure 13-1 illustrated a demonstration for a portrayal of the problem of effective photographic composition, and Figure 13-2 illustrated an application for a portrayal of this problem. Figure 14-1 illustrated a sample of portrayals, and Figure 14-2 illustrated the identification of the component skills required by each of the portrayals in the progression. Figures 15-1 through 15-6 illustrated instructional strategies for the required component skills distributed across the portrayals in the progression. While this sequence of instructional events represents only a part of the course, I will use this portrayal sequence to illustrate the finalization of my functional prototype. I decided to use this sequence of instructional events as the primary instructional events in a module of my course limited to photographs of individuals.

Design Overall Course Structure

Figure 17-1 is an outline of the course organization that resulted from my finalization of the instructional design. It is hard to illustrate a functional prototype in book format. In my prototype I have arranged all of the slides identified in this table in a PowerPoint presentation where I can make modifications as the design process unfolds. The animations described in the audio scripts have been implemented for the slides. Before I recorded the audio I used the notes capability of PowerPoint to include the scripts for the audio under the slide. These scripts included bookmarks indicating where animations were to occur as the audio message played. By going to Notes Page view in PowerPoint I can easily print out a preliminary version of my course for easy review and editing before recording the audio and connecting the animations to the bookmarks.

The thumbnail figures in each cell of Figure 17-1 will be represented by a slide in my functional prototype. The figures that show a larger illustration of each slide and the accompanying audio/animation are indicated under each thumbnail. This course sequence includes additional slides that I included in my course structure as a result of the finalization activity described in this chapter. These instructional events are described in the following paragraphs.

Design Missing or Inadequate Course Components

Table 15-3 showed that my instructional strategy for each of the component skills was incomplete. The Course Critique Checklist indicated that the strategy would be improved by the addition of instructional events: The step, viewfinder, needs an additional demonstration and both Do_{id} and Do_{ex} application. The condition, simplicity, needs an additional Do_{id} application. The step, edit, needs *Tell* and Guidance added to its demonstration and additional Do_{id} and Do_{ex} application. The conditions—line and framing—need additional *Show* demonstration and/or Do_{id} and Do_{ex} application. Some of the applications might benefit from coaching.

My first design activity in finalizing my instructional strategy was to design additional slides to implement some of the missing elements just identified. I added three application slides to the original sequence from Chapter 15. (See instructional events 12, 13, and 14 in Figure 17-1.) Figure 17-2 requires cropping and editing to implement simplicity, rule of thirds, and format. Figure 17-3 requires cropping to implement rule of thirds and framing. Figure 17-4 requires cropping to implement rule of thirds and line. These three slides provide additional application opportunities. I decided that the emphasis was on modifying existing photographs, so I did not include additional learning events for the step viewfinder.

Design Title Page and Introduction

I next added a title slide that included an opportunity for a student to register. (See instructional event 1 in Figure 17-1 and Figure 17-5.) In Chapter 18, I will illustrate how I will use this registration to keep track of student data for assessment and evaluation.

To introduce the course, I decided to show the whole problem, an effectively composed photograph, and overview the conditions for effective photographic composition by briefly defining and illustrating each of these conditions. I adapted the demonstration I had previously prepared (see Figure 13-4) as in introduction slide for this module (also see event 2 in Figure 17-1 and Figure 17-6).

Learners like to have an overview of the extent of a course: What is included? How long is the course? Where are different ideas taught in the course? A table of contents provide this function, but I decided to add a more interactive form of a table of contents. I added a Contents slide as an introduction to the course. (See event 4 in Figure 17-1 and Figure 17-7.) This slide shows the organization of course and is a menu that is part of the course navigation to be described later in this chapter.

FIGURE 17-1 Course Organization for Photographic Composition—Module 1

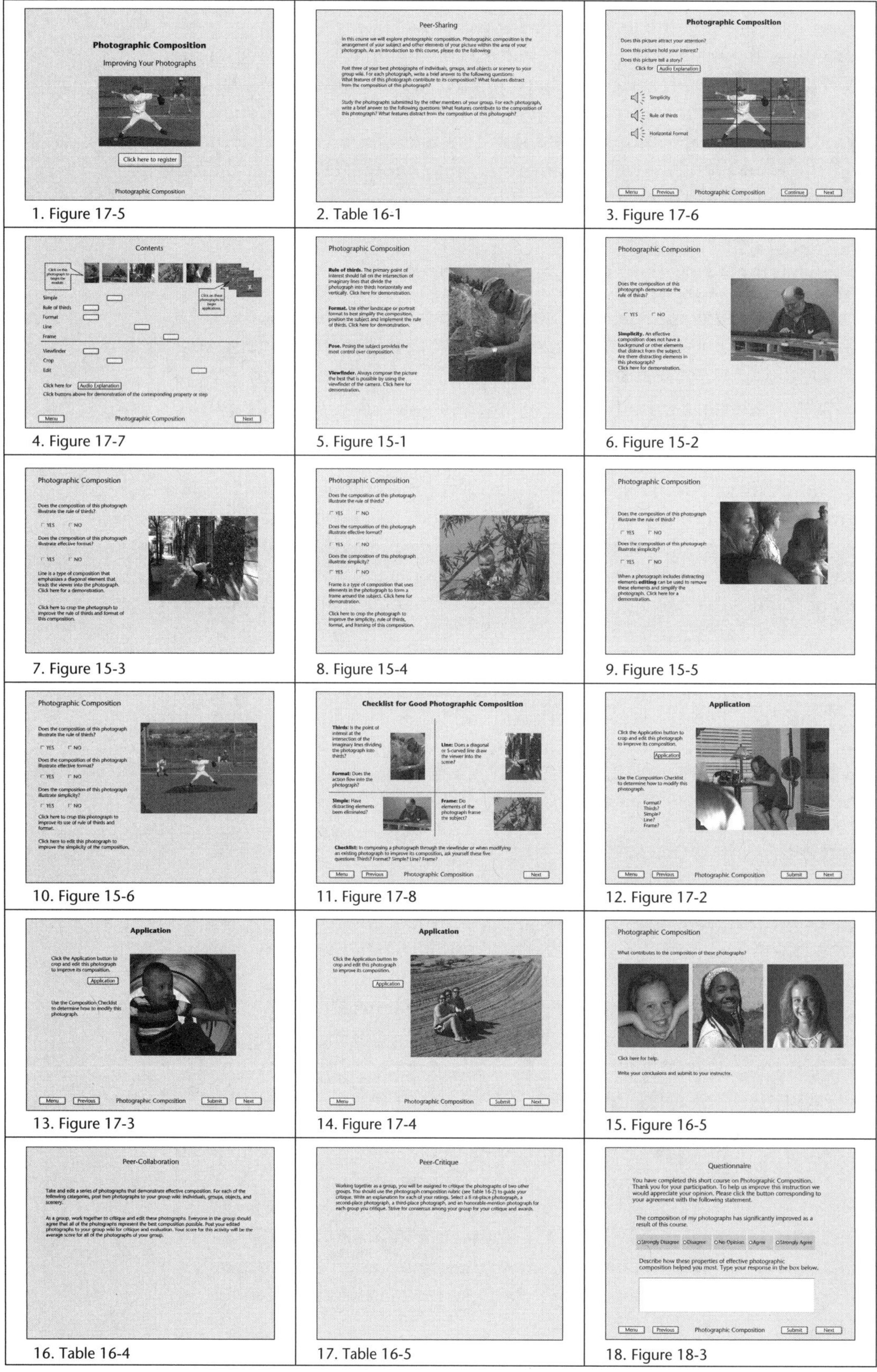

FIGURE 17-2 Application Slide for Photographic Composition

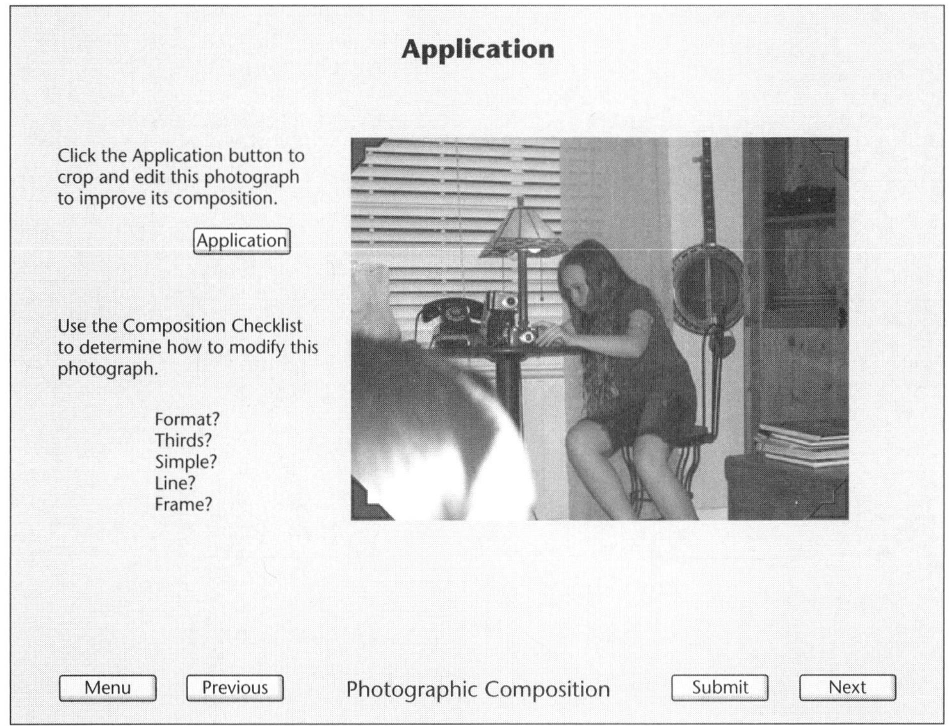

FIGURE 17-3 Application Slide for Photographic Composition

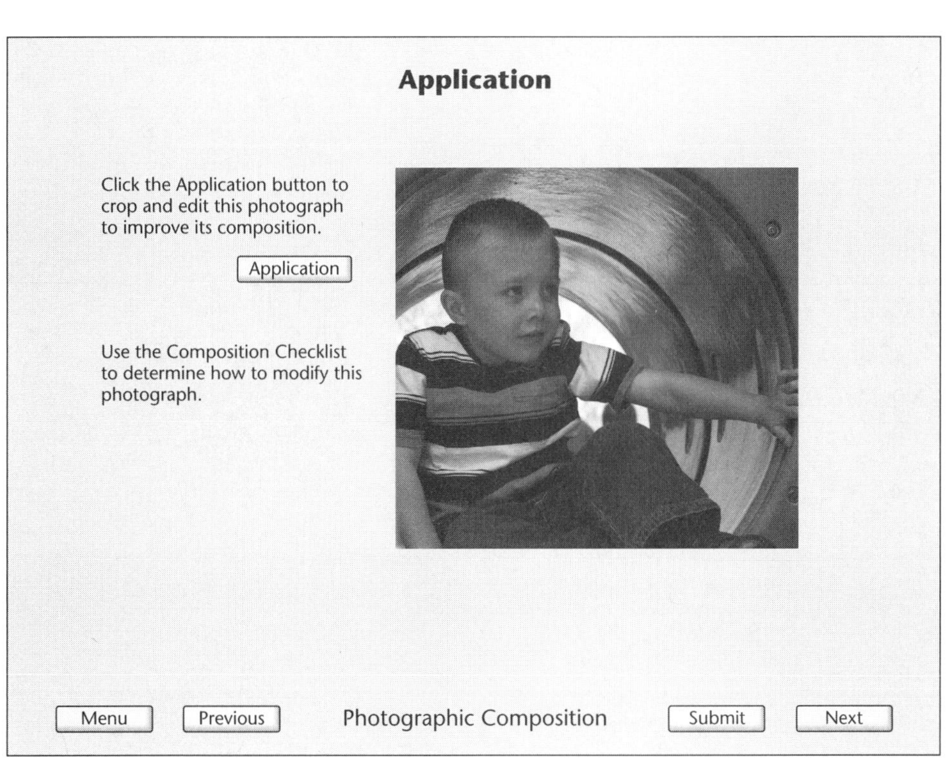

FIGURE 17-4 Application Slide for Photographic Composition

FIGURE 17-5 Title Page for Photographic Composition

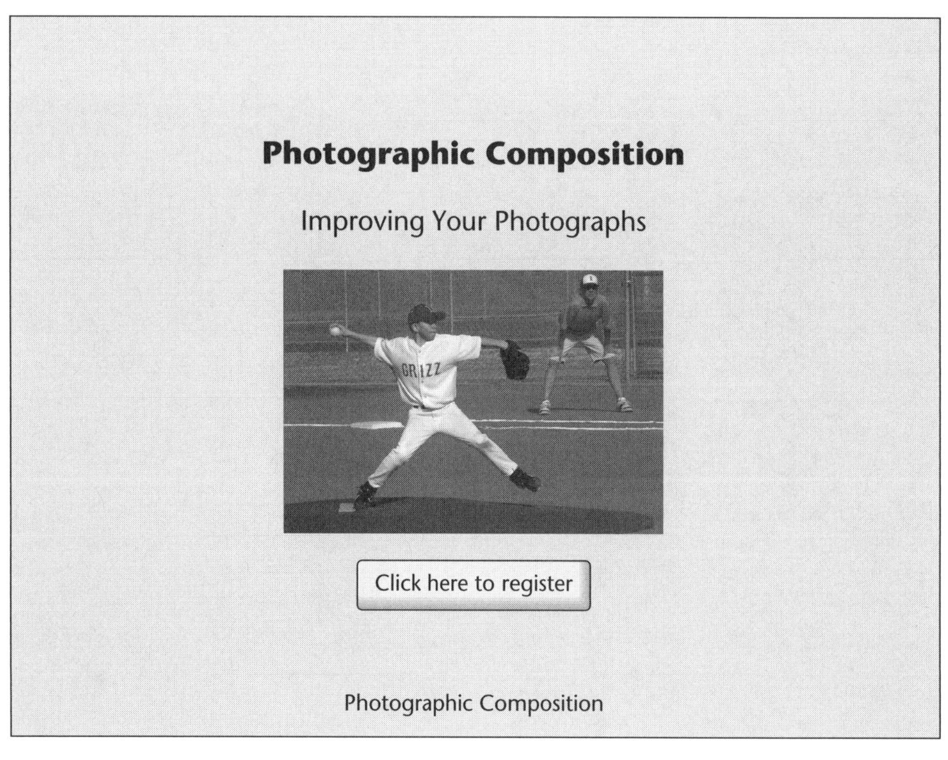

FIGURE 17-6 Introduction Slide for Photographic Composition

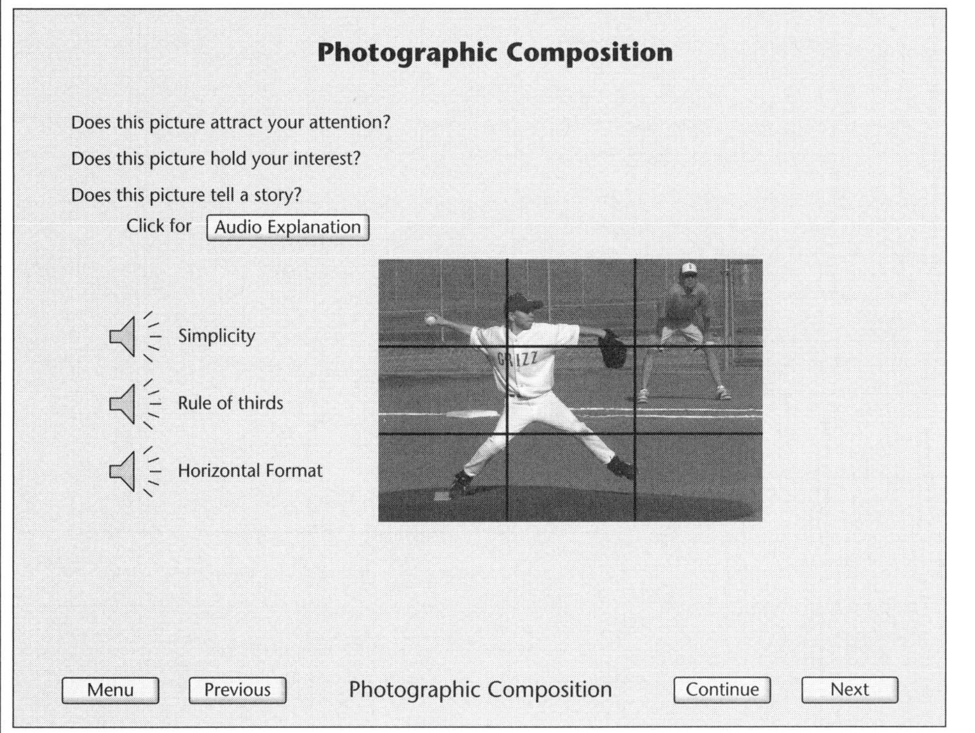

Audio

This picture tells a story. The pitch is about to be delivered. Will it be a strike? Or will the batter be out?

Several things that contribute to the composition of this photograph. [1 The word Simplicity appears and the pitcher is highlighted.] The pitcher is clearly the subject in the photograph. There is no distracting background except the coach, who contributes to the tension in the event. There is a clear and simple object of interest. [The Continue button is displayed.] Click Continue to go on.

[2 The words *Rule of thirds* appear and crossed lines that divide the picture into thirds are overlaid on the photograph.] The primary point of interest in the photograph is the pitcher's windup. A composition is more interesting when the point of interest falls on one of the points where these imaginary dividing lines cross. Click Continue to go on.

[3 The word Format appears.] Finally, the picture uses a horizontal format with the pitcher at the left of the photograph so that he is throwing into the photograph.

[The Next button is highlighted.] Click Next to go to the next slide.

Integrate Structural Framework Strategy Enhancement

A structural framework is an organization of previously learned information that learners can use to adapt an existing mental model or to build a new mental model for new content. A structural framework may enhance the e^3 quality of this module. I considered several alternatives but decided that, for this module, perhaps a Composition Checklist might be sufficient to provide coaching for the application exercises I had designed. Introducing the checklist at the beginning of the course felt awkward since learners had not yet seen demonstrations for the conditions of an effective composition. Therefore, I introduced the Checklist for Good Photographic Composition shown in event 11 of Figure 17-1 and in Figure 17-8 as a summary of the component skills they should have learned. This slide summarizes the conditions of an effective composition and provides a checklist for coaching the applications on the following screens.

FIGURE 17-7 Course Organization and Menu for Photographic Composition

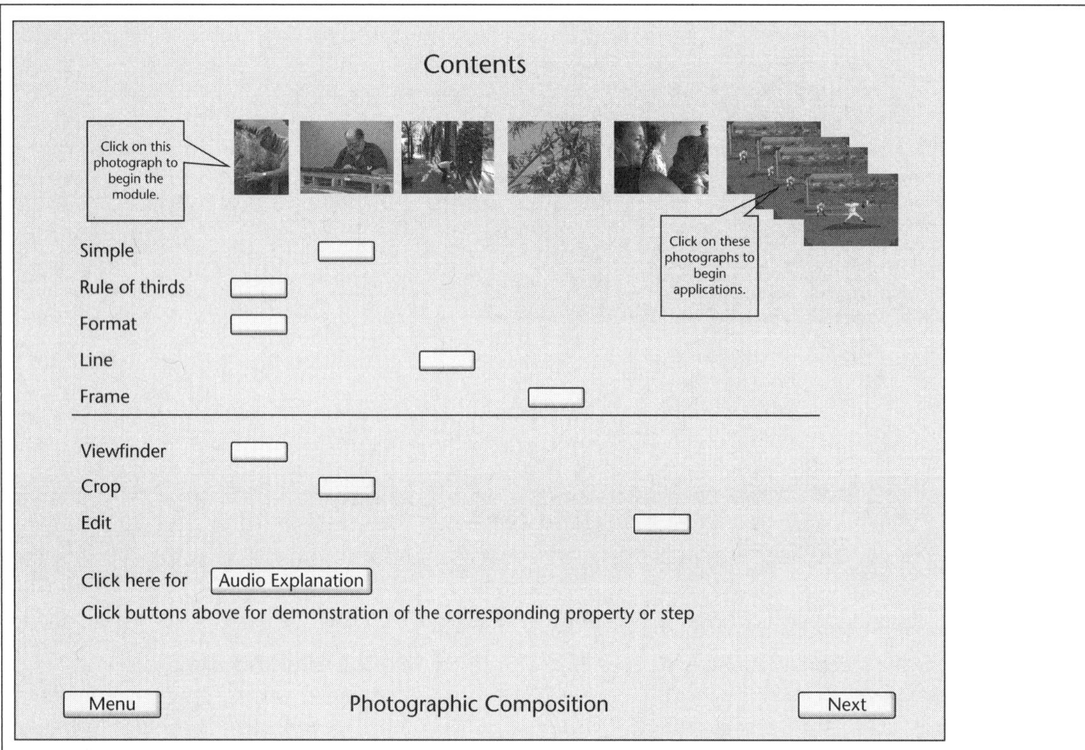

Audio

In this module you will learn about photographic composition. Photographic composition is the arrangement of your subject and other elements in your photograph to create a photograph that is interesting and appealing to the viewer.

In this module you will study the composition of a series of photographs. You will learn those properties of a photograph that contribute to a pleasing composition. While there are many things that contribute to a pleasing photographic composition, this module will concentrate on only five of these properties: simplicity, rule of thirds, format, line, and framing. In addition, this module will demonstrate two techniques that you can use to modify an existing photograph to improve its composition: cropping and editing. [Each of these words will be highlighted as the name of the property is spoken.]

This Contents slide illustrates the organization of this module. The photographs used in this module are shown in miniature. The five properties of a pleasing composition are listed down the left side. Using the viewfinder and the two techniques for modifying an existing photograph, cropping and editing, are listed below the properties of a pleasing composition. The buttons under each photograph indicate where in the course each property or each editing technique is demonstrated.

You are encouraged to study the photographs and corresponding composition properties and editing techniques in the order shown from left to right. After you have studied the module, you can return to this menu, where you can click on one of the buttons to review the demonstration of a given property or technique.

Click on the first photograph to begin your study of this module.

FIGURE 17-8 Photographic Composition Summary and Checklist

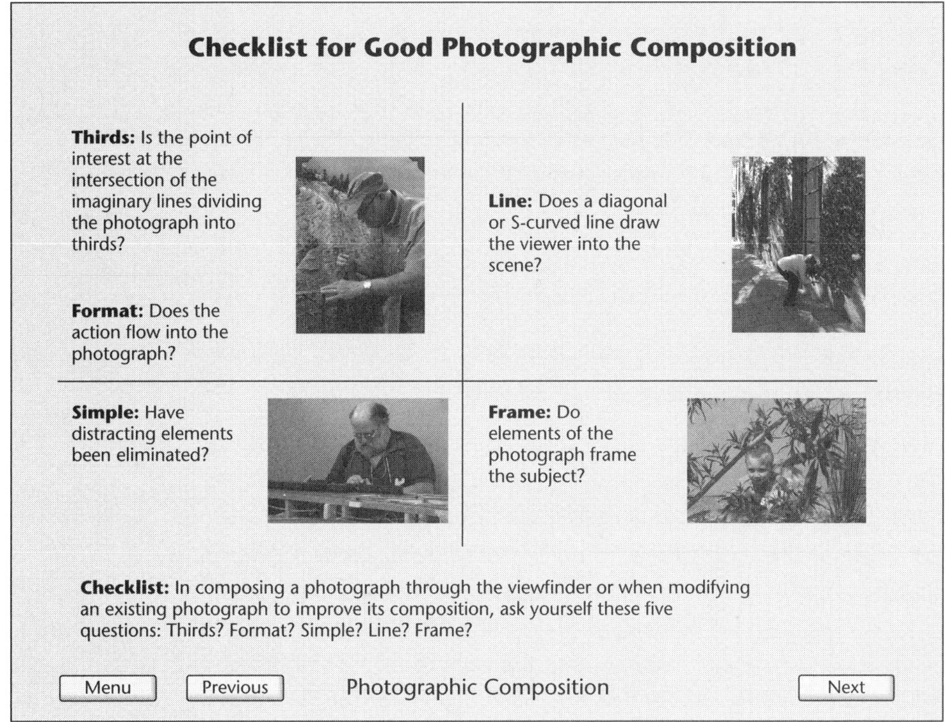

I used this checklist to provide coaching for the screens shown in events 12, 13, and 14 in Figure 17-1 and in Figures 17-2 through 17-4. Figure 17-2 reminds learners to use the checklist and lists the five conditions with a question mark. If learners have forgotten the questions, they can use the Previous button to return to the Checklist slide. Figure 17-3 also reminds learners to use the checklist but does not list the five conditions. By the time they reach Figure 17-4, it is hoped that learners will remember the checklist and apply it to the new photograph to be modified. This gradual reduction in the amount of coaching is consistent with the coaching principle.

Integrate Peer-Interaction Strategy Enhancement

Peer-interaction is an instructional activity in which learners teach one another via sharing, discussion, collaboration, or critique. The Photographic Composition course was designed primarily as a self-study online tutorial. However, when I do have an opportunity to teach this course to a group of students, I want to take advantage of peer-interaction to enhance the instructional strategy.

When teaching a group of students, I introduce the peer-sharing activity described in Chapter 16 as the first learning event for this course, as indicated in event 2 in Figure 17-1 and Table 16-1. The activity consists of having each learner post his or her three best photographs with a brief description of what he or she thinks contributes to the composition of each photograph and what features distract from good composition. Learners are encouraged to study the photographs of other members in their group.

I introduce the peer-reflection and discussion activity described in Chapter 16 after learners have completed the application exercises in Figures 17-1, 17-2, and 17-3 as shown in event 12 in Figure 17-1 and in Figure 16-5. As a final activity, I decided to include the peer-collaboration and peer-critique activities described in Chapter 16 as shown in events 13 and 14 in Figure 17-1 and in Tables 16-4 and 16-5.

The instructional event shown in event 18 in Figure 17-1 is a questionnaire that will be described as part of our assessment and evaluation in Chapter 18. I included it here so that Figure 17-1 included all of the instructional events in my functional prototype.

LEARNER INTERFACE

Design Course Appearance and Appeal

Until this point in the design process, I have not worried too much about the appearance of the slides that have been designed. My primary concern was to be sure that the content was correct and that the instructional strategies used were consistent with the prescriptions for e^3 instruction. The task now is to carefully edit all of the slides in the presentation to be sure that their appearance and appeal are appropriate and consistent with the principles of effective multimedia, as demonstrated in Chapter 9.

As I designed the slides I tried to use a layout that was simple and clear to the learners. I didn't want the slides to be too busy or to contain irrelevant information. At this point in the design process, I carefully examined each slide in the sequence and corrected any layout that I thought was unclear or distracted from the content. I checked to be sure that my font size and type were consistent within and across slides.

I wanted to improve the appearance of the slides. Since this was a module on photography, I tried to find a symbol that would represent photography but that would not distract from the content of the slides. I decided to use a gray matte background on each of the slides to resemble the paper one might find in a photograph scrapbook. This light gray background is very neutral and actually enhances the appearance of the color photographs (which are gray scale in this book). In keeping with my scrapbook appearance, I decided to include scrapbook photo corners on the photographs, as shown in the photo in Figure 17-9.

Design Consistent Location Indicators

An effective user interface provides consistent location indicators. A *location indicator* enables learners to know where they are in relation to the whole module. The Contents slide, Figure 17-7, was designed to provide a content map for the learner indicating the organization of the course. It lists the properties of an effective photographic composition that will be introduced and a miniature of the photograph that will be used to explain and illustrate each of these properties.

There are two location indicators available to learners. The first is the photograph featured on a given slide and the second is the name of the properties or steps illustrated. The name of the property or step illustrated is used as a title for each slide. In my original slides (see Chapter 16) I used the name of the course as a title on each slide, but since the name of the course is not a location indicator, I put it in a footnote at the lower center of each slide. I did this in the slide master so that the title would automatically appear on each slide. Figure 17-9 is a revision of Figure 15-1. This slide demonstrates rule of thirds, format, and the use of the viewfinder. The contents of the slide—Rule of Thirds, Format, and Viewfinder—appear as the title of this slide. The name of the course appears center bottom. The last three slides in the progression are application, requiring learners to use the steps of cropping and editing to modify each photograph to more effectively implement the properties of good composition. The title of each of these slides is merely Application. (See Figures 17-2, 17-3, and 17-4.)

FIGURE 17-9 Location Indicator and Within-Slide Navigation

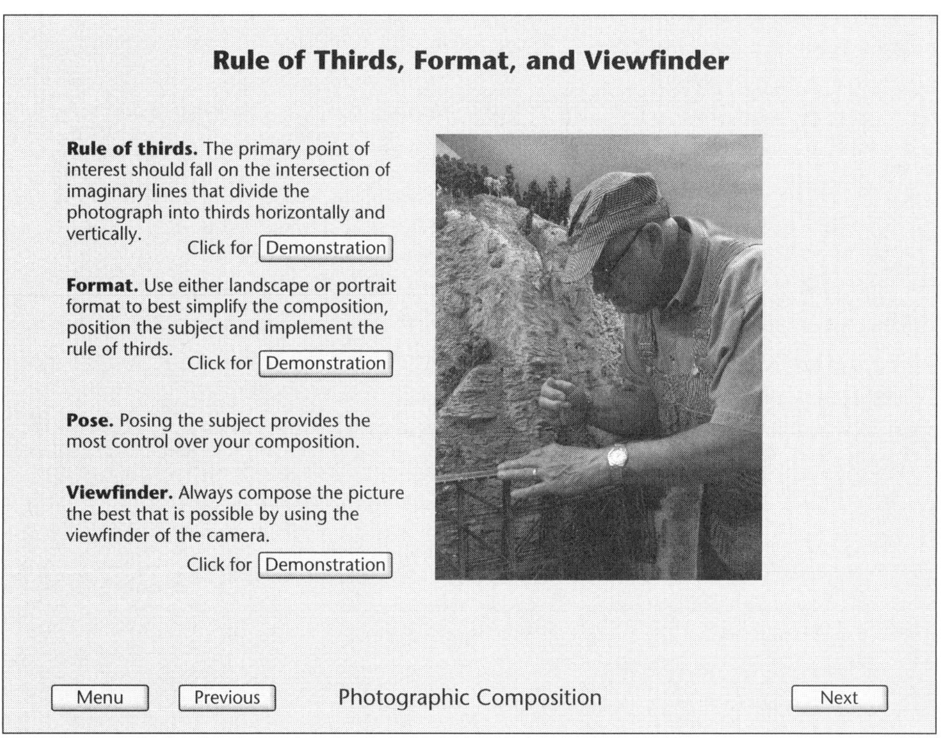

NAVIGATION

Navigation is a set of controls that enable learners to interact with learning events within a slide and to move to the next slide or a previous slide. Nothing distracts more from a course than poor navigation. Learners become frustrated very quickly when they can't figure out where they are, when they don't know what to do next, when the program does not react in a way that they anticipate, and especially when they find themselves lost and unable to recover. There are two levels of navigation: navigation within a given slide when interacting with a number of related learning events and navigation between slides moving to a different set of learning events, often with the next portrayal in the progression.

Design Consistent Within-Slide Navigation

When there are a number of related learning events all in the context of a given portrayal of the problem, it is critical that learners can easily engage in these events before moving forward to the next portrayal or next set of learning events on the next slide. What may seem obvious to the designer is too often obscure to the learners, especially if they are not familiar with the conventions often used for computer applications. Good within-slide navigation depends on (1) clearly marked controls over the presentation; (2) unambiguous directions for how to use these controls; (3) an opportunity to repeat any given learning event; and (4) being warned or prevented from proceeding to the next slide until all of the required learning events have been completed.

The next step in finalizing a functional prototype is to carefully study each slide to be sure that the controls are clearly marked, that the directions are unambiguous, and that learners are clearly warned or prevented from moving to the next slide prior to completing the available learning events. For teaching component skill in my progression of portrayals, I designed a number of slides that each contained several related instructional events. During this initial design effort I concentrated on the instructional events involved and didn't worry too much about within-slide navigation. But in this finalization phase of the design, it is critical that each slide be revised to facilitate the learner's interaction with all of the learning events.

Figure 17-9 is a revision of Figure 15-1. There are three demonstration instructional events on this slide. This revision is designed to improve the navigation within this slide. I added an obvious Demonstration button for each of the properties so that it is clear where the learner should click to see each demonstration. Learners can view the demonstrations in any order, and a given demonstration can be repeated when its Demonstration button is clicked again. The Next button does not appear until the last Demonstration button is clicked. If the learner views the demonstrations in order, then the Next button does not appear until after the learner has viewed the final demonstration. I made similar within-slide navigation modifications to other slides in my functional prototype, as illustrated in Figure 17-10.

The disadvantage of the above method is that the learner may not view the demonstrations in the order shown and would then be able to advance if he or she viewed only the last demonstration on the page. There is a more advanced approach for controlling the appearance of the Next button. As an alternative I can attach a short Visual Basic program to the Next button. This computer code provides a warning to the learner if the Next button is clicked before he or she has looked at each of the demonstrations. The warning is a pop-up message such as the following: "You have not studied Rule of Thirds. You may want to view this demonstration before you go to the next slide." The learner can override the warning by merely clicking the Next button a second time.

Figure 17-10 is a revision of Figure 15-4. This is an application/demonstration slide with even more instructional events. There are three Do_{id} application events, there is a *Show* frame event, and there is a Do_{ex} cropping application. We would like the learner to respond to the application events and complete the demonstration event before moving to the next portrayal in the progression. There is a Submit button that enables the program to record the learner's responses to the condition statements and also saves the learner's cropped version of the photograph. The method for saving this data will be explained in Chapter 18. The Next button appears when the Submit button is clicked. Additional computer code attached to the Submit button can also check to be sure that the learner has responded to each of the questions and has viewed the demonstration before recording the data or causing the Next button to appear.

FIGURE 17-10 Within- and Between-Slide Navigation

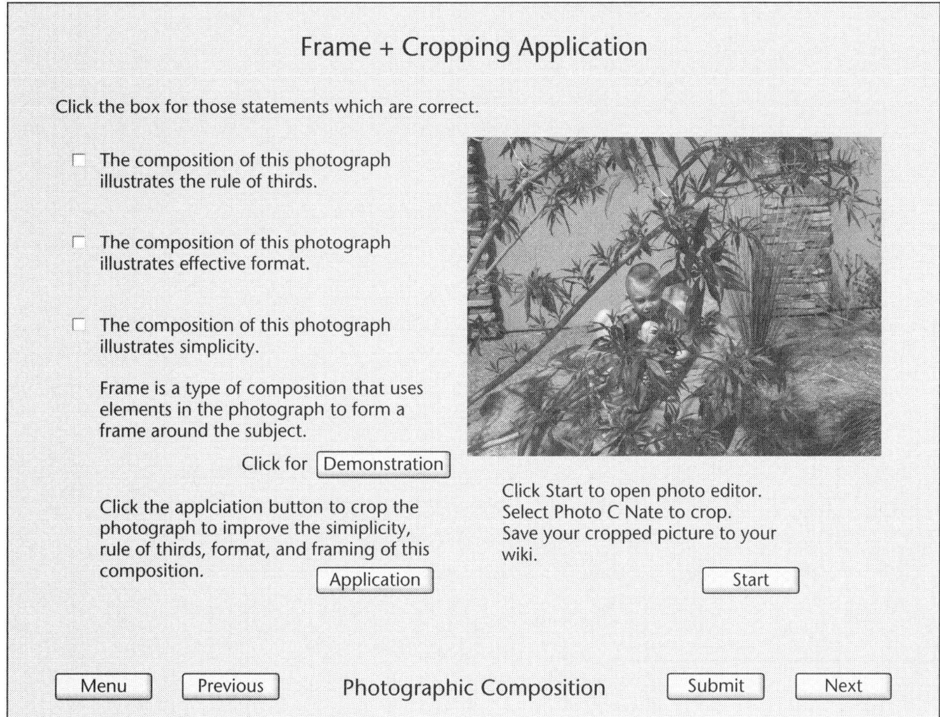

Design Consistent Between-Slide Navigation

Good between-slide navigation depends on (1) allowing learners to move forward; (2) allowing learners to return to a previous slide; and (3) encouraging learners to complete all of the instructional events before leaving a given slide.

Every slide has a Next button. However, when the slide has a number of different instructional events, it is important that there is some assurance that the learner does not skip some of these learning activities by clicking on the Next button before finishing the learning events provided by the slide. As explained in the previous paragraphs, in most cases the Next button does not appear until the learning events on the slide have been completed.

Every slide also has a Previous button that allows learners to return to the previous slide if they wish to repeat any of the learning events on this previous slide.

Design Consistent Content-Driven Navigation

The Contents slide (see Figure 17-7) in the Photographic Composition course attempts to allow learners to see the extent of the course and how it is organized. This slide is also a content-driven menu that allows learners to have control over the course, determine where they want to study, and review what they have already learned. Each slide in my functional prototype contains a Menu button in the lower-left corner of the slide. This button allows learners to return to the Contents page whenever they want to review. In this course, learners are encouraged and directed to study the course in sequence. However, because the audience is adult learners, I decided that they were mature enough to control their own sequence and so provided this option. Using the Content slide menu allows learners to study the component skills in any order they want. Adult learners often become annoyed when they are constrained by a linear sequence that they cannot override.

Learner Directions

An important rule for using an online or computer-based course is to never assume that the learner knows how to execute even the standard computer conventions. Always check to be sure that the directions for navigation for every slide are present, clear, and unambiguous. At this point, I examined every slide in the presentation to see whether there were any expectations for a student action that were not clearly explained on the slide itself. The best programs are those that do not require an extensive How to Use This Program set of directions.

The "Click here to register" button on the first slide (see Figure 17-5) should be obvious. There is really nothing else the learner can do on this slide since nothing will happen for any other click. When the learner clicks the "Click here to register" button, the message box appears with a box where the learner can type his or her name and an OK button. When the learner clicks the OK button, another message box appears that says, "Welcome <Learner's Name>" with an OK button to close the box. When this message box is closed, the Next button appears on the slide to allow the learner to move to the Introduction slide (Figure 17-6).

The directions for using the Introduction slide (Figure 17-6) also seem complete. The Continue and Next buttons do not appear until they are triggered by the audio script. The learner is clearly directed to click on the Audio Explanation button. After the audio/animation is complete, the Next button appears and the audio directs the learner to click this Next button to go to the next slide.

I continued this process of reviewing the directions on every slide to be sure that the directions were present when needed, unambiguous, and complete. I added directions where I thought there might be some confusion.

SUPPLEMENTAL MATERIALS

Design a Glossary

If a given course has many new terms, as is the case in many technical content areas, then it is advisable to provide learners with a glossary where they can check the meaning of a word when they encounter it during the course. This glossary can be added as a slide to your functional prototype with a link from the Contents slide. Be sure to add a return link on the Glossary page so that the learner can easily return to the Contents page after visiting the glossary. If there are many technical words, these words themselves can be linked to their definitions in the glossary or in a pop-up window for easy access by learners. I did not feel that a glossary function was necessary for the segment of the Photographic Composition course I have used as an illustration here.

Design Links to Lengthy Materials

The portrayals in some courses can be lengthy and not easily displayed using a computer screen. I chose examples for this book that mostly have portrayals that are brief and more easily displayed on a computer screen. However, some of the courses I have demonstrated do have lengthy portrayals that might best be provided to learners as supplemental off-line materials. For example, the Copyright course demonstrated in Chapter 9 had some rather lengthy examples. Those shown in this book are relatively short, but some of the examples could be too lengthy for convenient presentation in a slide. These materials could be made available external to the displays for the course. Some of these portrayals involved multimedia. The authors provided links to one or more computer websites for these portrayals.

The Entrepreneurship course demonstrated in Chapters 7 and 9 has some rather lengthy spreadsheets as the businesses becomes more complex. While many of these spreadsheets were presented using the computer screen, it might be advisable to make printed copies available for learners to study while they are interacting with the questions in the course or to link to Excel spreadsheets from within the course.

The course on the Persuasive Essay was designed for young students; hence the portrayals were relatively short and not difficult to display using the computer screen. But if a similar course were developed for older students, then the portrayals could run to several pages. In this situation it might be well to provide learners with printed copies of the essays or links to a website where they could download these essays to study and analyze them and then respond on the computer.

An important activity for the finalization phase of the design process is to identify and prepare those materials that might be best accessed either from other sites online or in takeaway format that learners can study while simultaneously viewing a discussion of these materials on the computer. Since most of the photographs included in this course were my own work, it was easy to include them in the PowerPoint slides. This course could also be designed to take advantage of the many photographs available on the Internet. However, if you link to portrayals for your course on the Internet, it is important to obtain permission from the copyright holders of this material or determine that your links are within the copyright guidelines for educators.

Design Takeaway Materials

Too often when learners complete a technology-based course, there is no takeaway material for them to review. In conventional courses that are textbook-based, students sometimes are able to retain the text for review at a later time. It might be advisable, even for a short course like Photographic Composition, to provide learners with a short takeaway summary of the important ideas from the course. For my course I prepared a card with the material from Figure 17-7 on one side and the rubric from Table 16-2 on the reverse side. This card then serves as a reminder of the conditions of effective photographic composition for use by learners when they are taking new photographs and when they are modifying existing photographs to improve their composition.

PRINCIPLES AND PRESCRIPTIONS

Functional Prototype: The Pebble-in-the-Pond model is a *prototyping approach,* that is, a functional prototype of the instruction is the primary design product rather than an abstract design specification.

Finalize your functional prototype by completing the following steps:

- Review your course using the Course Critique Checklist.
- Design missing course components.
- Design a title page and introductory learning events.
- Design a structural framework for guidance and coaching.
- Design peer-interaction for use with groups of learners.
- Design overall course structure.
- Design an appealing appearance.
- Design unambiguous navigation and directions.
- Design links or supplemental representations for extensive portrayals.
- Design takeaway materials for future learner review.

APPLICATION

Using the materials you designed as part of previous Application activities, finalize your functional prototype by designing missing strategy components, designing introductory material, and incorporating a structural framework and peer-interaction. Review and design easy-to-use, unambiguous navigation and associated directions. Design links or representations of lengthy portrayals, and design takeaway review materials for your course.

TO LEARN MORE

Allen, M. W. (2003). *Michael Allen's guide to e-learning.* Hoboken, NJ: John Wiley & Sons.
Many of the ideas in this chapter are elaborated in the following guide. See especially Chapter 3, The Essence of Good Design; Chapter 4, Getting There Through Successive Approximation; Chapter 6, Navigation; and Chapter 7, Instructional Interactivity.

See the Online Premium Content, "Demonstration Functional Prototype for Photographic Composition," to see the implementation of a functional prototype described in this chapter.

COMING NEXT

The sixth ripple in the Pebble model is to identify learner performance data opportunities in your functional prototype and to add computer code to your prototype that will enable you to record this data for analysis. Chapter 18 will guide you in identifying learning data opportunities and in preparing simple Visual Basic scripts that can be added to your functional prototype to enable you to record learner performance. Chapter 18 will also provide guidance in conducting one-on-one and small-group summative evaluation of your functional prototype. Finally, this chapter will guide you in the use of this data to revise your prototype to make it ready for final production.

CHAPTER 18

DESIGN ASSESSMENT AND EVALUATION

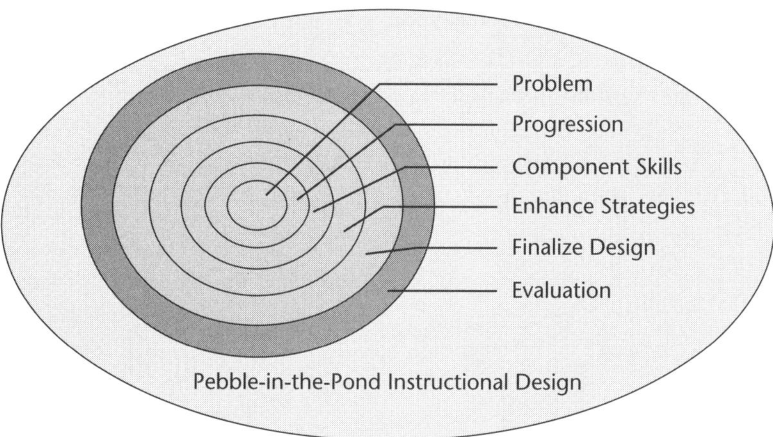

Quick Look

The final ripple in the Pebble-in-the-Pond model is to assess learner performance and evaluate the functional prototype. This chapter will guide you in the activities required to design assessment events, modify the functional prototype to enable it to record learner performance data, and conduct evaluation activities to determine what works. It will answer the following questions: What is assessment? When do you conduct assessment? How do you design or modify response events to facilitate data collection? What can you learn from a professional review, a one-on-one tryout, and a small group evaluation? How can you conduct mini experiments to determine what works?

Key Words

Assessment: the process for determining what learners know and are able to do, by which you determine whether your instruction is really effective, efficient, and engaging.

Macro: a piece of computer code designed to cause some action to occur; sometimes called a script.

INTRODUCTION

This chapter includes two parts: designing assessment activities and using the data collected from your assessment activities and other information to evaluate and revise your course. The chapter defines assessment and suggests when to assess learner performance. It provides guidance in identifying assessment opportunities in your functional prototype and guidance for designing appropriate response events. It provides guidance in adapting your functional prototype to collect and save learner performance data, time data, and attitude data. If you are using PowerPoint as a prototyping tool, the Appendix at the end of this book provides specific guidance in how to modify a PowerPoint prototype to enable it to collect assessment data.

The next section in this chapter then provides guidance for evaluating your course, including describing other data that you should gather in addition to learner performance data. Following that, I suggest ways that you can use your functional prototype to conduct mini experiments to determine which of two or more alternative learning events or strategies might be more effective. The final section provides some guidance in revising your prototype based on the data gathered from your ongoing evaluation of your course.

DESIGN ASSESSMENT

What Is Assessment?

Assessment is the process of determining what learners know or are able to do. This book proposes principles and prescriptions for designing e^3 instruction. Assessment is the process by which you determine whether the instruction you design really is effective, efficient, and engaging. It is effective if, as a result of the instruction, learners are able to solve a class of problems that they could not solve before the instruction? Efficiency is the time required to acquire a set of component skills for problem solving and the time required to solve an instance of the problem. Instruction is efficient if learners can solve an instance of the problem in less time following instruction than they could prior to the instruction and/or if learning from one instructional strategy requires less time than learning from an alternative instructional strategy, providing that the resulting problem-solving skill is the same. Instruction is engaging if learners are motivated to complete the instruction, are persistent in trying to solve a problem, and seek additional opportunities to engage in similar instruction. The purpose of assessment is to gather data that can be used to determine the effectiveness, efficiency, and engagement of your instructional product.

When to Assess Performance

You need to gather the data to determine instructional effectiveness, efficiency, and engagement at three distinct times: before the instruction begins, during the instruction, and after the instruction concludes. Observing a change in what a learner knows or is able to do requires a comparison of before-assessment data with after-assessment data. Determining the effectiveness and efficiency of different parts of the instruction requires assessment data gathered during the instruction. Determining engagement requires comparing the data gathered before the instruction with data gathered during and following the instruction.

Identify Assessment Opportunities

Are there instructional events that enable you to collect performance data? Application instructional events should be such that there are opportunities to collect data that reflects learner performance. Assessment must be valid, reliable, and objective. A measure is *valid* if it measures what it purports to measure. The prescriptions for application in this book are designed to increase the probability of valid application and, therefore, valid assessment. Such prescriptions as using unencountered examples, using classification for Do_{id} application, and using execution of a procedure for Do_{ex} application are all designed to contribute to valid application. A measure is *reliable* if it yields the same score every time. One way to increase reliability is to increase the number of times a given outcome is assessed. The greater-than-three prescription is designed to increase the probability of reliable application. Finally, an *objective* measure is one that is scored the same way every time. The use of rubrics is one way to increase the objectivity of a measure when a judgment is involved. The Photographic Composition Critique Rubric in Table 16-2 is designed to increase the objectivity when raters score photographic composition.

The first assessment activity is to carefully review each of the instructional events in the functional prototype that could be used to gather assessment data. Consider the sequence of instructional events outlined in Figure 17-1. Instructional event 2 in this prototype is a peer-sharing activity that requires each student to post three of his or her photographs taken before engaging in this module on photographic composition. These three photographs provide an opportunity to gather assessment data regarding learners' knowledge of photographic composition before the instruction begins. Instructional event 16 (Figure 17-1) is a collaboration activity that requires each student to post eight photographs following the instruction. Gathering data concerning the composition of these photographs, prior to students' collaboration with members of their group, enables me to determine what learners know and are able to do about photograph composition following the instruction. Comparing the score on the composition of their pre-instruction photographs with the score on their post-instruction photographs provides an indication of whether or not they acquired the skills taught in the course. Event 17 (Figure 17-1) provides a second source of assessment data for learning effectiveness. If each learner is required to submit his or her critique before collaborating with the group, then this critique can also be scored to determine each learner's ability to recognize the component skills of good photographic composition in the work of another. Comparing the critiques from instructional event 2 (Figure 17-1) and instructional event 17 provides another measure of how much they have learned from the course.

The effectiveness of given segments of the instruction can be assessed by gathering data for each of the application instructional events throughout the course (see Figure 17-1, instructional events 6 through 10). Performance on these application events provides information about the effectiveness of the preceding information and portrayal for the component skills.

Efficiency assessment is also possible by recording the time required for learners to complete each of the segments in the instruction. Gathering efficiency data on their ability to compose effective photographs is more difficult since these activities are off-line. Later in this chapter I will discuss comparing different instructional strategies to enable a comparison of learning efficiency.

Design or Revise Response Events

Having identified the assessment opportunities, it is now necessary to carefully examine each of these opportunities to identify the specific data that will be collected.

Data for pre-assessment will be gathered for the peer-sharing instructional event described in instructional event 2 from Figure 17-1. How will I score the photographs? What numbers will I collect to determine the effectiveness of the composition of each photograph? For each of the photographs submitted by each student, I decided to use the rubric from Table 16-2 to score the photograph as follows: strongly agree = 5, agree = 4, no opinion = 3, disagree = 2, and strongly disagree = 1. I will add the five scores together and divide by the number of conditions that are applicable to the photograph. This gives me a score from 1 to 5 for each photograph.

Data for the post-assessment will be gathered from the peer-collaboration event described in instructional event 16 (Figure 17-1). The photographs submitted by the students prior to collaboration will be scored also using the rubric from Table 16-2. Using appropriate statistical analysis, I can determine whether or not there is a significant increase in their scores as a result of the instruction.

I next examined each of the instructional events in my functional prototype to see which could be used to gather data about the effectiveness of the instruction for each of the conditions for an effective photographic composition. Instructional events 6, 7, 8, 9, and 10 (Figure 17-1) each of these slides included yes/no check boxes for one or more of the conditions of an effective photographic composition. Since one reason to design an easily modified functional prototype is to enable me, as the designer, to continually improve the instruction with each instructional activity, it occurred to me that I might be able to get more data on the three conditions of rule of thirds, format, and simplicity if the module asked learners to rate each of these five photographs on all three of these conditions. I also decided that it might be less confusing to merely have the learner check all of the conditions that apply to a given picture. Figure 18-1 shows how I modified each of these instructional events to include all three of the conditions for each photograph and how the yes/no questions from my original design were replaced by statements accompanied by the direction, "Check the box for each statement that is correct."

There are no Do_{id} events to measure framing or line in the segment of my functional prototype illustrated here; therefore, I have no data in support of the instruction for these conditions. This is a another revision I may want to make in my module, but I felt that including this addition here was not necessary for you to grasp the ideas being presented.

Design Assessment Prototype

An important advantage of a functional prototype over a design specification is that it becomes possible to have learners interact with the prototype as part of your formative evaluation. This enables you to collect data on learner performance and use this data to determine whether your instruction accomplishes its goal. In order to execute this evaluation activity, it is necessary that the functional prototype you design has the capability of recording and storing learner performance data to a file where it can be used for analysis. You may be using a rapid prototyping tool that has built-in data recording functions.

FIGURE 18-1 Revision of Application Slides in the Functional Prototype

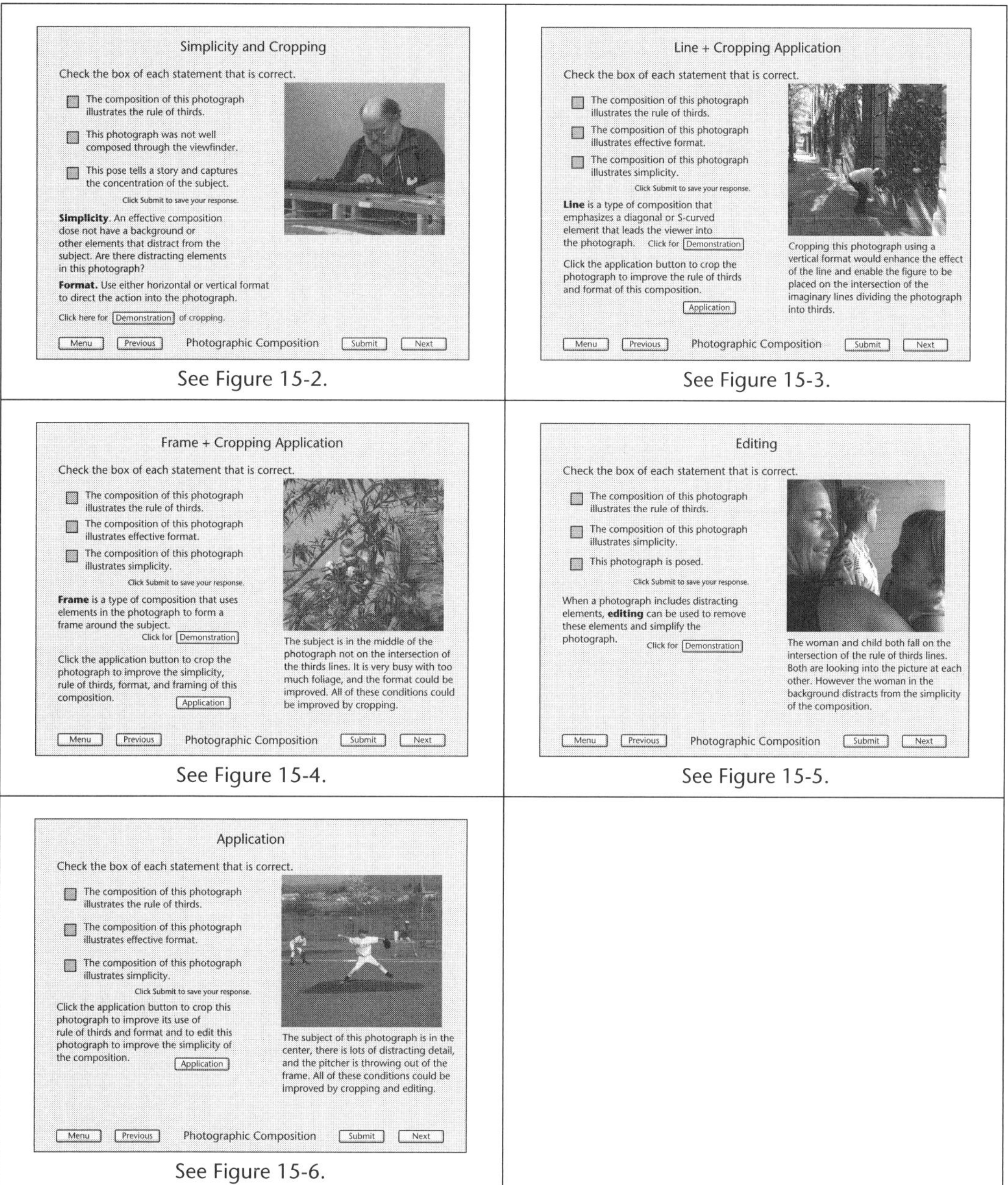

In my case I chose to use PowerPoint because at the time I'm writing this book it represents one of the most available and affordable tools to use for designing a functional prototype. However at this time, PowerPoint does not include built-in functions for data collection, so in order to use my functional prototype for formative evaluation it is necessary to extend PowerPoint to enable it to collect the learner performance data I have identified as necessary to enable me to evaluate the effectiveness, efficiency, and engagement of my course. PowerPoint is extensible, meaning that, by providing a bit of Visual Basic computer code you can add functions to PowerPoint and you don't have to be a computer programmer to do so. The Appendix at the end of this book describes the Visual Basic routines that I added to my PowerPoint functional prototype to enable assessment.

Recording Performance Data

The first requirement for recording assessment data is to obtain the learner's name so that his or her data can be identified and to identify the file where the learner data will be stored. The Appendix describes the macros required to get this data and set up a data file for the student using PowerPoint.

There are several slides (events 6 through 10 in Figure 17-1 and Figure 18-1) that require learners to judge a photograph to determine which of the conditions of an effective composition are used. To facilitate data collection, I designed a slide master that could be used for each of these slides so that I would only have to design Visual Basic code for the slide master rather than for each individual slide. I then used this slide master to modify each of these application slides. Figure 18-2 illustrates the placeholders on this slide master. The macros triggered by responses to these checkboxes are described in the Appendix. The Submit button on this slide master causes a number of events to occur. It is animated to trigger the contents of the feedback placeholder, to play any accompanying feedback audio, and to make the Next button visible. It also is animated to make each of the empty checkboxes visible so that the next frame that uses the slide master does not show an "x" in any of the checkboxes. It also triggers a macro that records the student responses and stores them to the student's response file. The macros that are triggered by the Submit button are also described in the Appendix.

Recording Time Data

I wanted to keep track of the time required for a learner to complete my program. On the last slide of the program I included an Exit button and requested the learners to click this Exit button when they have completed the program. I attached a very short macro to this Exit button to record the students' name, date, and time when they exited the program.

You may want more detailed time data, such as the amount of time it takes learners to complete the demonstration/application slides for a given component skill. You can easily record the time when a learner starts a given sequence of slides and when the learner completes this sequence of slides. You can save this time data to the student data file.

My course is very short and I anticipate that learners would complete the course in a single setting. For longer courses, I would include controls on a menu page that would allow learners to exit the course after completing a section of the course and require them to sign back in to the course when they return. I could record this exit and entry time data in the data file. The amount of data that is collected is limited only by what you feel would be worthwhile to enable you to determine the effectiveness, efficiency and engagement of your course.

FIGURE 18-2 Slide Master for Application Slides for Photographic Composition

Click to add Title

Check box of each statement which is correct.

Statement 1

Statement 2

Statement 3

Insert Picture Here

Insert Feedback message here.

Menu Previous Photographic Composition Submit Next

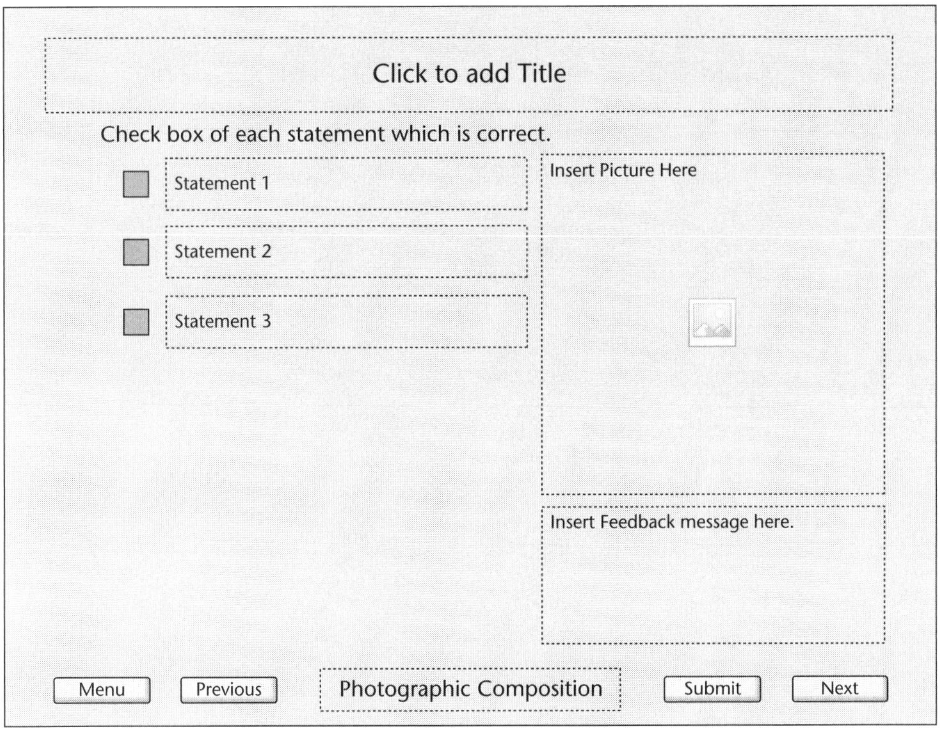

Recording Attitude Data

This chapter has already shown you how to adapt your course to enable you to collect relevant performance data from the application learning events. Performance data gives you a very important part of the evaluation data you need to evaluate your course, but it may not provide all of the data you would like to have. You may want to spend some time at this point preparing some interview questions to ask learners when they have finished taking the course to help answer the following formative evaluation questions: Do learners leave the course with a positive attitude about the content? Do they leave with a positive attitude about the media or technology involved in the delivery of the course? You can also use your functional prototype to gather other data about your course, as illustrated in Figure 18-3.

Figure 18-3 is a brief questionnaire concerning students' perception of how their photographic composition might have improved as a result of the course. It includes option buttons such that clicking one option sets it to true and the others to false. It includes a response box that enables learners to enter text of any length in response to my question. See the Appendix for the macros for recording data from this slide. You can include additional question slides in your functional prototype to gather additional data about student attitudes before, during, and after the instruction. However, you should be careful not to include so many questions that you distract from the learning experience for the learners.

FIGURE 18-3 Questionnaire Slide for Photographic Composition

Questionnaire

You have completed this short course on Photographic Composition. Thank you for your participation. To help us improve this instruction we would appreciate your opinion. Please click the button corresponding to your agreement with the following statement.

The composition of my photographs has significantly improved as a result of this course.

O Strongly Disagree O Disagree O No Opinion O Agree O Strongly Agree

Describe how these properties of effective photographic composition helped you most. Type your response in the box below.

Menu | Previous | Photographic Composition | Submit | Next

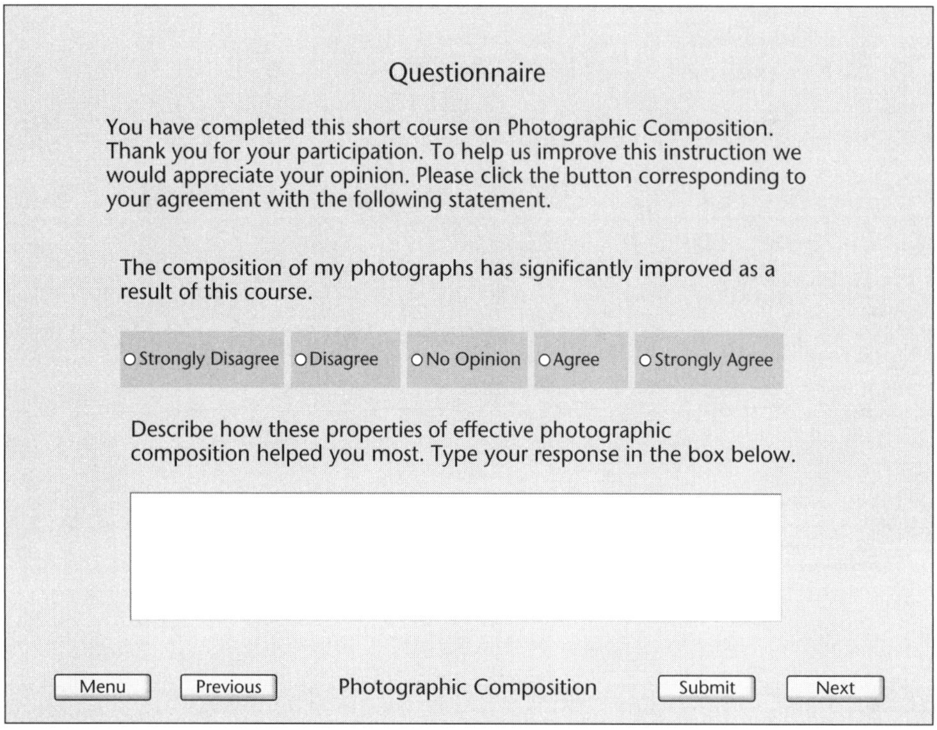

CONDUCT EVALUATION

Once you have adapted your functional prototype to be able to collect and save learner performance data, then it is time to conduct some formative evaluation of your module or course. The purpose of formative evaluation for First Principles of Instruction is the same as the purpose for more traditional instructional design. Before engaging in final development of your course and before putting your course to work with a large group of students, you will want to identify any design flaws that may hinder a learner's acquisition of the desired problem-solving skill.

Professional Review

A good first step in formative evaluation is to have other professionals review your course. An editor can help identify errors in grammar, spelling, sentence structure, and other formal communication mistakes. A subject-matter expert can help identify content inaccuracies or omissions. Another instructional professional can help identify limitations in your design or implementation of First Principles of Instruction that you may have overlooked.

One-on-One Trials

Learners have an uncanny ability to find design flaws that you may have overlooked in your several reviews of the course. A good second step in formative evaluation is to observe several learners one-on-one as they interact with your course. If you observe any of the following learner reactions, there is a pretty good indication that the design may need to be modified or adjusted. Does the learner find the content confusing or difficult to follow? Does the learner have difficulty following the navigation? Does the learner have difficulty following the directions for interaction? Is the learner confused by a demonstration or guidance? Does the learner have difficulty with an application or coaching?

A good procedure for these one-on-one observations is to prepare an observation checklist that identifies each slide in the course, includes a brief checklist of items to observe about the slide, and includes a place to write a comment after each item. Your checklist should at least include the following items for each slide: content, directions, navigation, demonstration, guidance, application, coaching, and other. If you observe a problem, check the item and write a brief comment.

Small Group Trials

Using the data-collection macros described previously, you can collect performance data for a small group of learners as they interact with the functional prototype of your course. This data will help answer the formative evaluation question, "Are learners able to solve instances of the problem following instruction better than they could before instruction?" For my prototype, my evaluation question is: "Are the composition scores for learning event 16 (Figure 17-1) higher than the composition scores for learning event 2?" Statistical analysis is required to determine whether the difference is greater than might occur by chance. If there is a significant gain, then I know that my module was successful in improving learners' ability to take photographs with effective composition, at least on the conditions taught in my module.

WHAT WORKS?

Do the demonstration/application strategies used in my module help learners acquire the ability to recognize effective composition involving rule of thirds, simplicity, and format? For my prototype learners have an opportunity to judge the condition of rule of thirds, format, and simplicity five times each. Do they show a pattern of improved performance over these five application opportunities? If so then it would appear that the demonstration/application for these skills is enabling learners to acquire DO_{id} skill in identifying new examples of these three conditions for an effective photographic composition.

First Principles of Instruction has provided principles and prescriptions for designing e^3 instructional products. This book provides a number of examples of how to apply the principles and prescriptions taught. However, every instructional situation is unique, and the application of these principles and prescriptions can take a wide variety of different forms and variations. The examples given in this book are merely illustrations of what could be done, and they are far from exhaustive. The prescriptions given in this book may require adaptation for other situations. How do you know whether your adaptation of these principles and prescriptions is more effective in your unique situation? Oftentimes you may think of two or more ways to implement a given principle or prescription in your course. How do you know which is best? "What works" evaluation may involve comparing two or more alternative approaches to a given instructional strategy to see which is more effective, efficient, or engaging.

One way to answer the above questions is to conduct a mini experiment, to actually compare two or more alternative strategies to see which works best in a given situation. Fortunately, a functional prototype can be used to conduct such an experiment. The first step is to design two or more alternatives for a given instructional strategy prescription. For example, for my prototype, one prescription is to provide audio rather than text guidance to help learners apply information to a given set of portrayals during a demonstration. Figure 18-4 illustrates comparing an audio approach with a text approach for providing guidance for the rule of thirds. Does this audio provide better guidance than the same guidance in text form? For this comparison I would create an audio and a text version for all of the conditions for an effective photographic composition.

FIGURE 18-4 Alternative Treatments for Audio Guidance Versus Text Guidance

<table>
<tr>
<td>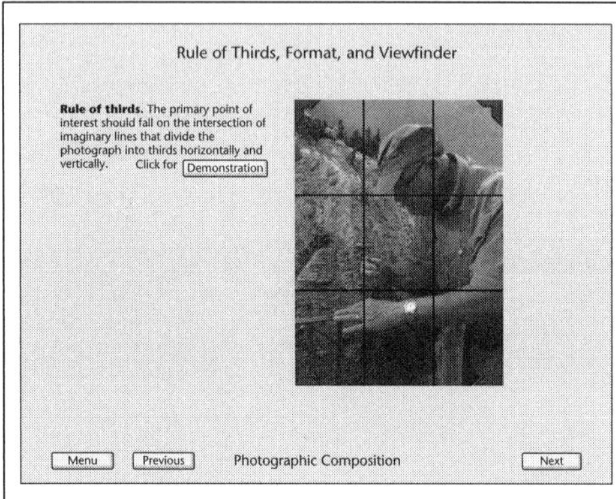
</td>
<td>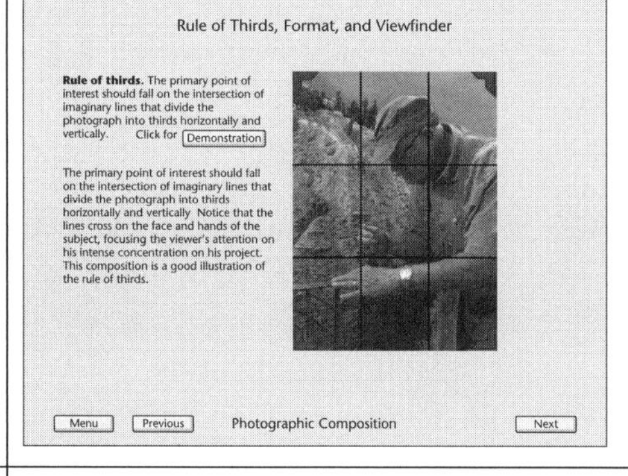
</td>
</tr>
<tr>
<td>Demonstration
[Grid lines are drawn over the photograph.]
The primary point of interest should fall on the intersection of imaginary lines that divide the photograph into thirds horizontally and vertically. Notice that the lines cross on the face and hands of the subject, focusing the viewer's attention on his intense concentration on his project. This composition is a good illustration of the rule of thirds.</td>
<td>Demonstration
[Grid lines are drawn over the photograph.]
[The second paragraph of text appears.]</td>
</tr>
</table>

The second step is to randomly assign learners to one of the two treatments during the small group evaluation of the course. This can be done within your functional prototype by adding some simple macros (see the Appendix). After completing the demonstration/application instructional events in one of the two treatments, the learners all receive the same application instructional events similar to those previously described.

After you have conducted your small group evaluation, you can then use the data files from the students to aggregate your data and apply the appropriate statistical analysis to determine whether there is a significant difference between the two strategy variations. Because it takes only a little more effort to design two or more alternative treatments and it requires almost no additional effort to collect comparison data during a small group evaluation of my functional prototype, I encourage you to always consider expanding your evaluation to include some what-works comparisons.

REVISE PROTOTYPE

One of the advantages of developing a functional prototype is that the revision of your course can be an ongoing process. In a rapid prototyping approach you should not wait until your course is almost finished before you conduct formative evaluation and make revisions. You should be conducting formative evaluation all along the way. When you have a section of the course completed, it is wise to try it out with one or two learners. You can use your observation checklist with a few slides at a time as well as with the whole course. Using this evaluate-as-you-go approach allows you to catch problems with directions, navigation, and format early so that you can incorporate these changes in the later sections of the course as it is developed. Performance data from even one or two students even for a small section of your course can help you identify obvious problems with insufficient or incomplete demonstrations, poorly constructed or confusing application, inadequate or unnecessary guidance, and inadequate or too much coaching. Identifying these problems early can help you as you design subsequent demonstrations and applications.

If you have adopted an evaluate-as-you-go approach, you should have a pretty reliable functional prototype by the time you complete your design. This is the point at which it is probably wise to engage in a more formal formative evaluation of the whole course by administering it to another small group of potential learners. If all goes well you are ready for prime time, but in case there are still some problem areas, this gives you one last opportunity to revise the course before it goes to final production and distribution.

PRINCIPLES AND PRESCRIPTIONS

e^3 learning. The purpose of instructional design is to ensure that the resulting instructional product really does promote e^3—effective, efficient, and engaging— learning. Effectiveness, efficiency, and engagement are in large part a function of the degree to which First Principles of Instruction are implemented.

The purpose of assessment is to determine the degree to which the resulting learning is efficient, effective, and engaging. Take the following steps to implement adequate assessment:

- Identify assessment opportunities and design response events for gathering learner performance data.
- Design or revise response events to identify specific data that will be collected.
- Design or modify your functional prototype so that it will collect and save learner performance data.
- Conduct ongoing evaluation to acquire learner interaction and performance data, including professional review, one-on-one trials, and small group trials.
- Use your evaluation data to engage in ongoing revision of your functional prototype.

APPLICATION

Using your functional prototype designed as part of previous application activities, design assessment activities, and modify your functional prototype to enable it to collect and record learner performance data. Conduct evaluation activities, including professional review, one-on-one trials, and small group evaluation. Using the data collected during the small group evaluation, determine whether your module teaches the problem-solving skill. Using the data collected, determine whether the individual sections of your module teach the desired component skills.

You may also want to modify your functional prototype to compare two or more instructional strategy alternatives and to randomly assign learners to these alternative treatments. Use the data collected to determine which alternative is most effective, efficient, and/or appealing.

TO LEARN MORE

Dick, W., Carey, L., & Carey, J. O. (2009). *The systematic design of instruction* (7th ed.). Boston: Pearson. (See Chapter 7, Developing Assessment Instruments; Chapter 10, Designing and Conducting Formative Evaluation; Chapter 11, Revising Instructional Materials; and Chapter 12, Designing and Conducting Summative Evaluations.)

Gagné, R. M., Wager, W. W., Golas, K., & Keller, J. M. (2005). *Principles of instructional design* (5th ed.). Belmont, CA: Thompson Wadsworth. (See Chapter 16, Evaluating Instruction.)

Marcovitz, D. M. (2004). *Powerful PowerPoint for educators.* Westport, CT: Libraries Unlimited. www.loyola.edu/edudept/PowerfulPowerPoint/. This book and website contain many suggestions for extending PowerPoint.

Mayer, R. E. (2011). *Applying the science of learning.* Boston: Pearson. (See Section 3, How Assessment Works.) This small book is a wonderful summary of research-based learning, instruction, and assessment principles.

See the Online Premium Content, "Demonstration Functional Prototype for Photographic Composition," to examine the animation and macros identified above in a live PowerPoint presentation.

COMING NEXT

Chapter 19 is the culminating chapter for the second part of this book. It presents a comprehensive checklist for the use of the Pebble-in-the-Pond model of instructional design. This checklist is cross-referenced with the prescriptions, tools, and examples of instructional design throughout the second part of the book.

CHAPTER 19

THE PEBBLE-IN-THE-POND INSTRUCTIONAL DESIGN CHECKLIST

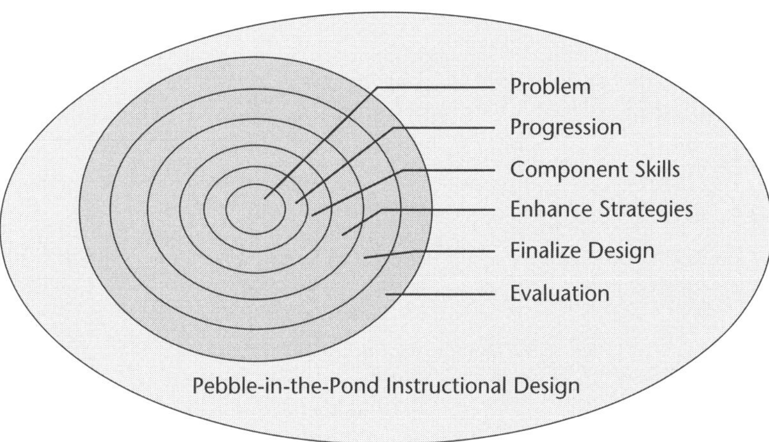

Quick Look

The previous chapters of the second part of this book have described and illustrated the instructional activities or ripples in the Pebble-in-the-Pond model for instructional design. This chapter is a checklist that provides a list of these steps, together with questions that you should answer as you complete each instructional design activity in the model.

INTRODUCTION

Part II of this book describes and illustrates the Pebble-in-the-Pond model for designing e^3 instruction based on First Principles of Instruction. This chapter provides a checklist organized around all of the instructional design activities or ripples in this model. For each instructional activity, this checklist contains a list of questions related to the details of the instructional design activity. Where instructional design tools or examples described in previous chapters are involved, these are cross-referenced in the checklist.

The checklist has two parts: Part 1 (Table 19-1) is an abbreviated checklist that lists each of the instructional design activities and then has checkboxes for the corresponding detail questions associated with each activity. This form can be used as a literal checklist during the instructional design process. Part 2 is an expanded checklist that lists each of the instructional design activities, the questions associated with each activity, and cross-references for tools and examples from previous chapters.

Table 19-1 Pebble-in-the-Pond Instructional Design Checklist

1. Design a Problem Prototype (See Chapter 13.)	
Identify the content area, primary goal, and learner population for the instruction.	☐ Goal ☐ Content ☐ Learners
Identify a class of problems that when solved accomplish the learning goal.	☐ Typical ☐ Portrayals ☐ Complete ☐ Ill-Structured ☐ Real-World
Collect a sample of problem portrayals.	☐ Divergent ☐ Range
Identify the content elements for the problem portrayals.	☐ Consequence (Q) ☐ Q properties ☐ Conditions (C) ☐ C Properties ☐ Steps (S) ☐ S Properties
Design a prototype demonstration for a portrayal of the problem.	☐ *Show*-Q ☐ *Show*-C ☐ *Show*-S
Design a prototype application for a portrayal of the problem.	☐ Do_{ex}-Q ☐ Do_{ex}-C ☐ Do_{ex}-S
2. Design a Problem Progression (See Chapter 14.)	
Identify the component skills required to solve each problem portrayal in the sequence.	☐ Component Skills Matrix
Design a progression of divergent problem portrayals from simple to complex.	☐ Skill Complexity Analysis
Adjust the progression to include sufficient opportunity for learners to acquire all of the desired component skills.	☐ Missing Portrayals ☐ Redundant Portrayals
3. Design Strategies for Component Skills (See Chapter 15.)	
Determine the distribution of demonstration and application for each condition and step required for the portrayals in the progression.	☐ Instructional Event Table

Table 19-1 *Continued*

Based on this strategy distribution chart, design demonstration and application instructional events for each condition and step of the portrayals in the problem progression.	For each component skill: Portrayal 1 ☐ *Tell*-C ☐ *Show*-C ☐ *Tell*-S ☐ *Show*-S Portrayal 2 ☐ Do_{id} -S ☐ Do_{id} -C Portrayal 3 ☐ Do_{ex} -S ☐ Do_{id} -C
Use the Course Critique Checklist to evaluate the adequacy of the instructional strategies you designed.	☐ Demonstration Checklist ☐ Application Checklist ☐ Revisions
4. Design Structural Frameworks and Peer-Interaction Strategy Enhancements (See Chapter 16.)	
Design a structural framework.	☐ Familiar ☐ Similar ☐ Simple
Design guidance based on this structural framework.	☐ Focus Attention
Design coaching based on this structural framework.	☐ Provide Help
Design reflection based on this structural framework.	☐ Extrapolate
Assign peer-interaction groups.	☐ Size ☐ Heterogeneous ☐ Directions ☐ Assignments
Design peer-sharing for activation.	☐ Prior Experience
Design peer-discussion for demonstration.	☐ Consensus
Design peer-collaboration for application.	☐ Group Solution ☐ Individual Contribution
Design peer-critique for integration.	☐ Rubric
5. Finalize the Functional Prototype (See Chapter 17.)	
Review the course using the Course Critique Checklist.	☐ Missing Elements ☐ Inadequate Elements

(continued)

Table 19-1 *Continued*

Design missing or inadequate course components.	☐ Revision
Design a title page and introductory learning events.	☐ Title Page ☐ Introduction
Integrate a structural framework for guidance and coaching.	☐ Structural Framework
Integrate peer-interaction for use with a group of learners.	☐ Peer-Interaction
Design overall course structure.	☐ Organization
Design an appealing appearance.	☐ Location Indicator ☐ Simple ☐ Relevant ☐ Multimedia Principles
Design unambiguous navigation and directions.	☐ Controls ☐ Directions ☐ Return ☐ Repeat ☐ Proceed
Design links or supplemental representations for extensive portrayals.	☐ Glossary ☐ Lengthy Materials
Design takeaway materials for future learner review.	☐ Takeaway Summary
6. Design Assessment and Evaluation (See Chapter 18.)	
Identify assessment opportunities and design response events for gathering learner performance data.	☐ Response Events
Design or revise your functional prototype so that it will collect and save learner performance data.	☐ User Name ☐ Data File ☐ Response Data
Conduct ongoing evaluation to acquire learner interaction and performance data.	☐ Professional Review ☐ One-on-One Trials ☐ Learner Sample ☐ Small Group Trial
Use your evaluation data to engage in ongoing revision of our functional prototype.	☐ Revision ☐ Evaluation Study

The Expanded Pebble-in-the-Pond Instructional Design Checklist

1. Design a problem prototype (see Chapter 13).

- Identify the content area, primary goal, and learner population for the instruction.

  Goal: Have you specified the change that needs to be promoted in the skill set of the learner population?

  Content: Have you identified the domain of skills that learners need to acquire?

  Learners: Have you identified the learner population that will engage in your instruction?

  Example: Goal, Content, Learners for Photographic Composition (Chapter 13, Identify Content, Goal, and Learner Population)

- Identify a class of problems that, when solved, accomplish the learning goal.

  Typical: Are the problems in this class typical of those learners will encounter in the real-world following instruction?

  Portrayals: Have you identified portrayals of specific problems not merely descriptions?

  Complete: Are the problem portrayals complete, including a consequence, the givens, and a set of activities that transform the givens into the solution?

  Ill-structured: Are the problem portrayals ill-structured with more than one correct solution and more than one way to solve the problem?

  Real-world: Are the problem portrayals in a real-world or simulated setting?

- Collect a sample of problem portrayals.

  Divergent: Are the problem portrayals divergent from one another?

  Range: Do the problem portrayals represent a range of quality from excellent examples to poor examples?

  Example: Sample Problem Portrayals for Photographic Composition (Figure 14-1)

- Identify the content elements—consequence, conditions, steps, and properties—for a portrayal of the problem.

  Tool: Content Elements for the Problem-Solving Event (Figure 6-7)

  Consequence (Q): Have you identified the specific consequence or solution for a specific portrayal of the problem?

  Q properties: Have you identified the property values that enable a learner to identify an instance of the consequence?

  Conditions (C): Have you identified the conditions that lead to this consequence?

  C properties: Have you identified the property values that enable a learner to identify an instance of each condition?

  Steps (S): Have you identified the step that leads to each condition?

  S properties: Have you identified the property values that enable a learner to identify an instance of the execution of the step?

  Example: Problem-Solving-Event Chart for Photographic Composition (Figure 13-3)

- Design a prototype demonstration for a portrayal of the problem.

  Tool: Prescribed Instructional Events for Whole-Problem Application (Table 13-2)

  Show-Q: Does your portrayal show the solution to the problem represented by the portrayal?

Show-C: Does your portrayal show each of the conditions that lead to the consequence?

Show-S: Does your portrayal show the execution of the step that leads to each of the conditions?

Example: Prototype Problem Demonstration for Photographic Composition (Figure 13-1)

- Design a prototype application for a portrayal of the problem.

  Tool: Prescribed Instructional Events for Whole-Problem Demonstration (Table 13-1)

  Do_{ex}-Q: Does your application require learners to predict a consequence from a set of conditions?

  Do_{ex}-C: Does your application require learners to find faulted conditions for an unanticipated consequence?

  Do_{ex}-S: Does your application require learners to execute the steps to create the conditions that lead to the consequence?

  Examples: Prototype Problem Application for Photographic Composition (see Figure 13-2). Additional Application Slides for Photographic Composition (Figures 17-2, 17-3, and 17-4).

2. Design a problem progression (see Chapter 14).

- Identify the component skills required to solve each problem portrayal in the sequence.

  Tool: Component Skills Matrix for Photographic Composition (Figure 14-2)

  Component Skills Matrix: Have you arranged the consequence for the portrayals in your progression in a preliminary order and identified the conditions and steps required to accomplish each consequence?

  Example: Component Skills Matrix for Photographic Composition (Figure 14-2)

- Design a progression of divergent problem portrayals from simple to complex.

  Tool: Skill complexity analysis (Chapter 14)

  Skill Complexity Analysis: Have you adjusted your sequence so that the consequence requiring the least number and most easily observed or executed conditions and steps occur early in the sequence, with subsequent portrayals increasing in the number and difficulty of the required conditions and steps?

  Example: Component Skills Matrix for Photographic Composition (Figure 14-2)

- Adjust the progression to include sufficient opportunity for learners to acquire all of the desired component skills.

  Missing Portrayals: Have you added portrayals to include any conditions or steps that are not represented in the progression?

  Redundant Portrayals: Have you eliminated portrayals that may be unnecessary because their conditions and steps are already included in a sufficient number of other portrayals?

  Example: Modify the Progression by Adding a Photograph (Figure 14-3)

3. Design Strategies for Component Skills (see Chapter 15).

- Determine the distribution of demonstration and application for each condition and step required for the portrayals in the progression.

  Instructional Event Table: Have you created a table to indicate when each condition or step will be demonstrated and when it will be applied?

Example: Instructional Event Table for Photographic Composition for Individuals (Table 15-1)

- Based on this Instructional Event Table, design demonstration and application instructional events for each condition and step of the portrayals in the problem progression.

  Tool: Checklist for Prescribed Instructional Events for Component Skills (Table 15-2)

  For each component skill:

  - *Tell-C:* Is there a demonstration instructional event describing the condition for portrayal 1?
  - *Show-C:* Is there a demonstration instructional event illustrating the condition for portrayal 1?
  - *Tell-S:* Is there a demonstration instructional event describing the step for portrayal 1?
  - *Show-S:* Is there a demonstration instructional event illustrating the execution of the step for portrayal 1?
  - Do_{id}-S: Is there an application instructional event requiring learners to identify an instance of the execution of the step for portrayal 2?
  - Do_{id}-C: Is there an application instructional event requiring learners to identify the adequacy of the condition that resulted from the execution of the step for portrayal 2?
  - Do_{ex}-S: Is there an application instructional event requiring learners to execute the step for portrayal 3?
  - Do_{id}-C: Is there an application instructional event requiring learners to identify the adequacy of the condition resulting from the execution of the step for portrayal 3?
  - *Show-C:* Is there an application instructional event requiring learners to identify the condition that results from the execution of the step for portrayal 3?

  Example: Prototype Application/Demonstration for Photographic Skills (Figures 15-1 through 15-6)

- Use the Course Critique Checklist to check the adequacy of the instructional strategies you have designed.

  Tool: Course Critique Checklist for Whole Problem (Table 10-14)

  Demonstration Checklist: Is there appropriate *Tell, Show,* Guidance, use of multimedia, and >3 examples for the demonstration of each condition, and step?

  Application Checklist: Is there appropriate Do_{id}, Do_{ex}, coaching, feedback and >3 examples for each condition and step?

  Revisions: Have you revised the instructional events for each condition and step to improve their rating on the Course Critique Checklist?

  Example: Prototype Application Demonstration (Table 15-3)

4. Design Structural Framework and Peer-Interaction Strategy Enhancements (see Chapter 16).

- Design a structural framework

  Familiar: Is the structural framework already familiar to the target learners?

  Similar: Does the structural framework contain elements and relationships parallel to the target content?

  Simple: Is the structural framework less complex than the target content?

  Example: Structural Framework for Photographic Composition (Figure 16-1)

- Design guidance based on this structural framework.
  Focus attention: Are the elements or relationships of the structural framework used to focus the learner's attention on the properties of the content exemplified in the portrayal of the content?
  Example: Presentation Guidance Based on Structural Framework (Figure 16-2)
- Design coaching based on this structural framework.
  Provide help: Do the elements or relationships of the structural framework help the learner identify parallel properties in the target content or help the learner modify the properties of the target content to help solve the problem?
  Example: Application Coaching Based on Structural Framework (see Figure 16-3)
- Design reflection based on this structural framework.
  Extrapolate: Does the reflection cause learners to apply their skills beyond the specific portrayals of the problem progression or even to different problems?
  Example: Reflection Based on Structural Framework (Figure 16-5)
- Assign peer-interaction groups.
  Size: Are the peer-interaction groups comprised of from three to five individuals?
  Heterogeneous: Are the peer-interaction groups comprised of individuals with different backgrounds, opinions, and skills?
  Directions: Are the peer-interaction groups given specific directions for interaction?
  Assignments: Does each member of a peer-interaction group have a specific role to play?
- Design peer-sharing for activation.
  Prior Experience: Do learners share with one another their prior relevant experience with the subject matter content?
  Example: Directions for Peer-Sharing for Photographic Composition (Table 16-1)
- Design peer-discussion for demonstration.
  Consensus: Is the group of learners required to reach consensus concerning the adequacy of one or more solutions for portrayals of the problem?
  Example: Peer-Discussion and Peer-Critique Rubric and Activity (Tables 16-2 and 16-3)
- Design peer-collaboration for application.
  Group Solution: Are learners required to work together to develop a group solution to the portrayal of the problem?
  Individual contribution: Can the individual contribution of each learner in the group be clearly identified and credited?
  Example: Peer-Collaboration Activity for Photographic Composition (Table 16-4)
- Design peer-critique for integration.
  Tool: Peer-Discussion and Peer-Critique Rubric (Table 16-2)
  Rubric: Are learners given some form of checklist to guide their evaluation of the work of their fellow learners?
  Example: Peer-Critique Activity for Photographic Composition (Table 16-5)

5. Finalize the Functional Prototype (see Chapter 17).

- Review the course using the Course Critique Checklist.
  Tool: Course Critique Checklist for Whole Problem (Table 10-14)
  Missing Elements: Have you identified missing instructional events that might increase the e^3 quality of your module or course?
  Inadequate Elements: Have you identified inadequate instructional events that, if revised, might increase the e^3 quality of your module or course?
  Example: Checklist for Component Skills in Photographic Composition for Individuals (Table 15-3)
- Design missing or inadequate course components.
  Revision: Have you revised the course to revise inadequate instructional events or include missing instructional events?
  Example: Application Slides for Photographic Composition (Figures 17-2, 17-3, 17-4)
- Design a title page and introductory learning events.
  Title Page: Have you designed an appropriate title page for your module or course?
  Introduction: Have you designed an appropriate introduction for your module or course?
  Example: Title Page for Photographic Composition (Figure 17-5) and Introduction slide for Photograph Composition (Figure 17-6).
- Integrate a structural framework for guidance and coaching.
  Structural Framework: Have you integrated a structural framework into the course and used this framework to enhance guidance and coaching?
  Example: Photographic Composition Summary and Checklist (Figure 17-8)
  Example: Application Slides for Photographic Composition (Figures 17-2 and 17-3)
- Design peer-interaction for use with groups of learners.
  Peer-Interaction: Have you integrated peer-interaction into the course including appropriate peer-sharing, peer-discussion, peer-collaboration, and peer-critique?
  Examples: Directions for Peer-Sharing for Photographic Composition (Table 16-1); Peer-Discussion Activity for Photographic Composition (Table 16-3; Peer-Collaboration Activity for Photographic Composition (Table 16-4); Peer-Critique Activity for Photographic Composition (Table 16-5)
- Design overall course structure.
  Organization: Have you included a slide that shows the organization and extent of the course?
  Example: Course Organization for Photographic Composition (Figure 17-7).
- Design an appealing appearance.
  Location Indicator: Is there an indication on each slide of where the learner is in the course with respect to the whole?
  Simple: Is the appearance of the course simple and clear?
  Relevant: Are all of the graphic elements relevant to the content?
  Multimedia: Are the principles for effective multimedia implemented?
  Example: Location Indicator and Within-Slide Navigation (Figure 17-9)
- Design unambiguous navigation and directions.
  Controls: Are controls over the presentation clearly identified?

Directions: Are the directions for using these controls unambiguous and easy to follow?

Repeat: Are learners allowed to repeat a dynamic demonstration or application?

Return: Are learners allowed to return to a previous demonstration or application?

Proceed: Are learners warned or prevented from proceeding until they have completed all of the learning events for a given slide?

Example: Location Indicator and Within-Slide Navigation (Figure 17-9)

Example: Within- and Between-Slide Navigation (Figure 17-10)

- Design links or supplemental representations for extensive portrayals.

  Glossary: If the content is technical or complex, is there a glossary for technical terms?

  Lengthy Materials: If there are lengthy materials that do not lend themselves to display on a computer screen, are there easily executed links to these materials?

- Design takeaway materials for future learner review.

  Takeaway Summary: Is there a takeaway summary of the important conditions and steps for solving the problem?

  Example: Peer-Discussion and Peer-Critique Rubric for Photographic Composition and Photographic Composition Summary and Checklist (Table 16-2 and Figure 17-8)

6. Design Assessment and Evaluation (see Chapter 18).

- Identify assessment opportunities and design response events for gathering learner performance data.

  Response Events: Have you identified and modified the application slides to facilitate the collection of learner performance data?

- Design or revise your functional prototype to acquire learner interaction and performance data.

  User Name: Have you included a means for obtaining the learner's name?

  Response Data: Have you included a means for collecting learner response data?

  Data File: Have you included a means for saving learner response data to a file?

  Tool: Macros for Collecting Performance Data (Appendix).

  Example: The macros YourName and CreateDataFile (Table A-1 Row 2 and Row 4)

- Conduct ongoing evaluation to acquire learner interaction and performance data.

  Professional Review: Have you had other professionals—editor, subject-matter expert, designer—review your course?

  One-on-One Trials: Have you conducted and observed one-on-one trials of learning events from your course as they are developed?

  Learner Sample: Have you identified a small sample of potential learners from the target learner population?

  Small Group Trial: Have you collected and analyzed student performance data with your learner sample to determine whether your course is effective, efficient, and engaging?

- Use your evaluation data to engage in ongoing revision of your functional prototype.

Revision: Based on the data from your trials, have you revised your course to improve any weak areas?

Evaluation Study: Have you conducted a trial of your course with a group of learners to see whether the revisions corrected the problems identified by earlier trials?

APPLICATION

As you have completed the applications for Part II of this book, you should have designed a functional prototype of your lesson or module. Using the checklist in this chapter, carefully review your work. Have you completed all of the steps in the Pebble-in-the-Pond model? Can you check off each of the detail questions in the checklist? You may want to revise your functional prototype to more adequately implement all of the prescriptions outlined in this checklist.

COMING NEXT

You have now completed the description and illustration of First Principles and the Pebble-in-the-Pond model for instructional design. Part III of this book includes two chapters that review both indirect support and direct support for First Principles of Instruction. Indirect support reviews instructional design prescriptions from the work of other researchers that are similar to those principles represented in this book. Direct support reports some of the research that has been done to verify the principles and prescriptions presented in this book. The final chapter discusses the possible role that First Principles may play in the future of instructional technology.

TO LEARN MORE

There are many instructional design checklists available (search the Internet for "instructional design checklists"). Many are based on the traditional ADDIE model of instructional design. You might want to compare some of these checklists with the checklist in this chapter.

A good exercise would be for you to apply this checklist to the Photographic Composition functional prototype. See the Online Premium Content, "Demonstration Functional Prototype for Photographic Composition."

PART III

SUPPORT FOR FIRST PRINCIPLES OF INSTRUCTION

Chapter 20, *Indirect Support for First Principles of Instruction,* is based on the premise that there is a set of principles that can be found in instructional design research, theories, and models. This chapter cites a sample of research findings and prescriptive principles for instructional design that provide indirect support for First Principles of Instruction.

Chapter 21, *Direct Research Support for First Principles of Instruction,* cites a sample of formal and informal research efforts to directly evaluate the effectiveness of First Principles of Instruction. It also includes a review of some projects that used First Principles but did not collect systematic research data.

Chapter 22, *First Principles of Instruction and the Future,* reviews my underlying motivation for presenting a theoretical approach to instructional design that includes very specific prescriptions for identifying and designing instructional strategies. It presents a science/technology model of instructional design and suggests how First Principles contribute to this model. It concludes by suggesting ways that you might contribute to a science/technology approach to instructional design.

CHAPTER 20

INDIRECT SUPPORT FOR FIRST PRINCIPLES OF INSTRUCTION

Quick Look

First Principles of Instruction is based on the premise that there is a set of principles that can be found in instructional design research, theories, and models. In this chapter I cite a sample of research findings and prescriptive principles for instructional design that provide indirect support for First Principles of Instruction. This chapter addresses the following questions: What are some of the research findings that support First Principles of Instruction? What research-based prescriptive principles, recommended by other researchers and designers, support First Principles of Instruction. What are some representative instructional design models that are similar to First Principles of Instruction?

INTRODUCTION

In this chapter I cite research findings and research-based prescriptive principles for instructional design that provide indirect support for First Principles of Instruction. This material is titled "Indirect Support" in that these findings and principles were developed independently from my statement of First Principles of Instruction. The research and prescriptive principles cited represent a sampling of the literature from which First Principles were derived and more recent literature that subsequently provides independent indirect support of these principles. In Chapter 21 I will cite research that attempts to provide *direct support* for First Principles.

The first part of this chapter includes research findings and prescriptive instructional design principles, which are summarized under the First Principles of Instruction: Problem-Centered, Activation, Demonstration, Application, and Integration. The prescriptive principles that are quoted in this chapter were all based on empirical research. You are encouraged to consult the sources cited for a review of the evidence that support these prescriptive statements.

PROBLEM-CENTERED

Learning Is Promoted When Learners Acquire Skill in the Context of Real-World Problems.

Much of the work in cognitive psychology has shown that students learn better when engaged in solving problems (R. E. Mayer, 1992a). Problem-centered learning is well represented by a number of instructional models, including Cognitive Apprenticeship (Collins, Brown, & Newman, 1989); Goal-Based Scenarios (Schank, Berman, & Macpherson, 1999); Constructivist Learning Environments (Jonassen, 1999); Problem-Based Learning (Savery & Duffey, 1995); Novel Problem Solving (Clark & Blake, 1997); and Whole Task Practice in the 4C/ID Model (van Merriënboer, 1997; van Merriënboer & Kirschner, 2007). The definition of *problem* varies among theorists. For some, a problem is engaging in some form of simulation of a device or situation. For others, it merely means being involved in some form of real-world task. My use of the word *problem* includes a wide range of activities, the most critical characteristic being that the activity is some whole task, rather than only components of a task, and that the task is representative of the problems the learner will encounter in the world following instruction.

Clark and Mayer (2003, 2008) review learning research and translate the findings of this research into prescriptive principles for instructional design. They state the following prescriptive principles related to the Problem-Centered principle.

> "Interactions should mirror the job." (Clark & Mayer, 2003, p. 53)
>
> "Use job contexts to teach problem solving processes" (Clark & Mayer, 2003, p. 251).
>
> "Focus training on thinking processes versus job knowledge" (Clark & Mayer, 2003, p. 256).
>
> "Incorporate job-specific problem-solving processes" (Clark & Mayer, 2003, p. 264).

Demonstrate the Whole Problem

It has become common practice to state learning objectives at the beginning of a module or lesson material. These objectives are usually some form of, "The learner will be able to. . . ." Objectives of this form are abstract and often only understood following the instruction. Most theorists suggest that a specific demonstration of the particular whole task similar to those the learners will be able to do following instruction provides a better orientation to the instructional material to follow than a list of abstract objective statements. van Merriënboer (1997) recommends that the first problem in a sequence be a worked example that shows the student the type of whole task that they will learn to complete.

Consider the following prescriptive principles:

> "When instruction provides clear (to the learner) and complete procedural 'how to' examples of the decisions and actions needed to solve problems and perform necessary tasks to be learned, then learning and transfer will be increased" (R.E. Clark, 2003, p. 16).
>
> "Instructional goals narrow what students focus on." (Marzano, Pickering, & Pollock, 2001, p. 94). This is probably because most objectives are topic-oriented rather than whole-problem-oriented.
>
> "Instructional goals should not be too specific" (Marzano, Pickering, & Pollock, 2001, p. 94). When objectives are very specific, they are usually

topic-oriented rather than whole-problem-oriented. Sometimes objectives are specific to only one instance of a problem, rather than to a class of problems.

Use a Progression of Problems

Some of the problems that learners must complete are very complex. Most theorists would agree that solving a single problem and receiving little or no guidance is not effective. To master a complex problem, learners must first start with a less complex problem. When the first problem is mastered, then learners are given a more complex problem. Through a progression of increasingly complex problems the learners' skills gradually improve until they are able to solve complex problems. Problem progression is advocated by Elaboration Theory (Reigeluth, 1999a); 4C/ID Model (van Merriënboer, 1997); Work Model Progression (Gibbons, Bunderson, Olsen, & Robertson, 1995); Scaffolding (Collins, Brown, & Newman, 1989); and Understanding-Performances (Perkins & Unger, 1999).

Consider the following prescriptive principle from Clark & Mayer (2008, p. 240):

> *"Design worked examples . . . to illustrate guidelines with differing contexts." The emphasis here is on a varied sequence of job-related tasks rather than on a single task.*

ACTIVATION

> *Learning is promoted when learners activate a mental model of their prior knowledge.*

It has long been a tenant of education to start where the child is. It is therefore surprising that many instructional products jump immediately into the new material without laying a sufficient foundation. If learners have had relevant experience, then the first phase of learning is to be sure that this relevant information is activated and ready for use as a foundation for the new knowledge. If learners have not had sufficient relevant experience, then the first phase of learning a new skill should be to provide hands-on experience that they can use as a foundation for the new knowledge. Too much instruction starts with abstract representations for which learners have insufficient foundation. First Principles borrowed the term *activation* from Andre (1997), who provides one of the best discussions of this principle. Ebert-May, Brewer, and Allred (1997) recommend asking students a question to probe their prior knowledge and to organize their thinking for what they are about to learn.

Consider the following prescriptive principles:

> "Cues and questions are ways that a . . . teacher helps students use what they already know about a topic" (Marzano, Pickering, & Pollock, 2001, p. 112).
>
> ". . . providing cues to encourage learners to activate relevant preexisting knowledge facilitates learning" (Andre, 1997, p. 246).

"Help students develop their background knowledge" (Rosenshine, 1997, p. 199).

"Review . . . relevant previous learning . . . prerequisite skills and knowledge" (Rosenshine, 1997, pp. 202, 216).

Provide a Structural Framework

Simple recall of information is seldom effective as an activating experience. Activation is more than merely helping learners recall previous experience or providing relevant experience. Activation also involves stimulating those mental models that can be modified or tuned to enable learners to incorporate the new knowledge into their existing knowledge. Helping learners recall or develop a relevant structure to organize the knowledge facilitates learning of complex tasks. If a learner has a mental model that can be used to organize the new knowledge, then he or she should be encouraged to activate this mental model. However, if the learner's mental model is insufficient to adequately organize the new knowledge, then learning is promoted if the instruction provides a structure that the learner can use to build the required organizational schema for the new knowledge.

Gagné (1985) suggests that new learning depends on previously learned entities. R. E. Mayer (1975) indicates that providing learners with a conceptual model can facilitate the acquisition of problem solving. He advocates giving learners a simple analogy to make it easier to learn details and finds that providing students with an organizing structure helps them organize and integrate new knowledge into their existing knowledge (R. H. Mayer, 1999). Collins, Brown, and Holum (1991) recommend providing learners with a conceptual model to help them organize new information. Clark and Blake (1997) recommend presenting dynamic schema and analog models to promote far transfer. Darabi (2002) suggests giving learners a visual model to organize their new learning. Andre (1997) cites theory and research supporting schema activation and advance organizers. He shows that themes can serve as an organizing structure if they are relevant to the content being taught.

Consider the following prescriptive principles:

"Being aware of the explicit structure of information is an aid to summarizing information" (Marzano, Pickering, & Pollock, 2001, p. 32).

"Graphic organizers are perhaps the most common way to help students generate nonlinguistic representations" (Marzano, Pickering, & Pollock, 2001, p. 75).

"The more we use both systems of representation—linguistic and nonlinguistic—the better [learners] are able to think about and recall knowledge" (Marzano, Pickering, & Pollock, 2001, p. 73).

"Advance organizers should focus on what is important as opposed to what is unusual. . . . 'Higher level' advance organizers produce deeper learning than the 'lower level' advance organizers. . . . Advance organizers are most useful with information that is not well organized" (Marzano, Pickering, & Pollock, 2001, p. 118).

". . . concrete AOs [advance organizers] seem to be more effective than more abstract AOs" (Andre, 1997, p. 248).

"Providing learners with a conceptual model can facilitate the acquisition of problem-solving skills" (Andre, 1997, p. 247).

". . .providing students with appropriate maps and diagrams has been shown to enhance their learning. . . . Concept or semantic mapping has promise of helping students acquire the interrelationships component of a knowledge domain" (Andre, 1997, p. 253).

"Provide and teach a checklist" (Rosenshine, 1997, p. 213).

DEMONSTRATION

Learning is promoted when learners observe a demonstration of the skill to be learned.

Knowledge to be learned exists at two levels: information and portrayal. Information is general and inclusive and refers to many cases or situations. Portrayal is specific and limited and refers to a single case or a single situation. Presenting information is by far the most common form of instruction. Instruction is far more effective when it also includes the portrayal level in which the information is demonstrated via specific situations. Learners can apply information far more readily when the information includes specific portrayals. van Merriënboer (1997) indicates that showing a learner what to do via a worked-out example, which shows the learner how to do the problem, is an important first step in an instructional sequence. Merrill (1994) cites research that shows presenting examples is more effective than merely presenting information and that presenting examples in addition to application promotes better learning than application alone.

Consider the following prescriptive principles:

"Start with a full worked example and gradually increase the amount of work the learner must perform, ending with a full practice assignment" (Clark & Mayer, 2008, p. 274).

". . . examples in teaching concepts, principles, and problem-solving procedures [result in] substantial benefits. . . . presenting learners with worked-out examples . . . led to more effective learning . . ." (Andre, 1997, p. 255).

Use a Consistent Demonstration

Gagné (1985) identified categories of learning and suggested that effective learning occurs when the conditions of learning were consistent with the desired category of learned performance. Merrill (1994) elaborated on Gagné's categories and prescribed primary and secondary presentation forms consistent with each outcome category. Dijkstra and van Merriënboer (1997) identify three classes of problems: problems of categorization, problems of design (plans and procedures), and problems of interpretation (principles, models, and theories). Each of these different classes of problems requires different knowledge structures (corresponding to the desired cognitive structure) and different constituent skills (concepts, activities, and processes) if learning is to be efficient and effective. Van Merriënboer (1997) has extended this work in the context of problem-centered instruction. These theorists agree that if demonstrations are inconsistent with the intended learning outcomes, then learning will be ineffective. The consistency criterion should be applied first because if the presentation is inconsistent with the intended learning outcome then it doesn't matter whether there is learner guidance or whether the media representation is effective.

Consider the following prescriptive principles for different types of skills:

Demonstration for Kind-of Skills

> *"New concepts should be taught by providing a definition of the concept, examples from the work environment, and practice exercises in which learners are asked to correctly classify many different work-relevant concept examples. If new concepts are presented with these supports, learning of concepts is enhanced. If highly novel applications of the concept are required, then provide practice on many different novel examples of the concept" (R. E. Clark, 2003, p. 24).*

> *"In teaching concepts or classification skills, it is important to provide students with a range of examples of particular concepts, and also to provide contrasts between examples of closely related concepts" (Andre, 1997, p. 256).*

> *". . . instruction should activate misconceptions and then induce learners to be in a state of disequilibrium or dissatisfaction about the misconception" (Andre, 1997, p. 257). One role of non-examples is to allow a student to see where the information does not apply or where he or she may have mistakenly thought it applied when it does not. This principle is an elaboration of the examples and non-examples prescription.*

Demonstration for How-to Skills (Procedures)

> *"When teaching procedures, the more that instruction is based on expert-based descriptions of the sequence of actions and decisions necessary for goal achievement, and is accompanied by a worked example and the opportunity for part-whole practice that is scaffolded to reflect the learner's prior knowledge and accompanied by a conceptual elaboration of the declarative knowledge base supporting the procedure, the more effective will be the learning and transfer of the procedure back to the job environment" (R. E. Clark, 2003, p. 30).*

Visualizations for What-Happens Skills

> *"When designing instruction for a process (how something works), give students a clear narrative description integrated with a visual model of the sequence of events that characterize the process, and describe each stage in the process and what key events or actions occur at each stage to produce a change that leads to the next stage" (R. E. Clark, 2003, p. 26).*

"When teaching causal principles, the more that the instructional presentation provides a statement about the cause and resulting effects, provides instruction using a worked, prototypical example drawn from the application setting, and helps the learner to first elaborate the elements and sequence of the causal chain and then to apply it to gradually more novel and complex examples, the more effective will be the learning and transfer to the job" (R. E. Clark, 2003, p. 28).

Provide Learner Guidance

Clark and Blake (1997) indicate that problem solving (far transfer) is promoted when the structural features are carefully identified and explicitly mapped for the student. This explicate guidance focuses the learner's attention on relevant information in the problem. Early in an instructional presentation, this attention-focusing function facilitates knowledge acquisition. However, as the instruction progresses, this information-focusing role should be faded and students expected to attend to and focus their own attention on the relevant aspects of the information (Andre, 1997).

Another form of guidance is to provide learners with multiple representations of the ideas being taught and the demonstration being provided. Spiro and Jehng (1990), Schwartz, Lin, Brophy, and Bransford (1999) and Clark and Blake (1997) all stress the importance of alternative points of view, especially for ill-defined domains and non-recurrent skills. Spiro, Feltovich, Jacobson, and Coulson (1992), in cognitive flexibility theory, stress the importance of coming at a given topic from multiple perspectives.

Gentner and Namy (1999) have demonstrated that merely presenting alternative representations is not sufficient. When learners are explicitly directed to compare different viewpoints, they are forced to tune their mental models to provide a broader perspective.

Consider the following prescriptive principles:

"People learn better from narrated animations when the narration highlights the key steps and the links between them" (R. E. Mayer, 2003b, p. 47).

"Presenting students with explicit guidance in identifying similarities and differences enhances students' understanding of and ability to use knowledge" (Marzano, Pickering, & Pollock, 2001, p. 15).

"Asking students to independently identify similarities and differences enhances students' understanding of and ability to use knowledge" (Marzano, Pickering, & Pollock, 2001, p. 15).

". . . use of signaling devices generally has positive effects on memory for the presented information" (Andre, 1997, p. 255).

Use Multimedia to Implement Prescribed Instructional Events

Consider the following prescriptive principles about the use of effective multimedia:

"Visual representation of text material is helpful in improving comprehension of complex material" (Dembo & Young, 2003, p. 60).

"People learn more deeply from corresponding words and graphics (e.g., animation, video, illustrations, pictures) than from words alone" (Clark & Mayer, 2008, p. 81; R. E. Mayer, 2003b, p. 37).

"The more we use both systems of representation—linguistic and nonlinguistic [graphic]—the better we are able to think about and recall knowledge" (Marzano, Pickering, & Pollock, 2001, p. 73).

"We recommend that corresponding graphics are placed near rather than far from each other on the screen" (Clark & Mayer, 2008, p. 93).

"People learn better when corresponding animation and narration segments are presented simultaneously" (R. E. Mayer, 2003b, p. 51).

Use an Organizing Structure to Provide Guidance

Consider the following prescriptive principles concerning the use of an organizing structure in demonstration:

"Encourage deeper learning through techniques such as self-explanations that promote deeper processing of worked examples" (Clark & Mayer, 2008, p. 231). If this self-explanation assists learners to relate the new information to previously learned information or the structure that was provided, then it will facilitate learning.

"Whether you adopt a part-task, a whole-task or some combination design, it will be important to use instructional methods that make invisible thinking processes explicit" (Clark & Mayer, 2008, p. 355). The processes that facilitate learning are those that help the student relate previous knowledge to new knowledge or to the structure that was provided.

"[Use] a variety of structured tasks to guide students through generating and testing hypotheses" (Marzano, Pickering, & Pollock, 2001, p. 106). Testing hypotheses is another way to relate specific cases to general information.

". . . relating to-be-learned instructional events to preexisting knowledge . . . leads to superior learning and performance" (Andre, 1997, p. 250).

"Give clear and detailed instructions and explanations" (Rosenshine, 1997, p. 202).

Avoid Misuse of Multimedia

Consider the following considering the misuse of multimedia:

"There is considerable evidence that presenting words in audio rather than on-screen text can result in significant learning gains" (Clark & Mayer, 2008, p. 115).

"People learn better from animation and narration than from animation, narration, and on-screen text" (R. E. Mayer, 2003b, p. 45).

"In general, do not add printed text to a narrated graphic" (Clark & Mayer, 2008, p. 133).

"People learn better from narrated animations when the narration has a human voice with a standard accent rather than a machine voice or an accented voice" (R. E. Mayer, 2003b, p. 53).

"People learn better from multimedia messages when extraneous words, pictures, and sounds are excluded rather than included" (R. E. Mayer, 2003b, p. 33).

"We summarize the empirical evidence for excluding rather than including extraneous information in the form of background sound, added text, and added graphics" (Clark & Mayer, 2008, pp. 151–152).

R. E. Mayer (1992b, 2001) has demonstrated that gratuitous illustrations make little or no instructional contribution and are often ignored by learners or may actually interfere with efficient learning. He has also demonstrated that some combinations of multimedia (for example, text and a graphic) compete for attention and therefore increase the cognitive load for the student. Other combinations of media, such as audio and graphic, support one another and promote more effective learning.

APPLICATION

Learning is promoted when learners apply their newly acquired skill.

Merrill (1994) cites research demonstrating that adding practice to information and examples increases learning. Most instructional design theories advocate application of knowledge and skill as a necessary condition for effective learning. Gagné (1985) describes eliciting performance and providing feedback as necessary instructional events. H. Gardner (1999) and Perkins and Ungner (1999) both emphasize the necessity of many opportunities for performance. Many of the problem-based models (Clark & Blake, 1997; Jonassen, 1999; Nelson, 1999; Savery & Duffy, 1995; Schank, Berman, & Macpherson, 1999; Schwartz, Lin, Brophy, & Bransford, 1999; van Merriënboer, 1997) emphasize the importance of being involved in doing real-world problems. It is astounding that, with this almost universal agreement on the importance of applying knowledge to real-world problems, so much instruction merely includes a few multiple-choice questions that are labeled practice. Such remember-what-you-were-told questions do little to promote learning.

Consider the following prescriptive principles:

"Adjust the amount of practice based on task criticality" (Clark & Mayer, 2008, p. 260).

"Provide a high level of active practice for all students" (Rosenshine, 1997, p. 202).

"Ask a large number of questions, check for student understanding, and obtain responses from all students" (Rosenshine, 1997, p. 202).

Use Consistent Application

Just as there are different components of knowledge, presentation, and learner guidance appropriate for different kinds of instructional goals, so there are different kinds of application appropriate for different instructional goals. Engaging in application that is inconsistent with the desired instructional goal will do little to improve performance. Gagné (1965, 1985) and Merrill (1994, 1997a) identify appropriate application for each of the kinds of knowledge and skill identified. Learning is promoted when the practice is consistent with the learning goal. The consistency criterion should be applied first. If the application is inconsistent with the intended goals of the instruction, then it will be ineffective and it doesn't matter whether or not there is appropriate coaching and feedback or a sequence of problems.

Show a Divergent Set of Examples

Applying knowledge to a single problem is insufficient for learning a cognitive skill. Adequate application must provide multiple opportunities for learners to use their new skill for a variety of problems. Andre (1986) indicates the importance of providing learners with a range of examples. Merrill, Tennyson, and Posey (1992) indicate that a necessary condition for effective concept instruction is a range of divergent examples. Tennyson and Park (1980) and Tennyson and Cocchierella (1986) reviewed research demonstrating the value of a sequence of varied examples in concept instruction, and van Merriënboer (1997) stresses variability of practice.

Use Coaching

One theory of effective instruction is Scaffolding (Burton & Brown, 1979; Collins, Brown, & Newman, 1989). The idea is that early in learning students need considerable support, but as the learning progresses this support is gradually taken away, leaving the students eventually on their own. Scaffolding involves having the instructor perform parts of the problem that the students cannot perform and gradually reducing the amount of guidance and shifting the control to the student.

Consider the following prescriptive principles:

> "Use effective on-screen coaches to promote learning" (Clark & Mayer, 2008, p. 191).
>
> "Guide students during initial practice. . . . Provide procedural prompts or facilitators. . . .Provide models of appropriate responses. . . . Think aloud as choices are being made. . . . Anticipate and discuss potential difficulties. . . . Regulate the difficulty of the material. . . . Provide a cue card" (Rosenshine, 1997, p. 212).
>
> "When teaching higher-level tasks, support students by providing them with cognitive strategies. . . . Help students learn to use the cognitive strategies by providing them with procedural prompts and modeling the use of these procedural prompts" (Rosenshine, 1997, p. 215).
>
> "Increase student responsibilities" (Rosenshine, 1997, p. 214).

Provide Feedback

Providing intrinsic or corrective feedback has long been recognized as the most important form of learner guidance. All theories advocate some form of feedback as a necessary condition for learning. Gagné (1985) includes feedback as one of the events for instruction. Andre (1997) includes feedback as one of his three phases of effective instruction. Numerous research studies have demonstrated the importance of feedback while investigating a number of variables about what type of feedback is most effective (Kulhavy, 1977; Kulhavy & Stock, 1989).

Making errors is a natural consequence of problem solving. Most learners learn from the errors they make, especially when they are shown how to recognize the error, how to recover from the error, and how to avoid the error in the future. Error diagnosis and correction is a fundamental principle of Minimalism (van der Meij & Carroll, 1998).

Consider the following prescriptive principles:

> "Effective feedback about learning progress results in better learning and transfer of such learning to the work environment" (R. E. Clark, 2003, p. 18).
>
> "Look for feedback that not only tells the respondent whether an answer is correct or incorrect, but gives an explanation as well" (Clark & Mayer, 2008, p. 275).
>
> "Feedback should be 'corrective' in nature . . . simply telling students that their answer on a test is right or wrong has a negative effect on achievement. . . . The best feedback appears to involve an explanation as to what is accurate and what is inaccurate in terms of student responses" (Marzano, Pickering, & Pollock, 2001, p. 96).
>
> "Feedback should be specific to the criterion" (Marzano, Pickering, & Pollock, 2001, p. 98).
>
> "Provision of [feedback] typically results in superior performance on later tests than no [feedback] and providing the correct response is usually more effective than simply saying right or wrong" (Andre, 1997, p. 259).
>
> "Provide systematic feedback and corrections" (Rosenshine, 1997, p. 202).

INTEGRATION

Learning is promoted when learners reflect on, discuss, and defend their newly acquired knowledge and skill.

McCarthy (1996) suggests that the fourth phase of effective instruction is creating personal adaptations of the new knowledge and skill. The Vanderbilt group (Schwartz, Lin, Brophy, & Bransford, 1999) includes reflecting back on the experience as a step in their Star Legacy system. Current instruction literature has much to say about the importance of motivation. Often glitz, animation, multimedia, and games are justified as motivational elements of an instructional product. However, for the most part, these aspects have a temporary effect on motivation. The real motivation for learners is learning. Learners have integrated instruction into their lives when they are able to demonstrate improvement in skill, when learners come to defend their new knowledge, and when learners modify their new knowledge for use in their everyday lives.

Whenever a learner acquires a new skill, the first desire is to show a significant other his or her newly acquired ability. Learning is the most motivating of all activities when the learner can observe his or her progress. One of the main attractions of computer games is the increasing skill level that is apparent to the player. Effective instruction must provide an opportunity for learners to demonstrate their newly acquired skills. This principle of going public with their newly acquired knowledge is emphasized in Teaching for Understanding (H. Gardner, 1999; Perkins & Unger, 1999) and for Vanderbilt's Star Legacy (Schwartz, Lin, Brophy, & Bransford, 1999).

Learners need the opportunity to reflect on, defend, and share what they have learned if it is to become part of their available repertoire. Nelson (1999) cites a number of problem-solving models that include synthesize and reflect as an important process activity for collaborative problem solving. Laurillard (1993) stresses the role of reflection in her Conversational Framework model of instruction. Boud, Keogh, and Walker (1985) present a model for reflection in learning.

Modifying new knowledge to make it their own is where learners move beyond the instructional environment and take their new knowledge and skill into the world beyond. McCarthy (1996) stresses creating, revising, editing, synthesizing, and re-focusing as important final phases of a learning experience.

Consider the following the following prescriptive principles:

> "The process of explaining their thinking helps students deepen their understanding of the principles they are applying" (Marzano, Pickering, & Pollock, 2001, p. 105).
>
> "Make assignments that require collaboration among learners" (Clark & Mayer, 2003, p. 207). Meaningful collaboration requires learners to discuss and defend their conclusions. The research reviewed by Clark and Mayer shows that effective collaboration depends on a number of factors such as type of collaboration and intended outcomes.
>
> "Heterogeneous teams that include high and low prior knowledge learners or homogeneous high prior knowledge teams are best" (Clark & Mayer, 2008, p. 289). Heterogeneous groups require more reflection and discussion than groups that easily agree.
>
> "Organizing groups based on ability levels should be done sparingly" (Marzano, Pickering, & Pollock, 2001, p. 87). Differing abilities promote more discussion.
>
> "Structure group assignments around products or processes" (Clark & Mayer, 2003, p. 208). This requirement encourages collaboration.
>
> "Cooperative groups should be kept rather small [three or four members] in size" (Marzano, Pickering, & Pollock, 2001, p. 88). In larger groups some learners are left out of the discussion.

INDIRECT SUPPORT SUMMARY

It would appear from the limited sources quoted in this chapter that First Principles are not only common to and prescribed by many instructional design theories and models, but that they are also consistent with empirical research on instruction. It is hoped that as instructional design matures this set of First Principles can form a foundation on which future instructional design models and prescriptions can build. These principles are deliberately general, and their implementation can take many forms. These principles do not require the adoption of any particular philosophical –ism. First Principles can be found in some form in almost all instructional design theories and models. I have not identified any principles that are contrary to these First Principles. And yet, with this general agreement on fundamental foundational principles of instruction, many of the instructional products I have reviewed fail to implement even the first level of these principles, that is, these products often fail to provide sufficient demonstration of worked examples, often fail to provide appropriate practice beyond remember-what-you-were-told questions, and seldom are centered in real-world problems. Few instructional products implement the activation and integration phases. Even fewer instructional products implement the next level of First Principles by providing demonstrations and practice that are consistent with a variety of different instructional outcomes. Almost none of the products we have reviewed involve a structure-guidance-coaching-reflection cycle. If these are the First Principles of Instruction, let's hope that they will become more widely applied, thereby resulting in instruction that is more effective, efficient, and appealing.

ANALYSIS OF REPRESENTATIVE INSTRUCTIONAL THEORIES

This section briefly reviews a small number of instructional theories that were originally cited in support of First Principles of Instruction. The instructional theories described in this section all implement some of the principles and their corollaries. Since the vocabulary is often different, in this chapter, I attempt to do some translation of theorists' terms to be consistent with the terms used in my statement of First Principles of Instruction. I have sometimes quoted these authors to provide the reader with the vocabulary of the theorists so that the reader can see firsthand how these statements have been interpreted as representative of the First Principles outlined in this book. This overview is representative only and does not present all of the principles specified by the theory but only enough for the reader to get a feel for the correspondence with the First Principles stated. The reader is encouraged to examine these and other theories in detail to determine for yourself whether or not the theory reflects the First Principles as stated.

Herbart (1776–1841)

The First Principles of Instruction presented in this book are not new. Johann Friedrich Herbart is often identified as the father of scientific pedagogy. He recommended that the teacher should first prepare the pupils to be ready for a new lesson. Further, he suggested that the pedagogy should associate the new lesson with ideas studied earlier. Both of the recommendations are consistent with the principle of activation. He also recommended that the pedagogy should use examples to illustrate the lesson's major points. Clearly, he also emphasized demonstration in addition to the presentation of information. Finally, he recommended that the pedagogy should test pupils to ensure they have learned the new lesson. This is the principle of application (Hilgenheger, 1993).

Vanderbilt Learning Technology Center—Star Legacy

The Learning Technology Center at Vanderbilt (Schwartz, Lin, Brophy, & Bransford, 1999) describes Star Legacy, a software shell for instruction. The Vanderbilt approach is a good illustration of the phases of instruction and the five general principles that have been identified. They describe a learning cycle that they believe involves important, yet often implicit, components of effective instruction. They emphasize making the learning cycle explicit. Their learning cycle is illustrated in Figure 20-1.

FIGURE 20-1 Learning Cycle of Star Legacy

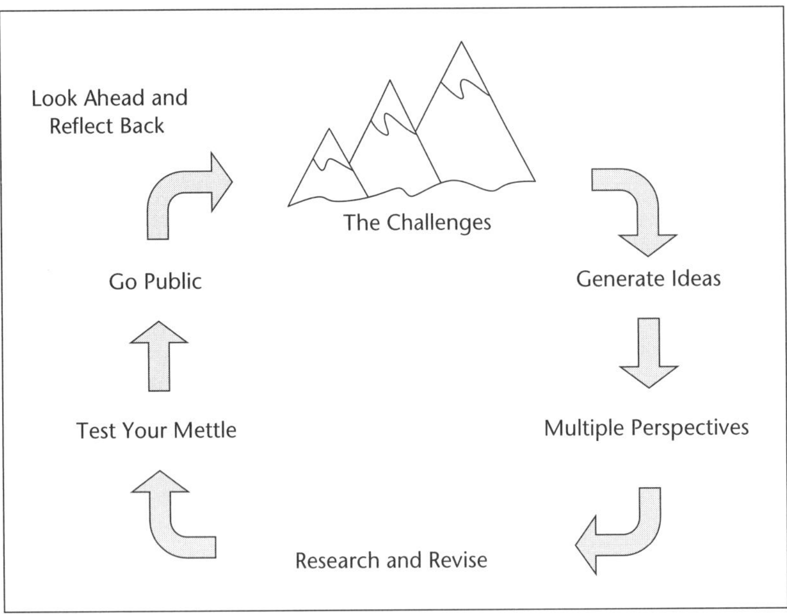

Look ahead provides the learning context and learning goals. The *challenges* are problems to be solved. They use the metaphor of successively higher mountains to represent a progression of increasingly difficult problems. *Generate ideas* is an activation activity whereby learners interact with other learners to share experiences and to share what they already know related to the challenges. *Multiple perspectives* provides an opportunity for students to identify or generate a variety of possible solutions and to compare their views of the problem and possible solutions with the views of other students and, more importantly, with the views of experts. During multiple perspectives concepts, procedures, and principles that the student may need to solve the problem are demonstrated. *Research and revise* continues the demonstration phase and moves into the application phase in that the learners gather lots of different ideas and try them out to see how they might solve the problem. *Test your mettle* is an opportunity for learners to apply their ideas and obtain feedback before they go public with their solutions.

Go public is a chance for the learners to demonstrate their solutions and to defend their ideas. This is an important component of the integration phase of instruction. *Reflect back* is an opportunity for learners to review their learning activities and is another important aspect of integration. Star Legacy is one of the most explicit representations of the learning cycle that forms the structure for the First Principles of Instruction. This same cycle of learning is also found in other theories and models, but it is frequently more subtle and not made as explicit as in Star Legacy.

McCarthy—4-MAT

McCarthy (1996) represents a model used by many teachers in K–12 education. Her work is important to our consideration of First Principles in that she also makes the learning cycle very explicit. McCarthy approached this idea from a consideration of learning styles but concluded that, while learners may have preference for various approaches to learning, effective instruction requires students to

FIGURE 20-2 4-MAT Cycle of Learning

Renewing refine, integrate, adapt, re-present, share, renew	**Meaning** connect, examine, share, dialogue, reflect
IF? 4	1 **WHY?**
HOW? 3	2 **WHAT?**
act, practice, tinker, try, extend **Operationalizing**	acquire knowledge, understand theory, imagine, define **Conceptualizing**

be involved in the whole cycle of learning activities. Figure 20-2 illustrates some of the ideas that she emphasizes in the 4-MAT approach.

McCarthy does not emphasize problem solving as much as the Learning Technology Center does. Her emphasis is on the various types of activities that might be appropriate for each of the learning phases and how these learning activities reflect learning preferences of various types of learners. Phase 1 serves the role of activation, in which the learners share what they know and try to find meaning related to the new material they will learn. 4-MAT Phase 1 is similar to Star Legacy's *generate ideas* but emphasizes a more learner-centered approach whereas Star Legacy is more problem focused. 4-MAT Phase 2 is the *demonstrate* phase where the learners acquire new knowledge and relate it to what they already know. McCarthy (1996) includes sub-phases, the description of which is beyond the scope of this presentation, but which provide practices and theory for making the transition from one phase to the next. Phase 3 is clearly the *application* phase, where learners use what they know to do something, make something, or play with the ideas. This phase is also related to the Star Legacy Research and Revise and Test Your Mettle components. McCarthy's Phase 4 is where learners make the knowledge their own. This is the *integration* phase of First Principles and I have borrowed McCarthy's term *integration* for this phase. The formulation of the learning cycle for First Principles and the graphic representation of these phases were influenced by McCarthy's work. She provides perhaps the most explicit articulation of the cycle of learning and the phases required for effective instruction.

Andre—Instructional Episode

Andre's (1997) work is focused on the research supporting instruction rather than a theory per se. He describes an instructional episode consisting of three major phases: *activation phase* (from which First Principles borrowed the term), *instructional phase*, and *feedback phase*. For Andre the instructional phase consists of presentation, discovery, and practice (the First Principles demonstration and application phase). His feedback phase is only part of the First Principles application phase as described above. Andre does not emphasize problem solving or integration following the practice/feedback phase. Andre describes research findings that support a number of the corollaries of First Principles of Instruction.

Gardner—Multiple Approaches to Understanding

H. Gardner's (1999) Performance Approach to Understanding emphasizes understanding content ("important questions and topics of the world," p. 73) rather than problem solving, but his approach does embrace each of the four phases of instruction as described in this book. He stresses that understanding can only be observed when students engage in "performances that can be observed, critiqued, and improved" (p. 73). He organizes his theory around phases he identifies as *entry points, telling analogies,* and *approaching the core.*

Entry points are a form of activation. "One begins by finding a way to engage the students and to place them centrally within the topic. I have identified at least six discrete entry points, which can be roughly aligned with specific intelligences" (p. 81). He then describes entry points from these six viewpoints: narrational, quantitative/numerical, foundational/existential, aesthetic, hands-on, and social.

Telling analogies forms a transition from activation to demonstration: "come up with instructive analogies drawn from material that is already understood, and that can convey important aspects of the less familiar topic" (p. 82).

Approaching the core includes some of the prescriptions for demonstration: "portray the topic in a number of ways [use] multiple approaches [that] explicitly call upon a range of intelligences, skills, and interests" (p. 85).

He also stresses application: "multiple representations are one component of effective teaching; the complementary component entails the provision of many opportunities for performance, which can reveal to the student and to others the extent to which the material has been mastered" (p. 86). "Although it is easy to fall back on the tried-and-true—the short answer test, the essay question—there is no imperative to do so. Performances can be as varied as the different facets of the topic and the diverse sets of skills of students" (p. 87). Gardner does emphasize entry points and multiple approaches to the topic consistent with different kinds of intelligences; however, in his paper, he does not explicitly identify practice consistency with these different intelligences.

Perhaps the primary emphasis of Gardner is on those prescriptions for integration that involve going public. "When students realize that they will have to apply knowledge and insights in public form, they assume a more active stance vis-à-vis material, seeking to exercise their 'muscles of performance' whenever possible" (p. 74).

Nelson—Collaborative Problem Solving

Nelson's (1999) theory emphasizes problem solving and includes all of the phases, but with more emphasis on application and less emphasis on demonstration. She attempts to provide "an integrated set of guidelines . . . to design and participate in authentic learning environments which invoke critical thinking, creativity, and complex problem solving while developing important social interaction skills" (p. 246).

She provides an extensive list of guidelines and the source for these guidelines, organized under nine process activities: (1) build readiness, (2) form and norm groups, (3) determine a preliminary problem definition, (4) define and assign roles, (5) engage in an iterative collaborative problem-solving process, (6) finalize the solution or project, (7) synthesize and reflect, (8) assess products and processes, and (9) provide closure (see Table 11.2, p. 258). Some of these activities are clearly related to collaboration.

Nelson is clearly problem-oriented, as reflected by the following guideline: "Develop an authentic problem or project scenario to anchor instruction and learning activities" (p. 258).

She promotes activation via the following learning activities: "[a] Negotiate a common understanding of the problem, [b] Identify learning issues and goals, and [c] Brainstorm preliminary solutions or project plans" (p. 258).

She provides guidelines for gathering information that may be required for the problem-solving process. I view these activities as part of application rather than demonstration per se: "[a] Identify sources of needed resources, [b] Gather preliminary information to validate the design plan, [c] Acquire needed information, resources, and expertise, and [d] Collaborate with instructor to acquire additional resources and skills needed" (p. 258).

Application activities include: "[a] Select and develop initial design plan, [b] Refine and evolve the design plan, [c] Engage in solution or project development work, [d] Conduct formative evaluations of the solution or project, [e] Draft the preliminary final version of the solution or project, [f] Conduct the final evaluation or usability test of the solution or project, [g] Revise and complete the final version of the solution or project, and [h] Evaluate the products and artifacts created" (p. 258).

Integration activities include: "[a] Identify learning gains, [b] Debrief experiences and feelings about the process, and [c] Reflect on group and individual learning processes" (p. 258).

Jonassen—Constructivist Learning Environments (CLE)

Jonassen's (1999) approach emphasizes problem solving and includes all four phases of instruction. The primary emphasis of Constructivist Learning Environments (CLE) is problem solving, as reflected by the following statements: "The goal of the learner is to interpret and solve the problem or complete the project (p. 217); . . . the problem drives the learning (p. 218); . . . Students learn domain content in order to solve the problem, rather than solving the problem as an application of learning" (p. 218); and ". . . you must provide interesting, relevant, and engaging problems to solve. . . . The problem should not be overly circumscribed. Rather, it should be ill defined or ill structured, so that some aspects of the problem are emergent and definable by the learners" (p. 219). Jonassen recommends problem progression: "Start the learners with the tasks they know how to perform and gradually add task difficulty until they are unable to perform alone" (p. 235).

Some attention is directed toward activation. "What novice learners lack most are experiences. . . . Related cases [demonstrations] can scaffold (or supplant) memory by providing representations of experiences that learners have not had" (p. 223).

Demonstration is stressed: "Carefully demonstrate each of the activities involved in a performance by a skilled (but not an expert) performer. . . . Modeling provides learners with an example of the desired performance. . . . Two types of modeling exist: . . . Behavioral modeling . . . demonstrates how to perform the activities identified. . . . Cognitive modeling articulates the reasoning . . . that learners should use while engaged in the activities" (p. 231). "A widely recognized method for modeling problem solving is worked examples" (p. 232).

Application is also stressed, with an emphasis on coaching and scaffolding: ". . . in order to learn, learners will attempt to perform like the model, first through crude imitation, advancing through articulating and habituating performance, to the creation of skilled, original performances. At each of these stages the learner will likely improve with coaching" (p. 232). "The most important role of the coach is to monitor, analyze, and regulate the learners' development of important skills" (p. 233). Jonassen suggests "three separate approaches to scaffolding of learning: adjust the difficulty of the task to accommodate the learner, restructure the task to supplant a lack of prior knowledge, or provide alternative assessments" (p. 235).

The reflection aspect of integration is suggested as one role of coaching: ". . . a good coach provokes learners to reflect on (monitor and analyze) their performance" (p. 233).

van Merriënboer—Four Component Instructional Design Model (4C/ID)

Van Merriënboer provides perhaps the most comprehensive model of instructional design that is problem-centered and involves all of the phases of instruction identified in this book (van Merriënboer, 1997; van Merriënboer & Kirschner, 2007). His model integrates more directive approaches to instruction with problem-based approaches, all in the context of what is known about cognitive processing. The model describes multiple approaches to analysis and how the products of these various analysis techniques lead to instructional design that focuses on whole-problem practice. This short summary is inadequate to illustrate the comprehensive nature of this model.

The model is clearly problem-based: "At the heart of this training strategy is whole practice, in which more and more complex versions of the whole complex cognitive skill are practiced. . . . In . . . the analysis phase . . . the skill is decomposed in a hierarchy of constituent skills; . . . classified as recurrent constituent skills, which require more-or-less consistent performance over problem situations, or non-recurrent constituent skills, which require highly variable performance over situations" (p. 8). "While learners practice simple to complex versions of a whole task, instructional methods that promote just-in-time information presentation are used to support the recurrent aspects of the whole task while, at the same time, instructional methods that promote elaboration are used to support the non-recurrent aspects of the task" (p. 10).

Demonstration is addressed at several levels. The first problems in a sequence should be worked-out examples of how to perform the problem. As the student progresses through the sequence of problems, other information is presented or demonstrated. These include part-task practice for development of "situation specific, automated rules" (p. 12). For just-in-time information, "Demonstration is usually needed to illustrate the application of rules or procedures and to exemplify concepts, principles, or plans that are prerequisite to a correct application of those rules or procedures [in solving the problem]" (p.13). The heuristic methods used by skilled performers are modeled for the learner. It should be noted that all of this demonstration occurs in the context of having the learner engage in problem solving.

Application and integration are at the center of the model. "The heart of the 4C/ID model concerns the design of whole-task practice. . . . The design of information presentation [demonstration] is always subordinate to, although integrated with, the design of practice" (p. 170). The emphasis of the model is on a sequence of problems so that demonstration and application are an integrated whole rather than distinct phases. The model describes in some detail both product-oriented problem formats and process-oriented problem formats. The model suggests that appropriate practice involves scaffolding of problems, but rather than leaving the definition of scaffolding somewhat unspecified, the model suggests how different types of problem formats relate to cognitive load and practice sequences that are likely to promote the most effective skill development. The whole-task practice model leads the learner toward a real-world task that van Merriënboer feels should promote maximum integration.

Schank—Learning by Doing

Schank's model is clearly problem-centered, with a very strong emphasis on the application phase of instruction (Schank, Berman, & Macpherson, 1999). In this model there is limited emphasis on activation and demonstration and, while integration is certainly the goal, there is very little in the model to direct the integration process per se. "GBS [goal-based scenario] is a learn-by-doing simulation in which students pursue a goal by practicing target skills and using relevant content knowledge to help them achieve their goal" (p. 165). "There are seven essential components of a GBS: the *learning goals*, the *mission*, the *cover story*, the *role*, the *scenario operations*, the *resources*, and the *feedback*, including coaches and experts" (p. 173).

Scenarios (problems) are carefully defined: ". . . the first step in creating a GBS is determining a goal or mission that will be motivational for the student to pursue. . . . The cover story is the background story line that creates the need for the mission to be accomplished . . . the most important thing to consider is whether the story will allow enough opportunities for the student to practice the skills and seek the knowledge you wish to teach. . . . The role defines who the student will play within the cover story. . . . it is important to think about what role is the best in the scenario to practice the necessary skills" (pp. 173–175).

Schank, Berman, and Macpherson stress that new cases (memories) are developed from existing cases (memories). Activation is elicited via *stories*: "The memories that contribute to our library of cases [memories] are of specific events in the form of stories. . . . the best way to convey information is . . . to embed lessons in stories [portrayal] that the learner can understand as an extension of the stories he or she already knows [activation]" (p. 177).

Demonstration is provided within the context of the scenario: ". . . the resources we provide are usually experts telling stories about the information the student needs" [demonstration] (p. 177). "Information is provided primarily via feedback during the operation of the scenario in three ways: . . . consequence of actions . . .

coaches [who] provide . . . a just-in-time source to scaffold the student through tasks . . . and domain experts who tell stories that pertain to similar experiences" (p. 178).

"The scenario operations [application] comprise all of the activities the student does in order to work toward the mission goal" (p. 175). "The scenario operations should . . . have consequences that become evident at various points throughout the student interaction. . . . It is important that . . . little time be spent talking to the student about the scenario, and much more time be spent with the student practicing the skills and learning the information that comprise the learning goals" (p. 176).

The model does not address integration directly but assumes that if the mission is motivating and of interest to the learner that the learner will internalize the case (memories) and that it will be available in later real-world or other instructional scenarios.

REVIEW OF INSTRUCTIONAL THEORIES

J. Gardner (in press) conducted an extensive review of instructional theories to more carefully determine the veracity of my assumption that most theories supported First Principles. An intensive literature search found only twenty-two theories that met the criteria set by Gardner. The theories included had to have been published between 1999 and 2009. Only theories that prescribed specific instructional events were included. Only theories that focused on cognitive instruction (see the five types of component skills in Chapter 3) were included. And only theories that referred to themselves as "instructional theory" were included.

Table 20-1 lists the twenty-two theories that were included in this review. Theories previously cited in this chapter are marked with an asterisk. All twenty-two of the theories emphasized one or more of the principles: seven theories emphasized all five principles; ten theories mentioned four of the principles; four theories mentioned three principles, and one theory mentioned only two of the principles. The demonstration principle was emphasized by twenty-one of the theories; application was emphasized by all twenty-two of the theories; problem-centered was emphasized by eighteen; activation by twelve; and integration by sixteen. The degree of emphasis was determined on a 0- to 3-point scale. The average emphasis for each of the principles was as follows: demonstration received 2.5; application 2.9; problem-centered 2.0; activation 1.0; and integration 1.8. Thus, First Principles has fundamental support from current instructional theories. Application and demonstration have the most emphasis, problem-centered somewhat less emphasis, while activation and integration seem to be the least emphasized. This is consistent with the discussion of relative contribution of the individual principles in Chapter 2. It would appear that the assumption that most theories include some or all of the First Principles of Instruction is justified by this review.

Table 20-1 Theories Reviewed by J. Gardner

Authors	Topic
*Nelson (1999)	Collaborative Problem Solving
Beielaczyc & Collins (1999)	Learning Communities
Corno & Randi (1999)	Self-Regulated Learning
*H. Gardner (1999)	Multiple Approaches to Understanding

Table 20-1 *Continued*

Gibson (2009)	Discussion Approach
Hannafin, Land, & Oliver (1999)	Open Learning Environments
Huitt, Monetti, & Hummel (2009)	Direct Approach
*Jonassen (1999)	Constructivist Learning Environments
Kovalik & McGeehan (1999)	Thematic Instruction
Landa (1999)	General Methods of Thinking
Larson, Johnson, Rutherford, & Bartlo (2009)	Quotient Group Concept
Lee & Paulus (2001)	Interactions in Web-Based Learning
Lindsey & Berger (2009)	Experiential Approach
R. H. Mayer (1999)	Constructivist Learning
Pogrow (1999)	Powerful Learning Environments
Savery (2009)	Problem-Based Approaches
*Schank, Berman, & Macpherson (1999)	Learning by Doing
*Schwartz, Lin, Brophy, & Bransford (1999)	Flexibly Adaptive Instruction
Snyder (2009)	Online Learning Communities for Adults
Wiske & Beatty (2009)	Fostering Understanding

CONCLUSIONS FROM REVIEW OF INSTRUCTIONAL DESIGN THEORIES

Do the theories and models reviewed in the last section of this chapter involve fundamentally different principles of instruction? The answer appears to be no.

1. All the theories and models reviewed incorporate some of these principles.
2. Only a few of the theories or models reviewed include all of these principles.
3. Some theories and models reviewed include principles or prescriptions that are not described in this book. These represent areas for further investigation.
4. No theory or model reviewed includes principles or prescriptions that are contrary to those described in this book.

The vocabulary used to describe these theories and their implementation details vary significantly. These theories and models tend to emphasize different principles. Gardner stresses public exhibition of understanding (integration) and different kinds of intelligence (that is not included in the prescriptions of this book). Nelson emphasizes collaboration. Jonassen emphasizes problem solving in learning environments. Van Merriënboer emphasizes problem sequence and the sequence of supporting information. Schank emphasizes stories (a form of demonstration) and problem solving (cases). This survey of research on instruction and instructional theories and models demonstrates that this literature does include principles of instruction that are similar to First Principles of Instruction regardless of philosophical orientation.

TO LEARN MORE

Some of the material in this chapter was originally published in the following sources:

Clark, R. C., & Mayer, R. E. (2008). *e-Learning and the science of instruction* (3rd ed.). San Francisco: Pfeiffer. These authors state many of the prescriptions that were quoted in this chapter and describe the empirical evidence that support these prescriptions.

Merrill, M. D. (2002a). First principles of instruction. *Educational Technology Research and Development, 50*(3), 43–59.

Merrill, M. D. (2007a). First principles of instruction: A synthesis. In R. A. Reiser & J. V. Dempsey (Eds.), *Trends and issues in instructional design and technology* (2nd ed.) (Vol. 2, pp. 62–71). Upper Saddle River, NJ: Merrill/Prentice Hall.

COMING NEXT

This chapter provided indirect support for First Principles of Instruction, that is, research and instructional design theory that support these principles but does not provide a direct test of them. Chapter 21 reviews research that does provide a direct test of First Principles of Instruction.

CHAPTER 21

DIRECT RESEARCH SUPPORT FOR FIRST PRINCIPLES OF INSTRUCTION

Quick Look

In this chapter I cite a sample of formal and informal research efforts to directly evaluate the effectiveness of First Principles of Instruction. This chapter addresses the following questions: Is learning from an instructional product that implements First Principles of Instruction more effective and efficient than learning from an instructional product that does not? Do learners perceive that they learn more from a course that implements First Principles of Instruction? Is a course that implements First Principles of Instruction more engaging for learners?

INTRODUCTION

Chapter 20 cited research and instructional design prescriptive principles in the literature that contributed to the specification of First Principles of Instruction. None of this research was conducted as a direct test of the First Principles but concluded with findings that support these principles. In this chapter I describe selected research efforts that were a deliberate attempt to evaluate First Principles as a whole. These research efforts fall into three categories: (1) experimental studies comparing instruction based on First Principles with existing instruction that does not attempt to implement these principles; (2) a study of student course evaluations designed to assess the use of First Principles in their classes and its correlation with their performance and engagement; and (3) informal case studies that implemented First Principles but did not record carefully controlled experimental comparisons.

EXPERIMENTAL STUDY—EXCEL

As a consultant to a major vendor of computer application software training packages, I supervised a study to evaluate the effectiveness of their off-the-shelf training package for Microsoft Excel. The study indicated that, when asked to solve Excel problems, the learners who had completed the Excel training were either hesitant to complete the problems or performed poorly on real-world Excel problems. (See Chapter 11 for a description of this course.)

In response to the findings from this study, I proposed that the vendor undertake a project to develop a task-centered approach to teaching Excel based on

First Principles of Instruction (Thompson Learning, 2002). I hypothesized that a problem-centered approach would be more effective and efficient than their existing off-the-shelf training course. My students and I developed a prototype problem-centered version of the Excel course. Using this prototype as a model, the vendor used their professional developers to develop a new problem-centered Excel course as described below. I served as a quality control consultant during this development to ensure that the new course implemented a problem-centered approach that implemented First Principles of Instruction. After the problem-centered course (the company's term for this version was *scenario-based*) was developed, a study was conducted comparing the new version of the course with the previous off-the-shelf version that was then being marketed by the vendor. This study is described in the following paragraphs.

Problem

Is a problem-centered Excel course more effective, efficient, and engaging than the existing off-the-shelf course offered by the vendor? Does the problem-centered course better prepare participants to engage in developing real-world spreadsheets?

Treatments

Topic-Centered Tutorial The vendor's off-the-shelf program is a topic-centered tutorial that teaches each Excel command in turn. (This was previously described as a Simon-says instructional strategy.) The spreadsheet is simulated; the learner is asked to complete a specific command. If the command is executed correctly, then the spreadsheet reacts as it would in the actual application. If the command is not executed correctly, then the learner is given a prompt and asked to execute the command again. If the learner's action is still incorrect, the spreadsheet executes the command and shows the learner the result. All of the commands of a given type are taught one-by-one.

Figure 21-1 illustrates a typical Simon-says interaction for entering text into a cell. The program gives a direction: "Type shoes in Cell A8." If the learner follows the direction exactly, then the program moves to the next step. If the learner makes an error, a strong prompt tells the learner what to do and provides a prompt as to where to carry out the action. The next instructional events in this program show learners how to enter the numbers in the cells opposite the label *shoes.*

FIGURE 21-1 Instructional Events from an Off-the-Shelf Topic-Centered Tutorial

Microsoft Excel Course

Audio:

Entering data into a worksheet is a simple process. You will be creating and manipulating inventory data for a fictitious company called Small World.

Start entering data in Cell A8 now.

As you type, text will display in the cell on the Formula bar. To lock text in a cell, press Enter. Type Shoes and press Enter now.

Display:

	A	B	C	D	E	F
1		Small World - 1996 Inventory				
2		Jan. - Mar.	Apr. - June	July - Sept.	Oct. - Dec.	Yearly Totals
3						
4	Dresses	100	200	200	100	600
5	Jackets	350	150	200	400	1100
6	Jeans	575	400	500	600	2075
7	Shirts	350	250	250	475	1235
8						
9	Shorts	150	425	250	100	925
10	Socks	600	500	500	750	2350
11	Sweaters	375	100	75	400	950
12	T-shirts	400	450	300	500	1650
13						
14						
15						

FIGURE 21-1 *Continued*

Note: If the learner does not follow the directions exactly, then a prompt appears to tell or show him or her what to do. The correct cell is highlighted for the learner.

Arial 12 | A11 | Pants

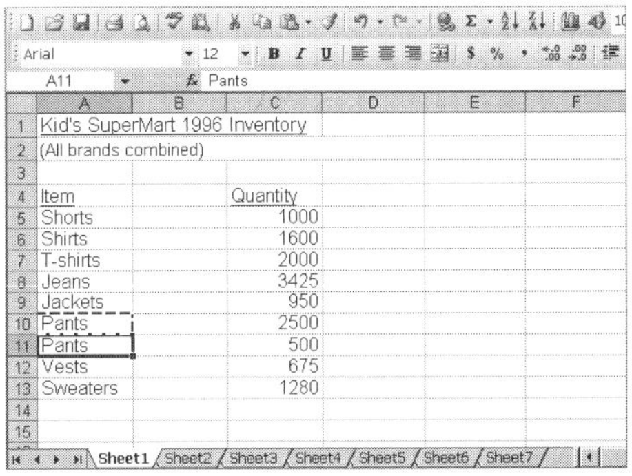

	A	B	C	D	E	F
1	Kid's SuperMart 1996 Inventory					
2	(All brands combined)					
3						
4	Item		Quantity			
5	Shorts		1000			
6	Shirts		1600			
7	T-shirts		2000			
8	Jeans		3425			
9	Jackets		950			
10	Pants		2500			
11	Pants		500			
12	Vests		675			
13	Sweaters		1280			
14						
15						

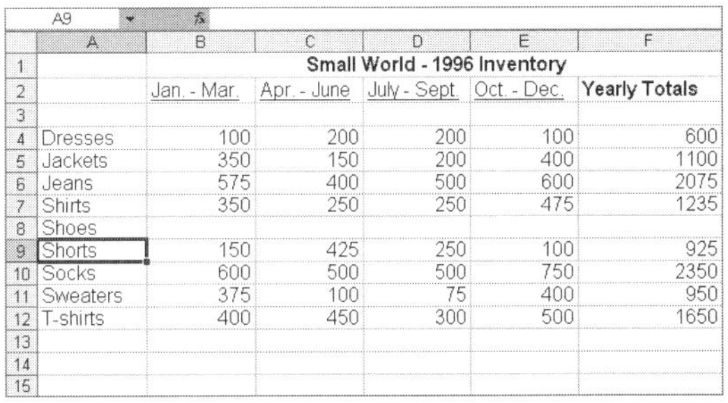

Sheet1 / Sheet2 / Sheet3 / Sheet4 / Sheet5 / Sheet6 / Sheet7

As you type data into the cell, the Cancel and Enter buttons display on the Formula bar. Clicking on the Enter button locks the data in a cell; clicking on the Cancel button removes the data that you have just entered.

A9

	A	B	C	D	E	F
1				Small World - 1996 Inventory		
2		Jan. - Mar.	Apr. - June	July - Sept.	Oct. - Dec.	Yearly Totals
3						
4	Dresses	100	200	200	100	600
5	Jackets	350	150	200	400	1100
6	Jeans	575	400	500	600	2075
7	Shirts	350	250	250	475	1235
8	Shoes					
9	Shorts	150	425	250	100	925
10	Socks	600	500	500	750	2350
11	Sweaters	375	100	75	400	950
12	T-shirts	400	450	300	500	1650
13						
14						
15						

The quiz at the end of the course tests a number of commands one-by-one. Figure 21-2 illustrates several questions from the quiz.

FIGURE 21-2 Sample Quiz Items from an Off-the-Shelf Topic-Centered Course

Microsoft Excel—Quiz

Sequence the listed steps for the Replace command by dragging each statement into the correct order starting at the top. When finished, click on the Page Forward button to continue.

Choose the Replace command.

Click on Close.

Click on the Replace button.

Click on the Find Next button.

Select the Edit menu in the Menu Bar.

Type the text string that will replace the first text string entered.

Type the text string to be replaced.

Select Column D of this worksheet.

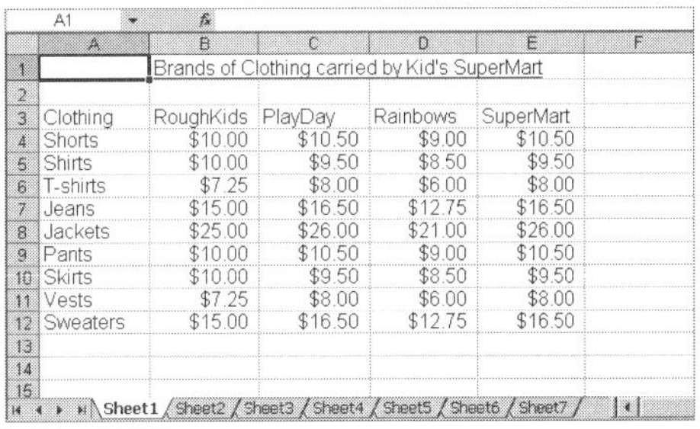

A1

	A	B	C	D	E	F
1		Brands of Clothing carried by Kid's SuperMart				
2						
3	Clothing	RoughKids	PlayDay	Rainbows	SuperMart	
4	Shorts	$10.00	$10.50	$9.00	$10.50	
5	Shirts	$10.00	$9.50	$8.50	$9.50	
6	T-shirts	$7.25	$8.00	$6.00	$8.00	
7	Jeans	$15.00	$16.50	$12.75	$16.50	
8	Jackets	$25.00	$26.00	$21.00	$26.00	
9	Pants	$10.00	$10.50	$9.00	$10.50	
10	Skirts	$10.00	$9.50	$8.50	$9.50	
11	Vests	$7.25	$8.00	$6.00	$8.00	
12	Sweaters	$15.00	$16.50	$12.75	$16.50	
13						
14						
15						

Sheet1 / Sheet2 / Sheet3 / Sheet4 / Sheet5 / Sheet6 / Sheet7

(continued)

FIGURE 21-2 *Continued*

Using the standard toolbar, copy Cell A10 to Cell A11. [The image shows the spreadsheet right after the learner has completed the command.]

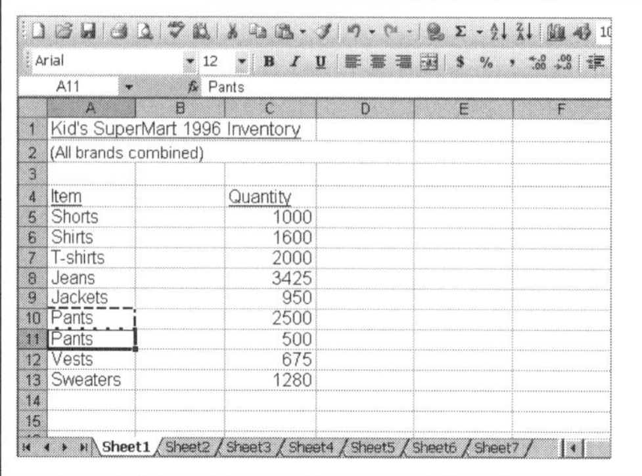

Problem-Centered Tutorial With our help the vendor developed a problem-centered strategy for this course. This new course used the following strategy:

The instruction consisted of a sequence of five increasingly difficult spreadsheet problems. Table 21-1 describes the first three of these problems.

Table 21-1 First Three Problems in Problem Progression

In the course, each of these problems was associated with a before-and-after spreadsheet. The before spreadsheet provided the data from which to construct the after spreadsheet. The after spreadsheet was used to provide feedback to learners after they completed their own version of the spreadsheet. To facilitate scoring, learners were provided some minimal directions for basic formatting and in which cell to start their data entry.

Problem 1. Susan has opened a small restaurant. She has been very successful and wants to expand her business. To finance this project, Susan needs a bank loan. She knows that an accurate and well-designed presentation will help her obtain the loan. You have agreed to prepare the last month's sales figures for Susan.

Problem 2. Susan has given the Total Lunch Earnings worksheet to Isaac, one of her main suppliers, who has been successful in getting bank loans for his business. He is impressed with your work and offers three improvements. First, include a column that calculates percentage of sales. Second, add some nice borders and shading formats. Finally, set up the page to give the printout a professional appearance.

Problem 3. Susan expanded her business. Her restaurant is busier, and she needs more staff. To judge her new staffing requirements accurately, Susan conducted a count of customers before and after the renovations. Each survey was taken over a four-week period. You have agreed to help Susan determine her new staffing levels by calculating statistics from her second survey.

The problems were then taught using demonstration and application according to the prescriptions for First Principles of Instruction described earlier in this book. The first two problems were worked examples or demonstration; Problems 3 and 4 were application problems with considerable coaching; and Problem 5 was an application problem with no coaching. This problem-centered strategy is described in the following paragraphs.

1. Present the first problem shown in the first section of Figure 21-3.
2. Study the commands that are required to solve the problem as shown in the second section of Figure 21-3. These are the Simon-says tutorials for each command from the original course. As contrasted with the original course,

instead of teaching all of the commands of one type and then going on to the commands for the next type, only the commands required to solve the problem are taught.

3. Present a step-by-step solution for the problem as illustrated in the third section of Figure 21-3.
4. Repeat instructional events 1 through 3 for the second problem.

FIGURE 21-3 Problem-Centered Demonstration Strategy—Problem 1

1

Problem 1

Directions: In this exercise, you apply your knowledge of Microsoft Excel 2000 to redesigning a worksheet. Given the information in the first spreadsheet (shown on the left), you will manipulate the spreadsheet to produce the information and format in the second spreadsheet (shown on the right).

Problem: Susan has opened a small restaurant. She has been very successful and wants to expand her business. To finance this project, Susan needs a bank loan. She knows that an accurate and well-designed presentation will help her get the loan. You have agreed to prepare the last month's sales figures for Susan.

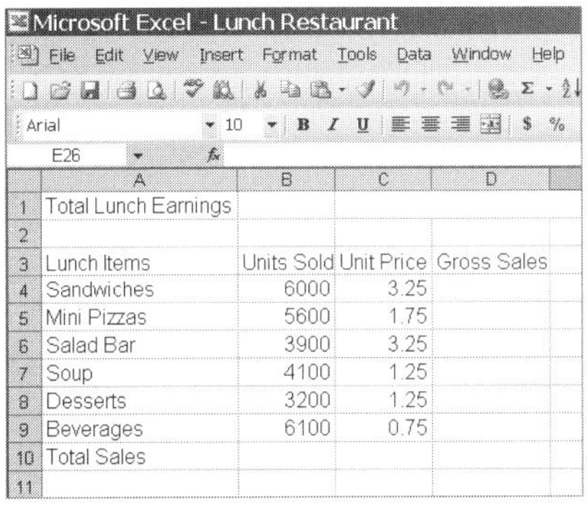

Microsoft Excel - Lunch Restaurant

File Edit View Insert Format Tools Data Window Help

Arial 10 B I U $ %

E26

	A	B	C	D
1	Total Lunch Earnings			
2				
3	Lunch Items	Units Sold	Unit Price	Gross Sales
4	Sandwiches	6000	3.25	
5	Mini Pizzas	5600	1.75	
6	Salad Bar	3900	3.25	
7	Soup	4100	1.25	
8	Desserts	3200	1.25	
9	Beverages	6100	0.75	
10	Total Sales			
11				

Microsoft Excel - Susan

File Edit View Insert Format Tools Data Window Hel

Arial 10 B I U $

I16

	A	B	C	D	E
1	**Total Lunch Earnings**				
2					
3	**Lunch Items**	**Units Sold**	**Unit Price**	**Gross Sales**	
4	*Sandwiches*	7200	$3.25	$23,400	
5	*Healthfood Salad Bar*	3900	$3.25	$12,675	
6	*Mini Pizzas*	5600	$1.75	$9,800	
7	*Soup*	4100	$1.25	$5,125	
8	*Beverages*	6100	$0.75	$4,575	
9	*Desserts*	3200	$1.25	$4,000	
10					
11	**Total Sales**			**$59,575**	
12					

2

Directions: The following commands are required to complete Problem 1. Click on each topic in the right-hand column and study these commands. [A different set of commands was required to study for Problem 2.]

Step 1	Creating the Gross Sales formulas	Formulas: Entering Formulas: Cell Referencing
Step 2	Creating the Total Sales formula	Fill Handle functions: An Introduction Basic functions
Step 3	Inserting a new row	Row and Column: Insertion
Step 4	Formatting fonts	Cell: Accommodating Text Formatting: Textual Data Formatting: Text Alignment
Step 5	Formatting numbers	Formatting: Numerical Data
Step 6a	Overtyping text and values	Data: Entering and Editing
Step 6b	Widening columns	Row and Column: Insertion

(continued)

FIGURE 21-3 *Continued*

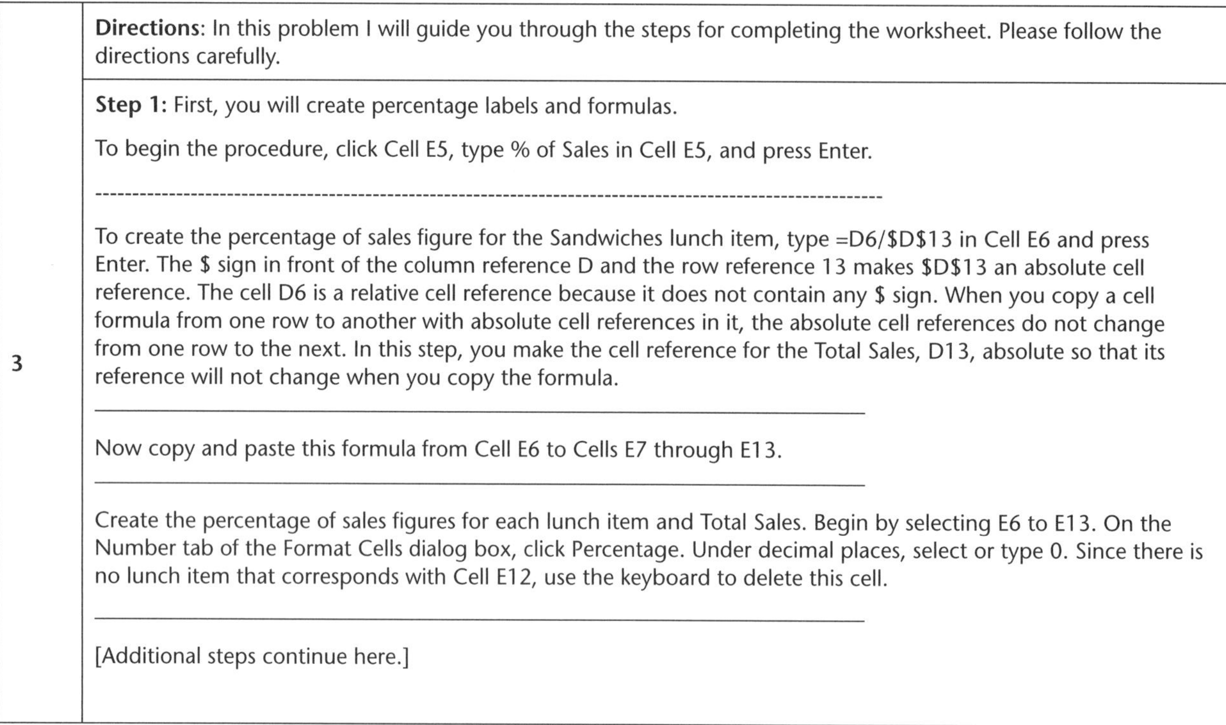

3	**Directions:** In this problem I will guide you through the steps for completing the worksheet. Please follow the directions carefully.
	Step 1: First, you will create percentage labels and formulas. To begin the procedure, click Cell E5, type % of Sales in Cell E5, and press Enter. --- To create the percentage of sales figure for the Sandwiches lunch item, type =D6/$D$13 in Cell E6 and press Enter. The $ sign in front of the column reference D and the row reference 13 makes $D$13 an absolute cell reference. The cell D6 is a relative cell reference because it does not contain any $ sign. When you copy a cell formula from one row to another with absolute cell references in it, the absolute cell references do not change from one row to the next. In this step, you make the cell reference for the Total Sales, D13, absolute so that its reference will not change when you copy the formula. ___ Now copy and paste this formula from Cell E6 to Cells E7 through E13. ___ Create the percentage of sales figures for each lunch item and Total Sales. Begin by selecting E6 to E13. On the Number tab of the Format Cells dialog box, click Percentage. Under decimal places, select or type 0. Since there is no lunch item that corresponds with Cell E12, use the keyboard to delete this cell. ___ [Additional steps continue here.]

Problems 3 and 4 were application problems with considerable guidance. These problems were taught using the directions in Table 21-2.

Table 21-2 Detailed Directions for Coached Application Problems 3 and 4

Problems 3 and 4

Directions: In the previous two problems, you were guided step-by-step in the application of the commands to complete the problem. In this problem, you will not be given this step-by-step guidance. You should first review the modules teaching the commands that you will need to complete this scenario. Then you should try to complete each task in the problems on your own. If you need help, there is learner guidance provided at the end of the exercise for each of the tasks. You will learn more if you try to do the task before you look at this guidance material and use this guidance only when you are unable to perform the required commands. After you have completed each task, you will be shown an interim spreadsheet that you can compare with your own work.

Directions: The following commands are required to complete Problem 3. Click on each topic and study these commands. [Each problem required learners to study the new commands that were relevant to the problem.]

Directions:

Enter your User ID in Cell D1.
Create Income formulas in Cells B9, C9, and D9.
Create Cost formulas in Cells B15, C15, and D15.
Create Profit/Loss formulas in Cells B17, C17, and D17 for the final worksheet.

If you have completed Problems 1 and 2, you are familiar with creating formulas, since this information was covered. The detailed guidance for creating formulas in this exercise is provided at the end of the problem in a section called Learner Guidance.

You must not simply type in the values. You need to apply the appropriate formulas. You have successfully created Income, Cost, and Profit/Loss formulas for Problems 1 and 2. At this point, your worksheet should contain the following data.

[Data is supplied here.]

After you have completed your worksheet, it should look like the following completed worksheet. If it does not, you may want to try again or go to the Learner Guidance section. [Learners are shown this correct final worksheet only after they have completed an attempt at designing the worksheet.]

[Final worksheet is shown here.]

The fifth problem in the problem progression is an application problem with no coaching. The pattern is similar to that shown for the earlier problems. Learners are first directed to study the relevant commands using the Simon-says tutorials for these commands. They are then directed to use the data given to complete a spreadsheet. The directions for Problem 5 are shown in Table 21-3.

Table 21-3 Directions for Problem 5

Problem 5

Directions: In this problem there is no Learner Guidance section. If your worksheets do not match the sample worksheets provided, you should return to the Excel course and review the appropriate modules.

Directions: The following commands are required to complete Problem 3. Click on each topic and study these commands. [Each problem required learners to study the new commands that were relevant to the problem.]

Directions:

Step 1: Enter your User ID in Cell D1. Add formulas to compute the totals in Column G and generate the expenses (with no decimals) in Row 18.

Step 2: Format the data. Use 12 point bold for table headings. Add months as column headings.

[Additional directions continued here.]

Assessment Problems Three real-world spreadsheet tasks provided the final three problems for the targeted content. These were also application problems with no coaching or guidance. Learners were required to apply what they had learned to these new spreadsheet problems. For these problems learners were not allowed to use the help system of Excel or to return to the component skill instruction for help. They were required to use the commands and operations as they remembered them and were able to apply them, based only on their previous instruction. Table 21-4 illustrates the directions provided for one of the final tasks. These tasks were developed to reflect real-world applications of Excel.

Performance Scoring Two researchers independently scored each of the final tasks using a set of standardized scoring sheets. The inter-rater agreement between the two raters was 98 percent, indicating a very high level of agreement and providing strong support for the accuracy of the scoring process. The internal consistency reliability for the three final tasks was 94 percent, which indicates that the tasks consistently measure what they purport to measure, ability to correctly design an Excel worksheet.

Table 21-4 Directions for a Final Spreadsheet Problem to Evaluate Learner Performance

Problem 6

Directions: In this problem you must apply your knowledge of Microsoft Excel 2000 to redesign a worksheet. Jake has returned from a holiday in France. He had set a budget for the vacation and wants to compare his actual and planned expenses. He is unsure of the correct exchange rate. You have agreed to work this out for Jake in return for a bottle of vintage French Chardonnay.

Jake has given you the basic information on the following worksheet named Holiday. [Worksheet appears here.]

You must create formulas and redesign the worksheet to make it look like the following example. [Final worksheet appears here.]

Objectives

- Refer to the target screen on the previous page to ensure that the columns and rows in that example and your final screen are identical.
- Insert a new row under Row 1.
- Calculate the value of goods purchased in $ terms.
- Calculate the variance of goods purchased in $ terms compared to the budget.
- Calculate the totals for each of the four columns of numeric data.
- Center and bold the title across the five main data columns and change the font size to 12 point.
- Italicize the Items row labels.
- Bold the Total row.
- Bold all column labels, except for the exchange rate column label.
- Right-align column labels over numeric data.
- Format the numbers, except for the Exchange Rate value, with thousand separators, two decimal places, and red negative.
- Create a double-line border around all the data, except for the exchange rate data.
- Shade the column labels—except for the exchange rate—with dark green background and white font.
- Change the exchange rate to 6.685. Is the total variance better or worse?
- Save the file with the name Finance Final.

Design

The experimental design consisted of three groups: Group 1 received the revised problem-centered strategy described above; Group 2 received the original off-the-shelf topic-centered strategy described above; Group 3 were asked to complete the three final problem-based spreadsheets without participating in either of the training strategies. None of the groups had access to online help. All three groups were required to complete the final three assessment problems. All groups had access to an online mentor and a set of frequently asked questions.

Participants

The vendor solicited volunteers from among their client companies to participate in the study. There were participants from aerospace, computing, retired executives, and U.S. and Irish graduate students. Participants were randomly assigned to groups. Group 1, the problem-centered group, had forty-nine participants; Group 2, the topic-centered group, also had forty-nine participants; Group 3, the no training group, had thirty participants.

Method

The course problems and the assessment problems were administered online through the company's website. Students participated from various locations. All participants received directions in how to operate the website, how-to interact with the course materials, how-to enter their responses into the actual Excel software application, and how-to submit their final projects online for evaluation. For the final three problems, the help system, normally available in the Excel application, was turned off, requiring students to rely only on what they had learned in the course to complete the tasks.

Results

On the three final application problems, the problem-centered group scored an average of 89 percent, the topic-centered group scored 68 percent, and the control group scored 34 percent. All differences are statistically significant beyond the .001 level. The times required to complete the three final application problems were twenty-nine minutes for the problem-centered group and forty-nine minutes for the topic-centered group. Most of the control group failed to finish the tasks, so no time data was recorded. These differences are also statistically significant beyond the .001 level. Finally, on a qualitative questionnaire, the problem-centered group expressed considerably more satisfaction with the course than did the topic-centered group.

Discussion

The problem-centered strategy implemented in the revised course is a clear demonstration of the problem-centered instructional strategy, as explained in Chapters 6 and 7. The course consisted of a progression of five increasingly complex tasks; each task was shown to learners and then the component *how-to* skills required by that task were demonstrated to the student via the Simon-says instructional strategy. These skills were demonstrated in the problem for the first two problems; learners were required to apply these skills to Problems 3 and 4 with coaching; and learners were required to apply these skills to Problem 5 without coaching. All media used in the course were relevant and presented adjacent to the explanatory text. There were five problems in the instructional progression and three additional problems in the application assessment. This study did not involve a structural framework for the activation principle, nor did it implement peer-interaction to facilitate the integration principle.

The results clearly show that revising the off-the-shelf course of this vendor to a problem-centered course based on First Principles of Instruction significantly increased the effectiveness, efficiency, and engagement of learners completing the course.

EXPERIMENTAL STUDY—FLASH PROGRAMMING

In a dissertation study, Rosenberg-Kima (2011) compared the effects of task-centered versus topic-centered instructional strategies to learning to program in Flash.

Problem

The purpose of this study was to investigate whether a task-centered approach might be superior to a topic-centered approach to teaching problem solving. The primary research question was: What are the effects of instructional strategy (task-centered versus topic-centered) on (1) skill-development performance, process-development performance (near and far transfer), (2) on time on task, and (3) attitudes toward learning?

Treatments

Two computer-based instructional strategies were employed. The treatments were presented in the computer lab in the form of a two-hour Flash module.

Task-Centered In the task-centered condition, the learners were presented with three whole tasks with increasing level of difficulty. Task 1 created a slideshow of animals (see Figure 21-4), Task 2 created a virtual "petting zoo" (see Figure 21-5), and Task 3 created a navigation system so that whenever the user clicks an animal, he will move to see the information page associated with this animal. Each of the three tasks included all of the elements of the whole-task, thus, in Task 1, for example, the learners learned the basics of timeline, texts, and buttons.

FIGURE 21-4 Flash Programming Task 1—Create Animal Slideshow

In this first task you will create a slideshow of animals (just like the one on the right).

Each slide includes text with the animal's name, a picture, and a Next button.

Dissertation, Florida State University, Rinat Rosenberg-Kima.

Topic-Centered In the topic-centered condition, on the other hand, no task was presented to the learners up-front. Instead, objectives were presented to the learners at the beginning of each topic section (timeline, dynamic texts, and buttons). Thus, in the topic-centered condition, each of the three steps referred to only one of the topics. It is important to note that, while the order and the context of the instruction are different, the content (for example, how to add static text) was identical for both conditions. Figure 21-6 illustrates how a Flash programming step was demonstrated in the topic-centered treatment, and Figure 21-7 illustrates how this same step was demonstrated in the task-centered treatment. Figure 21-8 illustrates the order of the individual topics within the two treatment conditions.

FIGURE 21-5 Flash Programming Task 2—Create a Virtual "Petting Zoo"

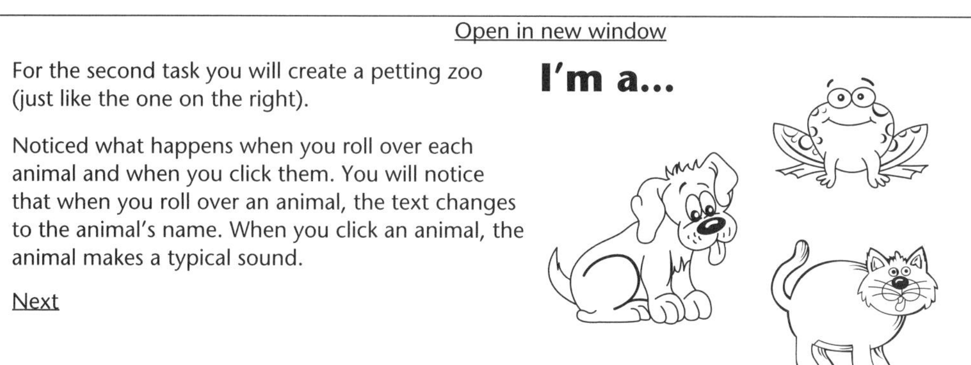

Dissertation, Florida State University, Rinat Rosenberg-Kima.

FIGURE 21-6 Topic-Centered Instructional How-to Demonstration Event

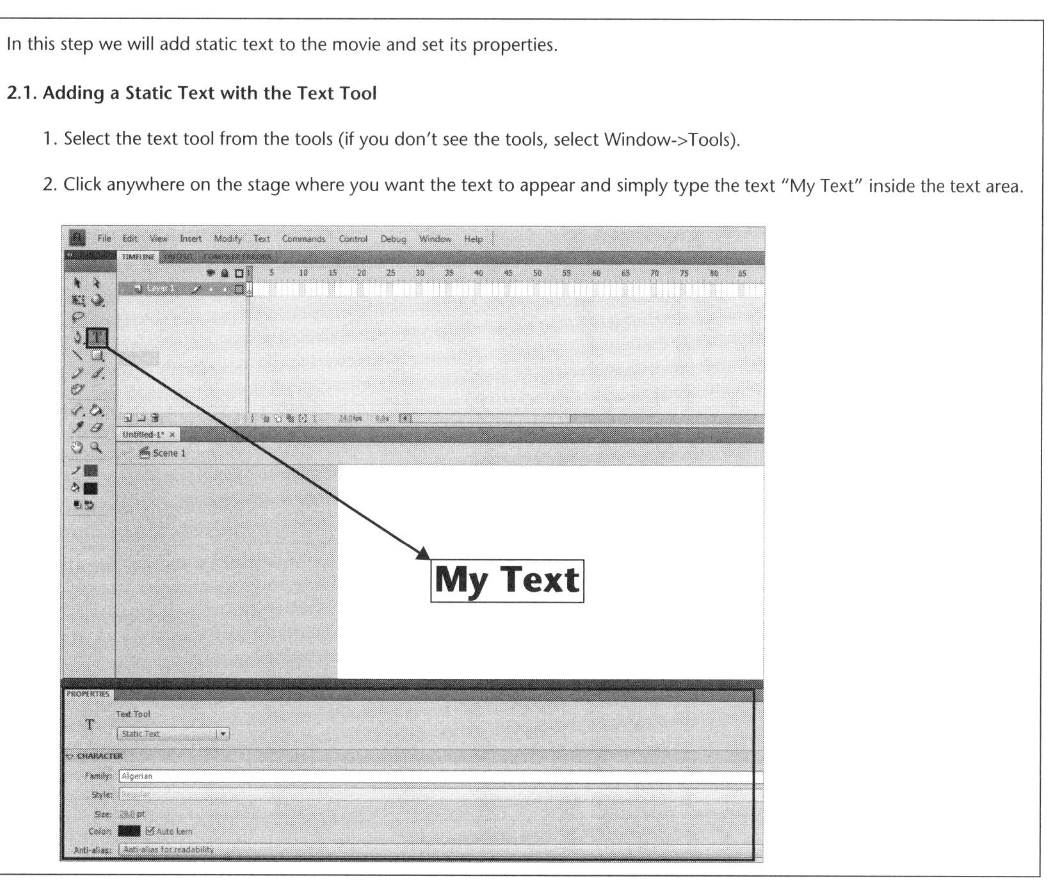

Dissertation, Florida State University, Rinat Rosenberg-Kima.

FIGURE 21-7 Task-Centered Instructional How-to Demonstration Event

In this step, we will simply insert a static text object and an image into the first frame.

1.1.a. Adding a Static Text with the Text Tool

Static text fields display text that doesn't change characters dynamically.

1. Select the text tool from the tools (if you don't see the tools, select Window->Tools).
2. Click anywhere on the stage where you want the text to appear and simply type the text "Cat" inside the text area.

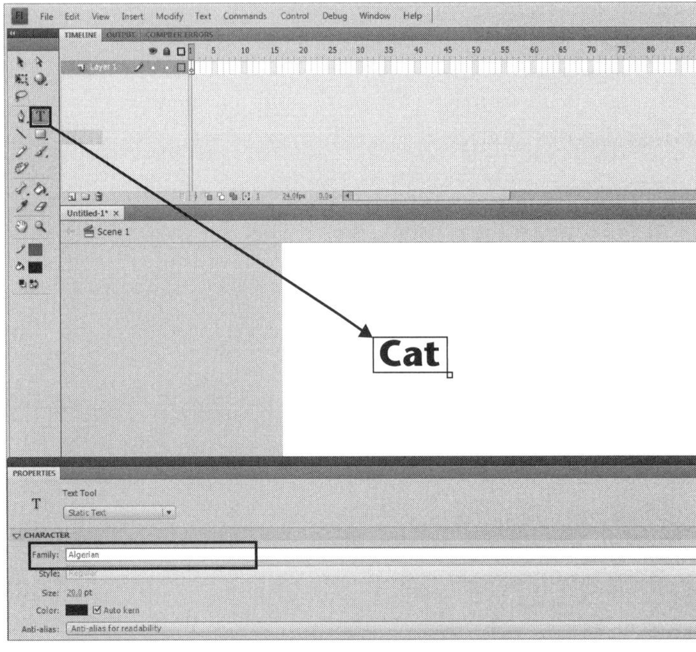

Dissertation, Florida State University, Rinat Rosenberg-Kima.

Dependent Variables

There were six dependent variables: performance on module tasks, posttest skill development, posttest near transfer process development, posttest far transfer process development, time on task, and attitude toward instruction.

For performance on module tasks, participants completed a Flash file at the end of each topic for the topic-centered condition and at the end of each task for the task-centered condition. Score reflected module completion and time. No differences were expected.

FIGURE 21-8 Sequence of Topics in Flash Programming Treatment Conditions

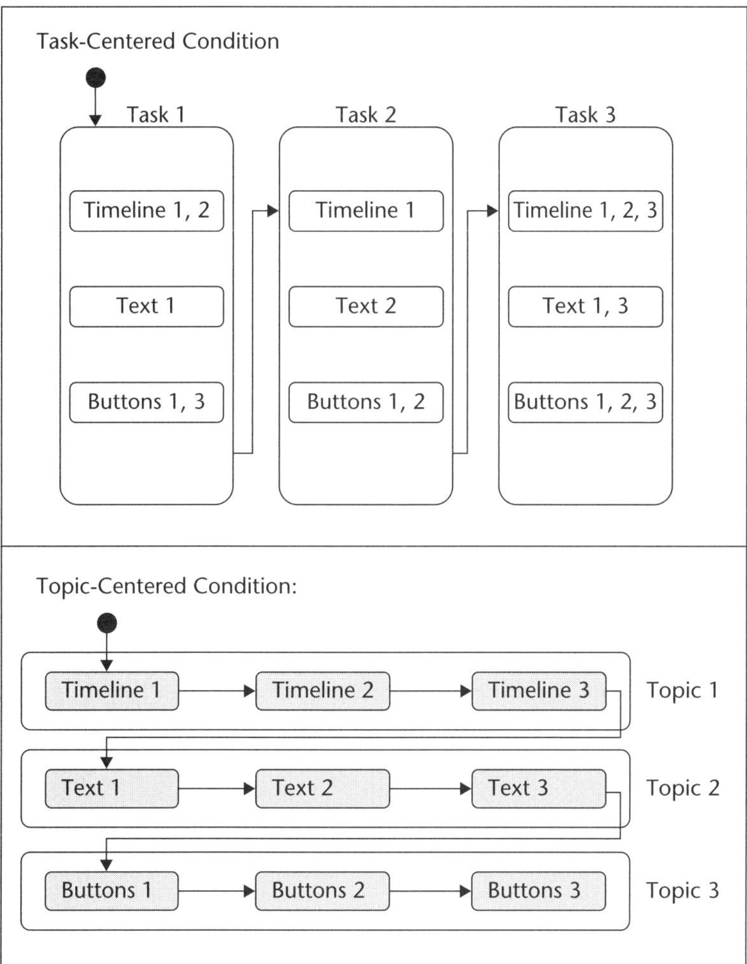

Dissertation, Florida State University, Rinat Rosenberg-Kima.

- For posttest skill development, students had to develop a simple Flash application by following specific instructions.
- For near transfer process development, students were given a Flash application similar to the examples they had seen and had to provide a narrative explanation on how to create this application.
- For far transfer process development, students were given a Flash application that was different from the examples they had seen, but required the same skills, and had to provide a narrative explanation on how to create this application.
- For time on task, six time measures were recorded: time on each of the three modules and time to compete each of the three posttest tasks.
- Attitude toward instructions was measured using Keller's Instructional Materials Motivational Survey (Keller, 1993).

Participants

Sixty-five students, both graduate and undergraduate, from a large southeastern university in the United States volunteered to participate in the study. No prior knowledge of computer programming was required to participate. The participants were randomly assigned to the two treatment conditions. Students received a small payment and academic credit for participating in a subject pool.

Results

On all three of the posttest performance measures the task-centered group performed better than the topic-centered group. All differences were statistically significant. Each of the measures was scored on a 10-point scale: on skill development the task-centered group scored 9.0 and the topic-centered group scored 7.5 ($p < 025$); on the near transfer posttest, the task-centered group scored 8.3 and topic-centered group scored 6.3 ($p < 001$); on the far transfer posttest the task-centered group scored 7.9 and topic-centered group scored 5.8 ($p < 001$).

There were no differences between the treatment groups for the time required to complete the posttest tasks; however, on the modules the task-centered group took longer on Part 1 and Part 2 than the topic-centered group, whereas the topic-centered group took longer on Part 3 than the task-centered group, but there was no difference in total learning time between the two groups.

On the attitude measure, the results revealed a statistically significant difference between the groups, with the task-centered group seeing more relevance and expressing more confidence than the topic-centered group. There were not differences on the attention and satisfaction scales.

Each of the treatments implemented the strategy prescriptions for a how-to task. The difference was the use of a problem-centered approach versus a topic-oriented approach. In this carefully controlled comparison, the data clearly supports the benefit of a problem-centered approach. Rosenberg-Kima also gathered data in support of a theoretical model that attempts to explain why a task-centered approach is superior. The details of this model and the supporting data are beyond the scope of this book.

STUDENT EVALUATIONS—FRICK

Student evaluations of faculty are a standard activity in most colleges and universities. However, these scales are notably general and do not contain items that would prescribe to a professor ways to improve the design of a course, even when students score a particular item low. Frick and his associates modified the typical student evaluation form to include items that were specific to First Principles of Instruction (Frick, Chadha, Watson, Wang, & Green, 2009; Frick, Chadha, Watson, & Wang, 2010; Frick, Chadha, Watson, & Zlatkovska, 2010).

The new Teaching and Learning Quality (TALQ) scales also included global items that enabled learners to rate the unspecified overall quality of the course; academic learning time items that allowed students to estimate the amount of effort put into a course; learning scales that allowed learners to indicate how well they felt they learned from the course; and learner satisfaction items that enabled learners to indicate how much they liked the course. Table 21-5 lists the items in each of the nine scales aggregated by category. Cronbach alpha (α) is a measure of internal consistency within each scale. Since the individual items within each scale are highly related, a single score was computed for each scale for purposes of analysis. The items were presented in random order as they were administered to the students.

Table 21-5 Teaching and Learning Quality Scales[1]

Item Stems[2]

Academic Learning Time (ALT): Cronbach α = 0.85

I frequently did very good work on projects, assignments, problems, and/or learning activities for this course.
I spent a lot of time doing tasks, projects, and/or assignments, and my instructor judged my work as high quality.
I put a great deal of effort and time into this course, and it has paid off—I believe that I have done very well overall.

Learning Progress (Kirkpatrick, Level 2): Cronbach α = 0.97

Compared to what I knew before I took this course, I learned a lot.
I learned a lot in this course.
Looking back to when this course began, I have made a big improvement in my skills and knowledge in this subject.
I learned very little in this course. (–)[3]
I did not learn much as a result of taking this course. (–)

Student Satisfaction (Kirkpatrick, Level 1): Cronbach α = 0.94

I am dissatisfied with this course. (–)
This course was a waste of time and money. (–)
I am very satisfied with this course.

Global Course Rating: Cronbach α = 0.94

Overall, I would rate the quality of this course as outstanding.
Overall, I would rate this instructor as outstanding.
Overall, I would recommend this instructor to others.

Authentic Problems (First Principles Problem-Centered Principle): Cronbach α = 0.81

I performed a series of increasingly complex authentic tasks in this course.
I solved authentic problems or completed authentic tasks in this course.
In this course I solved a variety of authentic problems that were organized from simple to complex.

Activation (First Principles Activation Principle): Cronbach α = 0.91

I engaged in experiences that subsequently helped me learn ideas or skills that were new and unfamiliar to me.
In this course I was able to recall, describe, or apply my past experience so that I could connect it to what I was expected to learn.
My instructor provided a learning structure that helped me to mentally organize new knowledge and skills.
In this course I was able to connect my past experience to new ideas and skills I was learning.
In this course I was not able to draw upon my past experience nor relate it to new things I was learning (–)

Demonstration (First Principles Demonstration Principle): Cronbach α = 0.88

My instructor demonstrated skills I was expected to learn in this course.
My instructor gave examples and counterexamples of concepts that I was expected to learn.
My instructor did not demonstrate skills I was expected to learn. (–)
My instructor provided alternative ways of understanding the same ideas or skills.

Application (First Principles Application Principle): Cronbach α = 0.74

My instructor detected and corrected errors I was making when solving problems, doing learning tasks, or completing assignments.
My instructor gradually reduced coaching or feedback as my learning or performance improved during this course.
I had opportunities to practice or try out what I learned in this course.
My course instructor gave me personal feedback or appropriate coaching on what I was trying to learn.

(continued)

Table 21-5 *Continued*

Integration (First Principles Integration Principle): Cronbach $\alpha = 0.81$

I had opportunities in this course to explore how I could personally use what I have learned.
I see how I can apply what I learned in this course to real-life situations.
I was able to publicly demonstrate to others what I learned in this course.
In this course I was able to reflect on, discuss with others, and defend what I learned.
I do not expect to apply what I learned in this course to my chosen profession or field of work. (–)
Assignments, tasks, or problems I did in this course are clearly relevant to my professional goals or field of work.

[1]Copyright Theodore Frick.

[2]Each item requires Likert scale ratings (strongly disagree, disagree, undecided, agree, and strongly agree).

[3]Items with (–) are negatively worded; thus rating scores are reversed for analysis of these items.

Study 1 A first study acquired evaluations using this new evaluation scale from 193 students who were enrolled in 111 different courses representing all subject areas, including business, medicine, education, English, and computer technology (Frick, Chadha, Watson, & Wang, 2010). Participants were one-third undergraduate students and two-thirds graduate students, about 60 percent female and 40 percent male. About 60 percent of the classes were face-to-face and 40 percent were online.

This study found the following statistically significant correlations: First Principles of Instruction is correlated with academic learning time ($r = 0.67$); with perceived learning ($r = .83$); with satisfaction ($r = 0.85$); and with outstanding instructor and course ($r = 0.89$).

Study 2 A second study included 140 students enrolled in eighty-nine different courses at multiple institutions (Frick, Chadha, Watson, Wang, & Green, 2009). These courses included business, medicine, education, computers and technology, and single instances of a number of other courses. There were ninety-three women and forty-three men, representing both graduate and undergraduate education at the university level. No difference were found between gender and any of the variables.

Data analysis indicated that the perception that a course contained First Principles of Instruction was highly correlated with academic learning time (ALT) (0.68), learning progress (0.82), satisfaction with the course (0.83), perceived mastery of the material (0.34), the global rating of the class (0.73), and overall instructor course rating (0.87). All correlations were significant ($p < 0.0005$).

"MAPSAT (mapping and analyzing patterns and structures across time) results indicated that students were three to five times more likely to agree or strongly agree that they learned a lot and were satisfied with courses when they also agreed that First Principles of Instruction were used and students were frequently engaged successfully. Students were nine times more likely to report mastery course objectives when both First Principles and ALT were reported to have occurred, compared with their absence. Results from this study provide the strongest empirical support thus far for First Principles of Instruction" (Frick, Chadha, Watson, Wang, & Green, 2009, p. 713).

Study 3 One criticism of previous studies was that students self-reported their level of learning. A third study was conducted with 490 students in twelve classes, including business, philosophy, history, kinesiology, social work, computer science, and nursing (Frick, Chadha, Watson, & Zlatkovska, 2010). In these classes the instructor rated the students' mastery of the course. The following significant correlations were found in this study:

1. First Principles is correlated with global ratings of course and instructor quality($r = 0.75$); with student satisfaction ($r = 0.77$); with academic learning time ($r = 057$); and with perceived learning progress ($r = 0.72$).
2. Academic learning time is correlated with global ratings ($r = 0.53$); with student satisfaction ($r = 0.56$); with perceived learning progress ($r = 0.51$); and with instructor rating of student mastery ($r = 0.39$).
3. Perceived learning progress is correlated with instructor rating of student mastery ($r = 0.43$).
4. Seventy percent of the students in this study agreed that First Principles occurred in the course they evaluated. Of these, nine out of ten indicated that they were satisfied with the course; that they learned a lot; and that it was an outstanding instructor and course.

In Chapter 2 I claim that learning will be promoted when First Principles of Instruction are utilized. Frick and his colleagues stated the following: "We would not have thought to put such items on our survey instrument without such a prediction." This prediction is supported by these studies.

INFORMAL APPLICATIONS

Shell EP

First Principles formed the basis of a tool used by Shell EP to evaluate and redesign their courses (Margaryan & Collis, 2005). Their instrument was applied to more than sixty-five courses, which were redesigned to be in greater compliance with First Principles. Twelve courses were studied in detail. The course-scan values (score on First Principles) were compared with participant evaluation data and instructors' reflections. The participants and the instructors indicated that the problem-centered First Principles courses were more relevant to their business, promoted more effective and deeper learning, and resulted in more application of the skills attained in the workplace (Margaryan, 2006).

Entrepreneur Course

An entrepreneur course for distance delivery for students in developing countries was developed at Brigham Young University–Hawaii using First Principles of Instruction and the Pebble-in-the-Pond approach (Mendenhall, Buhanan, Suhaka, Mills, Gibson, & Merrill, 2006). Six principles for starting a business were taught in the context of five small businesses (see Chapter 7). A final exam required students to evaluate a business plan for a sixth small business. A pilot study compared performance on this exam by eight business majors who had completed several previous business courses, to twelve non-business majors who had completed only this one new course. Seven of the twelve non-business majors scored as well as the business majors on this exam. While the course is still being used, to my knowledge no further formal evaluation has been conducted.

Biology 100 Course

BYU–Hawaii Biology 100 was revised based on First Principles of Instruction, as described in Chapter 7. This course underwent formative evaluation with eighty-nine students in two classes. The evaluation included classroom observation, instructor observations, a class survey, and online discussion observations. Classroom observations indicated that most students actively participated in group discussions about the problems. The instructor indicated that some of the online problem solutions by the students were similar to conclusions to similar problems by his more experienced biology students.

Marriage Relationship Courses

I am often told that First Principles of Instruction are well-known and frequently used. However, a study by Barclay, Gur, and Wu (2004) analyzed more than fourteen hundred websites in five countries that claimed to provide instruction on marriage relationships. The websites included in this study were all authored by marriage professionals, including counselors, clergy, and other professionals concerned with families. Each site was scored on a 15-point scale indicating the degree to which the First Principles of Instruction were implemented. The average scores by country indicate almost no implementation of these instructional principles. Table 21-6 lists the countries included in the study, the number of websites analyzed for each country, the highest score for any of the sites for each country, and the average score for each country.

The highest score on any site was 7.0, indicating that even the best site implemented less than half of these principles. The average scores indicate that most of these sites do not implement any of these principles. The result is that these so-called instructional websites fail to implement the principles that instructional design theorists have identified as fundamental for effective, efficient, and engaging instruction. However, this research merely indicates whether or not these principles are implemented; it does not provide information about the contribution of these principles to student performance or whether those sites that score low teach less than those sites that score high on the implementation of these principles.

Table 21-6 Use of First Principles of Instruction in Marriage Relations Courses (Possible Score = 15)

Country	Number of Sites	Highest Score	Average Score
Australia	202	6	0.11
China	551	2	0.02
France	257	6	0.12
Turkey	42	6	0.17
United States	410	7	0.13

SUMMARY

It is clear that more carefully controlled research directly evaluating the e^3 contribution of First Principles of Instruction is needed. However, the research reported here indicates that First Principles of Instruction do contribute to improved effectiveness, increased instructional efficiency, and increased learner engagement when compared with other forms of instruction. It is hoped that this book may provide sufficient incentive for researchers to undertake more carefully controlled studies of these principles.

COMING NEXT

Chapter 22 is the concluding chapter in this book. This chapter looks backward to indicate what led me to develop such a detailed approach to instructional design and then looks forward to how I hope that *First Principles of Instruction* will affect the future of instructional technology. The chapter concludes by suggesting some ways that you can contribute to the future of First Principles of Instruction and instructional technology.

CHAPTER 22

FIRST PRINCIPLES OF INSTRUCTION AND THE FUTURE

Quick Look

This chapter reviews my underlying motivation for presenting a theoretical approach to instructional design that includes very specific prescriptions for identifying and designing instructional strategies. This chapter will address the following questions: Why did I choose to present such a detailed approach to identifying and designing quality instructional? What prompted me to take this approach? How do I hope that this detailed approach to First Principles of Instruction will affect the future of the field of instructional technology? And finally, how can you contribute to the future of First Principles of Instruction and instructional technology?

Key Word

Designer-by-Assignment: a person selected by an organization to do instructional design based on his or her knowledge of the subject matter rather than on his or her training or skill in the process of instructional design.

INTRODUCTION

This book, *First Principles of Instruction*, presents a very detailed approach for identifying and designing effective, efficient and engaging instruction. Some reviewers of this work have wondered whether this detailed approach is really necessary. They have suggested that some readers will be turned off by the new vocabulary and the specificity of the prescriptions involved. In this chapter I first provide a brief history of the events in my life that that led me to this detailed approach to instructional design theory. I then provide a brief outline of my view of a scientific/technology approach to instructional design. I explain how I believe that the terminology, propositions, and theory presented here can contribute to a scientific/technology approach to instructional design. Finally, I suggest ways that you can contribute to the future of a scientific/technology approach to instructional design.

WHY THIS THEORETICAL APPROACH TO INSTRUCTIONAL DESIGN

My major in secondary education was a frustrating experience. I can only recall one or two lectures that dealt with the topic of effective instruction. I had a wonderful experience as an unconventional student teacher, but caused considerable consternation for the principal of the school where I was assigned. I was advised that I probably would not survive the public schools. It occurred to me that perhaps my decision to major in education was a mistake and that I should seek another career path. As I expressed my frustration to one of my professors, he gave me a challenge that put me on the career path that I have since pursued. In response to my suggestion that I abandon education, he simply stated, "You could pursue another career, or you could realize that there is much that needs to be done. Perhaps you could make positive change in the field." Not being one to back away from a challenge, I decided to take up the gauntlet and pursue a Ph.D.

In my final semester of undergraduate work, a check with the registrar showed that I was short one hour of credit for my minor in mathematics. Naturally, there were no one-hour math classes, so it was necessary to enroll in a three-hour class. The University of Illinois had already awarded me a fellowship for my Ph.D. study; therefore the completion of the additional math class assumed considerable significance for my future. A class in number theory appeared, on the surface, to be the easiest path to the necessary credit. The year was 1961. "New mathematics" in the public schools was still in the future. Computers were just coming on the scene. Binary arithmetic, base 8, base 16, and other representations of numbers were not in the repertoire of a small-town undergraduate student scrambling to complete his bachelor's degree.

This particular class in number theory was, for this student, a unique math class: no problems to work, no homework, and a very small textbook. At the end of each lecture the professor merely said, "Think about it!" Think about what? How do you think about mathematics? In desperation, and as a substitute for thinking, I read the textbook every week. It wasn't difficult; it had only ninety-seven pages. However, the concepts presented floated over my head like clouds in the sky. I had no idea what the course was about or what the text was about. Each week a lecture, the injunction to "Think about it!," and another read through the text.

The midterm exam was a disaster. There were no problems to work, only a single directive: "Invent a number system." Invent a number system? What in the world does that mean? In true survival mode I wrote for the whole two hours. However, it didn't fool the professor. There were seven students in the class; there were seven F's on the midterm. When we objected, the only explanation from the professor was, "Think about it!"

My anxiety was at an all-time high. My graduate career was about to be terminated before it began by the unnerving command, "Think about it!" I tried every avenue of escape: Another class? Getting the registrar to waive the credit? Home study? There were no other options. My bachelor's degree, and hence my entrance to graduate school, were both riding on a class in which I had received a failing grade on the midterm and, worse, a class that was to me completely incomprehensible.

Somewhere in the thirteenth week the light came on. Number systems are inventions. They are not natural phenomena. Number systems are like any other invention: an assembly line, an organization. A number system is merely a system of logic consisting of premises and conclusions. Base 10 is only one of many possible number systems. Base 10 numbers are useful for many everyday things, but other systems might be equally useful.

The day of the final arrived. My anxiety was still high, but at least I thought I understood. You guessed it, only one directive: "Invent a number system." Either I understood or it was too late. My future graduate studies depended on my ability to invent a number system. So I wrote, "Let there be an oar and a rubber boot." I proceeded to define a binary number system with two elements, an oar and a rubber boot. I was in the professor's office the next day to see whether I was going to graduate school or not. He handed me my paper with a large red *A* written across the top. I thanked him, breathed a sigh of relief, and vowed to never take another math class as long as I lived.

• • •

My first year of graduate school was very difficult. Not only was there a tremendous amount of work, but there also seemed to be too many contradictions. The content of learning psychology challenged many of my fundamental beliefs. There were numerous contending systems, each claiming to explain learning. I struggled for days trying to explain learning of the concept *green* using only *S-R* (stimulus-response) bonds. I found myself in the basement of the psychology building feeding rats that were on a deprivation schedule. Why was I feeding rats when I wanted to know how to teach children? I was about ready to give up and look for a real job.

About this time, B.F. Skinner visited the campus. Like my fellow classmates, I went to hear the great man. I don't remember any details of his lecture, but his response in the question-and-answer period changed my life. A member of the audience said, "Dr. Skinner, in your book [which he named] you said such and such [some detail of Skinner's theory]; but tonight you seemed to contradict yourself by saying such and such"—he quoted a part of Skinner's speech.

"Hell," said Skinner, "do you think I believe everything I ever wrote?"

This was a great insight for me. Here was a great author saying he changed his mind and now disagrees with his earlier self. However, what he said next changed my life.

"What I've tried to do," continued Skinner, "is to make only a few assumptions and then see how much of human learning we can explain with only these assumptions." He went on to defend his theory and the point he made in his speech. I stopped listening before he ended his explanation.

"Good grief," I thought, "psychology is just an oar and a rubber boot as well."

Psychological systems are not reality either, but merely logical systems that try to explain what we observe in the real world. Behavior is merely one logical system that is tested against reality to see how good a match can be found. Just as there can be many different number systems, there can be many different psychological systems. Each is tested against reality to see how closely it fits, but none are reality, merely inventions.

I returned to my studies with renewed enthusiasm. I looked upon all theories as artificial systems and found them fascinating. I stopped trying to make all theories agree and force them to form one great truth. It became a game to see whether I could identify the theorist's assumptions and conclusions. It was fascinating to observe that some systems were carefully constructed and logical, while other systems were very loosely constructed and often violated the canons of logic. I realized that theory building is our puny attempt to understand our world by inventing artificial systems and trying them out against the world.

Later in my graduate career I had one additional insight. We were studying learning and some instructional theories. It was apparent that learning theories tended to explain how persons acquire and store knowledge, but they have very little to say about how an instructor should structure and sequence knowledge to promote efficient and effective learning. It occurred to me that one could build a logical system, a theory, about instruction. So I said, "Let there by an instructional oar and a rubber boot" (from the preface of Merrill, 1994).

Over the next several decades what followed were *Component Display Theory* and more recently *First Principles of Instruction* as represented in this book. What led to First Principles of Instruction? My desire to try to build a logical theoretical system about instructional design using only a few fundamental components (see Chapters 3 and 4) and combining them into propositions about instructional strategies (see Chapter 5) and theoretical models (see Chapters 6 and 7).

THE SCIENCE AND TECHNOLOGY OF INSTRUCTIONAL DESIGN

I believe that students of instructional design should be involved in both science and technology (Merrill, 1980b, 2007b). Science activities involve theory development and experimental research to substantiate the theory. Technology activities involve the development of design procedures, instructional development, and evaluation (field research). I advocate a science-based approach in which the development of actual instructional materials should be done by the use of principle-based procedures that have been derived from theory that has been empirically verified via experimental research. It is my observation that my hope for a technology of instructional design grounded in empirically verified theory is still the exception rather than the rule. So after more than thirty years I return to this theme.

Table 22-1 suggests that the discipline of instructional design involves both science and technology. Science is the pursuit of understanding; technology is the creation of artifacts. The goal of science is knowledge about the physical world; scientists are interesting in understanding and predicting. On the other hand, the goal of the designer is the design of useful artifacts and predicting the performance of the products they design (Vincenti, 1990).

Table 22-1 The Science and Technology of Instructional Design

Science		Technology		
Research	Theory	Tools	Development	Evaluation
Experimental Research; Product or Research Review	Outcomes; Concepts; Propositions, Models, Theories	Technology-Based Tools; Conceptual Tools	Instructional Products	Field Research

The field of instructional design involves both theory and research. Theory is about describing phenomena and predicting consequences (hypotheses) from given conditions. Research is applying appropriate methodology to test these predictions. Instructional design theory is about understanding what conditions are necessary for a learner to acquire specific instructional goals, specific knowledge and skill, or specific learning outcomes. Research is the method by which these predictions are empirically tested and verified. A major role for instructional technology should be the study of instruction and instructional design. Instructional design theory involves the careful specification of the instructional conditions necessary in order for a student to acquire the desired learning outcomes. Instructional design research involves the application of empirical quantitative and qualitative research methods to test these predictions or prescriptions.

The technology of instructional design involves the application of empirically verified instructional design theory to the development of instructional products designed to enable students to efficiently and effectively acquire desired instructional outcomes. Instructional products can be, and often are, designed without sufficient consideration of the applicable verified instructional design theory. Such an approach is not a technology of instructional design but the art of instructional design. While an artistic approach sometimes results in effective and engaging instructional products, it is often not possible to understand why such products are effective, and too often it is not possible to replicate the success of a given product in a subsequent product.

The technology of instruction involves three distinct activities: (1) develop the necessary design tools, (2) demonstrate the use of these tools in designing/developing an instructional product, and (3) predict and then test the performance of the instructional product.

Since most instruction is developed by designers-by-assignment, rather than technologists, it is necessary that the principles of effective and efficient instruction (instructional design theory) be captured in tools that provide intellectual leverage to novice designers who may not know the required instructional design theory. Most of our current tools provide this kind of leverage for the technology skills required such as computer programming, but fail to provide equivalent intellectual leverage for the required instructional design theory required. These tools too often assume that everyone is a designer and that the difficult skills to provide within the tool are technical skills, such as computer programming.

The instructional scientist attempts to discover and test principles for instruction. The instructional technologist, using the principles discovered by the scientist, develops and tests conceptual tools or procedures and technology-based tools or design systems that can be used by instructional designers, either professional or lay, for the production of instructional products.

The primary purpose of this book is to provide a set of guidelines for identifying and designing effective, efficient, and engaging instruction. A secondary purpose of this book is to provide theory and hypotheses that support a science and technology of instruction. In the following paragraphs I will elaborate the role of theory, research, technology tools, development, and evaluation and identify those theoretical ideas and principles from this book that support these activities.

THEORY

The central activity of any scientific approach always involves theory construction. Thus, any generalization constitutes a form of theory, and any investigation requires some level of theory construction. Instructional design theory is prescriptive theory rather than descriptive theory. That is, the theory identifies instructional conditions required for particular instructional consequences or outcomes. We say that instructional design theory is goal-driven. The instructional consequences or learning outcomes constitute the goal. The theory then specifies learning conditions thought necessary for a learner to be able to acquire the learning goal in an efficient and effective manner.

It is important to distinguish learning outcomes from instructional outcomes. Learning always occurs. Human beings learn from every situation. Instructional goals are attained when the learning outcomes correspond with the specified instructional outcomes or instructional objectives.

How does instructional design theory arise? What is required to specify an instructional design theory? And why are there so many different instructional design theories? The following paragraphs explore the answers to these questions.

Outcomes and Concepts

"The cutting edge of science is reductionism, the breaking apart of nature into its natural components" (Wilson, 1998, p. 54). But what are these natural components? Where do these natural components come from? All science begins with the invention of concepts, that is, the operational definition of what in the real world will be observed. How does a scientist determine what to observe? Usually by paying careful attention in a qualitative way to the phenomenon under consideration. For instructional design theory, the instructional design scientist observes many instruction and teaching situations. The scientist tries to abstract from these situations those events, those conditions, that seem to be present when learning of a particular kind occurs. The scientist then carefully defines the event or characteristic of the teaching situation that he or she believes contributes to the learning performance. The scientist then quantifies this condition using some appropriate metric as simple as present or absent or as complex as numerical amounts on a ratio scale of measurement.

In Chapter 3 I argued that instructional science and technology needs a way to describe content that applies to all different subject-matter areas and that provides a vocabulary that allows instructional scientists and technologists to describe the details of the content of instruction we wish to critique or design. Chapter 3 introduces key terms or concepts that can be used to unambiguously describe instructional content for five types of learning outcomes. In Chapter 4 I argued that instructional technology needs a way to unambiguously describe instructional modes or learner interaction with subject-matter content. Chapter 4 introduces key terms or concepts that can be used to unambiguously describe instructional interaction. The identification of those components of instruction that can be combined into propositions about a given instructional situation is the fundamental first step in building instructional design theory. Chapters 3 and 4 provide a description of outcomes and concepts that provide a foundation on which to build instructional theory.

Propositions

The next step in science is to combine the defined concepts into propositions, if . . . then statements. If a given amount of some condition is present, then there will be a corresponding improvement in the learning that occurs. This set of propositions constitutes an instructional design theory.

Chapter 5 combines instructional mode concepts with instructional content concepts to provide prescriptive propositions for demonstration and application instructional events for five types of component skill. This set of instructional strategy prescriptions is an attempt to carefully define instructional propositions that are an example of instructional theory.

Models and Theory

An effective instructional design theory also specifies the relationships among the propositions of the theory so that the theory is not merely a set of conditions that stand in isolation, but rather a set of interrelated principles or models that act together to produce the desired learning outcome or consequence.

Chapter 6 goes further, showing how instructional strategy propositions for individual component skills are combined to form prescribed instructional events for teaching problem solving. Chapter 6 provides an instructional theory about problem solving. Chapter 7 goes one step further to prescribe a problem-centered instructional strategy that combines problem-solving prescriptions into a curriculum sequence for teaching problem solving. These chapters provide prescriptive instructional design theory for combining the strategies for individual component skill to form a prescriptive instructional theory and curriculum for teaching problem solving.

Learning Theory

Often the instructional design theory is linked to an underlying learning theory. The learning theory explains why the predicted relationship may occur. It should be noted that the instructional design theory is the set of if-condition then-consequence prescriptions. The learning theory is a linking of these conditions to underlying learning constructs that explain why a given instructional proposition or set of propositions result in more efficient or effective learning.

This book is directed primarily at those whose goal is to identify or design effective, efficient, and engaging instruction. This book is very prescriptive in nature and provides only a glimpse at underlying learning theory in answer to the question: Why does it work? I hope this book may serve as a catalyst for further research on the underlying explanations for the instructional design theory presented here.

Renat Rosenberg-Kima (2011) conducted a dissertation study testing problem-centered versus topic-centered instructional design, as described in Chapter 21. In addition to showing what works, she provided a detailed cognitive model for why a problem-centered approach works better than a topic-centered approach. She collected data that not only demonstrated the validity of the prescription but provided support for the underlying explanatory cognitive model. The details of this research are beyond the scope of this book but do provide a model for future research on theory that explains why instructional theory propositions work.

Why Are There So Many Different Instructional Design Theories?

The answer to this question lies in the nature of science. Different investigators may not feel that the concepts previously defined are the right things to observe.

Or they may feel that the terminology used to identify a given event or condition is not sufficiently descriptive so they use a different term. Instructional design theory is sufficiently immature that there has not yet been a general agreement on the conditions that have been found to be most useful, nor has there been a general agreement on the terminology used to identify these instructional events or conditions. There have been several attempts at providing definitions of terminology in the field, but to date none of these have been generally accepted by the majority of the field. Eventually, as more theory is defined and more research conducted to verify this theory, there will be a gradual coming together of the accepted terms and conditions that are thought to be important.

This book represents only one way to define instructional theory that implements First Principles of Instruction. It is a serious attempt to carefully define outcomes, concepts, and prescriptive propositions. Fortunately, there is some empirical and experiential support of the validity of these propositions. It is my hope that this book will serve as a starting point or at least a model for future attempts at defining instructional design theory and facilitating research of these propositions and relationships.

INSTRUCTIONAL DESIGN RESEARCH

Theory is the starting point for any scientific enterprise. Without at least a set of propositions that can be tested, it is not possible to do meaningful research. Theory may be as simple as an if . . . then statement or as complex as an underlying model explaining why a given proposition is true. Instructional research is the means by which theory at all levels is validated. Instructional research consists of two primary activities: first, finding out what has already been done and, second, conducting original investigations.

Product or Research Review

An important research activity is finding out what has already been done and what is known about what works and why. There are two primary sources of this information. One is to review the findings of original empirical studies and the second is to carefully extract from instructional products the explicit or implicit propositions built into their design.

It is often a challenge to find existing research investigations of a given instructional prescription because of the wide variety of vocabulary that is used in the field. A first step in locating relevant research studies is to first translate the treatments involved in a given study into some common vocabulary that will allow comparison with treatments in other studies. A second step is to identify the instructional propositions or prescriptions that underlie these treatments and to translate these propositions into a common vocabulary that will facilitate comparison with other studies and treatments. One of the advantages of the carefully defined concepts for content (Chapter 3) and the carefully defined concepts for learner interaction (Chapter 4) is that these concepts provide a vocabulary to facilitate this translation. This translation is often facilitated by focusing on what instructional activities were actually implemented rather than on the labels used by the author to describe the treatments or instructional events. Once the instructional events have been carefully identified and described using a common vocabulary, then comparison with the prescriptions provided in this book or the prescriptions from other sources is much more easily accomplished.

Reviewing instructional products is another source of information-about what works. The implementation of a given instructional product may not yield a comparison with alternative treatments, but often the evaluation data will indicate whether a given instructional product accomplished its instructional goal. As with research, being able to compare what was done in one instructional product with another product requires some translation of the instructional events and underlying propositions into some common vocabulary. I hope the concepts and vocabulary introduced in this book provide one tool for facilitating this translation.

Experimental Research

A second scientific research activity is to conduct empirical investigations comparing one treatment with an alternative treatment. There is a paucity of research conducted on instructional design. Instructional technologists are too often distracted by the plethora of new applications that constantly flood the market. Many instructional technologists find their fascination with the technology overrides their discipline in conducting carefully designed research studies. Many instructional technologists find joy in creating instructional products but have much less interest in verifying that they really work and why they work.

A detailed description of empirical research methodology is beyond the scope of this book. However, I strongly advocate the use of mini experiments as described in Chapter 18 as a step in this direction that can be relatively easily accomplished by most instructional designers. Almost any functional prototype can include alternative instructional events or alternative instructional strategies that can provide some data during the evaluation phase of a development project.

This book contains many prescriptions that are believed to lead to more effective, efficient, or engaging learning outcomes. While there is some general support for these prescriptions, there is the important question: Does it work? The principles presented here can be implemented in many ways. Does your implementation of a given prescription really work? Compared to what? I hope that this book provides many hypotheses that beg for empirical verification, especially in your particular instructional environment.

A large number of instructional design theory questions still do not have sufficient research support. The research on instructional design would investigate some of these questions. The two primary questions for instructional design are "What to teach" and "How to teach." There are still unresolved questions about knowledge (subject-matter content) selection. From all there is to teach, what should be included and what should be excluded from the instruction? What should be taught first? What second? Does order matter? How should the content be structured? What kinds of structure should we provide to learners to help them internally organize the new knowledge? What is a knowledge object? How should knowledge objects be combined?

An equally large number of unresolved questions exist about how to teach. These questions involve effective demonstration for different types of learning; effective practice for different types of learning; effective guidance during demonstration; effective coaching during application; how to effectively activate prior learning; how to integrate the learning with subsequent activities in the learners' real world; and how to effectively use media. While I have suggested answers to some of these questions, there remain many unresolved issues.

And finally, last but certainly not least, the prescriptive relationships described in this book, even those that have been shown to work in a number of different instructional environments, beg for an explanation for why they work. I hope that the future brings an increased interest in building cognitive models that explain why a given instructional prescription works in a given situation. Building and verifying a cognitive model for instructional prescriptions is a complex task. Nevertheless, I hope that providing a carefully defined systematic instructional theory, such as presented in this book, will generate not only studies to determine whether it works and when it works but, more importantly, investigation of why it works.

INSTRUCTIONAL DESIGN TOOLS

I have taught at a number of different universities. They often assume that if professors have published in their field, they know how to teach and design their courses. Most professors are not trained in pedagogy or instructional design. They are designers-by-assignment. When a company needs someone in the training department, where does it go? Usually to the folks who have knowledge about the content to be taught. Many of those who are tasked to design courses for industry have little or no formal training in instructional design. Many of these folks are designers-by-assignment. Designers-by-assignment often do not read the instructional research and theory literature. Having formulated and verified effective design theory is merely an academic exercise, unless this theory is transformed into tools that provide intellectual leverage for these folks who do the bulk of the actual instructional design.

In a previous paper (Merrill, 1997b) I described several levels of ID tools, including information containers, authoring systems, templates and widgets, learning-oriented tools, and adaptive learning-oriented tools. To date most of the ID tools available fall into the first three categories. *Information containers* enable the presentation of information and media, but usually utilize only the most rudimentary of instructional functions. Most *authoring systems* have concentrated on making programming skills easier, but have failed to provide sufficient support for important instructional design decisions. The inclusion of *templates, widgets, and other preprogrammed instructional algorithms* are structure-oriented rather than learning-oriented, that is, the focus is on how the interaction works, not on what learning outcome the interaction enables.

What is needed are learning-oriented tools, tools that have built-in instructional strategies that are based on scientifically verified principles of instruction. Tools that enable designers-by-assignment to not only easily use the technology but that provide them with extensive guidance in effective instructional design or provide them with verified, effective, predesigned instructional strategies.

Presentation software is usually considered merely as an information container; however, I have tried to illustrate that with a little effort it can be used as a tool to design a functional prototype that enables learner interaction and enables you, as a designer, to gather evaluation data. In Chapter 12 I demonstrated the use of the animation feature of presentation software to create slide master templates. In Chapter 18 I suggested what needed to be done to collect learner performance data to enable you to determine whether your functional prototype works. Since I used PowerPoint as a demonstration for how to design a functional prototype, in the Appendix, I included simple Visual Basic macros that can be added to PowerPoint to enable this tool to collect and store learner performance data.

As described in Chapters 13 and 18, a functional prototype can also be used to design instructional design tools or templates. I hope that you will experiment with creating strategy templates and actually trying these templates out with novice designers to see whether you can provide a tool with built-in instructional strategies that enable a designer-by-assignment to design more effective instruction than might have been designed without this design aid.

INSTRUCTIONAL DEVELOPMENT

Much of the current instructional design is done by designers-by-assignment. When this is the case, a different set of skills is required of professional instructional designers; rather than designing the instruction themselves, they are more likely to manage designers-by-assignment, who will do the actual design and development. If there are learning-oriented instructional design tools available, then a major role for professional instructional designers is training and supervising the use of instructional design templates and other tools by these novice designers. While the principles of effective management are beyond the scope of this book, I hope that you will nevertheless create some instructional design templates and use these templates to assist novice designers to design instruction. If you are a student, developing such management skills will serve you well in the training world.

INSTRUCTIONAL EVALUATION

The proof of the pudding is in the eating; the proof of a scientific approach to instructional design is in the final product implemented with real learners, in a real instructional environment, in the real world. This book has illustrated how you might obtain valuable evaluation data during the formative stages of your instructional design effort. More extensive evaluation methodology is beyond the scope of this book. If you are a student of instructional technology, you are encouraged to acquire these evaluation skills. You should engage in the whole process of instructional technology, including managing the implementation and evaluation of instructional products that are based on verified instructional theory and developed by designers-by-assignment with the aid of instructional design templates.

THE FUTURE

Let me conclude this chapter and this book with the questions posed at the beginning of this chapter. Why did I choose to present such a detailed approach to identifying and designing quality instructional? How do I hope that this detailed approach to First Principles of Instruction will affect the future of the field of instructional technology? And finally, how can you contribute to the future of First Principles of Instruction and instructional technology?

I believe that instruction can be submitted to a scientific and technological approach. A scientific approach depends on the careful identification of the concepts involved. In this book I have attempted to use everyday terms, but in a very carefully defined way, in the hope that such a technical vocabulary might help instructional scientists more carefully define their hypotheses and more adequately communicate with one another and technologists who rely on their findings.

A technology of instruction depends on the development of tools that facilitate the application of this technology by lay folks who are charged with selecting and designing instructional products. I have attempted to identify carefully defined instructional strategy prescriptions to facilitate the design of such instructional evaluation and design tools.

Designers-by-assignment who use such instructional design tools need carefully defined instructional strategies that they can understand as they use tools to design instructional products. I have deliberately used carefully defined everyday terms in describing these instructional strategies in the hope that the tools designed using these strategies will be more easily comprehended by lay persons who have limited training in instructional design.

And finally, how can you contribute to the future of First Principles of Instruction and instructional technology? If you have completed this book, you probably fall into one of several categories of instructional professionals. If you are charged with identifying effective instructional products for your organization, I hope that the prescriptions presented in this book will facilitate your decisions, resulting in the selection of instructional products that provide effective, efficient, and engaging learning experiences for your learners. I hope you will share what you have learned and that your efforts and those of your colleagues will improve the quality of instruction in all education and training environments as well as on the Internet.

If you are an administrator or consultant who supervises instructors or trainers, I hope that the prescriptions presented here will provide tools for you to use as you interact with these instructional professionals. Perhaps the carefully described instructional strategies presented here will help you prescribe revisions in existing instructional materials that will improve their effectiveness, efficiency, and engagement.

If you are an instructional designer who is charged with designing new instruction or working with a team to design new instruction, it is hoped that this book will enable you to design e^3 instruction. But more, it is hoped that this book will provide tools and encourage you to be an instructional technologist, one who designs instructional strategy templates for designers-by-assignment who may be part of your team. Further, it is hoped that you will also contribute to instructional science by building instructional strategy comparisons into your instructional materials to help contribute data in confirmation or refutation of the strategy prescriptions of First Principles of Instruction.

Thank you for your interest in improving instruction. Few activities are more rewarding than helping learners acquire problem-solving skills. And as I always tell my students—learning is fun, so keep smiling ☺.

APPLICATION

Modify your functional prototype to create instructional strategy templates that implement effective instructional strategies. Recruit one or more novice designers and mentor them in the use of your instructional strategy templates to design e^3 instruction.

Modify your functional prototype to implement two or more alternative treatments. Recruit a sample of representative learners. Administer your functional prototype to these learners, collect data on their performance, analyze the data, and write a brief research report on your findings.

TO LEARN MORE

Merrill, M. D. (1997b). Learning-oriented instructional development tools. *Performance Improvement, 36*(3), 5–7. This paper describes different types of instructional design tools.

Merrill, M. D. (2007b). The future of instructional design: The proper study of instructional design. In R. A. Reiser & J. V. Dempsey (Eds.), *Trends and issues in instructional design and technology* (2nd ed., pp. 336–341). Upper Saddle River, NJ: Pearson Education, Inc. Many of the ideas in this chapter were originally published here.

Merrill, M. D. (2008). Reflections on a four-decade search for effective, efficient, and engaging instruction. In M. W. Allen (Ed.), *Michael Allen's 2008 e-Learning annual* (pp. 141–167). San Francisco: Pfeiffer. This paper is a brief history of the author's career and principle contributions.

APPENDIX

ADDING ASSESSMENT CAPABILITIES TO POWERPOINT

As mentioned in Chapter 18, this Appendix will describe some simple scripts or macros you can utilize in a PowerPoint course for the purpose of gathering data for assessment.

WHAT IS A SCRIPT OR MACRO?

A script or *macro* is a piece of Visual Basic computer code designed to cause some action to occur. Macros can be attached to any object on a PowerPoint screen and can perform a wide variety of functions. The examples here are based on PowerPoint 2010.

To add macros to PowerPoint under the Developer menu, in the Code section, select Visual Basic. When you click the Visual Basic menu item, the Visual Basic for Applications editor will open. I pasted the macros shown from Table A-1 into this editor.

A macro can be attached to any object on a PowerPoint slide. To attach a macro, click on the object, click on *Insert* from the menu, and click on *Action* under Links. Check the check box for *Run Macro*. A drop-down menu lists all of the macros stored in the Visual Basic editor for your PowerPoint presentation.

Table A-1 lists some macros that can be used to add assessment capabilities to PowerPoint. Row 1 of this table is required and defines the variables that will be used by the computer code. Statements preceded by an apostrophe (') are comments and are not executed. I have used these comments to indicate the function of the macros and how they are called.

REGISTER MACRO

The macro in line 5, *Register*, gets the learner's name (*YourName)* and the drive where the data file will be stored (*GetDriveName*) and creates a data file for the student (*CreateDataFile*). The Register macro is executed when the learner clicks on the *Click here to register* button on the title slide (see Figure 17-1). As the functional prototype collects additional learner performance data during the formative evaluation, this data will be added to the learner's data file, as explained in the following paragraphs.

APPLICATION SLIDE DATA

The application slides in my functional prototype (see Figure 18-1) enable me to collect student performance data for the acquisition of component skills. Each check box is composed of two boxes, one empty and one containing an "x." I animated each of these boxes so when a learner clicked on an empty box it was hidden and the box with the "x" appears; if a learner clicks on a box containing an "x," this box is hidden and the empty box is again made visible. The macros shown in Rows 6, 8, and 10 of Table A-1 are each triggered by a click on the corresponding empty check box. The macros shown in Rows 7, 9, and 11 of Table A-1 are each triggered by the corresponding check box containing an "x." When a learner clicks on an empty check box, the macro assigns "true" to the variable *Ans1*. If the learner then clicks on a check box containing an "x," the macro assigns "false" to the variable *Ans1*. The macros in lines 6 through 13 are triggered by the check boxes on the slide master so that these same macros work for every slide developed using this slide master, in my case, the slides shown in Figure 18-1.

When the learner clicks on the Submit button on a slide constructed on the slide master shown in Figure 18-2, the *Submit* macro listed in Row 14 is executed. This macro displays a message box showing the learner the answers they submitted (true if the check box was clicked and false if it wasn't), it then executes the *SaveFile* macro from Row 12. Every slide in PowerPoint has a unique name, usually a number indicating the order in which the slides were created, not the order they appear in the show. The first line of the SaveFile macro gets this name. The next two lines open the student data file and prepare it so that more data can be added to the file. Each of the WriteLine statements adds a line to the file. As written, the macro does not indicate the correct answer but merely records what the learner did for each slide that uses the slide master. This code could be extended to indicate the correct answer and score the learner's responses.

The data is saved with the name of the slide and the values of the check boxes for this slide. The initialize macro makes sure that the value of Ans1, Ans2, and Ans3 are set to false for the next slide to use the slide master. If I registered as "Dave" and had responded to each of the five slides shown in Figure 18-1, the data file would appear as shown in Table A-2. The slide names from my PowerPoint functional prototype are shown and correspond to the slides in Table A-2.

TIME DATA

The *RecordTime* macro in line 15 is triggered by the Exit button in my prototype. This macro saves the following information to the student's data file: the learner's name with a message that the learner had finished the course, the date and time when the learner left the course, and a message thanking the learner for his or her participation. This macro can easily be modified to record additional time data throughout the course.

ATTITUDE DATA

Figure 18-3 contains option buttons which are available under Development Controls in PowerPoint. Clicking one option sets its value to true and the value of the other options to false. Macro *Slide18Submit* (Row 19 in Table A-1) calls macro

Slide18Questionaire (Row 16 in Table A-1) that stores the response corresponding to the option button selected in a variable *Option*; then calls Macro *Slide18SaveFile* in Row 17 that saves the learner's response and the text the learner enter into the text box on Figure 18-3 to the learner's data file and concludes by calling macro *Slide18ClearQuestionnaire* (Row 18) by resetting the option buttons and clearing the text box ready for the next student. Note that these macros are specific to Slide18, which is the name of the slide in my prototype. If you use this macro for your prototype you will have to change the name of the slide (Slide18) to correspond to the name of the slide in your prototype.

ASSIGN LEARNERS TO TREATMENTS

Learners can be randomly assigned to different treatment groups by the use of an *AssignGroup* macro (Row 20) and a *GoToTreatment* macro (Row 21). In my prototype I triggered these macros by adding them to the Register macro (Row 5). The *AssignGroup* macro uses a random number to assign each learner to either Group 1 or Group 2. The *MyNumber* variable is assigned a number from 1 to 6 by the second statement in the macro. The *If* statements assign learners receiving a number 1, 2, or 3 to Group 1 and those receiving a number 4, 5, or 6 to Group 2. The *GoToTreatment* macro then sends Group 1 students to Slide 3, which is the first slide in my audio guidance treatment, and Group 2 students to Slide 6, which is the first slide in my text guidance treatment. The slide number here is the sequence number of the slide in the presentation, not the slide name.

Table A-1 Visual Basic Macros for PowerPoint Assessment

Row	Macro
1	'Dim statements define variables Dim UserName As String 'Learner name Dim FileName As String 'File where learner data is stored Dim DriveName As String 'Drive where learner data file is located Dim Option As String 'Option from questionnaire Dim MyNumber As Integer 'Randomly generated number Dim MyGroup As Integer 'Group number Dim Ans1 As Boolean Dim Ans2 As Boolean Dim Ans3 As Boolean Dim fs Dim f Dim done As Boolean Dim N As Integer

(continued)

Table A-1 *Continued*

<table>
<tr><td>2</td><td>

```
'This macro gets the name of the learner.
'It is called from the Register macro listed below.
Sub YourName()
   done = False
   While done = False
      UserName = InputBox(prompt:="Type your name", _
         Title:="Input Name")
      If UserName = " " Then
         done = False
      Else
         done = True
         MsgBox ("Welcome " & UserName)
      End If
   Wend
End Sub
```

</td></tr>
<tr><td>3</td><td>

```
'This macro gets the drive where student data will be stored.
'It is called by the Register macro listed below.
Sub GetDriveName()
   done = False
   While done = False
      DriveName = InputBox(prompt:="Type the drive letter for the Data File")
      DriveName = Trim(DriveName)
      If DriveName = "" Then
         MsgBox ("You did not type anything and a data file will not be saved.")
      Else
         done = True
      End If
   Wend
   FileName = (DriveName & ":\\" & UserName & "ResponseFile.txt")
   MsgBox ("Your Data File will be saved to " & FileName)
End Sub
```

</td></tr>
</table>

Table A-1 *Continued*

4	'This macro creates a data file for a student. 'It is called by the Register Macro listed below. Sub CreateDataFile() FileName = (DriveName & ":\\" & UserName & " ResponseFile.txt") Set fs = CreateObject("Scripting.FileSystemObject") Set f = fs.CreateTextFile(FileName, True) f.WriteLine (UserName) f.WriteLine (Date & Space(2) & Time) f.WriteLine ("") f.Close End Sub
5	'This macro gets the learner's name and creates learner data file. 'It is called from the *Click here to Register* button on the title slide (see Figure 17-1). Sub Register() YourName GetDriveName CreateDataFile End Sub
6	'Sets correct answer for Question 1 when first checkbox clicked. Sub Question1() Ans1 = True End Sub
7	'Changes Question 1 to false if learner unclicks checkbox. Sub Q1unchecked() Ans1 = False End Sub
8	'Sets correct answer for Question 2 when first checkbox clicked. Sub Question2() Ans2 = True End Sub
9	'Changes Question 2 to false if learner unclicks checkbox. Sub Q2unchecked() Ans2 = False End Sub

(continued)

Table A-1 *Continued*

10	'Sets correct answer for Question 3 when first checkbox clicked. Sub Question3() Ans3 = True End Sub
11	'Changes Question 3 to false if learner unclicks checkbox. Sub Q3unchecked() Ans3 = False End Sub

12	'Saves the data for the check boxes.
	Sub SaveFile()
	  SlideName = ActivePresentation.SlideShowWindow.View.Slide.Name
	  Set fs = CreateObject("Scripting.FileSystemObject")
	  Set f = fs.OpenTextFile(FileName, ForAppending)
	  f.WriteLine ("")
	  f.WriteLine SlideName
	  f.WriteLine ("Answer 1 = " & Ans1)
	  f.WriteLine ("Answer 2 = " & Ans2)
	  f.WriteLine ("Answer 3 = " & Ans3)
	  f.WriteLine ("")
	  f.Close
	End Sub

13	Sub Initialize ()
	  Ans1 = false
	  Ans2 = false
	  Ans3 = false
	End Sub

14	Sub Submit()
	  MsgBox ("Answers submitted " & Ans1 & Ans2 & Ans3)
	  SaveFile
	  Initialize
	End Sub

15	Sub RecordTime ()
	  Set fs = CreateObject("Scripting.FileSystemObject")
	  Set f = fs.OpenTextFile(FileName, ForAppending)
	  f.WriteLine ("")
	  f.WriteLine (UserName & space(1) & "has finished the course.")
	  f.WriteLine (Date & space(1) & Time)

Table A-1 *Continued*

<table>
<tr><td></td><td><pre>   f.Close
   MsgBox (UserName & Space(1) & “Thanks for participating in this course.”)
End Sub</pre></td></tr>
<tr><td>16</td><td><pre>Sub Slide18Questionnaire()
   If Slide18.OptionButton1 = True Then Opinion = "strongly disagree"
   If Slide18.OptionButton2 = True Then Opinion = "disagree"
   If Slide18.OptionButton3 = True Then Opinion = "no opinion"
   If Slide18.OptionButton4 = True Then Opinion = "agree"
   If Slide18.OptionButton5 = True Then Opinion = "strongly agree"
End Sub</pre></td></tr>
<tr><td>17</td><td><pre>Sub Slide18SaveFile()
   Set fs = CreateObject("Scripting.FileSystemObject")
   Set f = fs.OpenTextFile(FileName, ForAppending)
   f.WriteLine ("")
   f.WriteLine ("Photo improved Question " & Opinion)
   f.Write Slide18.TextBox1
   f.Close
   Slide18.TextBox1 = ""
   Slide18ClearQuestionnaire
   MsgBox ("Thanks for your submission " & UserName)
End Sub</pre></td></tr>
<tr><td>18</td><td><pre>Sub Slide18ClearQuestionnaire()
   Slide18.TextBox1 = ""
   Slide18.OptionButton1 = False
   Slide18.OptionButton2 = False
   Slide18.OptionButton3 = False
   Slide18.OptionButton4 = False
   Slide18.OptionButton5 = False
End Sub</pre></td></tr>
<tr><td>19</td><td><pre>Sub Slide18Submit()
   Slide18Questionnaire
   Slide18SaveFile
   Slide18ClearQuestionnaire
End Sub</pre></td></tr>
</table>

(continued)

Table A-1 *Continued*

20	Sub AssignGroup( )
	Randomize
	MyNumber = Int((6 * Rnd) + 1)
	If MyNumber <= 3 Then
	MyGroup = 1
	Else
	MyGroup = 2
	End If
	End Sub

21	Sub GoToTreatment( )
	If MyGroup = 1 Then
	ActivePresentation.SlideShowWindow.View.GotoSlide (3)
	End If
	If MyGroup = 2 Then
	ActivePresentation.SlideShowWindow.View.GotoSlide (6)
	End If
	End Sub

22	Sub GetSlideName() MsgBox ActiveWindow.View.Slide.Name End Sub

Table A-2 Sample Data File

```
Dave
6/12/2012 1:59:14 PM

Slide23
Answer 1 = True
Answer 2 = True
Answer 3 = True

Slide24
Answer 1 = True
Answer 2 = True
Answer 3 = True
```

Table A-2 *Continued*

Slide25
Answer 1 = False
Answer 2 = False
Answer 3 = False
Slide26
Answer 1 = True
Answer 2 = True
Answer 3 = False
Slide27
Answer 1 = False
Answer 2 = False
Answer 3 = False

GLOSSARY

>3: The symbol used to indicate that demonstration and application instructional interactions should each include at least three different portrayals.

Abbreviated Text: Bullet points or short phrases displayed as text with elaboration provided by audio.

Activation Principle: Learning is promoted when learners recall existing knowledge and skill as a foundation for new skills.

Advance Organizer: Information presented prior to learning new material that can be used to help learners organize and interpret the new content. Structural frameworks are one type of advance organizers.

Alternative Representation: Information represented by a graphic in addition to a text representation of the information.

Analyze: An instructional design step to determine the needs of an organization, select goals to meet these needs, and determine the characteristics of the learner audience that might affect their ability to acquire the desired skills.

Application: *Do* instructional events with coaching and corrective or intrinsic feedback.

Application Principle: Learning is promoted when learners use their newly acquired skill to solve problems.

Ask: An instructional interaction that requests learners to recall or recognize information.

Assessment: The process for determining what learners know and are able to do; by which you determine whether your instruction is really effective, efficient, and engaging.

Assessment Instruments: An instructional design product that specifies learner activities for measuring each of the performance objectives.

Attention-Focusing Guidance: An instructional interaction that helps learners relate information to the details of a portrayal.

C: An abbreviation for a condition in a what-happens component skill.

Checklist Summary Frame: A form of structural framework that presents an outline and a set of questions to help learners see the structure in new content material.

Coaching: An instructional interaction that provides help to learners during *Do* instructional events.

Component Skill: A combination of knowledge and skill required to solve a problem or do a complex task.

Component Skills Matrix: A chart that represents the consequences for a progression of portrayals across the top and the conditions and steps that lead to the consequences down the first column. The cells in the matrix indicate which steps and conditions are required for each consequence in the progression.

Concept: Category words in any language; also called *kind-of.*

Concurrent *Tell-and-Show:* Information and portrayal appearing together to facilitate comparison.

Condition: A content element that is a property of a situation that can assume different values and which lead to a consequence.

Consequence: A content element that involves a property of a situation that changes when there is a change in the conditions.

Content Element: Individual parts of subject-matter content that are involved in instructional events.

Content Menus: Navigation buttons related to next content that requires learners to make a decision about what to preview, study, or review next.

Content-First: Instructional design that uses the actual content materials (portrayals) as the primary vehicles for design rather than descriptions of these materials (information).

Coordinate Concept: A set of categories that share the same properties but where the individual classes in the set have different values on these properties.

Corrective Feedback: Information following a response indicating the correct response and why it is the correct response.

Course Critique Checklist: Questions to evaluate the presence and adequacy of prescribed instructional events for teaching individual component skills and whole problems.

Cumulative Content Sequence: An approach that teaches steps and their subordinate skills in order until all of the subordinate skills and steps in the process have been taught.

Custom Animation: Simple programming that controls the display of objects on the screen, including appearance, disappearance, and the ability for a click on one object to cause an animation for another object.

Definition: A content element that is a list of property values that define class membership.

Demonstration: *Show* instructional events with guidance.

Demonstration Principle: Learning is promoted when learners are shown the skill to be learned.

Design: An instructional design step to create appropriate learning and assessment activities.

Designer-by-Assignment: A person selected by an organization to do instructional design based on his or her knowledge of the subject matter rather than on his or her training or skill in the process of instructional design.

Develop: An instructional design step to select or create multimedia materials to implement learning and assessment activities.

Display: A screen that contains multimedia, including text, audio, graphics, video, animation, and/or control.

Distracting Animation: Animation included to increase interest that has no other instructional function.

Distracting Multimedia: Media included for interest but that has no instructional function and that may interfere with e^3 learning.

Distributed Instructional Events: Instructional events are distributed when the demonstration of a given skill occurs in the early problem portrayals in a progression, and the application of this skill occurs in subsequent problem portrayals in the progression.

Divergent Guidance: An instructional interaction that provides a sequence of portrayals that are all examples of a component skill but which differ from each other in significant ways that reflect the range of difference that occurs in the real world.

Do: An instructional interaction that requires learners to apply information to a portrayal.

Do_{ex}: An instructional interaction requiring learners to execute a step for a how-to component skill.

Do_{id}: An instructional interaction requiring learners to identify an instance for a kind-of component skill.

e^3: Effective, efficient, engaging as a modifier for instruction.

Evaluate: An instructional design step to measure the outcomes of the instruction to determine whether the learning goals were accomplished.

Example: A content element that is a portrayal or an instance from a given category or class.

Excessive Text: An abundance of text without media that promote learning.

Faulted Condition: An inadequate or missing condition required for a desired consequence.

Final Instructional Product: A revised version of the instructional product that corrects the learning problems observed during the formative evaluation and that is ready for implementation with the target learner population.

Format: The structure and organization of a module or course.

Formative Evaluation: An instructional design product that reports learning effectiveness, efficiency, and engagement, as well as potential learning problems, observed in one-on-one, small group, and field trials with a sample of the learner population.

Functional Prototype: A mock-up of the instructional strategy that includes actual content material or placeholders for this material; that allows learner interaction with the instructional strategies; and that approximates the learner interaction available in the final product.

How-to: A component skill that requires learners to perform a sequence of steps to bring about some consequence; also called a procedure.

How-to Strategy Checklist: A set of questions to evaluate the instructional events for teaching procedures.

Implement: An instructional design step to deliver the instruction in real-world settings.

Information: A content element consisting of a description of the parts, properties, steps, conditions, or consequences for a class of objects, events, or processes.

Information-About: A component skill that requires learners to remember content associated with a specific entity, activity, or process.

Instance: A content element that is a specific member of a class; a specific procedure; or a specific process.

Instructional Analysis: An instructional design product that identifies the steps, supportive and prerequisite skills that will enable learners to accomplish the instructional goal.

Instructional Event: The combination of an instructional mode with a content element.

Instructional Event Table: A table that indicates when each condition or step should be demonstrated and when it should be applied.

Instructional Goal Statement: An instructional design product that identifies a population of learners and the skills they will acquire as a result of the instruction.

Instructional Interaction: The action component of an instructional event, including *Tell, Ask, Show,* and *Do.*

Instructional Materials: An instructional design product that includes the multimedia objects required to implement the instructional strategy and an instructional mock-up of the instructional course.

Instructional Mode: The four primary instructional interactions—*Tell, Ask, Show,* and *Do.*

Instructional Strategy: A set of instructional events that is appropriate for, and consistent with, a given type of component skill.

Instructional Strategy Template: A tool for developing a functional prototype that contains placeholders for media objects and interaction that is appropriate for a given instructional strategy.

Integration Principle: Learning is promoted when learners reflect on, discuss, and defend their newly acquired skill,

Intrinsic Feedback: An instructional interaction that shows the learner the consequence of his or her response.

Irrelevant Color: Colored text, backgrounds, and decorations included to increase interest that has no other instructional function.

Irrelevant Multimedia: Media that do not have an instructional function.

Kind-of: A component skill that requires learners to identify instances of a class of objects, events, or processes that are characterized by a set of common properties; also called a concept.

Kind-of Strategy Checklist: A set of questions to evaluate the instructional events for teaching concepts.

Knowledge: Information a learner has acquired.

Learner Characteristics: An instructional design product that identifies the entry skills, experience, attitudes, and motivation of the learner population.

Learner Control: Buttons that enable learners to select the next content to study; to control audio, video, and animation; and to control learning events.

Learning Context: An instructional design product that identifies the environment in which learners will be to receive the instruction.

Level-0 Instructional Strategy: Information-only.

Level-1 Instructional Strategy: Information plus demonstration.

Level-2 Instructional Strategy: Information plus demonstration plus application.

Level-3 Instructional Strategy: Problem-centered information, demonstration, and application.

Location Indicator: Information that enables learners to know where they are in relation to the whole module or course.

Macro: A piece of computer code designed to cause some action to occur; sometimes called a script.

Matching Guidance: An instructional interaction that pairs examples from two or more kinds of objects, events, or processes that are similar on many of their non-discriminating properties but differ only on their discriminating properties.

Media Control Bar: Start, pause, stop, and progress indicator to enable learners to control dynamic media.

Mental Model: An internal representation of some phenomena in the real world.

Metaphor and Analogy: A form of structural framework that helps learners relate the relationships in a familiar entity, activity, or process to similar relationships in the entity, activity, or process to be learned.

Mnemonic: A memory aid that helps learners remember information.

Navigation: A set of controls that enable learners to interact with learning events within a slide and to move to the next slide or a previous slide: learners' progress within and among instructional events.

Non-Example: A content element that is an instance from a category of objects, events, or symbols that is similar to the target concept and that may be easily confused with examples of the target concept.

Part-of: A component skill that requires learners to locate, name, or describe a piece of some object, event, or process.

Peer-Collaboration: A form of learner-interaction for which learners work together in small groups to solve problems.

Peer-Critique: An instructional event in which learners evaluate the problem-solving activities of fellow learners and provide constructive suggestions for improvement.

Peer-Discussion: A form of learner-interaction for which learners deliberate the proposed solution of example problems.

Peer-Interaction: An instructional activity in which learners teach one another via sharing, discussion, collaboration, or critique.

Peer-Sharing: An instructional event in which learners share with each other prior relevant experience with the subject-matter content under consideration.

Peer-Telling: An ineffective form of learner-interaction in which learners review and present information to other students.

Performance Context: An instructional design product that identifies the environment in which learners will be expected to use their newly acquired skills, including facilities, social interaction, and administrative support.

Performance Objectives: An instructional design product that identifies the performance, conditions, and criteria required for each of the steps; supportive and prerequisite skills identified in the instructional analysis.

Placeholder: A location on a slide master that can be replaced with a media object, including text, picture, chart, table, video, audio, or clip art.

Portrayal: A representation of a specific object, event, or process.

Practice: *Ask* instructional events with corrective feedback.

Presentation: *Tell* instructional events.

Principle: A relationship that is always true under appropriate conditions, regardless of the methods or models used to implement the principle.

Principle-Oriented: Instructional design that emphasizes the instructional design products (conditions) that lead to an e^3 learning consequence rather than the steps that bring about these conditions.

Problem Class: A set of problem portrayals that require the same set of component skills for their solution.

Problem-Centered: Instructional design that demonstrates and applies component skills in the context of problems to be solved rather than as a set of skills that will eventually be used to solve a problem toward the end of the instruction.

Problem-Centered Component Skill Instruction: Demonstration and application for each of the conditions and steps distributed across the portrayals in a problem progression.

Problem-Centered Instructional Strategy: An approach that teaches component skills in the context of progression of problem portrayals. Instructional events for each component skill are distributed across the problem portrayals in the progression; teach all of the component skills required for the first problem portrayal, and then revisit these component skills, adding additional component skills or elements as required, for each subsequent problem portrayal in the progression.

Problem-Centered Principle: Learning is promoted when learners acquire skill in the context of real-world problems.

Problem-Progression: A series of problem portrayals of the same type from a given content area; a straightforward version of the problem is presented first and each successive problem increases in complexity. A set of demonstrations or applications for problem prototypes arranged in a sequence from the least complex to the most complex.

Problem-Solving Event: One of a series of activities involved in solving a problem; consists of a step and the condition it brings about.

Problem-Solving-Event Analysis: The instructional design process for identifying the consequence, conditions, and steps required by the class of problems to be taught.

Process: A change in a consequence resulting from changes in the conditions that lead to the consequence. *What-happens* always involves a process.

Prototype Problem Application: A functional mock-up of the instructional events that require the learner to predict a consequence from a set of conditions, to find the faulted conditions for an unexpected consequence, or to execute the steps required to bring about the consequence.

Prototype Problem Demonstration: A functional mock-up of the instructional events that show the learner the consequence, conditions, and steps required for an instance of the problem.

Prototyping: Instructional design that develops a functional prototype as the primary design product rather than an abstract design specification.

Pseudo-Example: A content element that is an instance that fails to show the discriminating properties that determine class membership.

Q: An abbreviation for a consequence in a what-happens component skill.

Range-of-Difficulty Guidance: An instructional interaction that provides learners with a sequence of examples that vary from those that are easy to solve to those that are difficult to solve.

Reflection: An instructional event that requires learners to consider the skills they have acquired and attempt to extrapolate beyond these skills to other applications.

S: An abbreviation for a step in a how-to component skill.

Script or Macro: A piece of Visual Basic computer code designed to cause some action to occur for a PowerPoint functional prototype.

Sequence Cue: Presenting items in the same order when sequence is not the goal of the instruction.

Show: An instructional interaction that displays portrayals to the learner.

Simon-Says: A form of a *Tell-and-Show* instructional interaction in which learners interact with a representation of a real-world device. They are told a step to take; they execute the step; and, if they are correct, the device responds to their action. If they execute the wrong step, they are told that their response is wrong; the correct part of the device is highlighted; and they are directed to try the step again.

Skill: What learners are able to do with information they have acquired.

Skill Complexity Analysis: A procedure for sequencing a progression of portrayals from simple to complex determined by the number and type of conditions and steps required for each consequence in the progression.

Slide Master: A layout design that can be used for multiple slides in a presentation.

Structural Framework: An organization of previously learned information that learners can use to adapt an existing mental model or to build a new mental model for new content.

Structure-Guidance-Coaching-Reflection Cycle: Presenting a structural framework early in instruction and using this framework for guidance during demonstration, for coaching during application, and for reflection during integration.

Subject-Matter Content: What is taught; component skills from some area of interest.

Successive Disclosure: Showing text or graphic items synchronized with their audio elaboration.

Summary Critique: A chart indicating the presence or absence of prescribed instructional events in a given instructional module.

Summative Evaluation: A report that documents the learning effectiveness, efficiency, and engagement for the final instructional product.

Tell: An instructional interaction that provides information to the learner.

Topic-Centered Instructional Strategy: An approach that teaches each component skill in turn, often without reference to a final problem.

Unencountered Examples: New examples that are different from the examples used in previous instructional events.

Variable: A computer code container that can store a value and whose value can change.

What-Happens: A component skill that requires learners to predict a consequence from a set of conditions or to find faulted conditions for an unexpected consequence.

What-Happens Strategy Checklist: A set of questions to evaluate the instructional events for teaching processes.

REFERENCES

Allen, M. W. (2003). *Michael Allen's guide to e-learning.* Hoboken, NJ: John Wiley & Sons.

Anderson, D. L., Fisher, K. M., & Norman, G. J. (2002). Development and evaluation of the conceptual inventory of natural selection. *Journal of Research in Science Teaching, 39*(10), 952–978.

Andre, T. (1986). Problem solving in education. In G. D. Phye & T. Andre (Eds.), *Cognitive classroom learning* (pp. 169–204). New York: Academic Press.

Andre, T. (1997). Selected micro-instructional methods to facilitate knowledge construction: Implications for instructional design. In R. D. Tennyson, F. Schott, N. Seel, & S. Dijkstra (Eds.), *Instructional design: International perspective: Theory, research, and models* (Vol. 1) (pp. 243–267). Mahwah, NJ: Lawrence Erlbaum Associates.

Barclay, M. W., Gur, B., & Wu, C. (2004). The impact of media on the family: Assessing the availability and quality of instruction on the World Wide Web for enhancing marriage relationships. Paper presented at the World Congress of the Family: Asia Pacific Dialogue, Kuala, Malaysia.

Beielaczyc, K., & Collins, A. (1999). Learning communities in classrooms: A reconceptualization of educational practice. In C. M. Reigeluth (Ed.), *Instructional-design theories and models: A new paradigm of instructional theory* (Vol. 2) (pp. 269–291). Mahwah, NJ: Lawrence Erlbaum Associates.

Boud, D., Keogh, R., & Walker, D. (1985). *Reflection: Turning experience into learning.* London: Kogan.

Bunderson, C. V. (2006). Developing a domain theory. In M. L. Garner, G. Englehard Jr., W. P. Fisher Jr., & M. Wilson (Eds.), *Advances in Rasch Measurement* (vol. 1). Greenwich, CT: JAI Press.

Burton, R. R., & Brown, J. S. (1979). An investigation of computer coaching for informal learning activities. *International Journal of Man-Machine Studies, 11*, 5–24.

Clark, R. C. (2003). *Building expertise: Cognitive methods for training and performance improvement* (2nd ed.). Washington, DC: International Society for Performance Improvement.

Clark, R. C. (2008a). *Building expertise: Cognitive methods for training and performance improvement* (3rd ed.). San Francisco: Pfeiffer.

Clark, R. C. (2008b). *Developing technical training: A structured approach for developing classroom and computer-based instructional materials* (3rd ed.). San Francisco: Pfeiffer.

Clark, R. C., & Lyons, C. (2004). *Graphics for learning.* San Francisco: Pfeiffer.

Clark, R. C., & Mayer, R. E. (2003). *e-Learning and the science of instruction: Proven guidelines for consumers and designers of multimedia learning.* San Francisco: Pfeiffer.

Clark, R. C., & Mayer, R. E. (2008). *e-Learning and the science of instruction* (2nd ed.). San Francisco: Pfeiffer.

Clark, R. E. (2003). What works in distance learning: Instructional strategies. In H. F. O'Neil (Ed.), *What works in distance learning* (pp. 13–31). Los Angeles: Center for the Study of Evaluation.

Clark, R. E., & Blake, S. B. (1997). Designing training for novel problem-solving transfer. In R. D. Tennyson, F. Schott, N. Seel, & S. Dijkstra (Eds.), *Instructional design: International perspective: Theory, research, and models* (Vol. 1) (pp. 183–214). Mahwah, NJ: Lawrence Erlbaum Associates.

Collins, A., Brown, J. S., & Holum, A. (1991). Cognitive apprenticeship: Making thinking visible. *American Educator, 15*(3), 6–11.

Collins, A., Brown, J. S., & Newman, S. E. (1989). Cognitive apprenticeship: Teaching the crafts of reading, writing, and mathematics. In L. B. Resnick (Ed.), *Knowing, learning and instruction: Essays in honor of Robert Glaser* (pp. 453–494). Hillsdale, NJ: Lawrence Erlbaum Associates.

Corno, L., & Randi, J. (1999). A design theory for classroom instruction in self-regulated learning? In C. M. Reigeluth (Ed.), *Instructional-design theories and models: A new paradigm of instructional theory* (Vol. 2) (pp. 293–318). Mahwah, NJ: Lawrence Erlbaum Associates.

Crouch, C. H., & Mazur, E. (2001). Peer instruction: Ten years of experience and results. *American Journal of Physics, 9,* 970–977.

Darabi, A. (2002). Teaching program evaluation: Using a systems approach. *American Journal of Evaluation, 23*(2), 219.

Dembo, M., & Young, L. G. (2003). What works in distance education: Learning strategies. In H. F. O'Neil (Ed.), *What works in distance education.* Los Angeles: Center for the Study of Evaluation.

Dick, W., Carey, L., & Carey, J. O. (2009). *The systematic design of instruction* (7th ed.). Upper Saddle River, NJ: Pearson.

Dijkstra, S., & van Merriënboer, J. J. G. (1997). Plans, procedures, and theories to solve instructional design problems. In S. Dijkstra, N. Seel, F. Schott, & R. D. Tennyson (Eds.), *Instructional design international perspective: Solving instructional design problems* (Vol. 2) (pp. 23–43). Mahwah, NJ: Lawrence Erlbaum Associates.

Ebert-May, D., Brewer, C., & Allred, S. (1997). Innovation in large lectures: Teaching for active learning. *Bioscience, 47*(9), 601–607.

Foshay, W. R. R., Silber, K. H., & Stelnicki, M. B. (2003). *Writing training materials that work: How to train anyone to do anything.* San Francisco: Pfeiffer. These authors also elaborate teaching facts, concepts, principles, and problem solving.

Francom, G., Bybee, D., Wolfersberger, M., Mendenhall, A., & Merrill, M. D. (2009). A task-centered approach to freshman-level general biology. *Bioscene, Journal of College Biology Teaching, 35*(1), 66–73.

Francom, G., Wolfersberger, M., & Merrill, M. D. (2009). Biology 100: A task-centered, peer-interactive redesign. *TechTrends, 53*(3), 35–100.

Frick, T., Chadha, R., Watson, C., & Wang, Y. (2010). Theory-based evaluation of instruction: Implications for improving student learning achievement in postsecondary education. In M. Orey, S. A. Jones, & R. M. Branch (Eds.), *Educational media and technology yearbook* (Vol. 35) (pp. 57–78). New York: Springer.

Frick, T. W., Chadha, R., Watson, C., Wang, Y., & Green, P. (2009). College student perceptions of teaching and learning quality. *Educational Technology Research and Development, 57,* 705–720.

Frick, T. W., Chadha, R., Watson, C., & Zlatkovska. E. (2010). Improving course evaluations to improve instruction and complex learning in higher education. *Educational Technology Research and Development, 58,* 115–136.

Gagné, R. M. (1965). *The conditions of learning.* New York: Holt, Rinehart and Winston.

Gagné, R. M. (1985). *The conditions of learning and theory of instruction* (4th ed.). New York: Holt, Rinehart and Winston.

Gagné, R. M., Wager, W. W., Golas, K., & Keller, J. M. (2005). *Principles of instructional design* (5th ed.). Belmont, CA: Thompson Wadsworth.

Gardner, H. (1999). Multiple approaches to understanding. In C. M. Reigeluth (Ed.), *Instructional-design theories and models: A new paradigm of instructional theory* (Vol. 2) (pp. 69–89). Mahwah, NJ: Lawrence Erlbaum Associates.

Gardner, J. (in press). Investigating theoretical support for first principles of instruction: A systematic review. *Midwest Journal of Educational Communication and Technology.*

Gentner, D., & Namy, L. (1999). Comparison in the development of categories. *Cognitive Development, 14,* 487–513.

Gibbons, A. S., Bunderson, C. V., Olsen, J. B., & Robertson, J. (1995). Work models: Still beyond instructional objectives. *Machine-Mediated Learning, 5*(3&4), 221–236.

Gibbons, A. S., McConkie, M., Seo, K. K., & Wiley, D. (2009). Simulation approach to instruction. In C. M. Reigeluth (Ed.), *Instructional-design theories and models* (Vol. 3) (pp. 167–193). New York: Routledge.

Gibson, J. T. (2009). Discussion approach to construction. In C. M. Reigeluth (Ed.), *Instructional-design theories and models* (Vol. 3) (pp. 99–116). New York: Routledge.

Gordon, J., & Zemke, R. (2000). The attack on ISD. *Training, 37,* 43–53.

Hake, R. (1998). Interactive-engagement vs. traditional methods: A six-thousand student survey of mechanics test data for introductory physics courses. *American Journal of Physics, 66,* 64–74.

Hannafin, M., Land, S., & Oliver, K. (1999). Open learning environments: Foundations, methods, and models. In C. M. Reigeluth (Ed.), *Instructional-design theories and models: A new paradigm of instructional theory* (Vol. 2) (pp. 115–140). Mahwah, NJ: Lawrence Erlbaum Associates.

Hilgenheger, N. (1993). Johann Friedrich Herbart. Prospects. *The Quarterly Review of Comparative Education, 23*(3&4), 649–664.

Huitt, W. G., Monetti, D., & Hummel, J. H. (2009). Direct approach to instruction. In C. M. Reigeluth (Ed.), *Instructional-design theories and models* (Vol. 3) (pp. 73–97). New York: Routledge.

Jonassen, D. (1999). Designing constructivist learning environments. In C. M. Reigeluth (Ed.), *Instructional-design theories and models: A new paradigm of instructional theory* (Vol. 2) (pp. 215–239). Mahwah, NJ: Lawrence Erlbaum Associates.

Keller, J. M. (1993). Instructional materials motivational survey. Unpublished manuscript.

Keogh, R., & Walker, D. (Eds.). *Reflection: Turning experience into learning* (pp. 18–40). London: Kogan Page.

King, A. (1992). Facilitating elaborative learning through guided student-generated questioning. *Educational Psychologist, 27,* 111–126.

King, A., Staffieri, A., & Douglas, A. (1998). Mutual peer tutoring: Effects of structuring tutorial interaction to scaffold peer learning. *Journal of Educational Psychology,* pp. 134–152.

Kirschner, P. A., Sweller, J., & Clark, R. E. (2006). Why minimal guidance during instruction does not work: An analysis of the failure of constructivist, discovery, problem-based, experiential, and inquiry-based teaching. *Educational Psychologist, 41*(2), 75–86.

Kovalik, S. J., & McGeehan, J. R. (1999). Integrated thematic instruction: From brain research to application. In C. M. Reigeluth (Ed.), *Instructional-design theories and models: A new paradigm of instructional theory* (Vol. 2) (pp. 371–396). Mahwah, NJ: Lawrence Erlbaum Associates.

Kulhavy, R. W. (1977). Feedback in written instruction. *Review of Educational Research, 47,* 211–232.

Kulhavy, R. W., & Stock, W. A. (1989). Feedback in written instruction: The place of response certitude. *Educational Psychology Review, 1,* 279–308.

Landa, L. N. (1999). Landamatics instructional design theory and methodology for teaching general methods of thinking. In C. M. Reigeluth (Ed.), *Instructional-design theories and models: A new paradigm of instructional theory* (Vol. 2) (pp. 341–369). Mahwah, NJ: Lawrence Erlbaum Associates.

Larson, S., Johnson, E., Rutherford, F., & Bartlo, J. (2009) A local instructional theory for the guided reinvention of the quotient group concept. www.rume.org/crume2009/Larson_LONG.pdf.

Laurillard, D. (1993). *Rethinking university teaching: A framework for the effective use of educational technology.* New York: Routledge.

Lee, M., & Paulus, T. (2001). An instructional design theory for interactions in web-based learning environments. Paper presented at the National Convention of the Association for Educational Communications and Technology, Atlanta, Georgia.

Lindsey, L., & Berger, N. (2009). Experiential approach to instruction. In C. M. Reigeluth (Ed.), *Instructional-design theories and models* (Vol. 3) (pp. 117–142). New York: Routledge.

Mager, R. F. (1997). *Preparing instructional objectives: A critical tool in the development of effective instruction* (3rd ed.). Atlanta: The Center for Effective Performance, Inc.

Marcovitz, D. M. (2004). *Powerful PowerPoint for educators.* Westport, CT: Libraries Unlimited.

Margaryan, A. (2006). Work-based learning: A blend of pedagogy and technology. Unpublished dissertation, University of Twente. Twente: The Netherlands.

Margaryan, A., & Collis, B. (2005). Design criteria for work-based learning: Merrill's first principles of instruction expanded. *British Journal of Educational Technology, 36*(5), 725–738.

Marzano, R. J. (1998). *A theory-based meta-analysis of research on instruction* (ERIC Document Reproduction Service No. ED 427 087). Aurora, CO: Midcontinent Research Laboratory for Education and Learning.

Marzano, R. J., Pickering, D. J., & Pollock, J. E. (2001). *Classroom instruction that works: Research-based strategies for increasing student achievement.* Alexandria, VA: Association for Supervision and Curriculum Development.

Mayer, R. E. (1975). Different problem-solving competencies established in learning computer programming with and without meaningful models. *Journal of Educational Psychology, 67,* 725.

Mayer, R. E. (1992a). *Thinking, problem solving, cognition* (2nd ed.). New York: Freeman.

Mayer, R. E. (1992b). Illustrations that instruct. In R. Glaser (Ed.), *Advances in instructional psychology* (Vol. 4) (pp. 253–284). Mahwah, NJ: Lawrence Erlbaum Associates.

Mayer, R. E. (1998). Cognitive, metacognitive, and motivational aspects of problem solving. *Instructional Science, 26,* 49–63.

Mayer, R. E. (2001). *Multimedia learning.* London: Cambridge University Press.

Mayer, R. E. (2003a). *Learning and instruction.* Upper Saddle River, NJ: Pearson Education.

Mayer, R. E. (2003b). What works in distance learning: Multimedia. In H. F. O'Neil (Ed.), *What works in distance learning* (pp. 9–42). Los Angeles: Center for the Study of Evaluation.

Mayer, R. E. (2011). *Applying the science of learning.* Upper Saddle River, NJ: Pearson.

Mayer, R. H. (1999). Designing instruction for constructivist learning. In C. M. Reigeluth (Ed.), *Instructional-design theories and models: A new paradigm of instructional theory* (Vol. 2) (pp. 141–159). Mahwah, NJ: Lawrence Erlbaum Associates.

Mazur, E. (1997). *Peer instruction: A user's manual.* Upper Saddle River, NJ: Prentice Hall.

McCarthy, B. (1996). *About learning.* Barrington, IL: Excell Inc.

Mendenhall, A., Buhanan, C. W., Suhaka, M., Mills, G., Gibson, G. V., & Merrill, M. D. (2006). A task-centered approach to entrepreneurship. *TechTrends, 50*(4), 84–89.

Merrill, M. D. (1980a). Learner control in computer-based learning. *Computers and Education, 4,* 77–95.

Merrill, M. D. (1980b). Can the adjective instructional modify the noun science? *Educational Technology, 20*(2), 37–44.

Merrill, M. D. (1983). Component display theory. In C. M. Reigeluth (Ed.), *Instructional-design theories and models: An overview of their current status* (pp. 279–333). Mahwah, NJ: Lawrence Erlbaum Associates.

Merrill, M. D. (1984). What is learner control? In R. Bass & C. R. Dills (Eds.), *Instructional development: The state of the art II* (pp. 221–242). Dubuque, IA: Kendall/Hunt.

Merrill, M. D. (1987a). A lesson based on component display theory. In C. M. Reigeluth (Ed.), *Instructional-design theories in action* (pp. 201–244). Mahwah, NJ: Lawrence Erlbaum Associates.

Merrill, M. D. (1987b). The new component display theory: Instructional design for courseware authoring. *Instructional Science, 16,* 19–34.

Merrill, M. D. (1994). *Instructional design theory.* Englewood Cliffs, NJ: Educational Technology Publications.

Merrill, M. D. (1997a, Nov/Dec). Instructional strategies that teach. *CBT Solutions,* pp. 1–11.

Merrill, M. D. (1997b). Learning-oriented instructional development tools. *Performance Improvement, 36*(3), 5–7.

Merrill, M. D. (2001). A knowledge object and mental model approach to a physics lesson. *Educational Technology, 41*(1), 36–47.

Merrill, M. D. (2002a). First principles of instruction. *Educational Technology Research and Development, 50*(3), 43–59.

Merrill, M. D. (2002b). A Pebble-in-the-Pond model for instructional design. *Performance Improvement, 41*(7), 39–44.

Merrill, M. D. (2006). Levels of instructional strategy. *Educational Technology, 46*(4), 5–10.

Merrill, M. D. (2007a). First principles of instruction: A synthesis. In R. A. Reiser & J. V. Dempsey (Eds.), *Trends and issues in instructional design and technology* (2nd ed.) (Vol. 2) (pp. 62–71). Upper Saddle River, NJ: Merrill/Prentice Hall.

Merrill, M. D. (2007b). The future of instructional design. In R. A. Reiser & J. V. Dempsey (Eds.), *Trends and issues in instructional design and technology* (2nd ed.) (Vol. 2) (pp. 335–351). Upper Saddle River, NJ: Merrill/Prentice Hall.

Merrill, M. D. (2007c). A task-centered instructional strategy. *Journal of Research on Technology in Education, 40*(1), 33–50.

Merrill, M. D. (2008). Reflections on a four decade search for effective, efficient and engaging instruction. In M. W. Allen (Ed.), *Michael Allen's 2008 e-learning annual* (pp. 141–167). San Francisco: Pfeiffer.

Merrill, M. D. (2009a). Finding e^3 (effective, efficient, and engaging) instruction. *Educational Technology, 49*(3), 15–26.

Merrill, M. D. (2009b). First principles of instruction. In C. M. Reigeluth & A. Carr (Eds.), *Instructional-design theories and models: Building a common knowledge base* (Vol. 3). New York: Routledge/Taylor and Francis Group.

Merrill, M. D., Drake, L., Lacy, M. J., & Pratt, J. (1996). Reclaiming instructional design. *Educational Technology, 36*(5), 5–7.

Merrill, M. D., & Gilbert, C. G. (2008). Effective peer interaction in a problem-centered instructional strategy. *Distance Education, 29*(2), 199–207.

Merrill, M. D., & Tennyson, R. D. (1977). *Teaching concepts: An instructional design guide.* Englewood Cliffs, NJ: Educational Technology Publications.

Merrill, M. D., Tennyson, R. D., & Posey, L. O. (1992). *Teaching concepts: An instructional design guide* (2nd ed.). Englewood Cliffs, NJ: Educational Technology Publications.

Morrison, G. R., Ross, S. M., & Kemp, J. E. (2006). *Designing effective instruction* (5th ed.). Hoboken, NJ: John Wiley & Sons.

Nelson, L. M. (1999). Collaborative problem solving. In C. M. Reigeluth (Ed.), *Instructional-design theories and models: A new paradigm of instructional theory* (Vol. 2) (pp. 241–267). Mahwah, NJ: Lawrence Erlbaum Associates.

Perkins, D. N., & Unger, C. (1999). Teaching and learning for understanding. In C. M. Reigeluth (Ed.), *Instructional-design theories and models: A new paradigm of instructional theory* (Vol. 2) (pp. 91–114). Mahwah, NJ: Lawrence Erlbaum Associates.

Pogrow, S. (1999). Systematically using powerful learning environments to accelerate learning in disadvantaged students in grades 4–8. In C. M. Reigeluth (Ed.), *Instructional-design theories and models: A new paradigm of instructional theory* (Vol. 2) (pp. 319–340). Mahwah, NJ: Lawrence Erlbaum Associates.

Reigeluth, C. M. (Ed.). (1983). *Instructional-design theories and models: An overview of their current status.* Mahwah, NJ: Lawrence Erlbaum Associates.

Reigeluth, C. M. (1999a). The elaboration theory: Guidance for scope and sequence decisions. In C. M. Reigeluth (Ed.), *Instructional-design theories and models: A new paradigm of instructional theory* (Vol. 2) (pp. 425–453). Mahwah, NJ: Lawrence Erlbaum Associates.

Reigeluth, C. M. (Ed.). (1999b). *Instructional-design theories and models: A new paradigm of instructional theory* (Vol. 2). Mahwah, NJ: Lawrence Erlbaum Associates.

Reigeluth, C. M., & Carr-Chellman, A. (2009). *Instructional-design theories and models, volume III: Building a common knowledge base.* Florence, KY: Routledge/Taylor & Francis Group.

Rosenberg-Kima, R. (2011). Effects of task-centered vs. topic-centered instructional strategy approaches on problem solving—Learning to program in Flash. Dissertation, Department of Educational Psychology and Learning Systems, Florida State University.

Rosenshine, B. (1997). Advances in research on instruction. In E. J. Lloyd, E. J. Kameanui, & D. Chard (Eds.), *Issues in educating students with disabilities* (pp. 197–221). Mahwah, NJ: Lawrence Erlbaum Associates.

Savery, J. R. (2009). Problem-based approach to instruction. In C. M. Reigeluth (Ed.), *Instructional-design theories and models* (Vol. 3) (pp. 143–165). New York: Routledge.

Savery, J. R., & Duffy, T. (1995). Problem-based learning: An instructional model and its constructivist framework. In B. G. Wilson (Ed.), *Designing constructivist learning environments* (pp. 135–148). Englewood Cliffs, NJ: Educational Technology Publications.

Schank, R. C., Berman, T. R., & Macpherson, K. A. (1999). Learning by doing. In C. M. Reigeluth (Ed.), *Instructional-design theories and models: A new paradigm of instructional theory* (Vol. 2) (pp. 161–181). Mahwah, NJ: Lawrence Erlbaum Associates.

Schwartz, D., Lin, X., Brophy, S., & Bransford, J. D. (1999). Toward the development of flexibly adaptive instructional designs. In C. M. Reigeluth (Ed.), *Instructional-design theories and models: A new paradigm of instructional theory* (Vol. 2) (pp. 183–213). Mahwah, NJ: Lawrence Erlbaum Associates.

Slavin, R. E. (1995). *Cooperative learning*. Boston: Allyn & Bacon.

Snyder, M. M. (2009). Instructional-design theory to guide the creation of online learning communities for adults. *TechTrends: Linking Research and Practice to Improve Learning, 53*(1), 48–56.

Spiro, R. J., Feltovich, P. J., Jacobson, M. J., & Coulson, R. L. (1992). Cognitive flexibility, constructivism, and hypertext: Random access instruction for advanced knowledge acquisition in ill-structured domains. In T. M. Duffy & D. H. Jonassen (Eds.), *Constructivism and the technology of instruction: A conversation*. Mahwah, NJ: Lawrence Erlbaum Associates.

Spiro, R. J., & Jehng, J. C. (1990). Cognitive flexibility and hypertext: Theory and technology for the nonlinear and multidimensional traversal of complex subject matter. In D. Nix & R. Spiro (Eds.), *Cognition, education, and multimedia* (pp. 163–205). Mahwah, NJ: Lawrence Erlbaum Associates.

Tennyson, R. D., & Cocchierella, M. J. (1986). An empirically based instructional design theory for teaching concepts. *Review of Educational Research, 56*, 40–72.

Tennyson, R. D., & Park, O. (1980). The teaching of concepts: A review of instructional design literature. *Review of Educational Research, 50*, 55–70.

Thompson Learning. (2002). Thompson job impact study: The next generation of learning. www.delmarlearning.com/resources/job_impact_study_whitepaper.pdf.

van der Meij, H., & Carroll, J. M. (1998). Principles and heuristics for designing minimalist instruction. In J. M. Carroll (Ed.), *Minimalism beyond the Nurnberg funnel* (pp. 19–53). Cambridge, MA: MIT Press.

van Merriënboer, J. J. G. (1997). *Training complex cognitive skills*. Englewood Cliffs, NJ: Educational Technology Publications.

van Merriënboer, J. J. G., & Kirschner, P. A. (2007). *Ten steps to complex learning*. Mahwah, NJ: Lawrence Erlbaum Associates.

Vincenti, W. G. (1990). *What engineers know and how they know it: Analytical studies from aeronautical history*. Baltimore: The Johns Hopkins University Press.

Wilson, E. O. (1998). *Consilience: The unity of knowledge*. New York: Alfred A. Knopf.

Wiske, M. S., & Beatty, B. J. (2009). Fostering understanding outcomes. In C. M. Reigeluth (Ed.), *Instructional-design theories and models* (Vol. 3) (pp. 225–247). New York: Routledge.

ABOUT THE AUTHOR

M. David Merrill is professor emeritus at Utah State University. Dr. Merrill has been engaged in the study of effective, efficient, and engaging instruction for more than fifty years since he started the Ph.D. program at the University of Illinois in 1961.

He was honored to receive the AECT Distinguished Service Award 2001 for advancing the field of instructional technology through scholarship, teaching, and leadership. He received a lifetime achievement award from the Utah State University College of Education in 2010; and he was recognized as an Honored Alumni for the College of Education at BYU in 2011.

Since receiving his Ph.D. from the University of Illinois in 1964, he has served on the faculty of George Peabody College, Brigham Young University–Provo, Stanford University, the University of Southern California, Utah State University, Florida State University, and BYU–Hawaii (as a missionary volunteer). He served a service mission at BYU–Hawaii, where he helped faculty put courses online. Since retiring, he has taught online courses at Florida State University and BYU–Hawaii. He is currently teaching online courses at the University of Hawaii and Utah State University. He is internationally recognized as a major contributor to the field of instructional technology, has published many books and articles in the field, and has lectured internationally. Among his principle contributions: TICCIT Authoring System, Component Display Theory and Elaboration Theory, Instructional Transaction Theory, automated instructional design and ID based on Knowledge Objects, and First Principles of Instruction.

He and his wife Kate have a combined family of nine children, 37 + 8 (by marriage) grandchildren with more marriages expected and six great-grandchildren plus more on the way, which he claims as his most important accomplishment. He is the owner of the miniature Ascape Tennsion & Sulphur Gulch Railroad.

He can be contacted at professordavemerrill@gmail.com. His website is http://mdavidmerrill.com. His model railroad can be viewed at http://davesatsgrr.blogspot.com.

INDEX

f represents figure; t represents table.

A

Abbreviated text: audio and, 194, 200; definition of, 193; example of, 194f
Abstract ideas, using examples to show, 11
Acronyms: definition of, 174; example of, 174–175f
Activation phase, 409
Activation principle: definition of, 20, 398; description of, 21, 27–28, 44; implementation of, 172; peer-sharing and, 185, 186; research related to, 397–398; sample lessons demonstrating, 31–34; structural framework in, 188; structuring new knowledge and, 28; theories related to, 411, 413
Advance organizers: definition of, 173; research related to, 398–399; structural frameworks and, 346–347
After-class instructional events, 168
Allen, M. W., 270, 368
Allred, S., 397
Alternative representations: for kind-of instructional strategy, 101; research related to, 401
Analogies: definition of, 173; description of, 175–176; example of, 177–180; identification of structural frameworks and, 341
Analysis, design, development, implementation, and evaluation (ADDIE) model, 250
Andre, T., 27, 397, 398, 399, 400, 401, 402, 404, 405, 409–410
Animations: description of, 192; effective use of, 199; example of, 199f; finalizing, 355; to focus attention, 200–201; in functional prototypes, 276–280; media control of, 206; misuse of, in multimedia, 213; in multimedia coaching and guidance, 200; research related to, 401, 402; in slide masters, 281–282, 289, 290, 293; in what-happens demonstration, 114
Anxiety, 438–439
Appeal, of courses, 362
Appearance, of slides, 362
Application principle: adjustment of mental models and, 25; challenges of, 25; in combination with coaching, 26; in course critique checklists, 220; definition of, 11–12, 20, 24; description of, 21, 44, 312, 337; importance of, 24; versus questions, 11–12; theories related to, 411, 412, 413
Applications: definition of, 88; design of, for conditions and steps, 326–334; elements of, 70, 77–86; in functional prototypes, 277, 279f; for how-to instructional strategy, 106, 107; for kind-of instructional strategy, 96; matching guidance in, 80; for part-of instructional strategy, 93, 94–95; in Pebble-in-the-Pond model, 255, 257, 258–259f; in problem-centered instructional strategies, 152; research related to, 403–405; structural framework in, 173; summary of, 89t; versus traditional instructional objectives, 336; use of instructional event tables to design, 326–334; in what-happens instructional strategy, 112. *See also* Do interactions
Approaching the core phase, 410
Arrow symbol, 200
Artistic inclinations, 266
Ask interactions: definition of, 70; examples of, 154–155, 156t. *See also* Practice
Assessments: data collection for, 371, 372, 373; definition of, 369, 370; description of, 370; methods of, 30; prototypes for, 372–374;

purpose of, 370, 379; recording data for, 374–375; requirements of, 30; timing of, 370–372
Associative memory, 28
Attention-focusing guidance: definition of, 70; description of, 78; examples of, 78–79f; in kind-of demonstrations, 98, 101; multimedia for, 200; in presentations, 89
Attitude data, 375
Audio: abbreviated text and, 194, 200; common mistakes involving, 15, 24; in complex animations, 279; course format and, 203; for defining and ordering portrayals, 197–198; definition of, 192; evaluating, 378–379; example of, 194f; finalizing, 355; graphics and, 194, 195f; ineffective use of, 198; media control of, 206; misuse of, 212; in multimedia coaching and guidance, 200; in multimedia example, 216; research related to, 402, 403; in what-happens lesson directions, 114f, 117
Australian First Aid course, 30–43
Authoring tools, 275

B

Background color, 213
Barclay, M. W., 434
Bartlo, J., 415t
Beatty, B. J., 415t
Beielaczyc, K., 414t
Berger, N., 415t
Berman, T. R., 396, 403, 413–414, 415t
Biochemistry courses, 311–312
Biology courses, 165–168, 187, 434
Blake, S. B., 396, 398, 401, 403
Boldface, 203
Bookmarks, 289, 290, 292–293
Boring instruction, 8, 16
Boud, D., 406
Branching slides, 293
Bransford, J. D., 401, 403, 405, 407, 415t
Brewer, C., 397
Brigham Young University–Hawaii, 153–168, 308–309, 310, 311, 434
Brophy, S., 401, 403, 405, 407, 415t
Brown, J. S., 396, 397, 398, 404
Buhanan, C. W., 153, 169, 433
Bunderson, C. V., 30, 397
Burton, R. R., 404
Buttons: course format and, 201; illustration of, 204f; in multimedia example, 216; for navigation, 203–204
Bybee, D., 165, 169

C

Callouts, 200
Car sales simulation, 293–294
Carey, J. O., 250, 380
Carey, L., 250, 380
Carpet Cleaning Business course, 157, 159f
Carr-Chellman, A., 20
Carroll, J. M., 405
Case-based learning, 26
Category words, 51
CD-ROM courses, 42
Cell Phone Business course, 160–161f
Chadha, R., 430, 432
Challenges, 408
Checklist summary frames, 173
Checklists: for application and demonstration design, 327t; for critiquing component skills, 220–230, 242–244; description of, 180, 220; example of, 180–181, 181–183f; finalizing courses and, 359–360, 361; for one-on-one trials, 377; parts of, 180; for Pebble-in-the-Pond design, 381–391; for whole problems, 237–242. *See also specific checklists*
Choirs, instruction of, 310–311
Chunking information, 92–93
Clark, R. C., 6, 21, 120, 194, 212, 218, 351, 396, 397, 399, 400, 402, 403, 404, 405, 406
Clark, R. E., 185, 396, 398, 401, 403
Class of problems. *See* Problem classes
Classifying information, 96–98
Coaching: in combination with application, 26; common mistakes involving, 8; definition of, 25, 70, 344; description of, 83; design of, 262, 265f; for Do interactions, 83; examples of, 42, 83–84f; finalizing courses and, 360–361; hints as, 25; importance of, 25–26; for kind-of instructional strategy, 96, 101; multimedia for

elaboration in, 199–201; in Pebble-in-the-Pond model, 262, 265f; purpose of, 83; research supporting, 404; structural framework basis of, 344–345f; summary critique for, 226, 230; theories related to, 412; use of structural framework and, 173; in what-happens applications, 112, 114–115

Cocchierella, M. J., 404

Coconut leaf weaving course, 226–228

Collaboration. *See* Peer-collaboration

Collins, A., 396, 397, 398, 404, 414t

Collis, B., 433

Color: finalizing, 362; to focus attention, 200. *See also* Irrelevant color

Communication issues, 48

Complexity: components of, 317; increases in, 316

Component skill complexity analysis: definition of, 317; procedure for, 317–319

Component skills: application and demonstration design for, 326–334; checklist for, 334–336; consistency of, 53; definition of, 47, 49, 325; designing instruction for, 259–262, 271; finalizing, 355; identification of, 302–305; instruction in, versus traditional instructional design, 336; navigation of, 204–205; in Pebble-in-the-Pond model, 252, 259–262, 269, 336–337; in problem progressions, 317–319; problem solving and, 122; requirements of, 80; summary critiques of, 220–230, 242–244; in teaching tools, 309; types of, 49t; in whole problem analysis, 238–239, 241. *See also specific skills*

Component skills matrix: definition of, 315; description of, 317–319

Concepts, 49, 51

Conceptual models, 398, 399

Concurrent tell-and-show: course format and, 203; definition of, 192; in multimedia example, 216

Conditions: definition of, 53, 63, 123; designing demonstrations and applications for, 326–334; example of, 55–56, 64, 65; identification of structural framework and, 341–342; in problem-solving event analysis, 302–304; in problem-solving events, 123, 125, 126, 127f; in prototype problem applications, 307–308

Consequences: definition of, 53, 62; example of, 55–56, 64–65f; in how-to component skill, 62; in problems, 122, 123f, 126, 127f; in prototype problem applications, 307–308; in prototype problem demonstrations, 305; in what-happens component skill, 63–64, 65

Consistency: in application, 25; of component skills, 53; in demonstrations, 23; importance of, 25; research related to, 399–401, 403–404

Constructivist Learning Environment theory, 411–412

Content. *See* Subject-matter content

Content elements: definition of, 47, 53; for how-to component skill, 62–63; for information-about component skill, 56; for kind-of component skill, 57–62; for part-of component skill, 57; in problem-solving event analysis, 302–303; for problem-solving events, 122–123, 126–127; for what-happens component skill, 63–66; for whole problems, 126, 128f, 237

Content menus: definition of, 192; for navigation, 204–205

Content organization: format of, 201, 202f; in multimedia example, 216

Content sequence, 269

Content-driven navigation, 365–366

Content-first design: definition of, 249, 250; in Pebble-in-the-Pond model, 268–269

Contents page, 365–366

Control. *See* Learner control

Control bar, 204, 206

Conventional buttons: definition of, 203; for navigation, 203–204

Cooking classes, 309–310

Cooperative groups, 406

Coordinate concepts: demonstration of, 101–106; description of, 59; unencountered examples and, 60

Copyright and Fair Use course, 194f, 195f

Corno, L., 414t

Corrective feedback: definition of, 20, 25, 70; description of, 84; examples of, 39, 42, 83–84f; in kind-of demonstrations, 98, 206–207; for kind-of instructional strategy, 96; media control and, 206–207; research supporting, 405

Coulson, R. L., 401
Course critique checklist: for component skills, 335–336; definition of, 219; description of, 220–221; types of, 220–230
Cover stories, 413
Critiquing instructional strategies: component skill checklist for, 220–230; description of, 220; for whole problems, 230–242
Crouch, C. H., 184, 185
Cues, 397
Cumulative content sequences, 269
Custom animation: definition of, 276–277; in functional prototypes, 276–279

D

Darabi, A., 398
Data collection: for assessments, 371, 372, 373; in Pebble-in-the-Pond model, 267
Decontextualized instruction, 26
Definition content element: description of, 57; example of, 57, 58f
Definitions, 95
Dembo, M., 401
Demonstration principle: case study examples of, 34–36; in course critique checklists, 220; definition of, 20; description of, 21, 23–24, 44, 88, 312, 337; enhanced learning and, 95; motivation and, 43; peer-collaboration and, 186; peer-discussion and, 185; theories related to, 412–413, 414
Demonstrations: characteristics of, 23–24, 77–83; definition of, 23, 62, 88; design of, for conditions and steps, 326–334; effective graphic use in, 198; in functional prototypes, 277, 278f; for how-to instructional strategy, 106–107; for kind-of instructional strategy, 95–106; for part-of instructional strategy, 92–93; in Pebble-in-the-Pond model, 255, 257, 259–262; peer-discussion and, 185; in problem-centered instructional strategy, 151f, 152; in problem-solving events, 123–125; research related to, 399–401; sample courses of, 30–43; structural framework in, 173, 342–343f; summary of, 89t; versus traditional instructional objectives, 336; use of instructional event tables to design, 326–334; in what-happens instructional strategy, 111; for whole problems, 130, 134, 135–136f. *See also* Show interactions
Design specification: purpose of, 274; weaknesses of, 274–275
Designer-by-assignment, 437, 441, 447, 448
Dick, W., 250, 380
Difficulty, range of, 106
Dijkstra, S., 399
Directions: content menus and, 204; finalizing, 366
Discrimination: range-of-difficulty guidance for, 80–81; skills required for, 79
Discussion boards, 348
Distracting animation: definition of, 192; mistakes related to, 213
Distracting multimedia: definition of, 192; description of, 212
Distributed instructional events: definition of, 150; example of, 156t; in problem progressions, 152–153
Divergent guidance: definition of, 70; description of, 80; examples of, 81f
Do button, 210, 211
Do interactions: coaching for, 83; in course critique checklists, 220–221; definition of, 70; description of, 75–77; distribution of, 152–153; examples of, 76f, 77f, 154–155, 156t, 157, 168; in how-to presentations, 107; multiple versus single use of, 82–83; for problem-solving events, 123, 124f; in what-happens presentation, 112; in whole problem analysis, 239, 241; for whole problems, 130, 145. *See also* Applications
Douglas, A., 184
Drake, L., 7, 8, 88
Duffy, T., 396, 403

E

E^3 learning: definition of, xvii, 70; elements of, 70; purpose of, 379; skill relevance and, 151
Ebert-May, D., 397
Education, versus training, 6
Efficiency, of learning, 370, 371

E-learning characteristics, xvii, 77–86
Engaging instruction, 370, 371
Enhancing strategies: in Pebble-in-the-Pond model, 252; types of, 339–340
Entrepreneur courses: complexity analysis for, 320; direct research of, 433–434; example of, 153–165, 214–216; format of, 201, 202f, 203; navigation of, 204
Entry points, 410
Errors, learning from, 404–405
Essays, 311
Evaluation: benefits of, 377–378; call for, 447; continuous type of, 379; design of, 271; experimenting with, 378–379; in Pebble-in-the-Pond model, 252, 267; purpose of, 376; revising after, 379; steps in, 376–377
Example content element: definition of, 9–10; description of, 57; examples of, 58f; rationale for, 9–11
Examples: adding links to, 367; in kind-of demonstrations, 96–98, 105–106; learner control over, 210–211; in matching guidance, 79–80; research related to, 399, 404; slide masters with, 284, 285f, 286, 287f; use of multiple, 82–83
Excel spreadsheet courses, 254–267, 309, 310, 320, 417–425
Excessive text, 213
Executing steps, 123
Exit button, 374
Experiential environment, 117–118
Experimental research, 440, 445–446
Experiments, 114
Explaining, requirements of, 96
Exploring: in information-about presentations and, 89; in part-of presentations, 92, 93
Extrinsic feedback, 107

F

Facilitating, versus promoting, 193
Facts, 56
Faculty evaluations, 430–433
Famous Presidents demonstration, 90–92; course checklist for, 220–221, 277–280; slide masters for, 280, 281f, 282
Feedback: adjusting mental models and, 25; examples of, 39, 40, 42; in functional prototypes, 277; versus guidance, 25; in how-to presentations, 110, 111; importance of, 25; in kind-of demonstrations, 97f, 98; learner control over, 211; in master slides, 282; for part-of demonstration, 95; for practice, 90, 93; research supporting, 404–405; in structural framework design, 344, 345f; in summary critiques, 225, 228, 230; types of, 25, 84; for whole problems, 145, 146f. *See also specific types*
Feedback button, 211
Feedback phase, 409, 410
Feltovich, P. J., 401
Finalizing design: course organization and, 354–362; learner interface and, 362–363; navigation and, 363–366; in Pebble-in-the-Pond model, 252, 266; steps in, 271; supplemental materials and, 366–367
First button, 205
"First Principles of Instruction" (Merrill), xviii
Flash programming, 425–430
Focal Length summary critique, 228–230
Fonts, 202–203
Format, of course: definition of, 193; multimedia and, 201–203; in multimedia example, 216
Format, of slide masters, 281
Formative evaluations, 308, 376–377
Foshay, W.R.R., 67
Four component instructional design (4C/ID) model, 412–413
4-MAT cycle of learning, 408–409
Francom, G., 165, 169, 187
Frick, T., 430, 432–433
Friendly Approach problem-solving event, 127–128, 129f, 137–144f; complexity analysis in, 320; slide masters for, 288–290, 291f
Frustration, of learners, 363
Functional prototypes, 270; characteristics of, 279–280; definition of, 273; description of, 274; design of, 275–280; experimenting with, 296, 377–378; finalization of, 354–368; rationale for, 274–275; tools for development of, 280–296

G

Gagné, R. M., 88, 120, 380, 398, 399, 403, 404
Games: common mistakes involving, 8, 16; for information-about practice, 90; motivation and, 16; for practice, 90
Gantt charts, 54f, 78–79f
Gardner, H., 403, 405, 410, 414t
Gardner, J., 414
General content elements, 54–56
General Education course, 165–168
Generalizations, 80
Generate Ideas activity, 408
Gentner, D., 401
Gibbons, A. S., 397
Gibson, G. V., 153, 169, 433
Gibson, J. T., 415t
Gilbert, C. G., 351
Glossary, design of, 366–367
Go Public activity, 408
Goal-based scenarios, 413
Goals, instructional: analysis of, 304, 322; identification of, 300; principles related to, 396–397; in traditional education, 308
Golas, K., 88, 120, 380
Gordon, J., 250
Graphic designers, 266
Graphic devices: description of, 199; in multimedia coaching and guidance, 200
Graphics: as alternative to text, 196; audio reading and, 15, 194, 195f; in complex animations, 279; dynamic types of, 192; ineffective use of, 198; in information-about component skill, 56; learners' limitations and, 194; in Pebble-in-the-Pond model, 266; versus portrayals, 56, 196; research related to, 402, 403; shortcomings of, 24; types of, 192; for visual portrayals, 198
Green, P., 430, 432
Guidance: definition of, 23–24; in demonstrations, 23–24; description of, 78; versus feedback, 25; forms of, 78; in how-to presentations, 106–107; in master slides, 284; in multimedia example, 215; multimedia for elaboration in, 199–201; overreliance on, 14; in Pebble-in-the-Pond model, 262, 263–264f; for peer-interaction, 347; purpose of, 343; research related to, 401, 402; structural framework basis of, 343–344f; use of structural framework and, 173; in what-happens presentation, 111. *See also specific forms*
Guided case studies, 31, 34–36
Guided discovery lessons, 112–118
Gur, B., 434

H

Hake, R., 185
Hannafin, M., 415t
Headings, 203
Help button, 205
Helping relationships, 61–62f
Helping Relationships demonstration, 96–98, 224–225
Heterogeneous groups, 347, 406
Highlighting, 200
Hilgenheger, N., 407
Hints, 25
History, 310–311
Holistic design, 308
Holum, A., 396, 397, 398
Homogenous groups, 347
How-to component skill: content elements of, 62; definition of, 48; description of, 49t, 51; Do interaction for, 76; example of, 52–53f; instructional strategies for, 89t, 106–111, 119; instructional strategy templates for, 288–290, 291f; in problems, 122, 123, 125f, 126; research related to, 400; summary critique for, 225–228
How-to problems: application and, 24; demonstration and, 23
How-to responses, 207
How-to strategy checklist, 220
Huitt, W. G., 415t
Hummel, J. H., 415t
Hypotheses, 402

I

Icons, for navigation, 204, 276
If-then relationships, 64
Illustrations, 57
In-basket simulations, 209
Incidental learning, 6

In-class instructional events, 167–168
Incomplete examples, 60–61f
Individual differences, 210
Information: definition of, 54; versus instruction, 8–9, 70; versus portrayal, 55–56, 399
Information-about component skill: content elements of, 56; definition of, 48, 50; description of, 49–50, 49t; example of, 50f; games for, 90; instructional strategies for, 89–92, 118; instructional strategy template for, 282, 283–284f; practice for, 90; purpose of, 50
Information-about strategy checklists, 220–221
Information-only presentation. *See* Level-0 instructional strategy
Instances, of problems, 254
Instruction: common mistakes involving, 8; components of, 48; definition of, 6; versus information, 8–9, 70; for problem-solving events, 123; purpose of, 17; versus textbooks, 193
Instructional architecture, 21
Instructional design class, interaction in, 187–188
Instructional design theories, 407–416
Instructional Design Theories and Models series, 20
Instructional design tools, 446–447
Instructional development, 252
Instructional episodes, 409–410
Instructional event tables: definition of, 325, 326; demonstration and application design with, 326–334; example of, 326
Instructional events: in checklist example, 180–181, 181–183f; course format and, 202–203; definition of, 48, 53, 87, 88; example of, 165–168; finalizing, 355; learner control of, 210–211; in metaphor example, 176; in multimedia example, 215, 216; navigation among, 204–205; navigation within, 205; in prototype problem applications, 307–308; in prototype problem demonstration, 305, 306t; sequence of, 151f, 152; in traditional instruction, 152; in whole problem analysis, 237–238; for whole problems, 129t
Instructional interactions: definition of, 48, 69; design of, 184, 264–266, 276–280; examples of, 187–188; forms of, 71–77; in functional prototypes, 276–280; goal of, 71; illustration of, 187f; instructor's role in, 184; in learning cycle, 186; media control and, 207; motivation and, 184; multimedia and, 193, 205–211, 216; promoting mental processing with, 77–78; rationale for, 183–184; summary of, 85t; technical vocabulary for, 71; use of multiple examples in, 82–83. *See also specific types; specific types of interactions*
Instructional modes: definition of, 69, 71; types of, 71, 88. *See also specific modes*
Instructional objectives: abstract type of, 396; in Pebble-in-the-Pond design, 253–254; research supporting, 396–397; in traditional instructional design, 253, 336
Instructional phase, 409
Instructional principles: criteria of, 20–21; definition of, xix; requirements of, 7
Instructional professionals, 17
Instructional strategies: versus component skill instruction, 336–337; definition of, xix, 87, 88; for how-to component skill, 106–111; importance of, 88; for information-about component skill, 89–92; for kind-of component skill, 95–106; levels of, 22–29; for part-of component skill, 92–95; for problem-solving events, 123–125, 127–145; requirements of, 7; selection of, 88; summary of, 89t; technology's effect on, 7; for what-happens component skill, 111–118; for whole problems, 127–145
Instructional strategy templates: definition of, 273; description of, 280; for how-to component skill, 288–290, 291f; for information-about component skill, 282, 283–284f; for kind-of component skill, 284–288; for what-happens component skill, 292–294, 295f
Instructional systems design (ISD): content sequences in, 269; criticism of, 250, 253, 270; description of, 250; early steps in, 268; illustration of, 251f; peer-interactions in, 350; traditional versus Pebble-in-the-Pond model, 300, 322, 336–337
Integration principle: collaborative methods of, 29; definition of, 20; description of, 21, 29, 44; implementation of, 172; peer-collaboration in, 188; peer-critique in, 186; research supporting, 405–406; structural framework in, 173; theories related to, 413, 414

Interactions. *See* Instructional interactions
Interactive scenario, 31–33
Interface: example of, 156, 157f; finalizing, 362–363
Internet instruction, 8
Internet links, 367
Interview questions, 375, 376f
Intrinsic feedback: definition of, 20, 25, 70; description of, 84; examples of, 39, 42, 84–85f; for how-to demonstrations, 107; in summary critiques, 228; in what-happens applications, 112
Introductions: example of, 157, 158f; finalizing, 355, 359f
Irrelevant color: alternatives to, 213; definition of, 192; to focus attention, 200. *See also* Color
Irrelevant media, 212
ISD. *See* Instructional systems design
Isolated illustrations, 309
Italics, 203

J

Jacobson, M. J., 401
Jehng, J. C., 401
Job counseling demonstration, 96–101
Johnson, E., 415t
Jonassen, D., 396, 403, 411–412, 415t

K

Keller, J. M., 88, 120, 380, 429
Keogh, R., 406
Kind-of component skill: content elements of, 57; coordinate classes and, 59; definition of, 48; description of, 49t, 51; Do interaction for, 76; example of, 52f, 57–59; goal of, 60, 95; incomplete examples and, 60; instructional strategies for, 89t, 95–106, 118–119; instructional strategy templates for, 284–288; matching guidance in, 79–80; in problem-solving events, 123, 125f, 126; pseudo examples and, 61–62f; research related to, 400; summary critique for, 223–225; unencountered examples and, 59–60
Kind-of problems: application and, 24; demonstration and, 23; feedback for, 206–207
Kind-of responses, 206–207
Kind-of strategy checklist, 220
King, A., 184
Kirschner, P. A., 184, 185, 313, 337, 396, 412
Knowledge: definition of, 22; versus skills, 22; structured acquisition of, 28
Kovalik, S. J., 415t
Kulhavy, R. W., 404

L

Labels, in part-of practice, 92, 93
Lacy, M. J., 7, 8, 88
Land, S., 415t
Landa, L. N., 415t
Large groups, 347
Larson, S., 415t
Last button, 205, 216
Laurillard, D., 406
Layout, screen, 276
Learner control: definition of, 192, 193; individual differences and, 210; of instructional events, 210–211; multimedia and, 205–211; text and, 195; use of, 192
Learner interface. *See* Interface
Learner population, 300
Learners: frustration of, 363; individual differences among, 210; interaction among, 183–188; unchanging nature of, 7–8
Learning by doing theory, 413–414
Learning communities: considerations regarding, 15; definition of, 350; versus peer-interaction, 350
Learning cycle theories, 407–409
Learning phases: description of, 21; peer-interactions in, 186; in problem-centered instruction, 21, 22f
Lee, M., 415t
Level-1 instructional strategy: definition of, 20; description of, 23–24
Level-3 instructional strategy: definition of, 20; description of, 26–29
Level-2 instructional strategy: definition of, 20; description of, 24–26
Level-0 instructional strategy: definition of, 20; description of, 22–23

Lin, X., 401, 403, 405, 407, 415t
Lindsey, L., 415t
Linear representations, 275
Literature courses, 311
Live presentations, 253
Location indicators: definition of, 353, 362; description of, 57; finalizing, 362–363; in part-of demonstrations, 93
Location practice, 93
Look Ahead activity, 408
Lyons, C., 218

M

Macpherson, K. A., 396, 403, 413–414, 415t
Macros: definition of, 369; description of, 451; examples of, 451–459; for learner names, 374; to record performance data, 374
A Man for All Seasons (More), 311
Marcovitz, D. M., 380
Margaryan, A., 433
Marriage relationship course, 434
Marzano, R. J., 172, 180, 189, 351, 396, 397, 398, 401, 402, 405, 406
Mastery: in information-about practice example, 90–92; practice and, 90
Matched examples, 105
Matching guidance: in applications, 80; definition of, 70; description of, 79–80; examples of, 80f; non-examples in, 79–80
Mathematics, 438–439
Mayer, R. E., 6, 15, 24, 28, 150, 173, 194, 212, 218, 351, 380, 396, 397, 398, 399, 401, 402, 403, 404, 405, 406
Mayer, R. H., 415t
Mazur, E., 184, 185
McCarthy, B., 405, 406, 408, 409
McGeehan, J. R., 415t
Media control, 205–211
Media objects, 281
Mediated instruction, 206–208
Memories, 413
Mendenhall, A., 153, 165, 169, 433
Mental models: activation of, 27–28, 342; adaptation of, 173; adjustments to, 25; appropriate use of, 184; benefits of interaction for, 184; decontextualized instruction and, 26; definition of, 20, 24; formation of, 24; ineffective use of, 173; research related to, 397–399; versus structural framework, 173; structure of new knowledge and, 28; themes and, 13–14
Mental processing, 77–78
Menu button, 366
Menus. *See* Content menus
Merrill, M. D., xviii, xvii, 6, 7, 8, 20, 45, 86, 88, 153, 165, 169, 187, 202, 246, 271, 351, 399, 403, 404, 433, 440, 446
Metaphors: definition of, 173, 340; demonstration of structural frameworks and, 342; description of, 175–176; example of, 176–177f; identification of structural frameworks and, 341–342
Microworlds: definition of, 34, 209; multimedia for, 209
Mills, G., 153, 169, 433
Minus sign, 221
Missing components, 355
Mistakes, instructional, 8
Mnemonic: definition of, 88, 89, 173; description of, 173; example of, 174–175; in presentations, 89; types of, 173
Mock-ups. *See* Functional prototypes
Momentum demonstration, 112–118
Monetti, D., 415t
More, T., 311
Motivation: common mistakes involving, 8, 14; decontextualized instruction and, 26; demonstration of skills and, 43; description of, 29; peer interaction and, 184; through games, 16
Multimedia: checklist for, 214t; for coaching and guidance, 199–201; common instructional mistakes involving, 8, 24; course format and, 201–203; definition of, 192; description of, 192; effective use of, 191–192; example of, 214–216; for instructional interactions, 205–211; misuse of, 211–213, 402–403; for navigation, 203–205; portrayal properties and, 197–201; principles for, 217–218; purpose of, 24; research related to, 401–402, 403; shortcomings of, 82; for Show interaction, 82
Multiple perspectives, 408

Multiple representations, 410
Music: instruction in, 310–311; misuse of, 212

N

Names, 56, 57, 62; example of, 62–63; in how-to component skill, 62; ordering of, 207; in what-happens component skill, 63
Names, of learners, 374
Naming practice, 93
Namy, L., 401
Narration, 402
Navigation: among slides, 276, 363, 365; definition of, 193, 203, 353, 363; finalizing, 363–366; levels of, 363; in multimedia example, 216; multimedia for, 203–205; in Pebble-in-the-Pond model, 266; in presentation software, 276; within slides, 363, 364
Nelson, L. M., 403, 405–406, 410–411, 414t
New mathematics, 438
Newman, S. E., 404
Next button, 204, 205; finalizing, 364, 365; in multimedia example, 216; in presentation software, 276
Nice-to-know information: in information-about instructional strategy, 89; in part-of instructional strategy, 93
Non-examples, 60, 61–62f; in kind-of demonstrations, 96, 98; in matching guidance, 79–80; in range-of-difficulty guidance, 81; slide masters with, 284, 285f, 286, 287f; for whole problems, 134
Number theory, 438

O

Objective measures, 371
Objects, 286, 288, 294
Observations, 205, 377, 442
Ohm's Law demonstration, 209f
Oliver, K., 415t
Olsen, J. B., 397
One-on-one trials, 376–377
Online instruction, 8–9
Open-ended learning, 6
Opening scenarios, 30–33
Ordering items, 207
Organization, of content: course format and, 201, 202f; finalizing designs and, 354–362; in multimedia example, 216; research related to, 402
Outcomes, learning versus instructional, 442
Outlines, 354, 356f

P

Page-turner instruction, 204
Park, O., 404
Part-of component skill: content elements in, 57; definition of, 48; description of, 49t, 50; example of, 51f; goal of, 50; instructional strategies for, 89t, 92–95, 118; summary critique for, 222–223
Part-of problems, 23
Passive demonstrations, 111
Passive interactions, 205
Paulus, T., 415t
Pause symbol, 206
Pebble-in-the-Pond model: description of, 252–253; design checklist for, 381–391; illustration of, 247f, 252f; initial design steps in, 300; phases of, 249, 253–267; properties of, 249–250, 268–270; versus traditional instructional design, 300, 322, 336–337
Peer-collaboration: benefits of, 184; definition of, 172, 340, 349; description of, 44, 186; design of, 264–265; example of, 349t; in flow of learning cycle, 186; illustration of, 187f; importance of, 29; in Pebble-in-the-Pond model, 264–265; rationale for, 350; research supporting, 406; theories related to, 410–411
Peer-critique: definition of, 172, 340, 350; description of, 44, 186; example of, 350t; in flow of learning cycle, 186; illustration of, 187f; importance of, 29; rationale for, 350
Peer-discussion: definition of, 172, 340, 348; description of, 185; in flow of learning cycle, 186; questions for, 185; rubric for, 349t
Peer-interactions: characteristics of, 347; creation of, 347–348; definition of, 339, 347; design of, 265–266, 271; effectiveness of, 347; finalizing, 361–362; in Pebble-in-the-Pond model, 265–266; versus traditional instructional design, 350

Peer-sharing: definition of, 172, 339, 348; description of, 185; directions for, 348; in flow of learning cycle, 186
Peer-telling: definition of, 172; description of, 184–185; shortcomings of, 184–185
Perfection, 275
Perkins, D. N., 397, 403, 405
Persuasive Essay checklist example, 180–181, 181–183f
Persuasive Essay text example, 197f
Photographs, usefulness of, 36
Photography courses, 208, 210–211; assessment of, 371–376; complexity analysis for, 320; component skill checklist for, 334–336; component skill matrix for, 317–319; critique of, 229–242; designing demonstrations and applications for, 326–334; finalizing, 354–366; instructional event table for, 326f; modifying portrayals in, 321; peer-interaction for, 348–350; problem-solving event analysis for, 302–303, 304f, 305f; prototype demonstration for, 306–307f; sample portrayals in, 317f; slide masters for, 292–293; structural frameworks in, 342–347
Pickering, D. J., 172, 180, 189, 351, 396, 397, 398, 401, 402, 405, 406
Pig Farm entrepreneur course, 153–159
Placeholders: creation of, 280–296; definition of, 280; in how-to slide masters, 289; in kind-of slide masters, 284, 288; in what-happens slide masters, 292, 294
Play symbol, 206
Plus sign, 221
Poetic Meter demonstration, 101–106
Pogrow, S., 415t
Pollock, J. E., 172, 180, 189, 351, 396, 397, 398, 401, 402, 405, 406
Pop-up messages: course format and, 203; finalizing navigation and, 364
Portrayals: audio in, 194; collecting samples of, 301–302; component skill complexity analysis and, 317–318; course format and, 203; definition of, 54; effective multimedia use for, 194, 196, 197–201; example of, 55–56; versus graphics, 56, 196; identifying component skills for, 302–305; versus information, 55–56, 399; modification of, 321; in multimedia example, 215; in problem progressions, 316–317, 320; research related to, 399; sequencing of, 319–320; as supplemental materials, 367
Posey, L. O., 404
Post-assessments, 372
PowerPoint software: assessment prototypes and, 373–374; finalizing design in, 354–355; for functional prototypes, 275–280; for instructional strategy templates, 280; macros for, 451
Practice: definition of, 87, 88, 89; description of, 90; example of, 90–92; for part-of instructional strategy, 92, 93; research supporting, 403; summary of, 89t. *See also* Ask interactions
Practice case studies, 39–43
Practicum experiences, 42–43
Pratt, J., 7, 8, 88
Pre-assessments, 372
Pre-class instructional events, 165–166
Prescriptions, xix
Prescriptive principles, 396
Presentations: definition of, 87, 88, 89; example of, 90–92; experimentation with, 296; for how-to instructional strategy, 106–107; for information-about instructional strategy, 89–90; for kind-of instructional strategy, 95; for part-of instructional strategy, 92–93; parts of, 193; research related to, 399; software for, 275, 276, 277, 280, 446; summary of, 89t; in topic-centered instruction, 150f; in what-happens instructional strategy, 111
Previous button, 204, 205; finalizing, 365; in presentation software, 276
Principle-oriented design: definition of, 249, 250; in Pebble-in-the-Pond model, 268
Principles: definition of, xix, 19, 20; versus prescriptions, xix
Prior knowledge: activation of, 27–28; research related to, 397–399
Problem classes: definition of, 315; identification of, 300–301, 308–312; research related to, 399–400
Problem progression: adjusting sequence in, 319–320; challenges in identifying, 309–310; definition of, 150, 315, 316; description of, 151; designing of, 256–259, 270–271; example

of, 165; identifying component skills in, 317–319; instructional event distribution in, 152–153; in Pebble-in-the-Pond model, 252; portrayals in, 316–317, 321; qualities of, 316; research related to, 397; theories related to, 411; versus traditional instructional design, 322
Problem-based learning: component skills in, 122; versus problem-centered instruction, 26
Problem-centered component skill instruction: component skill checklist in, 334–336; definition of, 325; demonstration and application design in, 326–334; description of, 326; instructional event tables and, 326; versus traditional instruction, 336–337
Problem-centered design: challenge of, 308; definition of, 249, 250; in Pebble-in-the-Pond model, 269–270; principles of, 322; problem progression in, 256
Problem-centered instruction: versus case-based learning, 26; description of, 26–29, 146; learning phases in, 21, 22f; versus problem-based learning, 26; research supporting, 396–415; sequences for, 153; single versus multiple problems in, 27; versus traditional instruction, 153
Problem-centered instructional strategies: definition of, 149; description of, 151–152; distribution of, 152–153; examples of, 153–168; illustration of, 151f; steps in, 168–169
Problem-centered principle: definition of, 19; description of, 21, 44, 168
Problem-centered tutorials, 420–423
Problems: component skills in, 122, 126; definition of, 63, 396; description of, 26; designing, 253–255, 270; example of, 64; good types of, 301; in instructional interactions, 185; in Pebble-in-the-Pond model, 252; versus tasks, 22. *See also specific types*
Problem-solving event analysis: definition of, 299, 302; versus goal analysis, 304; problem portrayals in, 302–305
Problem-solving events: content elements for, 122–123, 126–127; definition of, 121, 123; examples of, 154–156; 124f; instructional strategies for, 123–125, 127–145; prescribed instructional events in, 154, 155t; sample diagram for, 154, 155f
Procedures, 49, 51; media control and, 207; in Pebble-in-the-Pond model, 252, 268; results of, 253
Processes, 49, 53; definition of, 63
Product reviews, 444–445
Professional reviews, 376
Promoting learning: definition of, 6; versus facilitating learning, 193
Prompted examples, 257
Properties: coordinate concepts and, 59; definition of, 57, 123; example of, 57, 58f; incomplete examples and, 60; in problem-solving events, 124, 125, 127f; pseudo examples and, 61
Propositions, 442–443
Prototype problem application: definition of, 299; design of, 307–308; versus traditional instructional objectives, 336
Prototype problem demonstration: definition of, 299, 305; design of, 305–307; example of, 302f; versus traditional instructional objectives, 336
Prototypes, assessment, 371–374
Prototyping: definition of, 249, 250, 368; description of, 270; evaluation of, 267; in Pebble-in-the-Pond model, 266, 267, 270; revisions in, 267
Pseudo examples: description of, 61; example of, 61–62f; in kind-of demonstrations, 97
Public performance, 408, 410

Q

Questions: versus application, 11–12; to collect attitude data, 375, 376f; in design evaluation, 267; for Do interactions, 76; in functional prototypes, 277; for peer-discussions, 185; for practice, 90
Quizzes, 150

R

Randi, J., 414t
Range-of-difficulty guidance: definition of, 70; description of, 80–81; examples of, 81–82f

Readability, 213
Reading assignments, 165–166
Reading on-screen text, 15, 213
Real-world activities, 301
Real-world problems: in after-class instructional events, 168; benefits of, 150; component skills in, 122; example of, 153, 154, 168; research supporting, 403
Recall: versus activation, 398; in information-only presentations, 23
Reflect Back activity, 408
Reflection: definition of, 346; structural framework basis of, 346; use of structural framework and, 173; in what-happens demonstration, 117f
Reigeluth, C. M., 20, 397
Relevance, of learning, 151
Reliable measures, 371
Remember-questions, 9f
Remember-what-I-told-you questions, 13f
Repetition, 90
Research, 440, 444–446. *See also specific topics*
Research and revise activities, 408
Responses, 206–208
Restaurant Business course, 162–163f
Reviewing products and research, 444–445
Revising courses, 267, 372, 373f, 379
Rhetorical questions, 71
Robertson, J., 397
Roles, 413
Rosenberg-Kima, R., 425, 443
Rosenshine, B., 172, 398, 399, 402, 403, 404, 405
Rubric: to increase objectivity of measures, 371; for peer-discussion, 349t
Rutherford, F., 415t

S

Sampling with replacement: definition of, 93; for part-of practice, 93
Savery, J. R., 396, 403, 415t
Scaffolding, 404, 413
Scenarios, 413, 414
Schank, R. C., 396, 403, 413–414, 415t
Schema, 398
Schwartz, D., 401, 403, 405, 407, 415t
Science, of instructional design, 440–441
Scope, course, 165
Scoring modules, 241–242
Screen layouts, 276
Scripts, 451
Self-contained courses, 253
Self-directed learning, 6
Self-explanations, 402
Selling Furniture demonstration, 131–134f, 135–136f, 198
Sequence cues: definition of, 88, 90; repetition and, 90
Shell EP, 433
Short-term memory, 193–194
Shovelware, 8
Show button, 211
Show interactions: definition of, 69; description of, 72; distribution of, 152–153; examples of, 73f, 74f, 154–155, 156t, 168; in how-to presentations, 106; in kind-of demonstrations, 96–98, 101; multimedia for, 82; multiple versus single use of, 82–83; in problem-centered instructional strategy, 151f, 152; in what-happens presentation, 112; in whole problems, 134, 136, 144–145. *See also* Demonstrations
Show-portrayal, 194
Silber, K. H., 67
Simon-Says demonstration, 34; definition of, 70; description of, 74–75, 201; examples of, 75f, 255; in how-to presentations, 107
Simple Circuit simulation, 209f
Simulations: benefits of, 74; examples of, 74f; guided case study examples of, 34–36; for how-to presentations, 107; multimedia for, 209; practice case study examples of, 39–43; versus real-world activities, 301; slide masters for, 293–294, 295f
Skill acquisition: consistent application and, 25; demonstration of, 43; rationale for, 6
Skills: definition of, 49; versus knowledge, 22; relevance of, 151
Skills complexity analysis, 315, 319–320
Skinner, B. F., 439
Slavin, R. E., 184

Slide masters: definition of, 280; for instructional strategy templates, 280–296
Small groups, 347, 377, 406
Snyder, M. M., 415t
Social networking, 8
Sound. *See* Audio
Sources, 175
Speaker symbol, 206
Specific content elements, 54–56
Specifying instances, 254–255
Spiro, R. J., 401
Sportsmanship mnemonic, 174–175f
Spreadsheet courses, 254–267
Spreadsheet demonstration, 107–111, 225–226
Staffieri, A., 184
Star Legacy, 405, 407–408
Stelnicki, M. B., 67
Steps: definition of, 62, 123; designing demonstrations and applications for, 326–334; example of, 62; media control and, 207, 208; in Pebble-in-the-Pond model, 252, 268, 269; in problem-solving events, 123, 124f, 125, 126, 127f; in slide masters, 289–290
Stock, W. A., 404
Stop symbol, 206
Stories, 413
Storyboards, 130, 131–134f
Strategy templates. *See* Instructional strategy templates
Structural framework: benefits of, 172–173; characteristics of, 340–341; coaching based on, 344–345f; definition of, 171, 173, 339, 340; design of, 262–264, 271, 342–343f; effective use of, 173; examples of, 174–183; finalizing courses and, 359–361; forms of, 173–183; guidance based on, 343–344f; identification of, 341–342; versus mental models, 173; in Pebble-in-the-Pond model, 262–264; principles related to, 350; reflection based on, 346; research related to, 398–399; versus traditional instructional design, 346–347; types of, 340; in whole problem analysis, 239
Structure for knowledge, 28
Structure-Guidance-Coaching-Reflection cycle, 172
Study skills, 201
Subject-matter content: definition of, 47; general versus specific representation of, 54–56; vocabulary for, 48–49
Subject-matter experts: common instructional mistakes involving, 8; for professional reviews, 376
Submit button, 364, 365
Successive disclosure, 192
Suhaka, M., 153, 169, 433
Summary critiques: of component skills, 220–230; definition of, 220; description of, 221; example of, 221, 222t; of whole problems, 231–242, 244–245
Summary frames. *See* Checklists
Superordinate class, 95
Supplemental materials: finalizing, 366–367; in Pebble-in-the-Pond model, 266
Survey courses, 308–309
Sweller, J., 185
Synchronized graphic devices, 200

T

Table of contents, 355
Tabs: for course format, 201; for navigation, 204
Takeaway materials, 367
TALQ. *See* Teaching and Learning Quality scales
Target content: definition of, 340; demonstration of structural frameworks and, 342; identification of structural frameworks and, 341
Targets, 175–176
Task-centered conditions, 426
Tasks: definition of, 62; example of, 62; versus problems, 22
Teaching and Learning Quality (TALQ) scales, 430–432
Technical vocabulary. *See* Vocabulary, technical
Technological changes: instructional strategies and, 7; interactive instruction and, 205–206; learning mechanisms and, 7–8
Technology: common instructional mistakes involving, 8; of instructional design, 440–441. *See also specific technology*
Tell interactions: definition of, 69; description of, 71; distribution of, 152–153; examples

of, 73–74f, 154–155, 156t, 157; in how-to presentations, 106, 110, 111; in kind-of demonstrations, 96–98, 101; in part-of presentations, 92, 93–95; in problem-centered instructional strategy, 151f, 152; in what-happens presentation, 112; in whole problems, 136, 144–145. *See also* Presentations
Tell-and-ask interactions: description of, 72; examples of, 12f, 72f, 73f, 74f
Tell-information, 193–194
Telling analogies, 410
Tennyson, R. D., 202, 404
Test Your Mettle activity, 408
Text: in complex animations, 279; for defining and ordering portrayals, 197; definition of, 192; effective use of, in multimedia, 193–194; evaluating, 378–379; example of, 194f; fundamental role of, 193; graphics as alternative to, 196; learner control over, 195; learners' limitations and, 194; media control of, 206; misuse of, in multimedia, 213; in multimedia coaching and guidance, 200
Text boxes, 277
Textbooks: versus instruction, 193; versus online courses, 213
Themes, 13–14
Theories: detailed explanations of, 414–416, 440, 441–444; proliferation of, 20. *See also specific learning theories*
Thompson Learning, 418
Time data, 374–375
Title pages, 355, 358f
Tools, teaching of, 309, 310
Topic outlines, 309
Topic-centered conditions, 426
Topic-centered instructional strategies: definition of, 149; description of, 150; illustration of, 150f; limitations of, 151; sequences for, 153
Topic-centered tutorials, 418–420
Training: developing courses in, 312; versus education, 6; money spent on, 70
Transistor metaphor/analogy, 176–180
Trials, 376–377
Tutorials: complexity analysis and, 320; direct research of, 418–423; examples of, 31, 36–39
Typeface, 202–203

U

Unencountered examples: definition of, 59; description of, 59–60; in kind-of demonstrations, 96–98
Unger, C., 397, 403, 405
University of Illinois, 438
Unprompted applications, 257, 258f
Utah Counties demonstration, 93–95, 222–223

V

Valid measures, 371
van der Meij, H., 405
van Merriënboer, J.J.G., 147, 184, 185, 271, 313, 337, 396, 397, 399, 400, 403, 404, 412–413, 415
Vanderbilt Learning Technology Center, 405, 407–408
Verbal information, 49
Video demonstrations, 130, 131–134f, 137–144f; for dynamic visualizations, 198–199; media control of, 208; slide masters for, 288–290, 291f, 292; summary critique of, 226–227
Vincenti, W. G., 440
Visual Basic program, 364, 374, 451
Vocabulary, technical: for different skill types, 49; of learning theories, 415; rationale for, 48–49, 71; variances in, 444
Volume, 206

W

Wager, W. W., 88, 120, 380
Walker, D., 406
Wang, Y., 430, 432
Warm Greeting problem-solving event, 125f, 127, 137–144f
Watson, C., 430, 432
What-happens component skill: appropriate use of, 53; content elements for, 63–66; definition of, 48; description of, 49t, 53; Do interaction for, 77; example of, 54f; instructional strategies for, 89t, 111–118, 119; instructional strategy templates for, 292–294, 295f; in problems, 122, 123, 125f, 126; research related to, 400–401; summary critique for, 228–230
What-happens problems, 23, 24

What-happens responses, 207–208
What-happens strategy checklist, 220
What's My Line practice, 90–92
Who Did What practice, 90–92
Whole problems: components of, 126; content elements for, 126–127, 237; critiques of, 231–242, 244–245; instructional events for, 129t; instructional strategies for, 127–145
Who's Who practice, 90–92
Wiki, 347–348
Wilson, E. O., 442
Wiske, M. S., 415t
Wolfersberger, M., 165, 169, 187
Worked examples, 257, 399
Wu, C., 434

Y

Young, L. G., 401
Your Own Business course, 163–164f, 164–165

Z

Zemke, R., 250